A Doctor's Guide to Prescribing Peptides

A No-Nonsense Compliance Manual for Physicians Prescribing Peptides

Safely, Legally, and Profitably

Jim Bock

Registered Nurse 20+ years | Investment Banker 11+ years

Paralegal 40+ years | Film Maker 28+ years

Copyright, AI Disclosure, and Professional Disclaimer

Author Use Disclosure. Portions of this book were created, researched, edited, organized, illustrated, and formatted with assistance from generative AI tools. The author reviewed, organized, edited, and assumes full responsibility for the final published content. Think of the AI like a research assistant who types fast but does not have a nursing license, a law degree, or a medical board to answer to. I checked the work. The mistakes, if any, are mine. The good advice came from forty years of watching what happens when smart people get lazy.

AI Disclosure. This guide describes the use of generative AI tools and AI-assisted workflows for preparation, editing, research support, organization, and formatting. Readers are responsible for independently verifying medical, legal, regulatory, pharmacy, advertising, patient-consent, and business requirements before relying on any workflow, form, checklist, or operational recommendation. Do not assume that because something is in print, it is current. Laws change. Board attitudes change. Pharmacy rules change. What was true in June 2026 may not be true next year. Verify everything before you act.

Important Medical and Legal Disclaimer. This book is educational. It is not medical advice, legal advice, a prescribing protocol, a regulatory opinion, or a substitute for physician judgment, malpractice counsel, healthcare counsel, pharmacy counsel, or state-specific legal review. If you need a lawyer, hire one. If you need medical advice, ask a doctor - preferably one with a license in your state who has examined you. Do not use this book as a shield. It is a guide. A map. A warning sign on the side of the road saying "Bridge Out Ahead." It will not stop your car if you keep driving.

Peptide medicine, hormone therapy, compounding, cash-pay practice, telehealth, advertising, patient consent, and office dispensing sit in a changing legal and clinical environment. FDA policy changes without warning. State medical boards change posture overnight when a local news station runs an expose. Pharmacy rules change. Compounded product availability changes. Insurance, advertising, and consumer-protection rules change. If you are looking for permanence, go read a chemistry textbook. This is a field in motion.

Verify everything before acting. A patient signature does not make bad medicine good. A hold-harmless clause does not cure poor judgment. A consent form does not replace a chart. A pharmacy shipment does not replace physician review. A patient request does not force a prescription. Do not hide behind forms. Do not hide behind this book. If you would not want to explain the decision to a state board reviewer at ten in the morning under fluorescent lights, do not make the decision in the first place.

Use this book as a thinking guide. Then use your own clinical judgment and your own legal counsel. If you read something in here and think "that doesn’t sound right for my state," trust that instinct. I am not licensed in your state. I do not know your board’s current mood. I am telling you what I have seen work and what I have seen destroy good careers. Your mileage may vary. Your board certainly will.

 I do not endorse anyone. I do not take money from pharmacies, peptide manufacturers, compounding facilities, or anyone else who sells the products discussed in this book. My only income from this project is what you paid for the book. If that.

Table of Contents

Preface: Read This Before You Prescribe a Single Peptide

The State Is Not Your Friend - They Are Waiting for You to Slip Up

Let me tell you something, and I want you to hear it because it might save your license someday: the state medical board is not your colleague. They are not your friend. They are not a resource you call when you have questions about whether something is okay. They are a regulatory body whose entire reason for existence is to protect the public from physicians who screw up. You are the public they are protecting people from. Never forget that.

I have been a registered nurse for more than twenty years. An investment banker for eleven. A paralegal for forty. I have sat in deposition rooms where good doctors - smart doctors, caring doctors, doctors who got into medicine for the right reasons - watched their careers get dismantled one document at a time. I have seen board investigators ask questions that sound innocent until you realize they already know the answer and they are measuring how far your explanation deviates from what is in the chart. I have seen physicians who did nothing clinically wrong spend two years and a hundred thousand dollars defending themselves because their documentation was garbage. The board does not care that you meant well. You think the board cares that you meant well? They don't. They care what the chart says. They care what the pharmacy records show. They care what your staff told the investigator when he showed up unannounced on a Tuesday morning.

You want to prescribe peptides? Fine. Peptides are interesting. Some of them have real therapeutic potential. Patients are asking for them, and they will keep asking because the internet has already told them what they want. But you need to understand something before you write that first prescription: every state medical board in this country has a file drawer, or more likely a database now, labeled "Alternative Medicine Complaints." Maybe they call it something fancier - "Integrative Medicine Oversight" or "Non-Standard Therapy Review" - but it is the same thing. It is where complaints about doctors who do things differently go to ferment. And peptide prescribing, hormone therapy, IV vitamin therapy, stem cell injections, and all the other things patients see on podcasts - those complaints go straight into that file.

You are already on a list you did not know existed just by reading this book. Act accordingly.

Why This Book Exists: Watching Too Many Good Doctors Lose Licenses Over Stupid Mistakes

This book exists because I am tired of watching good physicians lose everything over avoidable, boneheaded, completely unnecessary mistakes. I am not talking about doctors who committed malpractice. I am not talking about doctors who intentionally hurt patients. I am talking about doctors who got sloppy. Doctors who trusted the wrong pharmacy. Doctors who let their staff do things staff should never do. Doctors who thought a consent form with enough fine print could substitute for clinical judgment. Doctors who priced their services like a discount warehouse and then wondered why the board assumed they were running a vial shop. Doctors who prescribed controlled substances when they absolutely did not need to, painting a target on their backs that DEA investigators could see from space.

I watched a colleague in California - smart endocrinologist, good clinician, genuinely cared about his patients - get put on five years of supervised probation because his chart notes for a peptide patient consisted of three sentences and a prescription. Three sentences. The patient had a bad outcome, which happens, but the board did not discipline him for the outcome. They disciplined him because he could not prove he had done any clinical reasoning before writing the prescription. His chart said "Patient requests BPC-157 for recovery. Agreed. Dispensed." That was it. Two years of investigation. Five years of probation. A hundred and fifty thousand in legal fees. All because he treated clinical documentation like a nuisance instead of a shield.

Another physician in Texas, a functional medicine doctor who built a beautiful practice, lost her license over staff scope creep. Her unlicensed office manager was adjusting patient doses over the phone based on "how the patient sounded." The manager was well-meaning. The patients loved her. She had been doing it for three years. Then one patient had a reaction, went to the emergency room, mentioned the practice name, and suddenly there was an investigator in the waiting room asking questions. The board does not care that your staff are nice people. They care that your staff are practicing medicine without a license on your watch.

These stories are not rare. They are not cautionary tales from the fringe. They are what happens when physicians who want to help patients get so busy being helpful that they forget the system around them is hostile to anything that looks different. And peptides look different. To a board investigator who spent his career reviewing standard primary care, a peptide protocol looks like a foreign language. Your job is not to change his mind. Your job is to make your chart so bulletproof that even a skeptical stranger can follow your reasoning from the first page to the last.

What This Book Is Not: Cheerleading, Anti-FDA Propaganda, or a Legal Textbook

Let me be equally clear about what this book is not, because there is a whole ecosystem of peptide enthusiasm out there that I find professionally embarrassing. You have probably seen the social media accounts. The doctors with a hundred thousand followers who post daily about how peptides are going to revolutionize medicine while the FDA sits in the dark ages. The supplement companies masquerading as medical educators. The compounding pharmacies with affiliate programs and commission structures. The "thought leaders" who have never testified before a medical board in their lives and have no idea what happens when the letter arrives.

I am not one of them. This is not a cheerleading manual. I do not think peptides are magic. I do not think they are going to cure aging, fix every metabolic disease, or replace the entire pharmaceutical industry. Some peptides have interesting evidence. Some have modest evidence. Some have no human evidence at all and should not be prescribed outside a research setting. I am going to tell you which is which, and I am going to tell you without enthusiasm or dread. Evidence is evidence. Lack of evidence is lack of evidence. Your job as a physician is to know the difference and act accordingly.

This is also not an anti-FDA screed. The FDA has plenty of problems. They move slowly. They are influenced by political pressure and industry lobbying. They have made decisions about compounded medications that have been genuinely harmful to patient access. I get all of that.

But here is the thing: the FDA is not the one who takes your license. The state medical board takes your license. And the board does not care about your opinions on federal drug policy. They care whether your chart shows reasonable medical judgment. So we are going to deal with the FDA as it exists, not as we wish it would be. We are going to understand its categories- approved, off-label, compounded, investigational, research-use-only - and we are going to use them correctly in our documentation because precision in language is what separates defensible medicine from reckless experimentation.

And this is definitely not a legal textbook. I am a paralegal, not an attorney. Nothing in this book constitutes legal advice. Laws vary by state. Board attitudes vary by state. Pharmacy regulations vary by state. What is perfectly acceptable in Arizona might get you investigated in New York. You need a healthcare attorney who knows your state, and if you do not have one, get one before you prescribe your first peptide. What this book gives you is a framework - a way of thinking about risk, documentation, patient selection, and practice management that will make your attorney's job easier when and if you ever need them.

The Hard Truth About Peptides, Hormones, IV Vitamins, and Everything Else Big Pharma Doesn't Sell Now let me tell you the hard truth, and I want you to really hear this because it is the foundation of everything else in this book. The reason peptides and hormone therapies and IV vitamins and all the other alternative therapies are under constant scrutiny is not because they do not work. Some of them work just fine. The reason they are under scrutiny is because they threaten a system that is designed to protect pharmaceutical profits, regulatory certainty, and institutional control.

Big Pharma does not care about patient outcomes. I know that sounds cynical, but after eleven years as an investment banker, I can tell you exactly what pharmaceutical companies care about: patent protection, market exclusivity, FDA-approved indications, reimbursement codes, and shareholder returns. A therapy that cannot be patented, cannot be mass-marketed, and cannot be billed through insurance is not a therapy to them. It is a competitor. And competitors get eliminated.

The FDA's drug approval process costs hundreds of millions of dollars. No company is going to spend that money on a peptide that cannot be patented when they can spend it on a small molecule that can. This is not a conspiracy theory. It is business logic. It is the same logic that explains why we have seventeen varieties of erectile dysfunction medication but only a handful of antibiotics in development. The system rewards what is profitable, not what is medically interesting. Peptides, many of them, fall into the gap - too complex to patent easily, too niche for blockbuster returns, too threatening to existing therapeutic categories.

What this means for you, practically, is that you are practicing in a space that the institutional system does not protect. There is no pharmaceutical rep calling on your board members to explain why your prescribing is reasonable. There is no industry-funded defense fund when you get investigated. There is no powerful lobbying group going to bat for peptide physicians in your state capital. You are alone. Your protection is your chart, your consent forms, your pharmacy relationships, your clinical reasoning, and your willingness to say no when the risk is too high.

IV vitamin therapy has been around for decades and boards still question it. Bioidentical hormone therapy has millions of satisfied patients and boards still investigate it. Peptides are newer, less understood by the general medical community, and carry all the same regulatory suspicion. You need to go into this with your eyes open. The system is rigged against alternative therapies. Not because they are bad, but because they are alternative. The word "alternative" in medicine does not mean "different but equal." It means "not protected by the institutional structure that shields standard-of-care physicians from scrutiny." You are choosing to stand outside that wall. Fine. But do not pretend the wall is not there.

Who This Is For: Physicians Who Want to Help Patients Without Becoming Board Exhibits

This book is written for a specific kind of physician, and if you are not that kind, you should put it down now and go read something else. This is for the doctor who sees patients suffering from metabolic disease, chronic inflammation, poor recovery, cognitive decline, sexual dysfunction, weight gain, fatigue, and all the other conditions that standard medicine addresses with a fifteen-minute visit and a prescription for whatever the insurance formulary covers. This is for the doctor who knows there are tools outside the standard toolkit - some of them genuinely useful - and wants to offer those tools safely, legally, and responsibly.

This is for the physician who already runs or is considering a cash-pay practice because they are tired of insurance companies dictating what constitutes care. This is for the physician who is willing to charge premium prices because they understand that cheap alternative medicine looks like a product business, not a medical practice. This is for the physician who is willing to turn patients away - to say no to the demanding patient, the broke patient, the patient who wants miracles, the patient who argues about every recommendation - because they know that one bad patient can generate a complaint that costs them everything.

This is not for the physician who wants to get rich quick. If that is your motivation, go open a med spa and inject Botox for cash. The regulatory path is clearer and the liability is lower. This is not for the physician who thinks peptides are a magic bullet that will fix patients who will not change their diets, exercise, sleep, or stress levels. This is not for the physician who thinks they can skip documentation because their patients love them. Patients who love you will still file complaints when things go wrong. Love turns to litigation faster than you think.

If you are the kind of physician who wants to do this right - who wants to help patients explore therapies that might genuinely improve their lives while keeping your license, your reputation, and your sanity intact - then read on. I am going to show you exactly how to do that. It is not complicated. It is not easy either. It requires discipline, consistency, attention to detail, and a willingness to be the bad guy sometimes. But it works. I have watched physicians practice this way for decades without a single board complaint. And I have watched physicians who cut corners lose everything in six months.

The difference is not luck. The difference is not clinical skill. The difference is operational rigor. This book is the manual for that rigor. Read it. Use it. Keep it on your desk where you can see it. And when a patient pushes you to do something that does not feel right, open it to the section on saying no. That section will save you more often than any peptide ever will.

Executive Summary: The Rules of Flying Under the Radar

You want the whole book in ten rules? Here they are. Read them. Memorize them. Tape them to your desk. Violate any of them at your peril.

Patient Demand Is Not Medical Necessity - Ever

Let me say this as plainly as I can: a patient asking for a peptide is not a medical indication. It is the beginning of a conversation, not the end of one. The fact that a patient watched a podcast, read a forum post, or heard about something from their gym buddy does not create a clinical reason to prescribe. You are a physician, not a pharmacy vending machine. Your job is to evaluate, not to fulfill orders.

Every time a patient comes to you requesting a specific therapy, you have three questions to answer before you even think about writing anything. One: what is the clinical problem we are trying to solve? Two: what evidence supports using this specific therapy for this specific patient? Three: can I explain my reasoning to a skeptical stranger who has never heard of this peptide and already thinks I am a quack? If you cannot answer all three questions with a clear, chart-documented rationale, you do not prescribe. Full stop. Patient enthusiasm is not a substitute for clinical reasoning. The patient who "really wants to try it" is the same patient who will file a board complaint six months later when their expectations were not met. Demand starts the evaluation. It never completes it.

Your Chart Is Your Shield - Write It Like a Lawyer Will Read It

Here is a lesson I learned in forty years of paralegal work: the chart is the only thing that matters when your case goes sideways. Your memory is worthless. Your good intentions are worthless. Your patient's glowing testimonial is worthless. The only thing that counts is what you wrote down at the time, in the moment, when the decision was made.

Write your chart notes like a prosecutor is going to read them aloud at a hearing. Because someday, one might. Every chart note needs to tell a complete story: why the patient presented, what you evaluated, what you considered, what you decided, why you decided it, what alternatives were discussed, what risks were disclosed, what monitoring was planned, and what the patient agreed to. If your chart note is three sentences and a prescription, you might as well write "Please investigate me" at the top. I have seen board reviewers laugh at notes that thin -actually laugh, in the middle of hearings - while the physician's attorney sank lower in his chair.

The standard is not "did I document the prescription?" The standard is "can a stranger who knows nothing about this patient or this therapy follow my reasoning and conclude that the decision was medically reasonable?" If the answer is no, rewrite the note. Charts are written for reviewers, not for your convenience. Get that through your head now.

Controlled Substances Are for Doctors Who Want to Be Investigated

Let me be brutally clear about this: controlled substances are a magnet for regulatory attention. The DEA, the state medical board, the local prosecutor's office, the pharmacy auditor - they all have their eyes on controlled substance prescribing. Add peptide therapy to the mix and you have created a profile that screams "alternative medicine prescriber who might be over his head." You do not need that profile.

If you are running a peptide practice, there is almost no clinical reason to have controlled substances in the same prescribing record. Pain management is a different specialty. Benzodiazepines are a different specialty. Stimulants are a different specialty. If a patient needs those things, refer them to someone who does that work. Your job is metabolic health, recovery, optimization, anti-aging, weight management - whatever you call it - and none of those things require DEA-scheduled drugs. The moment you start prescribing testosterone cypionate, you need to be extra careful, and if you are adding anything scheduled beyond that, you are asking for a world of scrutiny you do not need.

Every controlled substance prescription goes into a database. Every database entry is searchable. Every search can trigger an audit. Every audit can lead to an investigation. Every investigation can cost you fifty thousand dollars in legal fees even if you did nothing wrong. Do the math. Is that prescription worth it? Almost never. Keep your prescribing profile clean.

Let the pain management doctors fight with the DEA. You have enough to worry about.

Insurance Is a Trap - Cash-Pay Is Your Only Protection

If there is one thing my eleven years as an investment banker taught me, it is this: when an insurance company is involved, the rules stop being medical and start being financial. Insurance companies do not care about patient outcomes. They care about claims denials, prior authorization requirements, formulary restrictions, and medical necessity criteria that change without notice. The moment you bill insurance for a peptide therapy - assuming you even can, which in most cases you cannot - you have invited a third party into your clinical decision-making who has no medical training and every financial incentive to deny your claim.

But it gets worse. Insurance creates a paper trail that cash-pay does not. Every claim generates a record. Every denied claim generates an audit opportunity. Every audit opportunity generates exposure. And here is the part most physicians miss: insurance companies share data with state medical boards. They have formal and informal reporting relationships. A pattern of unusual claims, a cluster of denied prior authorizations, a whistleblower phone call from a disgruntled claims processor - any of these can put your name in front of a board investigator faster than you think.

Cash-pay medicine is not about tax evasion or hiding income. It is about clinical autonomy. When a patient pays you directly, the only relationship that exists is between you and the patient. No third-party reviewer is questioning your medical necessity. No auditor is combing through your CPT codes. No insurance fraud investigator is looking for patterns. The board can still investigate you - they can investigate anyone - but the path is harder. They need a complaint. They need a patient who is unhappy enough to file one. They need a chart that looks suspicious when they request it. Cash-pay does not make you invisible. It makes you harder to see. In this business, harder to see is the difference between a quiet practice and a front-page story.

Charge premium prices. If you are the cheapest peptide clinic in town, you look like a vial shop. Expensive medicine looks like supervised clinical care. Cheap medicine looks like medication distribution. The board knows the difference. So do patients. Price yourself like a specialist because you are one.

Your PCP Relationship Is Your Secret Weapon

This rule is so simple and so powerful that I am amazed how many peptide physicians ignore it. Every patient you treat should have a primary care physician who knows what you are doing. Not as a courtesy. As a strategic defense.

When a patient has a PCP who is aware of their peptide therapy, several good things happen. First, the PCP becomes a second set of eyes monitoring for side effects, drug interactions, and changes in the patient's condition. Second, the PCP's awareness demonstrates to any reviewer that you were not practicing in secret or behind another doctor's back. Third, if a complaint ever arises, the PCP can be a witness - maybe not a friendly one, but at least an informed one- who can say "Yes, I knew about the therapy. I was monitoring. I was kept in the loop." That is worth its weight in gold.

Informed Consent Is Not a Piece of Paper - It Is Your Lifeline

I have seen thousands of informed consent forms over forty years, and I can tell you without hesitation that ninety percent of them are garbage. They are legal documents written by attorneys to protect the practice, not educational tools written to inform the patient. They are fifteen pages of dense text in eight-point font that no patient has ever read thoroughly. They cover everything and explain nothing. They create the illusion of protection while providing almost none.

Real informed consent is a conversation, documented. The paper is proof that the conversation happened. It is not the conversation itself.

Your consent process needs to cover the basics in plain English: what the therapy is, what it is supposed to do, what the evidence says, what the risks are, what the alternatives are, what the patient needs to do, what the monitoring looks like, what the stop criteria are, and - this is critical - what you are not promising. No results are guaranteed. No outcomes are assured. The therapy may not work. The patient may have side effects. The therapy is off-label, or compounded, or investigational, or whatever it actually is. Say it plainly. Write it plainly. Have the patient initial each section so you can prove they were told.

Document the discussion. Make the form a record of understanding, not a substitute for it.

And one more thing: consent does not rescue poor judgment. You cannot get a patient to sign away a bad prescription. If the therapy was not medically appropriate, no amount of consent language will save you. Consent is a necessary condition, not a sufficient one. It is the floor, not the ceiling.

Charge What You're Worth - Cheap Doctors Look Like Vial Shops

This is business advice, but it is also compliance advice, and if you do not understand why, you need to read this section twice. The board does not just look at your charts. They look at your pricing. They look at your business model. They ask a simple question: is this a medical practice that happens to sell therapies, or is this a product distribution business that happens to employ a physician?

If your pricing is $99 a month for unlimited access to injectable peptides, you are not a medical practice. You are a subscription vial service. The board can see that. A prosecutor can see that. A jury can see that. Your prices need to reflect the actual value of what you provide: evaluation, clinical judgment, informed consent, monitoring, follow-up, risk management, and ongoing supervision. That is what patients are paying for. The vial is incidental.

Price your program at a level that makes sense for the work involved. Initial consultations should cost hundreds of dollars. Monthly monitoring should cost hundreds of dollars. Labs should be billed separately. Supplements and adjunct therapies should be additional. The total cost of a three-month peptide program should be in the thousands, not the hundreds. Expensive care looks like supervised medicine. Cheap care looks like bulk purchasing. The line between those two perceptions is the line between a thriving practice and an investigation.

Patients who cannot afford your prices are not your patients. This is hard for compassionate physicians to hear, but financial stress creates complaints. A patient who goes into debt for peptide therapy is a patient who will blame you when their credit card bill arrives, regardless of whether the therapy worked. A patient who skimps on monitoring because they cannot afford follow-up visits is a patient who will have a bad outcome and then claim you never followed up. Price creates a filter. The right patients pay your prices and follow your protocols. The wrong patients argue about cost, skip appointments, and file complaints. Let them go to the cheap clinic down the street. That clinic will not be there in two years anyway.

No Headache Patients, No High-Maintenance Patients, No Patients Who Can't Afford You

This rule sounds harsh. It is. It is also one of the most important rules in this book. There are patients who are not worth treating, no matter how much they want what you offer. The headache patient who argues about every recommendation, questions every fee, calls your office three times a week with questions they could Google, demands discounts, complains about wait times, and second-guesses your clinical judgment - that patient is a complaint waiting to happen. They consume ten times the staff resources of a normal patient. They create stress in your office. They poison the culture. And when something goes wrong, even slightly wrong, they are on the phone to the medical board before you have finished your morning coffee.

High-maintenance patients are not necessarily bad people. Some of them are anxious. Some of them have been failed by the medical system and are understandably wary. Some of them just have personalities that require more energy than you have to give. It does not matter why they are high-maintenance. What matters is that your practice is not a charity and your emotional bandwidth is not unlimited. Every hour you spend managing a difficult patient is an hour you are not spending on patients who follow instructions, appreciate your care, and refer their friends. The math does not work.

Patients who cannot afford you are in the same category. This is not about elitism. It is about reality. A patient who cannot afford your program will skip labs to save money. They will stretch their vials to make them last longer. They will miss follow-up appointments. They will buy cheaper products online when your pharmacy charges too much. They will blame you when their compromised protocol does not work. And they will file complaints about the cost while they are doing it all. You cannot help everyone. You can help the patients who can afford to do it right. That is your market. Accept it and move on.

Happy Patients Refer Friends - Unhappy Patients File Complaints

This is the most important business principle in medicine, and it applies double to peptide practices. The vast majority of board complaints do not come from random audits. They come from patient complaints. And patient complaints come from unmet expectations. An unhappy patient with access to the internet and a state board website is a weapon pointed directly at your license.

Your entire practice should be designed around creating patients who are satisfied - not because you overpromise, but because you deliver what you promise with professionalism, transparency, and care. The patient who feels heard, respected, monitored, and informed will tell their friends. They will post positive reviews. They will defend you if anyone asks. They will tolerate a less-than-perfect outcome because they trust your process.

The patient who feels rushed, deceived, overcharged, ignored, or dismissed will tell everyone too. They will post bad reviews. They will call the board. They will talk to plaintiff attorneys. They will join online forums dedicated to complaining about practices like yours. And they will be believed, because boards and juries start from the assumption that patients are vulnerable and physicians are powerful. It is not fair, but it is reality.

You control which kind of patient experience you create. Return phone calls promptly. Answer questions patiently. Follow up without being reminded. Explain setbacks honestly. Adjust protocols thoughtfully. Document everything. Treat every patient interaction like it is being recorded, because in the age of smartphones, it might be. The patient experience is not a luxury in cash-pay medicine. It is your entire defense strategy.

When in Doubt, Say No - The Easiest Prescription to Defend Is the One You Didn't Write

I am going to end this executive summary with the single most valuable piece of advice I can give you, and I want you to tattoo it on the inside of your eyelids if necessary. When you are unsure whether to prescribe, the answer is no. When the patient's history is thin, the answer is no. When the patient argues with your screening criteria, the answer is no. When the patient cannot afford proper monitoring, the answer is no. When the patient will not involve their PCP, the answer is no. When the patient found you through a Reddit thread and already knows exactly what they want, the answer is no. When anything about the case feels off, the answer is no.

You do not need a reason to say yes. You need a reason. The default answer in peptide medicine is no. Every yes is a conscious, documented, defensible decision that you made because the clinical picture supported it, the patient was appropriate, the pharmacy was legitimate, the monitoring was in place, and the chart was ready to explain it all. If any of those conditions is not met, the answer is no.

Saying no costs you a patient. Maybe a few hundred dollars in lost revenue. Saying yes when you should have said no costs you your license. It costs you your reputation. It costs you your ability to practice medicine ever again. It costs you your house if the malpractice settlement is big enough. The math is not complicated. A lost patient is a rounding error. A lost license is your life.

The easiest prescription to defend is the one you never wrote. The easiest chart to explain is the one that says "Patient requested therapy. After evaluation, determined not medically appropriate at this time. Alternatives discussed. PCP follow-up recommended." That note takes five minutes to write and zero years to defend. Compare that to the note that says "Patient wanted BPC-157. Prescribed. Will follow up." That note takes thirty seconds to write and might cost you everything.

Learn to say no. Practice saying no. Get comfortable saying no. Your staff should know that "Dr. Smith will review and decide" means no until the doctor says yes. Your patients should know that your evaluation is real and your standards are high. The word no is the most powerful tool in your compliance arsenal. Use it liberally. Use it proudly. Use it every single time your gut tells you something is not right.

Welcome to peptide medicine. It is rewarding work. It helps patients who have nowhere else to turn. It fills gaps that the standard medical system leaves wide open. But it is not safe territory. It is regulated by people who do not understand it, scrutinized by boards who distrust it, and populated by patients who heard about it on the internet. You need to be smart. You need to be careful. You need to be disciplined. And you need this book.

Turn the page. Let us get to work.

PART I: THE LANDSCAPE

Understanding the peptide world, the regulatory framework, and why you need to pay attention.

1 - Peptides Are Here - Deal With It

Peptides are in your waiting room right now whether you like it or not

Let me tell you something you already suspect but maybe haven't fully accepted. That patient sitting in exam room three - the forty-seven-year-old executive who dropped thirty pounds last year and showed up looking leaner than you've ever seen him - he's not just doing CrossFit. That woman in room two who asked you about "something called semaglutide" three months ago and now wants to know about "these peptide things for recovery" because she started tennis again? She's already been online. That fifty-five-year-old man in room five who mentioned his "anti-aging protocol" in passing and said he feels great? He's injecting something you didn't prescribe, from a vial you've never seen, and he thinks he's being careful because the website had a certificate of analysis.

Peptides are already in your exam room. Right now. Today. This week. Not next year. Not when the medical societies figure out how to feel about them. Not when the FDA publishes a nice neat guideline that tells you exactly what to do. Today. And every day you pretend otherwise is a day you become less relevant to your own patients.

I have been a registered nurse for over twenty years, an investment banker for eleven, and a paralegal for forty. I have watched good physicians lose their licenses over stupid things they didn't think would matter. I have watched smart doctors get blindsided by complaints that started with a patient doing something the doctor refused to acknowledge. And I have watched even better doctors - careful doctors - get investigated because they had no idea what their patients were already doing until it was too late.

This chapter is not here to sell you on peptides. I don't care if you ever prescribe a single one. What I care about - what this entire book cares about - is that you understand what is happening in your own practice, to your own patients, whether you choose to participate or not. Because the world is not waiting for your permission. The internet does not pause because you haven't read the latest FDA policy update. Your patients are already making decisions, and if you are not in that conversation, they are having it without you.

Here is the first thing you need to internalize. A peptide is not a fringe compound used only by bodybuilders and biohackers anymore. Semaglutide changed the game. Tirzepatide changed it again. When millions of Americans started losing dramatic amounts of weight on GLP-1 receptor agonists, the word "peptide" went from obscure science talk to dinner table conversation. Your patients now know that some peptides are FDA-approved. They know that these drugs work. And they have drawn a logical conclusion from those two facts: maybe other peptides work too. Maybe the ones that aren't FDA-approved are just "held up in the system."Maybe the research chemicals they saw on that forum are basically the same thing, just"cheaper because you don't need a prescription."

That patient reasoning is wrong on several levels. But you will never correct it if you don't engage with it.

Let me give you a real scenario. I know a physician - internal medicine, very respectable practice, been at it twenty years - who had a patient develop a septic joint. The patient, a sixty-two-year-old accountant, had been buying BPC-157 online, reconstituting it himself, and injecting it into his knee for "tendon support." He wasn't some reckless kid. He was a careful, middle-class man who read reviews, compared vendors, watched YouTube tutorials on sterile technique, and genuinely believed he was being responsible. The vial he used that week was contaminated. Within forty-eight hours he had a joint infection that required surgical washout, six weeks of IV antibiotics, and permanent damage to his knee mobility. The patient didn't sue the online vendor - the vendor had a terms of service disclaimer, was located overseas, and accepted only cryptocurrency. The patient sued the doctor. Why the doctor? Because the doctor had been treating this man's knee pain for two years, had never asked what else the patient was doing, and the plaintiff's attorney argued that a reasonable physician in ongoing care for knee symptoms should have inquired about self-injection. The case settled. It settled for enough to make the doctor's malpractice carrier raise his premiums for the next five years. All because the doctor thought "I don't prescribe peptides" meant peptides weren't his problem.

You think that patient should have known better? Sure. He should have. But he didn't. And you think the board cares that you meant well? They don't. They care what the chart shows. And the chart showed a physician who never asked, never documented a warning, and never acknowledged a reality that every physician in America should recognize by now: patients are self-medicating with injectable compounds they buy on the internet, and pretending this isn't happening doesn't protect you - it makes you look willfully blind when it goes wrong.

So here's what you do. You ask. Directly. Shamelessly. Without judgment. You ask every patient with unexplained weight loss if they are using anything they bought online. You ask every patient with joint pain what they are injecting. You ask every patient interested in "anti-aging" or "recovery" or "metabolic health" what they are already doing. And you document the answer. Every time. Because even if the answer is "nothing," the question itself protects you. The chart that shows you asked, you warned, you educated, and you offered a safer pathway -that chart is your first line of defense when the board comes knocking.

And they come knocking for every single complaint. Every one. We'll get to that later.

Your patients are already buying research chemicals online and injecting themselves

Most patients won't wait for you. That's the reality, and no amount of professional indignation changes it. They read online. They join groups. They compare vendors. They watch videos of other people mixing powders with bacteriostatic water and injecting themselves in the abdomen. And they do all of this before they ever have a serious medical conversation with you. In many cases, they do it without ever intending to tell you at all.

Why would they hide it? For the same reason patients hide all kinds of things: shame, fear of judgment, belief that you won't approve, or simply the conviction that they have already done their homework and you will just tell them no. The internet has created a parallel medical education system, and it is not run by doctors. It is run by influencers, forum moderators, affiliate marketers, and people with no medical training who happen to look good on camera and have affiliate codes for three peptide vendors.

Your job is not moral outrage. Your job is not to clutch your pearls because a patient bought something labeled "research use only" and injected it anyway. Your job is risk assessment

-real, practical, documented risk assessment. And you cannot assess risk you refuse to acknowledge exists.

Let me walk you through what your patient sees when they go online. They type "BPC-157 tendon healing" into a search engine. The first page of results shows forum threads with hundreds of posts describing personal experiences. They find a Reddit community with fifty thousand members sharing "protocols." They find a YouTube video with a charismatic man in a lab coat - not a physician, a lab coat he bought online - explaining "the science" in confident terms that sound scientific enough to be convincing. They find three or four vendor websites with professional layouts, certificates of analysis, customer reviews, and discount codes in the video description. The prices are a fraction of what any legitimate medical program would cost. The whole experience feels like a community. Like research. Like taking control of their own health because the medical system is too slow, too expensive, and too dismissive.

Now, you and I both know that most of what they are reading is garbage. The forum posts are self-selected anecdotes from people who had good experiences - the ones who got infections or had no results stopped posting. The YouTube expert has a financial relationship with every vendor he recommends. The certificate of analysis proves chemical identity at best, and may be forged or outdated at worst. It proves nothing about sterility, endotoxin safety, handling, storage, or whether the powder that was tested is the same powder in the vial that arrived at the patient's door.

But your patient does not know that. Or if they suspect it, the suspicion gets drowned out by desperation, by hope, by the social proof of fifty thousand forum members, and by the reassuringly low price.

And here is what they don't have in that entire transaction: a physician evaluating whether the therapy makes sense for their specific medical situation. A pharmacist verifying sterility and handling. A medical record documenting what was used. An informed consent process explaining risks, unknowns, and alternatives. A monitoring plan with stop criteria and follow-up. An adverse-event reporting pathway. Any of the things that distinguish medicine from self-experimentation.

That is the void that the grey market fills. It is not a product problem. It is a supervision problem. And the only way to address it is for physicians like you to step into the gap - not by endorsing everything, not by becoming a peptide enthusiast, but by providing the medical supervision that these patients desperately need and are currently doing without.

The first questions you ask matter. They set the tone for everything that follows. When a patient mentions peptides, or recovery, or anti-aging, or metabolic optimization, here is what you ask: What did you buy? From where? What dose? What route? How often? Who told you to use it? What happened after? Any side effects? Any infection? Any allergic reaction? Any changes in blood work? Are you still using it?

That conversation is not approval. It is medicine. Basic, fundamental, cannot-protect-patients-from-facts-you-refuse-to-ask-about medicine. And when you have the answers, you document them. You document the specific products. You document the source. You document the dose and route. You document the warning you gave against unverified products. You document the risks you discussed. And you document the legitimate medical pathway you offered as an alternative.

Your chart needs to show a physician who did not ignore patient self-experimentation. Because the chart that shows ignorance is the chart that loses the board hearing.

Ignoring peptides doesn't make patients safer - it makes you irrelevant

Let me be blunt about what happens when you refuse to engage. The patient does not say,"Well, my doctor doesn't think peptides are appropriate, so I guess I won't use them." The patient says, "My doctor doesn't know anything about this stuff," and then goes right back to the internet where someone is always willing to take their money and tell them what they want to hear.

You become irrelevant. Not morally superior. Not medically conservative. Irrelevant. And irrelevance is a dangerous professional position. A physician who is irrelevant to their patients'health decisions is a physician who cannot practice preventive medicine, cannot catch problems early, cannot guide patients toward safer choices, and cannot document the kind of engaged, informed medical relationship that protects them when something goes wrong.

I have heard doctors say things like "I don't believe in peptides" or "I'm not getting involved in that" or "That's not real medicine." Those are opinions, and everyone is entitled to their opinions. But opinions do not change patient behavior. Patient behavior is driven by pain, hope, fear, vanity, social pressure, internet influence, and the fundamental human desire to feel better. If you think your disapproval is a sufficient deterrent, you have not been paying attention to the last twenty years of healthcare consumerism.

Here is what actually makes patients safer: a physician who knows what they are doing, who asks direct questions, who provides honest education about risks and benefits, who offers a supervised medical pathway when appropriate, and who documents everything. That physician has a chance to intercept a patient before they buy a contaminated vial. That physician has a chance to catch a contraindication that the internet forum never mentioned. That physician has a chance to say no - a documented, defensible, clinically reasoned no - when the risk is too high. And that physician has a chart that will stand up to scrutiny if the patient goes ahead with self-treatment anyway and something goes wrong.

The physician who ignores peptides has none of those protections. They are flying blind, and they don't even know it. They are seeing patients for weight management while those patients are already on compounded GLP-1s they bought through telehealth apps. They are treating knee pain while patients are injecting mystery powders from overseas. They are managing metabolic syndrome while patients are cycling through unregulated "fat loss peptides" they read about on a podcast. And every single one of those patients represents a potential adverse event, a potential complaint, and a potential board investigation - all happening in a blind spot the physician created themselves.

You want to know the real risk? It's not that you prescribe a peptide and something goes wrong. That happens, and we'll talk about how to manage it. The real risk is that you never prescribed anything, never asked anything, never documented anything, and a patient you've been seeing for years ends up in the emergency room with a problem you could have prevented if you had just been willing to have an uncomfortable conversation.

The board does not give credit for clean hands. The board reads the chart. And the chart that shows a pattern of ignoring patient behavior because the physician found it inconvenient or distasteful is the chart that looks like substandard care.

So get over it. Peptides are not a moral issue. They are a clinical reality. Treat them like one.

The internet is the new prescriber: influencers, forums, and discount codes

If you want to understand why patients choose the grey market over supervised medical care, you need to understand what they are actually experiencing online. Because it is not just information. It is a full ecosystem designed to convert curiosity into purchase as smoothly as possible.

The modern patient journey for peptide information typically starts with a social media post or a podcast mention. A fitness influencer talks about their "recovery stack." A longevity expert mentions a "breakthrough peptide for metabolism." A celebrity doctor - and I use the term loosely - discusses the future of regenerative medicine in terms so optimistic that they might as well be reading from a sales brochure. The patient hears something that resonates with their own health concerns. They search for more information.

The search results lead them to communities. Reddit's peptide communities have hundreds of thousands of members. Discord servers host real-time discussions with experienced users who are happy to answer questions and share "protocols." Facebook groups offer the veneer of community support, with members posting before-and-after photos, sharing vendor experiences, and encouraging newcomers to "do their research." The research, of course, consists of reading more forum posts.

Then comes the education layer. YouTube videos with impressive production values explain peptide mechanisms using animated graphics and confident narration. The hosts are often affiliated with peptide vendors - a fact disclosed in the video description in font size that would require a magnifying glass to read - but the content is presented as independent medical education. The science is real enough to be credible and oversimplified enough to be reassuring. Risks are mentioned briefly, if at all, usually framed as "mild and temporary" or"dose-dependent and manageable."

And then the conversion. The patient clicks an affiliate link. The vendor website looks professional. It has a certificate of analysis displayed prominently. It has customer reviews -which are, of course, unverified. It has a clean checkout process, discreet shipping, and prices that are a fraction of what any legitimate medical program would cost. The label on the vial says "research use only" or "not for human consumption," but the website's FAQ section explains - with a knowing wink - that this is "just for legal compliance" and that "many researchers choose to study these compounds in vivo." The patient understands exactly what that means. Everyone understands what that means. It is a fiction maintained by mutual pretense, and it exists specifically to transfer liability from the seller to the buyer.

Within a week, a vial of white powder arrives at the patient's door. The patient mixes it with bacteriostatic water they bought separately, draws it into an insulin syringe they bought at the pharmacy - the pharmacist didn't ask what it was for - and injects it into their abdomen based on instructions they read in a forum post.

This is the system your patients are using. Right now. While you are reading this book. The question is not whether this system is dangerous - it obviously is. The question is whether you are going to be part of the solution or whether you are going to pretend the system doesn't exist while your patients use it without you.

The internet may be the patient's first prescriber. It should not be the last adult in the room. That adult needs to be you. Not because you endorse everything the internet sells - you absolutely should not - but because you are the only person in this entire chain who is actually accountable for patient outcomes. The influencer is not accountable. The forum moderator is not accountable. The vendor is not accountable. You are. And accountability requires engagement.

Here is the practical reality. Every patient who walks into your office has been shaped by this ecosystem whether they know it or not. They have expectations set by forum anecdotes. They have risk perceptions shaped by YouTube hosts with financial conflicts of interest. They have price expectations set by grey market vendors. They have a sense of what is "normal" based on what fifty thousand internet strangers say they are doing. Your job is not to match the internet's enthusiasm. Your job is to provide a medical reality check, documented and defensible, that gives the patient actual information instead of marketing dressed up as community.

When a patient tells you they saw something online, ask them to show you. When they mention a forum, ask which one. When they reference a "protocol," ask where they found it. Not because you are investigating them - because you need to understand the information environment they are operating in. The patient who thinks reconstituting a vial with tap water is acceptable because someone on Reddit said it was fine needs very different education from the patient who found a relatively balanced discussion of risks and benefits. You cannot tailor your counseling if you don't know what they have already been told.

And always, always, document the warning you gave against research-use-only products. Document the risks you discussed. Document the legitimate medical pathway you offered. Because when that patient ends up in the emergency room with an infection, or a reaction, or a problem they didn't expect, the chart that shows you engaged, warned, and offered alternatives is the chart that keeps your license safe.

The chart that shows you had no idea what they were doing because you never asked? That chart is a professional liability waiting to happen.

Short chains of amino acids - that's it, that's the definition

I am going to give you the straight explanation, and then we are going to move on to what actually matters for your practice. A peptide is a short chain of amino acids. That's it. That's the definition. Amino acids are the individual building blocks. When you string a few of them together - usually somewhere between two and fifty - you have a peptide. When you string a lot of them together, you have a protein. Your body is full of peptides. It makes them naturally. It uses them as signals - chemical messengers that tell different parts of the body what to do. Some peptides control appetite. Some affect metabolism. Some regulate growth hormone release. Some modulate inflammation and immune response. Some help repair tissue.

Some influence sexual function. The list is long, and it gets longer every year as researchers identify new signaling pathways.

That is what a peptide is. It is not magic. It is not nanotechnology. It is not something from a science fiction movie. It is a short chain of amino acids that acts as a biological signal. Some of those signals are well-understood, well-studied, and FDA-approved for specific uses. Some are poorly studied, overmarketed, and used primarily by people who read too much internet. And some are in between - showing real promise in early research but lacking the kind of large-scale human trials that would make any responsible physician comfortable using them routinely.

The point I want you to carry through this entire book is this: the word "peptide" tells you what kind of molecule you are dealing with. It does not tell you whether that molecule is safe, effective, legal, appropriate for your patient, or worth the professional risk of prescribing it. Those are separate questions, and they need separate answers. Every time.

I have seen physicians get into trouble because they heard "peptide" and either got excited -"this is the future of medicine" - or got dismissive - "this is all internet nonsense." Neither posture is clinically useful. The useful posture is the one that treats each peptide as its own clinical entity, with its own evidence base, its own risk profile, its own regulatory status, and its own documentation requirements. Semaglutide is a peptide. So is BPC-157. They are not the same thing. They are not even in the same category of medical decision-making. And if you can't articulate exactly why they are different, you have no business prescribing either one.

Your body already uses peptides as signals. That is not a selling point. It is a biological fact. Insulin is a peptide, and it has saved more lives than probably any other medication in history. Modern GLP-1 receptor agonists like semaglutide and tirzepatide are peptides, and they are transforming obesity medicine in ways that would have seemed impossible ten years ago. Oxytocin is a peptide. Tesamorelin is a peptide. These are real drugs with real evidence, real FDA labels or legitimate clinical pathways, and real effects on real patients.

But the existence of legitimate peptide drugs does not legitimize every compound that happens to be made of amino acids. The grey market sells peptides that have never been through human clinical trials. The internet promotes peptides based on animal studies, theoretical mechanisms, or forum anecdotes. Compounding pharmacies operate in a constantly shifting regulatory environment where what is legal today may be restricted tomorrow. And patients routinely conflate all of these categories because they all share the same label: peptide.

Your job is to keep them separate. In your thinking. In your prescribing. In your documentation. And most importantly, in your patient counseling. When a patient says "I want to try peptides," your response should not be "yes" or "no." Your response should be "which peptide, for what purpose, based on what evidence, from what source, with what monitoring, and what is the regulatory status?" If you cannot answer those questions to your own satisfaction, you cannot prescribe. It is that simple.

Your body already uses them as signals - some control appetite, some affect metabolism, some repair tissue

Let me explain what I mean when I say peptides are biological signals. Think of your body as a vast communication network. Hormones are one type of signal. Neurotransmitters are another. Peptides are a third. They travel through the bloodstream or act locally at tissue sites, binding to specific receptors and triggering cellular responses. When a peptide binds to its receptor, it is essentially delivering a message: release growth hormone, reduce inflammation, increase insulin sensitivity, stimulate tissue repair, suppress appetite - whatever the particular signal happens to be.

This signaling function is why peptides are so attractive as therapeutic agents. If a patient's body is not producing enough of a particular signal, or if the signal is not reaching its target effectively, an exogenous peptide can potentially restore normal function. Semaglutide mimics a gut hormone called GLP-1 that signals satiety and slows gastric emptying. In patients whose natural GLP-1 signaling is insufficient, adding semaglutide can dramatically reduce appetite and improve glycemic control. That is not mysterious. It is physiology, applied therapeutically.

Sermorelin and tesamorelin mimic growth hormone-releasing hormone, signaling the pituitary to produce more of the patient's own growth hormone. They don't replace growth hormone directly - they stimulate the body to make more. This matters because the body's feedback systems still provide some regulatory control, unlike direct recombinant growth hormone which can push IGF-1 levels higher than the body would naturally allow.

BPC-157, which we will discuss extensively in this book, is thought to promote angiogenesis, fibroblast migration, and tissue repair through multiple signaling pathways. The evidence base is overwhelmingly preclinical - mostly animal studies - but the mechanism is biologically plausible, which is why it generates so much interest and why so many patients are already using it, supervised or not.

Thymosin beta-4 and its fragment TB-500 are involved in actin regulation and cell migration, processes fundamental to wound healing and tissue remodeling. Thymosin alpha-1 modulates immune signaling through T-cell maturation and cytokine pathways. MOTS-c appears to signal from mitochondria to the nucleus, influencing metabolic pathways including glucose handling and insulin sensitivity.

Each of these compounds has a different mechanism. Each targets different pathways. Each has different evidence, different risks, different regulatory status, and different appropriate clinical uses. The fact that they are all peptides is medically trivial compared to these differences. And yet patients routinely treat them as interchangeable because they share a category label.

Your job is to unpack that label. Every time. When a patient says "I heard peptides are good for recovery," you need to ask: what kind of recovery? Tissue repair? Muscle recovery after exercise? Recovery from surgery? Recovery from illness? Because the peptide that might be relevant for tendon healing is not the same as the peptide that might be relevant for immune modulation, and neither is the same as the peptide that affects appetite and weight loss. The word "recovery" is as medically specific as the word "treatment" - which is to say, not specific at all.

The same principle applies to "anti-aging," "metabolic health," "immune support,""performance enhancement," and all the other vague categories patients bring into your office. These are marketing concepts, not medical indications. Your job is to translate them into clinical problems with specific characteristics, specific evidence-based interventions, specific monitoring plans, and specific endpoints. If you cannot define the clinical problem precisely, you cannot select an appropriate therapy. And if you cannot select an appropriate therapy with a defensible rationale, you should not be prescribing.

This is where I see the most sloppiness in peptide practices. A patient comes in with a vague goal - "I want more energy" or "I want to lose weight" or "I want to recover faster" - and the physician reaches for a peptide because that is what the practice sells. No careful diagnostic reasoning. No systematic evaluation of alternatives. No clear endpoint for measuring success. Just product-matching to patient desire, documented with a vague note that provides no actual medical reasoning. That is not medicine. That is retail with a prescription pad. And it will not survive a board review.

A real medical evaluation for a patient interested in peptide therapy looks like this: define the clinical problem in specific terms; review what has already been tried; evaluate the patient's medical history for contraindications; assess the evidence for proposed interventions; explain the regulatory status, known risks, and unknowns; discuss alternatives including doing nothing; establish measurable endpoints; set a follow-up schedule with stop criteria; document everything; and obtain informed consent that actually informs. If that sounds like a lot of work, it is. But it is the difference between a medical practice and a vending machine. And the board knows the difference when they see it.

The word "peptide" is not a selling point - mechanism, evidence, and source matter

I need to hammer this point home because I see physicians make this mistake constantly. They use "peptide" as if it carries some automatic medical legitimacy. They put it on their website. They mention it in marketing. They talk about "peptide therapy" as a category, as if that phrase means something specific to patients. It doesn't. It means whatever the patient imagines it means, and what they imagine is usually wrong.

The word "peptide" is not a selling point. It is a chemical classification. You know what else is a peptide? Snake venom. Ricin is a peptide-like compound. The word tells you about molecular structure, not clinical value. What matters is mechanism, evidence, source, and appropriateness for the individual patient. Those four factors determine whether a particular peptide therapy is defensible, not the fact that it happens to be made of amino acids.

Mechanism matters because it determines what the peptide actually does in the body, which pathways it affects, and what the downstream effects might be. A physician who prescribes without understanding mechanism is prescribing blind. If you cannot explain to a patient, in plain English, how the proposed therapy works and what it is supposed to accomplish, you are not ready to prescribe it.

Evidence matters because it determines how confident you can be that the therapy works and how well-characterized the risk profile is. FDA-approved peptides with large randomized trials have strong evidence. Peptides with only animal studies have weak evidence. Both might have a role in clinical practice, but the documentation burden is radically different. A physician who prescribes a high-evidence therapy needs standard documentation. A physician who prescribes a low-evidence therapy needs extraordinary documentation - and the chart better show that the physician knew exactly how thin the evidence was and counseled the patient accordingly.

Source matters because it determines whether the product the patient receives is what it claims to be, whether it is sterile, whether it is properly compounded, and whether it was produced under conditions that meet minimum quality standards. A peptide from a licensed 503A compounding pharmacy is not the same as a peptide from a 503B outsourcing facility, which is not the same as a peptide from an internet vendor with a "certificate of analysis" that may or may not be genuine. Source is a safety issue. Source is a legal issue. Source is a documentation issue. And source is where a lot of physicians get sloppy because they assume the pharmacy has it handled. Maybe they do. Maybe they don't. Verify. Every time.

Appropriateness for the individual patient matters because even a well-evidenced, properly sourced peptide can be the wrong choice for a particular person. The patient with a history of medullary thyroid carcinoma should not receive a GLP-1 agonist. The patient with a pituitary tumor should not receive growth hormone secretagogues. The patient with active cancer should probably avoid pro-angiogenic repair peptides. The patient with uncontrolled hypertension should not receive melanocortin agonists. The patient who is pregnant, breastfeeding, or trying to conceive needs extra scrutiny for any peptide therapy. The patient with unrealistic expectations needs counseling before any therapy, not after they are disappointed.

These are medical basics. I am not telling you anything you don't know. But I am telling you that the hype around peptides makes some physicians forget these basics. They get excited about the new frontier. Or they get pressured by patients who want what they saw online. Or they build a business model around peptide sales and start treating every patient as a potential conversion. And slowly, imperceptibly, the medicine gets thinner while the marketing gets louder. That is the path to a board investigation. That is the path I am trying to keep you off.

Interest is not evidence. Patient demand is not medical necessity. A good chart explains the difference. Every single time.

Categories that must stay separate: FDA-approved, off-label, compounded, investigational, and research-use-only

This is the section that will keep you out of the most trouble if you internalize it. Because the single most common mistake physicians make with peptide therapy is conflating categories that are legally and clinically distinct. When you throw everything into one bucket labeled"peptides," you create documentation chaos, regulatory confusion, and clinical sloppiness that a board reviewer will tear apart.

Let me lay out the categories, and I want you to treat them like they are written on different-colored paper that can never be mixed together.

FDA-approved peptide or peptide-like drugs are medications that have gone through the full FDA approval process for a specific indication. Semaglutide, sold as Ozempic for type 2 diabetes and Wegovy for chronic weight management, is FDA-approved. Tirzepatide, sold as Mounjaro and Zepbound, is FDA-approved. Tesamorelin, sold as Egrifta for HIV-associated lipodystrophy, is FDA-approved. Bremelanotide, sold as Vyleesi for hypoactive sexual desire disorder, is FDA-approved. Insulin has been FDA-approved for over a century. These are real drugs, with real labels, real evidence packages, established safety profiles, and - this is crucial - institutional support structures. When you prescribe an FDA-approved drug, you have the FDA label to reference. You have post-marketing surveillance data. You have established protocols. You have manufacturer liability if something goes catastrophically wrong. And if a patient has a problem, your defense starts with "I prescribed an FDA-approved medication according to the labeled indication." That is a strong position.

FDA-approved drugs used off-label are a different category. Off-label prescribing is completely legal and extremely common. It means you are using an approved drug for a different indication, dose, route, or population than what the label describes. Physicians prescribe off-label every day. Gabapentin for anxiety. Trazodone for insomnia. Beta-blockers for performance anxiety. The list is endless. Off-label prescribing is legitimate when there is a reasonable medical rationale, when the physician documents that rationale, and when the patient gives informed consent. The key difference from labeled use is that your documentation burden is higher. You need to explain why you chose this therapy. You need to discuss the evidence supporting the off-label use. You need to document that the patient understood they were receiving an off-label treatment. And you need to accept that you do not have the same institutional support you would have for a labeled use. But off-label use of an approved drug is still, fundamentally, the use of an approved drug - and that matters to boards, to courts, and to malpractice carriers.

Compounded patient-specific medications are prepared by licensed compounding pharmacies according to a physician's prescription for a specific patient. 503A compounding pharmacies serve individual patients with customized formulations. 503B outsourcing facilities produce compounded medications in larger quantities for healthcare facilities. Compounded medications are not FDA-approved in the same way manufactured drugs are. They do not go through the FDA's New Drug Application process. But they can be lawful, clinically appropriate, and medically necessary when a patient needs a dose, formulation, or combination that is not commercially available. The key issues with compounded peptides are pharmacy quality, current legal availability, and documentation. You need to verify that the compounding pharmacy is legitimate. You need to confirm that the specific peptide can be legally compounded under current FDA policy. You need to document why the patient needs a compounded product rather than an approved alternative. And you need to understand that compounded products do not carry the same quality guarantees as FDA-approved manufactured drugs.

Investigational or limited-evidence peptides are compounds that have not been FDA-approved and are still being studied. They may have promising preclinical data. They may have early-phase human trials. They may have compelling mechanisms and enthusiastic advocates. But they have not completed the FDA review process, and their safety and efficacy profiles are not established. Using these compounds in clinical practice requires extraordinary documentation. The informed consent must be extensive. The patient counseling must be exhaustive. The monitoring must be close. The chart must show that the physician understood exactly how limited the evidence was and made a patient-specific decision anyway, with full disclosure. This is the category where I see the most physician hubris - doctors who read some early research, get excited, and start prescribing without appreciating how exposed they are if something goes wrong.

Research-use-only substances should not be confused with any of the above categories. These are products sold with labels that say "research use only," "not for human consumption,"or "for laboratory use only." They are not medications. They are not produced under pharmaceutical manufacturing standards. They are not overseen by a pharmacist. They are not part of any legitimate clinical pathway. When a patient buys these products and injects them, they are self-experimenting with unregulated substances. As a physician, you do not prescribe these. You do not endorse these. You warn against these. You document the warning. And you offer a legitimate medical alternative when one exists. Any physician who treats a research-use-only product as if it were a legitimate medication is asking for catastrophic professional consequences. I don't care what the patient says. I don't care what the forum told them. I don't care how cheap it is. Research-use-only is not a clinical category. It is a warning label. Treat it like one.

Now, here is where physicians get into trouble. They use imprecise language in the chart. They write "off-label" when they mean "compounded." They write "compounded" when the patient is actually using a research-use-only product. They describe everything as "peptide therapy"without specifying which category applies. And when the board reviews the chart, they find a physician who apparently cannot distinguish between FDA-approved drugs, legitimate compounding, and internet chemicals. That is not a defensible position.

Your chart must use precise language. Every time. The therapy is FDA-approved, used off-label, compounded, investigational, or the patient is using a research-use-only product against medical advice. Those are distinct categories with distinct documentation requirements, distinct consent standards, and distinct legal implications. Learn them. Use them correctly. Write them clearly. Because the physician who cannot keep these categories straight is the physician who looks sloppy under scrutiny - and sloppy is what boards discipline.

Clinical reasoning comes before product selection, always. The clinical problem comes first. The peptide comes second - if it comes at all. A patient does not need a peptide because they heard about it on a podcast. They need an evaluation. They need a medical reason. They need alternatives reviewed. They need a clear discussion of risks and uncertainty. If you cannot explain why this therapy makes sense for this patient, at this time, after these alternatives, with this monitoring plan - slow down. Say no. Wait until you have a clear, defensible rationale. Because a chart with no rationale is a chart with no defense.

How the pipeline works: bulk powder from overseas, repackaged, labeled "research use only"

Now let me pull back the curtain on the system that is actively competing with you for your own patients. The online grey market for peptides is not a conspiracy theory. It is not a marginal activity practiced by a few fringe enthusiasts. It is a massive, organized, international distribution system that moves bulk peptide powder from manufacturing facilities - primarily in China and other overseas locations - through repackagers, online vendors, and direct-to-consumer shipping channels, ultimately ending with a patient mixing a powder at their kitchen table and injecting it into their own body.

Nobody knows the exact numbers. It could be hundreds of thousands of consumers. It could be millions. The market is deliberately opaque because transparency would mean regulatory exposure. What we know is this: the demand for peptides has grown so dramatically that a vast parallel economy has emerged, and it operates with no physician oversight, no pharmacist verification, no medical records, no informed consent process, and no accountability when things go wrong.

Here is how the pipeline actually works. Bulk peptide powder is manufactured overseas, usually in facilities that are not subject to FDA inspection, not held to Current Good Manufacturing Practice standards, and not accountable to U.S. regulators in any meaningful way. These are chemical synthesis operations, not pharmaceutical manufacturers. They produce kilograms of powder at a time - semaglutide analogs, BPC-157, TB-500, CJC-1295, ipamorelin, and dozens of others - and sell it to distributors who repackage it into smaller quantities.

The distributors - often operating from warehouse spaces or even residential addresses -weigh the powder into vials, attach labels that say "research use only" or "not for human consumption," create professional-looking websites with certificates of analysis and customer reviews, and sell directly to consumers through e-commerce platforms. Payment is typically through credit card processors that specialize in high-risk merchants, or increasingly through cryptocurrency, which adds another layer of opacity and makes chargebacks and refunds difficult for consumers.

The customer - your patient - receives a vial of white powder, a separate vial of bacteriostatic water for reconstitution, and a set of instructions that may range from reasonably accurate to dangerously wrong. They mix the powder and water, draw the solution into an insulin syringe, and self-inject, typically subcutaneously into the abdomen, thigh, or other accessible area. They are now their own pharmacist, their own compounding facility, their own quality control department, and their own prescriber. What could possibly go wrong?

Everything. Everything can go wrong, and sometimes does.

The powder may not be what the label claims. Studies of grey-market peptide products have found everything from completely different compounds, to peptide fragments rather than full sequences, to products that contain no active compound at all. Some vials are significantly underdosed. Some are overdosed - which sounds like "getting more for your money" until you realize that a five-fold overdose of a growth hormone secretagogue can have serious physiological consequences. Mislabeling is not rare in this market. It is the expected baseline, with accurate products being the exception rather than the rule.

The powder may contain contaminants. Chemical synthesis produces byproducts. Impurities. Residual solvents. Heavy metals from the manufacturing process. These contaminants are acceptable in research-grade chemicals that will be used in laboratory assays. They are not acceptable in a product that will be injected into a human body. But the grey market has no mechanism for removing them. There is no purification step equivalent to pharmaceutical manufacturing. There is no sterility testing required. There is no endotoxin testing. The certificate of analysis that the vendor proudly displays may show peptide identity - and even that can be fabricated - but it does not prove the product is safe for injection.

Which brings me to the most dangerous misconception in the entire grey market ecosystem.

Purity is not sterility - that certificate of analysis is worthless for safety

I cannot tell you how many patients have shown me a certificate of analysis from an online vendor and said "See? It's 99% pure." As if that means anything for safety. As if chemical purity and biological safety are the same thing. They are not. They are fundamentally, categorically different, and the fact that patients don't understand this distinction is exactly why they need a physician who does.

Purity in the context of a certificate of analysis means that the powder contains approximately the stated percentage of the target compound, as measured by analytical techniques like high-performance liquid chromatography or mass spectrometry. It does not mean the product is sterile. It does not mean it is free from endotoxins - bacterial components that can trigger severe inflammatory reactions when injected. It does not mean it is free from particulate matter, viral contaminants, prions, or other biological hazards. It does not mean the manufacturing facility met any hygiene standards. It does not mean the powder was handled in a clean environment, stored at appropriate temperature, or shipped under conditions that maintain stability.

A certificate of analysis from a grey-market vendor is essentially meaningless for patient safety. It may be genuine or fabricated. It may test the actual batch the patient received, or a reference sample from months ago. It may show chemical identity while saying nothing about biological safety. And even if it is accurate and current, it only addresses one of many safety parameters that pharmaceutical manufacturing requires.

When you get a medication from a legitimate pharmacy - a 503A compounder or a licensed dispensing pharmacy - that product has been manufactured or compounded under conditions that address sterility, endotoxin levels, identity, potency, stability, and labeling accuracy. The pharmacy is licensed. The pharmacist is accountable. The facility is inspected. The processes are validated. If something goes wrong, there is a chain of accountability that leads back to a licensed professional who carries malpractice insurance and answers to a state board.

The grey market has none of that. The vendor is not a pharmacist. The facility is not inspected. The product is not manufactured to pharmaceutical standards. There is no chain of accountability. And when a patient develops an abscess, a systemic infection, a severe inflammatory reaction, or an unexplained medical problem after injecting a grey-market product, the vendor disclaims responsibility - "not for human consumption, you knew that when you bought it" - and the patient is left holding the bag. Sometimes literally holding a bag of IV antibiotics in a hospital room they never expected to occupy.

Here are the specific dangers you need to explain to every patient who mentions grey-market products:

Contamination. An injectable product can look clean and still be catastrophically unsafe. Bacterial contamination may not be visible. Endotoxin contamination may not produce immediate symptoms but can cause fever, inflammation, and in severe cases, sepsis. Heavy metal contamination from synthesis processes accumulates over time and may not produce obvious symptoms for months or years. The patient has no way to detect any of these problems before they inject.

Mislabeling and misdosing. The vial says BPC-157. Is it actually BPC-157? Maybe. Maybe it's a related peptide. Maybe it's a fragment. Maybe it's something else entirely. The dose on the label says 5 milligrams. Is it actually 5 milligrams? Maybe. Maybe it's 2 milligrams, and the patient is paying for product they are not receiving. Maybe it's 10 milligrams, and the patient who thinks they are taking a conservative dose is actually taking double. Without pharmaceutical-grade quality control, the patient has no way to know.

Patient error. Even if the product were perfect - and it usually is not - the process of reconstitution and self-injection introduces multiple points of failure. Patients make math errors calculating doses. They use non-sterile water because they ran out of bacteriostatic water and "it shouldn't matter that much." They reuse syringes. They store reconstituted vials at room temperature for weeks. They inject into the same site repeatedly, causing tissue irritation and increasing infection risk. They mix multiple peptides in the same syringe without understanding interactions. Every one of these errors is predictable, and every one has sent patients to the emergency room.

The halo effect. This is maybe the most insidious risk. Patients see that semaglutide works -dramatically, life-changingly works - and they assume that anything called a peptide must be in the same safety and efficacy class. Wrong. One FDA-approved peptide drug with a robust evidence base does not bless every compound sold online. The GLP-1 agonists went through years of clinical trials, post-marketing surveillance, and regulatory review before they reached patients. Grey-market peptides have gone through none of that. But the halo effect makes patients feel safe when they are not, and that false security is what leads them to take risks they would otherwise avoid.

You need to explain this to your patients. Not condescendingly. Not with technical jargon. In plain English that they can understand and remember. And you need to document that you explained it. Because the patient who gets hurt after you warned them is a very different legal and professional situation from the patient who gets hurt because nobody ever warned them at all.

No physician, no pharmacist, no medical record, no accountability - that's what your patients are doing without you

Let me spell out what a patient in the grey market system actually experiences, step by step, and I want you to compare it to what would happen in a legitimate medical practice.

In the grey market: the patient has a health concern. They search online. They find a forum or video that mentions a peptide. They research vendors - which mostly means reading forum posts about which vendors ship quickly and have good "bunk" rates. They place an order. A package arrives. They reconstitute the product themselves. They self-inject based on dosing recommendations from strangers on the internet. They monitor themselves - or don't. If they have side effects, they post in a forum asking if it is "normal." If they have serious problems, they may go to the emergency room, where the physician has no idea what they took, what dose, from where, or when, because there is no medical record and the patient may not even know the actual compound name.

In a legitimate medical practice: the patient has a health concern. They make an appointment. A physician takes a history, performs an examination, reviews medications and contraindications, evaluates whether the proposed therapy is appropriate. If it is, the physician writes a prescription to a licensed pharmacy. The pharmacy compounds or dispenses the medication under validated conditions. The patient receives medication with verified identity, potency, and sterility, along with instructions from a pharmacist. The patient is monitored by the physician on a defined schedule. Side effects are reported to the physician and documented. If serious problems occur, the physician knows exactly what was prescribed, what dose, from what source, and can respond appropriately. The entire process is documented in a medical record that provides accountability for every decision.

These two pathways produce radically different patient outcomes, and the difference is not the peptide. The difference is the system around the peptide. Medical supervision. Pharmacy quality. Documentation. Accountability. Follow-up. These are not bureaucratic luxuries. They are the structural features that make medicine safe instead of dangerous.

And yet the grey market thrives because it offers something the medical system often does not: speed, low cost, no gatekeeping, no waiting rooms, no judgment, and no requirement that the patient convince a skeptical physician that their request is reasonable. The grey market says yes to everyone. The medical system says no sometimes, requires evaluations always, charges more, and moves slower. For patients who are impatient, distrustful of the medical establishment, or simply unable to afford supervised care, the grey market is the path of least resistance.

That is why you need to be part of the solution. Not because you should say yes to every patient request - you absolutely should not. But because the only way to compete with the grey market is to offer a medical pathway that is safe, responsive, and accessible enough that patients choose it over self-experimentation. If your practice is so expensive, so judgmental, so slow, or so dismissive that patients would rather buy mystery powder online, that is a practice problem, not a patient problem. And it is a problem you can fix.

A responsible practice does several things that the grey market cannot match. It warns patients explicitly against research-use-only products, and documents those warnings. It encourages legitimate pharmacy channels and verifies that the pharmacies it uses are properly licensed. It explains that physician-supervised therapy is not just a way to get a vial - it is a safety system that includes screening, monitoring, stop criteria, and accountability. It prices its services to reflect that medical supervision, not to compete with grey-market vendors on price - because competing on price is a race to the bottom that no legitimate medical practice can win.

And most importantly, a responsible practice offers patients something the internet cannot: a real physician who knows their medical history, who will catch problems before they become emergencies, who can adjust therapy based on individual response, and who can say no when no is the right answer. That last part is crucial. The grey market never says no. It will sell peptide therapy to anyone with a credit card. A physician who provides appropriate screening and refuses unsafe requests is providing a service that no vendor can match, and patients who understand this value will seek it out.

Why patients choose the grey market: price, access, impatience, and your refusal to engage

Let me be honest about why the grey market exists, because understanding the demand side is essential to addressing it. The grey market does not persist because patients are stupid or reckless, though some certainly are. It persists because the legitimate medical system has created conditions that drive patients toward alternatives. And one of those conditions, frankly, is physicians who refuse to engage with the topic at all.

Price is the most obvious factor. A month of supervised semaglutide therapy through a legitimate medical program might cost several hundred to over a thousand dollars, including consultation fees, pharmacy costs, and monitoring. The same amount of semaglutide analog from a grey-market vendor might cost a fraction of that. For patients without insurance coverage, or with high deductibles, or who simply cannot afford ongoing medical supervision, the price difference is not trivial - it is existential. It determines whether they get treatment at all. And while I will argue forcefully in this book that you should charge premium prices for your services - cheap peptide practices look like vial shops and attract the wrong kind of attention - I also recognize that legitimate care needs to be accessible enough that patients don't feel forced into the grey market by economic desperation.

Access is another major factor. Not every patient lives near a physician who prescribes peptides. Not every physician who prescribes peptides accepts new patients. Some areas have no local compounding pharmacies that work with peptide therapies. Telehealth has improved access significantly, but state licensing restrictions, pharmacy relationships, and insurance limitations still create barriers that the grey market simply does not have. The grey market ships everywhere. It requires no appointment. It asks no questions. For patients in underserved areas, or patients whose schedules don't accommodate medical office hours, or patients who have been turned away by other physicians, the grey market is the only option that seems available.

Impatience is real. We live in a culture of immediate gratification. Patients who have been struggling with weight, pain, fatigue, or metabolic problems for years do not want to wait three months for an appointment, then another month for prior authorization, then another two weeks for pharmacy fulfillment. They want to start today. The grey market delivers today. The medical system often does not. This is not an excuse for self-experimentation - it is an explanation that physicians need to understand if they want to compete effectively.

And then there is your refusal to engage. This is the factor that physicians control directly. When a patient asks about peptides and the physician responds with a blank stare, a dismissive comment, or a flat "I don't do that," the patient does not go home and forget about peptides. They go home and order them online. Because the physician's refusal did not address their underlying health concern, did not offer an alternative pathway, and did not provide any reason to trust the medical system over the internet community that has been far more responsive to their questions.

I am not saying every physician should prescribe peptides. I am saying every physician should be able to have an informed conversation about them. Every physician should ask what patients are already using. Every physician should warn against grey-market products. Every physician should know which legitimate medical pathways might exist for a patient with a specific concern. And every physician should document these conversations. Because a physician who engages - who listens, evaluates, educates, and either provides a supervised pathway or explains clearly why one is not appropriate - is a physician who keeps patients out of the grey market. A physician who refuses to engage is a physician who drives patients straight into it.

The bottom line on the grey market is this: it is not medicine. It is self-experimentation with injectable products of uncertain identity, purity, sterility, dose, and long-term safety. Some patients will use it anyway. That does not make you responsible for their choices. But it does create an opportunity - actually, an obligation - for you to bring order, screening, consent, monitoring, and honest risk discussion into a space that badly needs adult supervision. The patients are already there. The question is whether you will meet them there, or whether you will leave them alone with influencers, forums, and discount codes.

There is no multi-billion-dollar company defending doctors who prescribe peptides

Now I need to explain the perspective of this book, because it is not neutral, and I am not going to pretend it is. This book takes a protective stance toward physicians who prescribe or are considering prescribing peptide therapies. It is written by someone who has spent decades in healthcare, finance, and law, who has watched how the system actually works when things go wrong, and who knows exactly how alone a physician is when the regulatory machinery turns against them.

Let me tell you the central fact that shapes every recommendation in this book: there is no multi-billion-dollar company standing behind doctors who prescribe peptides. None. Zero. When you write a prescription for semaglutide or tirzepatide as an FDA-approved drug, Novo Nordisk and Eli Lilly have teams of lawyers, regulatory affairs professionals, and lobbying operations that, indirectly and structurally, create a protective environment for your prescribing. The drug has been through FDA review. The label establishes a standard of care. The manufacturer carries product liability. The entire pharmaceutical infrastructure - from the FDA approval to post-marketing surveillance to continuing medical education to published clinical guidelines - provides a scaffold that supports your clinical decision.

When you prescribe a compounded peptide - BPC-157, CJC-1295, thymosin beta-4, or any of the others we will discuss - none of that exists. There is no billion-dollar company defending your prescribing decision. There is no FDA label establishing a standard of care. There is no post-marketing surveillance system catching adverse events. There is no pharmaceutical rep visiting your office with reprints of the latest clinical trials. There is no medical society guideline endorsing your treatment protocol. There is just you, your chart, your clinical reasoning, and your documentation.

When something goes wrong with an FDA-approved drug - and things do go wrong, regularly, with drugs from the biggest pharmaceutical companies in the world - the manufacturer steps in. Not out of generosity, but out of self-interest. They have lawyers who handle product liability claims. They have regulatory affairs teams who respond to FDA inquiries. They have public relations departments who manage media coverage. They have a massive financial interest in defending the drug's reputation because their stock price depends on it. They may not defend you personally - that is what your malpractice insurance is for - but they defend the drug, which indirectly defends the prescribing environment.

With peptide therapies, especially compounded and investigational ones, there is nobody. The compounding pharmacy may or may not stand behind their product. Their insurance may or may not cover your patient. They may or may not be in business next year. The regulatory environment may shift and suddenly make their compounding operation legally precarious. And you - the physician whose name is on the prescription - are the most visible, most accountable, and most vulnerable person in the entire chain.

I want you to understand this viscerally, not just intellectually. When a patient of yours has a serious adverse event after a peptide therapy, here is who the system will look at: you. The state medical board will investigate your prescribing. Your malpractice carrier will review your chart. If the patient files a complaint, the board will examine your documentation, your clinical reasoning, your informed consent process, your monitoring plan, and your pharmacy selection. They will not investigate the online forum that recommended the therapy. They will not investigate the influencer who promoted it. They will not investigate the overseas manufacturer who produced the powder. They will investigate you. Because you are the only person in this entire ecosystem who has a medical license that can be revoked.

That is why this book is protective. That is why every recommendation is designed to keep you safe while you provide legitimate medical care. I am not interested in expanding the peptide market. I am not interested in helping you get rich quick. I am interested in helping you keep your license, your reputation, and your ability to practice medicine while navigating an area that is clinically promising but professionally dangerous precisely because you have no institutional support.

When a dangerous FDA-approved drug harms patients, Big Pharma has the doctor's back - when a peptide causes a problem, you stand alone

Let me illustrate this with a concrete example that every physician will recognize. Vioxx. Rofecoxib. Merck's blockbuster COX-2 inhibitor that was on the market from 1999 to 2004, when Merck voluntarily withdrew it after studies showed increased cardiovascular risk. Vioxx caused real harm to real patients. Thousands of heart attacks and strokes. Billions of dollars in litigation. Congressional hearings. Regulatory reforms. A disaster by any measure.

But look at what happened to the physicians who prescribed Vioxx. They were prescribing an FDA-approved drug for labeled indications according to standard clinical practice. When the litigation came, their defense was straightforward: "I prescribed an FDA-approved medication according to the labeled indication and standard of care. The manufacturer withdrew the drug due to safety concerns that emerged post-marketing. My prescribing was consistent with medical standards at the time." That defense worked. The vast majority of prescribing physicians faced no personal liability because the standard of care was established by the FDA label, the manufacturer's marketing, the medical literature, and the clinical guidelines of the era.

Merck paid billions in settlements. The FDA changed labeling requirements for the entire NSAID class. But individual physicians were protected by the institutional infrastructure that surrounded their prescribing decisions. They had the FDA label. They had the manufacturer's promotional materials - which, as it turned out, understated cardiovascular risk, but that was Merck's problem, not the individual physician's. They had medical society endorsements. They had a defensible standard of care.

Now imagine a different scenario. Imagine you prescribe a compounded peptide - let's say BPC-157 for tendon healing - and the patient develops a serious adverse event. Maybe they have an allergic reaction. Maybe they develop a problem related to the pro-angiogenic mechanism that wasn't anticipated. Maybe the compounded product was contaminated and caused an infection. Whatever happened, it happened after your prescription, and now you are the defendant.

Your defense is what, exactly? There is no FDA label establishing a standard of care. There is no large-scale clinical trial proving safety and efficacy. There is no medical society guideline endorsing BPC-157 for tendon healing. There is no manufacturer with deep pockets standing behind the product. There is just your chart. And if your chart is thin - if it doesn't show a clear clinical rationale, exhaustive informed consent, careful patient selection, appropriate monitoring, and documented stop criteria - then you have no defense at all.

The board will ask: why did you prescribe a compound with no FDA approval and predominantly animal-study evidence? What was your clinical rationale? What alternatives did you discuss? How did you inform the patient of risks and unknowns? What monitoring did you provide? What was your source? How did you verify pharmacy quality? What did you do when the patient reported side effects? And if your chart does not have clear, thorough answers to every one of those questions, you are exposed in a way that no physician prescribing Vioxx ever was.

This is the asymmetry that defines peptide prescribing. Big Pharma has lawyers, lobbyists, regulatory capture, institutional influence, and billion-dollar balance sheets. When one of their drugs causes harm, the system absorbs the shock through corporate liability, insurance pools, regulatory processes, and political negotiation. When a peptide causes harm - especially a compounded or investigational peptide - there is no corporate liability to absorb the shock.

There is just you. Your license. Your chart. Your documentation. Your professional future.

I am not saying this to scare you away from peptides. Peptides have legitimate clinical applications, and I believe thoughtful physicians can use them responsibly to help patients who have exhausted other options. But I am saying this to make sure you understand the risk landscape before you write your first prescription. You are operating without a safety net. The normal institutional protections that surround conventional prescribing do not exist in this space. You need to build your own protections through documentation, patient selection, informed consent, pharmacy verification, monitoring, and conservative clinical judgment. This book is a guide to building those protections, one decision at a time.

The system is rigged. That is not paranoia. That is structural reality. Big Pharma operates within an infrastructure of regulatory approval, liability distribution, institutional support, and political influence that makes their prescribing environment predictable and defensible. Peptide physicians operate in a wilderness. That wilderness has opportunities - real opportunities to help patients who are not being served by conventional medicine - but it also has predators. State medical boards with investigatory authority. Malpractice plaintiffs with contingency fee arrangements. Regulatory agencies that can change policy overnight. And patients who may be grateful for your help until they are not, at which point your chart is the only friend you have.

The medical board investigates every single complaint - every single one

Let me tell you how state medical boards actually work, because most physicians have a dangerously vague understanding of the process. A board complaint can come from anyone. The patient. A family member. A pharmacist. Another physician. An employer. An insurance company. A journalist. In some states, board staff can initiate investigations on their own authority without any external complaint at all. There is no filing fee for complaining. There is no requirement that the complainant have standing, or credibility, or even a good faith basis for their concern. Anyone can file a complaint about any physician, for any reason, at any time.

And the board investigates every single one. Every single complaint gets reviewed. Not every complaint leads to formal disciplinary action - most do not. But every complaint creates a file. Every complaint triggers a review process. Every complaint requires a response from the physician. And every complaint has the potential to escalate from a routine inquiry into a full investigation that examines your entire practice, your charting, your prescribing patterns, your pharmacy relationships, your advertising, your staff supervision, and your financial practices.

I want you to understand what this means in practical terms. A patient who is unhappy with their results can file a complaint. A patient who is angry about pricing can file a complaint. A patient who had a side effect they didn't expect can file a complaint. A patient's family member who thinks their loved one was exploited can file a complaint. A pharmacist who has concerns about your prescribing patterns can file a complaint. A competing physician who doesn't like that you are offering services they don't offer can - and sometimes does - file a complaint. And every single one of these complaints starts a process that you will have to respond to, that will consume your time and energy, that will stress you and your family, and that has the potential to threaten your license.

Boards do not need to prove malpractice the way a civil plaintiff does. Board discipline is administrative, not criminal. The standard of proof is typically "preponderance of the evidence" - more likely than not - not "beyond a reasonable doubt." The board can discipline you for care that falls below the standard of the profession, even if no patient was actually harmed. They can place conditions on your license, require additional education, mandate supervision, suspend your practice, or revoke your license entirely. The process alone- the investigation, the hearings, the attorney fees, the stress, the damage to your reputation- can be professionally devastating even if the final outcome is favorable.

Most board cases involving peptide, hormone, weight-loss, and wellness practices don't start because a doctor used a controversial therapy. They start because a patient complained. The chart looks thin. The monitoring was poor. The advertising was reckless. The staff were operating outside their scope. The doctor cannot explain the decision in plain medical language. And when the board looks at the chart - which is all they have to go on months or years after the care was provided - they find a record that does not support the claim that real medicine was being practiced.

Cash-pay medicine attracts disproportionate scrutiny. I am not being cynical; I am being factual. Medical boards are politically accountable institutions. They respond to public perception, media coverage, and legislative pressure. When a newspaper runs an exposé about"pill mills" or "vial shops" or "med spas prescribing dangerous experimental drugs," the boards feel pressure to act. And they act by investigating physicians who fit the profile -cash-pay practices, aesthetic or wellness focus, non-traditional therapies, high patient volumes, aggressive marketing. You do not have to be doing anything wrong to attract attention. You just have to look like the kind of practice the board feels pressured to investigate.

That is why this book emphasizes flying under the radar. No controlled substances. No reportable medications where possible. Premium pricing that reflects medical supervision rather than medication markup. Bulletproof charts written for a skeptical board reviewer. Exhaustive informed consent. PCP involvement. Conservative marketing. Documentation that proves real medicine occurred. These are not optional extras. They are survival strategies in an environment where the physician prescribing peptides has no institutional protection and every complaint gets investigated.

You do not defend the care you remember. You defend the care the chart proves. And if the chart cannot explain the decision to a skeptical stranger reading it two years later, the decision was not ready to be made.

Controlled substances, inappropriate patient relationships, and non-Big-Pharma treatments attract the most scrutiny

Let me close this chapter with the practical reality of what gets physicians in the most trouble, because understanding the risk patterns will help you avoid them. After four decades in healthcare law and compliance, I can tell you with confidence that three categories of medical practice attract disproportionate regulatory scrutiny: controlled substance prescribing, inappropriate patient relationships, and non-mainstream treatments - which includes peptides, hormones, and the broader universe of alternative therapies that operate outside the Big Pharma infrastructure.

Controlled substances are the highest-risk category by a wide margin. Opioids, benzodiazepines, stimulants, testosterone in some classifications - these substances are tracked, reported, monitored, and aggressively investigated. State prescription drug monitoring programs create data trails that boards can analyze for patterns. Federal agencies maintain databases. The DEA has jurisdiction. If you are running a peptide practice, you should not be prescribing controlled substances at all unless there is a compelling, well-documented clinical reason that you can defend to a skeptical reviewer. The combination of controlled substances and alternative therapies is like painting a target on your back. Don't do it.

Inappropriate patient relationships cover a range of boundary violations that boards take extremely seriously. Romantic or sexual relationships with patients are automatic license-losers in every state. But the category also includes financial relationships that create conflicts of interest, inappropriate self-disclosure, treating friends and family, accepting extravagant gifts, and any conduct that suggests the physician is exploiting the patient relationship for personal benefit. In cash-pay practices, the financial relationship is front and center, and you need to handle it with absolute transparency. Your pricing should be clear, consistent, and defensible as reflecting medical services rather than medication markup. You should not have business relationships with pharmacies that create kickback or conflict-of-interest concerns. You should not be selling products out of your office in ways that look like retail rather than medical dispensing. Every financial arrangement should be documented, justifiable, and structured to withstand scrutiny.

Non-Big-Pharma treatments - peptides, bioidentical hormones, functional medicine protocols, IV nutrient therapies, and the broader category of alternative or integrative therapies- attract scrutiny because they operate outside the institutional structures that boards find reassuring. There is no pharmaceutical company standing behind the treatment. There is no FDA label establishing a standard of care. There is no major medical society guideline endorsing the practice. The physician is operating as a clinical individual, making decisions based on their own judgment and a thinner evidence base than what supports conventional care. That independence is exactly what makes these practices valuable to patients who are not served by conventional medicine. But it is also what makes them vulnerable to board investigation.

The combination of all three risk factors - controlled substances, boundary concerns, and non-mainstream treatments - is the most dangerous practice profile in medicine. A cash-pay practice prescribing opioids and testosterone alongside investigational peptides, with aggressive marketing, high patient volume, thin documentation, and staff operating outside their scope, is a practice that will attract board attention sooner or later. I can almost guarantee it. And when the board comes, they will find problems - not because the physician is necessarily a bad doctor, but because that combination of risk factors, operated at speed, with weak controls, produces substandard care as a statistical certainty.

This is why this book takes the protective stance it does. I am not interested in expanding the peptide market. I am not interested in helping you get rich quick. I am interested in helping you build a practice that helps patients, makes money, and survives regulatory scrutiny - in that order. Because a practice that helps patients but loses the doctor's license helps nobody. A practice that makes money but attracts board investigation loses the money eventually, along with the license. And a practice that tries to survive scrutiny by avoiding all risk ends up providing such limited services that it fails as a business.

The path through this thicket is narrow but navigable. You prescribe peptides when there is a legitimate clinical rationale. You document that rationale exhaustively. You obtain informed consent that actually informs. You use legitimate pharmacies and verify their credentials. You monitor patients closely and set clear stop criteria. You involve primary care physicians when appropriate. You charge prices that reflect medical supervision rather than medication markup. You market conservatively. You keep your charts clean and your staff in their lanes. You say no when the risk is too high or the evidence is too thin. And you build every clinical decision around the question that matters most: how will this look to a skeptical board reviewer reading my chart two years from now?

If you cannot defend it in that context, do not do it. That is the line. And this book will help you know where the line is, every time you face a prescribing decision.

The bottom line of this entire chapter is simple: peptides are here. They are in your exam room. Your patients are using them, or they will be soon. The internet is the most aggressive prescriber in America right now, and it operates with no medical supervision, no accountability, and no interest in patient safety beyond what is necessary to keep sales flowing. You can choose to engage - to provide the medical oversight, documentation, and safety infrastructure that patients desperately need - or you can choose to ignore the reality and hope it goes away. But it won't go away. It will just go around you. And when it goes around you, you lose relevance, you lose patients, and you lose the protections that come from being the adult in the room.

Be the adult in the room. Ask the questions. Document the answers. Warn against the grey market. Offer safer pathways. Say no when no is right. And build a chart that proves you were practicing medicine, not selling hope. That is what this book will teach you to do. The rest of the chapters are the details. But this chapter - this one right here - is the foundation. Peptides are here. Deal with it. Because how you deal with it will determine whether you keep your license, your reputation, and your ability to practice the kind of medicine that actually helps people.

Now turn the page and let's talk about the FDA, the medical boards, and the legal framework you are operating in. Because you cannot practice safely in a system you do not understand.

2 - The FDA, the Medical Board, and Who Actually Controls Your License

Let me tell you something that might save you from a very expensive lesson: the FDA is not your enemy. I know that sounds strange coming from someone who spends half this book warning you about regulators, but it's the truth. The Food and Drug Administration has exactly zero interest in whether Dr. Smith in Tulsa is prescribing BPC-157 for a rotator cuff issue. The FDA does not wake up in the morning wondering what you're doing in your exam room. They regulate drugs. They regulate manufacturers. They regulate labeling and interstate commerce and compounding pharmacies that step out of line. They do not regulate you. Not directly. Not personally. Not in the way that keeps you awake at 3 a.m. staring at the ceiling.

The people who regulate you - the ones who can walk into your office, seize your charts, suspend your license, and turn your life into a multi-year administrative nightmare - work for your state medical board. And here's the part that makes smart doctors do stupid things: most physicians have only a vague understanding of the difference. They hear "FDA" and they think that's the big regulatory boogeyman. They worry about FDA enforcement actions and FDA warning letters and FDA policy changes. Meanwhile, they treat their state medical board like a professional club that renews their license every two years for a fee. That's not what the board is. The board is the entity that can end your career over a chart that looks thin and a patient who complained to the right person at the right time.

This chapter exists because I've watched too many good doctors - smart doctors, caring doctors, doctors who genuinely wanted to help their patients - walk into board investigations completely unprepared. They didn't understand who had authority over them. They didn't understand how investigations started. They didn't understand that their consent forms, their charting habits, their pharmacy relationships, and their advertising language would be picked apart by people who answer to the public, not to the medical profession. By the time they called an attorney, the damage was already done. The chart was weak. The protocols were verbal. The staff had been running loose for two years. And the doctor was sitting in a conference room across from a board investigator trying to explain why a patient with no documented contraindication screening had been prescribed an investigational therapy that wasn't working out so well.

You want to prescribe peptides? Fine. But first you need to understand the regulatory landscape you're walking into. Not because I want to scare you - though a little healthy fear never hurt anyone - but because understanding who regulates what, and why, and how they actually exercise that power, is the foundation of everything else in this book. The prescribing decisions, the charting standards, the consent protocols, the pharmacy relationships, the pricing strategy, the patient selection criteria - all of it rests on this basic framework. Get this wrong, and you're building a practice on sand. Get this right, and you have a fighting chance when -not if, but when - someone decides to take a hard look at what you're doing.

The FDA regulates drugs - your state medical board regulates YOU

Here's the simplest way to think about it. The FDA is a federal agency. Its job, broadly speaking, is to make sure that drugs and biologics sold in the United States are safe and effective for their intended uses. The FDA reviews New Drug Applications. It inspects manufacturing facilities. It approves labeling. It monitors adverse events. It issues warning letters to companies that violate the Food, Drug, and Cosmetic Act. It goes after manufacturers who make false claims. It regulates compounding pharmacies through a complex framework that distinguishes between 503A traditional compounding and 503B outsourcing facilities. It has plenty of power, and it uses that power against companies, not individual practitioners.

Your state medical board is a completely different animal. It's a state-level regulatory body, usually housed within your state's department of health or professional regulation. Its members are typically appointed by the governor. Some boards include physician members, but many include public members - regular citizens with no medical background - who have equal voting power on disciplinary matters. The board's statutory mission, in nearly every state, is to protect the public from unsafe, incompetent, or unprofessional practitioners. Notice what word is missing from that mission statement: "you." The board does not exist to protect physicians. It does not exist to advocate for the medical profession. It does not exist to ensure that cutting-edge therapies reach patients who need them. Its sole purpose is to protect the public. And in the context of peptide prescribing, that means protecting the public from you if the board decides your care doesn't meet acceptable standards.

This distinction matters because physicians constantly confuse the two frameworks. I hear it all the time. "But the FDA hasn't made this peptide illegal." Irrelevant. The FDA doesn't make clinical decisions illegal - the board does, by deciding that your prescribing falls below the standard of care. "But the FDA allows compounding." Also irrelevant. The FDA's compounding framework and your state board's expectation of due diligence are two completely different standards. You can be operating squarely within FDA compounding guidance and still find yourself in front of a medical board that thinks you didn't do enough homework on your pharmacy source. "But the FDA says physicians can practice medicine."Yes, they do - and that doctrine, sometimes called the "practice of medicine exemption,"means the FDA generally defers to the states on how individual physicians prescribe. Which is exactly my point. The FDA's deference doesn't protect you. It just means the FDA isn't the one you need to worry about.

Let me be painfully clear about what this means in practice. When you prescribe a compounded peptide for a patient, you are operating in a space where the FDA has explicitly said that it generally does not interfere with the practice of medicine. The FDA is not reviewing your chart. The FDA is not monitoring your follow-up appointments. The FDA is not checking whether you obtained informed consent or documented your rationale or verified your pharmacy's licensing status. Your state medical board, on the other hand, may do exactly all of those things - and will do them with enthusiasm if a complaint lands on someone's desk. The FDA's hands-off posture toward physician prescribing is not a permission slip. It is a transfer of oversight authority from the federal government to the states. And state medical boards, let me assure you, take that authority very seriously.

Think about it this way: the FDA is concerned with whether a drug is what it claims to be, whether it was manufactured under proper conditions, whether its labeling is accurate, and whether its approved uses are supported by adequate evidence. Your state board is concerned with whether you, as an individual practitioner, exercised proper clinical judgment in your care of an individual patient. The FDA looks at products. The board looks at people - specifically, you. When a patient has a bad outcome from a compounded peptide, the FDA may or may not get involved depending on whether there's a product quality issue, a compounding violation, or an adverse event cluster. But your state board will absolutely get involved if that patient files a complaint, because the board's jurisdiction is your clinical conduct, not the drug's regulatory status.

Confusing the two will not save your license when the board comes calling

I want to spend a moment on this because it's the most common and most dangerous misconception I encounter among physicians who get into peptide medicine. They genuinely believe that if the FDA hasn't explicitly prohibited something, they must be on solid legal ground. They read FDA guidance documents. They follow FDA policy announcements. They track which peptides the FDA has placed on the bulk drug substances list and which ones are excluded. They do all of this with the earnest belief that FDA compliance equals clinical safety equals legal defensibility. And they're wrong on every count.

FDA compliance and clinical defensibility are related but separate concepts. The FDA can say that a particular peptide is eligible for compounding under certain conditions. That tells you something about the regulatory status of the substance itself. It tells you nothing about whether your specific prescribing decision for a specific patient will pass muster with your state medical board. The board doesn't care what the FDA's Bulk Drug Substances List says. The board cares whether you practiced good medicine. Did you take an adequate history? Did you perform an appropriate exam? Did you screen for contraindications? Did you discuss alternatives? Did you obtain informed consent? Did you establish a monitoring plan? Did you document all of this in a chart that tells a coherent story? Those are the questions that determine whether you keep your license, and not one of them is answered by FDA guidance.

I've seen doctors walk into board hearings waving FDA policy documents like a shield. "Your honor - or commissioner, or panel member, or whatever the title is - the FDA's 2018 guidance explicitly states that compounded drug products may be prepared outside of current good manufacturing practice requirements under certain conditions." And the board member looks at them with complete indifference and says, "Doctor, we're not investigating an FDA violation. We're investigating whether you met the standard of care in your treatment of this patient. Your FDA guidance is noted. Now let's talk about why this patient was prescribed a therapy with no documented medical necessity, no follow-up plan, and no informed consent."

That conversation goes badly for the doctor. Every single time. Because the doctor prepared for the wrong fight. They studied federal drug regulation when they should have been studying what their state medical board actually looks for in a disciplinary case. They confused regulatory permission with clinical protection, and that confusion cost them dearly.

Here's what you need to tattoo on your brain: FDA policy tells you what the federal government thinks about a drug substance. State medical board standards tell you what your peers, your public representatives, and your regulatory overseers think about your clinical judgment. These are not the same thing. They operate in parallel universes. And when those universes collide - when the FDA says a substance is legally available but your state board thinks your use of it was sloppy - the board's universe is the one that determines whether you keep practicing medicine.

Let me put this in concrete terms you'll remember. Say you're prescribing a compounded GLP-1 receptor agonist. The FDA's position on whether that specific compound can be compounded is a federal regulatory question. Your state board's position on whether you appropriately evaluated the patient, documented the indication, screened for contraindications, obtained informed consent, and established follow-up is a clinical practice question. You can be 100 percent compliant with FDA compounding policy and still lose your license because your state board decided you practiced sloppy medicine. The two frameworks are independent. Understanding one does not excuse you from the other. And in my experience, the physicians who get into the most trouble are the ones who obsess over FDA policy while ignoring the clinical standards that their state board actually enforces.

The FDA does not investigate individual doctors - state boards do

Let me give you the practical breakdown of who actually shows up at your door, because this is where theory meets reality and a lot of physicians get caught flat-footed.

The FDA Office of Criminal Investigations does, on rare occasions, investigate individual physicians. This typically happens in cases of clear criminal conduct - selling prescriptions for cash without medical evaluation, operating a pill mill, diverting controlled substances, importing drugs illegally for commercial resale, or participating in a conspiracy to distribute unapproved new drugs. These are criminal investigations. They involve federal agents with badges and search warrants. They are not the scenario we're talking about in this book. If you're running a criminal enterprise, you don't need a compliance manual - you need a criminal defense attorney, and I can't help you.

What we're talking about is the vast majority of peptide prescribing: legitimate physicians running legitimate practices who genuinely believe they're helping patients and who genuinely want to stay on the right side of the law. For these physicians, the FDA is essentially a non-factor in day-to-day practice. The FDA does not audit your charts. The FDA does not review your informed consent forms. The FDA does not investigate patient complaints about your prescribing practices. The FDA does not send you letters asking you to explain why you prescribed BPC-157 for tendinopathy or sermorelin for age-related growth hormone deficiency. Those tasks belong to your state medical board, and they perform them with varying degrees of thoroughness and aggressiveness depending on the state, the composition of the board, the political climate, and the volume of complaints they're processing.

A state board investigation typically starts with a complaint. That complaint can come from anyone: a patient, a patient's family member, another physician, a pharmacist, a hospital, an insurance company, or even a board staff member who spotted something concerning during a routine license renewal review. Every complaint gets logged. Every logged complaint gets some level of review. And complaints that allege specific problems - inappropriate prescribing, inadequate examination, failure to monitor, poor informed consent - trigger formal investigations that can consume years of your life and tens of thousands of dollars in legal fees.

The investigation process varies by state, but the general pattern is depressingly consistent. The board receives a complaint. A staff attorney or investigator reviews it and decides whether it falls within the board's jurisdiction. If it does - and prescribing complaints almost always do- the board sends you a letter. Not a friendly letter. A letter that says something like: "The Board has received a complaint regarding your medical practice. You are required to respond to the allegations within thirty days. Failure to respond may result in disciplinary action." That letter, by the way, is a public record in many states. It shows up in databases that credentialing committees, hospitals, and malpractice insurers can search. Even if the complaint is ultimately dismissed, that letter exists, and it doesn't go away.

You respond. You hire an attorney - or you're foolish enough to respond without one, which is its own category of mistake. The board reviews your response. If they're not satisfied, they request records. Your charts. Your consent forms. Your protocols. Your advertising materials. Your pharmacy agreements. Your staff training records. They want everything, and under most state laws, they have the authority to demand it. They interview your staff. They may interview the complainant. They may hire an expert reviewer - another physician in your specialty area- to evaluate whether your care met the standard of practice. That expert reviewer gets paid by the board, by the way. They are not your friend. They are looking for problems, and if they find them, they write a report that becomes the foundation for formal charges.

If the board decides there's enough evidence of a violation, they file formal charges. You get a hearing. You present your defense. The board - or an administrative law judge, depending on the state - makes a decision. That decision can range from dismissal to a letter of concern to required continuing education to probation to suspension to revocation. And here's the kicker: the board doesn't need to prove malpractice. They don't need to prove you harmed a patient. They don't need to meet the "beyond a reasonable doubt" standard or even the "preponderance of the evidence" standard that applies in civil lawsuits. Administrative disciplinary proceedings operate under their own standards, which are typically described as "clear and convincing evidence" of a violation of the Medical Practice Act. But in practice, "clear and convincing"means whatever the board thinks it means, and boards are notoriously unsympathetic to physicians who can't explain their own clinical decisions.

Let me say that again because it's the single most important sentence in this chapter: The board does not need to prove malpractice. They only need to decide your care was deficient. And deficient, in the context of a board proceeding, can mean a chart that doesn't tell a clear story, a consent form that doesn't cover the actual risks, a follow-up plan that exists only in your memory, or a prescribing rationale that sounds more like internet enthusiasm than clinical reasoning.

This is why I spend the entire book hammering on documentation. The chart is not a clinical convenience. It is a legal document. It is the only evidence that exists of your clinical reasoning, your patient discussions, your informed consent process, and your monitoring plan. You do not defend the care you remember. You defend the care the chart proves. And if the chart is thin, or sloppy, or missing, or filled with templated language that doesn't match the actual patient encounter, then you have no defense. None. The board will draw the worst possible inference from every gap, every omission, every inconsistency. That's their job. They're not there to give you the benefit of the doubt. They're there to protect the public from practitioners whose care doesn't meet acceptable standards.

DEA investigations: why controlled substances put you on their radar permanently

Now I need to talk about a related threat that doesn't come from the FDA or your state medical board but from an agency that has even more power to ruin your life: the Drug Enforcement Administration. The DEA regulates controlled substances. They register physicians to prescribe them. They inspect prescribing records. They investigate diversion, overprescribing, and suspicious prescribing patterns. And they have a particular interest in physicians who prescribe controlled substances outside what they consider to be the usual course of professional practice.

Here's why this matters for peptide prescribing, even though the peptides discussed in this book are not controlled substances: if you're already on the DEA's radar for any reason - if you prescribe testosterone, if you prescribe appetite suppressants, if you prescribe any Schedule III, IV, or V medication in your practice - the DEA is watching your prescribing patterns. They have databases. They have algorithms that flag unusual volume, unusual combinations, unusual patient geography. And if they decide to investigate you for your controlled substance prescribing, they will look at everything else you're doing too. Your peptide prescriptions. Your hormone protocols. Your compounding pharmacy relationships. Your patient population. Your cash-pay model. Everything.

I know physicians who thought they were being careful. They kept their controlled substance prescribing completely separate from their peptide practice. They had different charts, different protocols, different staff. They thought the firewall would protect them. It didn't. When the DEA executed a search warrant looking for evidence of controlled substance diversion, they seized every record in the office. Every computer. Every server. Every file cabinet. And when the forensic accountants started going through the records, they found the peptide practice too. Not because peptides are illegal - they're not - but because the DEA investigation triggered a referral to the state medical board, which then started its own investigation into the "unusual"prescribing patterns the DEA had uncovered.

This is what I mean when I say controlled substances put you on the radar permanently. The DEA doesn't just investigate and go away. They create records. Those records get shared. Other agencies get interested. And even if you ultimately clear yourself of any controlled substance violation, the mere fact of a DEA investigation can be enough to trigger board scrutiny, hospital privilege reviews, insurance panel terminations, and malpractice premium increases. Your name goes in a database. It stays there. And every credentialing application you fill out for the rest of your career will ask whether you've ever been investigated by a federal agency, and you'll have to answer yes, and then you'll have to explain, and the explanation will never sound as clean as you'd like it to.

This is why the "fly under the radar" philosophy that runs through this book is so important. Controlled substances are like beacon flares in the regulatory sky. They attract attention. They trigger reporting requirements - to prescription monitoring programs, to the DEA, to state health departments. Every controlled substance prescription creates a data trail that algorithms and investigators can follow. And once you're on the radar, you don't get off it. You're flagged. You're watched. You're a known entity in a database somewhere, and when the next investigation starts, your name comes up faster than you'd like.

I'm not telling you to stop prescribing controlled substances if they're clinically appropriate for your patients. Testosterone replacement therapy, for example, is a legitimate medical treatment with established indications and monitoring protocols. What I'm telling you is to understand the risk landscape. If you prescribe controlled substances and peptides from the same practice, you need to be exponentially more careful than a physician who prescribes neither. Your documentation needs to be bulletproof. Your protocols need to be written and followed. Your pharmacy relationships need to be clean and well-documented. Your informed consent needs to be exhaustive. Because the day someone comes looking, they're not going to examine your peptide practice in isolation. They're going to look at everything, and the controlled substance piece is what's going to bring them through the door.

Let me put it in the bluntest possible terms: the FDA doesn't investigate doctors for prescribing peptides. State medical boards do. And the DEA investigates doctors for controlled substances, but once they're in your practice, they look at everything. Know who your real enemies are.

Prepare for the right fight. Because walking into a board hearing armed with FDA guidance documents is like bringing a knife to a gunfight - except the gun is loaded, the other guy has been practicing for twenty years, and he doesn't care what you think the FDA allows.

The Five Legal Buckets Every Prescription Falls Into

Before you write another prescription for anything - peptide, hormone, vitamin, or otherwise- you need to be able to answer one question with absolute clarity: which legal bucket does this prescription fall into? I don't mean which bucket you wish it fell into, or which bucket would make your life easier, or which bucket your compounding pharmacy thinks it falls into. I mean which bucket it actually falls into based on the FDA status of the substance, the manner in which it's being supplied, the clinical context of the prescribing, and the documentation you've created to support the decision. Because when the board investigator shows up and asks you to explain why you prescribed what you prescribed, your answer needs to be precise, accurate, and consistent with every piece of documentation in the chart. If you call something"off-label" when it's actually "investigational," you've just told the board that you don't understand the regulatory framework you're operating in. And a physician who doesn't understand the regulatory framework is a physician the board will happily make an example of.

Let me walk you through the five buckets. These are not arbitrary categories I invented to fill pages. These are the practical distinctions that determine your documentation burden, your consent requirements, your monitoring obligations, and your defensibility if someone decides to question your judgment. Get these right and you have a foundation. Get them wrong and everything you build on top of it is shaky.

Approved use: drug used within FDA labeling - standard documentation

The first bucket is the simplest and the one every physician learned about in medical school: approved use. This means you're prescribing an FDA-approved drug for an FDA-approved indication at an FDA-approved dose in an FDA-approved population using an FDA-approved route of administration. The drug has an NDA - a New Drug Application - or a BLA - a Biologics License Application - that the FDA has approved. The label tells you exactly what it's approved for, how to use it, who can take it, and what the warnings are. You follow the label. Your documentation burden is standard medical documentation: chief complaint, history, physical, assessment, plan, rationale for the selected therapy, and follow-up.

In the peptide world, approved use is relatively narrow. Insulin is a peptide, and it's one of the most important drugs in the history of medicine. When you prescribe insulin for diabetes according to the label, you're in bucket one. Semaglutide (Ozempic, Wegovy) and tirzepatide (Mounjaro, Zepbound) are FDA-approved peptide-based medications for type 2 diabetes and, in some formulations, for obesity. When you prescribe them for their approved indications at approved doses, you're in bucket one. Liraglutide (Saxenda, Victoza), dulaglutide (Trulicity), teriparatide (Forteo), abaloparatide (Tymlos) - these are all approved peptide or peptide-like drugs with established indications, approved labeling, and extensive safety data. Prescribe them within label, and your regulatory risk is minimal.

But here's where physicians get themselves into trouble even within the approved-use bucket: they get lazy with documentation because they think the FDA approval means they don't have to work as hard. Wrong. Approved status doesn't absolve you from taking a history, screening for contraindications, documenting your rationale, obtaining informed consent, or establishing a monitoring plan. A board can still discipline you for prescribing an FDA-approved drug carelessly. If you write a semaglutide prescription without checking for personal or family history of medullary thyroid carcinoma or MEN2, and the patient develops a thyroid issue, your "but it's FDA-approved" defense isn't going to help you much. The drug's approval doesn't replace your clinical judgment. It just means the federal government has determined that, when used as labeled by appropriately trained practitioners, the drug's benefits outweigh its risks. You still have to be one of those appropriately trained practitioners, and you still have to act like one in your documentation.

The standard documentation for approved-use prescribing includes: a documented medical indication that matches the approved labeling; a history and physical appropriate to the condition being treated; contraindication and precaution screening consistent with the label warnings; informed consent that covers the drug's known risks and benefits; a monitoring plan that follows established guidelines; and follow-up documentation that shows you actually monitored the patient. This is not exotic. This is basic medicine. But you'd be shocked how many cash-pay practices treat FDA-approved drugs like over-the-counter products, writing prescriptions with minimal evaluation and calling it good because the drug itself is legitimate. The drug's legitimacy doesn't excuse sloppy prescribing. The board won't see it that way, and neither will a jury if things go badly enough to generate a malpractice claim.

I want to add one more point about approved use that trips up physicians in the peptide space. Just because a drug is FDA-approved doesn't mean every formulation of it is approved. Semaglutide is FDA-approved in specific branded formulations at specific doses. Compounded semaglutide is not FDA-approved. When a pharmacy compounds semaglutide, they are creating a product that is not the same as the FDA-approved branded version. The active ingredient may be the same, but the formulation, the excipients, the delivery device, and the quality controls are different. If you prescribe compounded semaglutide for an FDA-approved indication, you're not in bucket one anymore - you're moving toward bucket three, compounded use, with its own documentation requirements. Don't let your familiarity with the approved drug lull you into thinking the compounded version carries the same regulatory status. It doesn't, and your documentation needs to reflect that distinction.

Off-label use: approved drug used outside labeling - requires rationale, consent, alternatives

The second bucket is where most peptide prescribing actually happens, and it's the bucket that requires the most nuanced understanding. Off-label use means you're prescribing an FDA-approved drug - a drug that has an approved NDA or BLA - but you're using it for a purpose, dose, population, or route that is not included in the approved labeling. This is completely legal. It is common. It is an established and accepted part of medical practice. Oncologists prescribe chemotherapy off-label constantly. Pediatricians prescribe adult-approved drugs for children off-label every day. Psychiatrists, cardiologists, neurologists, rheumatologists - virtually every specialist uses approved drugs in ways that go beyond the label. The FDA has repeatedly acknowledged that it does not regulate the practice of medicine and does not restrict physicians from prescribing approved drugs for off-label uses.

But - and this is the biggest "but" in the entire book - off-label prescribing does not mean anything-goes prescribing. Just because a drug is approved for something doesn't mean any off-label use is automatically defensible. The off-label use must be supported by evidence, professional consensus, or at minimum a rational clinical justification that you can explain and document. "I read about it on a forum" is not a justification. "My patient really wanted it" is not a justification. "Another doctor said it worked for them" is not a justification. A defensible off-label prescribing decision needs three things: a legitimate clinical rationale based on the drug's known mechanism and available evidence; documentation that you've considered and discussed alternatives, including approved alternatives; and informed consent that specifically discloses the off-label nature of the use, what evidence exists, and what uncertainties remain.

Let me give you a concrete example from the peptide world. Semaglutide is FDA-approved for type 2 diabetes and for chronic weight management in adults with obesity or overweight with at least one weight-related comorbidity. If you prescribe semaglutide for a patient who meets those criteria at approved doses, you're in bucket one - approved use. But let's say you have a patient with polycystic ovary syndrome and insulin resistance who doesn't meet the formal BMI criteria for obesity but has significant metabolic dysfunction. You believe, based on the drug's mechanism and emerging evidence, that semaglutide could help her metabolic profile even though she's not formally obese. You prescribe it. Now you're in bucket two -off-label use. The drug is approved. The patient is real. Your rationale might be perfectly sound from a clinical perspective. But your documentation burden just increased substantially.

Your chart now needs to show: why you chose this drug for this patient despite the fact that she doesn't meet the approved indication; what evidence supports this use (published studies, clinical guidelines, professional consensus statements, mechanism-based reasoning); what approved alternatives you considered and why they were insufficient or inappropriate; what you told the patient about the off-label nature of the prescription; what risks you discussed; what monitoring you established; and what criteria you'll use to determine whether the therapy is working or should be stopped. Every one of these elements needs to be documented in real time, not reconstructed from memory six months later when someone asks questions.

The informed consent for off-label use is particularly important and particularly detailed. The patient needs to understand - and you need to document that they understand - that the drug is being used in a way that the FDA has not specifically approved. They need to understand what evidence exists and what the limitations of that evidence are. They need to understand that their insurance may not cover off-label use, which means they may be paying out of pocket. They need to understand that while off-label prescribing is legal and common, it carries a different risk profile than approved-use prescribing because the safety and efficacy data for this specific use may be limited. And they need to understand that they can always decline and pursue approved alternatives instead.

This is where I see doctors make catastrophic errors. They prescribe off-label and don't even tell the patient it's off-label. They just write the prescription, hand it over, and move on to the next patient. Then a complication occurs - maybe minor, maybe not - and the patient, who had no idea they were receiving an off-label therapy, feels deceived. They complain. The board gets involved. And the doctor's chart shows a prescription with no documented off-label disclosure, no alternative discussion, no evidence review, and no enhanced consent. At that point, the doctor isn't defending a clinical decision. They're trying to explain why they didn't bother to tell the patient something material about their treatment. And that explanation never goes well.

The key principle for off-label prescribing is this: the further your use deviates from the approved labeling, the stronger your documentation needs to be. A slight dose adjustment within a well-studied range requires less justification than a completely novel indication based on animal studies. An off-label use supported by multiple published human trials requires less justification than one based on a single case series. An off-label use within your specialty's established practice patterns requires less justification than one that no other physician in your area has ever heard of. You need to calibrate your documentation to the novelty and risk of the off-label use, and you always need to err on the side of over-documenting rather than under-documenting. When in doubt, write it down. When not in doubt, write it down anyway.

Compounded use: patient-specific medication from a licensed pharmacy - requires due diligence

The third bucket is compounded use, and this is where peptide prescribing lives for the vast majority of substances discussed in this book. Compounded medications are not FDA-approved in the traditional sense. They are prepared by licensed compounding pharmacies -either 503A traditional compounding pharmacies or 503B outsourcing facilities - on a patient-specific basis pursuant to a valid prescription from a licensed prescriber. The FDA does not review compounded drugs for safety and efficacy before they reach the patient. Instead, the regulatory framework relies on a combination of federal compounding rules, state pharmacy board oversight, pharmacy accreditation standards, and the prescriber's clinical judgment.

This is a legitimate pathway. Compounding serves an essential role in American medicine. It provides access to medications that are not commercially available, allows for customized dosing and formulation when standard products don't meet patient needs, and fills gaps in the pharmaceutical supply chain that FDA-approved manufacturers can't or won't address. The FDA recognizes this and has developed a regulatory framework that permits compounding within defined boundaries. State pharmacy boards license and inspect compounding pharmacies. Accreditation organizations like PCAB (Pharmacy Compounding Accreditation Board) provide additional quality standards. And physicians have been prescribing compounded medications safely and legally for decades.

But - there's always a but - compounded prescribing carries a documentation burden that goes beyond what's required for approved or off-label use of commercially manufactured drugs. Because the medication is not FDA-approved in the final compounded form, your due diligence regarding the pharmacy source becomes part of your clinical responsibility. You cannot simply write a prescription and assume the pharmacy will handle everything else. You need to know who is compounding the medication, whether they're properly licensed, whether they use appropriate quality controls, whether they source their active pharmaceutical ingredients from legitimate suppliers, and whether they have appropriate sterility testing, especially for injectable products.

Your chart needs to document: why a compounded medication is necessary for this patient (patient-specific need, allergy to commercial excipients, need for customized dosing, unavailability of commercial product, etc.); which pharmacy will compound it and that pharmacy's licensing status; your due diligence regarding the pharmacy's quality and reputation; what you told the patient about the compounded nature of the medication; and the same clinical documentation you'd create for any prescription - indication, history, contraindication screening, consent, monitoring plan, and follow-up.

Let me be specific about what I mean by pharmacy due diligence, because this is where a lot of physicians get sloppy. You should know whether your compounding pharmacy is a 503A or 503B facility. You should know whether they're licensed in your state - and yes, interstate compounding creates additional regulatory complexity that you need to understand. You should know whether they source their APIs from FDA-registered facilities or from who-knows-where. You should know whether they perform sterility testing on every batch of injectable products or only on representative samples. You should know whether they've had any FDA warning letters, state board actions, recalls, or adverse event reports. You should have a pharmacy agreement or at minimum documented communication about their quality standards. And you should review this information periodically, not just once when you first start working with them, because pharmacy status changes. A pharmacy that was clean two years ago may have had an FDA inspection last month that turned up serious problems. A pharmacy that was accredited may have lost accreditation. A pharmacy that sourced from legitimate suppliers may have switched to a cheaper, less reliable source. Your due diligence is not a one-time checkbox. It's an ongoing responsibility.

The consent discussion for compounded medications needs to cover: that the medication is being prepared specifically for the patient by a licensed compounding pharmacy; that the compounded product is not FDA-approved in its final form; that the pharmacy, not the FDA, is responsible for the quality of the preparation; what the patient should look for in terms of appearance, labeling, and packaging; what to do if the product looks different from what they expected; and the same risk-benefit discussion you'd have for any therapy. Patients often don't understand what compounding means. They think they're getting the same thing they'd get at CVS, just in a different bottle. You need to explain that compounded products are custom-made, that quality depends on the specific pharmacy, and that while compounding is a well-established practice, it carries quality risks that commercially manufactured products don't.

I want to emphasize something that physicians frequently misunderstand: compounded does not mean unregulated. A compounded medication from a properly licensed, well-run, accredited compounding pharmacy is a legitimate medical product prescribed through a legitimate medical pathway. But compounded also does not mean "anything goes." The FDA has placed restrictions on which bulk drug substances can be used in compounding. Some peptides are on the FDA's 503A bulk drug substances list. Some are not. Some are on the "do not compound" list. Some are in regulatory limbo. You need to know where your specific peptide stands, not because the FDA is going to arrest you for prescribing it, but because your state board may ask you to explain why you thought this specific compounded product was appropriate for this specific patient, and "I didn't know about the FDA list" is not an answer that inspires confidence in your clinical judgment.

Investigational use: drug not approved and still being studied - high documentation burden

The fourth bucket is investigational use, and this is where the ground gets really soft under your feet. An investigational drug is a drug that has not been approved by the FDA for any indication. It may be in clinical trials. It may have completed some trials but not enough for approval. It may have orphan drug status. It may have been studied in animals but not humans. It may have limited human data from small trials, case series, or foreign studies that the FDA hasn't reviewed. Whatever the specific status, the defining characteristic is this: the drug does not have an approved NDA or BLA in the United States.

Now here's the critical distinction that physicians mess up constantly: investigational use is NOT the same as off-label use. Off-label use means the drug is approved for something, and you're using it for something else. Investigational use means the drug isn't approved for anything. These are fundamentally different categories with fundamentally different legal and clinical implications, and confusing them in your chart is a gift to any board investigator who wants to make your life difficult.

When you prescribe an investigational therapy outside of a formal clinical trial, you are operating at the edge of - and in some cases beyond - established medical practice. This doesn't mean it's automatically illegal or unethical. Physicians have provided investigational therapies to patients under various frameworks for as long as medicine has existed: compassionate use, expanded access, treatment INDs, and in some cases, direct prescribing when no approved alternatives exist and the patient has provided fully informed consent. But the documentation burden, the consent burden, the monitoring burden, and the legal risk are all substantially higher than for approved, off-label, or even compounded therapies.

Your chart for an investigational therapy needs to be a masterpiece of clinical reasoning. It needs to show: that the patient has a genuine medical condition that warrants treatment; that all approved and established treatment options have been tried, failed, refused, or are contraindicated; that you've reviewed the available evidence for the investigational therapy and can articulate both its potential benefits and its known and unknown risks; that you've discussed FDA-approved alternatives with the patient even if the patient has already tried them; that the patient understands the investigational status of the therapy and what that means; that you've established a rigorous monitoring plan with clear stop criteria; that you've involved the patient's primary care physician or relevant specialists when appropriate; and that your prescribing decision is based on the specific patient's clinical situation, not on general enthusiasm for the therapy or pressure from the patient.

The informed consent for investigational therapy is exhaustive. It cannot be a standard form with a few extra sentences. It needs to be a comprehensive disclosure that covers: the investigational status of the drug and what that means; the complete evidence landscape -what's known, what's unknown, what's been studied in animals, what's been studied in humans, and what hasn't been studied at all; all known risks and side effects; the possibility of unknown risks; the fact that the drug is not FDA-approved for any use; alternatives including doing nothing; the voluntary nature of the treatment; the right to discontinue at any time; the monitoring plan; emergency procedures; cost and refund policy; and a clear statement that no results are guaranteed. The patient needs time to read this, time to ask questions, time to consult with other physicians, and time to change their mind. Rushing a patient into investigational therapy is malpractice waiting to happen.

Many peptides that are popular in the cash-pay and longevity spaces fall into this investigational bucket. BPC-157, despite decades of interest and a substantial body of animal research, has limited human clinical trial data and no FDA approval. TB-500 (thymosin beta-4) is in a similar position. Epitalon, FOXO4-DRI, humanin, and many of the other peptides discussed in anti-aging and biohacking circles have either no human trials or very limited human data. Prescribing these is not off-label prescribing. It is investigational prescribing. And if your chart uses the term "off-label" to describe what is actually an investigational therapy, you have just demonstrated to any reviewer that you don't understand the regulatory distinction between approved drugs used differently and unapproved drugs used at all. That is not a position you want to be in.

Before you launch any program built around investigational therapies - and I mean any program, even one patient - you need to have your protocols reviewed by an attorney who understands both medical board proceedings and FDA regulatory structure. Not because you're doing something wrong, but because investigational prescribing sits at the intersection of medical practice law, FDA regulation, malpractice liability, and informed consent doctrine, and the rules are not always clear. An attorney can help you structure your protocols, your consent forms, your patient selection criteria, and your documentation standards to maximize your defensibility. This costs money. It's worth every penny. The cost of a pre-launch legal review is a rounding error compared to the cost of a board defense.

Grey-market product: unverified source or research chemical - do not prescribe, period

The fifth bucket is the one where I have zero flexibility and zero sympathy for physicians who get this wrong:grey-market product. This means any substance that comes from an unverified source, is labeled "research use only" or "not for human consumption," is sold directly to consumers over the internet, or otherwise bypasses the legitimate pharmaceutical supply chain. These are not medications. They are not drugs in any legally or clinically meaningful sense. They are chemicals - maybe the chemical they claim to be, maybe not -sold through a parallel distribution system that exists specifically to avoid pharmaceutical regulation.

Let me be absolutely clear about your obligation here: you do not prescribe grey-market products. You do not recommend them. You do not wink at them. You do not tell patients "I can't prescribe that, but if you happen to find it online, I can't stop you." You actively warn patients against them. You document that warning. You explain the risks of sterility failure, contamination, mislabeling, unknown dosing, and absence of medical supervision. You offer a legitimate medical pathway when one exists. And if no legitimate pathway exists, you say no.

I don't care how much the patient begs. I don't care how many forum posts they've read. I don't care that their friend got "amazing results" from some website. I don't care that the vendor has a certificate of analysis that looks very official. A certificate of analysis proves chemical identity under specific testing conditions. It does not prove sterility. It does not prove the absence of endotoxins. It does not prove that the vial the patient actually receives contains what the certificate says it contains. It does not prove safe handling, proper storage, or accurate dosing. It is a piece of paper designed to give consumers false confidence while transferring liability from the seller to the buyer. And any physician who treats it as equivalent to pharmaceutical quality control has no business prescribing anything.

The grey market exists because demand outpaces legitimate supply. Patients want access to therapies they read about online. Compounding pharmacies may not stock certain peptides. Prices for pharmacy-compounded products are higher than grey-market alternatives. The internet fills the gap with a pipeline that runs from bulk chemical manufacturers - often overseas, often outside normal pharmaceutical inspection - through repackagers and resellers to consumers who reconstitute, measure, and inject themselves with no medical oversight whatsoever. It is self-experimentation. It is not medicine. And your role as a physician is not to facilitate it, tacitly or explicitly.

When a patient tells you they've been buying peptides online, your response needs to be: documented education about the risks of unverified products; documented warning against continued use; documented offer of a legitimate medical pathway if one is clinically appropriate; and documented discussion of why the unverified product is not equivalent to a pharmacy-compounded medication. If the patient insists on continuing to use grey-market products despite your warning, that needs to be documented too - not because it protects you from every possible liability, but because it demonstrates that you fulfilled your duty to advise, warn, and offer a safer alternative. A patient who ignores medical advice is a patient making their own choice. A patient who was never given proper medical advice is a patient you failed.

There is no grey area here. I have seen physicians try to split hairs. "Well, I don't prescribe the grey-market product, but I provide medical monitoring for patients who choose to use it independently." That's prescribing by another name, and every board in the country will see it that way. If you're reviewing a patient's self-directed peptide use, providing dosing advice, adjusting their protocol based on labs, and essentially acting as their medical supervisor for a product you know came from an unverified source, you are complicit in that patient's self-experimentation. You are lending your medical license to legitimize an illegitimate supply chain. And when something goes wrong - an infection, an adverse reaction, a batch contamination, a dosing error - your name is going to be on every document the patient can produce, and the board is going to ask you why a licensed physician was supervising the injection of research chemicals.

The answer to grey-market products is simple. It's not complicated. It doesn't require regulatory nuance or legal interpretation. The answer is no. No, I don't prescribe that. No, I don't recommend that source. No, I don't provide medical supervision for unverified products. Yes, I will help you through legitimate medical channels if you qualify. Yes, I will document everything. Yes, I will explain why this matters for your safety. That's it. That's the whole position. Any physician who tries to find a creative workaround is a physician who doesn't understand that the workaround is what the board will use to take their license.

State Medical Boards: The Real Enemy

Now that you understand the regulatory landscape and the five legal buckets, let me tell you about the entity that actually has the power to destroy your career. I've mentioned them throughout this chapter, but now we're going to look at state medical boards directly - how they work, why they exist, what triggers their investigations, what they look for, and how a routine prescribing practice can become a years-long administrative nightmare that costs you your license, your savings, your reputation, and your sanity.

I'm going to be blunt here in a way that some readers may find uncomfortable. State medical boards are not your friends. They're not your colleagues. They're not reasonable people who understand the pressures of modern medical practice and will give you the benefit of the doubt because you're a good doctor who cares about patients. They are regulatory bodies staffed by attorneys, investigators, and appointed members - some physicians, some not - whose statutory duty is to protect the public from practitioners who fall below acceptable standards. That's it. That's their whole job description. And they take it seriously, especially when a complaint gives them something specific to investigate.

Boards exist to protect the public, not you - remember this every single day

Let me say this again because it's the most important thing you can internalize about state medical boards: they exist to protect the public, not you. Every time you sit down to write a chart note, every time you draft a consent form, every time you select a pharmacy, every time you decide whether to accept or decline a patient, you need to remember that the board's loyalty is to the patient, not to you. They are not interested in your good intentions. They are not interested in how much you care. They are not interested in how frustrated you are with a broken healthcare system or how much you believe in peptide medicine or how many patients have told you that you changed their lives. They are interested in one question: did this physician meet the standard of care in their treatment of this specific patient? If the answer is no - or if the chart doesn't clearly demonstrate that the answer is yes - you have a problem.

The standard of care, by the way, is not some magical standard written down in a book that everyone agrees on. It's a fluid, evolving, jurisdiction-specific concept that generally means what a reasonably prudent practitioner in the same specialty, under similar circumstances, would have done. In a board proceeding, this usually gets defined by an expert witness -another physician, often in a related specialty, hired by the board to review your chart and opine on whether your care met acceptable standards. That expert is not your peer in any meaningful sense. They are an adversarial witness whose job is to find problems with your care and explain them to the board in language that supports disciplinary action. They get paid whether they find problems or not, but let's be honest: boards don't hire experts who consistently say "everything looks fine." The experts who get repeat business are the ones who find problems.

This is why I tell every physician I work with: build your chart for the skeptical reviewer. Don't build it for yourself. Don't build it for the patient. Don't build it for your staff. Build it for the board attorney, the expert reviewer, and the panel member with no medical background who are going to read it eighteen months from now after a complaint has been filed and emotions have soured and you're sitting in a hearing room trying to explain why you made decisions that seemed perfectly reasonable at the time but don't look so great under fluorescent lights across from a prosecutor.

The board's structure varies from state to state, but the general pattern is similar. There's a board of members - appointed by the governor, confirmed by the legislature in some states -that includes both physician and public members. The public members have equal voting power. Think about that for a moment. A retired accountant or a community organizer or a schoolteacher can sit on a panel that decides whether you keep your medical license, and their vote counts exactly the same as the orthopedic surgeon's vote next to them. I'm not saying public members are unreasonable people. Many of them are thoughtful and conscientious. But they don't have medical training. They don't understand clinical nuance. They understand what sounds bad, what looks sloppy, and what seems like something a doctor shouldn't have done.

Your chart needs to tell a story that makes sense to them, not just to another physician.

Beneath the board members is a staff - attorneys, investigators, administrative personnel -who handle the day-to-day work of complaint intake, investigation, and case preparation. These are career regulators. They see hundreds of cases a year. They've read every excuse, every justification, every story about what the doctor "really meant" to do. They're not impressed by your credentials, your publications, or your patient testimonials. They're impressed by documentation that shows you did what you were supposed to do, followed your own protocols, and maintained appropriate standards.

I want you to think about this from the board staff's perspective for a moment. They come to work every morning to a desk piled with complaints. Some are frivolous - patients angry about wait times, ex-spouses filing revenge complaints, competitors trying to cause trouble. But many are legitimate concerns about care that looked questionable. The staff's job is to sort through all of this and decide which cases warrant further investigation. When they read a complaint about a physician who prescribed investigational peptides without documented evaluation, without informed consent, and without follow-up, that case goes in the"investigate" pile. Not because the staff hates peptides. Not because they're in the pocket of Big Pharma. Because their statutory duty is to protect the public, and a physician prescribing investigational therapies without proper safeguards looks like a public protection problem. That's all it takes.

Boards do not need to prove malpractice - they only need to decide your care looks sloppy

This is the part that shocks physicians who have never been through a board proceeding. In a civil malpractice lawsuit, a plaintiff needs to prove four elements: that you owed them a duty of care, that you breached that duty, that the breach caused harm, and that damages resulted. It's a structured legal framework with burdens of proof, rules of evidence, and judicial oversight. Board discipline is nothing like that.

Board discipline is administrative, not judicial. The board is not a court. The investigators are not police. The hearing is not a trial, at least not in the way physicians understand trials from television. The board operates under its state's Administrative Procedure Act, which has its own rules about evidence, standards of proof, and due process. But those rules are designed for administrative efficiency, not for the protection of the accused. The board can compel you to produce records without a warrant. The board can interview your staff without your attorney present. The board can issue subpoenas, hire experts, and build a case against you using a standard of proof that is lower than what would be required in civil court.

Most states require the board to find "clear and convincing evidence" of a violation of the Medical Practice Act before imposing discipline. That sounds protective. It isn't. "Clear and convincing" in an administrative proceeding means whatever the board says it means. If your chart is thin, if your consent is weak, if your monitoring is undocumented, if your rationale is missing - that can be enough. The board doesn't need to prove you harmed a patient. They don't need to prove your therapy caused an injury. They only need to prove that your care fell below the standard - that you were sloppy, or careless, or insufficiently thorough, or failed to document appropriately. And "failed to document appropriately" is the board's favorite allegation because it's almost always true and it's almost impossible to defend against retroactively.

Let me give you a real scenario. A physician in a southern state - I'll leave out identifying details because I don't want to get sued, but this is a composite of several real cases I've reviewed - started a cash-pay peptide and hormone practice. Good doctor. Cared about patients. Genuinely believed he was helping people who'd been failed by conventional medicine. He prescribed BPC-157 for musculoskeletal issues, sermorelin for age-related decline, and a few other compounds that were popular in the longevity space. He charged reasonable prices. Patients loved him. Google reviews were glowing.

Then a patient didn't get the results she expected. She'd paid $400 a month for three months. Her shoulder still hurt. She asked for a refund. He said no - medical services were rendered, outcomes weren't guaranteed. She got angry. She posted negative reviews. He didn't respond well - got defensive, which is the worst thing you can do with an unhappy patient. She filed a complaint with the state medical board.

The board opened an investigation. They requested his charts. They requested his consent forms. They requested his protocols. They requested his advertising materials. They requested his pharmacy agreements. What they found was predictable: charts that were mostly templated notes with minimal patient-specific documentation; consent forms that were generic and didn't mention the specific investigational status of the therapies; no written protocols for patient selection, monitoring, or stop criteria; staff who had been trained informally and whose roles were not clearly defined; advertising that emphasized "cutting-edge therapies" and"transformational results" without the appropriate medical disclaimers; and pharmacy relationships that had never been formally vetted beyond a phone call and a few prescription orders.

The board's expert reviewed ten charts and found problems in all ten. Inadequate history-taking. No documented contraindication screening. No evidence that standard therapies had been tried or considered before investigational therapies were prescribed. Consent forms that didn't disclose the investigational nature of the drugs. No monitoring plans. No follow-up documentation. No PCP involvement. No specialist referrals for complex cases. The expert's report was devastating - not because the doctor had harmed anyone, but because his care looked sloppy. And sloppy, in a board proceeding, is enough.

The board filed charges. The doctor hired an attorney - $15,000 retainer. The hearing took two days. The board suspended his license for six months, required him to complete 100 hours of continuing education, placed him on probation for two years with quarterly chart audits, and made the suspension reportable to the National Practitioner Data Bank. That NPDB report followed him for the rest of his career. Every credentialing application, every malpractice renewal, every hospital privilege request - he had to explain it. The investigation, the hearing, the suspension, the whole ugly story. Over a patient complaint about a $1,200 treatment that didn't work. That's what a board can do to you. And they can do it without proving malpractice, without proving harm, and without caring one bit about your good intentions or your patient's signed testimonial letters.

Common board allegations: poor standard of care, inadequate history, inappropriate prescribing, failure to monitor

Board investigations in cash-pay peptide, hormone, weight-loss, and wellness practices tend to cluster around a predictable set of allegations. I want to walk you through these because understanding what the board is looking for helps you build systems that prevent problems before they start. The most common allegations are:

Poor standard of care. This is the catch-all allegation that covers everything from inadequate evaluation to inappropriate therapy selection to failure to follow up. It's the board's way of saying "you didn't practice good medicine," and it can be supported by virtually any deficiency in your clinical process. The board will look at whether your evaluation was thorough enough to support the therapy you prescribed, whether your therapy choice was reasonable given the patient's condition and history, whether you followed established clinical guidelines where they exist, and whether your overall approach met the expectations that a reasonable practitioner in similar circumstances would meet. For peptide prescribing, this often means the board asking: why did you choose this specific peptide for this specific patient? What evidence supported that choice? What alternatives did you consider? Why wasn't a more established approach tried first? If your chart can't answer those questions clearly, you're vulnerable to this allegation.

Inadequate history or examination. This one is devastating because it's so easy to prove and so hard to defend. The board expert reviews your chart, compares your history and physical to what's generally expected for the condition being treated, and identifies gaps. Did you document a complete medication list? Did you ask about allergies? Did you screen for contraindications? Did you take vitals? Did you review prior records? Did you involve the patient's PCP? For peptide prescribing specifically, did you ask about pregnancy status? Did you screen for cancer history when relevant? Did you review the patient's current medications for interactions? Did you document a physical examination appropriate to the complaint? Every "no" or "not documented" is a mark against you, and it doesn't take many marks before the board concludes that your evaluation was insufficient to support your prescribing decision.

Inappropriate prescribing. This allegation focuses on the therapy itself: was the drug appropriate for this patient at this dose for this indication? The board will examine your prescribing patterns, looking for red flags like: prescribing investigational therapies without adequate justification; prescribing multiple peptides simultaneously without clear rationale; doses that exceed usual ranges; failure to consider drug interactions; prescribing to patients with clear contraindications; and prescribing patterns that suggest you're treating requests rather than medical conditions. If your charts show that virtually every patient who walks through your door gets the same cocktail of peptides regardless of their individual clinical situation, the board is going to conclude that you're running a product-distribution operation, not a medical practice. And they're going to be right.

Failure to monitor. This is where a lot of otherwise careful doctors get caught. They do a good intake. They get appropriate consent. They make a reasonable prescribing decision. And then they drop the ball on follow-up. They don't schedule monitoring appointments. They don't order follow-up labs. They don't document phone calls or patient-reported side effects. They don't have clear stop criteria. They auto-refill prescriptions without clinical review. The board sees this as prescribing without supervision - essentially handing out medication and hoping for the best. For peptide therapies, especially investigational ones, monitoring is not optional. It's part of the prescribing decision. If you prescribe BPC-157 and don't follow up to see if it worked, didn't work, or caused problems, you haven't completed the clinical encounter. You've started something and abandoned it, and boards hate that.

Poor informed consent. We've covered this in detail elsewhere in this book, but it bears repeating here because inadequate consent is one of the most common allegations in board complaints. Consent that doesn't disclose the investigational status of a therapy. Consent that doesn't discuss alternatives. Consent that doesn't explain risks in understandable language. Consent that the patient signed without any evidence that a real discussion occurred. Consent forms that are just legal documents with no educational value. All of these are problems, and all of them are easy for a board expert to identify and criticize. Good consent is documented proof of a real conversation. Bad consent is documented proof that you didn't bother to have the conversation. Boards can tell the difference.

Misleading advertising. Cash-pay practices live and die by patient acquisition, which means advertising. But advertising that promises results, uses patient testimonials inappropriately, fails to include required disclaimers, or creates the impression that you're selling products rather than providing medical care is a magnet for board complaints. Another physician sees your ad and thinks it looks unprofessional. A patient has a bad outcome and pulls up your website to show the board all the promises you made. A competitor reports you because your advertising is aggressive. Any of these can trigger an investigation, and once the board starts looking at your advertising, they'll look at everything else too.

Failure to supervise staff. This is the allegation that turns a physician problem into a practice-wide problem. Unlicensed staff giving medical advice. Nurses operating outside their scope. Medical assistants making triage decisions. Receptionists discussing dosing. Staff writing chart notes that the physician never reviews. Password sharing for e-prescribing systems. No written protocols defining what staff can and cannot do. When the board finds staff problems, they don't just discipline the staff member - they discipline the physician who was responsible for supervision. And "I didn't know they were doing that" is the worst possible defense, because it proves you weren't supervising.

Bad records. Inadequate, incomplete, illegible, or missing medical records. Templated notes that don't reflect the actual encounter. Charts that contain no evidence of clinical reasoning. Records that can't be produced when the board requests them. This is the allegation that makes every other allegation worse, because without good records, you can't defend yourself against anything. The chart is your evidence. If your evidence is weak, your defense is weak, and the board knows it.

Every complaint gets investigated - controlled medication complaints get investigated more aggressively

Here's a fact that keeps me up at night: in most states, every complaint to the medical board gets some level of review. Not every complaint leads to a full investigation - boards don't have the resources for that - but every complaint gets logged, read, and evaluated. And complaints that involve specific allegations of inappropriate prescribing, inadequate evaluation, or patient harm get investigated. Period. There's no threshold. There's no "this complaint isn't serious enough to bother with." If someone files a complaint that alleges you did something below standard, the board has a statutory obligation to look into it.

The investigation process varies by state, but the general pattern is consistent. Complaint comes in. Staff attorney reviews it for jurisdiction - does this fall within the board's authority? If yes, the complaint is assigned to an investigator. The investigator may request records from you, from hospitals, from pharmacies, from other physicians. They may interview the complainant. They may interview you - and if they do, you should have an attorney present, because anything you say can and will be used against you. The investigator compiles a report. The report goes to a screening panel or committee that decides whether there's enough evidence to proceed. If there is, formal charges are filed. You get a hearing. The hearing panel makes a decision. The decision can be appealed through the administrative court system in some states, but appeals are expensive and rarely successful.

The entire process, from complaint to final decision, can take one to three years. During that time, you're practicing under a cloud. The complaint may be confidential at the initial stages, but it doesn't stay confidential forever. In most states, disciplinary actions are public. They're posted on the board's website. They're reportable to the NPDB. They're discoverable by malpractice insurers, hospitals, and credentialing committees. Even if you're ultimately exonerated, the process itself is punishing - financially, emotionally, and professionally.

Now let me talk about the special risk of controlled substances, because this is where investigations get really aggressive. Complaints that allege controlled substance overprescribing, diversion, or inappropriate prescribing get prioritized. They get the A-team investigators. They get board members who are specifically concerned about the opioid epidemic and who view every controlled substance prescriber with heightened scrutiny. They get referred to the DEA if there's any hint of criminal conduct. And they get prosecuted with a zealousness that non-controlled-substance complaints rarely receive.

If you prescribe testosterone, anabolic steroids, appetite suppressants like phentermine, sleep medications, anxiety medications, or any other controlled substance from your practice, you are in a higher-risk category than a physician who doesn't. It's that simple. Testosterone, in particular, has become a flashpoint for board scrutiny because the explosion of testosterone clinics - some legitimate, some barely more than vial shops - has created a regulatory backlash. Boards in multiple states have launched targeted investigations of testosterone-prescribing practices, and those investigations almost always include a review of everything else the practice does, including peptide prescribing.

The connection between controlled substances and peptide investigations is real and it's dangerous. A board investigator looking at your testosterone prescribing will also look at your peptide prescribing. They'll ask whether you're using peptides to augment or substitute for controlled substance therapies. They'll ask whether your peptide patients are also your testosterone patients and whether that creates a pattern of high-risk prescribing. They'll ask whether your informed consent for peptides is as thorough as your informed consent for controlled substances - and if it's not, they'll want to know why you think peptides deserve less scrutiny. They'll look at your overall practice pattern and ask whether it looks like comprehensive medical care or a medication-access business with a medical license attached.

This is why the "fly under the radar" philosophy matters so much. Controlled substances put you on the radar. Once you're there, everything you do is visible. The board doesn't compartmentalize. They look at the whole practice. And if the whole practice has weaknesses

- weak charts, weak consent, weak protocols, weak supervision - those weaknesses get magnified under the spotlight of a controlled substance investigation.

Every complaint gets investigated. Every investigation creates a record. Every record follows you. And controlled substance complaints get investigated faster, more aggressively, and with more resources than any other category. That's not paranoia. That's the reality of medical board regulation in the current environment. Plan accordingly.

Experimental and Investigational: When You Cross the Line

We're now at the most dangerous territory in the peptide prescribing landscape. I've talked about the five legal buckets. I've explained why state medical boards are the real threat. I've walked you through how investigations start and what they look for. Now I need to focus on the specific category of therapy that gets more physicians into trouble than anything else: investigational and experimental prescribing. This is where good intentions meet weak evidence, where patient desperation meets physician optimism, and where charts that seemed adequate at the time get torn apart by board reviewers who have the benefit of hindsight and no particular interest in your clinical philosophy.

Let me start with the most important distinction in this entire section, because getting this wrong has ended more careers than any other single error in peptide medicine.

Off-label is not investigational - know the difference, document it precisely

I cannot tell you how many charts I've reviewed where the physician describes a therapy as"off-label" when it is plainly, obviously, undeniably investigational. They are not the same thing. They are not close to the same thing. They are different categories with different legal implications, different documentation requirements, different consent standards, and different risk profiles. And confusing them in your medical record is like hanging a sign around your neck that says "I do not understand the regulatory framework in which I practice."

Let me state the distinction one more time, as clearly as I can: Off-label means the drug has been approved by the FDA for at least one indication, and you're using it for something else. The drug has an NDA or BLA. It has been through the FDA's review process. It has established manufacturing standards, labeling, safety data, and a known risk profile. When you use it outside that labeling, you're in off-label territory, which is legally and clinically well-established territory with recognized documentation requirements.

Investigational means the drug has not been approved by the FDA for any indication. It does not have an NDA or BLA. It has not completed the FDA's review process. It may have research data - animal studies, foreign trials, early-phase human trials, case reports - but it does not have the regulatory and evidentiary foundation that comes with FDA approval. Prescribing an investigational drug is not off-label prescribing. It is a different category entirely, and it requires a different level of justification, documentation, and consent.

Here's why this distinction matters so much to boards. When you call something "off-label,"you're implying that the drug has FDA approval for something. You're invoking the legitimacy of the FDA review process even while acknowledging that you're using the drug differently. The board understands off-label prescribing. They see it all the time. They know it's legal. They know it's common. They may have questions about your specific rationale, but they're not starting from a position of suspicion about the drug itself.

When you call something "investigational" - or worse, when you call an investigational therapy "off-label" - you're in different territory. The board knows that investigational therapies lack FDA approval. They know the evidence base is thinner. They know the risks are less well-characterized. And they know that physicians who prescribe investigational therapies need to have their ducks in a row, because the presumption of clinical acceptability that comes with FDA approval simply doesn't exist. A physician prescribing an investigational therapy is a physician who has consciously chosen to step outside the mainstream of medical practice, and boards scrutinize that choice with particular care.

So when your chart says "off-label" and the therapy is actually investigational, you've created two problems. First, you've mischaracterized the regulatory status of the therapy, which suggests either ignorance or intentional obfuscation - neither of which helps your credibility. Second, you've applied off-label documentation standards to what is actually an investigational therapy, which means your documentation is almost certainly inadequate for the real category you're operating in. You've used a consent form for an approved drug used differently when you actually needed a consent form for an unapproved drug used at all. You've documented monitoring appropriate for a therapy with established safety data when you actually needed much more rigorous monitoring for a therapy with unknown long-term effects. Every element of your clinical process is calibrated to the wrong standard, and a board reviewer will spot that mismatch instantly.

Let me give you the concrete examples, because this is where abstraction meets reality. Semaglutide for weight management in a patient who meets the BMI criteria - approved use, bucket one. Semaglutide for PCOS-related metabolic dysfunction in a patient who doesn't meet obesity criteria - off-label use, bucket two. The drug is approved. The evidence for metabolic benefits in PCOS exists, even if it's not the approved indication. Your documentation shows why the approved indication doesn't quite fit, what evidence supports your alternative use, and what alternatives you considered. That's a defensible off-label prescribing decision if your chart is good.

Now take BPC-157. No FDA approval for any indication. No completed large-scale human clinical trials. Substantial animal data suggesting benefits for tendon healing, gut mucosal repair, and vascular protection, but limited human pharmacokinetic data, no established dosing standards for human use, and no long-term safety profile. You prescribe it for a patient with chronic Achilles tendinopathy who's failed physical therapy, NSAIDs, corticosteroid injections, and is considering surgery. Is this off-label? No. It's investigational. The drug has never been approved for anything. There is no label to go "off" of. Calling it off-label in your chart is factually wrong and clinically misleading.

Your documentation for the BPC-157 prescription needs to reflect its investigational status clearly and accurately. The chart should state: "BPC-157 is an investigational peptide with no FDA-approved indications." It should summarize the available evidence, including its limitations: "Animal studies suggest potential benefits for tendon healing, but human clinical trial data is limited and no large-scale safety studies have been completed." It should document the patient's informed consent to an investigational therapy: "Patient counseled regarding investigational status, limited human data, unknown long-term risks, and absence of FDA approval. Patient verbalized understanding and elected to proceed." It should establish monitoring and stop criteria: "Patient to return in four weeks for reassessment. Therapy to be discontinued if no clinically meaningful improvement in pain or function at eight weeks." And it should document the entire clinical reasoning chain that led from the patient's problem to this specific therapy.

Compare that level of documentation to what you'd create for an off-label semaglutide prescription. The semaglutide chart needs a rationale, alternative discussion, and off-label disclosure, but it doesn't need to explain why you're using a drug that has no regulatory approval at all. The investigational BPC-157 chart needs all of that plus a much more extensive evidence review, a much more detailed consent process, a much more explicit monitoring plan, and a much clearer justification for why an unapproved therapy is appropriate for this patient at this time. The documentation burden is not the same. It is substantially higher. And treating it as the same - or worse, using the wrong category entirely - is a catastrophic error.

I want you to do something right now. Go pull ten charts from your peptide practice. Look at how you describe the therapies you're prescribing. Do you use the term "off-label" for drugs that have no FDA approval? Do you describe compounded peptides without mentioning their investigational status? Do your consent forms accurately state whether the therapy is approved, off-label, compounded, or investigational? If you find errors - and I suspect many of you will- fix them. Today. Not next week. Today. Because every chart with an incorrect regulatory characterization is a chart that will destroy your credibility in a board proceeding.

Patient desperation does not equal medical indication

Now let's talk about the scenario that pushes physicians across the line from careful to careless: the desperate patient. Every physician who practices peptide medicine has met this patient. They've been to five specialists. They've tried everything approved. They've spent years in pain, or fatigue, or metabolic dysfunction, or whatever their issue is. They come to you as the last stop before giving up. They've read about peptides online. They know the evidence is limited. They don't care. They'll sign anything. They'll pay anything. They just want a chance at something that might help when nothing else has.

I understand the impulse. I really do. You've got a suffering patient in front of you. You have a therapy that, based on mechanism and limited data, might help. The patient is begging you to try. Every fiber of your physician-being wants to help. You tell yourself you'll monitor closely. You'll document carefully. You'll stop at the first sign of trouble. You're not promising results- just a chance. What's the harm?

The harm is that patient desperation is not a medical indication. It is an emotional state. And while compassion is essential to good medicine, compassion without clinical rigor is how physicians end up in front of boards trying to explain why they prescribed an investigational therapy to a patient who had no documented evaluation, no contraindication screening, no alternative discussion, and no realistic understanding of what they were getting into. The patient's desperation became the physician's justification, and that's not how medicine works. That's how disciplinary proceedings start.

Let me be clear about what I'm not saying. I'm not saying you should never prescribe investigational therapies to patients who've exhausted standard options. That is a legitimate clinical scenario, and there are legitimate frameworks for approaching it. What I'm saying is that the patient's desperation cannot substitute for your clinical judgment. The fact that a patient is suffering and wants to try something does not relieve you of your obligation to evaluate, screen, discuss alternatives, obtain proper consent, establish monitoring, and document everything. If anything, a desperate patient requires more rigorous evaluation, not less, because desperate patients are vulnerable patients. They may not hear your warnings. They may not understand your disclosures. They may have unrealistic expectations that you need to identify and address before prescribing, not after.

The desperate patient scenario also creates special consent challenges. A patient who sees you as their last hope may not process risk information the way a less emotionally invested patient would. They may focus entirely on potential benefits and minimize potential risks. They may hear "this could help" and not register "but we really don't know if it's safe long-term." Your consent process with a desperate patient needs to be even more thorough than usual. You need to check for understanding. Ask them to explain back to you what the therapy is, what it might do, what it might not do, and what could go wrong. Document that conversation. If they can't articulate the risks accurately, they haven't given informed consent, and you shouldn't prescribe until they can.

There's another problem with the desperation justification: it creates a pattern. If your charts show that you consistently prescribe investigational therapies to patients who are "desperate"or who have "exhausted all options," the board will ask a simple question: did you actually verify that they'd exhausted all options? Did you review their records from the other specialists? Did you consult with those specialists? Did you confirm that the standard therapies were truly tried at appropriate doses for appropriate durations? Or did you accept the patient's self-report and move straight to investigational prescribing because it was easier and more profitable than doing the hard work of coordination and verification?

I've seen charts where the physician wrote "patient has failed all standard therapies" and the chart contained zero documentation of what those therapies were, who prescribed them, at what doses, for how long, and why they failed. The physician just accepted the patient's word and moved on. That's not clinical reasoning. That's chart fiction. And board experts can smell chart fiction from a hundred pages away. If you claim a patient has exhausted standard options, your chart needs to list those options, document your review of the patient's history with them, and explain why each one was insufficient. If you don't have that documentation, you don't have a justification for skipping to investigational therapy.

The bottom line on patient desperation is this: compassion is not a clinical protocol. Your obligation to a desperate patient is to provide the same rigorous evaluation, the same careful consideration of alternatives, the same thorough consent process, and the same meticulous documentation that you'd provide to any other patient. Desperation may make the patient more willing to accept risk, but it doesn't reduce your obligation to manage that risk appropriately.

And if you find yourself prescribing investigational therapies primarily because patients are asking for them and you hate to say no, you need to take a hard look at your practice patterns, because that's not medicine. That's something else, and boards have a word for it.

If the chart cannot explain the decision, the decision is not ready

This is the rule that should be carved above the door of every physician's office. If the chart cannot explain the decision, the decision is not ready. Not "the decision might be okay if I explain it verbally." Not "the decision is good medicine even though my charting is rushed."Not "I'll document it better next time." If the chart, as it exists right now, cannot tell a complete stranger why you prescribed what you prescribed to whom you prescribed it with what rationale and what safeguards - the decision is not ready. Go back and do the work.

I know what you're thinking. You're busy. You see thirty patients a day. Your EHR is a nightmare. The templates are clunky. The documentation burden is crushing. You do good medicine, and the chart is just administrative overhead that gets in the way of patient care. I hear this from every physician I work with, and I have limited sympathy for it, because I've also read the charts that result from this attitude, and they're indefensible.

The chart is not administrative overhead. The chart is the only permanent record of your clinical judgment. It is the evidence that will either save you or destroy you in a board proceeding. It is the document that a skeptical stranger - someone who doesn't know you, doesn't like you, and has no reason to give you the benefit of the doubt - will read to determine whether you're a competent practitioner or a sloppy prescriber who got lucky until the luck ran out. And if that chart is thin, templated, generic, or missing critical elements, that skeptical stranger will draw the worst possible inference from every gap. That's not paranoia. That's how board investigations work.

Let me tell you what a chart needs to contain to explain an investigational therapy prescribing decision. This is the standard. Not my standard - the standard that board experts apply when they review these cases. If your chart doesn't have these elements, you're not ready to prescribe.

First, the clinical problem. Why is this patient in your office? What condition are you treating? What is the severity? How long has it been present? What impact does it have on the patient's function and quality of life? This needs to be specific, not generic. "Patient wants peptides" is not a clinical problem. "Patient with chronic rotator cuff tendinopathy, unresponsive to six months of physical therapy and two corticosteroid injections, with MRI- confirmed partial-thickness tear, experiencing persistent pain at 7/10 that limits overhead activity and sleep" - that's a clinical problem.

Second, the treatment history. What has been tried? What were the results? Why were standard approaches insufficient? This needs to be documented, not assumed. If the patient says they tried physical therapy, your chart should note where, when, for how long, and what the outcome was. If you have records from the physical therapist, even better - reference them. If the patient was seen by other specialists, document your review of those records or your communication with those specialists. The board wants to see that you didn't just skip to the investigational therapy because it's what you sell.

Third, the rationale for the investigational therapy. Why this therapy for this patient? What is the mechanism of action? What evidence supports its use in this clinical scenario? What are the limitations of that evidence? Your rationale should connect the patient's specific clinical picture to the therapy's known or theorized effects. It should demonstrate that you thought about this decision rather than reflexively reaching for your standard prescription pad. And it should be written in your chart note, not in your head.

Fourth, contraindication and risk screening. What could make this therapy unsafe for this patient? What did you check? What did you find? Document your screening for pregnancy, cancer history, organ dysfunction, drug interactions, allergies, and any other relevant contraindications. If the patient's history is complex, document your consultation with relevant specialists. If screening reveals a relative contraindication, document your risk-benefit analysis and why you proceeded despite it, or why you decided not to proceed.

Fifth, alternatives discussion. What other options exist? Why were they not chosen? This includes approved alternatives, other off-label options, non-pharmacological approaches, and the option of doing nothing. Document that you discussed these with the patient and that the patient understood them. The board wants to see that the patient made an informed choice among real options, not that they were channeled toward the one therapy you happen to offer.

Sixth, informed consent. Documented proof that the patient understood the therapy's investigational status, the available evidence, the known and unknown risks, the monitoring plan, the stop criteria, the cost, the refund policy, and the right to discontinue. The consent should be specific to the therapy and the patient, not a generic form that the patient signed without discussion. If the consent form is ten pages of legal language that no patient could reasonably understand, it's not informed consent - it's liability theater, and boards can tell the difference.

Seventh, the monitoring plan. How will you follow this patient? What labs, if any? What clinical assessments? How often? What are the stop criteria? What are the warning signs that should prompt the patient to contact you urgently? Document this in the chart, not on a separate handout that may or may not make it into the record.

Eighth, PCP or specialist involvement. For investigational therapies, involving the patient's primary care physician is one of the strongest protective measures you can take. It demonstrates that you're not practicing in isolation, that you respect the patient's existing medical relationships, and that you've communicated your prescribing decision to another qualified practitioner who can provide ongoing monitoring and catch problems you might miss. Document that communication. If the PCP expresses concerns, document those too and your response to them.

If your chart doesn't contain all eight of these elements for an investigational therapy prescribing decision, your chart doesn't explain the decision. And if your chart doesn't explain the decision, the decision is not ready. It's that simple. No exceptions. No "I was busy." No"the patient was waiting." No "I'll document it later." Do the work before you prescribe, document it in real time, and sleep soundly knowing that if anyone ever asks questions, your chart will answer them.

Why investigational therapies require attorney review before program launch

I want to close this chapter with a recommendation that every physician hates to hear but every experienced practitioner eventually accepts: before you launch any program built around investigational therapies, you need to have your protocols reviewed by an attorney. Not just any attorney - a healthcare attorney who understands medical board proceedings, FDA regulatory structure, malpractice liability, informed consent law, and the specific legal environment of your state. This is not optional. It is not a luxury for practices with extra money. It is an essential protective measure that costs a fraction of what a board defense will cost you.

Let me explain why attorney review matters so much for investigational therapy programs, beyond the general principle that lawyers are useful when you're doing things regulators might question.

Investigational therapy prescribing sits at the intersection of multiple legal frameworks, and those frameworks don't always align cleanly. State medical practice acts govern whether your prescribing meets the standard of care. FDA regulations govern the legal status of the substances you're prescribing. Federal compounding rules govern how those substances can be prepared and distributed. State pharmacy laws govern the pharmacies you work with. Malpractice law governs your liability if something goes wrong. Informed consent law governs what you must disclose to patients. And in some cases, federal research regulations may even come into play if your prescribing program starts to look like an informal clinical trial rather than individualized patient care.

An attorney who understands this landscape can help you navigate it. They can review your patient selection criteria to make sure they're clinically appropriate and legally defensible. They can review your informed consent forms to ensure they meet your state's standards for disclosure of investigational therapies. They can review your protocols to identify gaps that a board expert would exploit. They can review your pharmacy agreements to make sure they're structured appropriately. They can review your advertising to make sure it doesn't create liability. They can advise you on whether your state's Medical Practice Act has specific requirements for experimental or investigational therapies that go beyond the general standard of care. And they can help you structure your documentation standards so that every chart in your practice tells a coherent, defensible story.

Here's what attorney review typically covers in a pre-launch assessment: your patient intake forms and clinical evaluation protocols; your informed consent forms for each investigational therapy you plan to offer; your prescribing protocols including dosing ranges, monitoring schedules, and stop criteria; your pharmacy selection and vetting procedures; your staff training materials and scope-of-practice definitions; your advertising and marketing materials; your fee structures and refund policies; your procedures for handling adverse events, patient complaints, and red flags; and your documentation templates to ensure they capture the elements that matter in a board proceeding. Every one of these documents should be reviewed, revised, and approved before you see your first patient.

The cost of this review varies depending on your location, the complexity of your program, and the attorney's experience level, but as a general range, you're looking at $5,000 to $25,000 for a comprehensive pre-launch review. That sounds like a lot of money until you compare it to the cost of a board defense, which typically runs $50,000 to $200,000 in attorney fees alone, not counting lost income from suspended practice, increased malpractice premiums, mandatory continuing education, and the incalculable cost to your professional reputation. Spending $10,000 upfront to avoid spending $100,000 later is not a luxury expense. It's risk management, and it's the smartest money you'll spend on your practice.

I also want to address a specific concern that physicians raise about attorney review: the fear that if they consult an attorney, it creates a record that they were worried about legal risk, and that record could be used against them if there's ever a proceeding. This is a misunderstanding of how attorney-client privilege works. Communications with your attorney for the purpose of obtaining legal advice are privileged. They are not discoverable by a board. They are not admissible in proceedings. The fact that you sought legal advice to ensure compliance is actually a point in your favor if it ever comes up, because it demonstrates that you took your regulatory obligations seriously and made a good-faith effort to operate within the law. The board is not going to discipline you for being careful. They're going to discipline you for being sloppy. Attorney review is the opposite of sloppy.

There's another reason attorney review is particularly important for investigational therapies: the line between clinical practice and research. The federal regulations governing human subjects research - 45 CFR Part 46 and 21 CFR Part 50/56 - impose strict requirements on clinical trials, including institutional review board approval, informed consent that meets specific federal standards, and ongoing oversight. If your "peptide program" starts to look like a systematic study - if you're collecting data on outcomes, if you're using standardized protocols across multiple patients, if you're planning to publish your results, if you're advertising your program as "participating in cutting-edge research" - you may cross the line from medical practice into human subjects research without even realizing it. And human subjects research without IRB approval is a serious federal violation that can result in criminal penalties, not just administrative discipline.

An attorney can help you structure your program to stay clearly on the clinical practice side of that line. They can advise you on what activities constitute research versus treatment. They can help you design data collection that supports clinical care without triggering research regulations. They can review your patient communications to make sure you're not making promises or representations that could be construed as research recruitment. And they can help you understand when a therapy has moved from investigational clinical use into a territory where IRB oversight is actually required.

Let me give you one final war story to drive this point home. A physician in the Midwest decided to launch a "longevity peptide program" featuring several investigational peptides. He was a smart guy. Board-certified. Well-intentioned. He'd done his research on the peptides, talked to compounding pharmacies, read the animal studies, and genuinely believed he could help patients. He didn't consult an attorney because he thought it was unnecessary - he was a physician, he knew medicine, what did a lawyer know about peptides?

He created a beautiful website advertising his "evidence-based longevity protocols." He offered a "comprehensive longevity assessment" that included genetic testing, biomarker analysis, and a personalized peptide stack. He hired staff to handle patient coordination. He developed a streamlined intake process that allowed him to see a high volume of patients efficiently. He charged premium prices - $500 for the initial assessment, $400-$600 per month for ongoing therapy. Business was excellent.

A year later, a patient developed an autoimmune condition that she believed was triggered by one of the peptides. She filed a complaint with the state medical board. The board opened an investigation. They requested his charts. They requested his protocols. They requested his advertising. They requested his staff training materials. They requested his pharmacy agreements. And they found what they always find in these cases: charts that were mostly templates with minimal patient-specific documentation; no written protocols for patient selection or monitoring; consent forms that didn't clearly disclose the investigational status of the therapies; advertising that promised "evidence-based" results without explaining the limitations of that evidence; staff who had never been trained on what they could and couldn't say to patients; and pharmacy relationships that had been established through informal conversations rather than formal due diligence.

The board filed charges. The physician hired an attorney - $75,000 over the course of the proceeding. The hearing was brutal. The board's expert systematically demolished every element of his practice. The "evidence-based" advertising was misleading because the evidence was animal studies, not human trials. The consent forms were inadequate because they didn't clearly explain that the therapies were investigational. The charts were insufficient because they didn't document clinical reasoning. The staff were unqualified because they'd never been properly trained. The pharmacy relationships were undocumented because he'd never done formal due diligence. Every weakness was exposed, every gap was highlighted, every good intention was irrelevant.

The board suspended his license for a year, placed him on five years of probation with mandatory quarterly chart audits by a board-approved monitor, required him to complete 200 hours of continuing education, fined him $10,000, and reported the suspension to the NPDB. His malpractice insurer dropped him. The hospitals where he had privileges revoked them. His referral sources dried up. He spent the next three years trying to rebuild a practice that would never again be what it was. All because he didn't spend $10,000 on an attorney review before he launched.

Don't be that doctor. Don't let pride or thrift or the illusion that you're too smart to get caught prevent you from doing the basic protective work that every investigational therapy program requires. Get an attorney. Review your protocols. Fix your consent forms. Train your staff.

Document everything. Build your charts for the skeptical reviewer who will read them in eighteen months. Because that reviewer is coming. Maybe not for you specifically, but someone, somewhere, is going to read your chart and ask hard questions. The only question is whether your chart will have answers.

This chapter has been long and, I suspect, uncomfortable. Good. Regulatory reality should make you uncomfortable. Comfort in this space is dangerous. Comfort leads to cutting corners, skipping steps, assuming everything will be fine because it always has been. The physicians who get in trouble aren't the ones who worried too much. They're the ones who didn't worry enough. They're the ones who thought the FDA's hands-off posture meant nobody was watching. They're the ones who thought state boards were bureaucratic paper-pushers who'd never bother with a cash-pay practice. They're the ones who thought their good intentions and their patients' gratitude would protect them if questions ever arose.

Those physicians were wrong. Every single one of them. And the ones who are still practicing- the ones who survived their board encounters and kept their licenses - will tell you the same thing I'm telling you now: understand the regulatory landscape, know which bucket every prescription falls into, respect the power of your state medical board, document like your license depends on it, and for the love of everything holy, get an attorney to review your investigational therapy protocols before you launch. Not after. Before. Because after is too late. After is when you're sitting in a hearing room watching a stranger pick apart your career while you wonder how something that started with so much promise ended with so much pain.

It doesn't have to end that way. Not if you're careful. Not if you're thorough. Not if you treat every prescribing decision as a decision you'll have to defend, because one day, you will. The chart you write today is the defense you'll present tomorrow. Write it like you mean it.

3 - Fly Under the Radar - The Core Philosophy of This Book

Let me tell you something, and I want you to hear me good, because everything else in this book depends on you understanding this one thing: the state is not your friend. I don't care how many years you went to medical school. I don't care how many diplomas you've got hanging on your wall. I don't care how many patients you've helped or how pure your intentions are. The moment a state investigator opens your file, you are a problem to be solved, not a healer to be defended. And I have watched too many good doctors - smart doctors, caring doctors, doctors who got into this business for all the right reasons - lose everything because they didn't understand that simple truth until it was too late.

This chapter is the heart of the entire book. Everything else is just details. You can memorize every dosing protocol, every informed consent form, every charting template I give you, and it won't matter a damn if you don't internalize the philosophy I'm about to lay out. Because the doctor who flies under the radar, who stays boring, who stays invisible, who gives the medical board no reason to look his direction - that doctor practices peptide medicine for twenty years and retires with his license intact. The doctor who thinks his good intentions and his medical degree are some kind of shield? That doctor gets a certified letter from the state one Tuesday morning, and his life changes forever.

I've seen it. I've watched it happen. And I'm going to do everything in my power to make sure it doesn't happen to you.

What Flying Under the Radar Actually Means

Let me start with what this concept does NOT mean, because I've heard too many doctors get this wrong. Flying under the radar does not mean cutting corners. It does not mean sloppy charting or skipping informed consent or prescribing irresponsibly and hoping nobody notices. It doesn't mean operating some kind of sketchy backroom practice with no records and cash stuffed in shoeboxes. You do that, and you deserve what happens to you, and I won't waste my breath trying to save you.

Flying under the radar means the opposite of all that. It means your practice is so clean, so meticulous, so boringly compliant that an investigator could read every chart you've written for the past five years and find nothing to get excited about. It means your documentation is so thorough that any board reviewer looking at your files thinks "this doctor is careful" and moves on to the next file - which is probably some sloppy train wreck of a chart that gives him the ammunition he actually came looking for. You want to be the chart that disappoints the investigator. You want him to yawn and close your file and go find some real malpractice to pursue.

That's what flying under the radar means. It means being the most boring, most compliant, most invisible peptide practice in your state. And I mean that as the highest compliment.

You do not want the state looking at you - period

Let me be crystal clear about this, because I know the type of doctor who's attracted to peptide medicine. You're probably a little bit of a maverick. You probably got tired of the fifteen-minute insurance appointment, the checkbox medicine, the drug rep telling you what to prescribe. You probably think of yourself as independent-minded, willing to explore therapies outside the mainstream. And that's admirable, it really is. But that independent streak is exactly what can get you in trouble if you let it convince you that the rules don't apply to you.

Here's the reality: your state medical board has hundreds, maybe thousands, of physicians under its jurisdiction. They've got limited staff, limited budget, and more complaints than they can possibly investigate. Most boards operate on a reactive model - they don't go out proactively looking for problems. They respond to complaints. Someone files a complaint, it gets triaged, and if it meets the threshold, an investigator gets assigned. That investigator opens a file, starts pulling charts, and begins building a case.

Now here's what you need to understand about that process. By the time you get the letter saying you're under investigation, the investigator has already done preliminary work. They've already looked at enough to think there's something worth pursuing. That letter isn't the beginning - it's the point where they decided they have enough to let you know they're coming. The train has already left the station. And from that moment forward, you are playing defense, and defense in a medical board investigation is expensive, exhausting, and emotionally devastating.

You know what the worst part is? The board doesn't have to prove you harmed a patient. They don't have to prove anyone died or even got sick. Medical boards operate under a"preponderance of evidence" standard in most states, which means they just have to show it's more likely than not that you violated some regulation, some standard of care, some administrative requirement. And the violations they get you on are almost never the big dramatic things. They're charting deficiencies. Informed consent failures. Documentation gaps. The boring stuff that you thought didn't matter because you were too busy being a healer to worry about paperwork.

Let me give you a scenario that plays out across this country every single month. Dr. Johnson-let's call her that - has been prescribing peptides for two years. She's helped a lot of patients. Her outcomes are good. Her patients love her. She's got a 4.9-star rating online. One day, a patient doesn't get the weight loss results he expected from his GLP-1 agonist peptide protocol. He's angry. He spent four thousand dollars out of pocket, and his brother-in-law lost thirty pounds on the same drug from a different clinic, and Dr. Johnson's patient only lost twelve. So he does what angry patients do in 2024: he goes online and leaves a scathing review. Then he calls the medical board and files a complaint. He says the treatment was ineffective, overpriced, and that Dr. Johnson never told him peptides weren't FDA-approved for his condition.

The board gets this complaint. It gets logged. And because it mentions peptides - which are on the board's radar as an emerging area of concern - it doesn't get dismissed at triage. It gets assigned. An investigator calls Dr. Johnson's office and requests fifty charts. Fifty. Dr. Johnson's staff panics. They pull the charts, and guess what? Half of them have informed consent forms that are generic - just a standard office consent, nothing specific to peptides. A third of them don't document the patient's baseline labs. Several don't have clear records of what specific peptides were prescribed at what doses. One chart has a phone prescription for a refill that isn't documented anywhere except a sticky note.

Now the investigator has moved from looking at one complaint to seeing systemic documentation failures across the practice. Dr. Johnson didn't get investigated because she hurt anyone. She didn't get investigated because she prescribed a dangerous drug. She got investigated because an unhappy patient filed a complaint, and when the board looked at her charts, they found the kind of sloppy documentation that makes any investigator's eyes light up. Six months and forty thousand dollars in legal fees later, Dr. Johnson accepts a consent order: probation, remedial education, a fine, and a public reprimand that shows up every time someone Googles her name for the rest of her career. All because she thought her good outcomes and her patients' love would protect her.

You think the board cares that she meant well? You think they care that forty-nine of her fifty patients got better? They don't. They care about the charts, the documentation, the process, the compliance. And Dr. Johnson failed on every one of those measures because she never thought anyone would be looking.

That's what I mean when I say you do not want the state looking at you. Not because you're doing anything wrong. Not because peptide medicine is illegal. But because once they open your file, they will find something. They always find something. Nobody's charting is perfect under a microscope. Nobody's documentation holds up to fifty-chart review without some gaps. The question isn't whether you're perfect - the question is whether you ever give them a reason to start looking.

And an angry patient, a billing dispute, a bad online review - that's all it takes. That's the spark that lights the fire. Your job is to be so unremarkable, so compliant, so meticulously documented that even if that spark happens, the investigator closes your file and moves on because there's no oxygen for the fire. That's flying under the radar.

You do not want the state monitoring your charts

There's a particular kind of hell that comes with being under board monitoring. I've talked to doctors who've been through it, and they all say the same thing: it's like having a probation officer for your medical practice. Every month, or every quarter, depending on your consent order, you have to submit charts for review. You have to document every prescription, every patient interaction, every clinical decision to a standard that goes beyond normal practice. You have to pay for this monitoring out of your own pocket - and it isn't cheap. Three to five thousand dollars a month is typical. And it goes on for a year, or two years, or sometimes longer.

But the financial cost isn't the worst part. The worst part is the psychological weight of knowing that everything you write, every decision you make, is being read by someone whose job is to find fault. You start second-guessing yourself on every prescription. You start documenting defensively, writing paragraphs where a sentence used to suffice, because you know someone's looking for gaps. Your charting time doubles. Your stress level triples. You start wondering if every patient is someone who might complain, if every treatment is one that might be questioned.

And here's the thing: once you're in monitoring, the threshold for extending it or escalating sanctions is low. The monitor finds a few charts with inadequate documentation - not bad medicine, just inadequate paperwork - and now your monitoring gets extended another six months. Or they flag that you're still prescribing peptides, and the board starts asking whether that's appropriate given your "history." The board doesn't say it explicitly, but the message is clear: we don't like what you're doing, and we're watching you until you give us a reason to stop you permanently.

Some doctors survive monitoring and come out the other side. Others break. They close their practices, or they stop prescribing anything interesting and go back to standard family medicine, or they leave the profession entirely. I've talked to doctors who sold their practices for pennies on the dollar because they couldn't face another month of having someone look over their shoulder. The state doesn't have to revoke your license to destroy your career. Monitoring does the job just fine.

So when I say you don't want the state monitoring your charts, I mean it at the deepest level. You want to structure your entire practice - your documentation, your prescribing, your patient selection, your consent process, your fee structure - so that if an investigator ever does request your charts, what they see is so clean, so thorough, so above reproach that there's no basis for monitoring. The investigator requests your charts, reviews them, and writes in his report: "No significant deficiencies identified. Case closed." That's the outcome you're playing for. That's the only winning move.

How do you get there? You write every chart like it's going to be read by a skeptical board reviewer, because someday it might be. You obtain informed consent like the patient's about to sue you tomorrow, because someday one of them might. You document your clinical reasoning like you're teaching a medical student, because someday you'll need to explain it to someone who knows nothing about peptides and suspects the worst. You select your patients carefully, avoiding the ones who smell like trouble, because one headache patient can bring the whole house down. Every piece of this book is about building a practice that survives scrutiny, because scrutiny comes for everyone eventually - the only question is whether you're ready when it arrives.

You do not want to prescribe anything controlled or reportable

We're going to get into controlled substances in detail in section 3.4, but I need to touch on it here because it's foundational to the fly-under-the-radar philosophy. Every time you write a prescription for a controlled substance - a Schedule II, III, IV, or V drug - you create a data point. That data point goes into the Prescription Drug Monitoring Program (PDMP) in your state. It's tracked. It's reported. It's available to regulators, to law enforcement, to other prescribers who look you up. Every controlled prescription you write adds to a digital footprint that says "this doctor prescribes controlled substances."

Now, maybe you're thinking, so what? I'm a legitimate physician. I prescribe responsibly. I don't overprescribe. I follow all the guidelines. And I'm sure you do. But here's what you need to understand: the PDMP doesn't just track individual prescriptions. It generates patterns. It flags outliers. If you're prescribing controlled substances at a rate above the 75th percentile for your specialty, the system may flag you for review. If a patient of yours is getting controlled substances from multiple providers, the system flags that too - and the investigator doesn't start by asking the patient why they're doctor-shopping. They start by asking you why you're one of the prescribers.

Every controlled substance you prescribe is a thread that regulators can pull. And when they pull it, they don't just look at that one prescription. They look at your entire prescribing history. They look at your peptide prescriptions too, because now they've got your attention. They start asking questions about everything you do. The controlled substance was the entry point, but once they're in your practice, they look at everything.

Compare that to peptides. Most peptides are not controlled substances. They're not tracked in the PDMP. There's no federal database logging every vial of BPC-157 or tesamorelin you prescribe. That's not because peptides are somehow below the law's attention - it's because the regulatory framework hasn't caught up yet. And I'll be straight with you: that could change. The FDA could move to classify certain peptides as controlled or regulated substances. Congress could pass legislation. But as of right now, in today's environment, peptides exist in a regulatory gray zone that, paradoxically, offers some protection from automated surveillance.

But that protection only holds if you don't create other reasons for scrutiny. If you're prescribing testosterone - which is Schedule III - alongside your peptides, now you've got controlled substance prescriptions that bring investigators in the door. If you're writing for tramadol or phentermine or any of the other common adjuncts in anti-aging and wellness practice, you're creating data points. And I'm telling you: you don't need to do it. You can run a successful, profitable, life-changing peptide practice without ever writing a single controlled substance prescription. It may require turning away some patients who want the quick fix of a controlled drug. It may require explaining to patients why you're not their source for testosterone or phentermine. But the peace of mind that comes from having no controlled substance footprint is worth it. Every single time.

Think about it this way: if an investigator comes looking at your practice and you've never prescribed a controlled substance, you've already narrowed what they can investigate. They can't hit you with overprescribing charges. They can't question your DEA registration. They can't use the PDMP to build a pattern of concerning prescribing behavior. You've removed an entire category of risk from your practice. That's not cowardice - that's strategic self-preservation. That's flying under the radar.

You want your practice to be boring, compliant, and invisible to regulators

I want you to picture two medical practices. Practice A is Dr. Stevens, who runs a busy anti-aging clinic in a major metropolitan area. He's got a billboard on the highway. His website promises "revolutionary peptide therapies" and "cutting-edge protocols you won't find anywhere else." He's advertising on social media with before-and-after photos. He's got a podcast where he talks about how mainstream medicine has it all wrong. He prescribes peptides, hormones, IV vitamin cocktails, the works. His waiting room is packed. He's making seven figures.

Practice B is Dr. Chen, who has a modest office in a medical office park. She doesn't advertise. Her website is professional but conservative - it explains that she offers "integrative wellness consultations" and "personalized therapeutic protocols." She doesn't promise miracles. She doesn't bash mainstream medicine. Her fees are premium - cash only, no insurance. She sees fewer patients, spends more time with each one, documents exhaustively, and obtains informed consent that reads like a legal brief. She doesn't prescribe controlled substances. She doesn't take headache patients. She requires every new patient to have a primary care physician involved in their care.

Which doctor do you think the medical board knows about? Which doctor do you think has patients who expect miracles and get angry when they don't happen? Which doctor do you think has a file at the board - maybe not open yet, but building - based on complaints from dissatisfied patients, competitive physicians in the area, or even just the sheer visibility of his marketing?

Dr. Stevens thinks he's untouchable because he's helping people and making money. Dr. Stevens is going to learn a hard lesson one day. Dr. Chen, on the other hand, is boring. Her practice is invisible to anyone who isn't one of her carefully selected patients. There are no billboards inviting scrutiny. There are no miracle claims attracting desperate patients who will turn on her when their unrealistic expectations aren't met. There are no controlled substance prescriptions creating data trails. Her charts are bulletproof. Her consent forms are exhaustive. Her patients are screened for reasonableness before they ever sit in her exam room.

Dr. Chen is flying under the radar. And Dr. Chen is going to practice peptide medicine for as long as she wants, and retire on her own terms, with her license and her reputation intact.

Boring doesn't mean bad medicine. Boring means no drama. No headlines. No complaints that escalate. No investigator who even knows your name. Boring means every patient interaction is professional, documented, consented, and above board. Boring means your charts could be published as textbooks on how to do this right. Boring means when - not if, but when - a patient complains about something, the board takes one look at your file and decides this isn't worth their time.

Let me tell you something about state medical board investigators. They're overworked. They're underpaid compared to what they could make in private practice. They've got backlogs measured in months or years. They don't want to build complex cases against meticulous doctors who have their paperwork in order. They want the easy wins - the docs with sloppy charts, missing consents, unlicensed staff doing medical work, and obvious violations they can document in a week and close out of their queue. When an investigator pulls your charts and sees fifty consecutive files that are comprehensive, well-organized, thoroughly consented, and impeccably documented, what do you think they do? They move on. They find easier prey. You are not worth their time.

That is the goal. That is the philosophy. Be so clean, so boring, so meticulously compliant that the people whose job it is to find fault can't find any. Be invisible to regulators not by hiding, but by being so obviously aboveboard that there's nothing to investigate. Fly under the radar not by avoiding the law, but by exceeding its requirements at every turn.

And understand this: the doctors who get in trouble are almost never the ones who were trying to do something egregiously wrong. They're the ones who got sloppy. They got busy. They cut corners. They assumed their good intentions would protect them. They thought the rules were for someone else, some bad actor out there, not for a healer like them. And the board doesn't distinguish between malicious prescribing and sloppy prescribing. The violation is the same on paper. The penalty is the same. The public reprimand reads the same way to anyone who Googles your name.

Every chart you write is a potential exhibit in a hearing you hope never happens. Every informed consent form is a potential piece of evidence that either protects you or hangs you. Every patient you accept into your practice is a potential complainant or a potential advocate-and you get to choose which through the rigor of your screening process. Every prescription you write is either a data point that supports your clinical judgment or a thread that unravels your entire defense. You are building your case for your license every single day, in every single patient encounter, whether you realize it or not. The doctors who understand this - who internalize it, who make it the operating system of their practice - those are the doctors who survive. The ones who don't? I can tell you stories that would keep you up at night.

Why Peptides, Hormones, and Alternative Therapies Put You in the Crosshairs

Now let's talk about the elephant in the room. You didn't pick peptide medicine because it was the safe, mainstream, board-approved choice. You picked it - or you're thinking about picking it - because you believe in therapies that work, even when the institutional machinery of American medicine hasn't caught up to them yet. You saw patients getting better on BPC-157 when nothing else helped their tendons heal. You read the research on CJC-1295 and ipamorelin and saw real data on growth hormone stimulation. You watched patients transform their body composition, their energy, their sleep, their lives on protocols that no insurance company covers and no pharmaceutical rep ever pitched you. And you thought, this is real medicine. This helps people. I want to do this.

I get it. I really do. I've seen the same things. I've watched patients respond to peptide therapies in ways that no conventional treatment matched. I've read the literature, talked to the researchers, followed the case reports. There is real science here, real clinical value, real potential to change lives. And it's a damn shame that the system doesn't recognize that yet.

But here's what you have to understand, and you have to understand it deep in your bones: the fact that peptides work is not protection. The fact that your patients love you is not a shield. The fact that the science is legitimate doesn't matter one bit to the state medical board investigator who's reading your chart and looking for a violation to write up. You are practicing medicine in a domain that has no institutional protection, no political cover, and no deep-pocketed defenders. And that makes you vulnerable in ways that conventional physicians- even the sloppy, careless ones - simply are not.

There is no billion-dollar lobbying group protecting peptide-prescribing doctors

Let me paint you a picture of how protection works in American medicine. When the FDA considers new regulations that might affect cardiology practices, the American College of Cardiology shows up with lobbyists. They have a Washington office. They have relationships with congressional staffers. They have a budget measured in tens of millions of dollars, and they know how to use it. When Medicare proposes reimbursement cuts that would hit orthopedic surgeons, the American Academy of Orthopaedic Surgeons mobilizes its members, its PAC, its media contacts. They buy ads. They schedule meetings with legislators. They make phone calls that get returned.

When there's a problem with an FDA-approved drug - let's say a statin gets linked to a slightly increased risk of some adverse event - the pharmaceutical company that makes it has a team of lawyers and lobbyists on the case before the news even breaks. They've got relationships with the FDA built over decades. They've funded studies, endowed chairs at medical schools, sponsored continuing medical education conferences. They know how to manage a crisis because they've done it before, and they've got the infrastructure to push back.

Now, who shows up when peptides are under scrutiny? Who's in the room when state medical boards discuss whether to issue guidance on peptide prescribing? Who lobbies Congress to make sure that compounding pharmacies can keep making the peptides your patients depend on? Who takes out full-page ads defending the doctors who prescribe these therapies?

Nobody. That's who. Nobody with money. Nobody with power. Nobody with institutional clout.

There are organizations that care about peptides, don't get me wrong. There are research groups, online communities, compounding pharmacy associations, individual physicians who advocate passionately. But passion doesn't buy lobbyists. Research grants from small foundations don't compete with pharmaceutical company PAC contributions. The peptide community is fragmented, underfunded, and politically naive compared to the machinery that protects conventional medicine.

The American Medical Association, for all its size and history, is not riding to your rescue if you get in trouble for prescribing peptides. The AMA has enough trouble staying relevant to practicing physicians; it is not going to spend political capital defending a fringe therapy that most of its members don't use and some actively oppose. Your state medical society? Maybe they'll send a letter. Maybe. If you're a member in good standing and you've paid your dues for twenty years. But they are not going to war for you. They are not going to jeopardize their relationships with the board over a peptide-prescribing physician who, in the eyes of the medical establishment, was playing outside the sandbox to begin with.

This is the reality: you are on your own. Your peptide practice is your responsibility to defend, and the institutions that protect conventional physicians will not extend that protection to you. Understanding this isn't paranoia. It's operational awareness. It's knowing the terrain you're operating in so you can take the precautions that the protected doctors don't have to worry about.

The cardiologist who writes a prescription for a drug that's later found to have killed a few dozen patients? He's got the American College of Cardiology issuing statements. He's got the drug company sending lawyers. He's got malpractice insurance with a team of defenders who've handled a thousand cases just like his. The system is built to absorb that damage, to spread it around, to protect the prescriber because the prescriber is part of a protected class -a class you're not in.

You? You prescribe a peptide, a patient has an adverse reaction - maybe not even a serious one, maybe just something unexpected - and you are alone. The compounding pharmacy might help, if they're reputable and still in business. A few colleagues might offer moral support. But there is no army of lobbyists. There is no pharmaceutical company with a vested interest in defending you. There is no professional association with the clout to make the board think twice. You are one doctor with a problem, standing against a system that has no particular reason to be fair to you.

That is why flying under the radar isn't just good advice. It's survival strategy. It's understanding that without institutional protection, your only defense is to give the system no ammunition to use against you. Your charting, your consent, your documentation, your compliance - those are your lobbyists. Those are your defense team. Those are the only protection you've got.

Big Pharma contributes millions to political campaigns - peptides contribute zero

Let me tell you how the world actually works, because I spent enough years in investment banking to see the machinery up close. When Pfizer wants something from Congress, they don't write a letter and hope someone reads it. They hire former congressmen as lobbyists. They host fundraising dinners. They make PAC contributions through subsidiaries so the numbers are spread across dozens of entities and hard to trace. They fund the campaigns of committee chairs and ranking members. They show up at town halls in legislators' districts and talk about jobs - how many jobs their facility provides, how many more jobs a favorable bill would create. They commission economic impact studies that show billions in value to the American economy. They do all of this through teams of professionals who've been doing it for decades, who know every staffer on the Hill by name, who can get a meeting with a senator's office faster than you can get an appointment with your own primary care doctor.

In 2022, the pharmaceutical industry spent over $370 million on lobbying. That's just lobbying- the reported, disclosed spending. The dark money, the PAC contributions, the indirect funding through trade groups, the sponsored research that shapes academic opinion, the continuing medical education that shapes practicing physicians' prescribing habits - that number is much, much larger, and much harder to measure. The pharmaceutical industry is one of the most powerful political forces in American life, and it has been for generations.

How much did the peptide industry spend on lobbying in 2022? I can tell you without looking it up: a rounding error by comparison. Maybe a few hundred thousand dollars, spread across a handful of small compounding pharmacy associations and advocacy groups. Maybe less. And what they spent it on was probably defending compounding pharmacy rights in general - not peptide-specific legislation, because there basically isn't any. No one on Capitol Hill is introducing the "Peptide Access and Innovation Act." No senator is giving floor speeches about the importance of preserving physicians' ability to prescribe BPC-157 off-label. It doesn't happen, because the political economy of peptides doesn't support it.

This matters for your practice in concrete, practical ways. When the FDA issues guidance that restricts compounding of certain peptides - as they've done and will continue to do - that guidance isn't being balanced against input from a powerful peptide lobbying force, because there isn't one. The FDA hears from pharmaceutical companies about safety concerns, about the need for rigorous approval processes, about the dangers of unapproved therapies. And they hear crickets from the other side. The guidance gets written, the restrictions get tighter, and physicians like you are left figuring out how to adapt.

When state legislatures consider laws that would regulate or restrict anti-aging medicine, hormone therapy, or integrative practices, who shows up to comment? The state medical society, which is often ambivalent or hostile to these practices. The insurance industry, which doesn't want to pay for them. Maybe, if you're lucky, a patient advocacy group or two. But there is no peptide Super PAC. There are no congressmen who got elected on a pro-peptide platform. This is not a constituency that anyone in power is afraid of alienating.

And that asymmetry shapes every regulatory decision that affects your practice. It means that when there's ambiguity about whether a particular use is appropriate, the ambiguity gets resolved against you - not because of malice, but because there's no countervailing pressure.

The system defaults to the position that benefits the entities with power, and that is not you.

Understanding this isn't about cynicism for its own sake. It's about calibrating your risk assessment. A conventional physician practicing entirely within FDA-approved indications, following standard of care guidelines, prescribing drugs from major pharmaceutical companies- that physician has the entire weight of the medical-industrial complex behind him, whether he realizes it or not. His prescribing habits are the default. They are normal. They are protected by sheer institutional inertia. Even when he makes mistakes, the system is structured to absorb them, to contextualize them, to say "this was standard practice" and move on.

You? You are outside that protection. Every prescription you write is a choice to deviate from the default, and deviation requires justification. The system doesn't give you the benefit of the doubt. It gives you scrutiny. And the only way to survive that scrutiny is to be so meticulous, so well-documented, so obviously careful that even a skeptical reviewer has to admit you did this right.

When an FDA-approved blockbuster drug kills patients, the system protects the prescriber - when a peptide causes a headache, the prescriber stands alone

This is the part that really steams me, because I've watched it happen too many times to count. Let me give you a concrete example - and I'm going to use a real one, though I won't name names because I don't need the legal headache. A few years back, a major pharmaceutical company got FDA approval for a new diabetes drug. Blockbuster potential - billions in projected revenue. The clinical trials showed some cardiovascular safety signals, but the drug got approved anyway because the advisory committee decided the benefits outweighed the risks. The company launched with a massive marketing campaign, directly to consumers on television, to physicians through their sales force, to payers with rebate programs. Within two years, hundreds of thousands of patients were on this drug.

Then the deaths started mounting. Patients with pre-existing heart conditions were having cardiovascular events at rates significantly above what the trials had suggested. The FDA added a black box warning - the most serious warning the agency can issue. The company paid billions in lawsuits. Congressional hearings were held. It was a scandal, no question about it.

Now, here's my question: how many prescribing physicians lost their licenses over this? How many had their charts reviewed by state medical boards? How many faced disciplinary action for prescribing an FDA-approved drug exactly as indicated, following the labeling, doing everything by the book - a drug that turned out to be killing people?

Virtually none. The system correctly identified the pharmaceutical company as the responsible party. The FDA took the heat for inadequate oversight. Congress grandstanded.

But the individual physicians who wrote those prescriptions? They were practicing standard of care. They were following guidelines. They were prescribing an FDA-approved drug for an approved indication. The system protected them because the system is built to protect them. They were inside the walls, and the walls held.

Now compare that to what happens when a peptide patient has an adverse outcome. Let's say you prescribe a growth hormone secretagogue to a patient for anti-aging purposes. You've done your workup. You've checked their IGF-1 levels. You've screened for contraindications. You've obtained detailed informed consent. You've documented everything meticulously. The patient does great for six months - more energy, better sleep, improved body composition. Then they develop a headache. Just a headache. They mention it at their follow-up. You evaluate, you adjust the dose, you monitor. The headache resolves over a few weeks, maybe related to the peptide, maybe not - there's no way to know for certain.

But this patient is a headache patient - the type I warn you about elsewhere in this book. They're never satisfied. They've got a complaint about everything. They decide the peptide caused their headache, that you should have warned them better, that you downplayed the risks. They file a complaint with the medical board. They post online about how your"experimental therapy" gave them a neurological problem. Maybe they even hire a lawyer and threaten a lawsuit.

Now the board opens an investigation. They pull your charts. They start asking questions. Why did you prescribe an unapproved drug? What training do you have in peptide medicine? Did you explain to the patient that this was off-label? Where's your informed consent? What monitoring protocol did you follow? How do you know the headache wasn't related to something more serious? Did you consult with the patient's primary care physician? Why not?

The headache resolved. The patient is fine. No permanent harm done. But you are now spending forty, fifty, sixty thousand dollars on legal defense, facing months of stress and uncertainty, wondering if your license is going to survive because a patient got a headache on a therapy that, by any rational assessment, was working well and causing no lasting harm.

Do you see the asymmetry? The blockbuster drug that killed people - the physicians were protected. The peptide that caused a temporary headache - the physician stands alone, exposed, vulnerable, with no institutional voice saying "this doctor was practicing responsibly within the accepted norms of his specialty." Because there is no accepted norm. There is no specialty organization that has established guidelines for peptide prescribing. There is no pharmaceutical company with a vested interest in defending you. There is only you, your charts, and your lawyer.

This is why I am so relentless about documentation, about consent, about screening patients, about involving primary care physicians, about every single protective measure in this book. Because I know that when things go sideways - and eventually, for every peptide prescriber, something will go sideways - you will be standing alone. The only thing standing between you and a consent order, a reprimand, or a revoked license is the quality of the chart you wrote before anyone was looking at it.

The system is not fair. I want you to know that. I want you to feel it in your gut. The system is not fair, it is not balanced, and it is not going to change anytime soon. The physician prescribing the latest obesity drug that was rushed through accelerated approval with questionable long-term data - that physician is fine. The physician prescribing a peptide with decades of research and a stellar safety profile - that physician is taking a risk that the conventional physician is not. It may not be right, but it is real. And you have to operate in the reality that exists, not the reality you wish existed.

IV vitamins, colonics, hormones, and peptides: popular, effective for millions, and politically undefended

There's a pattern here that I want you to see clearly, because it extends beyond peptides to a whole category of medicine that I sometimes think of as the "politically orphaned" therapies.

These are treatments that millions of Americans seek out, pay for out of pocket, and report benefiting from. They're treatments that have clinical evidence supporting their use, that are administered by licensed physicians in legitimate medical settings, that have safety profiles comparable to or better than many FDA-approved interventions. And they exist in a regulatory and political no-man's-land where no one with power is willing to stand up and defend them.

IV vitamin therapy - popular with athletes, executives, people recovering from illness, anyone who wants rapid nutrient repletion. Administered in clinics across the country by licensed professionals. Millions of infusions given every year with a safety profile that, honestly, is remarkable. The biggest risks are infiltration and infection at the IV site -standard risks of any IV administration. Yet if a patient has an adverse outcome from an IV vitamin infusion and complains to the board, that physician is on his own. There's no American Academy of IV Vitamin Medicine with lobbyists in Washington. There's no pharmaceutical company selling these vitamins at a 10,000% markup and defending the prescribers. There's just the physician, the chart, and the hope that his documentation was good enough.

Hormone replacement therapy, especially in the anti-aging and wellness context - millions of patients, mostly women but an increasing number of men, seeking treatment for symptoms that conventional medicine often dismisses or inadequately addresses. Bioidentical hormones compounded specifically for individual patients, based on lab work and clinical assessment, monitored with follow-up testing. This is personalized medicine at its most literal. And it works for an enormous number of people who couldn't get relief from standardized pharmaceutical hormone products. But the compounding pharmacies that make these customized formulations are under constant regulatory pressure. The physicians who prescribe them are practicing in a gray zone where standards of care vary wildly by jurisdiction and are often poorly defined. And when a board investigator comes calling, there is no endocrine society riding to the rescue with practice guidelines and expert witnesses. You're on your own.

Colon hydrotherapy, hyperbaric oxygen, ozone therapy, platelet-rich plasma, stem cell treatments - the list goes on. Some of these have more evidence than others. Some are more controversial than others. But they share a common characteristic: they are not part of the mainstream medical infrastructure that provides institutional protection to physicians. They are not taught in most medical schools. They are not covered by insurance. They are not prescribed by the majority of practicing physicians. And that means that the physicians who do prescribe them, who do offer them, who believe in them enough to build a practice around them - those physicians are exposed.

Now, I want to be clear about something. I'm not saying these therapies are above criticism. I'm not saying every IV vitamin clinic is run responsibly, or that every hormone prescriber is careful, or that every peptide practice is legitimate. There are bad actors in this space, just like there are bad actors in conventional medicine. There are clinics that oversell, overcharge, underdeliver. There are practitioners who don't do adequate workups, who don't monitor properly, who take shortcuts that endanger patients. Those practitioners deserve scrutiny, and if they're harming patients, they deserve to lose their licenses.

But the system doesn't distinguish between the careful practitioner and the sloppy one - not initially, not at the investigation stage. The system investigates based on complaints, and the complaint doesn't come with a label saying "this doctor is meticulous" or "this doctor is sloppy." The investigator pulls the charts, and what they find determines the outcome. The careful practitioner with bulletproof documentation survives and continues helping patients. The sloppy practitioner with gaps and failures in their charts gets sanctioned. And the therapy itself - whether it's peptides, hormones, IV vitamins, or anything else - is what brought the investigator in the door.

This is the burden you carry as a physician practicing outside the mainstream. Every therapy you offer that isn't part of the standard playbook is a potential point of scrutiny. Every patient you treat who could have been treated conventionally - by which I mean, every patient, because there's always a conventional alternative, even if it's "do nothing and live with the symptoms" - is a decision you'll have to justify if asked. And you will not have the protection of standard-of-care defenses, of specialty society guidelines, of institutional cover. Your defense is your documentation. Your protection is your meticulousness. Your shield is your chart.

I want you to sit with that for a moment. Really let it sink in. The cardiologist has the American College of Cardiology. The oncologist has the National Comprehensive Cancer Network guidelines. The family physician has the US Preventive Services Task Force recommendations. You have your pen, your EMR, your informed consent forms, and your clinical judgment. That's it. That's all. And if that sounds frightening, good. It should. Fear, properly channeled, is a powerful motivator. It should motivate you to be the most careful, most documented, most defensible practitioner you can possibly be. It should motivate you to read every chapter of this book, to implement every recommendation, to treat every chart like it's evidence in a trial that hasn't started yet.

Because that trial - that investigation, that complaint, that moment when someone official starts asking questions about your practice - it's not a matter of if. It's a matter of when. And when it happens, the only friend you've got is the chart you wrote when nobody was looking.

The Medical Board Minefield

If I could take every physician reading this book and give them one superpower, it wouldn't be the ability to heal instantly or diagnose perfectly or never lose a patient. It would be the ability to see their practice through the eyes of a state medical board investigator. Because the gap between how you see your practice - the warm exam rooms, the grateful patients, the careful clinical reasoning, the lives you've improved - and how an investigator sees it is enormous. To you, it's medicine. To them, it's a file full of potential violations waiting to be documented. And the sooner you close that gap in your own mind, the sooner you'll start making the decisions that keep you safe.

I've spent enough time around medical board proceedings - consulting, testifying, watching good doctors get dragged through processes that would break most people - that I can tell you exactly what investigators look for, exactly how cases develop, exactly where the bodies are buried. And I'm going to give it to you straight, because sugar-coating this doesn't help anyone. The medical board is a minefield. Every step you take in your practice is potentially on a mine. And the only way through is to know where the mines are and walk around them.

How board investigations actually start: a patient complaint, a chargeback, or a bad review

Let me destroy a myth right now. Most physicians think board investigations start with something big - a patient death, a serious injury, a hospital reporting a sentinel event, a criminal conviction. And yes, those things do trigger investigations. But they're not the majority. Not even close. The majority of board investigations start with things so small, so seemingly trivial, that the physician often doesn't even remember the incident that started it all.

Here's the most common trigger: a patient complaint. Not a lawsuit - a complaint. A letter or an online form submission to the state medical board, usually from a patient who's unhappy about something. Maybe they didn't get the results they wanted. Maybe they thought the fees were too high. Maybe they had a personality conflict with the physician or the staff. Maybe they expected a refund and didn't get one. The content of the complaint often has only a loose relationship to what the board actually investigates, because the complaint is just the entry point. Once the door is open, the investigator can look at anything.

I've seen investigations start because a patient was mad about a twenty-dollar copay. I've seen them start because a patient felt "rushed" during their appointment. I've seen them start because a patient's ex-spouse filed the complaint as part of a divorce strategy. The threshold for opening a complaint file at most medical boards is shockingly low, and there is no penalty for filing a frivolous complaint. A patient can say virtually anything, and if it contains the magic words - "unsafe care," "inappropriate prescribing," "lack of informed consent,""unprofessional conduct" - it gets logged and triaged.

Now, most complaints do get dismissed at triage. The board receives thousands of complaints a year, and the majority are from people with obvious axes to grind, or complaints about things that aren't within the board's jurisdiction (like billing disputes), or complaints so vague that there's nothing to investigate. But here's what you need to understand: the complaint that gets dismissed at triage for Dr. Conventional, the family medicine doc who writes for blood pressure meds and antibiotics, might get assigned to an investigator for you. Because your name is attached to a peptide practice, or an anti-aging clinic, or a cash-pay model, and that makes you interesting. That makes the complaint worth a second look. The board staffer doing triage sees "patient alleges inappropriate prescribing of unapproved peptide therapy" and that gets their attention in a way that "patient alleges inappropriate prescribing of amoxicillin" does not.

The second common trigger is a chargeback. This is one that catches a lot of cash-pay physicians off guard. You're running a credit card practice - patients pay upfront for their consultation, their labs, their peptides. Most of the time, it goes smoothly. But then a patient disputes the charge with their credit card company. Maybe they say the service wasn't what was promised. Maybe they claim they never received the product. Maybe they just changed their mind and want their money back, and when you refuse - because they signed a contract, because you delivered the service, because your no-refund policy was clearly disclosed - they file a chargeback.

Here's what a lot of physicians don't realize: significant chargeback activity gets reported to state authorities. If a medical practice starts showing a pattern of disputed charges, that can trigger attention from the board, from consumer protection agencies, even from criminal authorities in extreme cases. A chargeback rate above a certain threshold flags the merchant account. Multiple chargebacks from different patients starts to look like a pattern. And even if you win every single chargeback dispute - which you should, if your documentation and policies are solid - the pattern itself can draw attention. The board sees three or four complaints about your practice involving financial disputes, and now they're wondering: what is this practice doing that generates so many unhappy patients?

The third trigger, and one that's becoming more common every year, is a bad online review. A patient goes on Google or Yelp or Healthgrades and writes a scathing review. They say you pushed "unapproved" therapies on them. They say you were only in it for the money. They say you didn't explain the risks. Maybe the review contains enough detail - specific drugs, dates, clinical details - that it reads as credible to someone at the board doing routine monitoring. Or maybe the patient, having vented online, also decides to file a formal complaint. Or maybe a competitor physician sees the review and forwards it to the board with a note saying "is this the kind of medicine we want in our state?" Yes, that happens. Competitor complaints are a real thing, especially in markets where peptide and wellness practices are seen as taking patients away from conventional providers.

Once any of these triggers activates, the process follows a predictable pattern. The complaint gets logged and assigned a case number. A triage reviewer reads it and decides whether it meets the threshold for investigation. If it does, an investigator gets assigned. That investigator will start by requesting records - your charts, your billing records, your consent forms, your policies and procedures. They may interview the complaining patient. They may interview your staff. They will review everything with a checklist of potential violations in mind, and they will document every gap, every inconsistency, every failure to meet whatever standard they believe applies.

And here's the critical point: this process can take months. You might not know you're under investigation for weeks after it starts. Your staff might get a records request before you even know there's a case. The investigator has the power to subpoena records, to interview people under oath, to demand documentation of your policies, your training, your quality assurance processes. By the time you get the letter saying you're the subject of an investigation, the investigator may have already built a substantial file.

Do you understand now why I say the chart proves your case? Because when that investigator pulls your records, what they find determines everything. If they find fifty charts that are detailed, well-organized, thoroughly consented, and impeccably documented, they're going to write a report that says "insufficient evidence of violation" and move on. If they find charts with gaps, missing consents, undocumented phone prescriptions, and no evidence of monitoring or follow-up, they've got the foundation for a case. And the case they build isn't about the complaint that started the investigation - it's about the patterns of deficiency they find once they're inside your practice.

Cash-pay medicine is still medicine - the board doesn't care that you don't take insurance

This is one of the biggest misconceptions I encounter among physicians entering the cash-pay and peptide space. They think that because they're not dealing with insurance, they've escaped the regulatory oversight that comes with billing Medicare or accepting managed care contracts. They think the cash transaction puts them in some kind of free zone where medical board rules don't apply, or apply differently. And that belief is not just wrong - it's dangerously wrong.

Let me say this as clearly as I can: cash-pay medicine is still medicine. You are still a licensed physician. Your patients are still patients. The standard of care still applies. The medical practice act in your state still governs everything you do. The fact that payment flows directly from patient to physician rather than through an insurance intermediary changes absolutely nothing about your regulatory obligations, your liability exposure, or the board's authority over your practice.

In fact, in some ways, cash-pay medicine puts you under more scrutiny, not less. Insurance-based practices have institutional layers that absorb some regulatory attention - the credentialing process, the utilization review, the pharmacy benefit management restrictions, the malpractice insurance requirements. These layers are often maddening to deal with, and I understand why physicians want to escape them. But they also serve as evidence of a certain baseline legitimacy. A physician who's credentialed with three major insurers, who gets prior authorizations approved, whose prescribing passes pharmacy benefit manager review - that physician has institutional stamps of approval that cash-pay physicians lack.

You? You're on your own. There's no insurance company doing utilization review on your peptide prescriptions. There's no pharmacy benefit manager denying coverage for off-label uses. There's no hospital credentialing committee verifying your training. That independence is liberating, but it also means that when questions arise about your practice, there are no institutional layers to provide context or legitimacy. The board looks at you and sees a physician who has deliberately stepped outside the system, and that makes them inherently curious about whether you're operating responsibly or running some kind of operation.

I've heard cash-pay physicians say things like "the board can't tell me how to run my business" or "I have a right to set my own fees" or "my patients are adults who can choose to pay for whatever services they want." And there's a sense in which all of those things are true. You do have business rights. Your patients are adults. Fee-for-service medicine is a legitimate model. But the board isn't interested in your business philosophy. The board is interested in whether your medical practice complies with the medical practice act, and that act governs everything from informed consent to scope of practice to record-keeping to prescribing standards. Whether you take insurance or not is irrelevant to those standards.

What the board cares about is whether you're practicing medicine safely and responsibly. They care whether your patients are adequately informed about what you're prescribing and why. They care whether your documentation supports your clinical decisions. They care whether you're practicing within your scope and training. They care whether you're monitoring patients appropriately, obtaining appropriate labs, referring to specialists when indicated, maintaining adequate records, and following up on abnormal findings. These are medical standards, not insurance requirements, and they apply to every physician in the state regardless of payment model.

Now, there is one area where cash-pay status does create specific vulnerability, and I want you to be aware of it. Cash-pay practices, especially those offering premium services like peptide therapy, anti-aging protocols, and wellness optimization, are sometimes perceived - not without reason - as appealing to physicians whose primary motivation is financial rather than clinical. I'm not saying that's true of you. I'm saying that's the perception you have to overcome. When an investigator sees a practice charging five thousand dollars for a peptide protocol, not taking insurance, and prescribing therapies that most physicians don't offer, there's an automatic assumption that needs to be overcome. The investigator is thinking: is this about patient care, or is this about revenue?

You overcome that assumption through the quality of your documentation and the thoroughness of your process. You show, through your charts, that you did comprehensive workups. That you reviewed lab results carefully. That you discussed risks and benefits in detail. That you obtained informed consent that specifically addressed the off-label, non-FDA-approved nature of the therapy. That you established monitoring protocols. That you collaborated with the patient's primary care physician. That you turned away patients who weren't appropriate candidates. That you documented clinical reasoning for every decision. When an investigator reads charts that demonstrate this level of care and thoroughness, the"just in it for the money" narrative collapses. But when they read charts with minimal documentation, no evidence of informed consent, no lab monitoring, and no clinical reasoning? That narrative writes itself.

And I want to address one more thing about cash-pay medicine because it comes up constantly. Some physicians think that because patients are paying out of pocket, they have somehow waived their rights to complain or to hold the physician accountable. They think a cash transaction is somehow a release of liability. Let me be absolutely clear: that is nonsense. A patient paying cash has exactly the same rights as a patient whose insurance is paying. They can file complaints with the medical board. They can sue for malpractice. They can post negative reviews. They can report you to consumer protection agencies. The fact that they chose to pay you directly gives them no fewer rights and gives you no additional protection. None. Zero.

In fact, cash-pay patients may actually be more likely to complain, because they have a direct financial relationship with you that creates different expectations. When a patient pays a five-thousand-dollar fee and doesn't get the results they expected, that financial investment becomes part of their grievance. They feel personally invested in a way that insured patients don't. The money becomes evidence of their commitment, and your failure to deliver becomes a betrayal of that investment. I'm not saying this is rational or fair. I'm saying it's real, and you need to account for it in how you structure your practice, your consent process, your fee agreements, and your patient selection.

Consent issues, staff scope creep, documentation failures, prescribing problems, and system failures

When I talk to physicians who've been through board investigations, I always ask them the same question: what did the board actually get you on? And you know what? It's almost never the thing they were worried about. The physician who was terrified they'd be sanctioned for prescribing peptides off-label? The board got them on inadequate informed consent and unlicensed staff administering injections. The physician who worried about being questioned on their clinical judgment? The board got them on documentation failures and missing follow-up notes. The big scary thing - the peptide prescribing, the alternative therapy, the unconventional approach - usually isn't what generates the actual violation. It's the boring stuff underneath. It's the foundation crumbling while the physician was focused on keeping the roof pretty.

Let me walk you through the five categories where board investigations find actual violations, because if you understand these, you can build defenses against all of them.

Consent issues are probably the single most common violation in peptide and wellness practices. And when I say consent issues, I don't mean "the patient didn't sign a consent form."I mean the consent form was inadequate. It was generic - the same form used for every procedure in the practice, with nothing specific to peptides. It didn't explain that the therapy was off-label. It didn't explain that the peptide was not FDA-approved for the indication prescribed. It didn't list the specific risks of the particular peptide being used. It didn't document that the patient had the opportunity to ask questions and had them answered. It didn't confirm that the patient understood they were receiving an experimental or investigational therapy. It didn't include alternative treatments discussed. It didn't have a clear statement that the patient consented voluntarily and could withdraw consent at any time.

When a board investigator reads a consent form, they're reading it with one question in mind: would a reasonable patient, reading this form and having this conversation, understand exactly what they were getting into? If the answer is no - if the form is vague, generic, or missing key elements - you've got a consent violation. And consent violations are easy for boards to prove, because the evidence is right there in the chart. Either the consent is adequate or it isn't. It's binary. And "I had a verbal conversation with the patient" doesn't cut it. If it isn't documented, it didn't happen. That's the rule. Write it down.

Staff scope creep is the next landmine, and it's a big one in practices that do a lot of in-office administration. Your medical assistant starts giving peptide injections because she's seen you do it a thousand times and it looks easy. Your front desk person starts answering clinical questions from patients on the phone because she's heard you explain the protocols so many times. Your nurse starts adjusting doses based on patient feedback because she wants to be helpful and save you time. Every one of these scenarios is a potential scope-of-practice violation that can bring your entire practice down.

The board investigator who interviews your staff - and they will interview your staff - is listening for exactly this kind of thing. "Who gives the injections?" "Who answers patient questions about side effects?" "Who calls in refills?" "Who adjusts the protocol if a patient calls and says they're not tolerating the dose?" If your staff's answers suggest that anyone without the appropriate license is making clinical decisions, administering medications, or providing clinical advice, you have a problem. And it's not just your problem - it's your staff's problem too, because practicing medicine without a license is a criminal offense in most states.

The fix is simple in concept and demanding in execution: clear role definitions, written protocols, regular training, and constant vigilance. Every staff member should have a written job description that explicitly states what they are and are not authorized to do. There should be written protocols for every clinical task that specify who can perform it and under what circumstances. There should be regular training sessions where you reinforce these boundaries. And there should be zero tolerance for scope violations, because one incident of an unlicensed person making a clinical decision is all it takes to create a board case.

Documentation failures are the bread and butter of board investigations. Investigators live for documentation failures because they're objective, provable, and easy to write up. Missing follow-up notes? Documented. Gaps in the medication record? Documented. Phone conversations not recorded? Documented. Lab results reviewed but not acknowledged in the chart? Documented. Every failure to document a required element is a potential violation, and when you multiply them across dozens of charts, the investigator builds a pattern: this physician has a systemic problem with documentation.

I cannot stress this enough: your chart is your defense. Every entry you make is either building your wall or leaving a gap for the investigator to exploit. The follow-up note you didn't write because you were busy? That's a gap. The phone call you didn't document because it seemed routine? That's a gap. The lab result you reviewed mentally but didn't acknowledge in writing? That's a gap. The dose change you discussed with the patient verbally but didn't record? That's a gap. And an investigator with fifty of your charts and a checklist is going to find every single one of them.

The standard I teach is simple: if you did it, write it down. If you thought it, write it down. If you discussed it, write it down. If you reviewed it, write it down. If you decided it, write it down. The chart should tell the complete story of the patient's care, from initial encounter through every follow-up, in enough detail that someone reading it five years later - which is exactly what might happen - can reconstruct your clinical reasoning and see that you practiced responsibly.

Prescribing problems in peptide practices usually fall into a few predictable categories. Inadequate workup before initiating therapy - starting peptides without appropriate baseline labs, without a thorough history, without screening for contraindications. Inadequate monitoring - not following up with labs, not assessing response, not watching for adverse effects. Polypharmacy without documented rationale - prescribing multiple peptides, or peptides alongside hormones, or peptides alongside other supplements, without a clear documented plan and without evidence that you've thought about interactions. And inappropriate prescribing for the wrong patient - giving peptides to patients with contraindications, or to patients who clearly aren't going to comply with monitoring, or to patients whose complaints are vague and whose diagnoses are speculative.

Every one of these is avoidable with careful patient selection and rigorous protocols. You don't prescribe peptides to patients who won't do follow-up labs - period. You don't start multiple new therapies simultaneously without a clear plan for assessing what's doing what. You don't prescribe to patients whose primary complaints are "I just don't feel good" without a thorough workup that yields at least a working diagnosis. You don't let patients pressure you into prescribing something you're not comfortable with because they're paying cash and they expect to get what they want. When in doubt, say no. The patient you turn away might be annoyed. The patient you shouldn't have accepted can cost you your license.

System failures are the catch-all category that boards use when they can't quite pin a violation on one of the specific categories above. "Failure to maintain adequate systems for quality assurance." "Failure to implement appropriate policies and procedures." "Failure to supervise staff adequately." These are the kinds of findings that get tacked on when the board investigator sees a pattern of problems and concludes that the root cause is a practice that just isn't run well enough to ensure patient safety.

And here's the thing: in many cases, they're right. The physician who has consent failures AND documentation gaps AND staff scope issues AND prescribing problems probably does have a systems problem. The practice isn't structured properly. There aren't adequate checks and balances. There isn't a culture of meticulousness. The physician is doing too much himself, or delegating too much to people who aren't qualified, or cutting corners because he's busy and the shortcuts haven't caught up to him yet. When the board sees this pattern, they don't just issue a citation for the individual violations. They impose systemic remedies -practice monitors, mandatory training, operational audits, restrictions on practice activities -that are designed to force the physician to build the systems they should have had all along.

The lesson is clear: build the systems before the board makes you. Implement the quality assurance processes before an investigator finds the gaps. Write the policies and procedures before you're asked to produce them. Train your staff before someone testifies that they didn't know what they were allowed to do. The practice with robust systems survives scrutiny. The practice without them gets dismantled.

The board reads your chart after the story turns ugly - write it before it does

I want to leave you with an image that I hope will haunt you in the best possible way - the way that motivates you to do the right thing even when it's tedious, even when you're busy, even when nobody's watching.

Imagine this scene. It's two years from now. You're sitting in a conference room with your lawyer. Across the table is a board investigator, and she's got a stack of your charts in front of her. Fifty charts, pulled at random from your practice. She's been reviewing them for weeks. She knows your prescribing patterns. She knows your documentation habits. She knows which of your staff members do what. She's read your consent forms. She's looked at your lab monitoring. She's interviewed your patients. She's built a case, and now she's presenting it.

Your lawyer is looking through the same charts, trying to find the evidence that defends you. But your lawyer doesn't know medicine. Your lawyer doesn't know why you prescribed what you prescribed. Your lawyer is depending entirely on what you wrote in those charts to tell the story of your clinical reasoning, your careful patient selection, your thorough informed consent, your appropriate monitoring. If the charts tell that story - if they're detailed, organized, comprehensive, and clear - your lawyer has something to work with. If they don't, your lawyer is trying to defend you with both hands tied behind their back.

The board investigator flips to a chart and points to a consent form. "This is the practice's standard consent form," she says. "It's the same form used for every patient and every therapy. It doesn't mention peptides. It doesn't mention that the therapy was off-label. It doesn't mention that the peptide isn't FDA-approved for this indication. The patient signed it, but what exactly did they consent to?"

She flips to another chart. "This patient was started on three new therapies at the initial visit. There's no documentation of why these three were chosen, what the expected timeline for response was, or how the patient would be monitored. The first follow-up note is six months later, and it's a phone conversation with the medical assistant that isn't documented in the physician's note."

She flips to another. "This patient called the office four times with questions about side effects. The calls are logged, but there's no documentation of what advice was given or who gave it. The patient ultimately stopped the therapy on their own and never came back. There's no follow-up, no closure, no documentation of why they stopped or what their outcome was."

Your lawyer is wincing. You're sweating. This is your practice being dissected in front of you, and the only tools you have to defend it are the charts you wrote when you thought nobody was ever going to read them this way.

Now let me give you a different scene. Same conference room. Same investigator. Same stack of charts. But this time, when she opens the first chart, she finds a detailed informed consent form that is specific to the peptide prescribed. It lists the peptide by name. It explains that the use is off-label. It explains that the peptide is not FDA-approved for this indication. It lists the known risks and the potential unknown risks. It documents that alternatives were discussed. It confirms the patient had the opportunity to ask questions. It's signed, dated, and witnessed.

She flips to the clinical note and finds a comprehensive encounter note. Detailed history. Appropriate physical exam. Relevant lab results reviewed and acknowledged. Clear clinical reasoning documented in the physician's own words: "Patient presents with X, has failed conservative management including A, B, and C. Given the evidence for peptide Y in this condition (Smith et al., 2019; Jones et al., 2021), and after discussing risks, benefits, and alternatives with the patient, I am initiating therapy. Follow-up scheduled in four weeks with repeat labs."

She flips to the follow-up notes and finds them: timely, detailed, documenting response to therapy, any side effects, lab results reviewed, dose adjustments with clinical reasoning, collaboration with primary care physician noted. Every phone call documented with date, time, who spoke, what was discussed, and what action was taken. Every decision supported by chart evidence.

The investigator keeps looking, because it's her job to find problems. But chart after chart, the story is the same: this physician is careful. This physician documents thoroughly. This physician obtains genuine informed consent. This physician monitors appropriately. This physician collaborates with other providers. This physician runs a practice that may be unconventional in its therapies but is meticulous in its process.

She closes the last chart and writes in her report: "No significant deficiencies identified. No evidence of violation of the Medical Practice Act. Case closed."

That is the outcome you're writing for. Every single day, with every single chart, you are either building toward that outcome or building toward the first scenario. There is no neutral choice. There is no "I'll clean it up later." The chart you write today is the evidence that either saves you or sinks you, and you won't know which until the investigator shows up.

So write it like your license depends on it. Because someday, it might.

Controlled Substances: The Fastest Way to Get Investigated

I saved this section for last because I want it to land with the force it deserves. Of all the risk factors we've discussed in this chapter - the peptide prescribing, the alternative therapies, the cash-pay model, the politically undefended position - none of them, and I mean none of them, compares to the radioactive danger of controlled substances in your practice. A peptide practice without controlled substances is a practice that can fly under the radar indefinitely, with careful documentation and good judgment. A peptide practice with controlled substances is a practice with a target on its back, and that target gets brighter and more visible with every Schedule III testosterone prescription and every Schedule IV phentermine script you write.

I've watched enough physicians go down this road that I can tell you the pattern with depressing predictability. The physician starts a wellness or anti-aging practice. They're doing peptides, they're doing well, patients are happy. But then patients start asking for testosterone."Doc, I saw another provider who offers testosterone pellets. Can you do that?" Or they want phentermine for weight loss. Or they read online that low-dose naltrexone helps with inflammation. Or they're coming off their GLP-1 agonist and they need something for the transition. There are always reasons. The patients ask. The physician doesn't want to lose the patient to a competitor. The controlled substance seems relevant to the patient's goals. It seems like standard of care in the anti-aging and wellness space. Everyone else is doing it. What's the harm?

The harm is that every controlled substance prescription you write turns on a light that shines directly at your practice, and that light never turns off. You can't fly under the radar when you're carrying a flashlight. You can't be invisible when you're generating data that every regulator in your state can see in real time. And you can't claim to be a cautious, under-the-radar peptide practice when your PDMP record shows three hundred controlled prescriptions a year.

Let me walk you through exactly how this works, and why it's different from every other risk factor we've discussed.

Controlled substances are reportable, trackable, and investigatable

When you write a prescription for a controlled substance - any controlled substance, from Schedule V cough syrup up to Schedule II opioids - you are creating a record that enters multiple surveillance systems simultaneously. That record goes to the pharmacy, which reports the dispensed prescription to your state's Prescription Drug Monitoring Program (PDMP). The PDMP aggregates every controlled prescription dispensed in your state, linked to the prescriber's DEA number and the patient's identifying information. Law enforcement has access to this database. Medical board investigators have access. Other prescribers can query it to see what their patients are getting from other doctors.

Every single prescription. Every single time. There is no opt-out. There is no "this is just between me and my patient." The moment you write that prescription, it becomes data, and that data is available to anyone with the authority and the curiosity to look.

Now, the PDMP by itself doesn't generate investigations. It's a passive system - it collects data, and someone has to actively query it to find patterns of concern. But here's what you need to understand: queries happen all the time, and they happen for reasons you cannot control. When a patient of yours goes to an emergency room and the ER doctor checks the PDMP and sees controlled substance prescriptions from multiple providers, that ER doctor may report it. When another physician is considering prescribing a controlled substance to your patient and checks the PDMP to see what they're already getting, they may contact you- or they may report their concerns to the board if the pattern looks concerning. When a pharmacy notices that a patient is filling controlled prescriptions from multiple prescribers, they may file a report.

And beyond the PDMP, controlled substances have their own dedicated reporting requirements. Suspicious orders - unusually large or frequent prescriptions - must be reported by pharmacies to the DEA. Prescribers who write outside the norms for their specialty may be flagged by data analytics systems that the DEA and state authorities use to identify outliers. Individual states have their own reporting thresholds: some require reporting when a prescriber writes above a certain number of morphine milligram equivalents per patient. Others flag prescribers whose controlled prescribing volume exceeds the 90th percentile for their specialty.

Every one of these systems is designed to identify the small percentage of prescribers who are operating irresponsibly - the pill mills, the over-prescribers, the doctors who've become unwitting suppliers to diversion networks. And I know what you're thinking: that's not me. I'm not running a pill mill. I'm prescribing testosterone at physiologic doses to appropriate patients with documented lab abnormalities. I'm writing phentermine for thirty-day courses to patients with genuine obesity. I'm careful. I'm responsible. I'm not the problem these systems are designed to catch.

And you might be right. You probably are right. But here's the thing the responsible prescribers don't always understand: these systems catch you anyway. Not because you're doing anything wrong, but because you're doing something visible. You're generating data in a system that's designed to look for patterns, and the mere fact of your visibility makes you subject to scrutiny that invisible prescribers never face.

Let me give you an example. Dr. Martinez runs a peptide and wellness practice. She prescribes peptides - BPC-157, CJC-1295, ipamorelin, the usual array. She does good work. Her patients are happy. She also prescribes testosterone cypionate to her male patients who have documented low total testosterone with symptoms. She's careful about it - she checks baseline labs, confirms the diagnosis, discusses risks, monitors with follow-up labs every six months. By any reasonable clinical standard, she's practicing responsibly.

But Dr. Martinez is writing two hundred testosterone prescriptions a year. That puts her in the top 5% of testosterone prescribers in her state for her specialty classification. The state's data analytics system flags her as an outlier. Not because any patient was harmed. Not because anyone complained. Just because her prescribing volume exceeds the threshold that triggers review. An investigator gets assigned, pulls her PDMP history, sees the pattern, and requests fifty charts.

Now the investigator is in Dr. Martinez's practice. They're not just looking at testosterone prescribing - though that's what brought them in the door. They're looking at everything. The peptides. The consent forms. The documentation. The staff. The policies. The collaboration with primary care. And maybe Dr. Martinez's charts are perfect - maybe she survives the investigation with her testosterone prescribing intact. But maybe the investigator finds that her peptide consent forms are inadequate, or that her staff are performing clinical tasks without proper supervision, or that three charts have documentation gaps. Now what started as a controlled substance data flag has turned into a broader investigation with multiple potential violations.

This is what I mean when I say controlled substances are the entry point. They bring investigators in the door, and once the investigator is inside, they look at everything. The controlled substance wasn't the problem - it was the key that unlocked the door.

The PDMP tracks every controlled prescription you write

I want you to really understand what the PDMP is and what it means for your practice, because too many physicians treat it like some kind of background administrative system that doesn't affect them directly. The PDMP is one of the most powerful surveillance tools in American medicine, and it was built specifically to monitor controlled substance prescribing.

Every state has a PDMP, and while the specifics vary by jurisdiction, the core function is the same: collect data on every controlled substance prescription that is dispensed, link it to prescriber and patient, make it available to authorized users, and use analytics to identify concerning patterns. When you write a prescription for testosterone, the pharmacy enters it into their system, and that data flows to the state PDMP. When the prescription is filled, the dispensation is recorded. When the patient gets a refill, that's recorded too. Every date, every quantity, every strength, every prescriber, every pharmacy - it's all there.

And the analytics that run on this data are sophisticated. They can identify patients who are getting controlled substances from multiple prescribers - a classic sign of doctor-shopping. They can identify prescribers whose prescribing patterns are statistical outliers. They can identify pharmacies that are dispensing unusually high volumes of controlled drugs. They can track prescription-filling patterns that suggest diversion - patients who fill prescriptions far from home, who pay cash instead of insurance, who fill at multiple pharmacies.

Now, as a peptide prescriber, you might think: I'm not prescribing opioids. I'm not running a pain clinic. My testosterone prescribing is conservative and appropriate. The PDMP isn't looking for me.

But it is. The PDMP is looking for everyone who writes controlled substances. It's just a question of whether your data triggers the thresholds that generate human review. And those thresholds can change. States can and do lower their reporting thresholds when political pressure mounts around controlled substance abuse. A new attorney general gets elected on a platform of fighting the "opioid epidemic" - which sounds good to voters - and suddenly the state starts pulling records on every prescriber above the 75th percentile. A news story breaks about testosterone abuse in athletes, and the board starts looking at TRT prescribers.

A politician needs a healthcare issue for their reelection campaign, and "reining in unregulated hormone clinics" becomes their cause.

You cannot control any of this. You cannot predict when your prescribing pattern might go from unremarkable to statistically interesting. But you can control whether you're in the database at all.

That's the key insight. The PDMP only tracks controlled substances. It does not track peptides. It does not track vitamins. It does not track supplements, nutraceuticals, compounded non-controlled medications, or anything that doesn't have a DEA schedule assigned to it. If you run a practice with zero controlled substance prescriptions, you generate zero PDMP data. You are invisible to the most powerful prescribing surveillance system in American medicine. That is not a small thing. That is a fundamental structural advantage that every peptide-only prescriber has over every peer who also writes for controlled drugs.

And I want to address a specific scenario that comes up constantly, because I know the anti-aging and wellness space. You're treating a patient for peptide-based wellness optimization. Their labs show low testosterone. The clinical picture supports testosterone replacement. You know how to do this safely. You've been trained in it. The patient wants it. Every other wellness clinic in your market offers it. Why are you tying your own hands?

Because the patient with low testosterone who genuinely needs replacement therapy should be getting it from someone whose practice is structured around that therapy, who has the institutional support and the specialized focus to manage it defensibly. I'm talking about a urologist. An endocrinologist. A men's health specialist who builds their entire practice around hormone management, who has the relationships with the specialty societies, who knows the standard of care inside and out, whose documentation and protocols are designed specifically for hormone therapy. Send your patient to that doctor. Collaborate. Request a consultation. Get the hormone management handled by the specialist while you manage the peptide side of the patient's protocol.

This isn't passing the buck. It's practicing within your scope. It's recognizing that you don't have to do everything yourself to provide comprehensive care. And it's understanding that the testosterone prescription you refer out is one less thread that regulators can pull when they come looking at your practice.

Now, I know what some of you are thinking. "But my patients don't want to see another doctor. They came to me for comprehensive care. If I send them to an endocrinologist, they'll just go to the endocrinologist's peptide practice instead." That might happen. But you know what definitely won't happen? You definitely won't lose your license over a testosterone prescription you didn't write. You definitely won't get a board investigator digging through your peptide charts because your name popped up as a high-volume controlled substance prescriber in a database query. The patient you lose to a competitor is a financial hit. The patient who brings an investigator to your door is an existential threat. I'll take the financial hit every time.

DEA registrations invite federal scrutiny that peptide practices do not need

When you obtain a DEA registration, you are entering into a relationship with the federal government that most physicians don't fully appreciate. The DEA is not a professional licensing body like your state medical board. The DEA is a law enforcement agency. Its mission is to enforce the controlled substances laws and regulations of the United States. And when you sign that DEA registration application, you are agreeing to be subject to the DEA's authority - including unannounced inspections of your practice, audit of your prescribing records, and investigation of any suspected violation of the Controlled Substances Act.

Let me repeat that: unannounced inspections. The DEA can show up at your office without warning, present their credentials, and demand to review your controlled substance records. They can examine your security measures - how you store controlled substances if you keep them in the office, how you manage your prescription pads, how you secure your e-prescribing credentials. They can review your prescribing patterns. They can interview your staff. And if they find violations - inadequate security, improper disposal of expired controlled drugs, prescribing outside the usual course of medical practice - they can act immediately, without the slow deliberative process that state medical boards typically follow.

The DEA can suspend your registration on an emergency basis if they believe there is an imminent danger to public health and safety. Think about that. Not after a hearing. Not after a trial. On an emergency basis. Your DEA registration can be suspended by an administrative order, and now you cannot prescribe any controlled substance anywhere in the United States. You can appeal, of course. You can challenge the suspension. But while that process works its way through the system - weeks or months - you are unable to prescribe controlled substances, and your patients who depend on those medications are scrambling to find alternative care.

And here's the connection to peptide practice that a lot of physicians miss: once the DEA is in your practice for a controlled substance issue, they see everything. They're not limited to looking at your Schedule III testosterone prescriptions. If they're doing a comprehensive inspection, they're looking at your entire operation. They see the peptides. They see the IV vitamin therapy. They see the cash-pay model. They see the anti-aging marketing. And while the DEA doesn't have direct jurisdiction over peptides - most peptides aren't controlled substances - they have referral relationships with the FDA, with state medical boards, with other federal and state agencies. If they see something that concerns them, even if it's outside their jurisdiction, they can make a phone call. They can send a report. They can trigger the very state medical board investigation you've been working so hard to avoid.

I've seen this happen. A physician gets a DEA inspection because their testosterone prescribing triggered an algorithm. The DEA looks around, doesn't find anything egregious on the controlled substance side, but sees a practice model that makes them uncomfortable - high cash fees, aggressive marketing, patients who seem more like customers than medical patients. The DEA inspector files a report with the state medical board. Three months later, the physician gets a letter: "The Board has received information regarding your practice and has opened an investigation." The DEA inspection was the entry point. The board investigation is the main event.

Without a DEA registration, none of this happens. There is no DEA inspection of a practice that doesn't handle controlled substances. There is no federal law enforcement presence in your office. There is no automatic referral pipeline from federal drug enforcement to state medical regulation. You're just a physician practicing medicine with non-controlled therapies, subject to the same state board oversight as every other physician - but without the additional layer of federal scrutiny that the DEA registration brings.

And I want to be clear: I'm not saying DEA registration is inherently dangerous. Every physician who legitimately needs to prescribe controlled substances should have one, and most do so without ever attracting scrutiny. Internists prescribing blood pressure meds and occasional hydrocodone for acute pain. Surgeons prescribing postoperative opioids. Psychiatrists prescribing controlled anxiolytics. These are normal, necessary, appropriate uses of controlled substances, and the DEA generally leaves these prescribers alone because their prescribing patterns don't trigger the algorithms.

But you? You're running a peptide practice. You're already operating in a gray zone from the perspective of the medical establishment. You're already prescribing therapies that raise eyebrows at the state board. You're already politically undefended, institutionally unsupported, and practicing in a space where scrutiny is more likely than for your conventional colleagues. Why would you voluntarily add a federal law enforcement relationship to that already-complicated picture? Why would you invite the DEA into your practice when you have the option not to?

Some of you are reading this and thinking I'm being paranoid. You're thinking the DEA has bigger fish to fry than a wellness clinic writing a few testosterone scripts. And you're right -they do. Until they don't. Until your data crosses a threshold. Until a new administrator decides to make hormone prescribing a priority. Until a news story about "testosterone mills"prompts a crackdown. Until a pharmacy report flags your prescribing as suspicious for reasons you don't understand and might not even be valid. The point isn't that DEA scrutiny is likely on any given day. The point is that it's possible, and the consequences if it happens are severe, and you can eliminate the entire category of risk by simply not having a DEA registration.

If you can run your practice without controlled substances, you should

This is the bottom line, the practical conclusion, the action item I want you to take from this section. If you can run your peptide practice without prescribing controlled substances, you should. Full stop. No exceptions. No "but what about this one patient who really needs testosterone." No "but my competitor across town offers it and I lose patients." No "but it's standard of care in anti-aging medicine."

Those are business arguments, not safety arguments. And this book is about safety - the safety of your license, the safety of your practice, the safety of your career. You can build a successful, profitable, life-sustaining peptide practice without ever touching a controlled substance. Thousands of physicians do exactly that. They refer hormone management to specialists. They manage pain through non-pharmacological means or refer to pain specialists. They handle weight loss with peptides, with dietary protocols, with behavioral interventions -not with phentermine. They treat anxiety and sleep disorders with peptides, supplements, lifestyle modification, and referral to mental health specialists - not with controlled anxiolytics.

And their practices thrive. Because what draws patients to peptide medicine isn't access to controlled drugs. It's the promise of something different, something personalized, something that conventional medicine didn't offer them. Patients come to you because they're frustrated with the fifteen-minute insurance visit, the pill-for-every-ill approach, the dismissal of their symptoms because their labs are "normal." They come because they want someone to take the time to understand their whole picture, to craft a protocol tailored to them, to monitor their response and adjust accordingly. They come for peptides. They come for the relationship. They come for the attention and the personalization. They don't come because you're a source for testosterone.

Every patient you lose because you won't prescribe controlled substances is a patient who values the controlled substance more than they value your comprehensive care. That's not your ideal patient anyway. Your ideal patient is the one who says "I appreciate that you're careful about what you prescribe. That makes me trust you more." Your ideal patient is the one who understands that your caution is a feature, not a bug. Your ideal patient is the one who refers their friends because they know you run a practice that puts safety first, that doesn't take shortcuts, that doesn't hand out controlled drugs like they're samples at a trade show.

Let me tell you something I've learned from thirty-plus years in healthcare, in finance, in law: the physicians who last are the ones who say no. No to the patient who pressures them for a prescription they're not comfortable writing. No to the therapy that doesn't have adequate evidence for the indication. No to the business model that generates revenue at the cost of compliance. No to the controlled substance that brings federal scrutiny to a practice that otherwise flies beautifully under the radar.

Saying no is hard. I know it's hard. You didn't get into this business to turn patients away. You want to help people. You want to say yes to the treatment that might change their life. You want to be the doctor who offers what no one else will offer, who thinks outside the box, who finds solutions when conventional medicine has given up. That impulse is noble. It's why you're reading this book instead of writing standard-of-care prescriptions in a hospital-employed clinic somewhere.

But saying no to controlled substances isn't saying no to helping patients. It's saying no to a category of risk that can destroy everything else you've built. It's saying no to the data trail that leads investigators to your door. It's saying no to the federal law enforcement relationship you don't need. It's saying no to the single biggest threat to the under-the-radar practice that this whole chapter is about.

If you're currently prescribing controlled substances in your peptide practice, I want you to seriously consider a transition plan. Start referring testosterone patients to endocrinology or urology. Start managing weight loss without phentermine. Start handling anxiety without controlled anxiolytics. Communicate the change to your patients with a clear, confident explanation: "Our practice is focusing exclusively on non-controlled therapies to provide the safest, most sustainable care possible. I'm partnering with specialists who can manage your hormone needs with the focused expertise you deserve." Frame it as a practice enhancement, not a limitation. Because it is. It's a practice enhancement that removes an entire category of regulatory risk.

And if you're just starting out - if you're building your peptide practice from the ground up- make the decision now, before you have patients who are accustomed to getting controlled substances from you, before you've built a DEA registration into your operational workflow, before you've created expectations that are hard to unwind. Build your practice without controlled substances from day one, and you never have to have the difficult conversation about taking them away. You never have to transition. You never have to explain to a patient why something you used to offer is no longer available. You start clean, and you stay clean, and the investigator who looks at your practice sees a physician who made a principled decision to operate in the safest possible zone.

I want to close this section with a final story, because stories are what stick. Dr. Williams ran a successful peptide and hormone practice for four years. He prescribed peptides, he prescribed testosterone, he prescribed thyroid medication, he offered IV vitamins, he did well. He had two hundred active patients, revenues in the mid-six figures, a staff of four, and a reputation as one of the best wellness providers in his region. He was meticulous about his documentation -he'd read the early version of this book, actually, and took the charting advice to heart. His peptide consent forms were specific and thorough. His follow-up protocols were rigorous. He collaborated with primary care physicians. He did almost everything right.

Almost.

He kept prescribing testosterone because his patients wanted it, because it was clinically appropriate in most cases, because he'd been doing it for years without problems. And then one of his testosterone patients - a successful businessman in his fifties - had a myocardial infarction. The patient survived, thankfully. But in the course of his cardiac workup, the cardiologist noted that the patient was on testosterone replacement therapy prescribed by a"wellness clinic." The cardiologist didn't say the testosterone caused the heart attack. The medical literature on testosterone and cardiovascular risk is mixed and evolving. But the cardiologist documented it. And the patient, frightened and looking for someone to blame, filed a complaint with the medical board alleging that Dr. Williams's testosterone prescription caused his heart attack.

The board opened an investigation. They pulled Dr. Williams's PDMP records and saw hundreds of testosterone prescriptions. They requested fifty charts. And because Dr. Williams was meticulous about his documentation, they didn't find deficiencies in his testosterone prescribing - his workups were appropriate, his monitoring was consistent, his consent forms were specific. But they also looked at everything else, because that's what investigators do. And in three of his peptide charts, they found informed consent forms that were missing the patient's signature on the date line. In two charts, they found that follow-up notes were written by a medical assistant without physician co-signature. In one chart, they found a phone prescription for a peptide refill that wasn't documented in the medication record.

None of these were egregious violations. None of them caused patient harm. But they were violations, and the board documented every one. Dr. Williams ended up with a consent order: monitored practice for eighteen months, mandatory documentation training, a fifteen-thousand-dollar fine, and a public reprimand that appears in every search of his name for the rest of his career. He survived - his license wasn't suspended, he wasn't forced to stop practicing. But he's now paying four thousand dollars a month for a practice monitor. His malpractice insurance increased by 40%. He lost twenty percent of his patient base when the reprimand became public. And he stopped prescribing testosterone entirely - not because the board ordered him to, but because he finally understood what I'd been saying all along.

The testosterone prescription didn't cause the heart attack. But the testosterone prescription caused the investigation. And the investigation found the violations that generated the sanctions. That is the chain of causation I want you to understand. The controlled substance was the entry point. Everything else flowed from there.

If Dr. Williams had referred that patient to an endocrinologist for testosterone management, there would have been no testosterone prescription in his name when the cardiologist checked.

No PDMP record. No complaint linking the heart attack to his prescribing. No investigation. No chart review. No consent order. No monitor. No reprimand. No fine. Just a physician continuing to practice peptide medicine, helping his patients, flying under the radar where he belonged.

That's the choice in front of you. Controlled substances or invisibility. You cannot have both. And I have never, in all my years in this business, met a physician who chose controlled substances and invisibility and got both. You get one or the other. Choose wisely.

4 - Big Pharma Has Your Back - When It Makes Them Money

> **BLUNT RULE: The system is not fair. It is not designed to be fair. It is designed to protect profitable drugs and the doctors who prescribe them. You are not playing on a level field, and pretending otherwise will cost you your license.**

The Unequal Playing Field

Let me tell you something that took me thirty years in medicine, finance, and law to fully appreciate. The healthcare system in this country does not protect good doctors. It protects profitable drugs. Those two things overlap just often enough to create the illusion that the system works for physicians. It doesn't. It works for money. And if you understand that distinction - really understand it, deep in your bones - you will practice differently, document differently, and sleep better at night.

The unequal playing field is not an accident. It is architecture. Decades of regulatory design, lobbying investment, legal precedent, and institutional capture have built a system that wraps a warm blanket of protection around blockbuster pharmaceuticals and the physicians who prescribe them, while leaving alternative therapies - and the doctors who use them -standing naked in the cold. This is not paranoia. This is structural reality. And if you are prescribing peptides, compounded therapies, or anything else that lacks a billion-dollar corporate sponsor, you need to understand exactly what you are up against.

FDA-Approved Drugs with Billion-Dollar Revenues Have Armies of Lawyers and Lobbyists

When a pharmaceutical company gets FDA approval for a drug that generates a billion dollars a year in revenue, that company does not sit back and hope for the best. It builds a fortress. That fortress has multiple layers, and each layer exists to protect the drug, the company, and -by extension - the physicians who prescribe it.

First, there is the lobbying apparatus. The Pharmaceutical Research and Manufacturers of America - PhRMA - spends more on lobbying than any other industry in Washington. In a typical year, that is north of three hundred million dollars. That money does not buy direct protection for individual prescribers, of course. But it buys access. It buys influence over FDA advisory committees. It buys relationships with members of Congress who oversee FDA funding. It buys the kind of regulatory environment where blockbuster drugs get approved, post-marketing surveillance is manageable, and REMS programs are funded by the manufacturer rather than imposed as crushing burdens on individual practitioners.

Consider what happens when a blockbuster drug has a safety problem. The manufacturer fields a team of regulatory specialists, epidemiologists, and attorneys who work full-time on managing the FDA relationship. They submit safety reports, conduct post-hoc analyses, negotiate labeling changes, and manage the media narrative. When the FDA requires a Risk Evaluation and Mitigation Strategy - a REMS - the manufacturer pays for it. The REMS includes prescriber education, patient education, pharmacy controls, and ongoing monitoring.

The physician prescribing the drug is embedded in a system of institutional support that manages risk at scale.

You think the state medical board investigator knows any of this? Of course not. The investigator sees an FDA-approved drug, a physician prescribing within labeling, and a REMS program that the manufacturer funded. The investigator's report practically writes itself:"Prescriber followed standard of care. FDA-approved therapy. Manufacturer-managed risk mitigation." Case closed.

Now let me ask you a question. When you prescribe a compounded peptide, who funds your REMS program? Who manages your post-marketing surveillance? Who lobbies Congress on your behalf? Nobody. That is the point. You are the REMS program. You are the post-marketing surveillance. You are the regulatory defense. And if something goes wrong, you are standing alone in front of a board that has never heard of your therapy, has no framework for evaluating it, and has every institutional incentive to treat you as a problem rather than a victim of an unfair system.

The lobbying gap matters in ways that most physicians never consider. When a blockbuster drug is under review, the manufacturer submits thousands of pages of clinical data, conducts advisory committee presentations, funds continuing medical education, sponsors clinical conferences, and publishes in major journals. All of this creates an ecosystem of legitimacy. The drug is not just approved - it is embedded in the medical culture. Residency programs teach it. Board certification exams reference it. Clinical guidelines incorporate it. When a physician prescribes it, that prescription swims with the current of mainstream medical opinion.

Peptides swim against that current. Most state medical board members have never prescribed a peptide. Many have never heard of the specific peptides they are investigating. Their frame of reference is FDA-approved drugs, institutional guidelines, and standard-of-care protocols. When they encounter a physician prescribing compounded BPC-157 or CJC-1295, they do not see a practitioner operating at the edge of legitimate medicine. They see an outlier. And outliers attract scrutiny.

The pharmaceutical industry also funds the infrastructure of medical education in ways that create subtle but powerful bias. Continuing medical education - CME - is heavily sponsored by pharmaceutical companies. The ACCME has tightened rules on commercial influence, but the reality is that most major CME programs on diabetes, obesity, cardiovascular disease, and endocrinology receive significant industry support. This does not mean the education is corrupt. It means the educational ecosystem is shaped by the interests that fund it. New therapies from well-funded companies get robust CME programming. Alternative therapies without corporate sponsors get nothing. When a board investigator asks what CME you have completed on peptide therapy, and you have to say "none, because it doesn't exist," you have already lost credibility in that room.

This is the landscape you are practicing in. Not a neutral marketplace of ideas where the best therapy wins. A landscape where institutional support flows to profitable products, where regulatory infrastructure is designed around blockbuster drugs, where medical education follows the money, and where physicians who step outside that system must build their own defenses from scratch.

When Patients Are Harmed by Blockbuster Drugs, the System Is Designed to Minimize Prescriber Liability

Let me tell you a story that I have seen variations of a dozen times in my career. A patient is prescribed a widely used FDA-approved medication - let's say a COX-2 inhibitor for arthritis pain, or a thiazolidinedione for diabetes, or a statin at high dose. Six months or a year later, the patient suffers a serious adverse event. Maybe it is a cardiovascular event. Maybe it is liver failure. Maybe it is something else that the drug is eventually found to increase the risk of.

The patient or the family is angry. They want answers. They consider a lawsuit. They file a complaint with the state medical board. What happens next reveals everything about how the system actually works.

In the malpractice context, the prescribing physician is almost always shielded by what defense attorneys call the "learned intermediary doctrine." This legal doctrine holds that the manufacturer has a duty to warn the physician of known risks, and the physician then acts as a learned intermediary between the manufacturer and the patient. If the physician prescribed the drug within the standard of care - which, for an FDA-approved drug with clear labeling, is relatively easy to establish - the physician is typically dismissed from the malpractice case early. The lawsuit then proceeds against the manufacturer, which has deep pockets and a predictable legal playbook.

The state medical board process follows a similar pattern. The board receives the complaint and asks a series of standard questions. Did the physician prescribe within the labeled indication? Yes. Was the drug FDA-approved for this use? Yes. Did the physician follow standard monitoring protocols? Yes. Was the patient informed of risks? The labeling includes warnings. Was there a clear departure from standard of care? Usually not.

The board may open an investigation. It may request records. But the investigation rarely progresses to formal charges against the prescribing physician. Why? Because the system has a vocabulary for evaluating FDA-approved drug harm. The vocabulary includes terms like"known adverse event," "labeled risk," "risk-benefit ratio," and "standard of care." The physician's decision fits within a framework that the board understands and accepts. The patient was warned - by the manufacturer, by the label, by the pharmacist, by the prescribing physician. The risk was known. The drug was approved. The system moves on.

Compare this to what happens when a peptide patient has an adverse event. There is no learned intermediary doctrine protecting you in the same way because there is no manufacturer with a duty to warn in the same way. The compounding pharmacy has its own duties, but they are limited and differ by state. There is no FDA-approved label with standardized warnings. There is no manufacturer's legal department standing between you and the complaint. The board investigator does not have a framework for evaluating your decision. They have suspicion, discomfort with the unfamiliar, and institutional bias toward FDA-approved therapies.

The Vioxx story illustrates this perfectly. Rofecoxib was approved by the FDA in 1999. It generated more than two billion dollars in annual revenue for Merck. Physicians prescribed it millions of times. Post-marketing data eventually showed increased cardiovascular risk, and Merck withdrew the drug in 2004. The lawsuits that followed were primarily against Merck, not against individual prescribers. Merck paid nearly five billion dollars to settle litigation. Individual physicians? They were largely protected by the fact that they had prescribed an FDA-approved drug, following labeled indications, with the manufacturer's warnings in hand.

You think any peptide prescriber would get that kind of institutional protection? You think a compounding pharmacy is going to set aside five billion dollars to settle litigation? The very suggestion is absurd. And that absurdity reveals the structural inequality at the heart of this system.

The opioid epidemic provides another lens - though a more complex one. For years, physicians prescribed opioid pain medications based on manufacturer-funded education, flawed clinical guidelines, and FDA approval. The manufacturers built a system that promoted aggressive prescribing. When the disaster became undeniable, the legal system went after the manufacturers - Purdue Pharma, Johnson & Johnson, Mallinckrodt - and extracted tens of billions of dollars in settlements. Individual prescribers have faced discipline too, particularly those operating pill mills. But the primary legal and financial liability fell on the industry that created the system, not on every physician who prescribed within it.

The lesson is not that FDA-approved drugs are safe. The lesson is that the system has a designated villain when things go wrong with profitable drugs - and that villain is the manufacturer, not the prescriber. With peptides, there is no designated villain except you.

Post-Marketing Surveillance, REMS Programs, and Continuing Medical Education Are Funded by Manufacturers

The institutional support system for blockbuster drugs extends into every corner of medical practice. When you prescribe a drug that generates a billion dollars a year, you are not just prescribing a molecule. You are plugging into an infrastructure that manages risk, educates providers, monitors outcomes, and defends against complaints.

Post-marketing surveillance is the process by which adverse events are collected, analyzed, and reported after a drug is approved. For blockbuster drugs, this is a massive operation. The manufacturer employs pharmacovigilance teams that review adverse event reports, conduct epidemiological studies, publish safety updates, and communicate with the FDA. The FDA itself has post-marketing surveillance systems - MedWatch, the Sentinel Initiative - that aggregate data across millions of prescriptions. When a safety signal emerges, there is a systematic process for evaluating it, updating labeling, and communicating to prescribers.

This matters for prescriber liability because it creates a record. When a physician is accused of failing to warn a patient about a risk, the defense can point to the FDA-approved labeling, the manufacturer's risk communications, the CME programs, and the published literature. The physician is embedded in an information ecosystem. A court or a board can see that the physician had access to standardized, validated information and acted within that framework.

What post-marketing surveillance exists for compounded peptides? Almost none. There is no manufacturer collecting adverse events at scale. The FDA's systems are not designed to capture data on compounded products in the same way. The compounding pharmacy may have an adverse event reporting obligation, but the scale and sophistication are minuscule compared to a major manufacturer's pharmacovigilance operation. There are no large epidemiological studies, no Sentinel Initiative equivalent, no systematic safety signal detection.

This means that when a peptide prescriber is asked, "Did you know this risk existed?" the answer is often "There was no data." That answer does not help you. It sounds like ignorance rather than the absence of institutional infrastructure. A board investigator hears "no data" and thinks "reckless." They do not think "systemic gap in post-marketing surveillance for non-FDA-approved therapies." That distinction is lost on people who have never practiced outside the blockbuster system.

REMS programs are another layer of manufacturer-funded protection. A Risk Evaluation and Mitigation Strategy is required by the FDA when a drug's benefits outweigh its risks but the risks require active management. REMS programs can include prescriber certification, pharmacy certification, patient education, patient monitoring registries, and controlled distribution systems. The manufacturer designs the program, funds its implementation, and reports to the FDA on its effectiveness.

From a prescriber liability standpoint, REMS programs are a gift. They create a standardized protocol. If you follow the REMS, you have a powerful defense: "I did exactly what the FDA required." The REMS certification demonstrates that you were educated about the drug's risks. The pharmacy certification demonstrates that the medication was dispensed through a controlled system. The patient education materials demonstrate that the patient was informed. The monitoring registry demonstrates that outcomes were tracked. Each element is a building block in a defensible record.

No REMS program exists for peptides. There is no prescriber certification. There is no pharmacy certification for most peptides. There is no patient registry. There is no controlled distribution. You are building all of that yourself, practice by practice, patient by patient. And when a complaint comes, there is no institutional framework to point to. Just your chart, your consent forms, and your documentation. If those are weak, you are finished.

Continuing medical education is the third pillar of manufacturer-funded infrastructure. Major pharmaceutical companies spend hundreds of millions of dollars annually on CME. This includes sponsoring conferences, funding online education modules, supporting medical society programs, and underwriting journal supplements. Again, this is not necessarily corrupt- the ACCME has commercial support rules - but it creates an environment where blockbuster drugs have robust educational programming and alternative therapies have almost none.

When a physician prescribes a GLP-1 receptor agonist for diabetes, they have access to dozens of CME programs, clinical guidelines, medical society recommendations, and published evidence reviews. When a physician prescribes a compounded peptide for weight loss support, they have almost none of that. The board investigator who asks about your CME in peptide therapy is asking a question that has no good answer because the system has not created one.

This is the infrastructure gap. It is real. It is structural. And it puts you at a disadvantage that no amount of individual competence can fully overcome. You must be aware of it, account for it, and compensate for it with documentation that is better than anything the blockbuster prescriber needs.

The Legal and Regulatory Infrastructure Protects the Prescriber of Profitable Drugs

The final layer of institutional protection is the legal and regulatory infrastructure itself. The laws, regulations, court decisions, and administrative procedures that govern medicine in this country were built around a model of FDA-approved pharmaceutical products. When you operate outside that model, you step into legal territory that is less mapped, less certain, and less forgiving.

FDA approval creates a presumption of legitimacy. This is not written into any statute, but it operates as a practical reality in every courtroom and board hearing in the country. An FDA-approved drug has survived what courts describe as a "rigorous" review process. The label is treated as authoritative. The manufacturer's warnings are treated as adequate. The physician who prescribes within labeling is operating within a zone of presumed medical reasonableness.

This presumption affects every stage of legal and regulatory proceedings. In malpractice litigation, the plaintiff's attorney knows that prescribing an FDA-approved drug within labeling is hard to attack. The attorney will look for other angles - failure to monitor, failure to obtain informed consent, failure to diagnose a contraindication - but the basic decision to prescribe the drug is defensible. In board proceedings, the investigator knows that FDA-approved therapies are within the mainstream. The burden shifts to the complainant to show something else went wrong.

With peptides, there is no presumption of legitimacy. Quite the opposite. The compounded or investigational status of the therapy creates a presumption of suspicion. The board investigator does not start from "FDA-approved drug, physician prescribed within standard of care." The investigator starts from "What is this substance? Why is this physician using it? Where did it come from? Who made it? What evidence supports it?" Every question is a challenge. Every answer requires explanation. The burden is on you to prove that your decision was reasonable- not on the complainant to prove that it was not.

This reversal of the burden of practical proof is invisible to people who have never faced a board investigation. It is not written in any regulation. It is an operational reality created by institutional bias, unfamiliarity, and the human tendency to distrust what we do not understand. A physician prescribing semaglutide for diabetes is swimming with the current. A physician prescribing a compounded growth-hormone secretagogue for age-related metabolic decline is swimming against it. The current is invisible until you try to swim against it.

The FDA's own regulatory framework reinforces this disparity. Approved drugs have detailed labeling, established manufacturing standards, systematic adverse event reporting, and a legal framework that has been litigated and refined over decades. Compounded products exist in a more ambiguous space. The FDA's 503A and 503B regulations provide pathways, but they are not the same as the New Drug Application process. The legal boundaries shift. The FDA's enforcement discretion changes with administration. State pharmacy boards have their own rules. The prescriber who uses compounded products must navigate this complexity without the map that FDA approval provides.

Federal preemption is another legal protection that benefits blockbuster drugs but not peptides. When a drug is FDA-approved, the manufacturer can sometimes argue that federal law preempts state tort claims - that the FDA's approval and labeling decisions override state-level failure-to-warn lawsuits. The Supreme Court has addressed this in cases like Wyeth v. Levine and PLIVA v. Mensing, and the landscape is complex. But the key point is that this entire body of law exists around FDA-approved products. Compounded peptides have no such federal preemption shield. State law applies fully, and every state is different.

The learned intermediary doctrine, which I mentioned earlier, also operates differently. For FDA-approved drugs, courts have consistently held that the manufacturer's duty to warn is directed at the prescribing physician, not the patient. The physician is the learned intermediary who evaluates the risks and benefits and communicates with the patient. This doctrine protects physicians because it centralizes the manufacturer's duty on the physician's knowledge, which is assumed to include the FDA-approved labeling. For therapies without FDA-approved labeling, the doctrine's application is less certain. Courts have less precedent to rely on. The protection is thinner.

All of this adds up to a stark reality. The legal and regulatory infrastructure of American medicine was built for a pharmaceutical-centered, FDA-approved, manufacturer-funded model. When you practice outside that model - as you do when you prescribe peptides - you step into territory where the protections are thinner, the precedents are scarcer, the presumptions are reversed, and the burdens are heavier. This is not a reason to stop prescribing peptides. It is a reason to practice with your eyes open, to document with extraordinary care, and to understand that you are building your own institutional protection patient by patient, chart by chart, consent form by consent form.

The Peptide Paradox

Now that I have explained the fortress that surrounds blockbuster drugs, let me tell you the part that should make you angry. Angry enough to practice better. Angry enough to document like your license depends on it - because it does.

Peptides have helped millions of people. I am not exaggerating, and I am not engaging in marketing hype. The GLP-1 receptor agonists alone - semaglutide, tirzepatide, and their analogs - have transformed the treatment of obesity and type 2 diabetes in ways that were unimaginable fifteen years ago. Patients have lost life-changing amounts of weight. They have put their diabetes into remission. They have reduced their cardiovascular risk. They have improved their sleep apnea, their joint pain, their mobility, their self-esteem, and their lifespan. These are not trivial outcomes. They are among the most significant therapeutic advances in metabolic medicine in my lifetime.

And peptides have delivered benefits far beyond weight loss. Growth-hormone secretagogues have helped patients recover from injury, sleep better, regain functional capacity, and improve their body composition. BPC-157 and related repair peptides have been used by patients with stubborn soft-tissue injuries who failed conventional treatment. Immune-modulating peptides have been explored in contexts ranging from chronic infection to cancer adjuvant therapy. Sexual health peptides have provided options for patients who did not respond to conventional therapies. The list goes on.

The paradox - the maddening, unjust paradox - is that the same system that wraps protection around blockbuster drugs strips it away from the therapies that are helping patients outside the pharmaceutical mainstream.

Peptides Have Helped Millions of People Lose Weight, Recover Faster, Sleep Better, and Feel Younger

Let me be specific about what peptides have accomplished, because the contrast between clinical reality and institutional support is genuinely stunning.

The GLP-1 peptides are the most obvious example, and I will spend some time on them because they illustrate the paradox so clearly. Semaglutide, administered once weekly, produces average weight loss of fifteen to twenty percent of body weight in clinical trials. That is not a minor metabolic tweak. That is a transformation. Patients who have been obese for decades, who have failed every diet and every exercise program, who have watched their health deteriorate year after year - these patients are losing the equivalent of a person's worth of weight and keeping it off. Their blood pressure improves. Their cholesterol improves. Their inflammatory markers improve. Their risk of heart attack and stroke drops. Their sleep apnea resolves. Their knee pain diminishes. Their energy increases. Their depression lifts. I have seen it happen. You have seen it happen. It is real.

Tirzepatide, the dual GIP/GLP-1 agonist, produces even greater weight loss in some patients-upward of twenty percent in clinical trials, with individual patients losing more. The metabolic improvements are profound. The impact on quality of life is immeasurable. And this is happening at scale - millions of prescriptions, millions of patients, millions of lives changed.

Now consider the growth-hormone secretagogues. Sermorelin, CJC-1295, ipamorelin, tesamorelin - these are not magic anti-aging potions, and I am not going to pretend they are. But for appropriate patients, they produce meaningful improvements in sleep quality, recovery from exercise and injury, body composition, energy, and functional capacity. The evidence base varies by compound and indication, but the clinical experience is substantial. Patients report benefits. Physicians observe them. And the safety profile, when these compounds are used with appropriate monitoring, is manageable and well-understood within the clinical community that uses them.

The repair peptides - BPC-157, TB-500, thymosin beta-4 - occupy a more contested space, and I am not going to oversell the evidence. Much of the published literature is preclinical. Human trials are limited. But the anecdotal and small-study evidence of benefit in soft-tissue injury recovery is compelling enough that thousands of physicians use these compounds, and thousands of patients report improvement in tendon, ligament, and muscle complaints. The demand exists because the clinical need exists. Patients with chronic injuries have limited options, and the conventional toolkit of rest, physical therapy, anti-inflammatories, corticosteroid injections, and surgery does not solve every problem.

Immune peptides like thymosin alpha-1 have been used in millions of patients worldwide -just not in the United States, where they lack FDA approval. In countries where these peptides are approved, they are used for chronic hepatitis, cancer adjuvant therapy, immune dysregulation, and severe infection. The evidence base is stronger than most American physicians realize, because the studies were published in international journals and conducted outside the FDA framework. A drug approved in thirty-seven countries is not experimental. It is just not American.

Sleep and cognition peptides - from various growth-hormone secretagogues to cerebrolysin to selank - have helped patients with sleep disturbance, cognitive fatigue, anxiety, and post-injury neurological recovery. Again, the evidence varies. But the clinical reality is that patients report benefits, physicians observe them, and the demand for these therapies continues to grow because conventional medicine has not adequately addressed these needs.

The point of this recitation is not to create a sales pitch for peptides. I am deeply allergic to that. The point is to establish the factual premise of the paradox: peptides help patients, in large numbers, in clinically meaningful ways. They fill therapeutic gaps that conventional medicine has not filled. They address patient populations that have been underserved or ignored by the pharmaceutical mainstream. They represent a significant and growing area of clinical medicine.

And the system treats their prescribers like criminals.

There Is No Multi-Billion-Dollar Company Making Campaign Contributions to Protect Peptide Prescribers

This is where the righteous anger comes in. Every benefit I just described - every pound lost, every injury healed, every night of better sleep - exists in a clinical context that offers no institutional protection to the physician who made it possible.

When you prescribe semaglutide as Ozempic or Wegovy, you are prescribing a product of Novo Nordisk, a pharmaceutical company with a market capitalization that has at times exceeded four hundred billion dollars. Novo Nordisk spends millions on lobbying. It funds CME programs. It sponsors medical conferences. It employs thousands of people in regulatory affairs, pharmacovigilance, legal defense, and government relations. If a patient is harmed by semaglutide, Novo Nordisk has teams of lawyers to manage the litigation. It has relationships with the FDA to manage labeling changes. It has the financial capacity to settle lawsuits without threatening its existence.

When you prescribe a compounded semaglutide from a 503A pharmacy - which you may do for patients who cannot afford the branded product, or who need a different formulation, or who require a dose not commercially available - you are on your own. The compounding pharmacy has its own regulatory obligations, but they are limited and differ by state. There is no four-hundred-billion-dollar company standing behind that vial. There are no lobbyists in Washington arguing for your right to prescribe it. There is no CME program funded by a manufacturer to educate your colleagues. There is no medical conference sponsored by an industry player to normalize your clinical decision.

The political economy of this is staggering. Novo Nordisk can afford to spend millions lobbying Congress and the FDA to protect its interests. The compounding pharmacy industry, by comparison, has a fraction of that resources. The individual peptide prescriber has none. The playing field is not just tilted - it is vertical.

And the problem extends beyond compounding. Consider the non-GLP-1 peptides. BPC-157 has no corporate sponsor because it cannot be patented in its natural form. No pharmaceutical company is going to spend a billion dollars on clinical trials for a compound it cannot exclusively market. The same is true for many of the growth-hormone secretagogues, immune peptides, and repair peptides. They are either naturally occurring, or they were developed in academic labs, or their patent protection has expired, or they were never patentable in the first place. Without patent protection, there is no revenue stream to fund the trials, the lobbying, the CME, the legal defense, and the regulatory infrastructure that blockbuster drugs enjoy.

This is not a market failure in the conventional sense. The market is working exactly as designed. It allocates resources to profitable activities and starves unprofitable ones. The problem is that the regulatory system has conflated profitability with medical legitimacy. A drug that can generate a billion dollars gets the full infrastructure of American medicine. A therapy that helps patients but cannot be monetized gets nothing. And the physicians who use those therapies - the ones who are actually solving problems that the pharmaceutical industry has ignored - are left exposed.

The campaign contribution angle is not a joke. Pharmaceutical companies and their trade associations are consistently among the largest donors to federal political campaigns. They fund both parties. They fund incumbent committee chairs. They fund candidates who oversee FDA appropriations. They fund state-level political action committees. This money does not buy specific favors in most cases - the system is more subtle than outright bribery. But it buys access. It buys a seat at the table when regulations are being written. It buys the kind of relationship where a phone call gets returned, where a concern gets heard, where a proposed rule gets modified before it is finalized.

No one is making those phone calls for peptide prescribers. No one is sitting at that table representing your interests. When the FDA issued its policy on compounding GLP-1 receptor agonists, the voices in the room were pharmaceutical manufacturers, pharmacy trade groups, patient advocacy organizations funded by industry, and members of Congress who had received pharmaceutical contributions. The individual physician prescribing compounded peptides was not represented. Your interests were abstracted into categories - "compounding interests," "patient access concerns" - and addressed at a level of generality that missed the practical reality of your practice.

This is the political and economic reality. It is not going to change anytime soon. The pharmaceutical industry has too much money, too much influence, and too much institutional momentum. Peptide prescribers are a tiny fraction of the medical community, with a fraction of the resources, and none of the political infrastructure. If you are waiting for the system to become fair, you will be waiting a very long time. The only rational response is to understand the system as it is and practice accordingly.

When a Peptide Patient Complains, the Doctor Has No Institutional Defense

Here is where the rubber meets the road. All of the structural inequality I have been describing collapses into a single moment: the moment a patient complaint lands on a state medical board investigator's desk. In that moment, every advantage that the blockbuster prescriber enjoys is an advantage that you do not have. And the consequences can be devastating.

Let me walk you through what happens. A patient - maybe a patient with unrealistic expectations, maybe a patient who had a genuine adverse event, maybe a patient who is angry about cost, maybe a patient whose spouse convinced them they were experimented on - files a complaint with the state medical board. The board opens a file. An investigator is assigned. The investigator requests your records. And the process begins.

The investigator's first question is not "Did this physician help the patient?" It is "Is this physician's care consistent with the standard of practice in this state?" That question sounds neutral, but it is loaded. "Standard of practice" means "what most board-certified physicians in this specialty do." And most board-certified physicians do not prescribe peptides. They prescribe FDA-approved drugs for labeled indications. They follow clinical guidelines written by medical societies that are funded - directly or indirectly - by pharmaceutical companies. They practice within an institutional framework that you have deliberately stepped outside of.

So the investigator looks at your chart. What do they see? If you have followed this book's advice, they see a thorough evaluation, a documented rationale, an informed consent discussion, a monitoring plan, and appropriate follow-up. But they also see a therapy they do not recognize, prescribed for an indication that is not in the FDA labeling, sourced from a compounding pharmacy that they have never heard of, with a consent form that mentions investigational status and unknown risks. None of this is present in the blockbuster prescriber's chart. And none of it looks familiar to the investigator.

The blockbuster prescriber's chart, by contrast, is full of familiar elements. FDA-approved drug. Labeled indication. Standard monitoring. No special consent required. The investigator recognizes the drug, recognizes the indication, and recognizes the monitoring protocol. Even if the patient had a serious adverse event, the chart reads as standard care. The investigator's report practically writes itself.

Your chart requires explanation. The investigator needs to understand what the peptide is, why it was chosen, what the evidence is, where it came from, how the patient was monitored, and what the patient was told. Every element requires context that the investigator does not bring to the review. You are not just defending your care. You are educating the investigator about an entire field of medicine that they may have never encountered.

Now consider what happens when the investigator consults with the board's medical expert. Medical experts for state boards are typically senior physicians in conventional specialties - internal medicine, family medicine, endocrinology, depending on the case. These experts have spent their careers practicing within the pharmaceutical mainstream. They may never have prescribed a peptide. They may have negative assumptions about alternative therapies based on training, experience, or institutional bias. They are asked to opine on whether your care met the standard of practice. Their frame of reference is the standard they know - FDA-approved drugs, labeled indications, established guidelines. Your care does not fit that frame.

This does not mean the expert will condemn you. A fair-minded expert may recognize that alternative therapies have a legitimate place in medicine. But the burden is on you to demonstrate that. The blockbuster prescriber does not need to demonstrate that FDA-approved drugs are legitimate. That legitimacy is assumed. You must prove yours, case by case, chart by chart, to people who may start from a position of skepticism.

And then there is the media and public perception dimension. When a blockbuster drug causes harm, the story is about the drug. "Vioxx linked to heart attacks." "Opioid epidemic fueled by manufacturer marketing." The physician is rarely the villain. The narrative centers on corporate greed, regulatory failure, or systemic problems. Individual prescribers are portrayed as victims or unwitting participants in a larger system.

When a peptide prescriber is accused of harm, the story is about the physician. "Doctor accused of experimenting on patients with unapproved drugs." "State board investigates clinic using controversial weight-loss injections." The narrative is personal. It is about a rogue physician operating outside the boundaries of legitimate medicine. There is no corporation to blame. There is no systemic narrative to deflect attention. Just you, alone, facing a story that is framed to make you look reckless before any hearing occurs.

I have seen this happen. I have watched good physicians - careful, conscientious, patient-focused physicians - dragged through board investigations that consumed years of their lives, cost them hundreds of thousands of dollars in legal fees, damaged their reputations, and in some cases ended their careers. These were not bad doctors. They were doctors who prescribed therapies that the system was not designed to protect. And when complaints came, the system did what the system does - it treated them as outliers, as risks, as problems to be managed.

The absence of institutional defense is not abstract. It is the difference between a complaint that is dismissed in ninety days and one that drags on for two years. It is the difference between a chart that speaks for itself and a chart that requires expert explanation. It is the difference between a narrative that frames you as a practitioner of legitimate alternative medicine and one that frames you as a dangerous experimenter. These differences matter. They can cost you your license, your livelihood, and your peace of mind.

This Inequality Is Unfair, but It Is Reality - and You Must Practice Accordingly

I want to be very clear about something. Everything I have described in this section is unfair. It is unfair that therapies helping millions of patients lack the institutional support that blockbuster drugs enjoy. It is unfair that physicians who fill therapeutic gaps are treated as outliers while physicians who prescribe within a flawed mainstream are protected by layers of corporate and regulatory infrastructure. It is unfair that the system values profitability over patient benefit, patent protection over clinical innovation, and institutional power over individual competence. It is all unfair.

Fairness is not the operating principle of the system you practice in. The operating principle is power. Pharmaceutical companies have power. They have money, lobbyists, lawyers, regulatory specialists, and political access. You, as an individual peptide prescriber, have none of those things. Neither do your patients, many of whom are grateful for the care they receive but have no organized voice in the regulatory process.

Accepting this reality is not cynicism. It is pragmatism. The physician who rails against the unfairness of the system while failing to protect themselves within it is not a hero. They are a future cautionary tale. I have seen too many good doctors lose their licenses because they believed that doing the right thing for patients would somehow protect them. It does not. The system does not care about your good intentions. It cares about whether your chart, your consent, your documentation, and your practice structure can withstand scrutiny.

The pragmatic response to institutional inequality is not to abandon peptide prescribing. Your patients need you. The therapies you provide fill genuine gaps in care. The pharmaceutical industry has no interest in addressing many of these gaps because they cannot be monetized. If you step away, your patients do not go back to effective conventional treatment. They go to the grey market. They go to internet vendors. They go to unqualified practitioners. They self-experiment. You are not just protecting yourself by practicing well. You are protecting patients by providing a medically supervised alternative to chaos.

But you must practice with full awareness of the inequality I have described. Every clinical decision you make must be defensible without institutional support. Your chart must explain itself to a skeptical stranger. Your informed consent must be exhaustive because you have no manufacturer's warnings to fall back on. Your patient selection must be conservative because problem patients have no barrier to filing complaints and no institutional filter to prevent those complaints from reaching you. Your monitoring must be meticulous because there is no pharmacovigilance infrastructure catching what you might miss. Your pharmacy relationships must be bulletproof because a compounding problem will be laid at your door, not the manufacturer's.

This is the practice of medicine without a safety net. It is harder than conventional practice. It requires more documentation, more caution, more defensive thinking, and more willingness to say no when the risk is too high. But it is also some of the most rewarding medicine you can practice - because you are helping patients who have been failed by the system, who have nowhere else to turn, and who genuinely need what you can provide.

The inequality exists. It is real. It is unfair. And it is not going away. Practice accordingly.

Why the System Favors Some Treatments Over Others

Understanding the inequality is not enough. You need to understand why it exists - the structural, economic, and political mechanisms that create and sustain it. Because when you understand the why, you can anticipate the problems before they reach your door. You can see the regulatory train coming down the tracks. You can make decisions that protect you and your patients instead of reacting to a system that was never built for the work you do.

FDA Approval Costs Hundreds of Millions - Only Profitable Drugs Get Approved

The FDA approval process for a new drug is one of the most expensive undertakings in modern commerce. Estimates vary, but the consensus figure in the pharmaceutical industry is that bringing a new drug from discovery to FDA approval costs between one and three billion dollars. That includes preclinical research, the three phases of clinical trials, regulatory submission, advisory committee preparation, manufacturing scale-up, and post-approval commitments. It takes an average of ten to fifteen years from first discovery to pharmacy shelves.

Those numbers are staggering, and they create an economic filter that most physicians never think about. A pharmaceutical company will only invest that kind of money if the potential return justifies the risk. That means the drug must be patentable, marketable to a large patient population, and priced at a level that generates substantial revenue. The drug must treat a common condition - or a rare condition at an extremely high price - and it must do so in a way that can be protected from generic competition for long enough to recoup the investment.

This economic filter explains why certain categories of therapy are richly supplied with FDA-approved drugs and others are barren. Common chronic conditions - diabetes, hypertension, high cholesterol, depression, obesity - have dozens of approved drugs because the patient populations are large and the revenue potential is enormous. Rare diseases with orphan drug designation can also attract investment because the FDA provides incentives and the pricing can be set at astronomical levels.

But therapies that do not fit this economic model do not get developed. A naturally occurring peptide that cannot be patented is not going to attract a billion-dollar investment. A therapy that requires individual compounding rather than mass manufacturing is not going to generate the revenue needed to fund clinical trials. A treatment for a condition that already has adequate pharmaceutical options - even if those options are imperfect - is not going to attract investment unless the new therapy offers a dramatic advantage that can be monetized.

This is why so many peptides lack FDA approval. It is not because they are ineffective. It is not because they are dangerous. It is because no one has been willing to spend a billion dollars proving to the FDA that they work. And no one has been willing to do that because the economic return does not justify the investment. The system is not designed to approve therapies. It is designed to approve profitable therapies.

Consider BPC-157 as an example. The published evidence - mostly preclinical, but substantial - suggests genuine therapeutic potential in soft-tissue healing, gut mucosal protection, and anti-inflammatory applications. Patients report benefits. Physicians observe them. But BPC-157 was developed in an academic lab in Croatia, not by a pharmaceutical company. It is a short peptide sequence derived from a naturally occurring protein. Patent protection would be limited. The market for a soft-tissue repair peptide, while significant, is not large enough to justify a billion-dollar investment. So no one has funded the clinical trials needed for FDA approval. And without FDA approval, BPC-157 remains in regulatory limbo- used by thousands of patients, prescribed by thousands of physicians, and officially“unapproved” by the agency that only approves what is profitable to develop.

This is the economic reality of drug development. The FDA is not a medical organization evaluating therapies based on patient benefit. It is a regulatory gatekeeper that requires a massively expensive proof process that only profitable drugs can afford. The gatekeeping function is real and serves important safety purposes. But the cost of the gate creates a system where only wealthy applicants can pass through. The rest stand outside - effective or not, safe or not, needed or not.

Natural Compounds and Unpatentable Peptides Lack the Economic Incentive for Approval

The patent system is the invisible hand behind FDA approval decisions. The United States grants patent protection for new pharmaceutical compounds, typically for twenty years from the date of filing. During that period, the patent holder has exclusive rights to manufacture and sell the drug. This monopoly allows the manufacturer to charge prices far above manufacturing cost, generating the revenue needed to recoup the billion-dollar investment in clinical trials and regulatory approval.

Patent protection is the engine of pharmaceutical innovation. It is also the filter that excludes therapies that cannot be patented. A naturally occurring peptide - a sequence of amino acids that exists in the human body or in common foods - cannot be patented in its natural form. You cannot patent insulin as it exists in the human pancreas. You can patent a specific manufacturing method, a specific formulation, or a specific delivery device. But the molecule itself is a product of nature, and products of nature are not patentable under U.S. law following the Supreme Court's decision in Association for Molecular Pathology v. Myriad Genetics.

This legal principle has profound consequences for peptide medicine. Many of the most interesting peptides - BPC-157, thymosin beta-4, various growth-hormone secretagogues, fragments of larger proteins like KPV - are either naturally occurring or derived from naturally occurring sequences. They can be synthesized in a lab, but the underlying sequence exists in nature. Without patent protection on the molecule itself, there is no economic incentive to fund the clinical trials needed for FDA approval.

Some workarounds exist. A manufacturer can patent a specific formulation, a specific salt form, a specific route of administration, or a specific delivery device. But these patents are narrower and easier to design around. If a compound can be administered subcutaneously in a simple formulation, a competitor can do the same without infringing the patent. The economic incentive is reduced.

Compare this to a small-molecule drug like a statin or a kinase inhibitor. These are novel chemical entities that do not exist in nature. They can be patented in their molecular form. The patent provides broad protection that prevents competitors from selling the same molecule. The manufacturer has a genuine monopoly for the patent term, allowing high pricing and massive revenue. That revenue funds clinical trials, regulatory approval, and the entire infrastructure of institutional support I described earlier.

The result is a systematic bias in the FDA-approved drug portfolio toward novel, patentable, synthetic molecules and away from natural compounds and unpatentable peptides. The system is not biased by design - it is biased by economics. The FDA does not actively exclude natural compounds. It simply requires an approval process that only patented compounds can afford. The exclusion is structural, not intentional. But the effect is the same.

This explains why insulin - one of the most important peptide drugs in history - required decades of development by academic researchers and public funding before it became commercially viable. It explains why the most significant advances in GLP-1 therapy came from pharmaceutical companies that patented specific analogs with modifications that extended half-life and improved pharmacokinetics. The natural GLP-1 molecule has a half-life of minutes. Semaglutide is an engineered analog with a half-life of days. That engineering created patentable intellectual property and made the billion-dollar investment worthwhile.

For peptide prescribers, this economic reality means that many of the therapies you use will never have FDA approval - not because they do not work, but because no one can make enough money from them to fund the approval process. You are practicing in a space that the pharmaceutical business model has abandoned. That is not a value judgment. It is an economic fact. And it means that your practice must account for the absence of the infrastructure that FDA approval creates.

Insurance Reimbursement Drives Prescribing Behavior - Cash-Pay Therapies Are Automatically Suspect

Insurance reimbursement is the third structural force that shapes prescribing behavior and creates suspicion of alternative therapies. The American healthcare system is built on third-party payment. Patients receive care, providers bill insurers, and insurers pay according to complex fee schedules, coding systems, and coverage policies. This system has many flaws, but its influence on medical practice is enormous and underappreciated.

When a drug is covered by insurance, it enters the mainstream of medical practice in a way that cash-pay therapies cannot match. Coverage means accessibility. A patient with a twenty-dollar copay will fill a prescription that a patient facing a five-hundred-dollar cash price will not. Coverage means volume. Thousands of prescriptions are written for covered drugs for every cash-pay prescription of an alternative therapy. Coverage means legitimacy. The insurance company's decision to cover a drug is treated as a validation of its medical value -even though coverage decisions are driven by cost-effectiveness analysis, contractual negotiations, and actuarial calculations, not by clinical judgment.

The process by which drugs obtain insurance coverage reinforces the pharmaceutical infrastructure. A manufacturer seeking coverage submits clinical data, cost-effectiveness analyses, and pharmacoeconomic models to pharmacy benefit managers - PBMs - and insurance companies. The PBM evaluates the drug, compares it to alternatives, negotiates rebates, and decides where to place it on the formulary. A preferred formulary placement means lower copays for patients and higher prescribing volume for the manufacturer. The negotiation process is complex and opaque, but the outcome is clear: FDA-approved drugs with robust clinical data get covered. Alternative therapies without that data do not.

Cash-pay therapies exist outside this system. The patient pays the full cost. The physician does not bill insurance. The transaction is private, direct, and unfiltered by third-party review. From a clinical standpoint, this has advantages - no prior authorization delays, no formulary restrictions, no clawbacks, no audits. But from an institutional standpoint, it creates suspicion.

Why would a patient pay cash for a therapy when insurance covers alternatives? Why would a physician prescribe something that no insurance company will pay for? These questions may not be asked explicitly, but they operate beneath the surface of every board investigation, every malpractice review, every credentialing evaluation. The cash-pay nature of peptide therapy is treated as a signal that something is unconventional, and unconventional is treated as suspect.

This suspicion is compounded by the pricing of cash-pay therapies. A peptide program that costs three hundred to a thousand dollars a month seems expensive to patients, to investigators, to juries. The fact that branded GLP-1 drugs can cost even more when purchased without insurance is often lost in the analysis because those drugs have FDA approval, manufacturer support, and insurance coverage as contextual anchors. The cash-pay peptide program has none of those anchors. The price stands alone, stripped of institutional context, and is easily portrayed as exploitation.

Chapter 5 of this book addresses the insurance question in detail, and I will not repeat that analysis here. But the structural point is essential: the American healthcare system has built its legitimacy framework around insurance reimbursement. Therapies that exist outside that framework are automatically viewed with skepticism. This is not fair. Many cash-pay therapies are clinically valuable, patient-centered, and appropriately priced. But fairness is not the standard by which the system evaluates you. The system evaluates based on institutional norms, and cash-pay peptide therapy violates those norms.

The insurance gap also affects medical records and documentation. Insurance billing creates a structured record of care - diagnostic codes, procedure codes, units of service, prior authorizations, appeals. This record, whatever its flaws, provides a trail that investigators can follow. Cash-pay practices often lack this structure. The record is whatever the practice creates. If the practice's documentation is weak, there is no billing trail to fill in the gaps. The chart stands alone. And if the chart is thin, the defense is thin.

This is why documentation is so critical for cash-pay peptide prescribers. You do not have the structural support of insurance billing, pharmacy benefit management, manufacturer-funded education, or FDA-approved labeling. Your chart is your infrastructure. It must carry the entire weight of defending your clinical decisions. Every element - history, physical, rationale, consent, monitoring, follow-up, stop rules - must be present and must be strong. Not because you are more likely to make mistakes than a conventional prescriber. But because you have none of the institutional scaffolding that catches mistakes before they become disasters.

State Medical Boards Are Influenced by Mainstream Medical Opinion, Which Is Influenced by Pharmaceutical Funding

I saved the most politically sensitive point for last, and I am going to state it plainly without apology. State medical boards are influenced by mainstream medical opinion. Mainstream medical opinion is influenced by pharmaceutical funding. The influence is not corrupt in the criminal sense. It is structural, pervasive, and largely invisible to the people who operate within it.

State medical boards are composed of physicians. In most states, the majority of board members are practicing physicians appointed by the governor or by medical societies. These physicians are, by definition, successful within the current system. They have built careers in conventional medicine - academic medicine, hospital practice, group practice, or specialty practice. They have passed board examinations, maintained licensure, and practiced within the mainstream. They are not, as a group, rebels, innovators, or critics of the pharmaceutical industry.

The medical education these board members received was shaped by pharmaceutical funding. Their residency programs used textbooks and guidelines funded by industry. Their CME has been sponsored by pharmaceutical companies. Their medical societies receive industry support for conferences, journals, and educational programs. Their hospital formularies are managed by pharmacy committees that evaluate drugs based on FDA approval, insurance coverage, and manufacturer data. Their entire professional experience has been within a system where pharmaceutical companies are the primary source of new therapies, new knowledge, and new standards of care.

This is not a conspiracy. It is a professional culture. And cultures shape perception in ways that individuals rarely recognize. A board member who has never prescribed a peptide, who has never read the literature on growth-hormone secretagogues, who has only heard about

BPC-157 in the context of regulatory warnings - that board member is not starting from neutral. They are starting from a position of skepticism that is deeply embedded in their professional identity.

The influence operates at multiple levels. Board members attend medical conferences where pharmaceutical companies sponsor sessions, exhibit products, and fund speaker honoraria. They read medical journals that rely on pharmaceutical advertising. They participate in medical societies that accept industry funding. They serve on hospital committees that evaluate drugs based on manufacturer-supplied data. None of this makes them corrupt. It makes them human. It makes them products of a system that has been shaped by pharmaceutical interests for decades.

When these board members review a complaint about a peptide prescriber, they bring this entire framework of assumptions with them. The peptide is not FDA-approved - that is a red flag. The prescriber is not following established guidelines - that is another red flag. The therapy is not covered by insurance - another red flag. The consent form mentions investigational status - another red flag. Each of these factors, viewed in isolation, might be neutral or even positive. But viewed together, through the lens of mainstream medical culture, they create a picture of deviation. And deviation is what boards are trained to correct.

The pharmaceutical industry's influence on mainstream medical opinion also operates through the clinical guidelines that board members rely on. Clinical practice guidelines are written by medical societies, government agencies, and expert panels. These guidelines are supposed to be evidence-based and objective. In practice, they are heavily influenced by the available evidence, and the available evidence is heavily influenced by what gets funded. Pharmaceutical companies fund the vast majority of clinical trials. They control the data. They decide what gets published and what does not. Guidelines committees review the published literature and make recommendations. But the literature they review is a curated sample shaped by commercial interests.

This influence is well-documented in the medical literature itself. Studies have shown that guidelines committee members frequently have financial relationships with pharmaceutical companies, that industry-funded trials are more likely to show positive results, that negative trials often go unpublished, and that guideline recommendations tend to favor newer, more expensive therapies over older, cheaper alternatives. This does not mean that guidelines are worthless. It means they are products of a system with built-in biases - biases that favor FDA-approved, pharmaceutical-industry-supported therapies over alternative approaches.

For peptide prescribers, this means that the mainstream medical opinion that influences board decisions is itself influenced by the same pharmaceutical funding that shapes every other aspect of the system. The board member who reviews your case is not necessarily biased against you personally. They are biased against deviation from a mainstream that has been constructed, in part, by the industry that has the most to lose from the growth of alternative therapies.

Understanding this influence is not paranoia. It is strategic awareness. You cannot change the composition of state medical boards. You cannot eliminate pharmaceutical influence on mainstream medical opinion. You cannot rewrite clinical guidelines. What you can do is practice in a way that anticipates the biases you will face and builds defenses against them. Your documentation must be better than mainstream standard because the standard applied to you will be stricter. Your informed consent must be more thorough because the presumption of legitimacy that mainstream therapies enjoy will not be extended to yours. Your patient selection must be more conservative because the margin for error is narrower. Your monitoring must be more meticulous because the institutional safety nets that catch errors in conventional practice do not exist for you.

The system is rigged. Not by conscious conspiracy, but by decades of economic incentives, institutional capture, and cultural formation that have created a healthcare landscape where profitable drugs are protected and alternative therapies are exposed. You did not create this system. But you practice within it. And understanding it - really understanding it, in all its structural unfairness - is the first step toward protecting yourself and your patients within it.

What This Means for Your Practice

I have spent the bulk of this chapter describing a system that is tilted against you. That description is not meant to discourage you or to drive you out of peptide prescribing. Quite the opposite. I am describing the battlefield because you need to know the terrain before you step onto it. Physicians who understand the system they are operating in make better decisions, build stronger defenses, and keep their licenses. Physicians who pretend the system is fair get destroyed by it. The choice is that simple.

So let me now tell you exactly what the inequality I have described means for your daily practice. Not in abstract terms. In concrete, actionable, do-this-not-that terms that you can implement starting today.

You Are Practicing at a Disadvantage - Accept It and Compensate for It

The first thing you need to do - and I mean really do, not just intellectually acknowledge -is accept that you are practicing at a disadvantage. This acceptance is not defeatism. It is strategic clarity. You cannot compensate for a problem you refuse to acknowledge.

Every physician who prescribes peptides, compounded therapies, or any treatment outside the FDA-approved mainstream is practicing without the institutional armor that conventional prescribers take for granted. No manufacturer-funded REMS. No FDA-approved labeling. No CME infrastructure. No insurance coverage creating legitimacy. No lobbying apparatus. No learned intermediary doctrine with clear precedent. No post-marketing surveillance at scale. No board investigator's familiarity with your therapy. No presumption of legitimacy.

That is the reality. And the only rational response is to build your own defenses - stronger, more comprehensive, and more meticulous than anything the conventional prescriber needs. You are not just practicing medicine. You are practicing medicine while constructing the institutional infrastructure that conventional prescribers inherit from the pharmaceutical industry.

This means your standards must be higher. Your documentation must be better. Your consent must be more thorough. Your patient selection must be more conservative. Your monitoring must be more systematic. Your pharmacy relationships must be more carefully vetted. Your staff training must be more rigorous. Your marketing must be more restrained. Every element of your practice that can be strengthened must be strengthened, because you have no institutional backup for weaknesses.

Think of it this way. A physician prescribing an FDA-approved drug within labeling is swimming in a pool with a lifeguard, a safety net, lane lines, and a posted set of rules. If they stumble, the system catches them. You are swimming in the open ocean. No lifeguard. No net. No lane lines. The rules are unclear and subject to interpretation by people who may not understand what you are doing. If you stumble, you sink. The only way to survive is to be a stronger swimmer than anyone in the pool.

That is the mindset. Not resentment. Not wishful thinking. Not hope that the system will change. Just clear-eyed recognition that the bar is higher for you, and the consequences of falling are worse. Practice accordingly.

Let me give you a concrete example of what this acceptance looks like in action. A patient comes to you asking for a growth-hormone secretagogue for weight loss support, sleep improvement, and recovery from exercise. They heard about it on a podcast. They are not your patient yet - they are a prospective patient evaluating whether to work with you.

A physician who has not accepted the reality of their disadvantage might say yes quickly. The patient seems motivated. The therapy is reasonable for their goals. The pharmacy can compound it. Why not? The answer is: because the chart will not defend you if something goes wrong. The patient who hears about a therapy on a podcast has expectations shaped by marketing, not medicine. They do not understand the investigational status. They do not understand the monitoring requirements. They do not understand the stop rules. They have not been appropriately screened. They have not had their primary care involvement confirmed. They have not signed a comprehensive informed consent. If they have an adverse event -even a mild one - they may panic, complain, or worse.

A physician who has accepted the reality of their disadvantage says: "I understand your interest. Let me evaluate whether this is appropriate for you. We need a complete medical history. We need recent labs. We need to discuss what this therapy is and is not. We need to involve your primary care physician. We need to set clear expectations, monitoring, and stop rules. We need you to understand the FDA status, the evidence limitations, and the risks. Then we decide together." That physician might lose the patient to a less careful competitor. But the patients who stay are the ones who will not destroy the practice with a complaint.

Your Documentation Must Be Better Than the Doctor Prescribing the Blockbuster Drug

I have said this before, and I will keep saying it until it is burned into your consciousness: your documentation must be better than the chart of a physician prescribing an FDA-approved blockbuster drug. Not as good. Better. Significantly, unmistakably, defensibly better.

Why? Because the blockbuster prescriber's chart does not need to explain why the therapy was chosen. The FDA approval, the labeled indication, the insurance coverage, and the clinical guidelines do that work. The prescriber's chart needs to show that the patient had the condition, the drug was appropriate, and standard monitoring was followed. That is all. The institutional infrastructure carries the rest of the defense.

Your chart must carry the entire defense. It must explain what the therapy is, why it was chosen, what the evidence is, what the risks are, what the alternatives were, why they were insufficient, what the patient was told, what monitoring was established, what stop rules were set, and what follow-up was planned. Every element must be present. Every element must be clear. Every element must be written for a skeptical stranger who has never heard of your therapy and starts from a position of suspicion.

The standard for your chart is not "would a reasonable physician understand this?" The standard is "would a hostile board investigator, working from a complaint, without prior knowledge of peptide therapy, reading this chart for the first time, conclude that this was a thoughtful, defensible medical decision?" That is a much higher standard. And it is the standard you must meet every single time.

What does this look like in practice? It means your chart notes include the following elements for every peptide prescription:

A clear statement of the clinical problem. Not "patient wants weight-loss peptide." Something like: "Patient is a 47-year-old female with BMI 32.4, history of prediabetes, obstructive sleep apnea on CPAP, bilateral knee osteoarthritis limiting mobility, and failed trials of lifestyle modification, orlistat, and phentermine. GLP-1 agonist therapy considered." The problem is medical. The evaluation is thorough. The failed alternatives are documented.

A statement of the therapy's regulatory status. "Compounded semaglutide prescribed. Patient informed this is not FDA-approved in compounded form. Patient informed of FDA-approved branded alternative (Wegovy) and its cost. Patient elected compounded formulation due to affordability. Discussion documented." This is not a footnote. It is a clear, explicit statement that shows the patient knew exactly what they were getting.

A summary of the evidence discussion. "Evidence for GLP-1 receptor agonists in obesity reviewed with patient. Key trials discussed (STEP 1-5, SURMOUNT-1). Expected benefits described without guarantees. Common side effects reviewed (nausea, vomiting, diarrhea, constipation, injection-site reactions). Serious risks discussed (pancreatitis, gallbladder disease, thyroid C-cell tumors in rodents, potential medullary thyroid carcinoma contraindication)."This demonstrates that you did not just hand over a vial. You had a real medical discussion.

A description of the alternatives reviewed and why they were insufficient. "Lifestyle modification alone attempted for 18 months with minimal sustained weight loss. Orlistat discontinued due to GI intolerance. Phentermine effective for 3 months with weight regain after discontinuation. Branded semaglutide (Wegovy) not affordable at current pharmacy benefit. Bariatric surgery discussed; patient declined." This shows that the peptide was not a first-line shortcut. It was a considered decision after appropriate alternatives were tried or refused.

A description of informed consent. "Comprehensive informed consent obtained. Patient received written consent form documenting FDA status, evidence level, known risks, unknown risks, no guaranteed outcomes, cost, refund policy, monitoring requirements, stop rules, and emergency instructions. Patient had opportunity to ask questions. Patient signed consent. Copy provided." This is not a signature on a half-page form. It is a documented process of informed decision-making.

A statement about primary care involvement. "Patient's primary care physician, Dr. Smith, copied on prescription and monitoring plan. Patient advised to maintain regular PCP follow-up. PCP contact information documented." This is your secret weapon. PCP involvement demonstrates that you are not operating in isolation from the medical mainstream. You are coordinating care. The board investigator who sees PCP involvement sees a physician who respects the system, not one who is trying to circumvent it.

A monitoring plan with specific stop criteria. "Follow-up scheduled in 4 weeks, then every 12 weeks. Weight, vitals, HbA1c, fasting glucose, lipids, liver enzymes, amylase/lipase to be monitored. Stop criteria: pancreatitis symptoms, gallbladder disease, persistent severe GI side effects, weight loss exceeding 1.5 kg/week suggesting unsafe rate, patient request, or failure to follow up." This shows systematic medical supervision, not vial dispensing.

Each of these elements is a brick in a wall. The wall is your defense. If any brick is missing, the wall has a gap. A hostile investigator will find that gap. A plaintiff's attorney will find that gap. A medical expert reviewing your case for the board will find that gap. Your job is to build a wall without gaps, every single time.

This level of documentation takes time. It takes effort. It takes staff support. And it is not optional. If you cannot document at this level, you should not be prescribing peptides. The prescriber who cuts corners on documentation because "everyone knows this therapy is safe"or "the patient is fine with it" is building a time bomb. The complaint comes later. The chart is read then. And the chart either saves you or destroys you.

Your Informed Consent Must Be Bulletproof Because You Have No Institutional Safety Net

I have already discussed informed consent in other chapters, but the context of institutional inequality demands that I revisit it here with emphasis. Your informed consent is not a formality. It is not a legal checkbox. It is not something to get out of the way so you can move on to the medicine. For a peptide prescriber, informed consent is the single most important document in the chart after the clinical note itself. And it must be bulletproof.

What does bulletproof mean? It means the consent form - and the documented consent discussion - would survive scrutiny by a hostile board investigator, a plaintiff's attorney, a jury, and a medical expert witness who has never prescribed a peptide. It means the consent is so thorough, so clear, so explicit that no reasonable person could claim they did not understand what they were agreeing to.

The blockbuster prescriber does not need bulletproof informed consent in the same way. The patient receiving an FDA-approved drug within labeling has been warned by the manufacturer (labeling), educated by the pharmacist (medication guide), and protected by the learned intermediary doctrine. The physician's consent discussion is one layer in a multilayered warning system. If the patient's consent is imperfect, the other layers provide backup.

You have no other layers. Your consent is the warning system. It is the labeling, the medication guide, the REMS education, and the physician counseling all rolled into one document. If it is weak, the entire defense collapses.

A bulletproof consent for peptide therapy includes the following elements. I am not presenting these as bullet points for easy reading - I am weaving them into the analytical prose because each element requires understanding, not just checking off a list.

The consent must state the therapy's regulatory status in plain English. Not in a single sentence buried on page three. Prominently. Repeatedly. In language a patient can understand. “This medication is compounded by a licensed pharmacy. It is not FDA-approved in this form. The FDA has not evaluated its safety and efficacy for your specific condition.” That language is not scary. It is honest. And honesty is your best defense.

The consent must describe the evidence level accurately. “The active ingredient in this medication has been studied in clinical trials for [indication], and those trials showed [general results]. However, the specific compounded formulation you are receiving has not been evaluated by the FDA. The evidence supporting its use includes [specific trials if applicable, or preclinical data, or mechanism-based rationale].” This gives the patient context without overstating or understating what is known.

The consent must list known risks specifically. Not “some side effects may occur.” That is meaningless. List the actual known risks: nausea, vomiting, diarrhea, constipation, injection-site reactions, headache, fatigue, dizziness, potential pancreatitis, gallbladder effects, and any other risks specific to the therapy. The patient who experiences nausea and was warned about nausea in writing is much less likely to panic and complain than the patient who was told “side effects are rare.”

The consent must describe unknown risks explicitly. “Because this therapy has not been evaluated by the FDA in this compounded form, there may be risks that are not yet known. Long-term safety data are limited. You are assuming the risk of unknown adverse effects.” This is the language that protects you when a patient experiences something unexpected. If they signed a form acknowledging unknown risks, they cannot claim they were not warned.

The consent must state clearly that no outcomes are guaranteed. “This therapy may help with [clinical goal]. Individual results vary. No specific outcome is promised or guaranteed. Weight loss, if it occurs, varies by individual. Some patients experience significant benefit. Some patients experience minimal benefit. Some patients experience side effects without benefit.”This language inoculates you against the patient who expected miracles and got modest improvement.

The consent must describe alternatives, including doing nothing. “Alternatives to this therapy include [FDA-approved alternatives with pros and cons], lifestyle modification alone, other medical treatments, and no treatment. You may continue with your current management. The choice is yours.” This demonstrates that you are not pressuring the patient into an alternative therapy. You are presenting options and allowing an informed choice.

The consent must describe the monitoring plan. “This therapy requires follow-up visits at [interval], laboratory monitoring of [specific tests], and patient reporting of [specific symptoms]. Failure to follow up or report symptoms may result in discontinuation of therapy.”This establishes patient responsibility and creates a record that the monitoring plan was explained before therapy began.

The consent must include stop rules. “You must stop this medication and contact the practice immediately if you experience [list red-flag symptoms]. You must stop and seek emergency care if you experience [list emergency symptoms].” This protects the patient and protects you. A patient who ignores red-flag symptoms and suffers a serious adverse event cannot claim they did not know what to watch for.

The consent must address cost and the no-refund policy. “The cost of this program is [amount]. This includes [specific services]. Medication costs are [separate or included].

Refund policy is [specific policy]." Financial surprises turn satisfied patients into complainants. Transparency about cost prevents that.

The consent must clarify that you are not the patient's primary care physician. "This practice provides specialized evaluation and management of [condition]. We are not your primary care physician. You must maintain care with your PCP. We will coordinate with your PCP when appropriate. Any medical issues outside our scope must be addressed by your PCP or appropriate specialist." This boundary-setting protects you from complaints about unrelated medical issues and demonstrates responsible practice.

The consent must include patient certification language. "I certify that I have read this consent form, had the opportunity to ask questions, received answers I understand, and am choosing to proceed with full knowledge of the risks, benefits, alternatives, and uncertainties described above." This shifts the decision-making responsibility to the patient where it belongs.

A consent form with these elements is long. It may be eight to twelve pages. Patients will complain about the length. Staff will resist the workload. You will be tempted to use a shorter form to streamline the process. Resist that temptation. A long, thorough, well-explained consent form is your shield. A short, vague, inadequate form is an invitation to disaster. The patient who complains about reading twelve pages of consent will complain far more loudly when they have an adverse event and your defense is a one-page form with three paragraphs of fine print.

The consent discussion is as important as the consent document. The form is evidence that the information was provided. The documented discussion is evidence that the patient understood it. Your clinical note should describe the consent conversation: "Informed consent discussion conducted. Patient's questions addressed. Patient's understanding confirmed. Patient signed consent form after having time to review. Copy provided to patient." This closes the loop. The patient cannot later claim they signed without understanding what they were signing.

And let me add one more element that many physicians overlook. The consent must be updated when circumstances change. If new safety information emerges, the consent should be revised. If the patient's clinical situation changes, the consent should be reviewed. If the therapy continues beyond the initial expected duration, the consent should be reaffirmed. A consent form signed six months ago does not necessarily cover continued therapy today. Update it. Document the update. Show that your consent process is living and ongoing, not a one-time signature obtained on day one and forgotten.

Your Patient Selection Must Be Conservative Because Problem Patients Have No Barrier to Filing Complaints

The final practical implication of institutional inequality is the most uncomfortable one. You must be more selective about your patients than a conventional prescriber. Not because you are elitist. Not because you are greedy. Because problem patients - the demanding ones, the unrealistic ones, the unstable ones, the litigious ones - can destroy a practice that has no institutional armor. And you have none.

A physician prescribing an FDA-approved blockbuster drug can afford a certain percentage of difficult patients. The system absorbs the complaints. The manufacturer provides backup. The insurance company manages the financial disputes. The presumption of legitimacy protects the prescriber. A few unhappy patients are manageable within a large practice.

For a peptide prescriber, one unhappy patient can trigger a board investigation that consumes years of your life and hundreds of thousands of dollars in legal fees. One unrealistic patient who experiences a mild side effect and decides they were experimented on can generate a complaint that turns your practice upside down. One litigious patient who smells an alternative medicine payday can initiate a lawsuit that bankrupts you even if you ultimately win. The stakes are not just higher. They are catastrophically higher.

This means you must say no. More often than you want to. More often than your competitor down the street says no. More often than your business plan would prefer. Saying no is your most powerful risk management tool, and the physician who cannot say no should not be prescribing peptides.

Say no to patients with unrealistic expectations. The patient who watched an influencer lose fifty pounds in three months on a GLP-1 agonist and expects the same result regardless of their individual circumstances is a future complaint. They will lose weight more slowly. They will plateau. They will regain some weight. They will be disappointed. And disappointment turns to anger, which turns to complaints. Set expectations conservatively in the consultation. If the patient pushes back, if they insist on guarantees, if they quote social media testimonials as evidence - say no. You are not their obstacle. You are their protection from their own unrealistic thinking.

Say no to patients who will not involve their primary care physician. PCP involvement is not just good medicine. It is your institutional proxy. It demonstrates to any investigator that you are coordinating with the medical mainstream, not operating as a rogue practitioner. The patient who refuses to loop in their PCP - who wants secrecy, who says their PCP "doesn't understand," who insists on keeping this "just between us" - is waving a red flag. They are either hiding something, cutting corners, or preparing to blame you if things go wrong. Say no.

Say no to patients who cannot afford the program. Financial stress turns patients into complainants. The patient who stretches their budget to pay for therapy, who experiences a side effect, and who feels they wasted their money will complain, dispute charges, and post negative reviews. If a patient cannot comfortably afford your program, they should not be in it. This is not callousness. It is risk management. A patient who pays without financial strain can evaluate the therapy on its medical merits. A patient who pays with money they cannot afford will evaluate it on financial terms, and the slightest disappointment becomes a betrayal.

Say no to patients with complex psychiatric histories who are not under psychiatric care. Anxiety, depression, bipolar disorder, personality disorders - these conditions can interact unpredictably with peptide therapies. A patient with untreated anxiety who experiences a mild side effect may catastrophize. A patient with depression who does not experience immediate benefit may despair. A patient with a personality disorder may idealize you initially and then devalue you when you refuse an unreasonable request. The peptide prescriber without institutional armor cannot afford the volatility that a conventional practice with mainstream protection can absorb. Require psychiatric stability and ongoing care for patients with significant mental health histories.

Say no to patients who have complaints about every previous doctor. The patient who tells you their last five doctors were incompetent, uncaring, or harmful is telling you something important about themselves. They are either incredibly unlucky - possible, but statistically unlikely - or they are a chronic complainer who will eventually add you to their list. Listen carefully in the consultation. If the patient's history is a litany of grievances against previous providers, say no. You will not be the exception. You will be number six.

Say no to patients who want to self-direct their therapy. The patient who wants to adjust their own dose, add their own supplements, stack therapies without your input, or order their own labs is not a partner in care. They are a future adverse event with your name on it. Medical supervision means supervision. If a patient will not accept it, they do not belong in your program.

Say no to patients who are in a rush. The patient who demands to start therapy immediately, who pushes you to skip steps, who resists the thorough evaluation that good medicine requires- they are dangerous. They will also be the first to complain if anything goes wrong, claiming that you rushed them into therapy without adequate evaluation. A thorough evaluation protects you. A rushed evaluation exposes you. Do not let patient impatience override your medical judgment.

Patient selection conservatism is the hardest element of defensive peptide practice because it means turning away revenue. Every "no" is a patient who walks out your door and may go to a less careful competitor. Every "no" is a hit to your monthly numbers. Every "no" is a conversation where you must explain yourself to someone who does not want to hear it.

But every "yes" to the wrong patient is a potential complaint, a potential lawsuit, a potential board investigation, and a potential end to your career. The revenue from one problematic patient is not worth the risk they bring. Not when you practice without institutional armor. Not when one complaint can trigger a process that consumes everything you have built.

Conservative patient selection also means ongoing vigilance. The patient who was appropriate on day one may become inappropriate over time. They may develop new medical conditions. They may stop following up. They may start buying grey-market products online and stacking them with your prescribed therapy. They may have a life event that destabilizes them. Your patient selection process does not end at the consultation. It continues at every follow-up. And when a previously appropriate patient becomes inappropriate, you must be willing to say stop- to discontinue therapy, document your reasoning, and manage the consequences.

This is what it means to practice peptides without the institutional protection that Big Pharma provides. You must be better than mainstream physicians because you are judged by a harsher standard. You must document more thoroughly because you have no manufacturer's label to fall back on. You must consent more exhaustively because you have no REMS program to educate your patients. You must select patients more conservatively because one complaint can destroy you. You must monitor more meticulously because there is no pharmacovigilance infrastructure catching what you miss.

It is not fair. I have said that repeatedly, and I will keep saying it because it is true and because you need to feel the weight of that truth. The system protects profitable drugs and the physicians who prescribe them. It exposes alternative therapies and the physicians who use them. This is the reality. It is structural. It is economic. It is political. And it is not changing in your lifetime.

The only rational response is to accept this reality and build a practice that thrives within it. Document like your license depends on it - because it does. Consent like your freedom depends on it - because it might. Select patients like your livelihood depends on it - because it does. Monitor like your reputation depends on it - because it does. Build a practice that is so careful, so thorough, so obviously medical rather than commercial, that even the most hostile investigator would struggle to find fault.

You are not just practicing medicine. You are building a fortress. The pharmaceutical industry has its fortress - built with billions of dollars over decades, staffed with thousands of lawyers and lobbyists, protected by layers of regulatory and legal infrastructure. Your fortress is built one chart at a time, one consent form at a time, one careful patient selection at a time, one thorough follow-up at a time. It is smaller. It is humbler. But if you build it right, it will protect you. And it will protect the patients who depend on you when the system has nothing else to offer them.

That is the work. That is the reality. Now get to work.

5 - Why You Don't Take Insurance - And Never Will

Let me tell you something right now, and I want you to hear me good. If you're sitting there thinking about taking insurance in your peptide practice - if you're even considering it as a way to "get more patients" or "help people who can't afford it" - you need to close this book, walk over to your front door, and slam your hand in it. Hard. Because that thought, that little voice in your head telling you insurance might make things easier, is the same voice that's going to get your license stripped, your savings drained, and your name dragged through every database from here to the National Practitioner Data Bank.

I'm not being dramatic. I've watched it happen. Good doctors - smart doctors, caring doctors, doctors who got into this business to help people - have lost everything because they let an insurance company into their practice. The insurance industry doesn't partner with you. It doesn't collaborate. It colonizes. It inserts itself into the doctor-patient relationship, turns your clinical judgment into a billing code, and then - when it decides it wants its money back - it uses your own state medical board as its personal collections agency.

This chapter is about why cash-pay isn't some trendy boutique medical gimmick. It isn't about being elitist. It isn't about excluding patients. It's about survival. Cash-pay is a legal shield, a regulatory moat, and a structural firewall between your clinical decision-making and the institutions that exist to destroy you. By the time you finish this chapter, you will understand that taking insurance in a peptide practice isn't just unwise - it's professionally suicidal.

Insurance Companies Operate Hand-in-Hand with State Regulators

Here's the first thing you need to understand about the insurance industry, and I mean really understand it, deep in your bones. Insurance companies and state medical boards aren't two separate entities that occasionally bump into each other. They're part of the same ecosystem. They share information. They share incentives. And when it comes time to go after a physician- especially a physician doing something unconventional, something outside the standard playbook - they operate as a team.

You think your state medical board is an independent body of wise physicians carefully reviewing cases based on medical merit? Bless your heart. In many states, the medical board is underfunded, overwhelmed, and desperate for tips about doctors who might be doing something wrong. They don't have the staff to proactively investigate every practice. They need leads. They need complaints. And guess who generates those complaints by the truckload? Insurance companies.

The relationship works like this. An insurance company has a financial interest in not paying claims. That's its entire business model - collect premiums, deny claims, keep the difference. When an insurer reviews a claim and sees something it doesn't like - an unusual treatment, a high-cost medication, a diagnosis code that doesn't match the standard protocol - it doesn't just deny the claim and move on. It flags the provider. It builds a file. And if the dollar amounts get big enough, or if the treatment falls outside what the insurer considers "established medical practice," that flag gets passed along to the state medical board with a neat little bow on top.

Let me be very clear about what this means. The insurance company isn't calling the board because it cares about patient safety. It isn't calling because it has ethical concerns about your medical judgment. It's calling because it wants its money back, and it has learned - through years of successful practice - that the fastest way to recover money from a physician is to threaten their license. A clawback letter from an insurance auditor is one thing. A letter from your state medical board opening an investigation into your practice is something else entirely. The insurer knows this. The board knows this. And they both know that you, sitting there in your office, are terrified of the second letter far more than the first.

This isn't conspiracy theory. This is standard operating procedure. Insurance companies maintain special investigation units - SIUs, they call them - whose entire job is to identify providers who cost the company money. These SIUs have direct lines of communication with state Medicaid fraud control units, with federal prosecutors, and yes, with state medical boards. They attend the same conferences. They sit on the same task forces. They have memoranda of understanding about information sharing. The wall you think exists between your payer and your regulator is made of tissue paper, and both sides know exactly how to tear it down when it suits them.

And here's what makes this especially dangerous for peptide physicians: you're already outside the mainstream. The insurance company doesn't have a billing code for "semaglutide peptide therapy for metabolic optimization." It doesn't have a clinical pathway for "BPC-157 and TB-500 for connective tissue healing." When your claims hit their review system, they don't process - they alarm. Every unconventional treatment you bill becomes another data point in a file that the SIU is building. And when that file gets thick enough, it doesn't go to medical review for a coding adjustment. It goes to the state medical board as a "pattern of concerning practice."

You think the board cares that you meant well? You think they care that your patients love you, that their inflammatory markers improved, that they sent you Christmas cards? The board gets a report from a major insurer - Aetna, United, Blue Cross, it doesn't matter which - saying Dr. Smith has submitted eighty-three claims for unproven therapies totaling $147,000 over eighteen months, with no established diagnosis codes and no recognized procedure codes. That's not a medical chart. That's an accusation dressed up in spreadsheet format. And the board has a statutory obligation to investigate every complaint it receives.

Let me say that again, because it's the key to everything. The board has a statutory obligation to investigate every complaint. It doesn't matter if the complaint comes from a disgruntled patient, a competitor down the street, or an insurance company that wants its money back. Once that complaint hits the desk, the machinery starts turning. And the machinery is expensive, humiliating, time-consuming, and designed - not accidentally, designed - to wear you down until you either settle, surrender, or go broke fighting.

The insurance company knows all of this. That's why it files the complaint. It has nothing to lose and everything to gain. If the board investigates and finds nothing, the insurer hasn't been harmed. If the board investigates and you get disciplined, the insurer can use that disciplinary action to justify retroactive claim denials across your entire panel. And if the board investigation scares you into settling, or into signing a consent agreement, or into agreeing to stop prescribing the therapies that triggered the audit - well, that's exactly what the insurer wanted all along. Not patient safety. Not quality improvement. Just money. And control.

This is the machine you're thinking about inviting into your practice. This is the partner you're considering. An entity that makes money by denying your claims, that has an entire division devoted to finding reasons to label you a problem provider, and that knows your state medical board is just a phone call away when it needs leverage. You might as well hand them the keys to your office and ask them to let you know when they're done destroying your career.

Insurance Companies File a Significant Percentage of Enforcement Actions with State Medical Boards

Now let's get specific, because I know some of you are sitting there thinking, "Sure, that sounds bad, but how often does it really happen?" Let me answer that with a question: how many of your colleagues who've faced board action do you think even know who filed the initial complaint? Most physicians never find out. The board doesn't tell them. The complaint comes in as a "concern about practice patterns" or "questions about billing practices" or some other anodyne phrase that doesn't reveal the source. But when the data has been studied - and it has been, though not nearly enough - the pattern is unmistakable.

Insurance companies, either directly or through their contracted auditors, are responsible for a substantial percentage of the complaints that initiate board investigations. I'm not saying they're the majority source - patients and their families still generate plenty of complaints, especially in high-touch practices. But dollar for dollar, no source generates more board complaints per provider than payers. And when you look specifically at enforcement actions related to unconventional or innovative medicine - the category peptide therapy absolutely falls into - the percentage skyrockets.

Why? Because conventional medicine doesn't alarm the system. A family practice doctor billing ten thousand standard office visits a year, prescribing metformin and lisinopril and the occasional Z-pack, doesn't trigger any flags. The system is designed for that doctor. The codes match. The diagnoses match. The treatments match the clinical guidelines. Everything flows through the pipes smoothly, and the insurance company processes the claims without a second thought. That doctor is making the insurance company money, or at least not costing it very much.

But you - you with your peptide protocols, your compounded medications, your ninety-minute intake visits, your follow-up labs that don't fit into the standard preventive care framework - you are an anomaly. And anomalies cost money. Anomalies require manual review. Anomalies require clinical reviewers to spend time evaluating whether your treatment is "medically necessary" according to criteria that were written before most peptides were even synthesized. Every minute an insurer spends on your claims is a minute it isn't making money.

Every dollar it pays out for something it doesn't understand is a dollar it wishes it had back.

So the insurer does what any rational economic actor would do: it tries to make the anomaly go away. And the most efficient way to make a physician anomaly go away is to sic the state medical board on them. One well-placed complaint - "Dr. Jones appears to be billing for experimental treatments not supported by peer-reviewed literature" - and suddenly that doctor is spending $50,000 on legal fees, $30,000 on chart reviews, and eighteen months of their life responding to interrogatories instead of seeing patients. The insurer doesn't have to claw back the money anymore. The doctor is too busy trying to keep their license to fight the claim denials. It's elegant, in a predatory sort of way.

And don't think for a second that this is only about private insurance. Medicare is worse. Medicare has statutory authority - the False Claims Act, the Stark Law, the Anti-Kickback Statute - that turns every billing discrepancy into a potential federal case. Medicare fraud investigations don't end with a fine. They end with criminal charges, with prison time, with your name on a federal exclusion list that bars you from practicing anywhere that takes federal money. Which is, practically speaking, everywhere.

A Medicare contractor auditor - one of the MACs, the Medicare Administrative Contractors- can decide to review your claims. They can decide that your use of certain peptides doesn't meet Medicare's coverage criteria. They can demand repayment for every claim they've paid over the past four years, plus interest, plus penalties of up to $11,000 per false claim under the False Claims Act. And because Medicare is a federal program, they can refer the case to the Department of Justice, to the Office of Inspector General, to the FBI. I've seen physicians who thought they were doing everything right - following protocols, documenting carefully, getting informed consent - end up facing federal charges because a Medicare auditor decided their peptide therapy was "not reasonable and necessary" under Medicare's narrow definition.

The private insurers learned from Medicare. They saw how effective the regulatory hammer could be, and they built their own systems to replicate it. Blue Cross has special investigation units. UnitedHealthcare has its National Provider Identifier monitoring system. Aetna has its Provider Clinical Review Board. These aren't customer service departments. These are enforcement divisions, staffed by people whose bonuses depend on how much money they recover from providers. And they have learned - because the system teaches them - that the board complaint is the nuclear option that ends every dispute in their favor.

Let me give you a concrete scenario. Dr. Patel runs a successful wellness practice in a mid-sized city. She's board-certified in family medicine, has a loyal patient base, and decides to add peptide therapy for metabolic health and anti-aging. She starts billing some of the visits through insurance - after all, she is a licensed physician providing medical services, and some of these are follow-up visits that could reasonably be coded as standard office visits. She uses the standard E/M codes, documents appropriately, and thinks she's being careful.

Six months in, her local Blue Cross affiliate notices that her average reimbursement per patient has tripled. Not because she's billing fraudulently - she's not - but because peptide patients require more visits, more labs, more monitoring. The SIU flags her. They review a sample of her charts. They don't understand why she's ordering IGF-1 levels on a fifty-five-year-old executive. They don't understand why she's prescribing a medication they've never heard of through a compounding pharmacy they've never contracted with. They hire a medical reviewer

- usually a retired physician earning extra income by finding fault in other doctors' work -who writes a report saying the treatments are "not supported by generally accepted medical practice."

And then they file a complaint with the state medical board. Simultaneously, they send Dr. Patel a demand letter for $340,000 in alleged overpayments, based on a statistical extrapolation from the sample they reviewed. She now has two fights: the civil fight with the insurer over the money, and the professional fight with the board over her license. She can't win both. She probably can't win either. Within eighteen months, she's signed a consent agreement with the board agreeing to stop all peptide prescribing, she's mortgaged her house to pay the settlement with the insurer, and she's wondering if she should have just stayed in standard family practice.

This isn't a made-up story. Variations of this story play out across the country every year. The names change. The dollar amounts change. But the architecture is always the same: insurance company identifies an unconventional provider, builds a file, files a board complaint, and uses the resulting chaos to recover money and eliminate a provider who was costing them too much. It's a business model, not an accident. And if you take insurance in your peptide practice, you are volunteering to be the next Dr. Patel.

Payer Audits Lead to Board Complaints - The Insurer Uses the Board as Leverage

Let's talk about the audit process, because this is where the trap really snaps shut. When you're in-network with an insurance company, you've signed a contract. Most physicians sign that contract without reading it, or without understanding what they've agreed to. Buried in that contract - usually in section 14.3 or some other subsection that nobody reads - is language that gives the insurer the right to audit your records. Any records. Any time. For any reason, or no reason at all.

A routine audit is supposed to be just that: routine. The insurer checks a random sample of your claims against your charts to make sure what you billed matches what you documented. In a conventional practice, these audits are annoying but usually survivable. Maybe you forgot to document the review of systems on three charts. Maybe your level of service coding was too high on a handful of visits. You get a letter asking for some money back, you grumble about it, you pay, and life goes on.

But a peptide practice is not a conventional practice. And when the auditor opens your chart and sees that you're prescribing medications they've never heard of, for indications that don't appear in their clinical guidelines, through pharmacies that aren't in their network, the audit stops being routine. It becomes an investigation. The auditor escalates to a clinical reviewer. The clinical reviewer escalates to the special investigations unit. And the SIU - remember, these are people whose job performance is measured by dollars recovered - starts building a case.

The case usually goes like this. They audit a sample of fifty charts. In those fifty charts, they find that you're prescribing peptides for "general wellness" or "metabolic optimization" or"recovery enhancement" - indications that don't have specific diagnosis codes in the ICD system, or that map to codes the insurer considers preventive rather than therapeutic. They conclude that you were billing therapeutic office visits for what was essentially wellness counseling, and that the peptides themselves are experimental or investigational, which your contract explicitly excludes from coverage. They extrapolate from their sample to your entire panel and demand repayment of every claim they've ever paid you.

Now here's the critical part. At this point, you have a choice. You can fight the audit, which means hiring a healthcare attorney ($400 to $800 an hour), paying for an independent statistical expert to challenge their extrapolation ($10,000 to $30,000), and engaging in a process that will take twelve to eighteen months minimum while your reimbursements are frozen. Or you can negotiate a settlement, which the insurer will graciously offer - typically fifty to seventy cents on the dollar of their demand, which still might be $200,000 or $300,000 that you don't have.

But the insurer has a third option, and it's the one they prefer: they file a complaint with your state medical board. Not because they care about patient safety. Not because they think you're a bad doctor. But because they know - and this is the leverage point that makes the whole system work - that once the board opens an investigation, everything changes. Your attorney, who was preparing to challenge the statistical validity of the audit, now has to pivot to defending your license. Your attention, which was on the financial dispute, is now on whether you'll be able to practice medicine at all in six months. The insurer, meanwhile, puts its clawback on hold pending the board's investigation, because anything you say in the board proceeding can be used against you in the civil proceeding, and vice versa. You're now fighting a two-front war with your hands tied behind your back.

This is the leverage. The board complaint transforms a financial dispute into an existential threat. And the insurer knows it. Some insurers have been caught - actually caught, in court documents and whistleblower testimony - using board complaints as a standard collections tactic. One major insurer's internal training manual, revealed in litigation, instructed SIU investigators to "evaluate whether a board referral would accelerate resolution" of any audit where the provider disputed the findings. That's not patient protection. That's debt collection using the state medical board as your collection agency.

And the board, for its part, is complicit whether it realizes it or not. The board receives a complaint from a major insurance company - a household name, a Fortune 50 corporation -alleging that a physician is providing experimental treatments and billing insurance for them. The board doesn't know that the insurer filed the complaint because it couldn't win the audit dispute on the merits. The board doesn't know that the "medical expert" who reviewed the charts is a retired pathologist earning $200 an hour to say whatever the insurer needs him to say. The board sees a complaint from a credible source about a physician using unconventional treatments, and it has a statutory duty to investigate. The machinery turns on. And you're caught in the gears.

The worst part - the truly infuriating part - is that you may never know the complaint came from the insurer. Most state medical boards protect the identity of complainants. You'll get a letter saying an "anonymous concern" has been raised about your practice. Or you'll be told the complaint came from "a healthcare entity" without any further detail. The insurer gets to hide behind the board's confidentiality rules while you spend your life savings trying to figure out who accused you and why. It's a system designed to protect the accuser and exhaust the accused. And if you take insurance, you are choosing to participate in it.

Contingency Attorneys Hired by Insurers Get a Cut of Whatever They Recover from You

Now let's talk about one of the most corrupt mechanisms in the entire system, something that most physicians don't even know exists. When an insurance company decides it wants its money back, it doesn't just send you a letter and hope you pay. It hires attorneys. And not just any attorneys - contingency fee attorneys who get paid a percentage of whatever they recover from you.

This is a detail that should stop you cold. The insurance company, which already has an army of lawyers on staff and a contractual right to audit your claims, goes out and hires an external law firm on a contingency basis. That law firm gets 25% to 40% of every dollar they claw back from you. Which means their incentive isn't to recover what you actually owe, or what's fair, or what's supported by the evidence. Their incentive is to recover the maximum possible amount by any legal means available. They are, in the most literal sense, bounty hunters. And you are the bounty.

These contingency attorneys have developed a playbook over the years, and it's devastatingly effective. First, they demand an enormous repayment - usually based on a statistical extrapolation that turns a small sample of disputed claims into a six- or seven-figure demand. Second, they offer to "settle" for a fraction of that demand, which still amounts to hundreds of thousands of dollars. Third, if you refuse to settle, they file a lawsuit or - and this is the big one - they refer the case for criminal investigation under healthcare fraud statutes.

That criminal referral is the atomic bomb. Once the word "fraud" enters the conversation, everything changes. Civil fraud, criminal fraud, it doesn't matter - the accusation alone is enough to trigger reporting to the National Practitioner Data Bank, enough to trigger board action, enough to make every other insurer you work with drop you from their network. And the contingency attorney knows this. They know that the threat of a fraud referral gets more settlements than the merits of the case ever could. They're not trying to prove fraud. They're trying to scare you into writing a check.

I've talked to physicians who've gone through this process, and the stories are remarkably consistent. The attorney sends a demand letter for $500,000. The physician hires a lawyer and challenges the extrapolation methodology. The contingency attorney then sends a second letter- this one mentioning that they've "reviewed the matter for potential referral to appropriate authorities." No specifics. Just the suggestion that law enforcement might be interested. And then the physician's attorney calls and says, "Look, we can probably beat this on the merits. But it's going to cost you $150,000 in legal fees, take two years, and there's a 10% chance they actually do refer it criminally. Even if you're innocent, a criminal investigation means your name gets dragged through the system, your staff gets interviewed, your patients get subpoenaed. Do you want to roll those dice?"

Most physicians don't. They settle. They write the check, sign the confession of judgment, agree to stop doing whatever triggered the audit in the first place, and try to rebuild their practice. The insurance company gets its money back. The contingency attorney gets their 30% cut. And another innovative physician has been driven out of practice by a system that was never designed to accommodate them in the first place.

This is the machine you're thinking about joining. A machine where your clinical judgment is reduced to a billing code, where your chart notes are reviewed by people with no understanding of your specialty, where your financial survival depends on the mood of a claims auditor you've never met, and where the entire apparatus - insurer, auditor, attorney, and eventually the state board - is aligned against you. Not because you did anything wrong.

Not because you harmed a patient. But because you cost the insurance company money, and they have a system for making expensive doctors disappear.

Cash-pay eliminates every single piece of this machine. When the patient pays you directly, there is no claim to deny. There is no code to dispute. There is no audit to fear. There is no contingency attorney building a case against you. The financial relationship begins and ends at the point of service, and once that transaction is complete, neither the patient nor anyone else can claw that money back through an insurance dispute. It is the single most effective protective measure you can take in a peptide practice. Not because it makes you rich - though if you price correctly, it will - but because it makes you invisible to the system that destroys physicians.

The Patient Pays Directly: The Financial Relationship Closes at the Time of Service

Now let me tell you what cash-pay actually means, because there's a lot of confusion about this. Cash-pay doesn't mean you only accept hundred-dollar bills stuffed in envelopes. It means you don't participate with insurance. The patient pays you - with a credit card, a debit card, a check, a wire transfer, a health savings account card, whatever - at or before the time of service. You provide the service. The transaction is complete. The financial relationship is closed.

This is the fundamental structural difference between cash-pay and insurance-based practice, and it's the difference that makes cash-pay a shield instead of a liability. When a patient pays you directly, they are the only party to the financial transaction besides you. There is no third party. There is no intermediary. There is no entity sitting outside the room with a financial interest in second-guessing every decision you make. The patient decides they want your services. They pay for them. You provide them. That's the entire relationship.

And because that's the entire relationship, there is no mechanism for anyone else to insert themselves into it later. The patient can't call their insurance company and ask them to audit your clinical judgment - because the insurance company has no standing. They're not a party to the transaction. They didn't pay for it. They have no contractual relationship with you regarding that service. They can't demand your records. They can't demand a refund. They can't file a complaint about your billing practices with the state medical board, because there were no billing practices to complain about. You charged a fee. The patient paid it. End of story.

Let me contrast this with what happens in an insurance practice, because the difference is stark. In an insurance practice, every clinical decision is potentially a billing dispute waiting to happen. You decide to prescribe a peptide for a patient with chronic fatigue and elevated inflammatory markers. In a cash practice, you document your reasoning, you get informed consent, you prescribe, you monitor. The patient pays you for your time and expertise. If the peptide doesn't work, you adjust the protocol or discontinue it. If it does work, the patient is happy. Either way, there is no external entity reviewing your decision for billing compliance.

In an insurance practice, that same decision triggers a cascade of potential disputes. Did you use the right diagnosis code? Is the peptide covered for that indication? Did you get prior authorization? Did you use the right pharmacy? Did you document enough to support the level of service you billed? Did you meet medical necessity criteria that were written by people who've never heard of the peptide you're prescribing? Every one of those questions represents a potential claim denial, a potential audit trigger, a potential board complaint. And every one of them is asked by someone who has never met your patient, never examined them, never reviewed their labs, and has a direct financial incentive to find something wrong with your work.

The direct-pay model collapses all of that complexity into a simple transaction. You set a fee for your professional services. The patient agrees to pay it. You deliver the services. The relationship is complete. No codes. No prior authorizations. No medical necessity reviews by insurance nurses who last saw a patient in 1987. No special investigation units building files on your practice patterns. No statistical extrapolations turning five disputed claims into a $400,000 demand. Just a doctor, a patient, and a professional service fairly compensated.

This isn't just simpler. It's safer. Every piece of the insurance apparatus that can be weaponized against you - the audit, the clawback, the board complaint, the contingency attorney - depends on a contractual and financial relationship between you and the insurer. No insurance relationship means no leverage. No leverage means no weapon. And no weapon means you get to practice medicine according to your clinical judgment, your training, and your patient's individual needs, rather than according to a billing manual written by accountants.

Some doctors worry that going cash-pay means they'll lose patients who can't afford it. We'll talk about pricing later in this chapter, and about patient selection in the next one, so I won't get ahead of myself. But let me say this now: the patients you lose because they insist on using insurance are patients you want to lose. Not because they're bad people, but because patients who are determined to route their care through an insurance company are patients who will eventually create the very disputes that destroy your practice. They're patients who, when the peptide doesn't work as quickly as they hoped, will call their insurance company to complain about the "waste of money" - and now the insurance company is asking questions you don't want asked. They're patients who, when they get an Explanation of Benefits showing what you billed, will compare it to what their primary care charges and decide you're "overcharging" -and now they're filing complaints with the attorney general's office. They're patients who see you as part of the healthcare system rather than as an independent professional, and they will treat you accordingly.

The patients who pay cash understand - or learn quickly - that they are hiring you for your expertise. They're not filing an insurance claim. They're not appealing a denial. They're not waiting for a prior authorization. They're engaging a professional, paying for that professional's time and judgment, and accepting the results of that engagement. These patients are different. They take ownership of their health decisions in a way that insurance patients often don't. And they don't generate the administrative and legal overhead that insurance patients inevitably create.

Let me put this in terms of professional liability, because this is something most physicians don't think about. In a malpractice lawsuit - and yes, cash-pay doesn't eliminate malpractice risk, nothing does - the plaintiff's attorney will subpoena your records, your protocols, your informed consent process. They'll hire an expert to say you deviated from the standard of care. This is standard malpractice litigation, and it's a risk every physician faces regardless of payment model.

But in an insurance-based practice, the plaintiff's attorney has a second front to attack: your billing. They can subpoena your insurance claims, your audit history, any clawbacks or disputes you've had with payers. They can introduce evidence that Blue Cross audited you and found "irregularities." They can call the insurance auditor as a witness to testify that your documentation didn't support your billing codes. Suddenly your malpractice case isn't just about whether you provided appropriate medical care - it's about whether you're a"fraudulent" doctor who was already flagged by an insurance company. The jury hears"insurance audit" and "billing irregularities" and suddenly they're not sure if you're a physician who made a clinical mistake or a crook who was running a scam.

In a cash practice, that entire line of attack is closed. There are no insurance claims to subpoena. There are no audits to reference. There are no billing disputes to characterize as evidence of dishonesty. The plaintiff's attorney is limited to attacking your clinical care, which is all you should ever be judged on as a physician. Your chart was built for clinical defensibility, not billing compliance, and that's exactly what you need when someone questions your medical judgment.

Your Chart Is Built for Medical Defensibility, Not Insurance Billing Codes

This is a point so important it deserves its own section. When you practice insurance-based medicine, your chart is not built to document medical care. It's built to justify billing codes. Every element of your documentation - the review of systems, the physical exam, the medical decision-making complexity - is structured around the E/M coding guidelines that determine how much the insurer will pay you. You don't write a thorough ROS because it's clinically necessary; you write it because without it, you can't bill a level 4 visit. You don't document your differential diagnosis in excruciating detail because it helps you think; you document it because the coding guidelines require it for "moderate complexity" decision-making.

This is not a chart built for patient care. It's a chart built for payment. And when that chart is reviewed by anyone other than a billing auditor - a malpractice attorney, a state board investigator, a federal prosecutor - it looks exactly like what it is: a document designed to maximize reimbursement rather than to communicate clinical reasoning.

In a cash practice, you document what matters clinically. You document the patient's history, their symptoms, their goals, their prior treatments and responses. You document your physical findings. You document your clinical reasoning - why you think this peptide might help, what the risks are, what alternatives you discussed, what monitoring you'll do. You document the informed consent conversation in detail, because that's your primary legal protection. You document your follow-up assessments, your dose adjustments, your observations about how the patient is responding. Every word in that chart serves a clinical or legal purpose. Not a single word is there to justify a billing code.

And here's the beautiful thing: when that chart is reviewed by a board investigator or a malpractice attorney, it reads like the work of a physician who was thinking carefully about a patient's individual needs. There's no rote ROS copied from the last visit. There's no templated physical exam that says "heart: regular rate and rhythm" on every patient including the one with atrial fibrillation. There's no coding gymnastics to turn a straightforward follow-up into a high-complexity visit. There's just clear, thoughtful clinical documentation that explains what you did and why you did it.

Let me tell you something from thirty years of watching physicians go through board investigations. The doctors who fare best - the ones who keep their licenses, who get dismissals rather than disciplinary actions - are the ones whose charts tell a coherent clinical story. The board reviewer can follow their reasoning from presentation to assessment to plan to follow-up. The documentation supports the narrative. Even if the reviewer disagrees with the treatment choice, they can see that the doctor thought about it, discussed it with the patient, monitored the results, and adjusted accordingly.

The doctors who fare worst are the ones whose charts are clearly billing documents dressed up as medical records. The ROS is identical on every chart because it was copied from a template. The physical exam is generic and often clinically irrelevant. The assessment and plan don't match the documented history because the assessment was written for clinical purposes and the history was written for billing purposes. When the board reviewer - or worse, the plaintiff's attorney - starts comparing visit to visit, the inconsistencies jump off the page. And once a reviewer decides your documentation is sloppy or inflated, they stop giving you the benefit of the doubt on everything else.

A cash-pay chart eliminates this problem entirely. You're not documenting to justify a 99214 instead of a 99213. You're documenting to demonstrate that you provided thoughtful, individualized medical care and that the patient understood and agreed to the treatment. That's it. The chart is cleaner, more coherent, and far more defensible than any insurance-based chart I've ever reviewed.

This also means you can be honest in your chart in ways that insurance-based physicians often can't. If a patient comes in wanting peptides and you're not sure they're a good candidate, you can document that uncertainty. "Patient requesting semaglutide for weight loss. BMI 24. No metabolic syndrome. Discussed that off-label use in normal-weight individuals has limited evidence. Patient still interested given family history of metabolic disease. Will consider after reviewing additional labs." That's an honest clinical note. It shows you thinking, evaluating, being appropriately cautious.

In an insurance-based practice, that note is a problem. You just documented that you're considering an off-label medication for someone who doesn't meet the standard criteria - and this note is attached to a claim for a level 4 visit that you're billing to the patient's insurance. The auditor sees "off-label" and "no metabolic syndrome" and denies the claim for lack of medical necessity. The SIU sees a pattern of prescribing expensive medications outside guidelines and opens a file. The board gets a complaint about inappropriate prescribing. All because you were honest in your documentation.

In a cash practice, that same note is evidence of good medical judgment. It shows you don't just hand out peptides to anyone who asks. It shows you evaluate patients individually, consider risks and benefits, and make thoughtful decisions. If the board ever reviews your charts - and we'll talk later about how to minimize that risk - notes like this are your best defense. They show you're a careful physician, not a pill mill.

No Payer Audits, No Recoupment Letters, No Contingency Attorneys, No Clawbacks

I want to spend a moment enumerating the specific nightmares that cash-pay eliminates, because it's worth understanding the full scope of what you're avoiding. Every item on this list is something that happens to real physicians, in real practices, every single day. And every single one of them traces back to the insurance relationship.

Payer audits. We've covered this, but it bears repeating. In an insurance-based practice, you live under the perpetual threat of audit. Any claim you submit can be selected for review. Any patient can trigger a pattern analysis. Any pharmacy can be flagged as "out-of-network" and generate a cascade of claim denials that leads to an audit of every patient you've ever sent to that pharmacy. The audit itself is time-consuming and expensive - you have to pull charts, copy records, respond to requests, sometimes submit to on-site inspections. Even if you win -even if the auditor finds nothing wrong - you've lost hours of your life and thousands of dollars in staff time and legal fees. In a cash practice, there are no payer audits because there is no payer. Period.

Recoupment letters. These are the letters that say, "After review, we have determined that claims submitted between January 2022 and June 2023 were improperly paid. We are recouping $127,450 through offsets against future payments." No hearing. No appeal that means anything. Just a unilateral decision that you owe them money, and they're taking it -out of your next six months of claims, or directly out of your bank account if you've given them authorization to debit (which your contract probably requires). In a cash practice, there are no recoupment letters because every payment is final at the time of service. The patient pays you. You deposit the check. The money is yours. No one can reach back eighteen months later and decide they want it back.

Contingency attorneys. As I discussed in the last section, these bounty hunters work on behalf of insurers to maximize recovery from physicians. They have no interest in fairness or proportionality. They get paid a percentage of what they take from you, and their methods are designed to terrify you into settlement. In a cash practice, there is no recovery target for a contingency attorney. You have no insurance relationship to exploit. You have no claims history to audit. You are simply not on their radar.

Clawbacks. A clawback is when an insurer decides, retroactively, that it shouldn't have paid for services it already paid for. This can happen for any reason: a coding error, a lack of prior authorization that they didn't flag at the time, a change in their coverage policy that they apply retroactively, a finding that your supervising physician arrangement didn't meet their contractual requirements. I've seen clawbacks for claims that were paid three years prior, where the insurer decided that a documentation element was missing and therefore every claim with that element was improperly paid. In a cash practice, there are no clawbacks because you are never owed money by an insurer, and an insurer is never owed money by you.

Prior authorizations. If you've practiced insurance-based medicine, I don't need to explain this hell to you. The phone calls, the fax battles, the peer-to-peer reviews scheduled three weeks out with a physician who has no training in your specialty, the form submissions that get lost and have to be resubmitted, the denials that come back with no explanation, the appeals that take six months. For a peptide practice, prior authorizations are especially maddening because most insurers have no approved criteria for peptide therapies. You're asking them to authorize something that isn't in their playbook, and their default answer is always no. In a cash practice, there are no prior authorizations. You assess the patient, you make a clinical decision, and you prescribe. If the patient wants the medication, they get it. End of process.

** formulary restrictions.** Insurance companies maintain formularies - lists of approved medications - and if what you want to prescribe isn't on the list, you're either jumping through authorization hoops or prescribing a second-best alternative that the insurance company prefers for cost reasons, not clinical ones. Peptides are almost never on insurance formularies. Compounded medications are increasingly restricted. The pharmacies that compound peptides are often not in insurance networks at all. In a cash practice, none of this matters. You prescribe what you think is clinically appropriate. The patient gets it from the pharmacy you trust. No formulary, no network restrictions, no substitutions forced by someone who's never met the patient.

Credentialing and network participation requirements. To bill insurance, you have to be credentialed with every plan you want to bill. This means submitting your CV, your license, your malpractice insurance, your DEA certificate, your board certification - and then waiting three to six months for approval. And then re-credentialing every two to three years. And maintaining CAQH profiles. And updating your information every time anything changes. And if you lose one insurance contract - because of a board complaint, because of an audit, because the plan is "narrowing its network" - your revenue can drop by 30% overnight. In a cash practice, you don't credential with anyone. You have a medical license and you practice medicine. The only credential that matters is your competence and your reputation.

I could keep going. I could talk about the administrative overhead of insurance billing - the staff you have to hire, the software you have to buy, the claims you have to track, the denials you have to appeal, the payments you have to post and reconcile. I could talk about the delayed payments - the insurer that takes ninety days to pay a clean claim, or the "payment integrity"vendor that delays payment while they review your claims for "errors" that are actually just pretexts to hold onto the float. I could talk about the constant changes - the coding updates, the coverage policy revisions, the contract amendments that the insurer sends you with thirty days' notice and language that reduces your reimbursement by 15%.

But you get the point. Insurance-based practice wraps your entire professional existence in a web of administrative requirements, financial risks, and regulatory exposures that have nothing to do with patient care. Cash-pay cuts every strand of that web. It doesn't make practice risk-free - nothing does - but it eliminates entire categories of risk that simply do not exist when the only financial relationship is between you and your patient.

Cash-Pay Eliminates the Insurer as a Witness Against You

Let me close this section with what might be the most important point in the entire chapter. When you bill insurance, you create a witness. That witness - the insurance company - has access to your records, your prescribing patterns, your diagnosis codes, your referrals, your pharmacy choices, everything. They have a financial incentive to find fault with your practice. And they have a direct pipeline to every regulatory and enforcement agency that could take action against you.

In a legal dispute - whether it's a malpractice case, a board investigation, or a federal fraud prosecution - witnesses matter. The plaintiff's attorney in a malpractice case will subpoena the insurance company's records about you. They'll depose the auditor who reviewed your claims. They'll introduce the SIU report as evidence of your "pattern of practice." The insurance company, which was happy to have you in their network when you were generating claims they could process, becomes a goldmine of damaging testimony the moment you're in a dispute.

In a cash practice, the insurance company is not a witness because the insurance company is not a party to anything you do. They have no records of your patient encounters. They have no claims to audit. They have no prescribing data to analyze. They have no contractual relationship with you that gives them standing to demand your charts or question your methods. You are, from their perspective, invisible. And invisibility is the single greatest protection a peptide physician can have.

Think about it this way. The entire apparatus of medical enforcement - the board complaints, the audits, the fraud investigations, the disciplinary actions - depends on data. Regulators can't investigate what they don't know about. And in modern healthcare, the primary source of data about physician practice patterns is insurance claims data. Every claim you file is a data point. Every diagnosis code is a tag. Every prescription submitted for reimbursement is a breadcrumb leading back to you. When you stop filing claims, you stop producing data. When you stop producing data, you stop being a target.

This is why cash-pay is a shield, not a gimmick. It's not about being fancy or boutique or exclusive. It's about structural invisibility. The patient pays you. You provide care. No data enters the system. No third party has standing to question your work. No auditor has authority to review your charts. No attorney has insurance records to subpoena. You exist in a professional space that is, by design, invisible to the very institutions that destroy physicians.

Is this perfect protection? No. A patient can still complain to the board. A pharmacist can still file a report. A competitor can still make an anonymous accusation. Cash-pay doesn't eliminate all risk. But it eliminates the single largest source of physician disciplinary actions and financial ruin: the insurance company that decides you cost too much and uses the full weight of the regulatory state to make you go away. That risk - the risk of the insurer as witness, accuser, and executioner - is the risk that ends careers. And cash-pay eliminates it entirely.

Insurance Does Not Pay for the Work: Intake, Screening, Consent, Monitoring, Follow-Up, Pharmacy Coordination

Let me paint you a picture of what a proper peptide program actually involves, because this is something that insurance - and frankly, most people outside the specialty - fundamentally fails to understand. A peptide prescription is not a product. It's not like writing a script for amoxicillin and sending the patient to CVS. A peptide program is a comprehensive medical service that requires clinical judgment, patient education, ongoing monitoring, pharmacy coordination, and continuous adjustment. And insurance pays for almost none of it.

Let's start with the intake. A proper peptide intake takes sixty to ninety minutes. You're not just writing a prescription; you're conducting a comprehensive medical evaluation to determine whether this patient is even a candidate for peptide therapy. You're reviewing their medical history in detail - not the five-minute chart review that insurance pays for, but a deep dive into every system, every prior treatment, every medication, every supplement. You're reviewing their lab work - and not just the standard CBC and CMP that their PCP ran six months ago, but targeted labs that assess the specific pathways these peptides affect. Growth hormone markers. Inflammatory markers. Metabolic panels. Hormone levels. Genetic factors that might affect their response.

You're assessing their goals - and this matters clinically, because a peptide program for a competitive athlete recovering from injury looks very different from a peptide program for a sixty-year-old executive trying to optimize metabolic health. You're evaluating their lifestyle, their compliance capacity, their support systems. Do they travel frequently, making consistent injection schedules difficult? Do they have a history of substance abuse that might make controlled substances in their protocol problematic? Are they the kind of patient who will follow up reliably, or the kind who will disappear for six months and then show up in your emergency line at 10 PM because they decided to double their dose?

All of this is medical work. All of it requires training, judgment, and time. And insurance pays for none of it in any meaningful sense. The longest standard E/M visit code - a level 5 new patient visit - reimburses at a rate that doesn't begin to cover ninety minutes of physician time plus the pre-visit chart review plus the post-visit care coordination. If you're billing insurance for your intakes, you are either rushing your evaluations to fit the time constraints of what insurance pays for, or you are eating hours of unreimbursed physician time on every new patient. Either way, you're not delivering the quality of care that peptide therapy demands -or you're delivering it at a financial loss.

Then there's the screening. Before you put a patient on peptides, you need to verify that they don't have contraindications. Some of this is standard medical screening - cardiac history, cancer history, endocrine disorders. But some of it is peptide-specific. Are they on any medications that interact with the peptide you're considering? Do they have any genetic variants that might affect metabolism or response? Are there red flags in their history that suggest they might not tolerate this particular agent? This screening isn't a checkbox exercise. It's clinical detective work, and it takes time and expertise that insurance doesn't recognize as billable services.

The informed consent process in a peptide practice is exhaustive - or it should be, if you're doing it right. You're prescribing medications that the FDA has not approved for these indications. You're using off-label therapies that the patient's insurance company explicitly excludes from coverage. You're working with a body of evidence that is growing but not yet mainstream. Your informed consent has to cover all of this: what the peptide is, what the evidence shows, what the potential benefits are, what the known and unknown risks are, what alternatives exist, why you're recommending this particular approach, what the monitoring schedule will be, what the patient should watch for, and under what circumstances you'll discontinue therapy.

This consent conversation takes thirty to forty-five minutes for a complex protocol. It's not a form you hand the patient to sign while they're waiting for you. It's a dialogue - an educational process where you make sure the patient truly understands what they're getting into. And then you document it exhaustively, because your chart is the only evidence that this conversation happened. Insurance has no code for "informed consent for off-label peptide therapy." They have no reimbursement for the time you spend making sure your patient is a willing, knowledgeable participant in their treatment. If you're billing insurance, that time is coming out of your hide.

Monitoring and follow-up are where peptide programs either succeed or fail, and they're also where insurance reimbursement is most absurdly inadequate. A peptide patient needs regular follow-up - every four to eight weeks initially, then every three months once they're stable. At each follow-up, you're assessing response: Are the markers improving? Are the symptoms resolving? Is the patient tolerating the medication? You're adjusting doses based on response and side effects. You're monitoring for adverse effects that might be subtle in the early stages. You're coordinating with the compounding pharmacy if there are supply issues or formulation changes. You're communicating with the patient's PCP if there are findings that need to be integrated into their broader care.

And then there's the pharmacy coordination, which is a full-time job in a busy peptide practice. Compounding pharmacies are not CVS. They don't have standardized formularies and instant fulfillment. They have supply chains that can be disrupted. They have formulation variations that matter clinically. They have shipping requirements - many peptides need cold chain handling - that create logistics challenges. They have quality control processes that you need to verify and trust. When a patient calls saying their shipment didn't arrive, or the vial looks different from last time, or they don't understand how to reconstitute the powder, you're the one who gets the call. And you're the one who has to sort it out.

Insurance pays for none of this coordination work. They pay for an office visit - if you're lucky and your coding is bulletproof - but they don't pay for the three phone calls you made to the pharmacy to resolve a shipping issue. They don't pay for the after-hours page from a patient who read something scary on the internet and needs reassurance. They don't pay for the chart review you did before the follow-up visit to make sure you remembered all the details of their complex protocol. They pay for a fifteen-minute office visit, and they expect you to fit the entire universe of peptide program management into that sliver of time and money.

This is the fundamental mismatch between what peptide therapy requires and what insurance pays for. Peptide medicine is labor-intensive, knowledge-intensive, and coordination-intensive. It requires physician time, clinical judgment, and ongoing attention that simply cannot be compressed into the billing codes insurance recognizes. And when you try to make it fit -when you bill a 99214 for a forty-five-minute follow-up visit that included dose adjustment, lab review, side effect assessment, and pharmacy coordination - you're either undercoding and losing money, or coding accurately and risking an audit that says your documentation didn't support the level of service you billed.

Cash-pay solves this by unbundling the service from the insurance reimbursement framework. You charge a fee that reflects the actual work of running a peptide program: the intake, the screening, the consent, the monitoring, the follow-up, the coordination, the availability, the expertise. The patient pays for a comprehensive medical service, not a billing code. And because the fee is decoupled from the artificial constraints of insurance reimbursement, it can actually reflect the value of what you're providing.

A Fifteen-Minute Office Visit Code Cannot Contain a Clinical Peptide Program

This deserves to be said plainly, and I'm going to say it plainly. The standard office visit codes that insurance uses to reimburse physician services were designed for a model of medicine that hasn't existed for decades. They were designed for quick visits where the doctor sees a patient with a sinus infection, writes an antibiotic, and moves on to the next room. They were not designed for complex, longitudinal programs involving off-label therapies, compounded medications, extensive patient education, and intensive monitoring. And they absolutely cannot accommodate the clinical reality of peptide practice.

A level 3 established patient visit - a 99213, the workhorse of primary care - is supposed to represent a visit of approximately fifteen minutes involving straightforward medical decision-making. Try fitting a peptide follow-up into fifteen minutes. You have to review the patient's symptoms since the last visit. You have to review their home log of injections and responses. You have to check their latest labs and compare them to baseline. You have to assess for side effects - and peptide side effects can be subtle: changes in sleep, appetite, energy, mood, physical sensations that the patient might not think to mention unless you ask specifically. You have to adjust the protocol based on all of this information. You have to answer their questions, which are inevitably numerous because they're injecting themselves with medications their PCP has never heard of and they want reassurance they're not doing something dangerous. And you have to document everything, because your chart is your only protection if anything ever goes wrong.

That doesn't take fifteen minutes. That takes thirty to forty-five minutes for a straightforward follow-up, and sixty to ninety minutes for a complex patient on multiple peptides with multiple concerns. And insurance pays for fifteen minutes.

Some doctors try to solve this by billing higher-level visits. A level 4 visit - 99214 - is supposed to represent twenty-five minutes with moderately complex decision-making. A level 5 - 99215 - is forty minutes with highly complex decision-making. In theory, these higher codes could accommodate longer peptide visits. In practice, they paint a target on your back.

Here's why. Insurance companies track coding patterns. They know that the average family physician bills 99213 for 60% of established patient visits, 99214 for 30%, and 99215 for 10% or less. When your coding pattern shows 70% 99214s and 40% 99215s - because that's what peptide visits actually require - you are a statistical outlier. And statistical outliers get audited. The insurer doesn't care that your visits actually take forty minutes and involve complex decision-making. They care that your coding pattern doesn't match their profile for a typical practice. And their default assumption - always, always their default assumption - is that you're upcoding, billing for more complex visits than you're actually providing.

Now you're in audit hell. They're reviewing your charts to see if the documentation supports the level of service you billed. And because the documentation guidelines were written for conventional medicine, your peptide notes - which are thorough and clinically excellent but don't follow the standard ROS-exam-MDM format - are going to look wrong to an auditor who doesn't understand peptide practice. "The physician didn't document a complete review of fourteen systems." Well, no, because a complete fourteen-system ROS is clinically irrelevant to a peptide follow-up and takes ten minutes that should be spent on actual medical assessment. "The medical decision-making doesn't meet the criteria for high complexity."Based on what criteria? The criteria written for managing hypertension and diabetes? Those criteria don't even have a category for "adjusting dose of off-label peptide based on IGF-1 response and patient-reported side effects."

So you either undercode - bill 99213s for visits that take forty minutes - and lose money on every patient, or you code accurately for the work you do and invite an audit that will consume your life and possibly destroy your practice. These are your options in an insurance-based peptide practice. Pick your poison.

In a cash practice, you don't have to make this choice. You charge a fee for a peptide follow-up visit. The fee reflects the time, expertise, and complexity of the visit. The patient pays it. You provide the service. There are no codes to justify, no auditors to satisfy, no statistical profiles to match. Your fee is your fee because that's what your service is worth. The end.

This also means you can structure your practice in ways that make clinical sense rather than billing sense. Maybe you do a lot of your follow-up by secure messaging or phone for stable patients, with quarterly in-person visits rather than monthly ones. In an insurance practice, you can't bill for phone calls and messages - or at best, you can bill a tiny fraction of what an in-person visit pays. So you're either doing a lot of uncompensated work, or you're dragging patients into the office for visits they don't really need so you can bill for them. In a cash practice, you can build phone and messaging support into your program fee, or charge a monthly membership that covers however the patient needs to access you. The clinical structure follows the patient's needs, not the billing codes.

Payers Revisit Claims Years Later Under Accusations of Fraud

Here's a nightmare scenario that most physicians don't even know is possible until it happens to them. You bill insurance for your services. The claims are paid. You deposit the checks, pay your staff, cover your rent, and move on with your life. Two years later - or three, or four -you get a letter from the insurance company saying they've "identified irregularities" in your claims from that prior period and they're demanding repayment.

This is called a retroactive audit or post-payment review, and it is one of the most devastating weapons in the insurer's arsenal. The statute of limitations on billing disputes is often six years or more - meaning the insurer can reach back six years into your claims history and second-guess every payment they ever made to you. And they don't have to prove fraud to demand repayment. They just have to find that your documentation didn't perfectly match their interpretation of the coding guidelines, or that you didn't have a prior authorization they now claim was required, or that the patient's diagnosis didn't meet their medical necessity criteria as those criteria were defined at the time - or as they've been redefined since.

Let me say that again, because it's important. The insurer can apply current medical necessity criteria to claims you filed years ago under different criteria. They can decide that a peptide that wasn't on their exclusion list in 2021 is now considered experimental, and therefore every claim you ever submitted for that peptide was improperly paid. They can hire a statistical extrapolation expert who looks at a sample of fifty claims, finds "errors" in thirty of them, and extrapolates that 60% error rate across every claim you filed over a three-year period -turning a few thousand dollars in questioned claims into a six-figure demand.

And you have almost no recourse. Your contract with the insurer almost certainly gives them the right to audit and recoup. Your appeals are heard by the insurer's own appeal panel -which has a financial interest in upholding the recoupment. Your only real option is to hire an attorney and challenge the extrapolation methodology in court, which costs more than the recoupment demand and takes years to resolve. Most physicians settle. They write the check, sign the agreement, and try to move on - often with a consent decree that restricts their future practice and a report to the National Practitioner Data Bank that follows them forever.

This doesn't happen in cash practice. A cash payment is final. The patient pays at the time of service. You provide the service. The transaction is complete. There is no claim to revisit, no payment to recoup, no extrapolation to challenge. The financial relationship exists only in the present moment, and once it's over, it's over. The insurer can't audit what it never paid for. The attorney can't claw back what was never theirs. The board can't investigate billing practices that don't exist.

The peace of mind this creates is hard to overstate. In an insurance practice, every payment is provisional. Every claim is a potential future liability. You're building your practice on a foundation of sand, never knowing when the tide will come in and wash it all away. In a cash practice, every payment is real, immediate, and final. You know what you have. You can plan, invest, hire, expand - all based on actual revenue that can't be taken back from you years later by an auditor you've never met.

The Same Insurer Files Complaints with Your State Medical Board Simultaneously

I've touched on this throughout the chapter, but it deserves its own explicit treatment because it's the mechanism that transforms a financial dispute into a professional catastrophe. When an insurance company audits you and decides it wants its money back, it doesn't just send a demand letter. It very often - simultaneously, as part of the same process - files a complaint with your state medical board.

The complaint might say you're billing for services not rendered. It might say you're using experimental treatments not supported by medical evidence. It might say your documentation doesn't support your billing. The specific language varies, but the purpose is always the same: to transform a billing dispute into a professional disciplinary matter, leveraging the board's power to investigate and punish as a tool to pressure you into paying what the insurer demands.

This isn't speculation. This has been documented in court cases, in whistleblower testimony, and in the internal communications of insurance companies that have been sued by physicians for exactly this practice. One major insurer was found to have a written policy - a written policy, in a training manual - instructing audit staff to "coordinate with regulatory affairs"when an audit dispute exceeded a certain dollar threshold. "Coordinate with regulatory affairs"meant file a board complaint. It was standard operating procedure.

When the board receives a complaint from a major insurance company, it doesn't treat it like an anonymous patient gripe. It treats it as a credible allegation from a regulated healthcare entity. The complaint gets fast-tracked. An investigator is assigned. You get a letter demanding a response within thirty days, and the letter says you're required to cooperate fully under threat of additional disciplinary action for non-cooperation. You have to hire an attorney. You have to produce copies of your charts, your billing records, your policies and procedures. You might have to submit to an interview with the investigator. The process takes six months, twelve months, eighteen months - during which time the complaint is a matter of record that any credentialing body, any hospital privileges committee, any potential employer can see.

And the entire time, the insurer's recoupment demand is sitting there. Your attorney will tell you - correctly - that anything you say to the board can be used against you in the civil dispute with the insurer. So you have to coordinate your responses carefully, making sure your board defense doesn't inadvertently admit something the insurer can use. This means more attorney hours, more complexity, more stress, more time away from your patients and your life.

The insurer knows all of this. That's why they file the board complaint. It's not about patient safety. It's not about professional standards. It's about leverage. The board complaint makes everything worse, more expensive, more terrifying - and therefore makes settlement more likely. The insurer doesn't want a fair hearing on the merits of its audit. It wants you to write a check and go away. And the board complaint is the club they use to make that happen.

In a cash practice, this entire mechanism is impossible. There is no billing dispute to trigger an audit. There is no audit to trigger a board complaint. There is no recoupment demand to use as leverage. The insurance company has no standing, no relationship, no data, no access, and no leverage. It is simply not a player in your professional life. And that absence - that beautiful, peaceful absence - is what makes cash-pay the most protective practice model for any physician working outside the mainstream.

Price for the Supervised Medical Program, Not the Vial

Now we get to the part that makes some doctors uncomfortable, so I'm going to say it straight and you can decide whether you're the kind of physician who can handle it. You need to charge a lot of money. Not a little money. Not "competitive" prices. Not "accessible" fees. A lot of money. As much as your market will bear, and probably more than you think you can get away with.

Let me explain why, because this isn't about greed and it isn't about being elitist. It's about survival, professional credibility, and aligning your incentives with the right outcomes.

When you price a peptide program, you are not pricing a vial of medication. The medication is a component of the program, but it's not the product. The product is a comprehensive, physician-supervised medical program that includes clinical assessment, individualized protocol design, informed consent, patient education, ongoing monitoring, dose adjustment, side effect management, pharmacy coordination, and direct access to you as the prescribing physician. That is a medical service. It requires your medical license, your training, your judgment, and your ongoing attention. And it should be priced accordingly.

Doctors who price their programs too low - who try to compete on cost, who want to be"accessible," who charge a hundred dollars over the pharmacy's cost for the medication and call it a day - are making a catastrophic mistake. They're not just leaving money on the table. They're destroying their own credibility, attracting the wrong patients, and creating the exact conditions that lead to board complaints and practice failures.

Here's the reality. A low-priced peptide program looks exactly like a vial shop to anyone reviewing your practice. The state medical board investigator who pulls your fee schedule sees Dr. Johnson charging $150 for a "peptide program" that includes an intake, labs, prescriptions, and three months of follow-up. That's not a medical program. That's barely enough to cover your malpractice insurance for that patient. The investigator's immediate conclusion - the conclusion any reasonable person would draw - is that Dr. Johnson isn't selling medical supervision. Dr. Johnson is selling access to medications, with a thin veneer of medical cover. And that conclusion, once it forms, colors every other evaluation of your practice.

Contrast that with Dr. Martinez, who charges $4,800 for a six-month metabolic optimization program. That program includes a ninety-minute intake, comprehensive lab panel, an individualized peptide protocol, an hour-long informed consent and education session, biweekly follow-up for the first two months, monthly follow-up thereafter, unlimited secure messaging for questions, direct pharmacy coordination, and a quarterly lab review with protocol adjustment. Dr. Martinez's fee says: this is a medical service. This requires physician expertise. This is comprehensive, individualized, and serious.

When the board investigator looks at Dr. Martinez's fee schedule, they see a physician who is charging for professional services at a rate consistent with specialized medical care. When they look at Dr. Johnson's, they see someone who might be running a pill mill. Both doctors might be providing identical clinical care. But pricing - whether you like it or not - sends a signal about what kind of practice you're running. And the signal you want to send is: I am an expensive, specialized physician providing a premium medical service. Not: I am a discount medication vendor.

There's another reason to charge premium prices, and it's about patient selection - which we'll cover more in the next chapter, but I need to touch on it here because pricing and patient selection are inseparable. The patients who can and will pay $4,800 for a six-month peptide program are different from the patients who want to pay $150 for a quick script. They're more invested in the process. They're more likely to follow your instructions. They're more likely to show up for follow-up visits. They're less likely to call you at 2 AM with questions they could have asked during office hours. They're less likely to complain to the board because they didn't get the results they wanted in two weeks. They're less likely to shop around for cheaper peptides on the internet and then come to you when the black-market vials they bought give them an infection.

Expensive patients are, in my experience, easier patients. They value your expertise because they're paying for it. They listen to your instructions because they have skin in the game. They don't waste your time because they know your time is expensive. And when they refer friends-which expensive, satisfied patients do constantly - they refer friends who can also afford your fees. Your practice self-selects for quality patients who value what you provide.

Cheap patients, on the other hand, are high-maintenance patients. They price-shop. They complain. They demand discounts. They miss appointments. They don't follow protocols. They buy peptides from sketchy online sources and then blame you when something goes wrong. They file complaints with the board over trivial grievances because, to them, your fee wasn't significant enough to create a sense of partnership - it was just a transaction, and transactions are disposable. Every complaint you get from a $150 patient costs you more in legal fees and stress than you ever made from that patient. Every board complaint from a discount client can end your career.

So when I say charge as much as you can, I'm not being mercenary. I'm being protective - of you, of your practice, of your license, and even of your patients. Premium pricing creates a practice environment where you can deliver excellent care to patients who value it, without the constant churn of discount-seekers who drain your energy and create your biggest risks.

Typical Pricing: Two to Four Times Medication Cost, Depending on Market and Monitoring Burden

Let me get specific about numbers, because I know that's what you're actually wondering. What should you charge? What's the market? What's too low, what's too high, what's just right?

There is no single answer, because pricing depends on your market, your overhead, your experience, and the complexity of the programs you offer. But I can give you frameworks and ranges that will help you think about this correctly.

The general rule I teach physicians is this: your program fee should be two to four times the cost of the medication itself, depending on how labor-intensive your monitoring and follow-up is. If you're prescribing a relatively straightforward protocol - say, BPC-157 for connective tissue healing in a healthy patient who needs minimal monitoring - your fee might be on the lower end of that range, maybe 2 to 2.5 times medication cost. If you're running a complex metabolic optimization program with multiple peptides, frequent lab monitoring, dose adjustments, and intensive follow-up, your fee should be on the higher end - 3.5 to 4 times medication cost, or even more.

Let's work through some examples. Say you're prescribing a three-month BPC-157 protocol. The compounded medication costs you - or rather, costs the patient at the pharmacy - about $300. A reasonable program fee would be $600 to $900 for the three months. That covers your intake visit, your protocol design, your informed consent, your follow-up visits, and your availability for questions. At $750 - 2.5 times medication cost - you're charging enough to make it clear this is a medical program, but not so much that you're pricing out patients who could genuinely benefit from a relatively simple therapy.

Now let's look at a complex program. A six-month metabolic optimization program using GLP-1 agonists, growth hormone secretagogues, and anti-inflammatory peptides, with comprehensive lab monitoring every six to eight weeks, monthly follow-up visits, dose adjustments, lifestyle coaching integration, and unlimited messaging access. The medication costs over six months might be $1,200 to $1,800. Your program fee should be $3,600 to $7,200

- and in affluent markets, I've seen physicians charge $8,000 to $12,000 for comparable programs.

Are those numbers shocking to you? They shouldn't be. That's what specialized medical care costs. A cardiologist doing a comprehensive risk assessment and management program charges similar fees. An endocrinologist managing a complex hormone replacement protocol charges similar fees. A functional medicine physician running a six-month gut healing program charges similar fees. You are not selling vials. You are selling physician-supervised medical care, and you should price it like physician-supervised medical care.

Here's another way to think about it. What do you want to earn per hour of your time? Not what an insurance company thinks your time is worth - what do you think your time is worth? A highly trained physician with years of education, residency, and specialized knowledge in peptide therapy? My answer: at minimum $400 per hour, and ideally $600 to $800 per hour. That's what top specialists in other fields charge. That's what your expertise is worth.

Now work backward from that number. A new patient intake for a peptide program takes ninety minutes. At $600 per hour, that's $900 just for the intake. Add in pre-visit chart review (thirty minutes, $300), care coordination and pharmacy calls ($200), and the follow-up visits over the course of the program ($1,500 to $2,000), and you're at $2,900 to $3,400 in physician time alone. Add your overhead - rent, staff, malpractice insurance, software, continuing education - which typically runs 40% to 60% of revenue in a medical practice. Your program fee needs to be $5,000 to $7,000 just to hit a reasonable hourly rate after overhead.

This is the math that most physicians never do. They set their prices based on what they think patients will pay, or what the competition charges, or some vague sense of what's "fair." They don't calculate what their time actually costs and price accordingly. And then they wonder why they're working seventy hours a week and barely covering their overhead.

Don't be that doctor. Do the math. Value your time. Charge accordingly.

Market positioning matters too. If you're in Manhattan or Beverly Hills or Miami Beach, your fees should reflect your market. Patients in those markets expect to pay premium prices for premium services, and if you don't charge premium prices, they will assume your service isn't premium. A $15,000 annual optimization program in Manhattan is unremarkable. The same program in rural Ohio might be the most expensive medical service in the county. You need to know your market and price for it - but always on the high side of what your market will bear, not the low side.

And let me be very clear about one thing: do not try to be the lowest-priced option anywhere. Not in your city, not in your state, not on the internet. The lowest-priced physician attracts the most price-sensitive, highest-maintenance, most complaint-prone patients. The lowest-priced physician also signals - to patients, to regulators, to competitors - that they don't value their own expertise. You do not want to be known as the cheap peptide doctor. You want to be known as the best peptide doctor, and you want your prices to reflect that reputation.

If a patient tells you they found someone online who charges half what you charge, your answer should be: "That's great. I hope they provide excellent care. My fees reflect the level of monitoring, access, and expertise I provide, and I'm not able to discount that. If cost is your primary concern, that practice might be a better fit for you." Let them go. Wish them well. The patients you keep will be the ones who value what you provide enough to pay for it. And those are the patients who will build your practice, refer their friends, and never file a board complaint.

Explain What the Program Includes: Oversight, Screening, Education, Supplies, Pharmacy Coordination, Follow-Up

Pricing only works if patients understand what they're paying for. The most common objection you'll hear from potential patients is some variation of: "But the peptides only cost $300. Why am I paying $3,000?" And if you can't answer that question clearly and convincingly, you will lose that patient. Worse, you'll lose that patient with a bad taste in their mouth - they'll walk away thinking you're gouging them, and they might tell their friends, or complain online, or worst of all, mention your name to someone at the state medical board as "this doctor who wanted to charge me ten times what the medication costs."

So you need a clear, compelling, patient-friendly explanation of what your program fee covers. And it needs to be more than a list on your website. It needs to be a narrative you can deliver with confidence - because you genuinely believe it - that helps patients understand they're not buying medication. They're buying you.

Here's how I teach physicians to frame it. Your program fee covers four categories of service: clinical assessment, treatment management, ongoing monitoring, and access. Each of these categories represents real work that you do, real expertise that you provide, and real value that the patient receives. Let's break them down.

Clinical assessment is everything that happens before any medication is prescribed. It's your comprehensive intake, where you spend sixty to ninety minutes understanding the patient's medical history, their symptoms, their goals, their prior treatments. It's your targeted lab review, where you interpret specialized tests that their PCP never ordered - growth hormone markers, inflammatory panels, metabolic assessments - in the context of whether peptide therapy is appropriate for them. It's your screening process, where you identify contraindications, risk factors, and red flags that might make peptide therapy unsafe or ineffective for this particular patient. This is medical work. It requires your medical license, your training, and your judgment. And it often prevents inappropriate treatment that could have harmed the patient - which is valuable in itself.

Treatment management is the active oversight of the patient's peptide protocol. It's the informed consent conversation, where you spend thirty to forty-five minutes making sure the patient understands what they're taking, why you're prescribing it, what the evidence shows, what the risks are, and what to expect. It's your protocol design - selecting the right peptides at the right doses for this specific patient's goals and biology. It's your pharmacy coordination, where you work with a compounding pharmacy you trust to ensure the patient gets a high-quality product, properly formulated, with appropriate handling and shipping. It's your dose adjustments over time, based on the patient's response and lab results. This is ongoing medical management, not a one-time prescription.

Ongoing monitoring is the safety infrastructure of the program. It's your scheduled follow-up visits, where you assess how the patient is responding, check for side effects, review their latest labs, and adjust the protocol as needed. It's your review of the patient's home log, tracking their injections, their symptoms, their progress toward their goals. It's your vigilance for adverse effects - the ones you know about and the ones that haven't been fully characterized yet, because peptide therapy is still an evolving field. This monitoring is what separates a legitimate medical program from a vial shop. It's what keeps patients safe. And it's what protects your license, because it demonstrates that you're providing appropriate medical supervision, not just writing prescriptions.

Access is the ongoing relationship between you and the patient. It's the secure messaging for questions that come up between visits. It's the phone availability for urgent concerns. It's the peace of mind that comes from knowing your prescribing physician is available if something goes wrong. Patients on peptide protocols have questions - lots of them. Is this injection site reaction normal? Should I take my dose if I'm traveling across time zones? What if I missed a dose? Can I combine this peptide with the supplement I just read about? When you charge a program fee, you're charging for being available to answer these questions - which is medical work, even if it happens outside a formal office visit.

When you explain your fee structure this way, patients understand. The ones who are looking for a real medical program - the patients you want - will see the value immediately. They'll recognize that what you're offering is fundamentally different from the online peptide vendors who sell vials with no medical oversight. They'll understand that your fee isn't a markup on medication; it's payment for a comprehensive service that happens to include medication as one component.

Put this explanation in writing. Give every prospective patient a program overview document that lays out exactly what's included, exactly what the fee covers, and exactly what they can expect from the relationship. This isn't just good marketing - it's good legal protection. When a patient signs that document, they're acknowledging that they understand what they're paying for. If they ever complain that your fees are too high, or that they didn't understand what they were getting into, you have their signature on a document that says otherwise.

Handle Insurance Receipt Requests Carefully - Explain, Provide Receipts, Refuse to File Claims

Now we get to the practical reality that some of your cash-pay patients will have health insurance, and they'll want to use it. Maybe they want a superbill so they can try to get reimbursed out-of-network. Maybe they want you to submit a claim on their behalf. Maybe they have a health savings account and they need documentation to justify the expense. You need to handle these requests carefully, because there's a right way and a wrong way, and the wrong way can recreate exactly the insurance relationships you're trying to avoid.

Let's start with the superbill request. A superbill is an itemized receipt that includes diagnosis codes, procedure codes, and provider information - essentially everything a patient would need to submit a claim to their insurance company for out-of-network reimbursement. Patients love superbills because they think they might get some of their money back. And here's the thing: in many cases, if the patient submits a superbill for a peptide visit, the insurance company will deny it. Peptide therapy is almost always excluded as experimental or investigational. The patient won't get reimbursed, and that's the end of it.

But sometimes - not often, but sometimes - the insurance company pays something. And when they do, you've just entered their system. They now have a record of you as a provider. They have your NPI number, your diagnosis codes, your procedure codes, your fees. They can data-mine that information, compare it to other claims, flag you as an outlier. They can - and sometimes do - use that superbill submission as the basis for a network participation request, an audit, or a board complaint. The superbill that seemed harmless becomes the thread that unravels your protective cash-pay structure.

My advice? Don't provide superbills for peptide visits. Tell patients upfront, as part of your program overview, that you do not participate with any insurance plans, you do not provide superbills, and you do not assist with insurance reimbursement in any way. Explain why: because insurance reimbursement requires billing codes, and billing codes create a record with insurance companies that can compromise the privacy of their care and the structure of your practice. Most patients will accept this. The ones who don't - the ones who insist on superbills, who argue about it, who threaten to go elsewhere unless you accommodate their insurance needs - are patients you should let go. They're telling you, before they've even started treatment, that their relationship with their insurance company matters more to them than their relationship with you. That is not a patient who will be easy to manage, and it's not a patient worth the risk.

Now, what about health savings accounts and flexible spending accounts? These are different from insurance reimbursement. HSA and FSA funds belong to the patient. They're using their own pre-tax dollars, not asking an insurance company to pay. And in most cases, a simple receipt is sufficient for HSA/FSA documentation. You don't need diagnosis codes or procedure codes. You just need to provide a receipt that says "Medical Services - [Date] - $ [Amount]" with your practice name, address, and tax ID number. That's it. The patient submits that receipt to their HSA administrator, and unless the administrator is unusually demanding, the expense is approved.

Keep your HSA receipts simple. Do not include diagnosis codes. Do not include procedure codes. Do not include medication names or treatment descriptions. "Medical Services" is all the description you need. You're providing a medical service. The patient paid for it. The fact that it's tax-advantaged medical spending is between the patient and their HSA administrator. You are not a party to that transaction, and you should not create documentation that inserts you into it.

What if a patient asks you to submit a claim on their behalf? Even if they say they'll pay you directly and just want you to file the claim so they can get reimbursed? The answer is no. Flat, absolute, unequivocal no. Filing a claim creates a contractual and operational relationship with the insurance company. It gives them your NPI, your tax ID, your practice information, your coding patterns, and your patient volume. It gives them standing to audit you, to demand your records, to review your clinical decisions. It is the exact relationship this entire chapter has been explaining why you must avoid.

Be polite but firm with these requests. "I understand that you'd like to seek reimbursement from your insurance, and I wish you the best with that process. However, my practice policy is that I do not participate with any insurance plans and I do not submit claims or provide superbills. This policy protects the privacy of your care and allows me to focus entirely on your clinical needs without the administrative requirements of insurance billing. If you need documentation for your HSA, I'm happy to provide a simple receipt. But I cannot assist with insurance claims in any way."

If the patient pushes back, if they say every other doctor they've ever seen provides superbills, if they say they can't afford your program without insurance reimbursement - hold your ground. "I understand this may not work for your financial situation, and I completely respect that. There are other practitioners who may be able to accommodate your insurance needs. I'm not able to do so." Let them walk. The peace of mind that comes from maintaining your cash-pay integrity is worth far more than any single patient's fee.

One more scenario to address: what about Medicare patients? Medicare requires special caution, and honestly, my advice is simple and conservative: don't treat Medicare patients for peptide therapy unless you're absolutely certain you understand the legal landscape and are prepared to navigate it carefully.

Here's why. Medicare has something called the mandatory claims submission rule. If you are a licensed provider and you provide a covered service to a Medicare beneficiary, you are required to submit a claim to Medicare. You cannot opt out on a service-by-service basis. The only way around this is to formally opt out of Medicare entirely - which means you cannot treat any Medicare patients for any services for two years - or to provide only services that are statutorily excluded from Medicare coverage, which peptide therapy arguably is.

But "arguably" is the problem. If Medicare decides that some portion of your service to a Medicare patient is a covered benefit - a standard office visit, a preventive medicine consultation, something that could be billed under a standard E/M code - they can argue that you should have submitted a claim. And if you didn't, they can argue that you violated the mandatory claims submission rule. This is a federal violation. It can result in civil monetary penalties. It can trigger exclusion from federal healthcare programs. And it can lead to the kind of federal investigation that makes a state board complaint look like a parking ticket.

My conservative recommendation? Either formally opt out of Medicare - which allows you to treat Medicare patients on a cash-only basis for all services, but means you can't bill Medicare for anything for two years - or simply don't treat Medicare patients for peptide therapy. Refer them to a colleague who is comfortable with the Medicare landscape, or explain that your practice doesn't accept Medicare and you can't treat them. It's better to lose a patient than to gain a federal investigation.

For the patients you do treat, have a clear financial policy in writing that every patient signs before their first visit. This policy should state clearly: (1) payment is due at the time of service; (2) you do not participate with any insurance plans; (3) you do not submit insurance claims; (4) you do not provide superbills; (5) you can provide a simple receipt for HSA/FSA purposes only; (6) the patient is responsible for all fees regardless of any insurance coverage they may have. Have them sign this policy. Keep it in their chart. It is your protection when -not if, when - someone complains that you wouldn't take their insurance.

The Medicare Minefield - Special Considerations

I touched on Medicare in the last section, but it deserves its own dedicated treatment because Medicare is different from private insurance in ways that can destroy your life. Medicare isn't just another payer. It's a federal program with criminal enforcement authority, and the rules that apply to Medicare patients are stricter, more complex, and more dangerous than anything in the private insurance world.

The first thing you need to understand about Medicare is the mandatory claims submission rule I mentioned earlier. Under federal law, if you provide a Medicare-covered service to a Medicare beneficiary, you must submit a claim to Medicare. You cannot agree with the patient to skip Medicare and pay cash instead. You cannot provide the service "off the books" and just not bill. If you provide a covered service, you must bill. Period.

Now, peptide therapy services - the actual prescribing and monitoring of peptides - are not Medicare-covered services. Medicare doesn't cover off-label uses of medications, it doesn't cover experimental or investigational treatments, and it certainly doesn't cover anti-aging or wellness optimization. So in theory, if you're providing only peptide therapy services to a Medicare patient, you're not providing covered services, and the mandatory claims submission rule doesn't apply.

But here's the trap. Most Medicare patients don't come to you solely for peptide therapy. They have other medical issues. They need an office visit. They need a physical exam. They need lab work. They need you to manage their blood pressure medication or their thyroid replacement or their diabetes while they're also on peptides. And any of those services - the standard medical services - might be Medicare-covered. If you provide a covered E/M visit to a Medicare patient and don't submit a claim, you've just violated federal law. It doesn't matter that the main reason they came to you was the peptides. It doesn't matter that you spent most of the visit talking about their peptide protocol. If you provided a covered service and didn't bill Medicare, you're in violation.

The penalties for this are severe. Civil monetary penalties can run up to $10,000 per violation. Criminal penalties - yes, criminal - can include fines and imprisonment under federal healthcare fraud statutes. And a Medicare violation almost always triggers a state board complaint, because the board is required to investigate any physician who faces federal healthcare sanctions.

This is why my conservative recommendation is to either formally opt out of Medicare or decline to treat Medicare patients for peptide therapy. But if you choose to treat Medicare patients, you must understand the opt-out process and follow it precisely.

Opting out of Medicare is the only way to treat Medicare patients on a purely cash basis without triggering the mandatory claims submission rule. When you opt out, you submit a formal affidavit to Medicare stating that you will not treat any Medicare beneficiaries under Medicare for a two-year period. You must submit this affidavit at least thirty days before you start seeing Medicare patients on a cash basis. You must provide a copy to any Medicare patient before their first visit. The patient must sign a private contract acknowledging that they understand you have opted out of Medicare, that Medicare will not pay for any services you provide, and that they are responsible for your full fee.

Once you've opted out, you can treat Medicare patients for cash - including peptide therapy- and you have no obligation to submit claims to Medicare for any services. But you are locked into this decision for two years. You cannot change your mind and start billing Medicare next month. You cannot decide to treat some Medicare patients under Medicare and others on a cash basis. It's all or nothing for a full two-year cycle.

The opt-out process is manageable, and many cash-based physicians use it successfully. But you need to do it right. The affidavit has specific language required by statute. The private contract has specific required elements. If you mess up the paperwork, Medicare can invalidate your opt-out, and now you're back to the mandatory claims submission rule with all its attendant risks.

My strong advice: if you plan to treat Medicare patients in your peptide practice, hire a healthcare attorney who specializes in Medicare opt-out to handle the paperwork. It's not expensive - maybe $2,000 to $3,000 for a proper opt-out setup - and it is the single best investment you can make in protecting yourself from federal exposure. Do not try to DIY the Medicare opt-out. The stakes are too high and the rules are too specific to risk a mistake.

If you choose not to opt out and not to treat Medicare patients, you need a clear, respectful policy for how you handle inquiries from Medicare beneficiaries. "Thank you for your interest in our practice. I want to let you know upfront that I do not participate with Medicare, and I'm not able to provide services to Medicare beneficiaries due to federal billing requirements that are incompatible with my cash-based practice model. I'd be happy to refer you to a colleague who may be able to help you." Keep it simple, keep it respectful, and document the interaction. If a Medicare patient insists on being seen despite your policy, decline firmly and document the declination. Do not let sympathy or pressure lead you into a Medicare relationship you don't fully understand.

How to Talk to Patients About Cash-Pay

Let me close this chapter with some practical advice on the conversation itself - because all the theory in the world won't help you if you stumble and stammer when a patient asks why you don't take their insurance. You need to own this conversation. You need to deliver your explanation with confidence, clarity, and zero apology. The patient should walk away thinking,"This doctor knows exactly what they're doing and they're worth every penny," not "This doctor seems defensive about their prices and I wonder if they're legitimate."

The first rule of this conversation: never apologize for your pricing or your cash-pay model. You are not doing something wrong. You are not asking patients to participate in some sketchy arrangement. You are running a legitimate medical practice that happens not to participate with insurance - which is completely legal, completely ethical, and increasingly common in specialized medicine. If you sound apologetic or defensive, the patient will sense that you feel like you're doing something wrong, and they'll wonder if you are. If you sound confident and matter-of-fact, they'll accept your model as normal.

Here's the framework I teach physicians. When a patient asks about insurance, respond with three elements: explanation, value, and redirect.

Explanation: "I don't participate with any insurance plans. My practice operates on a direct-pay model, which means patients pay at the time of service and I provide them with a receipt they can use for HSA or FSA reimbursement if they have those accounts." Keep this brief and factual. Don't explain the entire insurance industry and its problems. Just state your policy clearly.

Value: "The reason I work this way is that it allows me to spend as much time as each patient needs, to design truly individualized protocols, and to be available for ongoing support without the administrative constraints that insurance companies impose. My patients find that the level of attention and customization they receive is very different from a standard fifteen-minute office visit." This is where you connect your payment model to the patient's experience. They're not just paying for medication. They're paying for time, access, and individualized care.

Redirect: "Does that make sense? Are there questions I can answer about the program or the fees?" Redirect the conversation away from insurance and toward the value of what you're offering. You want the patient thinking about their health goals and your expertise, not about their insurance reimbursement.

Some patients will push back. They'll say their friend got peptides from a doctor who takes insurance. They'll say they can't afford your fees without reimbursement. They'll say it seems like a lot of money for "just some injections." Here's how you handle each of these.

The friend who got insurance coverage: "That's wonderful for your friend. Different practices have different models. Some practitioners bill standard office visits through insurance, but that typically means they're working within the time constraints and clinical pathways that insurance allows. My approach is more comprehensive and time-intensive, which is why I work outside the insurance system." This acknowledges their point without criticizing the other doctor, and it connects your cash model to a clinical advantage.

The affordability concern: "I completely understand that this is a significant investment, and it's important that you feel comfortable with your decision. What I can tell you is that the program fee covers everything - the intake, all follow-up visits, lab review, protocol adjustments, and messaging access for questions. There are no surprise bills, no additional charges for phone calls, no claim denials to fight. Some patients find that the all-inclusive structure actually saves them money compared to practices where each visit and service is billed separately." Then pause and let them think. Don't pressure. If they genuinely can't afford it, refer them elsewhere. If they can afford it but are nervous about the investment, your calm confidence will reassure them.

The "just injections" objection: "I hear that, and let me clarify what the program actually involves. The peptides themselves are one component, but what you're paying for is my medical oversight of the entire process. I'm evaluating whether these medications are appropriate and safe for you specifically. I'm designing a protocol based on your individual biology and goals. I'm monitoring your response and your labs over time. I'm available if you have questions or concerns. That's medical care, and it's what ensures this is done safely and effectively. Without that oversight, you're not in a medical program - you're just buying medication on the internet." This is a powerful reframing. You're not selling vials. You're selling safety and expertise.

There will be patients who simply cannot accept your model no matter how well you explain it. Let them go gracefully. "I understand that my practice model isn't the right fit for everyone, and I respect that. I'd be happy to refer you to other practitioners in the area who may be able to work with your insurance. I wish you the very best with your health." Do not argue. Do not discount. Do not make exceptions. Every exception you make weakens your position with every other patient and creates the exact insurance entanglements this chapter has been warning you about.

Train your front desk staff on these conversations too. They'll get the insurance questions before patients ever reach you, and their response sets the tone. Give them a script."Dr. [Name] does not participate with insurance plans. Our program fees are all-inclusive and paid at the time of service. We can provide a receipt for HSA reimbursement. Would you like me to explain what's included in the program?" If the staff sounds unsure or apologetic, patients will sense it. If they sound confident and matter-of-fact, patients will accept it.

One final thought on this, and then I'm done. The way you talk about your fees communicates something powerful about your practice. If you whisper the number, if you rush past it, if you immediately start explaining why it's not really that much - you signal that you don't believe your own fees are justified. If you state the number clearly, pause, and then describe what it includes with genuine pride in what you offer - you signal that your fees are a fair exchange for genuine medical expertise. Patients respond to this. They can sense when a physician believes in their value, and they treat that physician differently than one who seems uncertain about what they're worth.

You are a highly trained medical professional providing a specialized service that very few physicians are qualified to offer. You are taking on clinical risks - medicolegal risks, regulatory risks, reputational risks - that standard primary care physicians don't face. You are providing comprehensive, individualized, labor-intensive medical care that insurance doesn't value but patients absolutely should. Your fees should reflect all of this. State them with confidence. Explain them with clarity. And never, ever apologize for running a practice that keeps you safe, keeps your patients well-cared-for, and allows you to practice medicine the way it should be practiced - without interference from anyone who doesn't have your patient's best interests at heart.

The Bottom Line

Let me bring this chapter to a close by stating the core principle as plainly as I can. Insurance is not a payment method. It is a surveillance system. Every claim you file is a data point. Every audit is an investigation waiting to happen. Every board complaint from an insurer is a leveraged attack designed to recover money and eliminate a provider who costs too much. The insurance industry and the state medical board system are not separate entities operating independently. They are parts of an ecosystem that feeds on physician compliance, and they have learned to use each other as tools of enforcement.

Cash-pay is your exit from that ecosystem. It is not a gimmick. It is not a boutique affectation. It is a structural firewall that eliminates the insurer as a witness, an adversary, and a threat. When the patient pays you directly, the transaction is complete at the moment of service. No clawbacks. No audits. No contingency attorneys. No board complaints triggered by billing disputes. No statistical extrapolations turning fifty charts into a $400,000 demand. Just a doctor, a patient, and a professional relationship based on mutual respect and fair compensation.

Price your programs for what they're worth - comprehensive medical care, not vials of medication. Charge two to four times your medication costs, minimum. Charge as much as your market will bear, and then push a little higher. Explain your fees in terms of clinical value- assessment, management, monitoring, access - so patients understand they're buying medical expertise. Handle insurance requests politely but firmly: no claims, no superbills, no exceptions. Be especially cautious with Medicare - opt out formally, or don't treat Medicare patients at all. Train yourself and your staff to discuss your model with confidence and zero apology.

The physicians who survive and thrive in peptide practice are the ones who understand that their payment model is their first line of defense. They don't take insurance because they know what insurance does to unconventional doctors. They charge premium prices because they know cheap medicine looks suspicious and attracts problematic patients. They keep their financial relationships simple because they know complexity creates vulnerability. And they sleep better at night because they know that the only person who can question their billing practices is the patient who paid them directly - and that patient, if you've done your job right, is too satisfied with their care to ever want to.

The next chapter is about patient selection - choosing who you treat and, more importantly, who you don't. And as you'll see, the principles in this chapter and the principles in that chapter are deeply connected. Cash-pay pricing selects for certain patients. Patient selection protects your practice from the patients who create the risks that insurance brings into your life. Together, these two chapters form the foundation of a practice that can deliver innovative care safely, legally, and sustainably for the long term. Pay attention to both. Your license depends on it.

PART II: THE MINDSET

The discipline, documentation, and defensive thinking that keep a peptide practice from becoming a regulatory circus.

The philosophy of flying under the radar and protecting your license at all costs.

6 - Patient Selection - Screening Out the Headaches

Unhappy patients file complaints - happy patients refer friends

Let me tell you something I have learned the hard way, watching good physicians lose licenses they spent decades earning. The patient sitting across from you is not just your customer. They are your biggest source of risk, your biggest source of revenue, and - if you choose wrong -the person who will walk into the state medical board office and tell a story that ends your career. Patient selection is not a soft skill. It is the hardest risk management tool you have, and most doctors treat it like an afterthought.

Here is the reality of this business. A happy patient tells three friends. An unhappy patient tells the internet, the credit card company, their attorney, and the state medical board. In that order. By the time the board letter lands on your desk, the patient has already posted three bad reviews, filed a chargeback, and written a complaint that makes you sound like you were running a pill mill out of a strip mall. You think the board cares that you meant well? You think they care that the therapy was clinically reasonable? The board cares about complaints, and complaints come from unhappy patients.

I have seen practices destroyed by one disgruntled patient who could not afford the program, felt slighted by staff, and decided to make the doctor pay. One patient. That is all it takes. The board does not need ten complaints. One well-written complaint from an articulate, angry patient with a thin chart on the other side is enough to trigger an investigation that consumes a year of your life and six figures in legal fees. The patient who felt respected, monitored, and heard? They never complain. Even when things go wrong medically, a patient who trusts you calls the office first. A patient who does not trust you calls the board first.

The math is simple but doctors refuse to do it. One bad patient costs more than ten good patients earn. I am talking about the patient who demands controlled substances, argues with your nurse, skips follow-ups, then files a complaint when something goes sideways. You could have forty compliant, respectful, cash-paying patients who love the program, and one headache patient will consume more staff time, more emotional energy, more legal exposure, and more board risk than all forty combined. It is not fair. It is the truth.

You want to know who files complaints? I will tell you exactly who. The patient who called three times demanding to speak to the doctor directly and was told the doctor would call back during clinical hours. The patient who argued about the price, asked for a discount, got one, and then decided they paid too much. The patient who did not read the consent, did not listen during the consult, experienced a side effect that was clearly disclosed, and then claimed nobody ever told them. The patient who was inappropriate with your front desk staff, yelled at your medical assistant, and then wrote a review calling the practice "rude and unprofessional."These are not medical failures. These are personality failures, and you invited them into your office because you were not willing to say no at the front door.

Headache patients, high-maintenance patients, and patients who can't afford you are the most likely to complain

Let me be blunt about something most doctors will not say out loud. Patients who cannot afford your program are the single highest-risk population in your practice. I am not talking about access to care in the abstract. I am talking about the practical reality of cash-pay elective medicine. When a patient stretches their budget to pay for peptide therapy, every side effect feels like a theft. Every pound not lost feels like fraud. Every follow-up visit feels like another bill they cannot afford. That patient does not see a medical program with ups and downs. They see an investment that is not paying off, and they want their money back. When they cannot get it, they complain.

Financial pressure turns minor dissatisfaction into formal complaints. A patient who paid two thousand dollars out of pocket for a supervised GLP-1 program and experienced nausea for two weeks does not think, "This is a known side effect that was disclosed." They think, "I paid two thousand dollars to feel sick and the doctor did nothing." That thought becomes a chargeback, which becomes a review, which becomes a board complaint. The same patient, if they were wealthy enough that two thousand dollars was incidental, would have called the office, gotten reassurance, adjusted the dose, and moved on. Money changes the emotional temperature of every interaction.

High-maintenance patients are the second-highest risk category. These are the patients who text your personal cell at 10 PM. They call the office four times a week. They want to talk to the doctor, not the nurse. They want answers now, not during business hours. They send long emails with eighteen questions. They expect you to manage their entire health history even though they have a primary care physician they have not seen in two years. Every one of these demands seems small in isolation. Cumulatively, they erode your staff, distract you from real medical decision-making, and create a relationship dynamic where the patient feels entitled to unlimited access. When you eventually set a boundary - and you must - the patient feels rejected, and rejected patients complain.

Then there are the outright headache patients. The ones who argue with your staff in the lobby. The ones who leave nasty voicemails because they had to wait twenty minutes. The ones who demand exceptions to every policy. The ones who treat your medical practice like a restaurant where the customer is always right. These patients are not looking for medical care. They are looking for a transactional relationship where their money buys them unlimited accommodation. When they discover that medicine has boundaries, they punish you for it.

Here is a war story. A physician I advised took on a patient who had been fired from two other peptide practices. Red flag number one. The patient came in demanding tirzepatide, arguing that the other doctors "did not know what they were doing." Red flag number two. He wanted compounded medication because it was cheaper than the brand name but expected brand-name results. Red flag number three. During the consultation, he questioned the doctor's dosing strategy, cited three internet sources, and insisted on a higher starting dose. Red flag number four. The doctor - against his better judgment, because the practice was new and needed revenue - said yes. Within six weeks, the patient was calling daily with side effects he had been warned about, demanding to speak to the doctor, refusing to follow the nurse's instructions, and threatening to "report this place if someone doesn't call me back in an hour."The staff was in tears. The doctor spent two hours managing one patient. Eventually the patient filed a complaint with the state board alleging inadequate supervision and failure to monitor. The board opened an investigation. The chart was thin because the practice was busy and distracted. Legal fees: forty thousand dollars. Emotional cost: incalculable. Revenue from the patient: twelve hundred dollars. That is the math of a bad patient.

Patient selection is the single most important risk management tool you have

You think your consent form protects you? It does not. You think your pharmacy relationship protects you? It does not. You think your monitoring protocol protects you? It helps, but it does not stop a determined complainer. The only protection that actually works is not letting the wrong patient through the door in the first place. Patient selection is your first, best, and cheapest line of defense. It costs nothing to say no. It costs everything to defend a yes that should have been a no.

Most doctors approach patient selection backward. They evaluate the clinical question: does this patient medically qualify for peptide therapy? That is the wrong starting point. The right starting point is: do I want this person in my practice? Not clinically - personally. Will this patient follow instructions? Will they respect my staff? Will they show up for follow-ups? Will they tell me the truth about their medical history? Will they understand that this is elective, cash-pay medicine with no guarantees? Will they call the office if something goes wrong, or will they call the board? These are not clinical questions. They are character assessments, and they matter more than any lab value.

A patient with a slightly elevated BMI who is respectful, compliant, wealthy enough that the program fee is not a burden, and willing to involve their primary care physician is a lower-risk patient than a patient with perfect labs who is demanding, argumentative, financially stretched, and treating your practice like a drive-through. The perfect clinical candidate with a terrible attitude is a lawsuit waiting to happen. The imperfect clinical candidate with a great attitude and realistic expectations is a referral source.

I want you to internalize this: every patient you accept is a patient you will eventually have to defend. The board investigator will read your chart. The plaintiff's attorney will depose your staff. The auditor will review your documentation. When that day comes, the clinical decision matters, but the patient's character matters just as much. A reasonable patient who had a bad outcome tells a story of informed consent and shared decision-making. An unreasonable patient tells a story of being rushed, ignored, and overcharged. The chart may be identical. The patient makes the story.

It is easier to say no at the front door than to defend a bad patient later

This is the simplest rule in the book and the most violated. Saying no at the front door costs you revenue in the short term and saves you everything in the long term. A refused patient cannot file a complaint against you. A refused patient cannot write a bad review. A refused patient cannot trigger a board investigation. A refused patient cannot sue you. The patient you never see is the safest patient in your practice.

Here is what happens when you do not say no. The patient who should have been declined gets through intake because your staff does not want to be rude. They get through the consult because you tell yourself you can manage them. They get prescribed because the pharmacy is ready to ship. They start therapy because you have already invested the time. Then the problems begin. Side effects they were warned about. Demands you cannot meet. Boundary violations you should have anticipated. And finally the complaint, the chargeback, the review, the board letter. At that point you are not managing a medical program. You are managing a crisis that you created by ignoring your instincts at the front door.

Train your staff to say no. This is non-negotiable. Your front desk, your patient coordinator, your intake nurse - they all need permission and language to decline patients who are inappropriate before they ever reach you. Scripts matter. "Based on the information provided, our practice does not feel this program is the right fit for you at this time. We are happy to provide you with a referral to another provider." That sentence, delivered calmly and consistently, prevents more board investigations than any consent form ever written. Your staff should not need to explain why. They should not need to justify the decision. They should simply need to deliver it professionally and hang up.

The patients who argue with the front desk before they ever meet the doctor are telling you exactly who they are. Believe them. The patient who calls three times in one day to ask if their prescription is ready is telling you they will be a management problem. The patient who fills out the intake form incompletely and argues when asked to complete it is telling you they do not follow instructions. The patient who says they "need this medication by Friday because I am going on vacation" is telling you their timeline matters more than your clinical judgment. Every one of these behaviors is a preview of the relationship. Ignore the preview and you deserve the movie.

Here is the practical standard I recommend. Before any patient schedules a consultation, they complete a screening questionnaire. Not the full intake - a brief screen designed to filter out the obvious nos. Do you have a primary care physician? Are you willing to provide medical records? Can you afford the program fee without financial hardship? Are you currently using any controlled substances? Have you been treated for substance abuse in the past year? Do you have stable psychiatric health? Are you willing to complete follow-up visits? Any patient who answers these questions in a way that raises red flags gets a polite decline. No consultation. No clinical time invested. No relationship formed. Just a clean no and a referral suggestion. The patients who pass the screen move to the full intake. The patients who refuse to complete the screen? That is a no. A patient who will not fill out a five-minute form will not complete a twelve-week monitoring program. Trust me on this.

Patients who have done their research and understand this is elective, cash-pay medicine

The ideal peptide patient is not the one who walked in off the street because they saw your ad. The ideal patient is the one who spent three months reading about GLP-1 receptor agonists, joined patient forums, compared practices, asked their primary care physician for input, and then called your office with specific, informed questions. That patient understands what peptide therapy is and what it is not. They know it is elective. They know it is not covered by insurance. They know results vary. They know there are side effects. They have realistic expectations because their expectations were formed by research, not by an influencer's before-and-after photo.

These patients are gold. They ask smart questions during the consultation. They read the consent form before signing it. They take notes. They involve their primary care physician without being pushed. They follow the dosing instructions. They report side effects accurately because they know what to look for. They show up for follow-ups because they understand monitoring is part of the program. When something goes wrong - and something goes wrong for every practice eventually - they call the office first because they trust the process. They do not panic, they do not threaten, and they do not complain to the board because they understood the risks before they started.

How do you find these patients? You do not find them. You attract them. Conservative marketing that emphasizes medical evaluation, individualized care, and realistic expectations draws informed patients. Flashy marketing that promises transformation, rapid weight loss, and revolutionary results draws desperate patients. Desperate patients make terrible peptide candidates. They want fast results, they want them cheap, and they want guaranteed outcomes. When they do not get those things - and they never do - they blame you. Informed patients want medical supervision, patient-specific protocols, and honest risk disclosure. When outcomes are modest, they are satisfied because the process matched their expectations.

During the consultation, ask the patient how they heard about peptide therapy and what research they have done. A patient who says "I read about semaglutide in the New England Journal and discussed it with my endocrinologist" is a very different candidate than a patient who says "I saw this TikTok where a guy lost forty pounds in two months." The first patient is making a medical decision. The second patient is shopping for a product. Your practice should attract the first patient and decline the second. Not because TikTok is wrong - sometimes the information is accurate - but because a patient whose decision is driven by social media hype has expectations you cannot meet. That gap between hype and reality is where complaints are born.

Patients with realistic expectations who understand there are no guarantees

I want you to tattoo this on your forehead: no guarantees. There are no guaranteed results in peptide therapy. There are no guaranteed results in any medicine, but especially not in elective, cash-pay, often off-label or compounded peptide prescribing. Every patient who walks through your door must understand this at a bone-deep level before they pay the first dollar. If a patient nods along when you say "results vary" but you can see in their eyes that they expect to lose thirty pounds in six weeks, you have a problem. That patient is not consenting to realistic medicine. They are consenting to their fantasy, and when the fantasy does not materialize, you become the villain.

The patients you want are the ones who say things like "I know this is a tool, not a magic bullet" or "I understand the goal is gradual improvement, not overnight transformation." They ask about the monitoring plan. They ask about what happens if side effects occur. They ask about the evidence level and what is still unknown. They do not ask "how much weight will I lose?" as if you have a crystal ball. They do not ask "will this work for me?" as if you can predict individual response. They understand that medicine is probabilistic, that individual results vary, that some patients respond well and some do not respond at all, and that the goal is the lowest effective dose monitored safely over time.

Screen for expectations during the consultation. Ask directly: "What do you expect to achieve with this therapy?" Then listen carefully. A patient who says "I want to lose weight, improve my energy, and work with my doctor to find the right approach" has realistic expectations. A patient who says "I need to lose fifty pounds for my daughter's wedding in eight weeks" has a deadline, not a medical goal. Deadlines create pressure. Pressure creates dose escalation. Dose escalation creates side effects. Side effects create complaints. Do not treat deadline-driven patients. They are not seeking health. They are seeking a quick fix, and when it does not work, they will blame you.

Here is a practical test. After explaining the therapy, the risks, the monitoring, and the uncertainty, watch the patient's reaction. The right patient leans in, asks follow-up questions, and says something like "That makes sense, I want to do this carefully." The wrong patient looks disappointed that you are not promising more, asks "But it works, right?" with anxiety in their voice, or says "I just really need this to work." That need is a warning sign. Needy patients are high-maintenance patients. They need results because they have emotional stakes that exceed medical reality. They will call constantly. They will demand adjustments. They will interpret every normal fluctuation as a failure of your care. Say no to needy patients.

Patients who have a primary care physician and are willing to involve them

This is the secret weapon that most peptide practices ignore, and it drives me crazy. A patient with an active primary care relationship is a safer patient. Full stop. When a patient has a PCP who knows their full medical history, manages their chronic conditions, and is willing to collaborate with your practice, you have backup. You have someone else watching the patient's labs. You have someone else managing the blood pressure, the diabetes, the thyroid, the psychiatric medications. You are not the patient's only doctor, which means you are not responsible for everything that goes wrong in their health.

Patients who refuse to involve their PCP are waving a red flag. Sometimes they say they "do not trust" their primary care doctor, which usually means they are doctor-shopping for someone who will give them what their PCP wisely refused. Sometimes they say they "have not seen a doctor in years," which means they have unmanaged conditions you do not know about. Sometimes they say they "do not want their insurance to know," which means they are trying to hide something. In every case, a patient who will not involve their PCP is a patient who wants your practice to operate in a vacuum, and vacuums are dangerous. When something goes wrong, there is no other physician to say "This was appropriate care with informed consent." There is only you, alone, explaining your decisions to a skeptical board reviewer.

Require PCP involvement for complex patients. If a patient has hypertension, diabetes, cardiovascular disease, psychiatric conditions, or is on multiple medications, their PCP should know they are starting peptide therapy. Send a clearance letter. Request recent labs. Ask the PCP if they have concerns. Document the response. Even if the PCP does not respond, you have a chart note showing that you tried to involve them. That note is worth its weight in gold during a board review. It shows you were not practicing in isolation. It shows you respected the primary care relationship. It shows you practiced collaboratively, not secretively.

The patients you want will say "I will call my PCP today" or "My doctor already knows I am looking into this." They will bring recent labs. They will sign a records release. They will welcome the collaboration because they understand that more doctors watching their care means safer care. These patients are not trying to hide anything. They are trying to get healthier, and they want their medical team coordinated. That attitude - collaborative, transparent, team-oriented - is the single best predictor of a patient who will not complain when outcomes are imperfect.

Patients who can afford the program without financial hardship

I have said it before and I will keep saying it until every doctor in this space listens: patients who cannot afford your program are your highest-risk patients. Not because they are bad people. Because financial pressure turns every medical disappointment into a financial grievance. When a patient pays five hundred dollars for a supervised program and does not lose the weight they hoped for, they do not think "Medicine is uncertain." They think "I wasted five hundred dollars on a scam." That thought pattern leads directly to chargebacks, bad reviews, and complaints.

The patients you want are the ones for whom your program fee is a comfortable investment in their health. They are not maxing out credit cards. They are not borrowing from family. They are not choosing between peptide therapy and their rent. They see the fee as comparable to a gym membership, a nutritionist, or other wellness expenditures. When these patients experience a side effect, they do not think about the money. They think about their health. They call the office, get guidance, and continue under supervision. They do not panic about wasted money because the money was never the primary driver of their dissatisfaction.

You must discuss cost openly before any patient starts therapy. Not in fine print. Not buried in a consent form. Openly, directly, and with enough detail that there are no surprises. "The initial consultation is this amount. The program includes this. Medication is separate and shipped by the pharmacy. Follow-up visits are this amount. Labs are this amount. If you need dose adjustments, that requires another visit. Total first-year cost is likely to be between X and Y. Are you comfortable with that investment?" Then be quiet and listen. A patient who hesitates, who asks about payment plans, who wants to know if insurance might cover it later - these are warning signs. Not because payment plans are wrong, but because a patient who is stretching to afford the program is a patient who will feel betrayed by any outcome short of spectacular success.

Charge premium prices. I covered this in the pricing chapter and I am repeating it here because it is a patient selection tool. Cheap programs attract price-sensitive patients, and price-sensitive patients are the most likely to complain. Premium pricing attracts patients who value medical supervision, who expect professional care, and who treat the relationship with respect. A patient paying two thousand dollars for a comprehensive program expects medical quality. A patient paying two hundred dollars for a quick prescription expects a product. When that product does not perform like they imagined, they feel cheated. The high-paying patient, by contrast, has already bought into the concept of supervised medicine. They are paying for your expertise, not just the vial. That mental frame makes all the difference when outcomes are less than perfect.

Patients who are compliant, communicative, and respectful of boundaries

Let me describe the ideal peptide patient in behavioral terms. They complete forms on time. They show up for appointments. They respond to check-in messages. They report symptoms honestly without drama or omission. They follow dosing instructions. They do not adjust their own doses. They do not share medication with friends. They treat your staff with respect. They understand that the doctor is not available 24/7 for non-urgent questions. They save non-urgent concerns for business hours. They understand that follow-up visits are required, not optional.

When given instructions, they follow them. When given boundaries, they respect them.

This sounds basic because it is basic. But a shocking number of patients fail these simple behavioral standards, and a shocking number of practices tolerate the failure because they need the revenue. Do not tolerate it. Noncompliance is not a personality quirk. It is a risk factor. A patient who skips follow-up visits, ignores symptom check-ins, adjusts their own dosing, and treats your staff poorly is not participating in a medical program. They are using your practice as a prescription source. That is not a patient-physician relationship. That is a transaction, and transactions are defensible only when everything goes perfectly. When something goes wrong- and it will - a transactional patient has no loyalty, no trust, and no hesitation about filing a complaint.

Communication style matters enormously. The patient who reports a side effect by saying "I have had mild nausea for two days after the dose increase, just like you warned me about, and I wanted to let you know" is a dream patient. They read the handout. They understood the risk. They are reporting appropriately. The patient who texts at midnight saying "This medication is POISON and you need to call me RIGHT NOW" is a nightmare. Both patients had the same side effect. One handled it like an adult participating in medical care. The other handled it like a customer demanding a refund at a retail counter. The clinical event was identical. The behavioral response was completely different, and that difference determines whether the side effect becomes a documented medical event or a board complaint.

Respect for boundaries is the final piece. Patients who demand your personal cell number, who show up without appointments, who expect same-day responses to non-urgent portal messages, who want to discuss their care while you are trying to leave the office - these patients do not understand the professional boundary between physician and patient, or they do not care. Either way, they will eventually violate a boundary that creates a problem. The patient who texts you at 11 PM with a non-urgent question and you do not respond within an hour is the patient who writes a review saying "Doctor does not care about patients. Ignores messages."Never mind that it was 11 PM. Never mind that the question could have waited until morning. The patient who does not respect boundaries creates their own narrative of neglect.

Set boundaries clearly from the first interaction. "Our office hours are this. Urgent symptoms require a call to this number or a visit to urgent care. Non-urgent questions are answered within one business day through the portal. The doctor does not respond to text messages. Follow-up visits are required every four weeks for the first three months. If you miss a follow-up, refills are paused until we reconnect." Say it. Put it in writing. Have the patient initial it. Then enforce it consistently. The patients who accept these boundaries are the patients you want. The patients who argue about them are telling you, before the relationship even starts, that they will be a management burden. Believe them.

Patients seeking controlled substances or reporting substances

Let me be absolutely clear about this, because I have seen too many physicians talk themselves into trouble. If a patient comes to your peptide practice asking for controlled substances -stimulants, benzodiazepines, opioids, testosterone they do not need, thyroid medication without indication, or any scheduled drug - you show them the door. Not because you are judgmental. Not because you are cruel. Because controlled substances in a peptide practice are like gasoline near a campfire. They attract the wrong patients, they attract board scrutiny, and they create a pattern of prescribing that you cannot defend when the investigator asks why a weight-loss clinic was also dispensing Adderall and Xanax.

I am not talking about legitimate hormone therapy managed within an appropriate protocol. I am talking about the patient who calls asking for semaglutide "and while I am there, can the doctor also write me for some phentermine?" Or the patient who mentions during the consult that they "really need their Klonopin refilled" and their psychiatrist "is hard to reach." Or the patient who wants testosterone pellets even though their levels are normal because they "just want to feel optimized." These are not clinical requests. These are drug-seeking behaviors disguised as clinical requests, and you are not sophisticated enough to tell the difference every single time. No one is. The only safe approach is zero tolerance.

Patients actively using illicit substances are an automatic decline. I do not care if it is "just marijuana" or "just occasional cocaine at parties." A patient who is using unreported substances is a patient who is already demonstrating dishonesty about what they put in their body. If they will lie to you about cocaine, they will lie to you about side effects. They will lie to you about how many injections they did. They will lie to you about whether they shared medication. Substance use disorder is not a moral failing - it is a medical condition that requires appropriate treatment. Your peptide practice is not that treatment. A patient in active recovery with a stable sponsor, regular monitoring, and transparent disclosure is a different conversation. A patient currently using? That is a no. Full stop. Document it and move on.

Here is what the board sees when they investigate a peptide practice that also prescribed controlled substances. They see a pattern. They do not see your careful clinical reasoning. They see a practice that prescribed semaglutide, tirzepatide, testosterone, HCG, phentermine, and Clonazepam to the same patient over six months. To you, each prescription had a rationale. To the board reviewer, that pattern looks like a one-stop shop for anyone willing to pay cash. And the board does not need to prove you did anything medically wrong. They only need to decide that your practice pattern looks like "indiscriminate prescribing." That phrase ends careers. Do not give them the ammunition.

Train your staff to screen for this during the initial phone call. "Are you currently taking any controlled substances? Are you being treated for substance use? Are you in recovery?" These are standard questions, not intrusive ones. A patient who gets angry about being asked is telling you everything you need to know. A patient who answers honestly and appropriately is demonstrating transparency. Document every answer. If a patient admits to active substance use, the response is: "Based on your current situation, our program is not appropriate for you at this time. We recommend you follow up with your primary care physician or an addiction medicine specialist." That is it. No argument. No negotiation. No exceptions because the patient seems nice.

Patients with unrealistic expectations who want guaranteed results

I have already touched on expectations, but this deserves its own section because it is the most common reason patients become complaints. A patient with unrealistic expectations is not just a difficult patient. They are a patient you cannot satisfy, and a patient you cannot satisfy will eventually become a patient who wants revenge. Revenge in the modern healthcare economy means chargebacks, one-star reviews, social media posts, and board complaints.

What do unrealistic expectations look like in practice? They look like the forty-five-year-old patient who has been overweight for twenty years, has tried nothing meaningful in terms of diet or exercise, and expects semaglutide to make them lose sixty pounds in three months without any lifestyle change. They look like the patient who wants BPC-157 to heal a chronic rotator cuff tear so they can avoid surgery they have needed for five years. They look like the patient who expects tesamorelin to give them a six-pack at age sixty without changing their diet or doing a single sit-up. They look like the patient who says "I will pay whatever it takes, just make me look like I did in college."

These patients are not medically unreasonable because of their goals. Everyone wants to be healthier and look better. They are unreasonable because they have divorced outcomes from effort, and they have divorced results from time. When you prescribe peptide therapy to a patient who believes the medication does all the work, that patient will fail. The weight loss will be modest because they did not change their eating. The body composition will not shift because they did not exercise. The recovery will be slow because they did not do physical therapy. And when they fail, they will not blame their own behavior. They will blame you. You sold them a miracle, they will say, and it did not work.

During every consultation, you must explicitly and repeatedly set expectations. Say it three times in three different ways. "This medication is a tool, not a guarantee." "Individual results vary significantly." "Your effort matters as much as the medication." "Some patients lose ten pounds a month. Some lose two. Some lose none." "The goal is gradual, sustainable improvement, not transformation." Watch the patient's face when you say these things. The realistic patient nods and says "I understand, I want to do this the right way." The unrealistic patient nods but you can see the disappointment. They are already planning their complaint. Do not give them the chance.

There is a specific category of unrealistic patient that deserves special attention: the patient who has already decided what medication they want, what dose they want, and what results they expect before they meet you. These patients often arrive with printed internet dosing schedules, forum posts, and influencer videos. They are not seeking medical evaluation. They are seeking a prescription pad. When you tell them that their requested dose is inappropriate, that the medication they want is not clinically indicated, or that their expectations are not realistic, they become angry. They will argue. They will cite their "research." They will accuse you of being "overly conservative" or "not understanding peptides." Do not engage. These patients have already decided that they know more than you. A patient who knows more than their doctor is a patient who will manage their own care, and self-managed peptide therapy leads to side effects, overdoses, and board complaints that you will have to explain.

The script for this patient is simple: "I appreciate that you have done research. My role is to evaluate whether this therapy is medically appropriate for you specifically, at a dose and monitoring level that is safe. Based on my evaluation, what you are requesting is not clinically appropriate at this time. I am happy to discuss alternatives that are within the standard of care, or I can refer you back to your primary care physician." Then stop talking. The patient will either accept your boundaries or leave. If they leave angry, you just prevented a complaint. If they stay, they have accepted that you are the physician and they are the patient. That power dynamic must be established for every patient, every time.

Patients who cannot afford therapy - financial pressure creates complaints

I know I sound like a broken record on this point, but I am going to keep repeating it because doctors keep ignoring it and then calling me when the board letter arrives. Patients who cannot comfortably afford your program are your highest-risk population. I am not being elitist. I am being practical. Financial stress changes how patients experience medical care. A side effect that a wealthy patient shrugs off becomes a catastrophic betrayal to a patient who put their therapy on a credit card they cannot pay off.

Here is the pattern I see over and over. A patient calls and asks about cost. Your staff gives them the price. The patient says "That is more than I expected" or "Can I do a payment plan?"or "Is there any way to make it cheaper?" These are not offensive questions. They are fair questions from people who are watching their budgets. But they are also signals. A patient asking about price reduction is a patient for whom the full price is a stretch. When that patient then pays the reduced price, starts therapy, and does not get the results they imagined, every dollar they spent feels like theft. The nausea they experience does not feel like a known side effect. It feels like suffering they paid for. The missed weight loss does not feel like normal variation. It feels like fraud.

You must have a frank affordability discussion before any patient pays. Not a passing mention. A real discussion. "The total cost of this program, including consultation, medication, follow-up visits, and required labs, is approximately X dollars over the first six months. This is a cash-pay service not covered by insurance. Are you comfortable with this investment? Will paying for this program create financial hardship for you?" If the patient hesitates, qualifies their answer, or asks about payment plans, you need to dig deeper. "It is important that you are comfortable with the cost because I want you focused on your health, not worried about money. If the cost creates stress, that stress will affect your experience and your outcomes."

Some doctors feel guilty about turning away patients who cannot afford care. I understand that feeling. But here is the reality: you are running a medical practice, not a charity. Charity care has its place, and if you want to do pro bono work, do it through a structured program with proper funding and legal protections. Ad hoc discounts in a cash-pay peptide practice create inconsistency, resentment, and documentation problems. The patient who got a discount tells their friend, who then demands the same discount and gets angry when refused. The patient who got a discount later claims they were "overcharged relative to other patients." The board investigator sees discounts as evidence of flexible standards. Do not create this mess. Set your prices. Charge them consistently. Decline patients who cannot afford the program. Refer them to their PCP, to community resources, or to programs with sliding scales. Your practice will be healthier, your patients will be happier, and your risk profile will be dramatically lower.

The exception that is not really an exception: patients who want cheaper compounded medication because the FDA-approved version is too expensive. This is a legitimate clinical conversation. Compounded semaglutide or tirzepatide, when lawfully available through appropriate pharmacy channels, can be discussed as an option. But the discussion must be clinical, not financial. "Compounded medication is not FDA-approved the same way as the brand name product. The manufacturing standards differ. The evidence base is different. The monitoring requirements are the same. If, after understanding these differences, you prefer the compounded option, we can discuss whether it is clinically appropriate for you." This framing puts the decision in clinical terms, not economic terms. The patient is choosing a different product category, not bargaining for a discount.

Patients who refuse monitoring, refuse PCP involvement, or refuse follow-up

This category of refusal is a gift wrapped in an inconvenience. When a patient tells you upfront that they will not do follow-up visits, will not get labs, or will not involve their primary care physician, they are doing you an enormous favor. They are telling you, before you ever write a prescription, that they are not willing to participate in the basic safety structure of your program. Believe them. Thank them for their honesty. And decline them.

Monitoring is not optional in peptide therapy. It is the difference between medicine and retail. When a patient says "I just need the prescription, I will be fine," what they are really saying is"I want the product without the supervision." That is not a patient. That is a consumer, and consumers do not participate in medical monitoring. They use the product until they do not like it, then they blame the seller. If you prescribe to a patient who refuses monitoring, you are not practicing medicine. You are selling a vial with a stethoscope around your neck, and the board knows the difference.

PCP refusals are equally revealing. A patient who will not let you contact their primary care physician is hiding something, or they are seeking care their PCP already refused to provide. In either case, you are entering dangerous territory. The patient whose PCP refused to prescribe GLP-1 therapy because of their pancreatitis history and then came to your practice hoping you would not ask about pancreatitis is a patient who will eventually have a pancreatitis episode on your medication. When that happens, the PCP will testify that they warned the patient. The board will ask why you prescribed without PCP involvement. Your answer - "The patient asked me not to contact their PCP" - will sound exactly as bad as it is. Patient preferences do not override clinical standards.

Follow-up refusals are the most obvious. A patient who says "I do not have time for follow-up visits" or "I live too far away to come in monthly" or "Can you just send me three months of medication at once?" is a patient who wants the convenience of self-directed care with the safety net of your medical license. No. Follow-up visits are where you assess tolerance, review side effects, check weight trends, evaluate labs, and make clinical decisions about continuing, adjusting, or stopping therapy. A patient who cannot commit to follow-up cannot safely participate in the program. "I understand your schedule is busy. Our monitoring protocol requires visits every four weeks for the first three months. If that schedule does not work for you, this program is not the right fit. I am happy to refer you to a practice with a different model or back to your primary care physician."

There is a dangerous temptation to make exceptions for patients who seem trustworthy. "This patient is a nurse, she can monitor herself." "This patient is very healthy, he does not need frequent follow-ups." "This patient lives three hours away, so telehealth follow-ups should be enough." Every exception you make weakens your standard of care and creates a chart that looks inconsistent. When the board reviews your records, they will see that most patients had monthly follow-ups but this one patient had quarterly visits. They will ask why. Your answer- "She seemed responsible" - is not a clinical rationale. It is an admission that you applied different standards based on personal impression. Boards hate that. Do not give them the opportunity.

Document every refusal and your response. "Patient declines follow-up visits as required by protocol. Patient educated that monitoring is required for safe therapy. Patient offered options. Patient declined. Decision made to not proceed with therapy at this time. Referral provided to PCP." That note takes thirty seconds to write and will save you hours of explanation if the patient later claims you "refused to treat them." You did not refuse treatment. You refused to practice unsupervised medicine. Those are very different things, and your chart must show the difference.

Patients who are argumentative, demanding, or disrespectful to staff

This is the section where I am going to make some of you uncomfortable, because I am going to tell you something that violates the customer-service culture that has infected medicine. The patient is not always right. In fact, in a medical practice, the patient is frequently wrong, and when they are wrong in ways that demean your staff, demand special treatment, or create a hostile environment, you fire them. Not reluctantly. Not after giving them three chances. You fire them the first time they disrespect your team, because disrespectful patients do not get better. They get worse.

Your staff are the front line of your practice. They answer the phones, they schedule appointments, they collect forms, they triage calls, they manage the logistics that keep your practice running. When a patient yells at your receptionist, demands to speak to the doctor immediately, insists on exceptions to policy, or treats your medical assistant like a servant, that patient is destroying your practice culture. Staff who are abused leave. Staff who are stressed make mistakes. Staff who feel unsupported stop caring about the quality of their work. One abusive patient can poison the environment for your entire team, and a poisoned team makes errors that lead to complaints and board actions.

More importantly, disrespectful behavior during the intake phase is a perfect predictor of disrespectful behavior throughout the relationship. The patient who argues with your scheduler about appointment availability will argue with you about dosing. The patient who yells at the front desk about forms will yell at your nurse about side effects. The patient who demands to be seen immediately will demand prescription changes immediately. This pattern does not change. People show you who they are in the first interaction. If they show you someone who believes their needs supersede everyone else's boundaries, believe them.

The staff script for this situation must be clear and practiced. "Our practice requires mutual respect between patients and staff. That language is not acceptable. If this continues, we will need to end the call and discontinue your care with our practice." Then follow through. If the patient continues, hang up. Document the interaction. Send a certified letter terminating the patient-physician relationship with thirty days of emergency coverage and a referral to another provider. Do not argue. Do not negotiate. Do not let the patient apologize their way back into your practice. Termination is final because it protects your staff, your culture, and your license.

I want to be very specific about what disrespect looks like, because some doctors tolerate behavior that they should not. Disrespect includes: raising one's voice to staff, using profanity, making personal insults, making racist or sexist comments, demanding immediate access to the physician, insisting on exceptions to written policy, threatening bad reviews or complaints, refusing to complete required forms and then berating staff for the delay, showing up hours early or late and expecting accommodation, and repeatedly calling after hours for non-urgent matters. None of this is acceptable in a medical practice. A patient who does any of these things is not a patient you want. They are a liability.

There is a special category of demanding patient that deserves attention: the patient who threatens bad reviews, board complaints, or legal action during routine interactions. This patient is not expressing dissatisfaction. They are attempting to coerce you through intimidation. Once a patient threatens a complaint to get what they want, the patient-physician relationship is permanently damaged. You cannot provide unbiased medical care to someone who is holding a metaphorical gun to your head. Every clinical decision becomes tainted by the threat. Terminate these patients immediately. "Given the nature of our interactions, I do not believe I can provide you with the objective medical care you deserve. I am terminating our physician-patient relationship effective immediately. Emergency coverage will be provided for thirty days. Here is a list of alternative providers." Document everything.

Patients with active eating disorders, unstable psychiatric conditions, or substance abuse

This is the clinical refusal category, and it is non-negotiable. Patients with active eating disorders, unstable psychiatric conditions, or active substance abuse disorders do not belong in an elective peptide therapy program. Not because they are bad people. Not because they do not deserve care. Because your peptide practice is not equipped to manage these conditions, because these conditions make peptide therapy unsafe, and because the board will hold you responsible when - not if - something goes wrong.

Let me start with eating disorders, because GLP-1 agonist therapy and eating disorders are a particularly dangerous combination. A patient with bulimia, anorexia, binge-eating disorder, or any disordered eating pattern should not receive appetite-suppressing medication from a peptide practice. Period. GLP-1 agonists suppress appetite. In a patient with anorexia, appetite suppression is not a feature - it is a medical catastrophe waiting to happen. In a patient with bulimia, the medication can mask purging behaviors or trigger new ones. In a patient with binge-eating disorder, the appetite suppression can feel like a miracle until it triggers restriction, obsession with the scale, and dangerous under-eating. These are psychiatric conditions that require psychiatric care, not a weight-loss peptide.

Screen for eating disorders in every patient seeking weight-management therapy. Ask directly:"Have you ever been treated for an eating disorder? Do you have a history of binge eating, purging, or restrictive eating? Do you become distressed about your weight or eating habits?"Patients may not disclose. That is why you also look for red flags: obsession with specific numbers on the scale, distress when weight plateaus, extreme dietary restriction beyond what is discussed, rapid weight loss celebrated without concern, body dysmorphia described in the consultation, and a history of multiple failed weight-loss attempts with extreme methods. If you suspect an eating disorder, the correct action is refusal and referral to an eating disorder specialist. Not "let's start low and see how it goes." Not "I'll prescribe but you have to promise to eat enough." Refuse and refer.

Unstable psychiatric conditions are equally disqualifying. A patient with uncontrolled depression, active suicidal ideation, untreated bipolar disorder, uncontrolled anxiety, recent psychiatric hospitalization, or psychotic symptoms needs psychiatric care, not peptide therapy. Some psychiatric medications interact with peptide therapies. Some psychiatric conditions are worsened by the metabolic changes that peptides cause. Some patients seek peptide therapy as a way to self-medicate psychiatric symptoms - energy, motivation, mood improvement -that should be managed by a psychiatrist. When you prescribe a peptide to a patient with unstable mental health and that patient later has a psychiatric crisis, the board will ask why you prescribed an elective therapy to a patient who needed psychiatric stabilization first. Your answer will not be good enough.

The screen is straightforward. Ask about psychiatric history on every intake. Ask about current medications. Ask about recent hospitalizations. Ask about suicidal ideation. If any answers are concerning, require psychiatric clearance before proceeding. "Given your history, I want to make sure peptide therapy is safe for you. I need clearance from your psychiatrist or mental health provider before we proceed." A patient who refuses psychiatric clearance is a patient who has something to hide. Decline them. A patient who obtains psychiatric clearance and the psychiatrist raises concerns? Follow the psychiatrist's advice. They know the patient's mental health better than you do.

Active substance abuse is the third disqualifier. I covered controlled substance seekers earlier. This is different. This is the patient who admits to regular alcohol abuse, recreational drug use, or a substance use disorder that is not in stable remission. These patients cannot safely participate in peptide therapy for several reasons. Substance use affects medication metabolism, increases side effect risk, impairs judgment about self-administration, and creates compliance problems. A patient who is drinking heavily cannot safely manage subcutaneous injections. A patient using stimulants is already affecting their cardiovascular system before you add any peptide with metabolic effects. A patient in active opioid use disorder is not going to prioritize your follow-up appointments or monitoring requirements.

The requirement should be clear: stable remission for at least twelve months, with verification from a substance use treatment provider, and ongoing monitoring. A patient who says "I used to have a problem but I am fine now" without documentation is not fine now. Require proof. "I am glad to hear you are doing better. For your safety, I need a letter from your treatment provider confirming stable remission before we can consider therapy." This is not punitive. It is protective - of the patient, of your staff, and of your license.

There is a final category that overlaps all of these: patients seeking peptides for body dysmorphia or muscle dysmorphia. These are primarily young men seeking growth hormone secretagogues, IGF-1 analogs, or "healing peptides" to achieve a physique that is not achievable naturally. They often have comorbid substance use, eating disorders, or psychiatric conditions. They frequently demand specific compounds at doses they found online. They argue about protocols. They are obsessed with results. These patients are psychiatric patients, not peptide candidates. Refer them to mental health care. Do not prescribe.

Require truthful disclosure - blank forms are dangerous forms

The intake form is where your relationship with the patient begins, and it is where you start building the documentation that will defend you if that relationship turns sour. A good intake form does two things simultaneously: it collects the clinical information you need to make safe prescribing decisions, and it creates a written record that proves you practiced medicine rather than operated a vending machine. Blank spaces on an intake form are not administrative oversights. They are legal vulnerabilities. Every blank space is an opportunity for a patient to later claim "I told them about my pancreatitis but they must not have written it down." Every skipped question is a gap in your defense.

Require patients to complete the entire intake form before scheduling a consultation. Not after. Not during. Before. If a patient submits an incomplete form, send it back. "We need all questions answered before the clinician can review your case. Please complete the missing sections and return the form." This may seem pedantic, but it establishes a critical pattern from the first interaction: this practice has standards, and those standards apply to everyone. Patients who complain about completing forms are patients who will complain about every other requirement you have. The form is a test, and patients who refuse to take it are already failing.

The certification section at the end of the intake form is where you separate patients who understand that this is real medicine from patients who think forms are meaningless paperwork. Require the patient to sign and date a statement that says, in plain English: "I certify that the information I have provided is complete and accurate to the best of my knowledge. I understand that providing false or incomplete information may result in harm to my health and may affect my eligibility for treatment. I agree to notify the practice immediately if any of this information changes." That signature matters. When a patient later claims they disclosed a condition that does not appear on the form, you point to the certification and ask whether they signed it. When a patient has an adverse event related to a condition they failed to disclose, your chart shows that they certified the accuracy of their information. That does not eliminate your duty of care, but it places responsibility where it belongs - on the patient who lied.

Train your staff to review every intake form for completeness before it goes to the clinician. A checklist approach works: medical history completed, medications listed with dosages, allergies specified, surgical history provided, family history answered, social history answered, substance use questions answered, psychiatric history answered, pregnancy status confirmed, PCP information provided, prior treatments documented, goals stated. If any section is blank or marked "N/A" inappropriately, the form goes back to the patient. This takes time. It is worth it. A complete intake form reviewed before the consultation allows the clinician to focus on clinical decision-making rather than playing detective with missing information.

Here is a scenario that illustrates why this matters. A patient completes an intake form and leaves the "medications" section blank except for "vitamins." Your staff sends it back. The patient resubmits with a full medication list that includes metformin, lisinopril, and atorvastatin. That resubmission just prevented a potentially dangerous drug interaction and a prescribing error that could have led to a complaint. The patient who refused to resubmit? That patient would have been declined, and rightfully so. A patient who will not list their medications is a patient who is hiding something, and hidden medications are how patients get hurt.

Ask about pregnancy, cancer history, pancreatitis, gallbladder, thyroid, mental health

The intake form must include targeted screening questions for the conditions that create the highest risk in peptide therapy. These are not general wellness questions. They are contraindication screens designed to identify patients who should not receive specific therapies before the clinician ever sees them. Every question must be answered. Every positive answer must trigger a flag for clinician review. Every flag must be documented as addressed.

Pregnancy and breastfeeding status is mandatory for every patient of childbearing potential. GLP-1 agonists, growth hormone secretagogues, and many other peptides have unknown or contraindicated safety profiles in pregnancy. The intake form must ask about current pregnancy, planned pregnancy, contraception use, breastfeeding status, and last menstrual period. A positive pregnancy screen is an automatic pause. No prescribing until pregnancy status is clarified. No exceptions because the patient says "I am pretty sure I am not pregnant."Document the screen and the outcome.

Cancer history must include personal history of any malignancy, current treatment, remission status, and family history of medullary thyroid carcinoma and Multiple Endocrine Neoplasia type 2 (MEN2). The GLP-1 class carries a boxed warning related to thyroid C-cell tumors in rodents. While human risk remains unclear, a patient with personal or family history of medullary thyroid carcinoma or MEN2 should not receive GLP-1 therapy. Ask specifically. Do not accept vague answers like "thyroid issues." Clarify the exact diagnosis. Document the clarification.

Pancreatitis history is critical for any patient considering GLP-1 or GIP/GLP-1 therapy. Ask about personal history of pancreatitis, including cause, severity, date, and hospitalization. Ask about gallbladder disease, gallstones, and biliary symptoms. Pancreatitis is the nightmare adverse event for incretin-based therapy, and a patient with prior pancreatitis has elevated risk. Some patients with remote, mild, non-recurrent pancreatitis may be appropriate candidates after specialist clearance. Most should be declined. The intake form must capture enough detail for the clinician to make that determination.

Gallbladder disease overlaps with pancreatitis risk and GLP-1 therapy specifically. Ask about prior cholecystectomy, gallstones, biliary colic, and any current right upper quadrant pain. GLP-1 agonists slow gastric emptying and can affect gallbladder motility. A patient with active gallbladder disease should not start GLP-1 therapy until the gallbladder issue is resolved. This is not optional screening. It is standard of care.

Thyroid history extends beyond cancer. Ask about hypothyroidism, hyperthyroidism, Hashimoto's disease, Graves' disease, thyroid nodules, and thyroid medication use. Thyroid dysfunction affects metabolism, weight, energy, and how patients respond to peptide therapy. A patient with uncontrolled thyroid disease needs endocrine management before starting elective metabolic therapy. The intake form should flag any thyroid history for clinician review and possible TSH, free T4, and free T3 testing.

Mental health history must be comprehensive without being intrusive. Ask about current or past psychiatric diagnoses, current psychiatric medications, psychiatric hospitalizations, substance use treatment, eating disorder history, and suicidal ideation. A patient with stable depression managed by a psychiatrist on stable medication may be an appropriate candidate. A patient with uncontrolled bipolar disorder, recent suicidal ideation, or an active eating disorder is not. The intake form must provide enough information for the clinician to distinguish between these scenarios and make a referral when indicated.

Each of these screening categories represents a known risk factor that has been associated with adverse outcomes in peptide therapy. A patient who screens positive in any category does not get an automatic decline. They get automatic escalation to clinician review with the specific positive screen documented. The clinician then decides whether the patient is appropriate, needs specialist clearance, or should be declined. That decision, and the reasoning behind it, goes in the chart. This process transforms a simple questionnaire into a documented safety system.

Screen for contraindications before you ever see the patient

The intake form should be reviewed by staff - or better yet, by an AI-assisted screening system - before the clinician ever sees the patient. This pre-clinical screen serves two purposes. First, it identifies obvious contraindications that make the patient inappropriate, allowing the practice to decline the patient before clinical time is invested. Second, it flags complex cases that require additional information, specialist clearance, or extended consultation time, allowing the practice to prepare appropriately.

A well-designed screening workflow looks like this. The patient submits the completed intake form. Staff or an AI system reviews the form against a checklist of hard contraindications and soft contraindications. Hard contraindications trigger an automatic decline with referral language. Soft contraindications trigger a request for additional information or a note for the clinician to address during the consultation. The clinician reviews the flagged form before the consultation, knows what to ask about, and enters the consultation prepared.

Hard contraindications that should trigger automatic decline or specialist clearance before any consultation include: active pregnancy or breastfeeding without specialist clearance; personal or family history of medullary thyroid carcinoma or MEN2 for GLP-1 therapy; history of pancreatitis for incretin therapy; active eating disorder; active substance use disorder; uncontrolled psychiatric condition; request for controlled substances; refusal to provide medical history or PCP information; and known allergy to the proposed medication class. A patient with any of these conditions is not necessarily banned forever. But they cannot proceed to standard consultation and prescribing without additional steps.

Soft contraindications that should trigger flagging for clinician review include: age over 65 for certain therapies; significant cardiac history; uncontrolled hypertension; significant renal or hepatic impairment; use of multiple medications with interaction potential; prior adverse reaction to similar therapies; unrealistic expectations expressed in the goals section; body mass index below the therapeutic range; recent major surgery; and active infection or inflammatory condition. These are not automatic declines. They are warnings that the standard protocol may need modification, additional monitoring, or specialist coordination.

The staff who conduct this pre-clinical screen must be trained to recognize red flags without making clinical decisions. Their job is to route cases appropriately, not to approve or decline patients. Clear protocols matter. "If you see X, flag for the clinician. If you see Y, request additional information. If you see Z, send the standard decline letter." Without these protocols, staff either route everything to the clinician - defeating the purpose of the screen - or make ad hoc decisions that expose the practice to liability. Write the protocols. Train the staff. Audit compliance.

Here is a practical example of why pre-clinical screening matters. A patient submits an intake form indicating they want semaglutide for weight loss. The form reveals a history of pancreatitis three years ago, no follow-up with gastroenterology, and current alcohol use of four drinks daily. Staff flags this for the clinician. The clinician reviews the flag before the consultation and knows to address pancreatitis risk and alcohol use directly. The consultation can focus on whether this patient is appropriate for therapy or needs referral - not on discovering these issues for the first time during the visit. If the clinician declines the patient, the decline is documented with specific clinical reasoning. If the patient later complains, the chart shows a thorough evaluation with identified contraindications. That chart defends the doctor. An unscreened intake form would have left the clinician scrambling during the consultation, and the chart would have shown it.

Make the patient certify accuracy - it matters later

I am going to end this chapter where I started it, with the simplest protection that most practices treat as an afterthought. The patient certification of accuracy is a legal document. Treat it like one. Every patient must sign, date, and initial a statement certifying that the information they provided is complete, accurate, and truthful to the best of their knowledge. They must acknowledge that providing false or incomplete information may result in serious harm to their health. They must agree to inform the practice promptly of any changes to their medical status, medications, or conditions. This is not fine print. This is the bridge between the patient's responsibility for honest disclosure and the physician's responsibility for safe prescribing.

The certification serves three distinct protective functions. First, it creates a legal basis for holding the patient accountable for misrepresentation. When a patient with a hidden history of pancreatitis experiences pancreatitis on GLP-1 therapy and claims "nobody asked," your certification form shows that they certified they had disclosed everything. This does not eliminate your duty of care, but it shifts the narrative from physician oversight to patient dishonesty. Boards and juries understand the difference between a physician who missed something and a patient who lied.

Second, the certification forces the patient to slow down and take the intake seriously. A patient who is mindlessly clicking through an online form treats it like a terms-of-service agreement they have never read. A patient who must physically sign and date a certification statement saying "I swear this is true" engages differently. The act of signing creates a psychological commitment to accuracy. Patients who are planning to hide something are slightly more likely to reveal it when they must sign their name to a truthfulness statement. Not always, but sometimes, and sometimes is better than never.

Third, the certification creates an audit trail that proves the intake was not a casual conversation but a formal medical documentation process. When the board investigator looks at your records, they see a completed form, a signed certification, and a dated clinician review. That sequence tells a story of systematic practice, not slapdash prescribing. The investigator compares your records to the bad actor down the street who has no forms, no certifications, and no documentation. Your practice looks controlled. Theirs looks reckless. Guess which one gets the board's full attention.

The certification language should be specific and should be included on the same page as the signature, not buried on page seven of a consent packet. "I certify that all information I have provided on this form and during my interactions with this practice is true, complete, and accurate to the best of my knowledge. I understand that my physician relies on this information to make safe medical decisions, and that providing false, misleading, or incomplete information could result in serious injury or death. I agree to notify the practice immediately if any of my medical information changes, including new diagnoses, medications, hospitalizations, or changes in my health status." That is the language. Put it in front of every patient. Make them sign it. Keep the original.

The final piece of the certification puzzle is the documentation of staff review. Someone on your team must review the intake form for completeness, initial the review, and date it. This creates a two-person chain: the patient certified accuracy, and staff verified completeness. If the patient later claims a section was blank when they submitted it, your staff initials show that the form was reviewed and appeared complete at the time of submission. If there were blanks, the staff initials document that the form was sent back for completion. Either way, you have a workflow, not a mystery.

Let me close with a war story that brings all of this together. A physician was investigated by the state board after a patient experienced severe side effects from a compounded GLP-1 agonist. The patient claimed they had disclosed their history of gallbladder disease and that the physician ignored it. The board reviewed the chart. The intake form showed no gallbladder history. The certification of accuracy was signed by the patient. The staff review initials were present, dated the day before the consultation. During the investigation, the patient admitted under oath that they had not disclosed the gallbladder history because they "did not think it mattered." The board closed the investigation with no action against the physician. The intake form, the certification, and the staff review created a documentation chain that proved the physician practiced appropriately. That is what a bulletproof intake system looks like in action. Build yours the same way.

7 - The Chart Is Your Shield - Make It Unbreakable

Let me tell you something I have learned from four decades of watching doctors go through board hearings, malpractice depositions, and criminal investigations: the physician almost always remembers being careful. They remember having a good conversation with the patient. They remember explaining the risks. They remember thinking it through. What they cannot produce is a chart that proves any of it happened. And without that chart, their memory might as well be a bedtime story they tell themselves to feel better. The board does not care what you meant. The plaintiff's attorney does not care what you intended. The Department of Justice does not care how many years you practiced without a single complaint. They care what the paper proves. The chart is your shield. Make it unbreakable, or do not bother picking up the pen in the first place.

I have sat in conference rooms with defense attorneys who looked like they wanted to cry because the doctor they were trying to protect handed them a chart that read like a grocery receipt. "Patient wants semaglutide. Prescribed." That is not a medical record. That is evidence of a vending machine with a medical license. I have also sat with the same attorneys when they opened a chart that was so clean, so thorough, so obviously the product of real clinical thinking that they smiled before they said a word. That chart did not just document care. It defended care. It explained the decision to a skeptical stranger so clearly that the stranger had nowhere to go. That is what you are building every time you touch a keyboard or pick up a pen. You are not doing paperwork. You are constructing a legal defense in real time, before you even know you need one.

Months later, nobody cares that you meant well - they care what the chart proves

Here is the hard truth that every physician needs to tattoo on the inside of their eyelid: your intentions are legally worthless. I do not care if you are the most caring doctor in your state. I do not care if you volunteer at free clinics on weekends. I do not care if patients write you love letters. When the board investigator opens your chart six months after a patient complaint, they are not reading it to find evidence of your good heart. They are reading it to see if the care looks sloppy, thoughtless, or commercially motivated. The chart either proves you practiced medicine, or it proves you processed a transaction. There is no middle ground.

Let me paint you a picture. A forty-seven-year-old woman comes to your clinic asking about BPC-157 for a rotator cuff issue that has been bothering her for eight months. She saw it online. She read the forums. She watched the videos. She is motivated, polite, and willing to pay cash. You talk to her for twenty minutes. You explain that the evidence is mostly preclinical. You explain that it is compounded, not FDA-approved for this indication. You go over the risks. She seems to understand. You prescribe a twelve-week course. She leaves happy. Three months later she has not improved much, she is annoyed at the money she spent, and she mentions your name in a Facebook group where another member tells her to file a complaint with the state board because "that stuff isn't even approved." Now the board opens a file.

Six months after you saw that patient, you get the letter. The investigator asks for the chart. You pull it up. What does it say? If it says "CC: shoulder pain. Wants BPC-157. Discussed risks. Patient consented. Rx sent to pharmacy," then you are in trouble. Deep trouble. Because what you remember as a thoughtful twenty-minute conversation looks on paper like a sales transaction. The board reviewer - who does not know you, does not like peptide therapy, and has seen a hundred charts just like this from doctors who turned out to be pill mills - reads that note and sees a pattern they already believe exists. You meant well. The chart makes you look like a vial shop.

The board reviewer is not your enemy personally, but they are not your friend either. They have a caseload. They have seen charts from doctors who were genuinely reckless. They have seen charts where patients died because nobody screened for anything. They have seen charts where staff wrote the notes and the physician signed without reading. When they open your chart, they are looking for confirmation that you fit the pattern or evidence that you do not. A thin chart is an admission that you fit the pattern. A thick, thoughtful, clinically detailed chart is the beginning of a different conversation.

Think about it from the reviewer's perspective. They are sitting in an office with a stack of charts. They have a checklist. Was there a history? Was there an exam? Was there documented clinical reasoning? Were alternatives discussed? Was consent obtained? Was follow-up planned? If your chart answers every one of those questions before they even ask them, you have changed the tone of the entire review. Now they are looking at a physician who takes documentation seriously. Now they are looking at someone who might actually be practicing medicine. That does not guarantee they close the file - nothing guarantees that - but it means the conversation starts from a completely different place.

The problem is that physicians confuse their internal experience with the external record. You know you had a good conversation. You know you screened her. You know you explained the limits of the evidence. But the chart does not know what you know. The chart only knows what you wrote down. And what you wrote down is the only thing that exists in the legal universe. Memory fades. Witnesses change their stories. Patient recollections shift to suit their current grievance. The chart is the only permanent record, and it had better tell the whole story because nobody else is going to tell it for you.

I have heard doctors say, "But my patients trust me. They would never complain." That is adorable. Really, it is touching. Let me introduce you to reality. Patients complain when they are disappointed. Patients complain when a side effect they were not prepared for hits them at two in the morning. Patients complain when their spouse asks how much they spent and the answer makes them feel foolish. Patients complain when they join an online group where everyone is trashing the doctor they just saw. Trust evaporates when the bill feels too high and the result feels too low. The patient who hugged you on the way out the door is the same patient who will write a complaint that triggers a board investigation if things do not go the way they expected. Your only protection is the chart you built while they still liked you.

Here is another scenario to keep you up at night. A patient files a complaint not about you, but about your nurse practitioner. Or your physician assistant. Or your "wellness coordinator" who has been giving medical advice over the phone without your knowledge. The board investigates the whole practice. They pull every chart. Not just the one that triggered the complaint. Every chart. The one you wrote carefully matters, but so do the seventeen your staff wrote while you were seeing other patients. If those charts look like sales receipts, the investigation expands. Now they are looking at your whole operation. The one careful chart gets lost in the sea of thin documentation. Your practice looks like a vial shop with one good note. That is not a defense. That is evidence of inconsistency at best, and the good note starts to look like the exception that proves the rule.

The chart is not just a record of what happened. It is the proof that what happened was medicine. The distinction between medical practice and retail transaction is documentation. That is it. That is the whole difference. Two doctors can make the exact same clinical decision. One documents the reasoning, the screening, the alternatives, the consent, the follow-up, and the stop criteria. The other writes "Rx sent." If both get investigated, one goes home and the other hires a lawyer they cannot afford. Which one do you want to be?

The time to care about your chart is not when the letter arrives. By then it is too late to fix anything. The time to care is while you are still in the room with the patient, or while you are finishing the note that same day before the details blur. Every note you write should be written as if a stranger with authority over your license is going to read it and question every word. Because someday, one will.

A good defense lawyer works with a clean chart; a bad chart forces reliance on memory and hope

I want you to imagine something. You are sitting in a conference room with mahogany furniture and bad coffee. Across from you is a defense attorney who costs eight hundred dollars an hour. They are looking at your chart because a patient filed a complaint six months ago and the state board wants answers. The attorney turns to you and says, "Walk me through what happened." You start talking. You remember the conversation. You remember the patient's questions. You remember explaining that the peptide was investigational. You remember going over the side effects. You sound credible because you are telling the truth.

Then the attorney holds up the chart and says, "Where is any of this?"

That is the moment everything changes. A good defense attorney can take a clean chart and build a fortress around it. The chart speaks for itself. It shows evaluation. It shows reasoning. It shows consent. It shows follow-up. The attorney does not need your memory because the chart proves the care was thoughtful. The attorney can point to specific entries and say, "Look here. The physician documented the chief complaint. Look here. The physician documented prior treatments and why they failed. Look here. The physician documented the alternatives discussed. Look here. The patient signed an informed consent after a documented conversation." That attorney is playing offense. They are showing the board that this doctor did everything right and wrote it down.

But if the chart says "Patient wants BPC-157. Rx sent to pharmacy. F/u PRN," that attorney is now playing defense with nothing but your word against a complaint. They cannot point to the documented clinical reasoning because there is not any. They cannot show the board that alternatives were discussed because the chart does not mention alternatives. They cannot demonstrate that informed consent was meaningful because the chart has no record of what was said. Now the attorney is hoping that you are a good witness, that the patient does not show up with a sympathetic story, that the board reviewer is having a good day, and that no other complaints surface. That is not a legal strategy. That is prayer.

Memory is the worst possible foundation for a legal defense. I have been a paralegal for forty years. I have watched witnesses who were absolutely certain about what happened crumble under cross-examination when confronted with documents that said something different. You might remember telling the patient about the risks. But if the chart does not say so, and the patient testifies that you never mentioned risks, now we have a he-said-she-said situation that rarely ends well for the physician. The patient is the consumer. The patient is the one the board is theoretically protecting. When the patient says "He never told me" and the chart is silent, the patient wins that argument almost every time.

And here is something most physicians do not think about: your memory gets worse under stress. When you are sitting in a deposition room with a court reporter typing every word, when the plaintiff's attorney is asking you the same question five different ways to see if your story changes, when you have not slept well in weeks because your license is on the line -that is when you need your memory to be perfect. It will not be. Stress degrades recall. Time degrades recall. The chart does not degrade. The chart is exactly what it was the day you wrote it. If it was thorough then, it is thorough now. If it was thin then, it is devastating now.

A clean chart does something else that physicians rarely appreciate: it signals professionalism to everyone who touches the case. The board reviewer sees it and thinks, "This doctor takes documentation seriously." The defense attorney sees it and thinks, "I can work with this." The plaintiff's attorney sees it - and yes, they see it during discovery - and thinks, "This might be harder than I thought." Even the expert witness the board hires to review your care looks at a clean chart differently. They can disagree with your clinical judgment, but they cannot credibly say you were careless if every note shows thought, screening, and patient education. A clean chart does not guarantee victory, but it shifts the burden. Instead of you proving you were careful, the other side has to prove you were not. That is a completely different fight.

I have watched attorneys spend forty hours preparing a doctor for deposition when the chart was thin. They have to reconstruct the conversation. They have to coach the physician on how to explain why the note does not reflect the care. They have to prepare for every possible attack on the physician's credibility. That preparation costs a fortune. It also puts the physician in the position of having to testify about what they remember, which opens them up to impeachment if they get a single detail wrong. Compare that to the attorney who spends four hours reviewing a clean chart with the physician and says, "Just tell them what the chart says."The chart does the talking. The physician confirms it. End of story.

The financial difference is staggering. A board investigation with a bad chart can cost fifty thousand dollars in legal fees before you even get to a hearing. A malpractice case with a thin chart can settle for amounts that would make you sick, not because the care was bad but because the chart made it impossible to prove the care was good. A clean chart can end an investigation before it ever reaches a hearing. I have seen it happen. The board gets the chart, sees that everything was documented properly, and closes the file with a letter saying no further action is needed. That letter is worth more than every minute you spent writing thorough notes.

You do not defend the care you remember - you defend the care the chart proves

This is the foundational principle of medical-legal defense, and if you remember nothing else from this chapter, remember this: you do not defend the care you remember. You defend the care the chart proves. Period. Full stop. The end. Your memory is not evidence. Your good intentions are not evidence. Your reputation is not evidence. The chart is the only evidence that counts, and the chart either proves you practiced medicine or it proves you processed orders.

Think about what that means in practical terms. It means every note you write is a legal document. It means the standard for your documentation is not "did I remember to write something down?" The standard is "if a stranger read this note without knowing me, would they conclude that I practiced thoughtful, individualized medicine?" If the answer is no, you have not finished the note.

This principle applies to every single entry in the medical record. The initial consultation note. The follow-up phone call. The lab review. The refill decision. The email exchange. The text message. All of it. Every piece of documentation is either building your defense or creating a vulnerability. There is no neutral ground. A note that says "Patient called with question.

Answered." is a wasted opportunity and a potential liability. A note that says "Patient called reporting mild nausea since dose increase to 1.0 mg tirzepatide. Advised to increase fluid intake, take with food, hold dose for 48 hours and resume at 0.5 mg. Follow-up call scheduled in 72 hours. Patient verbalized understanding." is a completely different document. Both notes take about the same time to write if you are in the habit of writing thoroughly. But one of them proves you practiced medicine, and the other proves you answered a phone.

The distinction matters because board reviewers and plaintiff attorneys look for patterns. One thin note among fifty thorough notes is a bad day. Twenty thin notes among thirty thorough notes is a pattern. Fifty thin notes is a practice standard, and not a good one. When I review charts for physicians who are worried about their liability exposure, the first thing I look for is consistency. Does every note show the same level of care? Does every patient get screened? Does every consultation document the same elements? Or does the quality of documentation vary wildly depending on how busy the physician was, how interested they were in the case, or whether the staff wrote the note instead of the doctor?

Inconsistent documentation is actually worse than consistently mediocre documentation. Consistently mediocre documentation suggests a physician who does not understand documentation standards. Inconsistent documentation suggests a physician who understands the standards but only applies them when it is convenient. The board reviewer looks at the good notes and the bad notes and asks a devastating question: "If this doctor knows how to document properly - and these good notes prove they do - then why didn't they document properly for this patient?" Now the argument becomes selective care. Now the argument becomes that this particular patient did not get the same careful evaluation that other patients received. That is a much harder defense than simply being sloppy all the time.

The chart also has to prove continuity of care. A single excellent note is not enough. The board wants to see that the care was supervised over time. That means your follow-up notes matter just as much as your initial consultation. I have seen initial notes that were beautifully written- thorough history, detailed clinical reasoning, excellent consent documentation - followed by follow-up notes that said "Doing well. Refill sent." That follow-up note destroys the credibility of the initial note. If you were so careful at the beginning, why are you so casual now? Did the patient's payment clear, so now you do not need to be as thorough? That is what the reviewer wonders. The follow-up note has to show the same level of attention. What did the patient report? What symptoms? What side effects? What labs were reviewed? What was the clinical assessment? What was the plan? What are the stop criteria? Every single follow-up is an opportunity to reinforce that you are supervising medical care, not processing refills.

Here is something else that physicians miss: the chart has to prove that the physician was the one making the decisions, not the staff. I will cover this in more detail later, but it belongs in this discussion because it is central to what the chart proves. If your chart has notes written in the voice of a salesperson - "Patient excited to start program. Coordinated pharmacy shipment." - then the chart proves that your practice operates like a wellness retail business, not a medical practice. Medical notes should sound like medical notes. They should reflect clinical thinking, not customer service. The physician's name on the note means the physician's judgment is in the note. If the note sounds like it was written by someone whose previous job was selling gym memberships, that is a problem whether the physician signed it or not.

The chart should not sound defensive - it should sound clinical and thorough

Now I need to tell you something that might seem contradictory given everything I just said about building a legal defense: your chart should not sound like it was written by a lawyer. It should sound like it was written by a careful physician. There is a difference, and that difference matters a great deal.

A defensive-sounding chart is almost as bad as a thin chart. When a note reads like the physician was trying to cover their posterior rather than document clinical care, it sends a message. It says, "This doctor was worried about being sued when they wrote this." That is not the impression you want to create. A note that says "Due to the investigational nature of this compounded peptide therapy which is not FDA-approved for this indication and carries unknown risks, the patient was extensively counseled regarding all possible adverse outcomes including but not limited to..." sounds like a legal document, not a medical record. It sounds like you were afraid of the therapy. It sounds like you were documenting for a lawyer, not for patient care.

Compare that to a note that says: "Patient presents with chronic shoulder tendinopathy, eight months duration, failed physical therapy and NSAID trial. Imaging shows partial-thickness supraspinatus tear. Patient is not a surgical candidate due to preference and occupational constraints. Discussed BPC-157 as a compounded option with limited human evidence but reasonable preclinical support for soft-tissue healing. Reviewed that this is not FDA-approved for this indication, that evidence is primarily animal studies, that results are variable, and that standard options including continued PT and corticosteroid injection remain available. Patient elects to proceed after discussion. Baseline pain score 6/10. Stop criteria: no improvement at 8 weeks, any new neurological symptoms, or patient request to discontinue. Follow-up in 4 weeks with pain score and functional assessment." That note does not sound defensive. It sounds clinical. It sounds like a physician thought about the patient, evaluated the options, made a reasoned decision, documented the rationale, and set clear parameters. It also happens to be a legal fortress.

The difference is subtle but critical. The defensive note is written to avoid blame. The clinical note is written to document care. The defensive note uses legal language because the physician is thinking about the board. The clinical note uses medical language because the physician is thinking about the patient. Paradoxically, the clinical note is the better legal defense because it proves that the physician was practicing medicine, not practicing law. Board reviewers are physicians too, most of the time. They know what a good note looks like. They can smell a note that was written to survive a hearing from a mile away, and it makes them suspicious.

Write for patient care, and let the legal protection be a byproduct. That is the secret. When you document because you want to provide excellent, continuous, thoughtful medical supervision, your notes will naturally contain everything a defense attorney needs. The clinical reasoning will be there because you actually did the reasoning. The alternatives will be documented because you actually discussed them. The consent will be thorough because you actually educated the patient. The follow-up will be specific because you actually planned to follow up. The chart is unbreakable not because you were trying to build a legal shield, but because you were practicing medicine at a high standard and documenting it honestly.

The best notes I have ever reviewed - the ones that made me confident a physician could survive any investigation - shared one quality: they read like the physician cared about the patient and wanted the next provider to understand exactly what was going on. That is clinical documentation at its best. It serves patient care first, and the legal protection emerges naturally. If you write notes thinking only about the board, your notes will sound like you were thinking only about the board. If you write notes thinking about the patient, your notes will sound like medicine. And medicine, practiced well and documented thoroughly, is the strongest legal defense there is.

The tone of the chart matters in another way too. Notes that are judgmental, dismissive, or angry create their own problems. I have seen notes that said "Patient is demanding and unreasonable, refused all sensible options." Maybe the patient was demanding. Maybe they were unreasonable. But writing that in the chart makes you look unprofessional. It makes it look like you let your emotions affect your care. A better note: "Patient expressed strong preference for specific therapy after online research. Discussed limitations of available evidence, regulatory status, and standard alternatives. Patient declined standard options and requested time to consider. Offered follow-up appointment to continue discussion." Same situation, completely different tone. One note creates a problem. The other documents a boundary while maintaining professionalism.

Remember this: the chart is a permanent record that can be read by anyone with a subpoena. The patient can read it. Their attorney can read it. The board can read it. The media can read it if things go badly enough. Every word you write should be a word you are comfortable having read back to you in a deposition room, on a witness stand, or in a newspaper article. If you would not say it out loud in a professional setting, do not write it in the chart. If it sounds defensive, angry, or dismissive, rewrite it. The chart should sound like the work of a physician who takes their work seriously, treats patients with respect, and documents with precision. That is the voice of someone who keeps their license.

What Every Chart Must Contain

Now that I have beaten you over the head with why the chart matters, let me tell you exactly what needs to be in it. Not in vague, academic terms. In specific, concrete, "here is what you write down" terms. Every chart for every peptide patient must contain certain elements. Skip any of them and you have created a gap. Gaps are where investigations find purchase. Gaps are where plaintiff's attorneys drive trucks through your defense. Gaps are where board reviewers conclude that your care was incomplete. Fill every gap, every time, for every patient. No exceptions.

Chief complaint or patient goal - why are they here

The first line of every note should answer the most basic question in medicine: why is this person in front of you? Not what medication do they want. Not what program are they buying. Why are they here? What is the clinical problem they are trying to solve? This sounds so elementary that you might think it goes without saying. It does not. I have read hundreds of charts from peptide practices where the opening line was "Patient enrolled in weight-loss program" or "Patient requesting semaglutide." That is not a chief complaint. That is a purchase order.

A proper chief complaint identifies the clinical problem in medical terms. "Patient presents with obesity, BMI 34.2, weight-related hypertension and knee osteoarthritis, seeking medical weight management after failed dietary modifications." That is a chief complaint. It identifies the condition, gives it clinical context, and frames the visit as medical care. Or: "Patient reports chronic tendonopathy of right rotator cuff, eight months duration, interfering with sleep and work as construction supervisor, failed conservative management including eight weeks physical therapy and oral NSAIDs." That is a chief complaint. It tells the story. It sets up the clinical reasoning that will follow.

The chief complaint also needs to include the patient's goal, but that goal needs to be framed clinically. "Patient's stated goal is 40-pound weight loss to improve mobility and reduce joint pain" is very different from "Patient wants to lose weight." The first version gives you clinical endpoints to measure. The second version gives you nothing. When you document the patient's goal specifically, you create the basis for measuring outcomes. You also create the basis for managing expectations. If the patient's goal is forty pounds and your clinical assessment suggests that twenty pounds would be a success given their medical history, that conversation belongs in the note. "Discussed realistic weight-loss expectations based on patient's age, medical history, and prior attempts. Patient agrees that 15-20 pound reduction with maintained lean mass would represent meaningful success. Will reassess at 12 weeks." Now you have documented expectation management. That single sentence can prevent a complaint from ever happening, because when the patient loses eighteen pounds instead of forty, the chart shows they agreed that eighteen was success.

I also want you to document where the patient heard about the therapy. This is not idle curiosity. It is clinically relevant and legally protective. "Patient reports learning about BPC-157 through online research and a podcast. States she has read forum discussions but has not purchased any products online. Advised against research-use-only products and grey-market purchases. Patient verbalizes understanding." That sentence does two things. It explains why the patient is asking about a specific therapy, and it documents that you warned them against the grey market. If the patient later buys something online and gets hurt, the chart shows you told them not to. If the patient testifies that they thought your prescription was just like what they saw online, the chart shows you distinguished legitimate pharmacy channels from internet vendors. That is protective documentation.

Relevant history, prior treatments, and why standard options failed or were refused

This section is where you prove that you did not just hand over a vial because the patient asked for it. This is where you demonstrate medical reasoning. The history must be relevant to the clinical problem, but "relevant" in peptide therapy is broader than many physicians think. You are not just documenting the shoulder pain or the weight history. You are documenting the clinical journey that brought this patient to your door. And that journey matters because it explains why a non-standard therapy is being considered.

For a weight-loss patient, the relevant history includes: current weight and BMI, highest adult weight, weight history over the past five years, prior weight-loss attempts with specific methods and outcomes, current diet and exercise patterns, relevant medical conditions (diabetes, hypertension, sleep apnea, joint disease, cardiovascular risk), current medications including anything that affects weight, family history of obesity and related conditions, and psychological factors including eating disorder history. That is a lot of information. It is all relevant. A patient who has tried commercial diets, medically supervised programs, exercise programs, and medication without sustained success has a very different clinical picture from a patient who has never tried anything and wants an injection to avoid trying. The chart needs to show which patient you are treating.

For a soft-tissue injury patient, the relevant history includes: mechanism of injury, duration of symptoms, prior treatments tried and for how long, imaging results, specialist consultations, current functional limitations, occupational demands, medication trials, physical therapy course and outcomes, injection history, and surgical considerations. If the patient saw an orthopedist, that belongs in the chart. If the patient had an MRI, the result belongs in the chart. If physical therapy was prescribed but the patient only went twice, that belongs in the chart with the reason for poor compliance. "PT prescribed x8 weeks, patient attended 2 sessions citing work schedule, elected to discontinue. Discussed importance of rehabilitation, patient requests to explore peptide option before returning to PT." That sentence tells the story honestly and completely.

The critical element here is documenting why standard options failed or were refused. This is the foundation of your clinical rationale for considering a peptide. If standard options have not been tried, you need a reason why they are not appropriate, why they are not desired, or why the patient is not a candidate. "Patient declined corticosteroid injection due to concern about tendon weakening and prior negative experience with steroid injection in contralateral shoulder. Understands risks and limitations of alternative approach." That documents a reason. It does not just say the patient said no. It says the patient said no for a specific reason that you discussed and that makes clinical sense in the context of their case.

This documentation also protects you against the most common board criticism of peptide prescribing: that you skipped standard care to sell a cash-pay product. When the chart clearly shows that standard care was tried, failed, refused for good reason, or was not appropriate, you have answered that criticism before it is ever made. The reviewer sees the history and thinks,"This physician did not just jump to peptides. This patient had a journey, and the peptide was considered after that journey." That is exactly what you want them to think.

Clear clinical rationale for why this therapy is reasonable for this patient at this time

This is the heart of the note. This is where you prove you are a physician, not a distributor. The clinical rationale connects the patient's problem to the therapy you are prescribing in a way that makes medical sense. It does not need to be a dissertation. It needs to be a clear, logical chain of reasoning that a competent physician could follow and agree with.

Let me give you an example of a good clinical rationale. "Patient with chronic rotator cuff tendinopathy, 8 months, failed PT x8 weeks and NSAID trial. MRI shows partial-thickness tear <50%, not surgical candidate by orthopedist evaluation dated 3/15. BPC-157 discussed as compounded option with preclinical evidence for tendon healing and limited human safety data. Patient understands investigational status. Rationale for selection: specific soft-tissue injury with functional limitation, standard options exhausted or declined, patient motivated and compliant, no contraindications identified, PCP aware and supportive. Monitoring plan: pain score, range of motion, reassessment at 4 and 8 weeks with stop criteria defined." That is maybe eight sentences. It tells the whole story. It shows thought. It shows that the physician considered the patient as an individual and made a reasoned decision.

Compare that to "Patient wants BPC-157 for shoulder. Prescribed." That is not clinical reasoning. That is order entry. And if you think the difference does not matter, go back and reread section 7.1.

The clinical rationale needs to be patient-specific. It cannot be a boilerplate paragraph that you copy and paste into every note. Board reviewers can smell boilerplate from across the room. If your rationale for every single patient says the same thing, it proves you are not actually thinking about individual patients. You are filling in a template. A template is not clinical reasoning. It is documentation theater.

Patient-specific means tying the rationale to this person's actual medical situation. "Given patient's history of GLP-1 intolerance with prior semaglutide trial (discontinued at 0.5 mg due to severe nausea and dehydration requiring urgent care visit), tirzepatide microdosing at 0.5 mg weekly selected to assess tolerability of dual-incretin mechanism at lower exposure." That is specific to this patient. It references their actual history. It explains the clinical thinking behind the dose selection. It shows that the physician is not just following a protocol but adapting the protocol to the individual.

The clinical rationale also needs to address timing. Why now? Why is this the right moment to start this therapy? "Patient reports weight gain of 25 pounds over past 18 months following job change to sedentary position. BMI now 32.4. Fasting glucose elevated at 108. Hypertension newly diagnosed by PCP. Family history of type 2 diabetes in both parents. Patient motivated after recent health scare and ready to commit to lifestyle changes. Clinical window is favorable for aggressive intervention before metabolic syndrome fully develops." That explains why now. It shows medical urgency without being dramatic. It frames the peptide as part of a broader medical plan, not as an isolated product sale.

Alternatives discussed, risks explained, no-guarantee language documented

Every chart must contain evidence that the patient was given a real choice. That means alternatives were discussed, not just mentioned in passing. The discussion of alternatives needs to be documented specifically enough that a reviewer can see what the patient was actually told. "Discussed alternatives including continued physical therapy, corticosteroid injection, PRP injection, surgical evaluation, and doing nothing with activity modification. Patient declined PT due to prior poor response and work schedule constraints. Declined steroid injection due to concern about tendon integrity. Declined PRP due to cost. Declined surgery per orthopedist recommendation that tear is not surgical. Elected to proceed with BPC-157 after understanding investigational status and variable outcomes." That is a real discussion. It shows the patient had options. It shows the patient made an informed choice. It shows the physician did not just present one path.

The risk discussion needs to be equally specific. Do not write "risks discussed." That is worthless. Write what risks were discussed. "Discussed known risks including injection-site reaction, potential for angiogenesis-related concerns in patients with active or recent cancer (patient denies, no history), limited human safety data, unknown long-term effects, and possibility of no clinical benefit. Patient verbalizes understanding and accepts these risks." That is a risk discussion that proves you actually had the conversation.

The no-guarantee language is not just about protecting you legally, though it does that. It is about setting realistic expectations so the patient does not become a complainant later. "Patient counseled that BPC-157 does not guarantee healing, that results are variable, that some patients experience no benefit, that improvement if it occurs is typically gradual over 4-8 weeks, and that therapy will be discontinued if no meaningful improvement at 8-week reassessment." That language belongs in the chart. It also belongs in the informed consent, which we will cover in the next chapter. But the chart must show that this conversation happened during the clinical encounter, not just that the patient signed a form.

I want to emphasize something about alternatives: doing nothing is always an alternative, and you need to document that you discussed it. "Alternative of observation and continued conservative management discussed. Patient understands that partial-thickness tears can remain stable for long periods without intervention. Patient elects active treatment due to occupational demands requiring full range of motion and quality-of-life impact of current limitations." That sentence proves the patient knew they did not have to do this. They chose to. That distinction matters enormously when a patient later claims they felt pressured or that no alternatives were presented.

FDA or regulatory status disclosed in plain language

This element is non-negotiable and it belongs in the chart, not just on a consent form. The chart must reflect that you told the patient, in plain English, exactly what category their therapy falls into. FDA-approved? Off-label? Compounded? Investigational? Limited evidence? Say it clearly. Document that you said it. Document that the patient heard it and understood it. "Discussed FDA status: BPC-157 is not FDA-approved for any human indication. It is a compounded medication prepared by a licensed 503A pharmacy. Evidence for tendon healing is primarily preclinical animal studies with limited human data. Patient verbalizes understanding that this is not an FDA-approved treatment and that they are choosing to use a compounded product with investigational elements." That paragraph does several things. It uses the right regulatory language. It explains compounding status. It sets the evidence level honestly. And it documents patient understanding.

Different therapies require different disclosure language, and your chart needs to match the therapy to the language. For an FDA-approved drug used off-label, the disclosure might read:"Semaglutide is FDA-approved for type 2 diabetes and chronic weight management. Use for patient's specific goal of metabolic improvement with BMI 27.3 falls within approved indications. Discussed on-label status and appropriate use." For a compounded therapy that is not FDA-approved: "Tirzepatide is FDA-approved under branded products for specific indications. Patient's compounded formulation is prepared by a licensed 503A pharmacy and is not FDA-approved in this form. Patient understands difference between branded FDA-approved product and compounded formulation." For an investigational peptide: "Retatrutide is investigational and not FDA-approved. No FDA-approved dose exists. Any use is off-label and investigational. Patient understands they are participating in a therapy that has not completed FDA review." Each of these is honest, specific, and appropriate to the therapy category.

Do not use vague language like "patient informed of status." Status of what? Do not say"patient understands risks" without documenting which risks and which status. The disclosure needs to be specific enough that a reviewer can tell exactly what the patient was told. If the patient later claims they did not know the therapy was not FDA-approved, and your note says"Discussed that BPC-157 is not FDA-approved, is compounded by licensed pharmacy, evidence is limited, and patient verbalized understanding of investigational nature," the patient has a very hard time claiming ignorance.

Monitoring plan, follow-up schedule, and stop criteria before medication ships

This is where you prove that your peptide program is a medical supervision program, not a shipping service. The chart must contain a specific monitoring plan with concrete follow-up appointments and clear stop criteria before the patient ever receives their first dose. Not after. Before.

A monitoring plan needs to answer three questions: What are you measuring? When are you measuring it? What makes you stop? If your note does not answer all three, you do not have a monitoring plan. You have a wish.

For a GLP-1 weight-loss patient, the monitoring plan might look like this: "Monitoring: weight weekly by patient log, follow-up visit at 4 weeks with vitals and weight, 8-week visit with metabolic panel and assessment, then monthly while on therapy. Stop criteria: failure to lose >3% body weight by 12 weeks with good adherence, intolerable GI side effects at any effective dose, new gallbladder symptoms, signs of pancreatitis, pregnancy, patient request to discontinue, or new contraindication. Patient given written emergency instructions for severe abdominal pain, persistent vomiting, or signs of dehydration." That is a monitoring plan. It has measurements, timelines, and stop criteria. It proves medical supervision.

For a soft-tissue repair peptide, the monitoring plan might be: "Follow-up at 4 weeks with pain score (VAS), range of motion assessment, functional status questionnaire. Repeat at 8 weeks. Stop criteria: no improvement in pain or function by 8 weeks, new neurological symptoms, patient request to discontinue, or failure to comply with concurrent physical therapy. Will obtain repeat imaging at 12 weeks if clinical improvement plateaued." Again: measurements, timelines, stop criteria. Specific enough that anyone reading the chart knows exactly how this patient is being supervised.

The follow-up schedule must be actual scheduled appointments, not "follow up as needed" or"patient will call if problems." Those are not plans. Those are abdications. Even if the follow-up is a phone call or telehealth visit, it needs to be scheduled at a specific interval with a specific purpose. "Follow-up telehealth visit scheduled for 4 weeks to assess tolerance, side effects, and clinical response. Patient provided with direct clinical line for urgent concerns between visits." That is a follow-up plan.

The stop criteria are especially important because they prove that you are not just shipping medication indefinitely. You have defined the conditions under which therapy ends. Failure to respond. Intolerable side effects. New medical conditions. Noncompliance with monitoring. Patient request. Pregnancy. These are all legitimate stop criteria, and they need to be documented before therapy starts so it is clear you had a plan and the patient knew the plan. If the patient is still on therapy six months later with no follow-up documented, the chart makes it look like you abandoned supervision. Stop criteria documented up front prevent that appearance.

Before medication ships means this monitoring plan must be in the chart at the time of the initial prescription. Not added later when someone reminds you. Not documented at the first follow-up visit. In the initial note, where the prescription decision is made. Because if the board ever looks at your chart, the first thing they will check is whether the monitoring plan was contemporaneous with the prescription or was it added after a complaint arose. Contemporaneous documentation is credible. Retroactive documentation is suspect. Write it down when you write the prescription. Not tomorrow. Now.

Write as if a board reviewer who doesn't like you will read it

Let me ask you a question. When you write your chart notes, who do you picture reading them? Yourself, six months later? Your billing staff? Your partner if they cover for you? That is the wrong audience. Completely wrong. The person reading your chart is someone you have never met, who may have already decided they do not like peptide therapy, who has seen a hundred charts from doctors who turned out to be careless, and who is looking for a reason to close your file or escalate it. That is your audience. Write for them.

A skeptical stranger is not someone who wants to find you guilty. They are someone who has no reason to assume you are innocent. They are neutral-to-negative by default. They have a job to do, and that job is to protect the public from bad doctors. The fact that you are not a bad doctor is not their starting assumption. It is what your chart has to prove. So every note you write should be written with this question in mind: if a skeptical stranger read this, would they conclude that I practiced careful, individualized medicine? If the answer is anything less than an enthusiastic yes, the note is not done.

This mindset changes how you write. It changes what you include. It changes what you assume. You cannot assume the reader knows anything about the patient. You cannot assume the reader understands why you made a particular decision. You cannot assume the reader knows what was discussed in the visit. You have to tell them everything, clearly and concisely, in language that a physician outside your specialty can understand and respect.

The skeptical stranger test is simple. Before you close a note, read it out loud and pretend you are the board reviewer. Does the note explain why this patient, with this problem, at this time, got this therapy? Does it show that alternatives were considered? Does it show that risks were discussed? Does it show that the patient was screened for contraindications? Does it show a follow-up plan? Does it show that a physician was thinking, not just prescribing? If any of those questions get a no or a maybe, go back and add what is missing.

Here is what the skeptical stranger does not want to see. They do not want to see notes that read like sales receipts. They do not want to see identical notes for every patient. They do not want to see vague language that could apply to anyone. They do not want to see medical decisions without clinical reasoning. They do not want to see follow-up plans that say "PRN"or "as needed." They do not want to see risk discussions that say "risks discussed" without specifics. Every one of those patterns triggers suspicion, because those are the patterns they see from doctors who eventually get disciplined.

What they do want to see is documentation that reflects real clinical work. A history that is relevant and complete. An assessment that shows reasoning. A plan that is specific and patient-centered. A follow-up schedule that proves ongoing supervision. Education and consent that is documented in detail. When a skeptical stranger reads a note like that, even if they personally think peptides are nonsense, they have to acknowledge that the physician practiced medicine. They might not agree with the clinical decision, but they cannot say the decision was careless, thoughtless, or commercially motivated. And that is the standard you need to meet. Not "will they agree with me?" but "will they believe I was practicing medicine?"

Every note must show thought, screening, education, consent, follow-up, and boundaries

These six elements are the pillars of defensible documentation, and every single note should touch every single pillar. Not just the initial consultation. Every note. The follow-up visit, the phone call, the lab review, the refill decision, the email response. Every entry in the chart is an opportunity to demonstrate one or more of these pillars. Miss a pillar and you have created a gap. Gaps are what investigations exploit.

Thought means clinical reasoning. The note shows that the physician was thinking, not just reacting. "Patient reports 3-pound weight loss in week 3, mild nausea after dose increase to 1.0 mg. Clinical assessment: early response is encouraging, nausea is expected side effect at this dose level. Plan: hold dose at 1.0 mg for additional 2 weeks to allow GI adaptation rather than escalating to 1.7 mg as originally planned. Patient agrees. Reassess tolerance and weight at week 5 before considering further increase." That is a note that shows thought. It shows assessment. It shows a clinical decision based on patient response. It shows adaptation of the plan. Compare to: "Patient doing okay. Continue dose." Which one would you rather defend?

Screening means documented evidence that you checked for problems before making decisions. Every note should reflect ongoing screening, not just the initial intake. "Reviewed current medication list. No new medications. No drug interactions identified. No new medical conditions reported. Patient denies chest pain, shortness of breath, severe abdominal pain, or neurological symptoms. BP 128/82, HR 72. Screening negative for red flags." That is thirty seconds of documentation that proves you are paying attention. It also creates a contemporaneous record that the patient denied specific symptoms, which protects you if they later claim they told you about a symptom you ignored.

Education means documenting what you told the patient. Not just "educated patient." What did you educate them about? "Educated patient on proper injection technique, including site rotation, needle disposal, and hand hygiene. Observed patient perform practice injection. Technique acceptable. Reinforced importance of consistent dosing schedule and not double-dosing if a dose is missed." That is education. It proves you did more than hand over a vial. It proves you invested time in making sure the patient could use the medication safely.

Consent means documenting that the patient is participating voluntarily with understanding."Patient confirms ongoing satisfaction with therapy, reports understanding that therapy is not FDA-approved, confirms no new questions at this time, wishes to continue." That is a consent check-in. It does not need to be long. It just needs to show that the patient is still informed and still participating by choice. This is especially important at follow-up visits where patients might be tempted to claim later that they did not really understand what they were getting into. The chart shows they were reminded, they confirmed understanding, and they chose to continue.

Follow-up means specific, scheduled, purposeful next contact. I have hammered this point already but I will hammer it again because it is that important. Every note must end with a specific follow-up plan. Not "follow up as needed." Not "patient will call if problems." A date, a method, and a purpose. "Follow-up visit scheduled for 3/15, telehealth, 20 minutes, purpose: review 4-week weight log, assess side effects, review metabolic panel, discuss dose adjustment." That is a follow-up plan. Anyone reading it knows exactly what is supposed to happen next. If the patient no-shows, you document that too. "Patient no-showed for scheduled 3/15 follow-up. Staff called patient, left voicemail. Text sent with rescheduling link. Will attempt contact again in 48 hours. Refill on hold pending follow-up visit." Now the chart shows that you tried to supervise and the patient did not comply. That protects you.

Boundaries means documenting what your practice is not doing. This is the most overlooked element of documentation, and it is one of the most protective. "Patient reminded that this practice provides peptide therapy oversight and is not a substitute for primary care. Patient's PCP, Dr. Smith, copied on care summary. Patient directed to PCP for hypertension management and routine preventive care." That sentence establishes boundaries. It shows that your practice knows its role and stays in its lane. It shows that the PCP is involved. It shows that you are not trying to be the patient's everything doctor. Board reviewers love this because it demonstrates professional maturity and appropriate scope.

Staff may gather information but the physician must review, own, correct, and sign every note

This is where a lot of practices get into trouble they never saw coming. Staff gathering information is fine. Staff taking vital signs is fine. Staff administering questionnaires is fine. Staff entering data into the chart is fine. But the medical note - the clinical assessment, the plan, the rationale, the prescription decision - belongs to the physician. Not the nurse practitioner acting on autopilot. Not the physician assistant with a loose protocol. Not the"wellness coordinator" who used to sell supplements. The physician.

Board reviewers can smell a staff-written note from across the room. The language is wrong."Patient is super excited to start their wellness journey! We got them all set up with their peptide program and the pharmacy will ship tomorrow!" That is not a medical note. That is a customer service email. It does not belong in a medical chart. Ever. If that note is signed by a physician, the board reviewer assumes one of two things: either the physician wrote it and does not know what a medical note sounds like, or the physician signed something they did not write and probably did not read. Neither assumption is good for the physician.

The rule is simple and non-negotiable: staff may gather information, but the physician must review it, own it, correct it if necessary, and sign it personally. That signature means "I reviewed this. I agree with it. I stand behind it." If the physician cannot honestly say those three sentences about a note, they should not sign it.

I understand that you are busy. I understand that chart review takes time. I understand that your staff is competent and well-trained. None of that matters. Your signature on a medical note is a legal attestation that you reviewed the information, made the clinical judgment, and documented your own thinking. If the staff did the thinking and you just signed, that is not physician oversight. That is delegation of medical decision-making, and it is exactly what board investigators look for when they are building a case against a practice.

The practical workflow should look like this. Staff completes intake, enters data, takes vitals, and prepares a note template with the gathered information. The physician reviews the template, adds their own clinical assessment, modifies the plan based on their medical judgment, completes the clinical reasoning section, and signs the note. If the physician disagrees with something the staff documented - "Patient denies all medical problems" when the patient actually told the staff about their diabetes - the physician corrects it before signing. That correction is itself evidence of physician review. It shows the physician was paying attention.

What you must never allow is a practice where staff write the clinical note and the physician signs a stack of them at the end of the day without reading. I have seen this. The physician gets a pile of twenty notes to sign. They sign them all in ten minutes while thinking about dinner. If one of those patients later complains and the note contains errors, inaccuracies, or language that makes the practice look like a retail operation, the physician's signature is on it. The physician cannot then claim they did not write it. The signature says they reviewed and approved it. They are bound by what it contains.

Electronic health records make this problem worse in some ways. The copy-and-forward function, the smart phrases, the templates - they all make it easy for staff to create notes that look physician-generated but are actually staff-assembled. A board reviewer who looks closely can often tell. The vitals section is perfect but the assessment section is generic. The plan section references a medication the physician has never prescribed. The follow-up plan contradicts something in the practice's own protocol. These inconsistencies suggest that the note was assembled by someone who did not fully understand the clinical context. If the physician signed it anyway, that is on the physician.

The fix is straightforward but requires discipline. Every note gets physician review before it is signed. No exceptions. No batch-signing without reading. No rubber stamps. If the note does not reflect the physician's own clinical thinking, the physician rewrites it. If the staff consistently produces notes that require heavy correction, the staff needs retraining. The chart is too important to trust to someone who treats it like customer service paperwork.

Never let the chart look like a sales receipt

This is the cardinal sin of peptide documentation, and I see it constantly. Notes that read like invoices. Notes that document what the patient bought, not what the physician evaluated. Notes that list products and prices instead of diagnoses and plans. If your chart could be mistaken for a sales receipt from a supplement store, you are doing it wrong, and you are creating evidence that will be used against you.

A sales receipt chart has certain telltale features. It starts with the product, not the patient."Semaglutide 2.5 mg vial, 10-week supply, $1,200." That is not a chief complaint. That is a line item. It does not contain a medical history. It does not contain clinical reasoning. It does not document alternatives or consent. It documents a transaction. The follow-up notes are equally empty. "Refill approved." "Patient wants to continue." "Sent to pharmacy." None of those are medical supervision notes. They are order processing logs.

The problem with sales receipt charting is that it proves exactly what you do not want to prove. It proves that your practice operates as a product distribution business with a medical license attached. Board investigators see those charts and their eyes light up. This is easy, they think. This doctor is not practicing medicine. This doctor is selling peptides. And once that impression is formed, everything else gets scrutinized more aggressively. The pharmacy relationships. The advertising. The pricing. The staff roles. The physician's prescribing patterns compared to their medical training. The investigation expands because the chart gave them reason to expand it.

The opposite of a sales receipt is a medical record. A medical record tells the patient's story. It documents the clinical problem, the evaluation, the reasoning, the decision, the consent, the plan, the follow-up, and the outcomes. It reads like medicine because it is medicine. Even when the therapy itself is controversial or the evidence is limited, a medical record proves that the physician approached the patient as a patient, not as a customer.

I want to give you a concrete example of how to transform a sales receipt note into a medical note. Here is the sales receipt version: "New patient consult. Wants semaglutide for weight loss. BMI 33. No contraindications. Rx semaglutide 0.25 mg weekly, titrate per protocol. Sent to pharmacy. F/u in 4 weeks."

That note takes thirty seconds to write. It also takes thirty seconds for a board reviewer to conclude that no real medical evaluation occurred. Now here is the medical version: "Patient presents for medical weight management. Chief complaint: 35-pound weight gain over 3 years, BMI now 33.2, associated with new-onset hypertension and knee pain. History: tried commercial diet programs x2 without sustained success, walking program limited by knee pain, no prior obesity pharmacotherapy. Medical history: HTN, OA bilateral knees. Medications: lisinopril 10 mg daily. Family history: mother with type 2 diabetes. Assessment: obesity class I with weight-related comorbidities, metabolic risk, functional limitation. Discussed treatment options including structured lifestyle modification, GLP-1 therapy with semaglutide, and referral to bariatric surgery evaluation. Patient declines surgery, requests medical therapy. Semaglutide selected: FDA-approved for chronic weight management, appropriate for BMI >30 with comorbidity, strong evidence base, manageable side effect profile. Discussed mechanism, expected benefits, common side effects (nausea, constipation, GI upset), rare but serious risks (pancreatitis, gallbladder disease), need for injection self-administration, dietary modifications required, no guarantee of specific weight loss. Patient verbalizes understanding, agrees to trial. Rx: semaglutide 0.25 mg subcutaneous weekly, titrate 0.25 mg every 4 weeks as tolerated to target 1.7-2.4 mg. Baseline weight 198 lbs, BP 138/86. Monitoring: weight log weekly, follow-up visit at 4 weeks with vitals and side effect review, metabolic panel at 8 weeks. Stop criteria: <5% weight loss at 6 months, intolerable side effects, new contraindication, patient request. PCP Dr. Martinez notified and supportive. Patient given written emergency instructions and injection training materials. Follow-up scheduled 3/15."

That note takes maybe five minutes to write. It proves that the physician practiced medicine. It documents every element we have discussed. It would survive any board review because it leaves nothing to imagination or memory. It is not defensive. It is clinical. It is thorough. It is the difference between keeping your license and hiring an attorney.

The sales receipt note costs you thirty seconds and potentially your career. The medical note costs you five minutes and protects everything you have built. You tell me which one is the better investment.

Common Charting Mistakes That Sink Doctors

I have spent four decades watching physicians destroy themselves with documentation that ranged from sloppy to reckless. Most of them were not bad doctors. Most of them were careless about paperwork because they thought their clinical skill would protect them. It does not. This section is where I tell you the specific mistakes that show up again and again in board investigations, malpractice cases, and criminal prosecutions. Every single one of these is avoidable. Every single one has ended a career. Learn from other people's disasters so you do not become one.

Notes that only say "patient wants medication" - that's not clinical reasoning

This is the most common and most deadly charting mistake in peptide practice. A note that identifies the patient's request but never documents the physician's clinical reasoning. "Patient wants semaglutide. Prescribed." "Patient interested in BPC-157. Rx sent." "Patient heard about peptides online. Started on program." These notes prove one thing and one thing only: the patient asked for something and the physician gave it to them. That is not medicine. That is a vending machine.

When the only documented indication for a prescription is patient desire, you have no defense. None. The board reviewer reads that note and thinks, "The patient wanted it and the doctor prescribed it. Where is the medical evaluation? Where is the clinical assessment? Where is the reasoning?" If those elements are not in the chart, they do not exist. The patient wanted something, the doctor sold it to them. That is the story the chart tells. And that story ends with a disciplinary hearing.

The fix is clinical reasoning. Every single prescription note must contain a sentence that starts with "Rationale for selection..." or "Clinical indication..." or "Therapy selected because..."That sentence must connect the patient's medical condition to the prescribed therapy through a logical chain that any competent physician could follow. Not "Patient requested." Not "Patient interested in." The clinical problem drives the therapy. The patient's request starts the conversation, but the physician's clinical judgment justifies the decision. If the chart does not show that transition from patient request to medical decision, it has failed its most basic purpose.

Here is the pattern I see over and over. A patient comes in asking about a peptide they saw online. The physician, wanting to be helpful and recognizing that the therapy might actually benefit this patient, has a good clinical conversation. They screen for contraindications. They discuss risks. They set expectations. They make a reasoned decision. Then they write the note in sixty seconds and it says "Patient wants BPC-157 for shoulder. No contraindications. Rx 500 mcg daily x6 weeks. F/u PRN." Everything that made it good medicine - the evaluation, the reasoning, the education, the consent - is gone. Erased by laziness. The physician remembers the good medicine. The chart proves a transaction. And when the complaint comes, the chart wins every time.

Staff writing physician notes - board reviewers can smell copy-paste from a mile away

I covered this in principle earlier, but now I want to show you exactly how it destroys physicians in practice. Staff-written or staff-assembled physician notes are a gift to board investigators. They are like a neon sign that says "We delegate medical decisions around here."And here is the thing: even if your staff is clinically sharp, even if they have been with you for years, even if you trust them completely - a note that sounds like it was written by someone other than the physician is a problem. Because the signature at the bottom says the physician wrote it, reviewed it, and stands behind it. If that is not true, you are lying on a medical record.

Copy-paste is the specific sin that reviewers spot instantly. The same assessment paragraph on twenty consecutive notes. The same plan language for every patient regardless of their individual situation. The same risk discussion, word for word, for every therapy. The same follow-up plan no matter what the patient's condition. This does not look like clinical documentation. It looks like a mail merge. And when a board reviewer sees identical clinical notes for different patients, they conclude - correctly - that the notes do not reflect individualized medical judgment. They reflect a template.

Template use is fine. Template abuse is lethal. A template should provide structure: the sections you need to fill in, the elements you need to address, the standard language for common disclosures. But the clinical content - the rationale, the assessment, the individualized plan -must be written by the physician for that specific patient. If I can take your note, change the patient's name, and have it make equal sense for a completely different patient, your note is not specific enough. If the board investigator can do the same thing, you are in trouble.

Let me give you a war story. A physician I consulted for had beautiful charts. Beautiful. Detailed histories, thorough consent documentation, excellent pharmacy due diligence. The problem was that every single assessment and plan section was identical for every patient receiving the same therapy. Word for word identical. The board investigator noticed on chart three. By chart ten, the investigator had concluded that the physician was not actually evaluating individual patients. The physician was applying a protocol and documenting it as individual care. The investigation expanded from a single patient complaint to a practice-wide review. The physician spent eighteen months and over a hundred thousand dollars defending what was actually good clinical care, because the documentation made it look like assembly-line medicine.

The rule is this: templates for structure, physician writing for substance. The chief complaint might start from a dropdown menu. The medication list might be entered by staff. But the clinical assessment, the rationale for therapy, the individualized elements of the plan - those must be in the physician's voice, reflecting the physician's thinking, specific to that patient on that day. If your note does not pass the "name swap test" - if swapping patient names does not create obvious nonsense - then your note is too generic and needs to be individualized.

I also want to address the "smart phrase" problem that electronic health records have created. Smart phrases are convenient. They let you insert pre-written text with a few keystrokes. They are also dangerous if they contain clinical content that you did not actually verify. I have seen smart phrases that say "Patient denies all red flag symptoms including chest pain, shortness of breath, severe abdominal pain, and neurological changes" get inserted into notes where the patient actually reported abdominal pain but the staff did not update the smart phrase. Now the chart says the patient denied something they actually reported. That is not just sloppy. That is a false medical record, and it is devastating when a patient later claims their symptoms were ignored.

If you use smart phrases - and most physicians do - they should contain only general, universally true language. "The risks, benefits, and alternatives of this therapy were discussed." That is fine because it is something you do every time. But "Patient denies chest pain, shortness of breath, severe headache, vision changes, and neurological symptoms" is only fine if you actually asked about every one of those symptoms and the patient actually denied them. If you inserted that phrase without asking, your chart is lying. And a lie in a medical record, even an accidental one created by a template, can destroy your credibility in a hearing.

Vague follow-up plans - "follow up PRN" is not a plan

Of all the sloppy habits I see in peptide practice, vague follow-up documentation is the one that causes the most preventable damage. "F/u PRN." "Patient will call if problems." "Follow up as needed." "See in 4-6 weeks." None of these are follow-up plans. They are abdications of medical supervision disguised as documentation. And they are read by board reviewers exactly that way. "Follow up PRN" means nothing. It means you have no plan. It means you are waiting for the patient to decide when they need you. That is not medical supervision. That is a suggestion box. A proper follow-up plan has three elements: a specific timeframe, a specific method, and a specific purpose. Without all three, you do not have a plan. "Follow-up visit scheduled for 4 weeks, telehealth, purpose: review weight log and side effects, assess clinical response, review labs, determine dose adjustment." That is a plan. It says when, how, and why. If the patient does not show up, you document the no-show and your attempts to reach them. Now the chart shows you had a plan and the patient did not comply. That protects you. "F/u PRN" with a no-show just looks like you did not care enough to schedule proper follow-up.

The purpose element is especially important because it proves medical intent. "Follow-up in 4 weeks" could be anything. It could be a social visit. It could be billing-driven. But "follow-up in 4 weeks to assess GI tolerability after dose escalation, review patient-kept weight and symptom log, obtain CMP to monitor metabolic markers, and make dose continuation or adjustment decision" proves that the follow-up is clinically driven. It is part of a medical supervision program. It is not just checking in to see if the patient wants more medication.

Stop criteria need to be documented as part of the follow-up plan. When does this therapy end? Under what conditions do you stop? If the chart shows ongoing refills with no reassessment documented, it looks like you are shipping medication indefinitely without medical oversight. But if the chart shows "Stop criteria: therapy to be discontinued if <3% weight loss by week 12, if intolerable side effects occur at any effective dose, if new contraindication develops, if patient becomes pregnant, or if patient misses two consecutive follow-up appointments" -now you have a framework for responsible prescribing. The patient knew the criteria. You documented the criteria. And if the patient kept getting refills past week 12 without documented reassessment, the chart at least shows you had a plan even if you failed to follow it. Having the plan and failing to follow it is a problem, but not having a plan at all is a much bigger problem.

I also want to address the specific problem of refill documentation. Every refill decision is a medical decision and must be documented as such. "Refill sent" is not documentation. "Refill approved after review of patient's 8-week follow-up visit: weight down 12 lbs, BP improved to 128/80, no significant side effects reported, labs within normal limits. Patient compliant with monitoring. Continue current dose. Next follow-up in 4 weeks." That is a refill decision. It shows review. It shows assessment. It shows ongoing supervision. The board reviewer reads that and thinks, "This physician is paying attention." They read "Refill sent" and think, "This physician is auto-shipping." Which impression do you want to create?

Cleaning up the chart after the complaint arrives - that's obstruction

Now we come to the mistake that transforms a bad situation into a potential crime. I am going to be very clear about this, and I want you to hear me because I have seen physicians go to prison for this one. When a complaint arrives, when you get the board letter, when the attorney sends the preservation notice - the chart is frozen. It is evidence. Touching it, changing it, adding to it, "clarifying" it, or "fixing" it is evidence tampering. It is obstruction. It is a crime in most jurisdictions. And it destroys your defense more completely than any original mistake ever could.

Here is how it happens. The physician gets the board letter. Panic sets in. They pull up the chart and realize the note is thin. They remember having a much more detailed conversation than what they documented. They think, "If I just add a few details, that will make the chart more accurate. I am not lying. I am correcting the record to reflect what actually happened."They add a paragraph. They update the risk discussion. They insert the alternatives they now remember discussing. They save the note.

Congratulations. They just committed a felony.

The electronic health record timestamps everything. Every edit, every revision, every addendum is logged with a date and time. When the board's forensic analyst pulls the audit trail - and they will - they will see that the note was modified three days after the complaint letter was received. They will see exactly what was added. They will see the original version and the revised version. And now the physician is not just defending the original care. They are defending why they altered a medical record after receiving notice of an investigation. That is a separate, additional charge. And it is much harder to defend than a thin note ever was.

The original thin note might have gotten you a reprimand or a fine. The altered note gets you a suspension or a revocation plus a criminal referral. I am not exaggerating. I have seen it happen. A physician who would have received a six-month probation for sloppy documentation instead lost their license permanently and faced criminal charges because they panicked and tried to fix the chart. The board does not tolerate record tampering. No regulator does. It goes to the heart of their authority. If physicians can alter records after complaints, the entire regulatory system collapses. They will make an example of anyone who tries.

The rule is absolute and has no exceptions. When you know or should know that a chart is subject to investigation, litigation, or regulatory review, you do not touch it. Period. You do not add an addendum. You do not correct a typo. You do not "clarify" anything. You call your attorney and you let them handle it. If your attorney wants you to create an addendum - and they might, for strategic reasons - they will tell you exactly how to do it, what to say, and how to document that it was created after the fact at counsel's direction. Doing it on your own is legal suicide.

Here is what an attorney-authorized addendum looks like: "Addendum prepared 4/3/2026 at direction of counsel after review of original note dated 9/15/2025. Original note is unchanged and appears above. This addendum is provided to clarify that at the time of the original visit, I also discussed [specific topic] with the patient, which I failed to document in the original note. This addendum does not alter the original record and is dated contemporaneously with its creation." That is a transparent, honest, legally supervised addendum. It does not hide that it was added later. It does not pretend to be part of the original note. It is a separate entry with its own date and context.

Compare that to what panicked physicians actually do: they open the old note, insert two paragraphs in the middle, save it, and hope nobody notices. The audit trail notices. The forensic analyst notices. The board notices. And your life gets destroyed over a documentation mistake that would have been survivable if you had just left it alone.

Let me tell you about the audit trail, because most physicians do not understand what it actually captures. Every modern electronic health record logs: when a note was created, when it was last modified, how many times it was modified, the date and time of each modification, which user made each modification, and in many systems, a complete before-and-after version history. Some systems even track what specific text was added, deleted, or changed in each edit. The board investigator does not just get your chart. They get the audit trail. They can see that you opened the note at 9:47 PM on Tuesday, spent fourteen minutes in edit mode, saved it at 10:01 PM, and the complaint letter was received on Monday. They know what you did. And when you sit in the deposition and deny changing anything, they produce the audit trail and your credibility evaporates.

The only thing worse than a bad chart is a bad chart that you tried to fix after the complaint arrived. If your chart is thin, your attorney works with a thin chart. Good attorneys have dealt with thin charts before. They know how to contextualize them, how to supplement them with affidavits and testimony, how to explain that documentation standards vary and that a thin note does not mean thin care. What they cannot fix is a chart with an evidence trail showing the physician tampered with it. That is unfixable. It is case-ending. It is license-ending. It is potentially freedom-ending.

So hear me on this. The day you get the letter, you stop editing charts. You call your attorney. You preserve everything. You let the professionals handle it. A thin chart is a problem. An altered chart is a catastrophe. If you remember nothing else from this entire chapter, remember this: do not clean up the chart after the complaint arrives. Your attorney would rather defend an honest mistake than a dishonest cover-up. Every single time.

Now let me circle back to where we started. The chart is your shield. Not your memory. Not your good intentions. Not your reputation. The chart. Build it strong from day one. Write every note as if a skeptical stranger will read it, because someday one will. Fill it with clinical reasoning, patient-specific assessment, documented education, specific consent, concrete follow-up plans, and clear stop criteria. Make it sound like medicine, not retail. Make it thorough enough that a defense attorney can build a fortress around it. Make it honest enough that you never need to alter it later.

The physicians who lose their licenses over peptide therapy rarely lose them because the therapy itself was indefensible. They lose them because the chart could not prove that anything medical actually happened. The difference between a physician who survives a board investigation and one who does not is almost never the clinical decision. It is the documentation of the decision. Write it down. Write it completely. Write it honestly. Write it like your license depends on it. Because it does.

8 - Informed Consent That Actually Protects You

Let me tell you something I have seen destroy more good physicians than bad medicine ever did: a consent form that nobody read, signed in a rush, and waved around like a magic shield the moment something went wrong. I have watched board investigators flip through thirty pages of legal gibberish, look up at the doctor, and ask the simplest question in the world:"Doctor, can you prove this patient understood what they were signing?" And when the doctor stammered something about the signature being on page twenty-eight, the investigator just nodded and made a note. That note turned into a consent-failure finding. That finding turned into a sanction. That sanction turned into a headline. And another good doctor's name got dragged through the mud because a piece of paper was treated like a get-out-of-jail-free card.

This chapter is about informed consent that actually works. Not consent that looks impressive. Not consent that fills a folder. Not consent that satisfies some lawyer's fantasy of what a lawsuit-proof document should look like. I am talking about consent that proves - to a skeptical board investigator, to a plaintiff's attorney, to a jury of regular people who have never injected anything in their lives - that your patient made a real, informed, voluntary choice to proceed with therapy. The kind of consent where, when someone asks what the patient understood, you can look them in the eye and say, "Let me show you what we discussed, what they acknowledged, and what questions they asked."

This is one of the three most important operational chapters in this book. Read it twice. Then build your consent process like your license depends on it - because it does.

Consent is proof that the patient made an informed voluntary choice

Here is the fundamental truth that too many physicians forget: informed consent is a process, not a document. The document is just the evidence that the process happened. It is the photograph of the conversation, not the conversation itself. And like any photograph, it only captures what was actually there. If the conversation was shallow, rushed, or delivered by a staff member who read from a script they did not understand, the photograph - no matter how many pages it contains - proves nothing except that paper got signed.

The legal standard for informed consent, which varies by state but follows a consistent pattern, asks whether a reasonable patient in those circumstances would have had enough information to make an informed decision about their care. Some states use a physician-based standard -what would a reasonable physician have disclosed? Others use a patient-based standard -what would a reasonable patient want to know? Either way, the question is about understanding, not about signatures. You think the board cares that you meant well? They care whether the patient knew what they were getting into. They care whether the risks were explained in a way that mattered. They care whether the patient had a real choice - not just a theoretical one, but a practical one where they could have said no and walked away without pressure.

Let me paint you a picture of what consent failure looks like in the real world. A forty-seven-year-old man comes to your clinic asking about semaglutide for weight loss. Your staff hands him a packet. It is twelve pages, single-spaced, written in language that would make a contracts professor proud. He signs it in four places, initials in six more, and hands it back. Nobody asks if he has questions. Nobody checks whether he understood that compounded semaglutide is not FDA-approved the same way Ozempic is. Nobody explains that pancreatitis is a real risk, not just a line item on a form. Three months later he is in the emergency room with severe abdominal pain. His wife finds the consent form in a drawer and shows it to a plaintiff's attorney. The attorney takes one look at it and sees exactly what I would see: a document designed to protect the clinic's lawyer, not to inform the patient. The lawsuit names the physician, the clinic, the staff member who handed over the form, and the pharmacy. And the consent form that was supposed to be your shield becomes Exhibit A in the case against you.

Now let me paint the opposite picture. Same patient, same therapy, different process. The physician sits down with him and says, "Let me explain what this medication is, where it comes from, what we hope it does, what could go wrong, and what your other options are. I want you to ask questions. I want you to think about it. I want you to talk to your primary care doctor before we move forward." The conversation takes twenty minutes. The consent form is clean, readable, and written in plain English. Every major risk has a checkbox the patient initials after the physician explains it. The form documents that alternatives were discussed, that the patient had time to ask questions, that they understood emergency warning signs, and that they voluntarily chose to proceed. Six months later, the same pancreatitis scenario occurs. But this time, when the attorney looks at the file, they see a patient who was informed, who acknowledged risks, who had a real conversation, and who made a choice with open eyes. The case settles for nuisance value or goes away entirely. That is the difference between consent theater and real consent.

The voluntary part matters just as much as the informed part. A patient who feels pressured -by staff urgency, by pricing that expires today, by social proof that "everyone is doing it," by the implicit message that declining means missing out - is not making a voluntary choice. They are making a compliance choice. And when things go wrong, that pressure becomes evidence that the consent was coerced, not voluntary. I have seen clinics where the intake process feels like a timeshare sales pitch: the patient arrives, gets swept through a beautiful presentation, meets a charismatic "consultant," and before they know what hit them, they have committed to six months of therapy and signed five documents. That is not medicine. That is a conveyor belt, and conveyor belts produce terrible consent.

Your consent process must demonstrate three things: that the patient was given sufficient information to make an informed decision, that they understood that information well enough to appreciate the risks and benefits, and that they made their choice freely without coercion or undue pressure. The document supports all three, but the document alone proves none of them. What proves them is the totality of the record: the chart note describing the conversation, the consent form with the patient's initials and signature, the documentation of questions asked and answered, the time allotted for decision-making, and the absence of any red flags suggesting pressure or haste.

A consent form that nobody understands is not strong - it's just long

I want to say this slowly so it sinks in: length is not strength. A twenty-page consent form written at a college reading level does not provide better consent than a four-page form written at a sixth-grade reading level. In fact, it almost certainly provides worse consent, because the longer and denser the document, the less likely the patient is to read it, understand it, or remember anything in it. You are not writing a legal brief. You are writing proof that a human being understood what they were agreeing to.

The research on health literacy is clear, and it is humbling. Roughly one-third of American adults have limited health literacy. That means they struggle to understand basic medical information, medication labels, and discharge instructions. Now hand that same person a consent form with sentences like "The patient acknowledges that the proposed therapeutic intervention carries risks including but not limited to those enumerated herein and that the enumerated risks may not be exhaustive." You might as well hand them a document in Sanskrit. They will sign it because they do not want to look stupid, because they trust you, or because they just want to get on with their day. But they do not understand it. And a signature on a document the patient did not understand is worth approximately nothing when the board comes calling.

Plain English is not dumbing things down. Plain English is respecting your patient's right to understand what is happening to their body. When you write "You could feel sick to your stomach, throw up, or have diarrhea" instead of "Gastrointestinal adverse events including nausea, emesis, and loose stools may occur," you are not insulting anyone's intelligence. You are speaking like a human being to another human being. The smartest patients in the world appreciate plain language because it leaves no ambiguity. The least literate patients need it because without it, they are signing blind. Everyone wins.

Let me give you a concrete example of what I mean. Here is how a bad consent form describes risk: "The administration of exogenous GLP-1 receptor agonists has been associated with pancreatitis, a potentially life-threatening inflammation of the pancreas, the incidence of which in clinical trials ranged from 0.1 to 0.4 percent depending on the comparator group and duration of exposure." Here is how a bulletproof consent form describes the same risk: "This medication can cause pancreatitis - swelling of the pancreas that can be serious and requires emergency care. Call us immediately or go to the emergency room if you have severe stomach pain that spreads to your back, especially with vomiting. This has happened in a small number of patients." Which one do you think the patient remembers? Which one do you think protects you when the plaintiff's attorney asks what the patient was told? The second version explains what pancreatitis is, what it feels like, and what to do about it. The first version reads like a textbook footnote that the patient skimmed over.

Every sentence in your consent form should pass a simple test: could a reasonably educated twelve-year-old understand it? If not, rewrite it. Could you explain this out loud to a patient in a way that makes them nod and say "Okay, I get it"? If not, rewrite it. Would you want your own mother signing this document without anyone walking her through it? If not, rewrite it. These are not low standards. These are the standards that separate physicians who keep their licenses from physicians who become cautionary tales.

The structure matters too. Dense paragraphs stacked on top of each other create visual fatigue. Patients stop reading after the second page. They start checking boxes without reading the text. They sign at the bottom because that is what the receptionist is pointing at. Your form should use short paragraphs, clear headings, white space, and checkboxes that force the patient to engage with each major point. Initials next to critical risks are better than a single signature at the end, because initials show the patient encountered each specific disclosure along the way.

And here is something most physicians never think about: the consent form should be written in the first person from the patient's perspective. "I understand that..." "I have been told that..." "I agree to..." This does two things. First, it forces the patient to mentally inhabit each statement, which improves comprehension and memory. Second, it creates a document where the patient is actively acknowledging understanding, not passively receiving information. When the board reads "I understand that compounded medications are not FDA-approved the same way branded medications are," they see a patient who claimed to understand a specific fact. When they read "The patient has been informed that compounded medications differ from FDA-approved products," they see a clinic that checked a box. The first version is stronger. Always.

A signature cannot turn a weak medical decision into a strong one

This is the hardest lesson for physicians to accept, and I am going to be blunt about it because I have seen too many doctors learn it the expensive way. If your medical decision was careless, poorly documented, or clinically indefensible, no consent form in the world will save you. The consent form is not a force field. It does not neutralize bad judgment. It does not transform a reckless prescription into a careful one. It does not convince a medical board that a patient who should have been screened out was actually appropriate because they signed on the dotted line.

I have heard physicians say things that make my blood run cold. "Well, the patient signed the consent." As if that erases a missed contraindication. As if that excuses a failure to review labs.

As if that makes up for prescribing an investigational compound to a patient with active cancer because they really wanted to try it. Let me be absolutely clear: a signature on a consent form is evidence of the patient's understanding and agreement. It is not evidence of your medical judgment. The board will evaluate your judgment separately, and if your judgment was poor, the consent form just becomes the document that proves the patient trusted you enough to say yes to something they should have been protected from.

Think about it from the board's perspective. Their job is to protect the public from unsafe practitioners. When they see a chart where a physician prescribed a compounded, limited-evidence peptide to a patient with multiple red flags - recent hospitalization, unmanaged diabetes, no PCP involvement, no prior conventional treatment attempts, unrealistic expectations - the board does not think "Well, at least the consent form was thorough." They think "This physician used a consent form to make an unsafe patient feel comfortable with an unsafe decision." And they are not wrong. That is exactly what a weak physician hiding behind a strong form looks like.

The consent form supports good medicine. It does not rescue bad medicine. If you would not want to explain this prescription to the board without a consent form, do not prescribe it with one. If the patient's history makes you uncomfortable, do not let a signed document soothe that discomfort. Your clinical gut exists for a reason. Trust it before you trust paper. I have said this before and I will say it again: when in doubt, say no. No consent form changes that rule.

Here is a practical test. Before you hand any patient a consent form for peptide therapy, ask yourself: if this patient's chart were reviewed tomorrow by a skeptical board investigator who already thinks peptide medicine is fringe, would the chart stand on its own? Would the medical reasoning be clear? Would the patient selection be defensible? Would the monitoring plan be appropriate? If the answer to any of those questions is no, fix the medicine first. Then write the consent. The consent documents a good decision. It does not create one.

This distinction matters in malpractice litigation too. A plaintiff's attorney will depose your patient and ask what they understood. If the patient says "I just signed what they told me to sign" or "I didn't really read it, it was a lot of pages" or "They made it sound like nothing could go wrong," your thirty-page consent form collapses like a house of cards. But if the patient says "The doctor sat with me for twenty minutes, explained every risk, told me to call my PCP, and said I could think about it and come back" - now you have something. The consent form supports a story about informed choice. But the story has to be true, and the medicine has to be sound, for the consent to matter.

The consent form does not replace the chart - both must be strong

This is where a lot of physicians create a dangerous gap. They invest enormous energy into their consent forms - beautiful documents, lawyer-reviewed, multi-page, comprehensive -and then they write chart notes that say "Consent obtained. Patient agrees to proceed." That is it. Two sentences. As if the consent form somehow did the charting for them. Let me disabuse you of that notion right now. The consent form and the chart serve different purposes, and both must stand independently.

The consent form is the patient's acknowledgment. It shows what the patient understood and agreed to. The chart is the physician's record. It shows what the physician thought, evaluated, decided, disclosed, and planned. The consent form is written from the patient's perspective -"I understand..." The chart is written from the physician's perspective - "I explained... I evaluated... I recommended..." Together they create a complete picture of the informed consent process. Either one alone leaves a hole that a skilled attorney or investigator will drive straight through.

Your chart note for every new peptide patient should document, at minimum: the patient's presenting concerns and goals; your evaluation including history, relevant screening, and contraindication review; the specific therapy discussed and why it was chosen over alternatives; the FDA status or regulatory status of the therapy and how you explained it; the risks discussed and how you explained them; the alternatives presented including doing nothing; the cost disclosed; the patient's questions and your responses; any recommendation to consult their PCP and the patient's response; the follow-up plan and monitoring schedule; emergency stop rules provided; and the patient's decision to proceed. That is a paragraph, maybe two. It takes five minutes to dictate. And it transforms your chart from a silent document into a speaking witness that tells the whole story.

I have seen board cases where the consent form was excellent but the chart was empty. The investigator's conclusion: "The clinic had a good template but no evidence the physician actually used it in a meaningful conversation with this patient." I have also seen cases where the chart was detailed but there was no signed consent. The investigator's conclusion: "The physician may have explained things well, but there is no proof the patient acknowledged understanding." You need both. The form proves the patient's participation. The chart proves the physician's process. Together they are bulletproof. Separately they are vulnerable.

This also means your consent forms and your chart templates need to align. If the consent form lists five specific risks and the chart note says "Risks discussed," there is a mismatch. If the consent form has the patient acknowledge they discussed the therapy with their PCP but the chart note says nothing about PCP outreach, there is a mismatch. These mismatches do not look like thorough care to a reviewer. They look like template-driven checkbox medicine where the left hand does not know what the right hand is doing. Align your documents. Make them tell the same story from complementary angles. That is how you build a record that survives scrutiny.

Let me close this section with a story that still keeps me up at night. A physician I knew -smart, caring, genuinely wanted to help his patients - got into peptide therapy because he saw people getting results. He had beautiful consent forms. Twenty pages, attorney-drafted, covered every risk under the sun. His charts, on the other hand, were two-line notes: "Patient counseled. Consent signed. Prescribed BPC-157." When a patient developed a serious adverse event and the board investigated, they found a disconnect that destroyed him. The consent form showed the patient checked a box acknowledging "unknown long-term risks with investigational therapies." But the chart showed no discussion of why an investigational therapy was chosen, what evaluation supported that choice, or what monitoring would catch problems. The board's finding: "The physician used comprehensive consent forms as a substitute for clinical reasoning and documentation. The consent does not explain the medical decision. The chart does not demonstrate medical judgment." His license was restricted. His practice closed. And all because paper that looked strong could not compensate for a chart that was weak.

Do not let that be you. The consent form is one half of a two-part system. Treat it that way. Build both halves with equal care, and you have a defense that actually defends.

What Bulletproof Consent Must Include

Now let me walk you through the specific elements that must be in every informed consent document for peptide therapy. I am not giving you template language to copy and paste - that is what the appendices are for, and besides, your lawyer needs to review anything a patient actually signs. What I am giving you is the architecture: the load-bearing walls that every consent form must have, the rationale for why each element matters, and practical guidance on how to explain these elements to patients in ways they will understand and remember. Skip any one of these elements and you have a gap. Gaps get filled by plaintiff's attorneys and board investigators, and they never fill them in your favor.

Nature and purpose of treatment explained in plain English

The first thing your patient needs to understand is what you are actually doing. Not the marketing name, not the internet hype, not the podcast they listened to - what you, as their physician, are prescribing and why. This sounds obvious, but I have seen consent forms that open with regulatory language before the patient even knows what the therapy is. That is backwards. Start with the basics. Name the substance. Explain what it is in simple terms. Describe what you expect it to do for this specific patient. Connect the therapy to their specific concerns and goals.

For example, if you are prescribing sermorelin, do not start with "Sermorelin acetate is a synthetic analog of growth hormone-releasing hormone that stimulates endogenous growth hormone secretion via the pituitary somatotroph cells." Start with: "Sermorelin is a medication that tells your own pituitary gland to release more growth hormone. The goal is better sleep, more energy, and gradual improvement in body composition over several months. It is not the same as taking growth hormone directly, and the effects are usually modest and gradual." That is something a patient can understand, repeat back to you, and remember when they talk to their family about it.

The purpose statement needs to be patient-specific. A generic description of what sermorelin does in general is better than nothing, but a description of what you are prescribing it for in this particular patient is much stronger. "You came in because of poor sleep and low energy. Sermorelin may help with those issues by supporting your body's natural growth hormone production. I am not prescribing it for weight loss, athletic performance, or anti-aging - I am prescribing it because your symptoms, history, and lab pattern suggest your growth hormone axis may be underactive, and this is a physiologic approach to supporting it." Now the consent form documents a specific clinical purpose tied to a specific patient. That is harder to attack.

You also need to be clear about what the therapy is not. This is the conversation where you set boundaries and manage expectations. Peptide therapy is not a miracle cure. It is not a substitute for lifestyle changes. It is not covered by insurance. It is not FDA-approved for many of the reasons patients are seeking it. It does not replace their primary care physician. It does not treat conditions outside the scope of what you evaluated. These "not" statements are protective because they prevent the patient from later claiming they were led to believe something that was never true. Every "not" statement you document is a potential lawsuit that never gets filed because the patient's expectations were grounded in reality from day one.

The route of administration matters too and needs to be explicitly stated. If it is a subcutaneous injection, say so. If the patient will self-inject, say so. If they need training, document the training. If the medication comes from a compounding pharmacy and requires reconstitution, explain that. I have seen patients who thought they were getting pills show up for their first injection completely unprepared. That is a consent failure even if they signed a form that technically mentioned "subcutaneous administration" in a list of ten other things. Plain English means the patient knows they are going to stick a needle in their belly twice a week. If they are not comfortable with that, better to find out during the consent conversation than at the first injection appointment.

FDA status disclosed plainly: approved, off-label, compounded, or investigational

This is the section where most consent forms get weak, and it is the section where the board will focus most intensely if something goes wrong. The FDA status of the therapy must be disclosed in language that cannot be misunderstood. Not buried in fine print. Not alluded to with vague phrases like "may not have undergone the same review as other medications."Named clearly, explained directly, and acknowledged by the patient with an initial or checkbox.

Let me break down what each status means and how you explain it, because these distinctions matter enormously both clinically and legally.

FDA-approved means the FDA has evaluated safety and efficacy data for a specific indication under a specific brand name. If you are prescribing an FDA-approved product for its labeled indication, the disclosure is straightforward: "This medication is FDA-approved for [indication]. I am prescribing it for that purpose." Simple. But if you are prescribing it at a different dose, for a different population, or through a different route, you need to say so: "This medication is FDA-approved at higher doses for diabetes. I am prescribing a lower dose for weight management, which is not the exact labeled use. This is called off-label prescribing, and it is legal and common, but it means the FDA has not specifically reviewed the dose I am recommending."

Off-label means you are using an FDA-approved medication in a way that differs from the approved labeling - different dose, different indication, different patient population, or different duration. Off-label prescribing is legal and common; oncologists do it constantly, and primary care physicians do it every day when they prescribe blood pressure medications for anxiety or antidepressants for sleep. But off-label status must be disclosed because the patient is entitled to know that the FDA has not reviewed the specific use you are recommending. Your consent should say: "I understand that this use is off-label, meaning the FDA has not specifically evaluated this medication for the exact way it is being prescribed to me. My clinician has explained why they believe this is appropriate for my situation."

Compounded means the medication was prepared by a compounding pharmacy rather than manufactured by a pharmaceutical company under FDA oversight. This distinction matters because compounded products are not subject to the same manufacturing standards, batch testing, and quality controls as FDA-approved branded products. Your consent must say this plainly: "I understand that compounded medications are prepared by specialized pharmacies and are not FDA-approved in the same manner as branded, mass-manufactured medications. Product quality, concentration, sterility, and availability may vary. My clinician has explained the pharmacy source and why a compounded product is being used."

Investigational means the therapy has not been approved by the FDA for any indication and is still being studied in clinical trials. Retatrutide, as of this writing, falls into this category. Investigational status requires the strongest disclosure: "I understand that this medication is investigational, meaning it has not been approved by the FDA for any use. Safety and efficacy data are still being collected. I am choosing to proceed despite this uncertainty, and my clinician has explained the limited evidence, unknown risks, and why investigational therapy is being considered after other options have been discussed."

The patient must acknowledge each status specifically. Do not combine them into a single catch-all statement. If the therapy is both compounded and off-label, the patient should acknowledge both separately. If it is investigational and compounded, same thing. Each status carries different implications for risk, evidence, and legal defensibility, and the patient needs to understand each one. When the board investigator asks the patient "Did you understand this was not FDA-approved?" you want the patient to say yes because they specifically acknowledged it, not because they sort of remember something about it being in the paperwork somewhere.

Expected benefits without any guarantee of specific results

This section walks a delicate line, and a lot of physicians get it wrong. You need to explain what the therapy might do - that is the whole point of prescribing it - but you must do so without promising any specific outcome. The moment your consent form, your chart note, or anything your staff says implies a guaranteed result, you have created a contractual expectation. And when that result does not materialize, you have a breach of that expectation, which sounds an awful lot like the beginning of a malpractice claim.

The language should focus on goals, not promises. "Possible goals include..." "Some patients experience..." "The intended effect is..." These are therapeutic intentions, not outcome guarantees. Follow every benefit statement with explicit no-guarantee language: "I understand that these are goals, not promises, and that my results may be mild, delayed, absent, or different than expected." The patient should initial this statement. It should not be buried in a block of text; it should be a standalone acknowledgment that forces the patient to engage with the uncertainty of medicine.

Be specific about the range of possible outcomes. Do not just say "results may vary." Say what that variation looks like. For semaglutide: "Some patients lose significant weight in the first three months. Others lose weight more gradually. Some cannot tolerate the medication and stop within the first month. Some lose weight initially and then plateau. The amount of weight lost varies widely depending on diet, activity, starting weight, other medical conditions, and individual response. No specific amount of weight loss is guaranteed." That level of specificity does two things: it genuinely informs the patient, and it documents that the patient was prepared for a range of outcomes rather than sold a fantasy.

Be especially careful about staff conversations and marketing materials. Your consent form can be perfect, but if your front desk staff told the patient on the phone that "most people lose twenty pounds in the first month" or if your website shows before-and-after photos that suggest dramatic transformation, your consent form becomes irrelevant. The patient's expectation was set before they ever walked in the door, and no amount of careful consent language will fully reset it. Your marketing, your staff scripts, your social media, and your consent forms must all sing the same tune: hopeful but realistic, encouraging but honest. If there is a gap between what attracted the patient and what the consent form says, the consent form loses. Every time.

Known risks and common side effects in language the patient understands

This is where overexplaining becomes your best friend. Most consent forms list risks. Bulletproof consent forms explain them. The difference is enormous. A list says "nausea, vomiting, diarrhea, constipation, headache, fatigue." An explanation says "You may feel sick to your stomach, especially when you first start the medication or when the dose increases. You might throw up, have loose stools, or the opposite - you might get constipated. Most people find these symptoms get better after a few days to a couple weeks, but some people cannot tolerate them and need to stop the medication. If the nausea is severe or you cannot keep fluids down, that is not normal - call us or go to urgent care."

See the difference? The list informs. The explanation informs and educates and prepares. The patient who received the explanation knows what to expect, knows what is normal versus what is alarming, and knows what to do. The patient who got the list knows only that some gastrointestinal things might happen. When they get nausea, they do not know if it is the"normal" kind or the "call the doctor" kind. So they either panic and call your office ten times, or they ignore a serious symptom because they thought it was just the expected side effect. Neither outcome is good.

For every risk you list, explain: what it feels like, how common it is, how long it typically lasts, what the patient can do about it, and when it crosses the line from expected to emergency. This takes space on the form, and I know you do not want a fifty-page document. But you can balance thoroughness with readability by organizing risks into categories -common and usually mild, less common but important, rare but serious - and giving each category the appropriate level of detail. Common side effects get the full explanation because the patient is likely to experience them. Rare but serious risks get a clear warning sign and action step because the patient needs to recognize them even if they are unlikely to occur.

Here is what I mean by overexplaining. Take the risk of gallbladder disease with GLP-1 therapy. A weak consent form says: "Gallbladder disease." A decent form says: "Possible gallbladder problems including gallstones." A bulletproof form says: "This medication can cause gallbladder problems including gallstones. Watch for severe pain in the upper right side of your abdomen, pain that spreads to your back or right shoulder, fever, yellowing of your skin or eyes, or clay-colored stools. These symptoms can mean a gallbladder attack or a blocked bile duct and require emergency medical attention. Call 911 or go to the emergency room." The patient who read that paragraph will recognize the emergency if it happens. The patient who only saw "gallbladder disease" on a checklist will not.

You should also include risks that are specific to the patient population you serve. If you treat a lot of patients on multiple medications, include drug interaction risk. If you treat patients who travel frequently, include the risk of running out of medication or needing care while away. If you treat patients who get their supplements from the internet, include the risk of unreported supplement interactions. Think about your actual patient population and the risks they actually face. Template language is a starting point, not an ending point. Every patient population has unique risk factors, and your consent should reflect them.

Serious warning signs and when to stop and seek emergency care

This is the section that saves lives and saves licenses. Every consent form must include explicit, unmistakable instructions about when to stop the medication and seek emergency care. Not "contact your provider if you experience concerning symptoms." That is useless. Patients do not know what "concerning" means. They worry about bothering you. They hope the symptom will go away. They do not want to look like anxious patients. So they wait, and sometimes waiting turns a manageable problem into a catastrophe.

You need to give them permission to act and clear criteria for when to act. Use the words "Stop the medication and call 911 or go to the emergency room if..." Then list the specific symptoms that constitute an emergency for the therapy you are prescribing. For GLP-1 therapy: severe abdominal pain with vomiting. Signs of dehydration you cannot correct at home. Fainting or severe dizziness. Signs of an allergic reaction: rash, hives, swelling of the face or throat, difficulty breathing. Signs of low blood sugar if they are on diabetes medications: confusion, sweating, shaking, rapid heartbeat. For peptides involving injection: signs of serious infection at the injection site - spreading redness, warmth, pus, fever.

Each warning sign needs three components: what to look for, what it might mean, and exactly what to do. "Severe abdominal pain that radiates to your back, especially with vomiting, can be a sign of pancreatitis. This is a medical emergency. Stop the medication immediately and go to the emergency room. Do not wait to call our office. Do not try to ride it out." That is unambiguous. That is actionable. That is what protects you when the patient later says nobody told them what to do.

You also need to explain what to do for less-than-emergency problems. "If you have mild nausea that comes and goes, try eating smaller meals, avoiding fatty foods, and staying hydrated. If it lasts more than three days, gets worse, or interferes with your ability to eat and drink, call our office." This prevents every mild side effect from becoming an after-hours panic call while also ensuring that worsening symptoms get appropriate attention. Patients need a decision framework, not just a list of scary possibilities.

The emergency instructions must include your after-hours contact process. Is there a number they can call? Is it answered by an answering service, an on-call clinician, or a voicemail system? How quickly can they expect a response? If you do not have after-hours coverage, say so: "If you have an emergency outside our business hours, call 911 or go to the nearest emergency room. Do not leave a voicemail and wait for a callback - emergency symptoms require immediate evaluation." Patients need to know the limits of your availability so they do not rely on you for something you cannot provide.

Alternatives discussed, including doing nothing

A choice is only informed if the person knows what their other options are. Consent without alternatives is not consent; it is acquiescence. Your patient needs to know that peptide therapy is not their only path, and they need to hear it from you directly, not figure it out later when they talk to their PCP and learn there were three other options nobody mentioned.

The alternatives you discuss must be genuine alternatives - things that could actually address the patient's concerns, even if they are not your preference. For a patient seeking weight loss, alternatives include: lifestyle modification with nutrition counseling and exercise; FDA-approved weight-loss medications; structured behavioral therapy; bariatric surgery evaluation; referral to an endocrinologist or obesity medicine specialist; and doing nothing - accepting their current weight and focusing on health metrics instead. Each alternative should be presented with a fair description of its pros and cons relative to the therapy you are recommending.

The "doing nothing" alternative is especially important and often overlooked. Patients need explicit permission to decline treatment without feeling pressured. Your consent form should say: "I understand that doing nothing is a valid choice. I can choose not to take any medication and instead focus on lifestyle changes, or I can choose to accept my current health status without active intervention. My clinician has explained the risks and benefits of this choice compared to the proposed therapy." When a patient acknowledges that doing nothing was presented as a real option, it proves the conversation was not a sales pitch. It was a medical discussion among options.

Documenting alternatives also protects you from the patient who later claims they were never told about other options. "You never told me about Wegovy - I would have tried that first."Your chart note says: "Alternatives discussed: FDA-approved semaglutide (Wegovy) at standard doses - patient declined due to GI intolerance history and cost. Tirzepatide -patient interested but wants to start with lower-cost option. Lifestyle-only approach - patient states they have tried this repeatedly without success and wants pharmacologic support. Patient elected to proceed with compounded semaglutide microdose after discussion of risks, benefits, and alternatives." That paragraph makes the patient's choice look like exactly what it was: an informed selection among real options.

Costs explained clearly with no hidden fees

Cost disclosure is part of informed consent. A patient who does not know what they will pay cannot make an informed decision about whether the therapy is worth it to them. This is especially true in cash-pay peptide practices where costs can be substantial and insurance does not help. Your consent must clearly state what the patient will pay, what is included, what is extra, and what the refund policy is.

Be specific. Do not say "Costs vary depending on treatment plan." Say: "Your initial consultation is $350. Your medication is $450 per month, which includes shipping. Labs ordered by this office are billed separately by the lab and typically cost $150-250. Follow-up visits are $200 each and are required every four weeks for the first three months, then every eight weeks. Total estimated first-year cost is between $5,000 and $6,500 depending on medication dosing and lab frequency." That level of specificity prevents sticker shock, prevents the "nobody told me it would cost this much" complaint, and demonstrates that the patient made a financial decision with open eyes.

The refund policy must be clear and fair. If you do not offer refunds, say so: "I understand that fees for consultation, medication, and services are not refundable once services are rendered or medication is dispensed." If you have a limited refund policy, state the conditions. If you offer a satisfaction guarantee - and I would think long and hard about that, because satisfaction guarantees in medicine create impossible expectations - state exactly what it covers and what it does not. Ambiguity around money creates angry patients, and angry patients file complaints.

Also clarify what insurance will and will not cover. Most peptide therapy is not covered by insurance. Say so plainly: "I understand that this treatment is not covered by my health insurance, Medicare, or Medicaid. I am responsible for all costs. I will not receive a superbill for insurance submission unless specifically offered and requested." Some patients will try to submit your receipts to insurance anyway, and when insurance denies the claim, they will be angry at you unless you clearly told them upfront that coverage was not available.

Patient responsibilities: truthful disclosure, compliance, no sharing medication, follow-up attendance

Informed consent is a two-way street. The patient consents to treatment, but they also accept responsibilities that make treatment safe and effective. These responsibilities must be stated explicitly, acknowledged by the patient, and enforced by your practice. A patient who violates these responsibilities and suffers harm as a result cannot reasonably claim the practice is solely responsible.

Truthful disclosure means the patient must provide accurate and complete information about their medical history, current medications, supplements, allergies, and substance use. Your consent should say: "I certify that the information I have provided about my health history, medications, supplements, allergies, and substance use is truthful and complete. I understand that withholding information or providing false information can lead to serious harm, and I agree to immediately notify the practice of any changes in my health status, new diagnoses, or new medications."

Compliance means the patient must follow the prescribed dosing, administration, and monitoring instructions. They cannot adjust their own dose, skip follow-up appointments, ignore lab orders, or decide on their own when to stop or restart medication. Your consent should say: "I agree to follow the dosing, administration, and monitoring instructions provided by my clinician. I will not change my dose, frequency, or schedule without clinician approval. I will not share my medication with anyone else or use medication prescribed for someone else."

No sharing medication deserves its own emphasis because it happens more than you think. Patients talk to friends. Friends express interest. The patient gives them a vial, or sells it to them, or both. When that friend has a bad reaction, everyone involved is in legal jeopardy, and the trail leads back to your prescription. Your consent must explicitly prohibit sharing: "I understand that sharing my medication with any other person is dangerous, illegal, and grounds for immediate discontinuation of my treatment. I agree never to share, sell, or give my medication to anyone else."

Follow-up attendance is a patient responsibility because monitoring is what makes peptide therapy safe. A patient who skips follow-ups, ignores lab orders, or goes radio silent for months is not participating in supervised care. They are self-medicating with your prescription pad. Your consent should say: "I agree to attend all scheduled follow-up appointments, complete requested laboratory tests, and respond to communications from the practice within a reasonable timeframe. I understand that failure to do so may result in discontinuation of my medication."

Each of these responsibilities should have its own checkbox or initial line. Bundling them into a single "I agree to all patient responsibilities" statement is weak because it does not demonstrate that the patient encountered and considered each responsibility individually.

Separate checkboxes create a record of specific acknowledgments that is much harder to attack.

The Enhanced Consent Requirements

Everything I have described so far applies to every informed consent process in every medical practice. These are the fundamentals. But peptide therapy - especially compounded, off-label, investigational, or limited-evidence peptide therapy - demands more. The enhanced consent requirements in this section are what separate a standard consent process from one that can withstand the extraordinary scrutiny that comes with prescribing therapies that regulators, insurers, and the mainstream medical establishment view with suspicion. When you step outside the well-worn path of conventional medicine, your documentation must be correspondingly more robust. Not because you are doing something wrong - you are not - but because you are doing something unusual, and unusual attracts attention.

Compounded or investigational therapies require stronger consent language

The moment you prescribe a compounded or investigational therapy, the consent burden increases. This is not optional. This is not lawyer overkill. This is the reality of practicing at the edge of conventional medicine, and you need to embrace it fully because every shortcut you take will be magnified under scrutiny.

Compounded therapies require enhanced consent because the patient is receiving a product that was not manufactured in an FDA-regulated facility, was not subject to batch-level quality testing by the FDA, and may vary in potency, purity, and sterility from batch to batch. None of this means compounded products are unsafe - a good 503A or 503B pharmacy produces high-quality medication. But it does mean the patient is accepting a different risk profile than they would with a branded FDA-approved product. Your consent must explicitly address this:"I understand that compounded medications are prepared individually by a licensed compounding pharmacy and are not subject to the same FDA manufacturing oversight, batch testing, and quality assurance processes as commercially manufactured, FDA-approved medications. My clinician has explained the pharmacy source and why a compounded product is being used in my case."

Investigational therapies require the strongest consent of all. An investigational therapy has no FDA approval. The long-term safety data may not exist. The efficacy may be uncertain. The patient is essentially participating in clinical exploration without the protections of a formal clinical trial protocol. Your consent must be brutally honest about this: "I understand that this medication is investigational, meaning it has not been approved by the FDA for any indication. Human safety data may be limited or incomplete. Long-term effects are unknown. I am choosing to proceed with this therapy despite these uncertainties, and my clinician has explained the available evidence, the unknowns, and why investigational therapy is being considered rather than established alternatives."

The enhanced language for compounded and investigational therapies should be prominently placed, not hidden at the bottom of the form. It should use bold text or a separate section header that draws the patient's attention. It should require a separate initial or checkbox that the patient cannot miss. And it should be reinforced by the physician in the conversation, not left for the patient to discover while reading.

I also recommend including a statement about regulatory change risk: "I understand that the legal and regulatory availability of compounded and investigational therapies can change. If FDA policy, pharmacy rules, or state law changes and this therapy is no longer legally available, my treatment may be discontinued without notice." This protects you from the patient who claims you breached a contract when a peptide becomes unavailable due to regulatory changes beyond your control.

The patient must acknowledge they discussed this with their primary care physician

This is your secret weapon, and I want you to use it every single time. The patient must acknowledge - in writing, with a checkbox, on the consent form - that they have discussed the proposed peptide therapy with their primary care physician or appropriate treating specialist. This one element transforms your consent from a document about your relationship with the patient into evidence of a collaborative care approach that includes the broader medical community.

Here is why this matters so much. When a board investigator looks at a peptide practice, one of their concerns is that the practice operates in isolation - that patients are being drawn away from their established care, that PCPs are being circumvented, that the peptide doctor is functioning as a shadow healthcare system. When your consent form shows that the patient discussed the therapy with their PCP and the PCP had no objection, that narrative collapses. You are not a rogue operator. You are a specialist consulting on a specific aspect of the patient's care with the knowledge and at least tacit approval of their primary doctor.

The language should be specific: "I certify that I have discussed the use of this specific peptide medication with my primary care physician or appropriate treating specialist. My PCP or specialist knows I am considering this treatment and has no objection based on the information available to them." Some practices go a step further and require PCP clearance in writing before initiating therapy. That is even stronger if you can get it, though many PCPs will not provide written clearance for therapies they are not familiar with. At minimum, the patient's acknowledgment that the conversation occurred is essential.

If the patient does not have a PCP, this is a red flag that requires additional documentation. Your consent should address this: "I do not currently have a primary care physician. My clinician has recommended that I establish care with a PCP and has provided me with a referral list. I understand that peptide therapy is not a substitute for comprehensive primary care and I agree to establish PCP care within [timeframe]." This prevents the patient from later claiming nobody told them they needed a PCP, and it demonstrates that your practice recognizes the limits of its role.

If the patient's PCP objects to the therapy, that does not necessarily mean you cannot proceed, but it changes the risk calculus and must be documented carefully. Your chart note should reflect: "Patient reports PCP Dr. Smith is not supportive of peptide therapy due to limited evidence. Patient has elected to proceed despite PCP's reservations after extended discussion of risks, benefits, and alternatives. Patient understands they can return to Dr. Smith for conventional care at any time. Copy of consent and monitoring plan offered to Dr. Smith at patient's request." This documents that the patient made an autonomous choice against their PCP's advice, not that you secretly treated a patient behind their PCP's back.

The patient must acknowledge they attempted conventional treatments first

This element addresses one of the most common attacks on peptide therapy: that it is being prescribed as a first-line treatment when established, FDA-approved alternatives exist. The patient must acknowledge that they have tried conventional approaches - or at least been offered them - before turning to peptides. This demonstrates that peptide therapy in your practice is not a shortcut around conventional medicine but rather an option for patients who have already traveled the conventional road without adequate results.

The language should be realistic about timeframe without being rigid: "I certify that I have repeatedly and professionally attempted, for a clinically reasonable period, to address my symptoms or condition through traditional FDA-approved medications, standard medical care, lifestyle changes, nutrition, exercise, sleep improvement, behavioral modification, physical therapy, specialist care, or other conventional approaches, without adequate relief or acceptable results." The phrase "clinically reasonable period" is important because it gives you flexibility- a patient with severe, debilitating symptoms may have a shorter reasonable period than a patient with mild, chronic complaints.

Your chart note should document what the patient actually tried. If they tried three different diets, two weight-loss programs, metformin from their PCP, and six months of working with a nutritionist, write that down. Specificity strengthens the record. "Patient reports eighteen months of lifestyle modification including Weight Watchers, intermittent fasting, and walking program. Lost 8 pounds initially, regained 12. Tried metformin 500mg from PCP for three months - discontinued due to GI intolerance. Declined phentermine from PCP due to anxiety history. Now seeking peptide therapy as next step after conventional options exhausted or declined." That paragraph tells a story of a patient who did the work, tried the standard options, and is now reasonably exploring alternatives. That is exactly the story you want your chart to tell.

If the patient has not tried conventional treatments, this is not an automatic disqualification, but it requires a different conversation and documentation. Some patients come to you precisely because they want to avoid the side effects or limitations of conventional therapies. That is a valid choice, but you need to document that the choice was informed: "Patient has not previously tried FDA-approved weight-loss medications. Alternatives discussed including orlistat, phentermine/topiramate, naltrexone/bupropion, and liraglutide. Patient specifically wishes to avoid stimulant-based therapy due to anxiety history and prefers peptide-based approach after independent research. Patient understands FDA-approved options are available and has elected to proceed with compounded semaglutide instead." This shows the patient made a choice among alternatives, not that alternatives were never presented.

The patient must acknowledge they independently researched the therapy

This element serves two purposes. First, it demonstrates that the patient is an active participant in their care decision, not a passive recipient of whatever the clinic sells them. Second, it insulates you from the claim that the patient relied solely on your marketing or staff representations and had no other source of information. When the patient acknowledges they did their own research, they are admitting they sought out information beyond what you provided - which undermines any later claim that they were misled by your practice.

The language should be specific: "I certify that I have independently researched the specific peptide or wellness medication named in this consent, including its possible benefits, limits, risks, regulatory status, off-label or compounded status when applicable, and available alternatives. I am not relying only on advertisements, social media, influencers, internet forums, or statements from clinic staff. I have sought information from multiple sources and have had the opportunity to ask my clinician questions based on my research."

This also opens the door for an important clinical conversation. When you ask the patient what they have read or watched, you learn what expectations they have formed and where those expectations came from. If they watched a TikTok video claiming BPC-157 cures everything from tendonitis to depression, you now know you need to address that specifically. If they read a research article about semaglutide cardiovascular outcomes, you know they have a more sophisticated understanding and you can have a deeper conversation. The independent research acknowledgment is not just a legal protection - it is a clinical tool that helps you meet the patient where they are.

Be realistic, though. Some patients have done extensive research. Others have done almost none beyond seeing a friend's results on Instagram. Your consent language should work for both, but your conversation should adapt. For the heavily researched patient, acknowledge their effort and add clinical context: "You have done a lot of reading, which is great. Let me add what I see from a medical perspective that may not have been in the articles you read." For the lightly researched patient, slow down and provide more education: "Before we go further, let me make sure you understand what this medication actually does, what it does not do, and what the real risks are."

Emergency stop rules and after-hours contact procedures

I touched on this in the basic consent section, but for compounded and investigational therapies, the emergency protocols need to be even more detailed and explicit. The unknown risk profile of these therapies means patients need crystal-clear guidance on when to stop and what to do.

Your enhanced consent should include what I call "hard stop" rules - specific, non-negotiable criteria for immediate cessation of therapy and emergency evaluation. These are not "call the office if you are concerned" guidelines. These are "stop the medication right now and seek emergency care" directives. Examples: Stop immediately and seek emergency care for severe abdominal pain with vomiting (possible pancreatitis). Stop immediately for signs of allergic reaction including difficulty breathing, swelling of face or throat, or widespread hives. Stop immediately for chest pain, shortness of breath, or fainting. Stop immediately for severe injection site reaction with fever. Stop immediately for any neurologic symptoms: severe headache, confusion, vision changes, weakness, or numbness.

Each hard stop rule should include the same three elements: the symptom, the possible meaning, and the exact action. "Stop the medication. Do not take another dose. Go to the emergency room or call 911. Do not wait for our office to open." This level of directive language removes ambiguity and protects both the patient and you. A patient who waits twelve hours because they were not sure if their symptom was "serious enough" is a patient whose outcome may be worse - and who may blame you for not being clear about what to do.

The after-hours contact process must be spelled out in detail. If you have an answering service, give the number and explain how it works: "After hours, call [number]. The answering service will take your message and contact the on-call clinician, who will return your call within 30 minutes. If you do not receive a callback within 30 minutes and your symptoms are worsening, go to the emergency room." If you do not have after-hours coverage, be explicit about that:"Our office does not provide after-hours telephone or messaging consultation. If you have symptoms that concern you outside our business hours, go to urgent care or the emergency room. Do not wait for our office to open if you believe your symptoms are serious."

I also recommend including a medication hold protocol for situations that are not emergencies but require pausing therapy. "If you develop a fever over 101 degrees, hold your injection until the fever resolves. If you are scheduled for surgery, hold your medication for one week before and do not resume until your surgeon clears you. If you become pregnant, stop the medication immediately and contact our office and your obstetrician." These practical instructions prevent problems that are not emergencies but could become problems if the patient keeps injecting through a situation that calls for a pause.

Hold Harmless, Arbitration, and Patient Responsibility

Now we get into the documents that accompany informed consent but are not the same thing. Hold-harmless language, arbitration agreements, and patient responsibility documents serve important purposes, but they are widely misunderstood by physicians who think these documents create magical protection against all liability. They do not. What they do is clarify the framework within which care is provided, establish shared expectations, and create efficient mechanisms for resolving disputes if they arise. Used correctly, they are valuable tools. Used incorrectly - or worse, used as substitutes for good medicine - they become evidence of a practice that cared more about legal defense than patient care.

Hold-harmless language acknowledges shared responsibility - it does not erase negligence

Let me say this as clearly as I can because it is the most misunderstood concept in this entire chapter. A hold-harmless clause does not protect you from a malpractice lawsuit. It does not prevent a board complaint. It does not excuse negligent care, reckless prescribing, or failure to meet the standard of care. If you prescribe the wrong medication to the wrong patient, miss a glaring contraindication, or fail to monitor for a known serious risk, no hold-harmless clause in the world will save you. And any attorney who tells you otherwise is selling you snake oil.

What hold-harmless language does do is establish that the patient understands there are risks inherent in the therapy, that the patient has responsibilities in managing those risks, and that the practice should not be held responsible for harms that result from the patient's own actions or from known, disclosed risks that materialized despite appropriate care. It is a shared-responsibility document, not a get-out-of-jail-free card.

The core language of a hold-harmless agreement for peptide therapy should address several specific points. First, the patient acknowledges that they were informed of risks and chose to proceed anyway: "I understand that the peptide therapy I am receiving carries known risks, unknown risks, and uncertainties. I have been informed of these risks in detail, I have had the opportunity to ask questions, and I am voluntarily choosing to proceed with full knowledge of the potential for adverse outcomes." This establishes informed choice, which supports the validity of the document.

Second, the patient acknowledges their own role in safety: "I understand that my truthful disclosure of medical history, compliance with dosing instructions, attendance at follow-up appointments, completion of recommended laboratory tests, and prompt reporting of adverse symptoms are essential to my safety. I agree to fulfill these responsibilities as a condition of receiving treatment." This establishes that the patient shares responsibility for the safety of their own care.

Third, the patient acknowledges limits of what the practice can control: "I understand that this practice cannot control how my individual body will respond to therapy, cannot guarantee specific results, cannot prevent all adverse outcomes, and cannot be responsible for problems caused by my failure to disclose relevant information, my failure to follow instructions, my sharing of medication with others, or my use of non-prescribed substances not disclosed to my clinician." This narrows the scope of what the patient can reasonably blame on the practice.

The language must never suggest that the patient is waiving their right to sue for negligence. That is not legally enforceable in most jurisdictions and makes the entire document look predatory. Instead, the language should focus on assumption of known risks and acceptance of shared responsibility. "I am not waiving any right to pursue a claim for negligent care. I am acknowledging that I understand the risks of this therapy, that I accept my share of responsibility for my own safety, and that I am proceeding voluntarily despite those risks."

This is honest, fair, and far more defensible than language that tries to strip patients of their legal rights.

I want to emphasize the tone of this document because tone matters enormously. A hold-harmless agreement that reads like a legal assault - aggressive, one-sided, designed to intimidate - creates the exact impression you do not want. It suggests a practice that expects things to go wrong and is more concerned with protecting itself than with caring for patients. A hold-harmless agreement that reads like a mature conversation between adults - honest about risks, clear about responsibilities, fair to both parties - supports the impression of a practice that takes its obligations seriously and expects patients to do the same. Write the second kind. Always.

Arbitration agreements must be reviewed by counsel and explained in plain English

Arbitration agreements are among the most legally complex documents a medical practice can use, and they vary dramatically in enforceability from state to state. Some states strongly favor arbitration and will enforce well-drafted agreements. Other states view pre-dispute arbitration in healthcare with skepticism and impose specific requirements - separate signatures, cooling-off periods, conspicuous language, attorney review opportunities - that must be met for the agreement to be valid. If you use an arbitration agreement without having it reviewed by counsel in your state, you may have a document that creates more problems than it solves.

The fundamental principle of a medical malpractice arbitration agreement is straightforward: the patient and the practice agree that any disputes arising from the care relationship will be resolved through binding arbitration rather than through litigation in court. Arbitration typically involves a neutral arbitrator or panel, limited discovery compared to court, no jury, and limited appeal rights. The goal is faster, more private, less expensive resolution of disputes. But here is what arbitration does not do: it does not change the standard of care. It does not excuse negligent medicine. It does not prevent a board complaint - boards are not bound by arbitration agreements. It does not stop the patient from reporting concerns to government agencies. And it does not eliminate the practice's obligation to carry malpractice insurance.

Your arbitration agreement must be presented separately from the consent form, not buried inside it. It must be titled clearly: "Medical Malpractice Arbitration Agreement." It must include a plain-language notice at the top explaining what the patient is agreeing to: "Please read carefully. By signing this agreement, you agree that certain disputes, including medical malpractice claims, will be resolved through binding arbitration instead of a lawsuit in court. This means you may be giving up your right to a jury trial."

The patient should initial specific acknowledgments: that they read the agreement or had it read to them; that they understand arbitration is different from court; that they understand they may be waiving the right to a jury trial; that this agreement is separate from medical informed consent; that this agreement does not prevent them from filing a complaint with a licensing board or government agency; that this agreement does not excuse negligent care; and that they had the opportunity to ask questions before signing. These initial requirements force engagement with the document and demonstrate that the patient encountered each key concept.

The agreement should specify what claims are covered - typically all claims arising from or related to medical care, treatment, prescribing, monitoring, and clinical services provided by the practice. It should also specify what is not covered: the patient's right to file board complaints, either party's right to seek emergency injunctive relief in court, and any claims that cannot legally be required to proceed in arbitration under applicable law. This balanced approach shows the agreement is not trying to strip the patient of all rights, which strengthens enforceability.

The arbitration procedure should be described in enough detail to be useful but not so much detail that the document becomes unreadable. Who selects the arbitrator? What organization administers the process? Where will arbitration take place? What law governs? These basics matter because they show the process is real and fair, not a sham designed to favor the practice.

The fee structure requires careful attention. Arbitration must not be structured in a way that prevents the patient from bringing a claim due to cost. If the arbitrator's fees, filing fees, and administrative costs are so high that a patient with a legitimate claim cannot afford to pursue it, the agreement may be deemed unconscionable and unenforceable. Consider including language that the practice will advance or pay fees necessary to preserve the patient's access to arbitration, subject to the arbitrator's final allocation of costs.

I strongly recommend including an opt-out or rescission period. "You may cancel this agreement by sending written notice to the practice within thirty days after signing. Cancellation will not affect medical care already provided, payment obligations, or any separate medical consent." This voluntary feature demonstrates that the agreement was not coerced and that the patient had a meaningful opportunity to reject it without losing access to care. Courts look favorably on opt-out provisions, and they transform the agreement from something that feels imposed into something the patient actively chose to keep.

Finally, and I cannot stress this enough, have your malpractice carrier review the arbitration agreement before you use it. Some carriers strongly support arbitration because it can limit exposure. Others object to it because arbitration decisions can be harder to appeal and may result in unexpected outcomes. If your carrier has not approved your arbitration language, you may find yourself without coverage for a claim that gets arbitrated contrary to their expectations. That is a conversation you want to have before the agreement is signed, not after a claim arises.

Patient duties: no sharing, no self-adjusting, reporting requirements

The patient responsibility document - whether it is a standalone form or integrated into your consent - is where you establish the behavioral expectations that keep therapy safe. These are not suggestions. These are conditions of continued treatment, and your practice must be willing to enforce them by discontinuing patients who violate them. A responsibility document that you never enforce is a responsibility document that weakens your position when you actually need it.

No sharing medication must be stated in the strongest possible terms. "I understand that the medication prescribed to me is for my use only. Sharing, selling, or giving this medication to any other person is dangerous, illegal, and strictly prohibited. If I share my medication with anyone, my treatment will be immediately discontinued and my prescription will not be renewed." This language establishes a clear rule with a clear consequence. When you actually discontinue a patient for sharing medication - and you must be willing to do this - the documentation shows the patient was warned and the consequence was applied as stated.

No self-adjusting dose addresses one of the most common sources of harm in peptide therapy. Patients read online forums where other patients discuss their doses. They decide their dose is too low or too high. They change it without consulting you. Then they show up to follow-up either sicker than they should be or demanding a refill sooner than expected. Your responsibility document must say: "I will not change my dose, frequency, injection schedule, or medication source without explicit written or verbal approval from my prescribing clinician. If I self-adjust my dose, my treatment may be discontinued." When you catch a patient self-adjusting and you follow through on the consequence, you are protecting both the patient and your license.

Reporting requirements establish the patient's obligation to communicate with your practice about matters that affect their safety. This includes: new symptoms or side effects; changes in other medications or supplements; emergency room visits, hospitalizations, or urgent care visits; new diagnoses; planned surgeries; pregnancy or attempts to conceive; and any other significant health changes. The language should be specific: "I agree to notify the practice within 48 hours of any emergency room visit, hospitalization, new diagnosis, or significant change in my health status. I agree to report side effects or symptoms promptly rather than waiting for my next scheduled appointment. I understand that failure to report relevant information may result in harm that could have been prevented."

Follow-up compliance must be explicitly tied to continued prescribing. "I understand that follow-up appointments and laboratory tests are medically necessary to monitor my safety and response to therapy. If I miss two consecutive follow-up appointments, fail to complete ordered laboratory tests without explanation, or become unreachable for more than thirty days, my medication may not be renewed and my treatment may be discontinued." This is not punitive. This is medical necessity. A patient who disappears for three months while continuing to self-inject is not receiving supervised care. They are engaging in unsupervised experimentation with your prescription attached. You have a duty to stop that, and your responsibility document gives you the contractual basis to do so.

Each of these duties should have its own checkbox and require a separate initial. The patient should not be able to scroll past them in a block of fine print. They should encounter each duty individually, acknowledge it specifically, and understand that these are binding conditions of their continued participation in treatment.

These documents show voluntary participation, informed choice, and cost disclosure

Let me pull back and explain what all these documents - the informed consent, the hold-harmless language, the arbitration agreement, and the patient responsibility document -actually accomplish when they work together as a system. They do not prevent lawsuits. They do not prevent board complaints. They do not excuse bad medicine. What they do is create a comprehensive record of a relationship built on transparency, shared understanding, and mutual responsibility. And that record, when the medicine behind it is sound, is extraordinarily powerful.

When these documents are aligned and complete, they show: that the patient voluntarily sought out peptide therapy, not that they were solicited or pressured; that the patient was informed of the therapy's nature, risks, benefits, alternatives, and costs in plain language they could understand; that the patient understood the FDA status and regulatory situation of the therapy they were receiving; that the patient discussed the therapy with their PCP and considered conventional options first; that the patient independently researched and actively chose to proceed; that the patient acknowledged specific responsibilities including truthful disclosure, compliance, no sharing, and follow-up attendance; that the patient understood emergency warning signs and what to do; that costs were disclosed clearly with no hidden fees; that the patient understood there were no guarantees of specific results; and that any disputes would be resolved through a fair, explained process rather than emotional escalation.

That is a story. It is a story about a patient who made a grown-up decision with open eyes and a physician who provided the information necessary for that decision to be truly informed. It is a story that survives scrutiny because every element of it is documented, consistent, and grounded in the actual care that was provided. When a board investigator or plaintiff's attorney encounters this kind of record, their case gets harder. Not impossible - nothing is impossible- but harder. Much harder. Because the patient cannot credibly claim they did not know what they were getting into. The chart shows they knew. They acknowledged. They chose.

But here is the final truth I need you to hear, and I want you to hear it from someone who has seen the best and worst of medical practice over decades. These documents are only as good as the medicine and the relationships behind them. A patient who feels respected, heard, genuinely cared for, and honestly informed does not sue their doctor when things go wrong. They call the office. They ask questions. They work with you. Lawsuits and complaints come from patients who feel betrayed, ignored, misled, or abandoned. Your consent documents can be perfect, but if your staff is rude, your follow-up is spotty, your pricing surprises people, or you disappear when problems arise, those documents will not save you.

The best protection is not a better form. The best protection is a practice where patients feel so well-treated, so well-informed, and so genuinely cared for that even when the outcome is not what they hoped for, they believe you did your best and told them the truth. Build that practice. Use these documents to support it. And you will spend your career practicing medicine instead of defending it.

9 - The Primary Care Physician - Your Secret Weapon

BLUNT RULE: A primary care physician who knows what you are doing and agrees with it is worth more than every consent form in your filing cabinet combined. Treat that relationship like the insurance policy it is. You need to document that patient's PCP has no objections to treatment you are providing and that he/she will follow-up with patient every six months. Your patient must sign off on this in your intake forms.

In cases of complex medical histories and or multiple medications prescribed or chronic medical conditions (neurologic, GI, cardiac, hepatic etc.) you must contact PCP with a letter. Otherwise don't accept unhealthy patients at your practice.

Let me tell you something I have learned watching doctors go through board investigations over thirty years. The physician who walks out of that hearing room with their license intact is almost never the one with the fanciest consent forms or the most aggressive lawyer. It is the one who can point to another doctor - a real doctor with a real practice and a real chart -who knew what was happening and thought it was reasonable. That is your secret weapon. That is the primary care physician.

You are running a specialized practice. Maybe it is weight management. Maybe it is hormone optimization. Maybe it is metabolic medicine or longevity or recovery protocols. Whatever niche you occupy, you are not the patient's primary doctor. You do not manage their diabetes, their hypertension, their thyroid medication, their cardiac risk factors, their cancer screenings, their vaccinations, or the hundred other things that make up primary care. And the moment you pretend you do - or the moment you act like those things do not matter because you are focused on your peptide protocol - you have become exactly the kind of cowboy the board loves to make an example of.

The PCP relationship is not a courtesy. It is not a formality. It is not something your staff checks off on intake and never thinks about again. It is the structural backbone of defensible specialized care. Without it, you are a doctor prescribing interesting medications to a patient nobody else is watching. With it, you are a specialist providing coordinated care within a broader medical ecosystem that another physician has reviewed and endorsed. Those are two completely different positions to defend. One gets you in trouble. The other gets you home for dinner.

Let me be very clear about what this chapter is going to teach you. I am going to explain why PCP involvement matters more than almost any other single factor in your compliance picture. I am going to show you exactly how to get PCP buy-in - including the actual language to use in your consultation letters. I am going to tell you when PCP involvement is absolutely non-negotiable, which means you stop the evaluation until it happens. And I am going to show you how to document every aspect of PCP coordination so thoroughly that a skeptical board reviewer has nowhere to poke holes. By the end of this chapter, you will understand that your PCP relationship is not a checkbox. It is your insurance policy. Treat it that way.

A PCP who knows what you are doing and agrees with it is your best defense witness

Picture this scenario because it happens more often than you think. A patient develops a problem six months into their peptide protocol. Maybe it is an elevated glucose that went unnoticed. Maybe it is a cardiac event that nobody connected to the therapy because nobody was looking at the whole patient. Maybe it is just a bad outcome in a patient who had risk factors that your specialized intake never uncovered because it was not designed to find them. The patient complains. The board opens an investigation. Now you are sitting in a conference room with your lawyer, looking at a chart that shows you prescribed an interesting therapy to a patient with complex medical history - and you are the only doctor who knew about it.

That is a lonely chair to sit in. Do not sit in it.

Now picture the alternative. Same patient. Same complaint. Same board investigator looking through your chart. But this time your chart contains a consultation letter to the patient's PCP dated before therapy started. It explains what you are proposing and why. The PCP wrote back. Maybe they said it looked fine given the patient's history. Maybe they raised a concern about the patient's blood pressure, and you documented that you addressed it by adding monitoring. Maybe they just said they had no objection and asked you to keep them informed. Whatever the response, there is now a second doctor in the record - a doctor who knows that patient better than you do, who manages that patient's overall care, and who agreed that your specialized intervention was reasonable in the context of that patient's complete medical picture.

You think the board cares that you meant well? They do not. They care that another doctor with ongoing responsibility for that patient's overall health reviewed your plan and did not object. That is called coordinated care, and it is the difference between looking like a responsible specialist and looking like a vial shop operating in the shadows.

I have seen board investigators' entire demeanor change when they realize there is PCP coordination in the chart. The posture shifts from "What was this doctor hiding?" to "This appears to have been coordinated care between two physicians." That shift is worth everything. It does not make a bad decision good. Nothing does that. But it makes a reasonable decision look exactly like what it was: reasonable, coordinated, supervised care with appropriate involvement of the patient's primary medical home.

And here is something most peptide doctors do not think about until it is too late. If things go really wrong - I am talking malpractice litigation, not just board inquiry - your defense attorney is going to ask you a very simple question under oath: "Did the patient's primary care physician know about this therapy?" If the answer is yes, and you have the documentation to prove it, your attorney now has a witness list that includes another physician who can testify that the care was coordinated and appropriate. If the answer is no, your attorney is explaining to a jury why a doctor prescribed an injectable therapy to a patient without telling the doctor who actually manages that patient's overall health. Which position would you rather be in?

They are the doctor who can look a board investigator in the eye and say, "Yes, I knew about it. Yes, I reviewed it. Yes, I thought it was appropriate for this patient, with the following precautions." There is no marketing material, no consent form, and no amount of informed consent disclosure that carries the weight of another physician's professional judgment backing up yours.

PART III: BUILDING A BULLETPROOF PRACTICE

Operational systems, follow-up, pharmacy handling, pricing, and consultation habits that protect the physician and the patient.

BUILDING A BULLETPROOF PRACTICE

The operational foundation: patients, charts, consent, PCPs, monitoring, pharmacy, and pricing.

10 - Follow-Up and Monitoring - The Follow-Up IS the Defense

No Monitoring Means No Medical Program

Let me tell you something I've seen too many times. A doctor sets up a beautiful cash-pay peptide program. Nice website. Good intake forms. Licensed compounding pharmacy. Direct ship. Everything looks professional. The patient pays, the pharmacy ships, and that patient disappears into the void. No follow-up. No check-in. No symptom review. No lab work. Nothing. Six months later, the patient shows up in an emergency room with severe abdominal pain, or a board complaint lands on the doctor's desk, or a chargeback hits because the patient never lost the weight they expected and now they're angry. And the chart? The chart shows a prescription and a payment. That's it. You think the board cares that you meant well? You think the malpractice carrier cares that you were busy? Let me answer that for you: they don't.

A peptide program without monitoring is not a medical program. It is a transaction. And transactions are what vial shops do. Transactions are what grey-market internet vendors do. Transactions are not what licensed physicians do. The moment you take money and ship medication without a follow-up system, you have crossed a line that every state medical board in this country cares about. They may not catch you tomorrow. But they catch enough doctors every year to make this worth your attention. I have sat in enough legal proceedings, reviewed enough charts, and watched enough colleagues lose licenses to know that the follow-up gap is where practices die.

I have been a registered nurse for over twenty years, an investment banker for eleven, and a paralegal for forty. I have watched regulatory investigations unfold in real time. I have seen the charts that get doctors suspended and the charts that get doctors cleared. The difference is almost never the therapy itself. The difference is the documentation that proves a medical relationship existed. Monitoring is where that proof lives. The follow-up visit, the symptom check, the lab review, the note that says "patient tolerating well, continue current plan" - that is the evidence that you were practicing medicine. Without it, you were just selling access to a vial.

Let me be blunt about why this matters so much in peptide practice specifically. Peptides sit in a regulatory and evidentiary gray zone. Some are FDA-approved. Some are off-label. Some are compounded. Some are investigational. Some are barely past the animal-study stage. When you prescribe in this space, you are operating without the institutional protection that Big Pharma enjoys. Novo Nordisk has a billion-dollar legal department. Eli Lilly has regulatory affairs teams in Washington. You have your chart. That's it. Your chart is your only defense lawyer, and the follow-up notes are the most important paragraphs in that entire file. Because the follow-up is where you prove you were watching. You prove you were thinking. You prove you weren't just collecting payments and writing prescriptions.

The board investigator's playbook is predictable. They start with the chart. They count the visits. They read the notes. They look for evidence of ongoing clinical supervision. If they find a robust follow-up system with dated notes, symptom reviews, lab tracking, and documented decision-making, they move on to easier targets. If they find a prescription pad and a credit card receipt, you become the target. It is that simple. The follow-up system is not a clinical nicety. It is a survival mechanism.

Let me walk you through what happens when a practice skips monitoring. The patient starts semaglutide. They lose ten pounds in the first month. Great. They feel a little nauseated but they're motivated. Month two, the dose goes up. They feel more nauseated. They start skipping meals. They get dehydrated. They don't call the office because nobody told them to, or because they texted the staff and got an emoji back. Month three, they develop persistent abdominal pain. They still don't call because they're afraid the medication will be stopped and they don't want to lose momentum. Month four, they end up in the ER with pancreatitis. Now there's an adverse event report. The hospital asks what physician is supervising their GLP-1 therapy. The patient gives your name. The state health department forwards it to the board. The board requests the chart. The chart shows an initial consult note, a consent form, and a prescription. Four months of therapy. One visit. You think that ends well for you? It doesn't.

Here's another war story. A practice in the Southwest started offering sermorelin for "anti-aging and wellness." No baseline IGF-1. No glucose monitoring. No stop criteria. Patients paid a flat fee, got their vials shipped monthly, and were told to "check in if they had any problems." One patient, a 58-year-old male with undiagnosed prediabetes, started the therapy.

Three months later his fasting glucose had climbed from 108 to 174. He didn't know because nobody checked. He developed polyuria, polydipsia, and blurry vision before finally seeing his PCP, who discovered the diabetic conversion and the sermorelin prescription in his medication list. The PCP filed a complaint with the board alleging failure to monitor. The board investigator opened the chart and found a single intake note, a consent form, and six months of refill authorizations with zero follow-up documentation. The physician received a one-year suspension with probationary terms that included mandatory chart audits and supervised practice. All because there was no system. No follow-up. No monitoring. Just vials and payments.

Contrast that with a practice that has a real follow-up system. The patient starts semaglutide. They get a written handout explaining nausea, what to eat, when to call, and when to go to the ER. At week two, an automated check-in asks about symptoms. At week four, a clinician calls to review. Nausea is documented. Dietary advice is given. At week eight, dose escalation is discussed and a joint decision is made to hold at the current dose because of tolerability. At week twelve, the patient mentions some mild upper abdominal discomfort. The clinician flags it, orders lipase, and holds the dose pending results. The lipase is mildly elevated. The medication is stopped. The patient recovers. The chart shows eleven touchpoints over three months, two clinician reviews, one lab order, and a documented hold decision with rationale. Which chart would you rather defend? I'll tell you which one I'd rather defend - and I've spent forty years reading medical records for legal proceedings.

Monitoring is also where you prove the patient understood what they were getting into. Informed consent is not a one-time event. It is a continuous process. Every follow-up conversation where you ask about side effects, every check-in where you confirm the patient knows when to stop, every reminder about red-flag symptoms - that is reinforcement of the informed consent. The patient who signed a form on day one and never heard from you again has a pretty good argument that they were left alone with a risky medication. The patient who received regular check-ins, symptom tracking, and documented education has a much harder time claiming they didn't understand the risks. The follow-up system protects the patient clinically and protects you legally. Both matter.

The pricing discussion connects directly here. If you are charging a premium for the program- and you should be - then follow-up is part of what the patient is paying for. A patient paying $400 a month for a supervised medical program expects supervision. If they wanted unsupervised medication access, they would buy from the internet for $99. The premium price creates an expectation of premium care. Meet that expectation and you have a happy patient who refers friends. Fail that expectation and you have an unhappy patient who files complaints. Happy patients refer friends; unhappy patients file complaints. That is not a marketing slogan. It is a law of clinical practice.

Let me also address the physicians who think that because this is cash-pay, because there is no insurance company auditing the chart, they can be less rigorous about follow-up documentation. That thinking is exactly backwards. Insurance audits look at billing codes and medical necessity. Board investigations look at standard of care and whether you were practicing medicine or running a retail operation. The cash-pay physician faces a different kind of scrutiny - one that asks, "If this patient was paying out of pocket for supervised care, where is the evidence of supervision?" The absence of documentation in a cash-pay practice doesn't look like efficient care. It looks like you took the money and disappeared. Don't let your chart look like that.

What does a proper monitoring system actually look like in practice? At minimum, it includes these elements, and I want you to think of them as non-negotiable: baseline assessment before medication ships; structured symptom tracking at defined intervals; clinician review before every refill; documented decision-making at every touchpoint; stop criteria established upfront and revisited at each follow-up; emergency instructions provided in writing; and a mechanism to identify patients who miss follow-up and escalate them to clinical review. If your practice does not have all seven of these elements, you have a gap. Fill it before the board finds it for you.

The patient should not disappear after payment. That is the simplest, most direct way to think about this. If your system allows patients to pay and vanish, your system is broken. Fix it. Because when the board investigator opens your chart and sees a patient who paid six months ago, got three shipments of medication, and has zero follow-up documentation, they do not see a physician practicing medicine. They see a vending machine with a medical license. And vending machines get unplugged.

Let me address the objection I hear from busy physicians: "I don't have time to follow up with every peptide patient every month." That's a resource problem, not a clinical problem. And the solution is not to skip follow-up. The solution is to build systems. Staff-supported check-ins. Automated symptom tracking. Structured 15-minute follow-up visits. Technology-assisted monitoring. A nurse or medical assistant can handle the routine check-in. The clinician reviews the flagged items. The physician makes the decisions. This is not revolutionary. Primary care has been doing team-based care for decades. The only difference is that in a cash-pay peptide practice, you're building it yourself instead of inheriting it from a hospital system. And here's the thing - once you build it, it runs. The upfront investment in systems pays dividends in protected licenses, satisfied patients, and defensible charts for years to come.

I also want to address the "it's just a wellness peptide" mentality that I see with certain compounds. A physician prescribes BPC-157 for tendon recovery, tells the patient to "let us know how it goes," and schedules nothing. Six weeks later the patient's tendon pain is actually worse because what they thought was tendinitis was actually a partial tear that needed imaging and surgical evaluation. If that patient had a scheduled week-three check-in with functional assessment questions, the lack of improvement would have been flagged. Imaging would have been ordered. The tear would have been diagnosed promptly. Instead, the patient lost six weeks, the tendon condition worsened, and the physician who prescribed peptide therapy without proper orthopedic follow-up now has a chart that looks like experimental treatment delayed standard of care. That is not a good position to defend.

The follow-up is also where you catch the patients who never should have been in the program to begin with - the ones who slipped through your initial screening. Maybe they didn't disclose their eating disorder history until week six when the appetite suppression triggered old behaviors. Maybe they didn't mention the antidepressant they started in month two because they didn't think it was relevant. Maybe they developed a new medical condition between baseline and follow-up that changes the risk profile entirely. These discoveries happen in follow-up. Without follow-up, they don't get discovered until something goes wrong. And by then, you're not catching a problem early. You're responding to a crisis.

Baseline Assessment

Before a single vial ships, before a single syringe is uncapped, before a single peptide molecule enters your patient's body, you need a baseline. I am not talking about a vague sense of how the patient is doing. I am talking about documented, dated, specific baseline data that you can compare against later. Weight. Vitals. Relevant labs. Pregnancy status. Medication review. Allergy review. Contraindication screen. And if you choose not to collect something - if you decide labs are not needed for this particular patient on this particular therapy - you document why. Because "I didn't think it was necessary" does not sound nearly as professional as"Baseline labs deferred given patient's age, absence of risk factors, and low-risk therapy selection; patient counseled to report symptoms and obtain labs if clinical situation changes."One of those sentences protects you. The other one invites questions.

Collecting baseline labs and vitals when clinically appropriate is not busywork. It is the starting line of your defense. Let me explain why with a real-world scenario I have seen variations of many times. A 52-year-old woman comes in for a weight-loss peptide program. She's enthusiastic. She's done her research. She wants semaglutide. Her BMI is 32. She has no significant medical history that she mentions. The physician prescribes. She starts. She loses weight. Three months in, she develops fatigue and jaundice. Workup reveals elevated liver enzymes. The board complaint alleges the medication caused hepatic injury. The physician's defense is that the patient must have had underlying liver disease. The board asks: what were the baseline liver enzymes? The physician has no idea, because they were never checked. Was the liver injury pre-existing or drug-related? Nobody knows. And when nobody knows, the physician loses the benefit of the doubt. Every single time.

Here's another case from the files. A 47-year-old male started a CJC-1295 and ipamorelin stack at a clinic that did not check baseline IGF-1. The patient had an undiagnosed pituitary microadenoma - completely asymptomatic, no visual changes, no headache history. Six weeks into therapy he developed significant headaches and visual field changes. MRI showed the microadenoma had enlarged, likely stimulated by the GHRH agonist. He needed neurosurgical evaluation and eventual transphenoidal resection. The lawsuit alleged that baseline IGF-1 and pituitary screening would have identified the elevated baseline growth-hormone axis activity and contraindicated the therapy. The clinic had no baseline IGF-1, no pituitary history documentation beyond a single checkbox on a form, and no follow-up until the patient called with severe headaches. The case settled. Expensively. All because nobody checked the starting point.

Baseline labs serve two purposes. Clinically, they identify problems before therapy starts. A patient with an undiagnosed HbA1c of 8.2 probably shouldn't start a GH-axis peptide without endocrine discussion. A patient with an ALT of 120 needs that evaluated before any hepatically metabolized therapy. A patient with a hematocrit of 54 who wants to start testosterone needs a very different conversation. But beyond the clinical value, baseline labs serve a legal and defensive purpose. They establish what was true before your medication entered the picture. If a patient's liver enzymes go from normal to triple the upper limit of normal three months after starting therapy, that is a pattern. If you have no baseline, you cannot demonstrate the pattern. The difference between "this drug caused liver injury" and "this patient had pre-existing liver disease that worsened" often comes down to one number on one lab slip from three months ago. Get that number.

What labs and vitals should you collect? That depends on the therapy, the patient, and the risk level. Let me give you practical guidance, not vague generalities. For any GLP-1 or incretin-based therapy, you want baseline weight, BMI, blood pressure, heart rate, fasting glucose or HbA1c when diabetes risk exists, and a basic metabolic panel to assess renal function. If the patient is on insulin or sulfonylureas, you need to know that before the first dose ships. Consider a lipid panel for patients with metabolic syndrome. Consider liver enzymes if the patient has any risk factors for hepatic disease. For GH-axis peptides - sermorelin, tesamorelin, CJC-1295, ipamorelin - you want baseline IGF-1, fasting glucose or HbA1c, and blood pressure. IGF-1 is non-negotiable for GH-axis therapy because it is your primary monitoring parameter and without a baseline you have no way to assess whether therapy is producing an appropriate or excessive response. For repair peptides like BPC-157 or TB-500, you want to know about cancer history, bleeding risk, and current medications. For immune peptides like thymosin alpha-1, a CBC with differential is reasonable. For metabolic peptides like MOTS-c or AOD-9604, glucose, lipids, and body composition metrics make sense. For PT-141, blood pressure is essential. For any peptide therapy in a patient over 50 or with cardiac risk factors, baseline EKG consideration is not excessive caution.

The point is not to order every lab for every patient. The point is to think about what this specific patient on this specific therapy needs, document that thought process, and collect what is clinically appropriate. When you document why you ordered what you ordered, you demonstrate clinical reasoning. When you document why you deferred something, you demonstrate that you considered it and made a judgment. Both are defensible. What is not defensible is collecting nothing and documenting nothing and hoping for the best.

Pregnancy status must be established and documented before any peptide therapy ships. This is non-negotiable. Most peptide therapies have insufficient safety data in pregnancy. Many carry theoretical risks. A pregnancy test for women of childbearing potential is baseline standard of care. Document the result. Document the discussion about pregnancy prevention. Document that the patient knows to stop therapy immediately if pregnancy is suspected. If you skip this because it feels awkward or because the patient says "I'm not pregnant," you are gambling with your license. I've seen board cases where the entire complaint hinged on a physician's failure to assess pregnancy status before starting a contraindicated medication. Don't be that case. A simple urine or serum hCG test takes minutes and costs almost nothing. The protection it provides is worth a hundred times its cost.

The medication review at baseline is where you catch interactions and contraindications that the patient forgot to mention or didn't understand were relevant. Patients are terrible historians. They don't think of supplements as medications. They don't think of over-the-counter NSAIDs as relevant. They don't think of the thyroid medication their PCP prescribed three years ago that they stopped taking on their own. Your job is to dig. Ask specifically: what prescription medications are you taking? What over-the-counter medications? What supplements? What hormones? What peptides did you buy online last month? Ask it all. Document it all. And when you find something concerning - a GLP-1 prescribed by another doctor they're still seeing, insulin they didn't mention, a thyroid disorder they forgot about - you address it before your medication ships, not after they develop hypoglycemia in week three.

I once reviewed a chart where a patient failed to disclose they were on warfarin because "it's just a blood thinner, not a real medication." They were prescribed a repair peptide protocol that included a compound with theoretical anticoagulant effects. The interaction was never caught because the medication review was a checkbox form, not a conversation. The patient's INR climbed to 5.2. They developed a significant bruising episode that required emergency evaluation. The board complaint wrote itself. A thorough medication review - one that specifically asks about anticoagulants, antiplatelets, and bleeding risk - would have caught this. But the practice used a generic intake form and never followed up with a clinician interview.

Allergy review is similarly critical and frequently superficial. "Are you allergic to anything?""No." That is not an allergy review. Ask about medication allergies, specifically. Ask about injection-site reactions to prior therapies. Ask about reactions to preservatives, because some compounded products contain preservatives that can trigger sensitivities. Ask about latex if you're providing syringes with latex components. Document the answers. If the patient has no known allergies, document "NKA confirmed" or "NKDA reviewed." If they have allergies, document the allergen, the reaction, and the severity. A patient who had anaphylaxis to a prior injectable therapy needs a very different risk discussion than a patient who got mild itching from one antibiotic ten years ago. The severity matters. The documentation matters.

The contraindication screen is where you earn your medical license. Every peptide has specific contraindications and cautions. Your job is to screen for them systematically. Family history of medullary thyroid carcinoma or MEN2 before starting a GLP-1. Active or recent cancer before starting GH-axis or repair peptides. Uncontrolled hypertension before PT-141. Autoimmune disease before thymosin alpha-1. Pancreatitis history before incretin therapy. Gallbladder disease before weight-loss peptides. History of eating disorder before any appetite-suppressing therapy. The contraindication screen is not a formality. It is where you decide whether this patient belongs in the program at all. And if they have a relative contraindication - not an absolute one, but a caution - you document your clinical reasoning for proceeding, the enhanced monitoring plan, and the patient's informed consent to accept that enhanced risk. This is medicine. This is what separates licensed physicians from internet vendors.

Let me talk about something that separates professional practices from amateur operations: setting stop criteria before the first dose ships. This is one of the most powerful defensive tools you have, and most practices skip it entirely. Stop criteria are the conditions under which therapy is paused, reduced, or discontinued. They should be established at baseline, documented in the chart, communicated to the patient in writing, and revisited at every follow-up. What does this look like in practice? For a GLP-1 patient, your stop criteria might include: hold dose and contact clinic if severe abdominal pain, persistent vomiting, or signs of dehydration occur; discontinue if lipase >3x upper limit of normal; hold if patient cannot maintain adequate protein intake below 800 calories daily; discontinue if pregnancy occurs. For a GH-axis peptide, your stop criteria might include: discontinue if IGF-1 rises above age-adjusted upper limit; hold if fasting glucose rises above a defined threshold; discontinue if new edema, carpal tunnel symptoms, or headaches are intolerable. For a repair peptide, your criteria might include: discontinue if no measurable improvement in target symptoms after one full cycle; escalate to imaging or specialist referral if symptoms worsen despite therapy.

Why does this matter so much? Because stop criteria prove you were thinking ahead. They prove you didn't just write a prescription and hope for the best. They prove you established a clinical framework for decision-making before emotions and patient pressure entered the equation. When a board investigator sees a chart with documented stop criteria, they see a physician who was practicing medicine with foresight and discipline. When they see a chart with no stop criteria and a patient who stayed on therapy for eight months with worsening side effects, they see negligence. The difference is that stark. I have testified in proceedings where the presence of documented stop criteria was the difference between a dismissed complaint and a consent order. Do not skip this step.

Emergency instructions must be provided in writing, not just verbally. I cannot stress this enough. Verbal instructions are worthless in a regulatory or legal proceeding. The patient will claim they were never told. Your staff will have no record of what was said. The board will assume the worst. Written instructions, signed or acknowledged by the patient, create a contemporaneous record. These instructions should be specific. Not "call if you have problems." That's useless. Instead: "Call the clinic immediately or seek emergency care if you experience: severe abdominal pain that does not resolve within two hours; repeated vomiting more than three times in 24 hours; yellowing of the skin or eyes; chest pain or shortness of breath; severe allergic reaction including swelling of the face, lips, or tongue; severe mood changes or thoughts of self-harm; signs of infection at the injection site including redness, warmth, swelling, or fever." That level of specificity serves two purposes. It guides the patient to appropriate action. And it proves in the chart that you took emergency education seriously.

The baseline assessment is also where you establish the patient's primary care involvement. PCP relationships are your secret weapon. At baseline, document the patient's primary care physician's name and contact information. Document whether you have spoken with or sent records to that PCP. Document the patient's understanding that you are not replacing their primary care. If the patient does not have a PCP, address that. Either require them to establish one as a condition of therapy, or document your clinical reasoning for proceeding without one and the specific limitations that places on the program. A patient without a PCP is a higher-risk patient. You need to account for that risk in your baseline documentation. When

I review charts where the PCP was looped in from day one, I see practices that survive scrutiny. When I see charts where the PCP was never mentioned, never contacted, and never informed, I see practices that look like they were trying to operate in the shadows. Don't operate in the shadows. Loop in the PCP.

Let me close this section with a practical example of a good baseline note, because I know physicians learn from examples. Here is what a solid baseline note looks like for a semaglutide patient: "Patient is a 44-year-old female with BMI 33.2, history of hypothyroidism on levothyroxine 88mcg daily, no diabetes, no pancreatitis history, no gallbladder disease, no MEN2 or medullary thyroid carcinoma family history. PCP is Dr. Smith at Westside Internal Medicine; records request sent. Baseline vitals: BP 128/82, HR 72, weight 192.4 lbs. Baseline labs: HbA1c 5.6%, CMP within normal limits, TSH 2.4. Pregnancy test negative; patient on oral contraceptives, counseled on pregnancy prevention and immediate discontinuation if pregnancy suspected. Medication review completed: levothyroxine 88mcg daily, occasional ibuprofen for headaches. No allergies. Contraindication screen negative. Informed consent completed and signed; patient counseled on GLP-1 mechanism, expected benefits without guarantee, common side effects including nausea, constipation, reflux, and dehydration, and serious risks including pancreatitis and gallbladder disease. Emergency instructions provided in writing and acknowledged. Stop criteria established: discontinue for severe abdominal pain, persistent vomiting, jaundice, pregnancy, or lipase >3x ULN. Hold dose for intolerable nausea or inability to maintain protein intake >800 cal/day. Follow-up scheduled at 4 weeks with symptom check-in at 2 weeks. Patient understands and agrees to plan."

That note tells a story. It shows evaluation. It shows screening. It shows risk assessment. It shows patient education. It shows planning. It shows documentation of the clinical reasoning process. A board reviewer reading that note knows this physician was practicing medicine. Compare that to the alternative: "Patient wants semaglutide for weight loss. Prescribed 0.25mg weekly. Pharmacy notified." One of these charts gets you through an investigation. The other one gets you a consent order. You decide which one you want to write.

The Follow-Up System

So you've done the baseline. The medication shipped. The patient started. Now comes the part that separates real medical practices from everything else: the follow-up. And I want to be very clear about what I mean by follow-up. I do not mean a text message that says "How are you doing?" I do not mean an automated email that asks for a star rating. I mean structured, documented, clinician-reviewed follow-up that asks specific questions, captures specific answers, and leads to a documented clinical decision. Every. Single. Time.

Let me start with the cardinal rule of refills in peptide practice: no check-in, no automatic refill. A refill is not a logistical event. It is a clinical decision. The decision to continue therapy requires evidence that the patient is tolerating the medication, responding appropriately, following the plan, and not developing problems that require intervention. If you do not have that evidence, you do not refill. It does not matter that the patient paid. It does not matter that they sent an angry email saying they need their medication before vacation. It does not matter that your staff is busy and auto-refilling is easier. If there has been no clinical check-in, there is no basis for a refill decision. Full stop.

I have reviewed charts where patients received six consecutive months of semaglutide refills with zero symptom documentation between the initial consult and month seven, when the patient finally complained of intolerable side effects and demanded a refund. Those charts are indefensible. Not difficult to defend. Indefensible. Because every refill along the way was a missed opportunity to catch problems early, adjust the plan, and document clinical judgment. Six refills without review does not look like medicine. It looks like subscription commerce. And if that chart lands on a board investigator's desk, the investigator will not struggle to find a problem. The problem is the entire structure of care.

I want to tell you about a case I reviewed that still makes me angry. A physician in a cash-pay practice had built a beautiful weight-loss program. Beautiful website. Compelling marketing. Competitive pricing. Patients were pouring in. The physician hired staff to handle the administrative load, and somewhere along the way, the refill process got delegated. Not to a clinician. To an office manager. The office manager's instructions were simple: "If the patient paid and it's been four weeks, authorize the refill." No symptom review. No weight tracking. No clinician oversight. For eighteen months, this system ran on autopilot. Then a patient developed intractable vomiting, severe dehydration, and acute kidney injury after six months of escalating GLP-1 doses. The patient had reported worsening nausea at week eight, week twelve, and week sixteen. Nobody had reviewed those reports because nobody was required to. The office manager saw the payment, authorized the refill, and moved on. The board complaint was devastating. The physician's defense - "I didn't know my staff was doing that" - made it worse. You are responsible for your practice. Build systems that enforce clinical oversight, not systems that bypass it.

So what should symptom tracking look like before every refill? It should be systematic. It should cover the domains that matter for the specific therapy. And it should produce documentation that a clinician reviews before authorizing the refill. For a GLP-1 patient, the pre-refill check-in should ask about: nausea, vomiting, and abdominal pain; constipation or diarrhea; hydration status and fluid intake; appetite and protein intake; weight change; dizziness or fatigue; injection-site reactions; new medications; pregnancy risk; and whether the patient has visited an emergency room or urgent care since the last check-in. For a GH-axis peptide, you want to know about: sleep quality; energy and recovery; edema or joint stiffness; carpal tunnel-type symptoms; headaches; mood changes; and any new medical issues. For repair peptides, you want to know about: target symptom changes; pain levels or functional improvement; any new lumps, masses, or concerning symptoms; and whether standard care like physical therapy or imaging has been pursued as planned.

The method of check-in can vary. Some practices use online forms that patients complete before each refill. Some use phone calls from nursing staff. Some use portal messaging. Some use a combination. The method matters less than the consistency and the documentation. What does not work is asking the patient at the front desk when they come to pick up medication whether they're doing okay. That is not symptom tracking. That is social conversation. And it creates zero documentation.

Let me talk about red-flag escalation, because this is where practices save lives or lose licenses. Red flags are symptoms that require immediate clinician review and possible hold or discontinuation of therapy. They are not "watch and see" symptoms. They are not "schedule an appointment next week" symptoms. They are "stop the medication and call now" symptoms. Every patient must know them. Every staff member must know them. And your system must have a clear escalation pathway that routes red-flag reports directly to a clinician for same-day review.

What are the red flags? I've organized them by category because different peptide classes have different risk profiles, but there is a core set that applies broadly. Severe or persistent abdominal pain requires immediate evaluation and likely hold of any GLP-1 or incretin therapy until pancreatitis is ruled out. Persistent vomiting or signs of dehydration requires same-day clinician contact and possible IV fluid evaluation. Jaundice or clay-colored stools requires immediate discontinuation and liver workup. Allergic symptoms - rash, hives, facial swelling, difficulty breathing - require immediate discontinuation and emergency evaluation if severe. Chest pain, shortness of breath, palpitations, or fainting require emergency department evaluation. Severe mood changes, suicidal thoughts, or new psychiatric symptoms require immediate clinician review and likely discontinuation of any neuroactive therapy. Signs of infection at injection sites - spreading redness, warmth, pus, fever - require evaluation and possible antibiotic therapy. Pregnancy or suspected pregnancy requires immediate discontinuation of most peptide therapies. And any patient who admits to sharing medication, obtaining it from other sources, or self-escalating dose requires immediate clinician review and likely program termination.

Your staff must understand that red-flag symptoms do not get a "we'll let the doctor know tomorrow" response. They get a same-day clinician callback. They get a documented hold on refills until the clinician reviews. They get clear instructions to the patient about seeking emergency care when appropriate. If your staff is treating red-flag reports like customer service tickets, you have a dangerous practice. Train them. Test them. Document the training. And audit their responses periodically to make sure the escalation pathway actually works.

I remember reviewing a chart where a patient called the office on a Tuesday afternoon and told the receptionist they were having "really bad stomach pain" after starting tirzepatide. The receptionist took a message and put it in the physician's inbox. The physician was seeing patients all day Wednesday. The message was still in the inbox Thursday morning when the patient called back, this time from the emergency room, with confirmed pancreatitis and a lipase of 1,800. The gap between first report and clinical evaluation was forty-eight hours. That gap should have been two hours. The receptionist needed training to recognize that severe abdominal pain on a GLP-1 agonist is a same-day escalation, not a routine message. The practice needed a protocol. They had neither. The board settlement was significant.

Now let me walk you through the 15-minute follow-up visit, because this is the workhorse of peptide practice monitoring. A follow-up visit does not need to be an hour. It does not need to be comprehensive. It needs to answer three questions, and only three questions. Is it working? Is it safe? What's next? That's it. Three questions. Fifteen minutes. Done properly, this is the most efficient clinical encounter in medicine. "Is it working?" means: has the patient achieved measurable progress toward the goal we established at baseline? For weight-loss therapy, this means weight change, BMI change, waist circumference if tracked, and patient-reported functional improvement. For repair peptides, this means pain scale changes, range of motion changes, functional status changes. For GH-axis peptides, this means sleep quality, energy, recovery, and body composition metrics. The key word is measurable. "I feel better" is nice. "Pain decreased from 7/10 to 4/10, and I can walk two miles without stopping" is clinical evidence. Track measurable outcomes. Document them. Compare them to baseline. "Is it safe?" means: is the patient tolerating therapy without concerning side effects? This is where your symptom review happens. Nausea level. Injection-site status. Hydration. Energy. Mood. Any new symptoms since the last visit. Any red flags. Any labs that need review. This is also where you check adherence - is the patient actually taking the medication as prescribed? Dose confusion is shockingly common in peptide practice because patients are drawing up their own injections from compounded vials with varying concentrations. Ask them what dose they're taking. Ask them to show you if there's any confusion. A patient who has been injecting the wrong dose for six weeks because they misunderstood the units on the syringe is a patient safety incident waiting to happen. "What's next?" means: based on the working and safe assessment, what is the clinical decision? There are only four options, and you must document which one you chose. Continue: therapy stays at current dose, next follow-up scheduled. Adjust: dose goes up, dose goes down, or frequency changes based on response and tolerability; document the rationale. Hold: therapy paused because of side effects, upcoming procedure, intercurrent illness, or pending labs; document the reason and the plan for restart or reassessment. Stop: therapy discontinued because of adverse effects, lack of efficacy, patient request, safety concern, or completion of treatment course; document the reason, the discontinuation plan, and any follow-up needed. Those four words - continue, adjust, hold, stop - should appear in every follow-up note. They prove a decision was made. They prove the decision was thoughtful. They prove the physician was steering the ship.

Let me give you a concrete example of a good 15-minute follow-up note for a GLP-1 patient at week eight: "45-year-old female, week 8 follow-up for semaglutide program. Current dose: 0.5mg weekly. Weight: baseline 192.4 lbs, week 4 visit 187.2 lbs, today 183.6 lbs. Total loss: 8.8 lbs in 8 weeks. Patient reports improved portion control, less food noise, able to maintain protein intake per dietary guidance. Nausea: mild, 2/10, occurs day after injection, resolves within 24 hours. No vomiting. No abdominal pain. No constipation - reports regular bowel movements with increased fiber and fluid intake. Hydration: adequate, drinking 64+ oz daily. No dizziness. No injection-site reactions. No new medications. Pregnancy status: negative today, remains on OCPs. BP: 124/78. HR: 68. No ER or urgent care visits. Assessment: therapy is working -steady weight loss with tolerable side effects. Therapy is safe - mild nausea only, no red flags. Plan: ADJUST. Increase to 1.0mg weekly given good tolerability at 0.5mg and continued weight-loss progress. Counseled on expected transient increase in nausea with dose change. Reinforced protein intake and hydration targets. Red flags reviewed. Refill authorized for 4 weeks. Follow-up scheduled for week 12 with symptom check-in at week 10. Patient agrees and understands plan."

Read that note again. It tells a complete story. It shows the trend. It shows the assessment. It shows the decision. It shows patient education. It shows follow-up planning. A board investigator or malpractice attorney reading that note knows exactly what happened, why it happened, and what the plan is. The physician who writes notes like this does not get blindsided by complaints because the chart proves competent, continuous care.

Contrast this with what I too often see: "Patient doing well. Continue semaglutide. Refill x4 weeks." That note proves nothing. It does not show what "doing well" means. It does not document weight change. It does not document side effects. It does not show clinical reasoning. It does not establish a follow-up plan. If that patient develops pancreatitis two weeks later, that note does not help the physician. It hurts them, because it demonstrates superficial care in a space where careful monitoring is expected.

The documentation of continue, adjust, hold, or stop should be explicit, not implied. Do not write "patient tolerated medication, will continue current plan" and leave the reader to infer that you chose "continue." State it directly: "Plan: CONTINUE current dose." This small habit creates clarity in the chart that pays enormous dividends during any review. The explicit decision word proves you made a decision. It proves you were thinking. It proves you were not on autopilot.

Let me also address the hold decision specifically, because many physicians struggle with this. Holding therapy feels like failure. It feels like admitting defeat. It feels like the patient will be disappointed and might leave a bad review. Get over it. A hold decision is often the most clinically appropriate decision you can make. A patient with moderate nausea at week four who you hold at current dose for two more weeks before reassessing is a patient who might have developed intolerable nausea if you had escalated on schedule. A patient with a pending vacation who you hold for a week is a patient who won't be calling you from a hotel room in panic. A patient with an intercurrent illness who you hold until recovery is a patient you're protecting from risks. Hold decisions demonstrate clinical judgment. They do not demonstrate weakness. Document them with confidence and clear rationale.

The follow-up system also needs to account for patients who do not follow up. This is a critical and frequently overlooked element. What happens when a patient misses their scheduled check-in? What happens when the symptom form goes unanswered for two weeks? What happens when a patient requests a refill but has not had a clinician visit in four months? Your system must have a defined response. At minimum: unanswered symptom forms should trigger a staff outreach call. Missed follow-up appointments should trigger a second outreach and a chart note documenting the attempt. Refill requests without adequate follow-up should be paused pending clinician review. And patients who repeatedly miss follow-up despite outreach should be considered for program discontinuation with documentation of the noncompliance. A patient who will not participate in monitoring is a patient who cannot safely participate in therapy. When in doubt, say no - and that includes saying no to continuing therapy for patients who refuse the follow-up structure.

I once reviewed a chart where a patient missed three consecutive follow-up appointments and failed to complete six symptom check-ins over a four-month period. The practice kept shipping medication because the patient kept paying. When the patient eventually developed significant side effects and filed a complaint, the board investigator had a simple question: "If the patient was not participating in monitoring, why did you continue therapy?" The practice had no good answer. They had a policy about follow-up but no enforcement mechanism. They had expectations for patient participation but no consequences for non-participation. The chart showed that the practice knew the patient was noncompliant and continued anyway. That is not defensible. If a patient won't follow the program, they can't be in the program. Document the outreach, document the noncompliance, document the program discontinuation or the clinical decision to continue with enhanced monitoring and informed consent. But do not just keep shipping vials into a void.

Let me close this section with a word about the cadence of follow-up, because physicians always ask how often is often enough. The answer depends on the therapy, the patient, and the phase of treatment. For GLP-1 therapy, I recommend a symptom check-in at week two, a clinician follow-up at week four, and clinician follow-ups every four weeks during active dose titration. Once stable on maintenance dose, every eight to twelve weeks may be appropriate for low-risk patients. For GH-axis peptides, a check-in at week two and clinician review at four to six weeks is reasonable, with follow-up every eight to twelve weeks if stable. For repair peptides, follow-up at the midpoint and end of the treatment cycle - typically weeks three and six for a six-week cycle - with reassessment before any renewal. For investigational or higher-risk therapies, more frequent follow-up is warranted. Monthly clinician review is not excessive for a patient on an investigational peptide where the safety profile is still developing.

These are guidelines, not rigid rules. The key is not the exact interval. The key is that you establish the interval at baseline, document it, stick to it, and escalate when things change. A patient who develops new symptoms mid-cycle does not wait for the next scheduled visit. A patient who tolerates well and is stable does not need excessive visits that drive up cost and burden. Use your judgment. Document your judgment. And build a system that enforces whatever schedule you set.

Using Technology Wisely

I have spent enough time in this business to be deeply skeptical of technology that claims to solve medical problems. I have seen practice management systems that promise to streamline everything and instead create seventeen new passwords and a support line that nobody answers. I have seen telehealth platforms that crash during patient visits. I have seen AI chatbots that give patients dangerous advice and then disclaim responsibility. Technology in medicine is a tool, not a solution. It can make a good practice better and a bad practice worse. The key is knowing what to automate, what to augment, and what requires the human judgment of a licensed clinician.

AI-assisted intake and symptom tracking can organize information, but it cannot practice medicine. This distinction is not philosophical. It is legal, regulatory, and clinical. Artificial intelligence can summarize a patient's questionnaire responses. It can flag missing information. It can identify keyword patterns that suggest contraindications. It can remind staff that a patient's follow-up is overdue. It can prepare a draft note for clinician review. What it cannot do is diagnose, prescribe, adjust doses, discontinue therapy, reassure patients that their symptoms are normal, or make clinical decisions. Any system that allows AI to cross that line is creating liability that the physician will own when something goes wrong.

Let me explain how AI-assisted intake should work in a peptide practice. The patient completes an online questionnaire before their initial consultation. The AI system organizes the responses into a structured summary: chief complaint, medical history, current medications, allergies, prior therapies, goals, and flagged concerns. It cross-references medication lists against known peptide interactions. It highlights contraindication responses - the patient who checked "family history of medullary thyroid carcinoma" or "prior pancreatitis." It flags missing required information - the patient who skipped the pregnancy question or left the PCP field blank. It presents all of this to the clinician in a clean, readable format before the patient ever enters the exam room or joins the video call.

What the AI system does not do is approve the patient for therapy. It does not calculate a dose. It does not generate a prescription. It does not tell the patient they are a good candidate. It does not provide medical advice through a chat interface. It organizes information and says, in effect, "Here is what the patient reported. Here are the items that need your attention. A clinician needs to review this." That is the correct role for AI in medical intake. Information organization. Risk flagging. Workflow efficiency. Nothing more.

I want to be very clear about something because I see this mistake repeatedly. A practice buys an AI intake system. The system generates a "patient summary" that includes language like"patient is appropriate for semaglutide therapy based on BMI and absence of contraindications." The clinician reads that summary, agrees, and prescribes. The problem? The AI made a medical judgment. The AI does not have a medical license. The AI does not carry malpractice insurance. The AI cannot be named in a board complaint. But you can. And when the board investigator sees that your prescribing decision was based on an AI recommendation rather than your own independent clinical assessment, your defense just got a lot harder. AI-generated summaries should contain no clinical recommendations. They should present data. The clinician makes the recommendation. If your AI vendor claims their system can "approve" patients or "recommend" therapies, find a different vendor.

Automated reminders for follow-up, labs, and check-ins are one of the highest-value technology applications in peptide practice. The most common reason patients miss follow-up is not resistance. It is inertia. They forget. They get busy. The medication is working and they don't feel urgent about checking in. Your system should not allow this. Automated text reminders three days before a scheduled check-in. Automated email reminders when labs are due. Automated phone calls for patients who have not completed their symptom form three days after it was sent. Automated flags in your dashboard for patients with overdue follow-up who have pending refill requests. These are not annoying bureaucratic steps. They are the infrastructure of a medical program. A patient who misses a follow-up and then has an adverse event is a much bigger problem than a patient who gets an extra text reminder.

Let me give you a specific example of how reminder technology should work. A patient is due for their four-week follow-up. Three days before, they receive a text: "Your follow-up for your semaglutide program is due. Please complete your check-in form here: [link]. Your clinician will review your responses before authorizing your next refill." The patient clicks the link and completes a symptom questionnaire. The AI system summarizes their responses: weight down 6 lbs, mild nausea reported, no red flags, no new medications, no ER visits. The summary appears in the clinician's dashboard. The clinician reviews it, sees no concerns, and authorizes the refill with a brief note: "Week 4 follow-up reviewed. Weight loss appropriate. Mild nausea tolerated. No red flags. Plan: CONTINUE current dose. Refill x4 weeks. Next follow-up week 8." The patient receives confirmation that their refill is authorized. The entire interaction took the clinician three minutes. But it created a documented clinical review that proves supervision occurred.

Every AI-flagged item requires clinician review and documentation. This is non-negotiable. If your AI system flags a patient's report of severe abdominal pain, a clinician must review that flag the same day. Not tomorrow. Not when the staff gets around to it. Same day. And the review must be documented. If the clinician reviews the flag, calls the patient, determines the abdominal pain was actually mild cramping that resolved, and advises continuing therapy with close monitoring - that entire interaction belongs in the chart. The AI flag alone is not documentation. The clinician review is the documentation. Without it, you have a flagged symptom and a silent record. That gap is exactly what plaintiff attorneys and board investigators look for.

Let me be very specific about what constitutes proper documentation of AI flag review. A good note looks like this: "AI symptom check-in flagged: patient reported 'severe stomach pain, 8/10, since yesterday morning.' Clinician reviewed flag at 2:15 PM same day. Called patient at 2:22 PM. Patient describes crampy periumbilical pain, 8/10 at worst, now improving. No vomiting. No fever. No jaundice. Pain began after large fatty meal. Currently

3/10 and continuing to improve. Assessment: likely GI upset, not consistent with acute pancreatitis. Plan: HOLD semaglutide for 48 hours, clear liquid diet, monitor. If pain worsens, vomiting develops, or jaundice occurs, seek emergency care immediately. Will reassess by phone in 48 hours before restarting. Patient verbalizes understanding." That note took five minutes to write. It proves the flag was reviewed, the patient was contacted, an assessment was made, a plan was established, and the patient was given emergency instructions. The AI started the process. The clinician completed it. Both roles are clear. Both are documented.

Now let me talk about audit trails, because this is where technology becomes your surveillance system for your own practice. An audit trail is a chronological record of who did what, when, and why. In a peptide practice, your technology should track several critical data streams. Overdue labs: which patients have pending lab orders that have not been completed, how long have they been pending, and what action has been taken? Unanswered forms: which patients have not completed their required symptom check-ins, how many reminders have been sent, and have they been escalated to staff outreach? Adverse events: what symptoms have been reported, which were flagged as serious, how were they handled, and what is the resolution status? Complaints and refund requests: which patients have expressed dissatisfaction, what was the nature of the complaint, how was it resolved, and is there a pattern that suggests a systemic problem? And finally, refill authorization patterns: which refills were approved without clinician review, which were held pending follow-up, and what is the compliance rate with your own follow-up-before-refill policy?

These audit trails serve multiple purposes. Clinically, they help you identify patients who have fallen through the cracks. A patient with three overdue lab orders is a patient who needs immediate attention. A patient who has skipped four consecutive symptom check-ins is a patient who should probably not receive their next refill. Legally, audit trails prove that your practice had systems, that those systems were followed, and that exceptions were identified and addressed. A board investigator who sees a dashboard with 200 active patients, 12 overdue labs, 8 unanswered forms, and notes that each has been escalated to staff with dated outreach attempts sees a practice that is monitoring itself. A board investigator who sees 200 active patients and no tracking system sees a practice that is flying blind.

The technology you choose matters, but not as much as how you use it. I have seen practices with expensive enterprise EHRs that still have terrible documentation because the physicians don't use the tools properly. I have seen practices with basic practice management software that have bulletproof charts because the staff is disciplined and the protocols are followed. Technology amplifies your operational quality. It does not create quality where none exists. If your practice culture is sloppy - if staff skip steps, if clinicians don't review AI flags, if reminders are ignored - no amount of technology will save you. Fix the culture first, then layer on the tools.

Let me address the specific question of AI-generated chart notes, because this is an area of intense interest and significant risk. An AI system can draft a note based on patient responses. It can suggest language. It can format the note in your preferred structure. But the clinician must review every word, correct every error, and sign the note only after confirming its accuracy. An AI-drafted note that the clinician signs without review is a dangerous document. AI systems hallucinate. They misinterpret patient responses. They miss nuance. They cannot detect when a patient is minimizing symptoms or when a seemingly routine report actually contains a critical red flag. The clinician who treats an AI-drafted note as ready-to-sign without review is delegating clinical judgment to a machine. That delegation is indefensible.

A proper workflow for AI-assisted documentation looks like this: patient completes check-in form; AI summarizes responses and drafts a preliminary note; the summary and draft note appear in a clinician review queue; the clinician reads the original patient responses, not just the AI summary; the clinician evaluates any flagged items directly; the clinician edits, corrects, or rewrites the note as needed; the clinician documents the clinical decision explicitly; the clinician signs the note. Every step matters. Skipping the direct review of patient responses and relying solely on the AI summary is where errors happen. The summary is a starting point, not a substitute.

Let me also address the patient-facing side of AI technology, because patients are increasingly interacting with chatbots, symptom checkers, and automated response systems. The rule is simple: any patient-facing AI that could be interpreted as providing medical advice must include clear disclosure that it is not a substitute for clinician judgment. The chatbot that answers questions about injection technique is fine. The chatbot that tells a patient their symptoms are normal and they don't need to worry is practicing medicine without a license -and you're facilitating it. Patient-facing AI should provide educational information, logistical support, and triage guidance that directs patients to clinician contact for any medical concern."That's a great question about your injection technique. Here's a video guide. If you develop any redness, swelling, or fever at the injection site, please contact your clinician immediately through this link." That is appropriate. "Your nausea sounds normal, don't worry about it." That is dangerous. That crosses the line from information to medical advice, and when something goes wrong, the liability lands on the physician who deployed the chatbot.

The transparency of your AI system matters for regulatory and trust reasons. Patients should know that AI is involved in their care workflow. A simple disclosure - "We use technology to help organize your information and identify items that need your clinician's attention. All decisions about your care are made by your physician." - sets appropriate expectations. If a patient later claims they thought an AI chatbot was their doctor, that disclosure becomes evidence. If you never disclosed the AI's role, you face a harder conversation. This matters particularly in cash-pay practices where patients may have different expectations about the level of direct physician contact.

I want to raise one more issue about technology that I see practices getting wrong: the integration between your practice systems and your pharmacy. If your practice management system automatically sends refill authorizations to the pharmacy without clinician review, you have created an automated prescribing pipeline. That is not medicine. That is distribution. Every refill authorization should require a deliberate clinician action. The clinician reviews the follow-up data, makes a decision, and then authorizes the refill. The technology should facilitate this workflow, not bypass it. If your system allows one-click refill authorization without requiring the clinician to at least view the patient's recent check-in data, you have a dangerous shortcut. Build friction into the system where clinical judgment is required. Friction around clinical decisions is not inefficiency. It is patient safety.

One more thing about technology that I need to address, because I see practices getting this wrong with alarming frequency: the patient portal message that becomes a medical visit. A patient messages their provider through the portal: "I've been having some nausea since my dose went up. Is this normal?" The nurse responds: "Yes, nausea is common when increasing semaglutide. Try eating smaller meals and let us know if it doesn't improve." Sounds harmless, right? It's not. That exchange is a medical encounter. It contains a clinical assessment ("nausea is common"), patient education ("try eating smaller meals"), and a triage decision (monitor, don't escalate). But it is almost never documented in the chart as a clinical note. It sits in the portal message log, separate from the formal medical record. If that patient later develops pancreatitis and the board investigator reviews the chart, they may never see that portal exchange. Or worse, they see it and ask why a triage decision about a GLP-1 side effect was documented as a casual message instead of a clinical note. Every clinical interaction belongs in the chart. Portal messages that contain clinical judgment must be copied, summarized, or imported into the formal medical record. If your technology doesn't do this automatically, your staff must do it manually. This is tedious. It is also essential.

I also want to address the temptation to use AI to handle the "simple" patient questions - the ones that seem repetitive and straightforward. "When should I take my injection?" "Can I travel with my medication?" "What if I miss a dose?" These seem like perfect chatbot questions. And maybe they are, if the chatbot is strictly limited to educational information from your approved patient materials. But the moment the chatbot starts interpreting patient-specific situations - "I missed my dose three days ago and I still haven't taken it, should I take double?" - it has crossed into clinical territory. That question requires a clinician. It requires assessment of where the patient is in their treatment cycle, what medication they're on, what dose they missed, and what the specific protocol says. A chatbot that answers that question without clinician involvement is making a clinical decision without a license. Program your patient-facing technology with hard boundaries. Educational questions get automated responses. Clinical questions get routed to a clinician. No exceptions.

Let me close this section with a practical framework for evaluating whether your technology is helping or hurting your practice. Ask these questions honestly: Does our technology create documentation that proves clinical supervision, or does it create the appearance of supervision without substance? Does every AI flag get clinician review with dated documentation, or do flags sit in queues for days? Do our automated reminders actually reach patients and produce completed check-ins, or do they get ignored? Can we produce an audit trail of every touchpoint for any patient within five minutes if a board investigator asks? Does our staff understand which decisions the technology can support and which decisions require clinician judgment? If you cannot answer every one of these questions confidently, your technology needs attention. Because in a regulatory proceeding, a sophisticated system that wasn't used properly looks worse than no system at all. It looks like you had the tools to do it right and chose not to.

The follow-up system is your defense. The baseline assessment is your foundation. The monitoring structure is your proof. The technology is your amplifier. Put them together with discipline, consistency, and genuine clinical attention to your patients, and you have a peptide practice that can withstand scrutiny. Build it halfway, automate around missing judgment, or treat follow-up as optional, and you have a practice that will eventually face the kind of regulatory attention that ends careers. I have seen it happen. I have read the charts that couldn't defend the care. I have read the charts that could. The difference is never the peptide. The difference is always the follow-up. Document like someone will question it, because someone eventually will. The physician who builds a real follow-up system doesn't just protect their license - they practice better medicine. And at the end of the day, that's what matters.

11 - Pharmacy, Compounding, and Why Direct Ship Saves Your Skin

> **BLUNT RULE: A cheap vial from a weak pharmacy is not a bargain. It is a future board exhibit.**

Let me tell you something I've watched happen more times than I care to count. A physician builds a perfectly reasonable peptide practice. Good intake. Solid consent. Decent monitoring. Then a patient gets a vial from a pharmacy that cut corners, and everything goes sideways. An infection. A strange reaction. A label that doesn't match what's inside. And suddenly the board isn't asking about the pharmacy - they're asking about you. They're asking why you prescribed medication from a source that couldn't prove what was in it. They're asking why your patient ended up in the ER with an abscess from a contaminated injection. They're asking why your chart shows a prescription to a pharmacy with a history of warning letters and recalled products.

The pharmacy you choose is not a purchasing decision. It is a medical decision. It is a liability decision. It is a license-protection decision. And most physicians treat it like they're ordering office supplies.

This chapter is about fixing that. We're going to walk through how to choose a compounding pharmacy, why direct ship keeps you cleaner than office dispensing, and what happens if you decide to store and hand medication to patients yourself. Spoiler: if you can't run a mini-pharmacy, don't dispense. But we'll get there.

A Cheap Vial From a Weak Pharmacy Is a Future Board Exhibit

Here's the thing about compounding pharmacies - not all of them are created equal. Some are sophisticated operations with clean rooms, trained pharmacists, rigorous testing, and FDA oversight appropriate to their category. Others are barely holding it together. And when you're prescribing injectable peptides, the difference between those two categories isn't a minor quality distinction. It's the difference between a patient who gets sterile medication and a patient who gets bacteria, endotoxin, or something that isn't even the right compound.

The board doesn't care that you saved thirty dollars a vial. The board cares that your patient was harmed by a product you prescribed. And when they trace that vial back to a pharmacy with expired licenses, FDA warning letters, or a history of recalled sterile products, your chart starts looking very thin indeed.

Let me paint you a picture. A physician in the Southwest prescribed compounded semaglutide from a pharmacy he'd never actually vetted. He found them online. They had a professional website. Good pricing. Quick turnaround. Six months later, a cluster of patients reported injection-site infections. The state pharmacy board investigated. The pharmacy's sterile compounding certification had lapsed. Their environmental monitoring - the testing that catches contamination before it reaches patients - hadn't been performed in months. The FDA had already sent a warning letter the physician never bothered to look up.

You think the medical board cared that the physician "didn't know"? You think they accepted"the pharmacy seemed legitimate" as a defense? Not even close. The board's position was simple: you prescribed the medication, you chose the source, you own the outcome. That physician spent eighteen months and six figures defending a license that should never have been at risk.

This is why pharmacy due diligence isn't paperwork. It's survival.

The peptide space attracts vendors like flies. Everyone wants to compound GLP-1s now because that's where the money is. New pharmacies pop up overnight. Existing pharmacies add peptide compounding to services they've never offered before. Some are excellent. Some are dangerous. And the only way to know the difference is to verify - not assume, not trust a sales rep, not rely on a colleague's recommendation without checking yourself.

The red flags are usually there if you look. A pharmacy that won't provide their license number promptly. A pharmacy with no 503A or 503B status you can independently confirm. A pharmacy that can't explain their sterile compounding process. A pharmacy that ships nationwide but only holds licensure in one state. A pharmacy whose website makes therapeutic claims about peptides - which, by the way, is the pharmacy practicing medicine, not pharmacy. These aren't subtle warning signs. They're flashing neon lights that say "future board exhibit."

And here's what makes this worse: the patient doesn't know the difference. To a patient, a vial is a vial. They don't know that one pharmacy tests every batch for sterility and endotoxin while another cross their fingers. They don't know that one compounder sources raw materials from audited suppliers while the other buys from a broker who imports from a warehouse overseas.

They trust you to make that distinction. That's literally why they came to you instead of buying research chemicals online.

When you prescribe from a weak pharmacy, you betray that trust. And you create a chain of liability that leads straight back to your license.

The financial temptation is real, I get it. Good compounding pharmacies charge more. They have to - sterility testing, environmental monitoring, pharmacist oversight, proper storage, and legitimate raw material sourcing all cost money. The cheap pharmacy undercuts them because they skip steps. And when you choose the cheap option because it lets you price your program competitively, you're trading patient safety for margin. The board will see that. A plaintiff's attorney will see that. And your defense will sound like exactly what it is: you cut corners to save money.

So the first rule of pharmacy selection is this: source is not a detail. It is a safety issue. Treat it like one, or prepare to explain why you didn't.

Verify Licensure, 503A/503B Status, Sterile Capabilities, Inspection History

Let me walk you through what actual pharmacy verification looks like. This isn't a five-minute phone call. This is structured due diligence that you document in your compliance files. Because when the question comes - and it will come - you need to show that you did real work, not just checked a box.

Start with licensure. Every pharmacy must hold a current license in the state where they operate. That sounds obvious, but I've seen physicians prescribe from pharmacies whose license had been suspended or restricted and the physician never checked. Go to the state pharmacy board's website. Look up the license. Verify it's active. Note the expiration date. Check whether any disciplinary actions, restrictions, or conditions are listed. Do this for every state the pharmacy operates in - not just their headquarters state. If they're shipping to your patients across state lines, they need appropriate licensure and shipping authority for each destination state. Some states have specific requirements for out-of-state pharmacies shipping compounded medications to their residents. Know what your state requires. Document that you checked.

Confirm 503A versus 503B status. This distinction matters legally and operationally. A 503A pharmacy compounds patient-specific prescriptions pursuant to a prescription for an identified patient. They're primarily regulated by state pharmacy boards, though federal law still applies.

They cannot compound in large batches for office stock or wholesale. A 503B outsourcing facility registers with the FDA, complies with Current Good Manufacturing Practice (cGMP) standards, and can compound sterile medications in larger batches for office use under certain conditions. They undergo FDA inspection. They're held to higher standards.

You need to know which category your pharmacy falls into because it determines what they can legally compound, how they can ship it, and what regulatory framework applies. If a 503A pharmacy is offering you "office use" products or bulk quantities that sound more like distribution than patient-specific compounding, that's a red flag. If a 503B facility can't show you their FDA registration or their most recent inspection report, that's a red flag too. The status isn't just a label - it defines the legal boundaries of what that pharmacy can do for you.

Verify sterile compounding capabilities. You're prescribing injectable medications. That means sterility isn't optional - it's everything. Ask the pharmacy directly: do they perform sterile compounding? What clean room classification do they use? ISO 5? ISO 7? How often do they perform environmental monitoring - that's the air and surface testing that catches contamination? Do they test every batch for sterility, or do they use process validation with periodic testing? What's their endotoxin testing protocol? Endotoxin from bacterial cell walls can cause serious reactions even in sterile products, and injectable medications require it.

A legitimate pharmacy will answer these questions without hesitation. They'll provide certificates of analysis. They'll explain their quality program. A pharmacy that hedges, deflects, or acts like you're being unreasonable for asking - that's a pharmacy with something to hide. Walk away.

Check FDA inspection history and warning letters. The FDA publishes warning letters and inspection observations online. Go look. Search the FDA's warning letter database for the pharmacy's name. Search the FDA's 483 observation database if you're working with a 503B facility. A warning letter isn't an automatic disqualifier - good facilities can have issues and correct them. But a pattern of warnings? Repeated sterility observations? Unresolved violations? That's a pharmacy that doesn't take compliance seriously. And if they don't take their compliance seriously, they're not going to take your patient's safety seriously either.

Also check for recalls. Has the pharmacy recalled products in the past? Why? How did they handle it? A recall process that was prompt and transparent is actually a positive sign - it means their quality systems caught a problem. A pharmacy with recalls they didn't initiate themselves, or recalls they tried to minimize, is a different story.

Confirm shipping authority and practices. Can the pharmacy legally ship to your state? Do they require signature confirmation? How do they handle temperature-sensitive products? Peptides often require cold chain shipping - refrigerated or frozen transport with temperature monitoring. A pharmacy that ships semaglutide in an envelope with an ice pack that melted three days ago is creating a liability that lands on you. Ask about their packaging, their temperature monitoring, their delivery confirmation process. Ask what happens if a shipment is delayed, damaged, or lost. Their answer tells you whether they've thought this through or whether they're winging it.

All of this verification gets documented. Not in your head. Not in an email you can't find later. In a pharmacy due diligence file that you maintain and update. Because the board doesn't care what you knew. They care what you can prove you checked.

The Pharmacy Dispenses, Ships, Labels, and Counsels - You Handle Medical Supervision

Now let's talk about the model that keeps you cleanest: pharmacy direct ship. The pharmacy receives your prescription. The pharmacist reviews it. The pharmacy compounds the medication. The pharmacy labels it with dispensing information. The pharmacy provides medication-specific counseling - how to store it, how to reconstitute it, how to administer it, common side effects, when to call. The pharmacy ships it directly to the patient. And you -you do what you're licensed to do. You evaluate the patient. You make the medical decision. You supervise the therapy. You monitor for efficacy and safety. You handle follow-up, refill review, dose adjustments, and stop rules.

That's separation of duties. That's what the system is designed to look like. The pharmacist owns dispensing. The physician owns medical supervision. Each professional stays in their lane. And when something goes wrong, the liability chain is clear - which protects both of you.

Direct ship preserves the professional boundaries that regulators expect to see. The board understands a model where the pharmacy dispenses and the physician supervises. It's the standard arrangement for virtually all outpatient prescribing in the United States. When you walk into your PCP's office and they prescribe lisinopril, the PCP doesn't hand you a vial from a cabinet in exam room two. They send a prescription to CVS or Walgreens, and the pharmacy handles the rest. That model exists for a reason. It works. It's understood. It's defensible.

When you hand medication to a patient from your office, you've stepped into a different role. You're no longer just the prescriber. You're also the dispenser. And regulators start asking dispenser questions. How was it stored? Who labeled it? Who counseled the patient? How do you track inventory? What's your recall process? Those aren't medical questions - they're pharmacy questions. And if you can't answer them with the same rigor a licensed pharmacist would, you're exposed.

Direct ship lets you avoid all of that. The pharmacy's licensed pharmacists handle dispensing-level obligations. Their name is on the label. Their counseling documentation is in their records. Their sterility testing is on their certificates. Their storage is in their controlled environment. If there's a product problem, the pharmacy is the first point of regulatory contact- not you. That doesn't eliminate your responsibility for the prescribing decision.

Nothing does. But it keeps you out of dispensing liability, which is an entirely separate category of risk.

And let's be clear about what your role still is. Even with direct ship, you still educate the patient clinically. You explain why you prescribed this therapy. You explain what symptoms to watch for. You explain when to stop and when to seek emergency care. You explain your follow-up plan and your monitoring requirements. You don't abdicate patient education to the pharmacy. But you also don't try to replace the pharmacist's dispensing counseling with your own casual instructions. The pharmacy tells them how to reconstitute and inject. You tell them why they're doing it, what to expect, and when to call you. Different jobs. Different expertise. Both necessary.

The cleanest direct-ship practices document this separation explicitly. Their consent forms state that the pharmacy handles medication dispensing, labeling, and pharmacy-level counseling. Their chart notes reference the pharmacy by name. Their patient education materials explain who to call for what - pharmacy questions go to the pharmacy, medical questions come to the practice. That clarity protects everyone. The patient knows where to direct questions. The pharmacy knows their role. The practice knows theirs. And if the board ever reviews the chart, they see a clear separation of duties that looks professional, controlled, and compliant.

Direct Ship Avoids Turning Your Office Into a Dispensary, Storage Site, and Retail Counter

Let me describe what office dispensing actually looks like in practice. You need a secure, temperature-controlled storage area - refrigerator for the peptides, maybe a freezer for some products, locked cabinet for anything that could be diverted. You need an inventory management system - what's in stock, what expires when, what was dispensed to whom, when. You need labeling capability - printing labels with patient name, drug name, concentration, instructions, expiration date, lot number. You need a counseling process -someone has to hand the medication to the patient, explain it, document that counseling occurred. You need a recall process - if a product gets recalled, you need to know exactly which patients received which lots, and you need to contact them. You need security - access controls, theft prevention, diversion monitoring. You need staff training - everyone who touches medication needs to know what they're doing and what they can't do.

Now let me ask you: does that sound like your office? Or does it sound like a pharmacy?

Most physician offices are not built for this. They're built for examination, consultation, and clinical procedures. The storage is a closet with a mini-fridge that may or may not maintain temperature. The inventory tracking is a spreadsheet that gets updated when someone remembers. The labeling is a printed sticker from an office printer. The counseling is a nurse saying "here you go, the doctor explained this" while handing a bag over the counter. The security is a cabinet that three people have keys to. The recall process is hoping nothing ever gets recalled.

This isn't criticism - it's reality. Running a dispensary is a specialized skill. Pharmacies train for it. They're inspected for it. They're regulated for it. They have pharmacists whose entire job is making sure dispensing happens correctly. Your office doesn't have that infrastructure, and trying to create it on the fly is how mistakes happen.

Temperature excursions are a perfect example. Semaglutide and tirzepatide require cold storage - typically 2 to 8 degrees Celsius. If your office refrigerator drifts above that range because someone left the door open, overloaded it, or the unit is aging, you've potentially degraded every vial inside. Do you have a temperature logger that alerts you when the range is exceeded? Do you have a protocol for quarantining products after an excursion? Do you document the excursion and your response? Most offices don't. Most offices have a fridge with a dial that says "cold" and a vague sense that it probably works.

Then there's the retail counter problem. When patients pick up medication from your office, they start treating your office like a pharmacy. "Can I get a refill while I'm here?" "Do you have any samples?" "My friend wants to try this - can you sell her a vial?" "I ran out early -can I buy an extra?" Each of these requests creates a boundary-testing moment. Your staff, wanting to be helpful, may say yes to things they shouldn't. Or they say no and the patient gets annoyed. Either way, you've created a transactional dynamic that undermines the medical relationship. Direct ship eliminates this entirely. The pharmacy is where patients go for medication transactions. Your office is where they go for medical care. The distinction matters.

And here's the optics problem. An office with shelves of medication looks like a vial shop. I'm not saying it is one - I'm saying it looks like one. To a board investigator. To a patient who files a complaint. To a journalist doing an exposé on cash-pay peptide practices. To a plaintiff's attorney taking photographs for a lawsuit. The visual of medication stacked in a physician's office creates an impression that the practice is selling products, not providing medical care. Direct ship avoids that visual entirely. Your office is clinical. Clean. Professional. No shelves of vials. No refrigerator humming behind the front desk. No staff counting inventory between patient visits. Just medicine.

Patients Self-Administer at Home After Education - No In-Office Injections

There's another layer to direct ship that doesn't get discussed enough: the injection question. When medication ships from the pharmacy, patients self-administer at home. They learn injection technique from pharmacy-provided materials, video instruction, or your practice's education process. They don't come to your office for shots. And that matters more than you might think.

In-office injections create liability. Needle sticks. Fainting episodes. Adverse reactions requiring immediate management. Syncope with injury. Anaphylaxis - rare but not impossible. Each of these events can happen in your office, with your staff, on your watch. Your malpractice carrier needs to know you're doing injections. Your facility needs protocols for managing acute reactions. Your staff needs training in emergency response. Your insurance may need to reflect the additional risk. And if something goes wrong during an in-office injection, the question isn't just whether the medication was appropriate - it's whether your office was equipped and staffed to handle the administration.

Self-administration at home, by contrast, is the standard model for subcutaneous peptide therapy. Patients with diabetes have been injecting insulin at home for decades. GLP-1 receptor agonists are designed for self-administration. The subcutaneous route is forgiving - it's not intravenous, not intramuscular in a dangerous location, not requiring aspiration or advanced technique. A reasonably educated patient can learn to self-inject safely. The pharmacy provides the supplies, the instructions, and the counseling. Your practice provides the clinical education, the monitoring, and the follow-up. It's a proven model that works at scale.

That doesn't mean you abdicate injection education entirely. A good practice still provides clear guidance - either directly or through vetted educational materials - on technique, site rotation, hygiene, and safety. You document that the patient was educated. You confirm they received pharmacy counseling. You make sure they have appropriate supplies - the right syringes, alcohol swabs, sharps disposal. But you do this as clinical education, not as hands-on administration. The patient administers at home. You supervise medically. The separation holds.

There are limited exceptions where in-office injection makes clinical sense. A first-dose observation for a patient with significant anxiety or medical complexity. A patient with demonstrated inability to self-administer safely. A medication that requires clinical monitoring during or immediately after injection. But these are exceptions, not the model. If your default is in-office injections for routine peptide therapy, you need to ask yourself why - and whether the reason justifies the additional liability, staffing burden, and operational complexity.

Let me also address the patient who says "I don't want to inject myself." That's a reasonable concern, and it should be addressed with education, support, and clear instructions. But it shouldn't automatically become your staff's job to inject them. If a patient genuinely cannot self-administer, that raises a question about whether this therapy is appropriate for them. Subcutaneous self-injection is part of the treatment. A patient who can't or won't do it may need a different therapy, a different route, or a different level of care. Don't let patient reluctance convert your practice into an injection clinic.

Direct Ship Is Not Lazy - It's the Cleaner Risk Model

I hear this sometimes from physicians who pride themselves on being hands-on. "Direct ship feels impersonal." "I like being able to hand the patient their medication." "It shows we care.""Other clinics dispense - shouldn't we?"

Let me be blunt about this. Direct ship is not lazy. It is not a shortcut. It is not a way to avoid patient contact. It is a deliberate structural choice that keeps the practice in its proper lane and keeps the physician out of dispensing liability. The physician who chooses direct ship isn't doing less - they're doing differently. They're focusing their time and expertise on medical evaluation, patient education, monitoring, and follow-up. They're letting the pharmacy do what pharmacies do. That's not lazy. That's smart.

The "I like handing medication to patients" argument is dangerously sentimental. You know what the board thinks when they see a physician enthusiastically dispensing medication from their office? They wonder whether the financial incentive is driving prescribing. They wonder whether the physician is making money on the medication markup. They wonder whether the medical evaluation is as thorough as it should be, or whether the practice has become a distribution channel with a medical veneer. I'm not saying that's what you are. I'm saying that's what it can look like to someone who doesn't know you and is paid to be skeptical.

Cash-pay peptide practices already operate under suspicion. You're prescribing compounded medications that aren't FDA-approved in the traditional sense. You're taking payment directly from patients. You're operating outside the insurance system that most regulators understand. In that environment, optics matter enormously. Direct ship is one of the most powerful optics tools you have. It says: "We are a medical practice. We evaluate patients. We make medical decisions. We send prescriptions to licensed pharmacies. The pharmacy handles dispensing.

This is normal medicine, just with different medications."

Compare that to the office that stores vials, hands bags to patients, rings up charges at the front desk, and has a refrigerator full of medication behind the reception area. Even if the medicine is identical, even if the care is excellent, even if the chart is perfect - the appearance is different. And appearances drive complaints. They drive board investigations. They drive media stories. They drive plaintiff attorney interest.

Direct ship also makes financial sense for most practices, once you account for the true cost of dispensing. Staff time for inventory management. Storage equipment. Security. Labeling supplies. Waste from expired products. Liability insurance adjustments. The salary of a dispensing coordinator (which we'll discuss in the next section). The time you spend managing dispensing problems instead of seeing patients. When you add it all up, the margin on office dispensing often isn't what it appears to be on a spreadsheet. And the risk-adjusted return -the profit after you account for the additional liability - is frequently negative compared to direct ship.

The practices that do office dispensing well are the exception. They have dedicated pharmacy-trained staff. They have proper storage and security. They have robust inventory and recall systems. They treat it like the serious operational commitment it is. If that's not your practice- if you don't have the infrastructure, the staff, the systems, or the will to run a mini-pharmacy - then direct ship isn't lazy. It's the responsible choice.

One final point about direct ship that many physicians miss: it creates a natural boundary that protects your staff from scope creep. When medication comes from the pharmacy, patients call the pharmacy with pharmacy questions. "My shipment hasn't arrived." "The vial looks different from last time." "How do I reconstitute this?" "The label says something I don't understand." These questions go to the pharmacist - where they belong. In an office dispensing model, patients ask your front desk staff these questions. And your staff, wanting to help, may try to answer. They may give advice about storage, administration, or side effects that drifts into medical territory. They may troubleshoot problems they're not qualified to address. Direct ship keeps those questions where they belong - with the pharmacy - and protects your staff from wandering into liability they don't need.

If You Cannot Run It Like a Mini-Pharmacy, Do Not Dispense From the Office

Let me say this as clearly as I can, because physicians keep ignoring it and then calling me when the damage is done: if you cannot run your dispensing operation like a licensed mini-pharmacy, you should not be dispensing from your office. Full stop. No exceptions. No"but it's more convenient for patients." No "but we make more money." No "but everyone else does it." If you do not have the systems, the staff, the training, the storage, the security, the documentation, and the discipline of a pharmacy, then dispensing medication from your office is an accident waiting to happen - and when it happens, it will have your name on it.

The moment you store medication on-site and hand it to a patient, you have crossed a line that regulators take very seriously. You are no longer just a prescriber. You are a dispenser. And dispensing - the physical handling, storage, labeling, and transfer of medication to a patient-is a regulated activity with its own rules, its own standards, and its own liability. State pharmacy boards have jurisdiction over dispensing. State medical boards have opinions about it. Your malpractice carrier cares about it. Your facility liability policy may or may not cover it. And if something goes wrong with a dispensed product - a labeling error, a temperature excursion, an expired vial, a contaminated product, a theft or diversion - you are the responsible party because it happened in your facility, under your supervision, with your name on the chart.

I've seen the aftermath. The practice in Florida that kept compounded GLP-1s in a break room refrigerator next to someone's lunch. The temperature logger - they didn't have one, by the way - would have shown excursions every time the door opened. When a patient developed a severe injection-site infection and the culture came back with environmental bacteria, the board investigator asked about storage. The answer was a mini-fridge in the staff kitchen. That case didn't end well. It never does.

Or the practice in Texas that had a "helpful" front desk coordinator who kept a few extra vials in her desk drawer for patients who "needed them right away." No inventory tracking. No temperature control. No documentation of lot numbers. When a recall notice came through for a specific lot of compounded semaglutide, the practice had no way to know which patients had received that lot. They had to contact every patient who'd ever received semaglutide from them - hundreds of people - and tell them to stop using it immediately. Three patients had already reported adverse reactions. The dispensing coordinator had given them recalled product from her desk drawer because it was faster than checking the main inventory. That coordinator didn't have a pharmacy license. She didn't have dispensing training. She had a friendly personality and a key to the cabinet. That was enough to create a patient safety event and a board complaint.

These aren't hypothetical scenarios. These are real cases with real consequences. And they share a common thread: the physician thought dispensing was simpler than it actually is. They thought storing a few vials and handing them to patients was just customer service. They thought the pharmacy rules didn't apply to them because they were doctors.

They were wrong.

The threshold question isn't whether you want to dispense. It's whether you can dispense with the same rigor a pharmacy would apply. That means secure, temperature-controlled storage with continuous monitoring. It means an assigned dispensing coordinator with defined responsibilities and proper training. It means written policies covering every aspect of the operation. It means inventory management with lot tracking. It means labeling that meets dispensing standards. It means patient counseling documented in writing. It means recall procedures that actually work. It means regular audits. It means theft and diversion controls. It means staff who understand their boundaries. And it means a physician-owner who treats all of this as seriously as they treat clinical care - because it is clinical care. The medication that comes out of your dispensing cabinet goes into a patient's body. If you wouldn't tolerate sloppy technique in your exam room, you shouldn't tolerate sloppy handling in your storage area.

Most practices, if they're honest with themselves, cannot meet this standard. Not because they're bad practices, but because they're medical practices, not pharmacies. Their infrastructure is built for patient care, not pharmaceutical distribution. Their staff are trained in clinical support, not inventory management. Their systems are designed for charting, not lot tracking. Trying to bolt on a dispensing operation without fundamentally changing how the practice operates is like trying to perform surgery in a conference room - you might get through it, but the environment isn't designed for what you're doing, and the risk is higher at every step.

So the first rule of office dispensing is the simplest and the hardest: be honest about whether you can actually do this right. If the answer is no - and for most practices, it should be no -then direct ship is your answer. Use it without apology. The patient gets their medication from a licensed pharmacy with proper systems. You stay in the medical lane. Everyone is safer.

If the answer is yes - if you genuinely have the infrastructure, the staff, the systems, and the discipline to run a mini-pharmacy - then keep reading. Because the next sections will show you exactly what that looks like. And if any of it feels excessive, refer back to the first rule: if you can't do it right, don't do it at all.

Written Policies, Assigned Coordinator, Staff Training, Secure Storage, Temperature Logs

Let's assume you've decided to dispense and you're committed to doing it properly. Here's what "properly" actually means in operational terms. Not vague aspirations - specific systems that you build, document, train, and audit.

Written policies come first. Before a single vial enters your office, you have a dispensing policy manual. It covers what products you dispense and what you don't. It defines who can handle medication and who cannot. It specifies storage requirements by product type -refrigerated, frozen, room temperature, protected from light. It details the labeling process -what goes on every label, who prints it, who checks it, how errors get caught. It outlines the dispensing workflow from prescription to patient handoff. It documents counseling requirements - what must be explained, what must be documented. It establishes your inventory management system - receiving, logging, tracking, counting. It defines your recall and adverse event process. It covers waste disposal - expired product, damaged product, patient returns. It addresses theft and diversion - security controls, access restrictions, suspicious activity monitoring. And it specifies your audit schedule - daily, weekly, monthly, quarterly checks with assigned responsible parties.

This manual isn't a draft you keep on your computer. It's a living document that your staff are trained on, that you review and update at least annually, and that you can produce on demand if a regulator asks. It's the evidence that you took dispensing seriously enough to build a system around it.

The dispensing coordinator is the linchpin. Someone in your practice - one specific person, named in writing, with this as part of their official job description - owns the dispensing program. Not "everyone helps out." Not "whoever is free." One person. Accountable. Trained. Authorized. Their name is on the policy. Their signature is on the training records. Their initials are on the logs.

The dispensing coordinator manages inventory. They receive shipments, verify contents against packing slips, check for damage or temperature excursion, log lot numbers and expiration dates, and store products according to policy. They monitor storage conditions -daily temperature checks with documented readings, immediate response to any excursion, quarantine procedures for affected product. They manage the dispensing workflow - prepare labels, verify prescriptions against labels, double-check drug name and concentration, confirm patient identity, document counseling, obtain patient signature. They handle recalls - tracking lot numbers, identifying affected patients, executing notification, documenting response. They conduct regular audits - daily log reviews, weekly expiration and tampering checks, monthly inventory counts, quarterly comprehensive audits. They train other staff on what they may and may not do. And they escalate immediately when something is wrong - temperature excursion, labeling error, suspected theft, suspicious patient behavior, product defect.

This coordinator needs training. Not just a five-minute conversation when they start - actual structured training on pharmacy practices, medication handling, sterile product storage, temperature monitoring, patient counseling, documentation requirements, and error recognition. If you can send them to a pharmacy technician training program or hire someone with pharmacy experience, do it. The cost of proper training is trivial compared to the cost of a dispensing error.

And here's the key: the dispensing coordinator does not make medical decisions. They don't approve prescriptions. They don't counsel patients on clinical matters. They don't interpret side effects. They don't recommend dose changes. They handle the operational aspects of dispensing and nothing more. Any question that requires clinical judgment gets escalated to the prescriber. This boundary protects the coordinator from practicing beyond their scope and protects the physician from delegation errors.

Secure storage is non-negotiable. Medication must be stored in a locked area accessible only to authorized personnel. The dispensing coordinator controls access. Not the office manager. Not the front desk staff. Not the medical assistants. The coordinator decides who gets keys or combinations, documents authorized access, and reviews access periodically. If someone leaves the practice, their access is revoked immediately - not next week, not when someone remembers. Same day.

Refrigerated and frozen products need dedicated, pharmacy-grade refrigeration - not the break room fridge, not the one you use for vaccines, not a dormitory mini-fridge from Amazon. These units must maintain required temperature ranges continuously. That means continuous temperature monitoring with digital loggers, not a thermometer you glance at when you think of it. The logger records temperatures at regular intervals - every few minutes - and alerts when thresholds are exceeded. Those alerts go to the dispensing coordinator and the practice manager, and they require immediate response. Every temperature reading gets logged. Every excursion gets documented with time, duration, product affected, assessment, and disposition. If product has to be discarded, it's documented as discarded with lot numbers and reasons. This log is auditable evidence that you maintained the cold chain - or that you caught and addressed problems when the cold chain failed.

Injectable peptides and compounded sterile products have no margin for error on temperature. A vial of semaglutide that's been sitting at room temperature for three days because the refrigerator failed over the weekend isn't just "probably fine." It's potentially degraded, potentially unsafe, and potentially the basis for a complaint if a patient uses it and has an unexpected outcome. Your policy must be clear: temperature excursion means automatic quarantine, assessment, and probable discard. No "let's see if it still works." No "it was only a little warm." The policy is the policy, and the coordinator enforces it without exception.

Staff training extends beyond the coordinator. Every person in the practice who might touch medication, enter the storage area, or interact with patients about dispensed products needs training on their role and their boundaries. Front desk staff need to know that they don't answer clinical questions about medication. Medical assistants need to know that they don't dispense, don't label, and don't counsel without specific authorization. Nursing staff need to understand where their clinical role ends and the dispensing coordinator's operational role begins. Everyone needs to know the basic safety rules - report temperature alarms immediately, don't leave medication unattended, don't share access codes, don't override procedures for convenience.

Training is documented. Everyone signs. The coordinator keeps the records. Annual refresher training is required. New staff get trained before they have any access. And if someone violates policy - even once, even "accidentally" - there's a documented corrective conversation and, if necessary, removal of access. You're running a mini-pharmacy, not a neighborhood swap meet. The standards are high because the stakes are high.

Inventory Counts, Expiration Checks, Labeling, Counseling, Recall Processes

Now let's get into the daily, weekly, and monthly operational grind. This is the work that separates a real dispensing program from a vial shop pretending to be a medical practice. It's boring. It's repetitive. It's essential.

Inventory counts happen on a schedule. Daily: the dispensing coordinator verifies that the dispensing log matches physical inventory. What went out, what's still on the shelf, any discrepancies are investigated immediately. Weekly: a more thorough count of all products by lot number, cross-referenced against the dispensing log. Monthly: full physical inventory -every vial, every lot number, every expiration date, matched against the log. Quarterly: comprehensive audit that the medical director reviews and signs off on. Discrepancies at any level trigger investigation. Missing product is a security event. Extra product is a receiving error. Both get documented, explained, and corrected.

The monthly inventory count includes a critical task: expiration date review. Every product gets checked. Anything expiring within 30 days gets flagged. Anything expired gets immediately quarantined, documented, and disposed of according to your policy and applicable regulations. You do not "use it up" before it expires. You do not give expired product to a patient who "really needs it." Expired medication is medical waste, and it gets handled as such. The coordinator documents what was discarded, why, the lot number, and how it was disposed of. That documentation is part of your audit trail.

The expiration check also identifies slow-moving inventory. If you have vials of a peptide that haven't moved in three months, you need to ask why. Is it because demand changed? Is it because you overordered? Is it because the product is less popular than expected? Slow inventory ties up capital, risks expiration waste, and suggests your ordering practices need adjustment. More importantly, it might signal that a product has become less available or that regulatory changes have affected what you can legally compound. The coordinator flags slow inventory for the medical director's review.

Labeling is where many dispensing errors originate. A label with the wrong patient name, the wrong drug concentration, the wrong instructions, or a missing warning can cause serious harm. Your labeling process must have a double-check built in. The coordinator prepares the label from the prescription. A second authorized person - another trained staff member or the physician - verifies the label against the prescription before the product is released. Name, drug, concentration, quantity, instructions, expiration date, lot number, prescriber name, practice contact information. Every element checked. Every discrepancy resolved before the patient touches the product.

Labels must meet the standards that apply to dispensed medication in your state. That typically includes patient name, drug name and strength, quantity, directions for use, prescriber name, dispensing date, expiration date, lot number, and pharmacy or practice identification. If you're compounding peptides that require special storage, the label should include storage instructions. If there are known risks - "refrigerate, do not freeze" or "protect from light" -those go on the label too. The label is your patient's primary source of information about what they're holding. Make it accurate, complete, and legible.

Patient counseling is mandatory and documented. When medication is dispensed, the patient receives counseling from an authorized staff member - ideally the dispensing coordinator, who has specific training. The counseling covers: what the medication is, how to store it, how to reconstitute it if applicable, how to administer it, common side effects, serious warning signs that require immediate medical attention, when to follow up with the practice, and how to contact the practice with questions. The patient has an opportunity to ask questions. Their questions and the answers get documented. The patient signs an acknowledgment that counseling was provided. That signature goes in the record.

This counseling is distinct from the clinical education the physician provides. The physician explains the medical rationale, the expected benefits, the risks in context, the monitoring plan, and the follow-up schedule. The dispensing counselor explains the practical aspects of handling and using the medication. Both are necessary. Both get documented. The separation reinforces the distinction between medical supervision and dispensing.

The recall process is where dispensing programs live or die. When a recall notice arrives -from your pharmacy supplier, from the FDA, from a state board - you need to act fast and act precisely. Your dispensing coordinator immediately checks inventory against the recalled lot numbers. Any recalled product in stock gets quarantined immediately - removed from active inventory, clearly marked, physically separated. The coordinator pulls the dispensing log for the affected product and identifies every patient who received a recalled lot. The medical director is notified within hours, not days. Each affected patient is contacted - by phone, with documentation of the call, followed by written notice if required. The contact includes: what was recalled, why, what the patient should do (stop using, discard, return), how to report any adverse effects, and how to reach the practice with questions. Every patient contact is documented - date, time, method, who made contact, what was said, patient response.

If a patient reports an adverse event related to recalled product, that's escalated immediately to the medical director and documented as a potential adverse event requiring follow-up. The pharmacy supplier gets notified per their adverse event reporting requirements. The FDA MedWatch system may need to be used depending on the event severity. Your malpractice carrier may need notification. The state medical board may need to be informed if the event is serious. All of this happens according to a written protocol that the coordinator can execute without having to figure it out in the moment.

The recall process is one of those things that seems theoretical until it isn't. And when it isn't theoretical anymore - when the FDA issues an alert and you have two hundred patients who might have affected product - your system either works or it collapses. I've seen practices that handled recalls beautifully because they had the system, the coordinator, and the documentation. I've seen others that took weeks to contact patients, lost track of lot numbers, and had no idea who got what. Guess which ones ended up with board complaints?

Adverse event handling deserves its own mention. When a patient reports a problem - an injection-site reaction, unexpected symptoms, a product that looks wrong, anything out of the ordinary - the dispensing coordinator captures the details immediately. What product? What lot number? When was it dispensed? When did the symptoms start? What happened? This information goes to the medical director for clinical assessment and to the pharmacy supplier for their quality investigation. The coordinator maintains a log of all reported events, whether they turn out to be product-related or not. Patterns get flagged. Three patients reporting similar reactions from the same lot is a signal, not a coincidence. Your adverse event log is early warning system, quality improvement tool, and legal protection all in one.

If This Checklist Feels Excessive, Use Direct Ship Instead

I've laid out a lot of requirements in this section. Written policies. Assigned coordinator. Staff training. Secure storage. Temperature monitoring with digital loggers. Daily, weekly, monthly, and quarterly audits. Inventory counts. Expiration checks. Double-checked labeling. Documented patient counseling. Recall procedures. Adverse event tracking. Theft and diversion controls. Continuous documentation.

If you're reading this and thinking, "This is insane, there's no way my practice can do all of this" - good. That means you're being honest with yourself. And the honest answer for the vast majority of peptide practices is: you shouldn't be dispensing from your office. You should be using direct ship. Let the pharmacy handle dispensing. Let them carry the operational burden, the liability, and the regulatory scrutiny. You focus on medicine.

I'm not trying to talk you out of office dispensing if you genuinely have the infrastructure and commitment to do it right. Some practices do. Large integrated wellness clinics with dedicated operations staff, facilities built for it, and the volume to justify the overhead can run excellent dispensing programs. Practices in rural areas where pharmacy access is genuinely limited may have good reasons to dispense certain products. Practices with specific office-use arrangements under 503B authority may have a defensible model. The exceptions exist.

But for the typical cash-pay peptide practice - a physician or two, a small support staff, a leased office suite, a focus on patient evaluation and monitoring - office dispensing is more risk than reward. The margin you think you're making gets eaten by staff time, storage equipment, waste from expired inventory, liability adjustments, and the opportunity cost of managing a pharmacy operation instead of seeing patients. And if something goes wrong - a temperature excursion you didn't catch, an expired vial that gets dispensed, a labeling error, a theft, a recall you mishandle - the cost of defending that error far exceeds whatever profit you made on the dispensing operation.

Let me give you the decision framework I use with practices. Ask yourself these questions, honestly:

Can you assign one person - one specific, named, trained person - as dispensing coordinator with no other conflicting priorities? Not "Sally does it when she's not at the front desk." Not"whoever has time." One person whose job description includes this accountability and whose performance review reflects it.

Can you install pharmacy-grade, temperature-controlled storage with continuous digital monitoring and alerting? Not a dorm fridge. Not the break room refrigerator. Purpose-built units with validated temperature ranges and automatic logging.

Can you implement and maintain an inventory management system that tracks every vial by product, lot number, expiration date, quantity in, quantity out, and patient dispensed to? A system that gets reconciled daily and fully audited monthly? A system that can produce a patient contact list by lot number within hours of a recall notice?

Can you create and enforce written policies covering every aspect of dispensing - receiving, storage, labeling, counseling, documentation, recalls, adverse events, waste disposal, theft prevention, and audits? Can you train every staff member on these policies, document the training, and hold people accountable for following them?

Can you conduct documented patient counseling for every dispensed product, with the patient signing an acknowledgment? Can you ensure that counseling happens consistently even when the practice is busy, even when the coordinator is out, even when the patient is in a hurry?

Can you execute a product recall within 24 hours - identifying affected inventory, pulling it from stock, identifying every patient who received it, and contacting them all with documented instructions?

If you answered "no" or even "I'm not sure" to any of these questions, you should not be dispensing from your office. Direct ship is your answer. It keeps you in the medical lane. It lets the pharmacy own dispensing. It gives you the cleanest liability profile. And it frees you to focus on what you were trained to do - evaluate patients, make medical decisions, and provide clinical supervision.

There's no shame in choosing direct ship. None. The physician who recognizes their operational limits and structures accordingly is making a smart, mature, defensible decision. The physician who dives into office dispensing without the systems to support it is gambling-with patient safety, with their license, and with their future.

Let me close this chapter with a story from a physician I advised a few years back. He was running a successful hormone and peptide practice, doing well, good patient outcomes, solid reputation. He decided to add office dispensing because a vendor showed him a spreadsheet suggesting he'd make an extra hundred fifty thousand a year. He bought a refrigerator, designated a staff member as "dispensing coordinator" (she was also the front desk lead, medical assistant, and social media manager - but sure, she could handle it), and started stocking vials.

Six months later, a state pharmacy board inspector walked in on a routine complaint follow-up. The refrigerator was at twelve degrees Celsius - above the required range. Three products were expired but still in active inventory. The dispensing log hadn't been reconciled in eleven days. The coordinator couldn't produce training records. Labels had been printed with the wrong concentration on two occasions - caught by patients, not by staff. The inspector wrote a report that triggered a full investigation. The medical board got involved. The malpractice carrier raised questions. It took eighteen months, seventy thousand dollars in legal fees, and two independent audits to resolve. The extra revenue from dispensing? About forty thousand dollars before the trouble started. Net result: a thirty thousand dollar loss, a tarnished reputation, a staff member who quit under stress, and a physician who told me later, "I wish I'd just stayed with direct ship."

The lesson isn't complicated. Source is a safety issue. Pharmacy selection matters. Direct ship is usually safer. And office dispensing - if you do it at all - must be run like the serious pharmaceutical operation it is. If you can't do it right, don't do it. Your license, your patients, and your peace of mind will all be better for it.

The pharmacy dispenses. You supervise the medical plan. That's the model that works. That's the model that defends. And that's the model that keeps you practicing medicine instead of explaining to a board investigator why a broken refrigerator and a missing log led to a patient getting harmed medication from your office.

Choose wisely.

12 - The Money: Pricing Like Your License Depends On It

Let me tell you something I have seen too many times. A good physician - smart, well-trained, genuinely cares about patients - decides to add peptides or hormone therapy to his practice. He looks at what the local competition charges, undercuts them by thirty percent to"get established," fills up his schedule in six weeks, and twelve months later he is explaining himself to the state medical board. The investigator is looking at his charts, and the charts are thin. The consent forms are a single page of legal jargon nobody read. The follow-up notes say"doing well, refill approved" eight times in a row. The patients who complained - and there are always patients who complain - say they never saw a doctor, never got proper monitoring, and paid a lot of money for a vial that showed up in the mail.

The doctor is stunned. He meant well. He really did. But meaning well does not fill out a chart, and it certainly does not impress a medical board investigator who has already seen ten of these cases this month. The problem started with the price. Not because the price was too high- because it was too low.

This chapter is about the money. Not how to get rich. How to price your program so you can afford to run it correctly, so the board sees a medical practice instead of a vial shop, and so you keep your license. Everything in this chapter connects back to one truth: underpricing is not a competitive strategy. It is a compliance death wish.

Charge for Supervised Medical Care, Not the Vial

The single biggest mistake physicians make when they start a peptide or hormone program is they price it like they are selling a product. They call the pharmacy, find out what the semaglutide or the tirzepatide or the testosterone cypionate costs per vial, add a modest markup that feels "fair," and call that the price. Then they tack on an office visit fee that barely covers the front desk staff's time. This is not a medical program. This is retail with a DEA number. And it will destroy you.

When you price at medication cost, you cannot afford proper follow-up. You cannot afford the thirty-minute intake that screens for contraindications. You cannot afford the nurse who calls the patient after the first injection to ask about side effects. You cannot afford the clinician review of every refill request. You cannot afford the documentation that explains why this patient, at this time, with this medication, after these alternatives were considered. You cannot afford the compliance infrastructure - the protocols, the audits, the staff training, the chart reviews - that keeps a practice out of trouble. So you skip it. You tell yourself you'll tighten things up once the practice is bigger. Except the practice gets bigger, the patients keep coming, the revenue looks good on paper, and the corners you are cutting become invisible until the board shows up with a subpoena.

Let me be very clear about what I am saying here. You want to charge as much as the market will bear. You do not want to try to be the lowest price anywhere. The lowest-priced peptide clinic in your market is not your friend - it is a warning sign. That clinic is either cutting clinical corners you cannot see, or it will be investigated soon, or both. Price competition in peptide medicine is a race to the bottom, and the bottom is a board hearing where you explain why your charts look like receipts.

A properly run peptide program is priced at two to four times the acquisition cost of the medication. Some programs go higher depending on the market, the therapy complexity, the monitoring burden, and the regulatory risk. That sounds like a lot until you actually list out what the patient is getting. Medical oversight and clinical consultation. Comprehensive screening and intake. Patient education on administration, side effects, storage, and emergency stop rules. Syringes and supplies. Pharmacy coordination and verification of compounded product integrity. Follow-up visits or structured check-ins. Refill review by a clinician before every shipment. Side-effect monitoring through a systematic reporting system. Staff time for patient communication, form processing, and care coordination. Documentation and compliance overhead that would make a hospital administrator proud. Risk management infrastructure, including complaint handling protocols and the legal framework that protects both doctor and patient. When you lay it all out, two to four times medication cost is not a markup - it is barely enough.

The psychology of pricing in medicine is counterintuitive. Patients do not trust cheap doctors. They may say they want a lower price, but what they actually want is confidence that they are in competent hands. A low price signals that the service is a commodity. A high price, explained properly, signals that the program is serious, personalized, medically supervised, and worth the investment. Think about the last time you chose a surgeon. Did you pick the cheapest one? Of course not. You picked the one who made you feel safe. Patients are not smarter than you - they operate on the same instincts. They want to feel that their doctor has time for them, that the program is thorough, that they will not be abandoned when they have a question. A low price makes those promises impossible to keep.

Here is how the conversation should go when a patient asks what the program costs. You explain that this is a supervised medical program, not a medication order. You walk through what is included: the intake, the screening, the education, the follow-up, the monitoring, the refill reviews, the access to clinical staff. You explain that cheaper options exist but that those options may not include the clinical support, the systematic follow-up, and the documentation that makes this medicine rather than retail. You let them decide. Some will go shop for a lower price. Let them. The patients who leave because your price is too high are often the same patients who will be unhappy no matter what you charge. The patients who stay understand that supervised medical care costs what it costs, and they are paying for your time, your judgment, and your commitment to doing this right.

If you price at medication cost, you will skip steps. It is not a character flaw - it is arithmetic. You cannot spend forty-five minutes on an intake, thirty minutes on education, fifteen minutes on every refill review, and an hour on follow-up monitoring per patient per month when you are making fifty dollars above drug cost. You will start batching refills. You will let staff approve renewals without clinician review. You will stop calling patients who miss their check-ins. You will accept thin charts because thorough charts take time and time is money you do not have. The board will notice. The board always notices. And when they do, your explanation that you "couldn't afford to do it right" will not save your license. It will accelerate its loss.

The other problem with underpricing is that it makes you look like a vial shop to everyone who matters. The state medical board investigator, the malpractice plaintiff's attorney, the pharmacy board auditor - they all know what a legitimate medical program looks like, and they all know what a discount medication operation looks like. A legitimate program has charts that explain clinical reasoning. A discount operation has charts that say "patient wants refill, approved." A legitimate program has follow-up. A discount operation has automatic refills. A legitimate program prices for the work. A discount operation prices for the product. You want to be unmistakably in the first category.

I am not telling you to gouge patients. I am telling you that doing this work correctly requires resources, and those resources have to come from somewhere. The pharmacy gets paid for the vial. The staff gets paid for their time. The landlord gets paid for the space. The malpractice carrier gets paid for the policy. You need to get paid for the clinical judgment, the risk you are assuming, and the infrastructure you are maintaining. If any of those pieces is missing, the whole system collapses. Underpricing does not make you competitive. It makes you vulnerable.

There is also the practical matter of patient accessibility. Now this sounds like it contradicts everything I just said, but hear me out. You want the patient to always feel as though you are accessible. That does not mean you are cheap. It means your staff answers the phone. It means questions get answered within a reasonable timeframe. It means patients are not left alone for weeks with a side effect they are scared about. Accessibility is a function of staffing, and staffing is a function of revenue. A practice priced at drug cost plus a tip cannot afford the staff to be accessible. So the paradox is that charging more actually makes you more accessible, because you can afford the infrastructure that responsiveness requires. The cheap clinic has a voicemail system and a two-week callback window. Your clinic has a human being who answers the phone. Which one keeps patients safe? Which one keeps patients happy? Which one keeps patients from filing complaints?

Let me give you a war story. I knew a physician in Texas who started a GLP-1 weight-loss program at $199 a month, medication included. He called it his "loss leader" to build the practice. Within four months he had six hundred active patients. His staff was drowning. Refills were approved by a receptionist clicking a button. The physician had not personally reviewed a chart in six weeks. Three patients ended up in the ER with dehydration and vomiting - they had been escalating their own doses based on internet advice, and nobody from the practice had called them back. Two of those patients filed board complaints. The investigator asked to see ten charts at random. Eight of them had no documented follow-up for three months. The ninth had a note that said "patient doing fine" with no vitals, no weight, no symptom review. The tenth was actually decent - one out of ten. The board restricted his license for eighteen months, required remedial education, and imposed monitoring conditions that cost him more than the entire program had generated. He told me later that the $199 price point was the single worst decision he had ever made. He could not afford to do the work, so he did not do the work, and the board noticed.

That is the reality. Underpricing is how practices cut corners that get doctors in trouble. If you price at medication cost, you cannot afford proper follow-up and documentation. You will skip steps, the board will notice, and your license will suffer. Charge as much as the market will bear. Do not try to be the lowest price anywhere. Your price should signal that this is medical care, supervised and documented, not a clearance sale on vials.

What the Program Price Must Include

When a patient hands over their credit card, they need to understand exactly what they are paying for. Not just in a vague "our program includes comprehensive care" sense. I mean itemized, explained, documented. Because when a patient feels confused about what they paid for, they complain. And when they complain, the board asks to see what was explained. If your explanation is murky, you lose. If it is clear, you win. It really is that simple. The program price is not just a number. It is a contract, a communication tool, and a compliance shield all at once. Let me walk through what belongs in that price and why each component matters to your license.

Medical oversight and clinical consultation are the foundation. This is what differentiates a peptide program from an internet order form. The patient is paying for a physician's judgment- the evaluation of whether this therapy is appropriate, the review of contraindications, the assessment of whether the potential benefit outweighs the risk for this particular patient at this particular time. That judgment does not happen once at intake and then disappear. It happens at intake, at every refill, at every follow-up, and whenever the patient reports a symptom or concern. The physician's time to review cases, make decisions, and document reasoning is the single largest cost in a properly run program. If your price does not cover physician time, you are subsidizing your patients with your future license.

Screening and intake work is substantial and often underestimated. A proper intake for a peptide or hormone program takes thirty to sixty minutes of staff time plus fifteen to thirty minutes of physician review. The patient completes a detailed medical history, medication list, allergy review, symptom questionnaire, and contraindication screen. Staff verify information, flag concerns, and route complex cases to the physician. The physician reviews everything before any medication is ordered. This is not busywork. This is where you find the patient with a family history of medullary thyroid carcinoma before you prescribe semaglutide. This is where you discover the patient is on warfarin before you introduce a therapy that could interact. This is where you learn the patient has a pituitary tumor before you start GH-axis stimulation. Skip this step because you cannot afford the time, and you are prescribing blind. Charge enough to do it right.

Patient education is another component that gets shortchanged in underpriced practices. The patient needs to understand what the medication is, what it is not, how to inject it, how to store it, what side effects to expect, what side effects require stopping the medication immediately, when to seek emergency care, and what realistic outcomes look like. Education takes time. It takes staff time to prepare materials and walk through administration. It takes physician time to answer questions and confirm understanding. It takes documentation time to record that education occurred. All of this is billable work that belongs in the program price. The patient who understands what to expect is less likely to panic, less likely to complain, and less likely to end up in the emergency room because they did not recognize a warning sign. Education is risk management, and risk management is worth paying for.

Syringes and supplies seem like a small line item, but they add up and they matter clinically. Patients need the right syringes for the right concentration. They need alcohol swabs, sharps containers, and sometimes mixing supplies if the medication requires reconstitution. Providing these through the practice ensures the patient has the correct equipment, understands how to use it, and is not improvising with the wrong needles from a farm supply store. It also demonstrates systematic care to any reviewer who examines your program. The patient got the right supplies, with the right instructions, as part of a comprehensive package. That is what a medical program looks like. A vial shop tells the patient to figure it out themselves.

Pharmacy coordination is an invisible but critical service. Your staff communicates with the compounding pharmacy to verify prescriptions, confirm concentrations, track shipments, handle insurance rejections, manage recalls, and resolve any issues that arise. When a pharmacy shipment is delayed, your staff follows up. When the pharmacy changes a concentration, your staff notifies the patient and updates the education. When a recall occurs, your staff handles it immediately. This coordination prevents medication errors, ensures continuity of care, and demonstrates to any reviewer that the practice is actively managing the therapy rather than simply routing orders. Patients do not see this work, but they benefit from it constantly, and it requires dedicated staff time that must be funded.

Follow-up visits are where the medicine actually happens. I do not care how good your intake is - if you are not following up, you are not practicing medicine. You are dispensing. Follow-up means structured check-ins where the patient reports symptoms, weight, vitals, and any concerns. It means a clinician reviewing those reports and deciding whether to continue, adjust, hold, or stop therapy. It means documenting that review and the clinical reasoning behind the decision. Follow-up visits happen at scheduled intervals - typically every four to twelve weeks depending on the therapy and patient risk - and they are essential to both patient safety and chart defensibility. The program price must cover this cost. If you are not charging enough to afford systematic follow-up, you are not running a medical program. You are running a subscription medication service, and that is a board complaint waiting to happen.

Refill review is the most dangerous place to cut corners, and it is the first place underpriced practices start improvising. Every refill should be reviewed by a clinician before it is approved. That means looking at the patient's recent symptom reports, checking for red flags, verifying that follow-up requirements have been met, confirming the dose is still appropriate, and documenting the review. Automatic refills - where the pharmacy ships because it is the third Tuesday of the month regardless of patient status - are indefensible. They say the practice cares more about continuity of revenue than continuity of care. Your program price must fund the clinical time to review every refill properly. If that sounds expensive, consider the alternative: a patient who develops a contraindication - say, a new pregnancy or a new cancer diagnosis - and receives an automatic shipment because nobody checked. That one shipment could cost you your license.

Side-effect monitoring is not optional. Every peptide and hormone therapy has potential adverse effects, and patients need a systematic way to report them and a guarantee that those reports will be reviewed promptly. This requires infrastructure: a reporting system, staff trained to triage reports, clinician availability to evaluate serious concerns, and documentation of every report and every response. Patients who experience side effects and cannot reach anyone become frustrated patients. Frustrated patients file complaints. A robust monitoring system funded by the program price prevents this. The patient knows they can report a problem and get a response. That confidence alone reduces complaint risk significantly.

Staff time encompasses everything the patient does not see directly but benefits from constantly. Phone calls answered. Forms processed. Charts maintained. Labs tracked.

Appointments scheduled. Pharmacy communications handled. Supplies inventoried. Complaints resolved. Protocols updated. Staff training conducted. Chart audits performed. Compliance documentation maintained. Every one of these tasks requires a human being with training and judgment. Underpriced programs run on skeleton crews where one overwhelmed employee does five jobs poorly. Properly priced programs run on adequate staffing where each person can do their job thoroughly. The difference shows up in patient satisfaction, clinical quality, and board defensibility.

Documentation and compliance overhead is the category most physicians resent and most investigators scrutinize. Every patient interaction must be documented. Every decision must have a rationale. Every consent must be complete. Every protocol must be written and followed. Every staff member's role must be defined. Every audit trail must be maintained. This documentation is not natural - it is learned, practiced, and enforced. It requires time, systems, and sometimes software. It requires someone in the practice whose job includes making sure the charts are defensible. This is overhead in the purest sense, and it is absolutely necessary. The program price pays for the systems and the people who keep your chart ready for the day - and that day will come for every peptide physician - when someone asks to see it.

Risk management and complaint handling deserve their own line item because they are real costs that underpriced practices simply cannot absorb. When a patient is unhappy - wrong expectations, side effects, financial pressure, family criticism - someone has to handle it. Properly staffed practices have protocols: the complaint is documented, the patient is heard, the clinical record is reviewed, a response is crafted, and if necessary a refund or credit is issued. This takes time and emotional energy and sometimes legal consultation. Cheap practices ignore complaints because they do not have the staff to address them. Ignored complaints become board complaints. Board complaints become investigations. Investigations become restrictions, probations, or worse. Fund complaint handling in your program price. It is cheaper than the alternative.

Here is the bottom line on what the program price must include. When you explain your pricing to a patient, you should be able to walk through every component: the physician oversight, the screening, the education, the supplies, the pharmacy coordination, the follow-up visits, the refill reviews, the side-effect monitoring, the staff support, the documentation systems, and the risk management infrastructure. You should be able to explain it without embarrassment, without defensiveness, and without apologizing. This is what supervised medical care costs. If you cannot afford to provide all of it, you cannot afford to run the program. Charge accordingly.

Why Cheap Doctors Get Investigated

There is a pattern I have seen repeat itself across state after state, and it goes like this. A physician opens a peptide or hormone practice with aggressive pricing - often at or barely above medication cost. The low price attracts a flood of patients, many of whom are price-shopping rather than relationship-seeking. The volume overwhelms the practice. Corners get cut. Charts get thin. Follow-up becomes optional. Refills become automatic. Then a patient has a bad outcome - maybe a side effect that went unmonitored, maybe an expectation that was not met, maybe a shipment that arrived after they tried to cancel. That patient complains to the state medical board. The board investigator pulls ten charts at random and finds the same problem in all of them: documentation that proves the practice was selling medication with medical supervision in name only. The board does not need to prove malpractice. They only need to decide the care looks sloppy. And sloppy, in their eyes, is enough.

Let me be direct about why low prices attract investigations. It is not because the board cares about your business model. It is because low prices correlate with high volume, thin margins, inadequate staffing, and poor documentation - and those are the things the board cares about. An investigator looking at a practice that charges $150 a month for a semaglutide program including medication knows, before opening a single chart, that the practice cannot afford proper clinical oversight at that price. They know the physician is seeing too many patients to review cases individually. They know the staff is too thin to provide systematic follow-up. They know the documentation is likely inadequate because there is no time and no infrastructure to make it adequate. The price tells the story before the chart confirms it.

Low prices attract price-shoppers, and price-shoppers are the highest-maintenance, highest-complaint patients in medicine. These are not patients who value a relationship with their physician. These are patients who treat healthcare like a commodity purchase. They compare vial prices on Reddit. They hop from clinic to clinic chasing the lowest monthly fee. They expect miracles because they have been sold miracle stories online, and when those miracles do not materialize, they blame the doctor. Not themselves for having unrealistic expectations. Not the internet for lying to them. The doctor. And a cheap doctor, running a high-volume practice with no time for thorough documentation, is the easiest target imaginable. You think the board cares that you meant well? The board cares that your chart explains the decision. If your chart is thin because you were too busy managing six hundred patients at $150 a month, the board will not be sympathetic.

There is a second, less obvious problem with low pricing. It signals to everyone - patients, regulators, competitors, and pharmacy partners - that your program is not serious. Patients interpret low prices as a signal that the service is basic. They do not expect thorough follow-up because they are not paying for it. They do not report symptoms because they assume nobody is listening. They do not follow instructions carefully because the whole interaction feels transactional. The low price creates a self-fulfilling prophecy: the patient treats the program like a product purchase because the price told them it was a product purchase. Then when something goes wrong, they treat it like a defective product complaint. This is how board complaints are born.

Cheap practices also cannot afford proper systems, and the absence of systems is visible in the chart. Thin charts with no documented follow-up. Rushed consent forms that the patient signed without reading because nobody took time to explain them. Refill approvals that happen without clinician review because the physician is seeing new patients and has delegated refills to administrative staff. Missing labs because the practice cannot afford the staff time to track them down. Absent stop criteria because the practice never set any. These are not minor documentation deficiencies. These are the exact deficiencies that board investigators are trained to find, because they are the deficiencies that predict patient harm.

Let me give you another war story. A physician in Florida was running a testosterone clinic at $99 a month, medication and labs included. He told me he was "disrupting the market." What he disrupted was his own career. He had eight hundred active patients. His "labs" were a single total testosterone drawn at a discount lab chain, reviewed by nobody - the patient got an automated email saying "labs acceptable, refill approved." His consent form was two pages of legal language copied from an online template. His follow-up was a text message sent by a scheduling bot. Three patients developed polycythemia - hematocrits above fifty-four - with no documented follow-up, no therapeutic phlebotomy, no physician awareness. One of them had a thrombotic event and ended up in the hospital. His family hired an attorney, the attorney filed a board complaint, and the board investigator found twenty-two other patients with dangerously elevated hematocrits that had been flagged by the lab but never acted upon because there was no system for reviewing abnormal results. The $99 price point could not fund a system to catch abnormal labs. The board revoked his license.

I want you to think about something. The board notices patterns. They do not generally investigate isolated incidents. They investigate patterns of care that suggest a systematic problem. And the pattern of cheap peptide practices with sloppy documentation is so common that many boards have seen it dozens of times. They know the profile: cash-pay, low price, high volume, online marketing, compounded medications, minimal follow-up, thin charts, patient complaints. When your practice fits that profile, you go on a list. Once you are on the list, every complaint gets scrutinized more closely. Every chart request gets expanded. Every patient interview gets broader. The low price that brought you all those patients also brought you the exact profile the board is watching for.

Your price signals your seriousness. Charge like a medical practice, not a discount store. A medical practice charges enough to fund the infrastructure of care. A discount store charges enough to move product. When the board investigator looks at your pricing and sees a number that could not possibly cover supervised medical care, they do not think "what a generous doctor." They think "this is a medication vendor, not a medical practice." And medication vendors get disciplined.

The "your competitor charges less" conversation comes up in almost every practice. Here is how you handle it. First, never apologize for your price. Your price reflects the cost of doing this work correctly, and you do not negotiate the cost of competence. Second, explain what the competitor's lower price likely means: fewer follow-up visits, less clinician involvement, thinner documentation, less accessibility, more risk for the patient. Do not disparage the competitor specifically - that invites problems - but explain the difference between supervised medical care and a medication subscription. Third, offer the patient a choice. They can choose thorough medical supervision at your price, or they can choose a less expensive option elsewhere with the understanding that less expensive means less oversight. Most patients who are serious about their health will choose oversight. The ones who choose the cheaper option were never going to be good patients for you anyway. Let them go. They are doing you a favor by self-selecting out of your practice before they become a complaint.

There is one more angle on pricing that physicians rarely consider until it is too late. Cheap doctors attract the attention of other regulators beyond the state medical board. Pharmacy boards notice when a physician is routing massive volumes of compounded prescriptions at discount prices - it suggests to them that the prescriber may not be exercising appropriate clinical judgment. The FDA notices when complaint patterns emerge around certain prescribing behaviors. Even the Drug Enforcement Administration, though peptides are not controlled substances, pays attention to high-volume cash-pay practices that look like pill mills in structure even if the substance is different. You do not want to be on any of these agencies'radar screens. The simplest way to stay off them is to charge a premium price, maintain premium documentation, and run a practice that is unmistakably medical in character rather than commercial.

Here is what I want you to take away from this section. Low prices do not protect you. They expose you. They expose you to volume you cannot manage. They expose you to patients who treat medicine like retail. They expose you to staffing shortages that force corner-cutting. They expose you to charts that cannot defend your decisions. They expose you to board investigators who know exactly what a discount vial shop looks like. Your price is a compliance tool. Use it like one. Charge enough to do the work right. Charge enough to fund the infrastructure. Charge enough to make it unmistakably clear to anyone who examines your practice that this is medicine, not merchandising.

Hormones and Testosterone: Same Model, Same Rules

Now we need to talk about testosterone and hormone optimization, because everything I have said about peptide pricing applies with equal force here - and in some ways, hormone therapy demands even more rigorous pricing discipline. Testosterone is not a peptide. It is a controlled substance in some contexts, it is a Schedule III anabolic steroid under federal law, and it carries a regulatory profile that peptides do not. But the business model is identical. Patients pay cash. They receive a prescription for a medication that requires ongoing monitoring. They need baseline labs, follow-up labs, symptom assessment, contraindication screening, and clinical oversight. The same pricing principles apply: charge for the program, not the vial; price high enough to fund proper care; use the program fee to build infrastructure that keeps you out of trouble. The difference is that testosterone mistakes get you in worse trouble faster, because testosterone is on every regulator's watch list.

Let me start with the clinical reality. Men come to testosterone clinics because they feel tired, have low libido, have gained weight, have lost muscle, have mood changes, or have seen an online ad promising to restore their vitality. Some of these men have genuine hypogonadism with clinically low testosterone levels, significant symptoms, and a clear medical indication for therapy. Others have normal levels for their age, unrealistic expectations, and a desperation to feel twenty-five again. Telling the difference - and documenting how you told the difference- is the foundation of defensible hormone practice. The man with a total testosterone of 280 ng/dL, fatigue, low libido, and depression symptoms is a different clinical conversation than the man with a total testosterone of 580 ng/dL who "just wants an edge." Your chart needs to show that you know the difference and that you treated them differently.

Baseline labs are non-negotiable. Before any testosterone prescription, you need a complete picture. Total testosterone, drawn in the morning on two separate days at minimum. Free testosterone, because total levels can be misleading when sex hormone-binding globulin is abnormal. Estradiol, because aromatization matters and elevated estradiol causes its own problems. Complete blood count with hematocrit, because polycythemia is the most common dangerous side effect of testosterone therapy and a hematocrit above 54 percent requires immediate intervention. Prostate-specific antigen when age-appropriate, with documented discussion of what elevated PSA means and when urology referral is indicated. Liver function tests. Lipid panel. Pregnancy test for women when relevant - and yes, women do receive testosterone in some clinical contexts, and pregnancy exposure is a serious concern. Baseline digital rectal exam when indicated by age and risk factors. These labs cost money. The staff time to order them, track them, review them, and document them costs money. The physician time to interpret them and make a clinical decision costs money. All of this belongs in your program price. If you are charging $99 a month for testosterone "all inclusive," you are losing money on the labs alone, which means you are either skipping labs, using the cheapest possible lab with questionable quality, or not reviewing the results properly. Any of those paths leads to a board complaint.

Symptom review is the clinical partner to lab review. Testosterone therapy should never be prescribed on numbers alone. The patient must have symptoms consistent with hypogonadism, those symptoms must be documented, and the rationale for linking those symptoms to testosterone deficiency must be explained in the chart. I see too many charts that say "low T, prescribed testosterone." That is not clinical reasoning. That is a lab value followed by a reflex. A proper chart says: "Patient reports progressive fatigue over 18 months, decreased morning erections, loss of interest in activities previously enjoyed, and difficulty maintaining lean mass despite consistent resistance training. Baseline AM total testosterone 245 ng/dL on two draws. Free testosterone 45 pg/mL. Symptoms and labs consistent with primary hypogonadism. Patient counseled on risks, benefits, alternatives including no therapy, and monitoring requirements. Patient elects to proceed." That chart tells a story. That chart defends a decision.

That chart takes time to write, and the time costs money that must be in your program price.

Contraindication screening for testosterone is particularly important because the consequences of missing a contraindication can be severe. Active prostate cancer is an absolute contraindication. Severe lower urinary tract symptoms from benign prostatic hyperplasia require careful assessment. Hematocrit above 50 percent at baseline requires evaluation before starting therapy. Untreated severe sleep apnea can worsen with testosterone. Uncontrolled heart failure is a contraindication. Severe lower urinary tract symptoms require consideration. Desire for fertility is a major issue - testosterone suppresses spermatogenesis, and the man who wants children in two years should know that exogenous testosterone may impair that goal. There are alternatives - clomiphene, hCG - that preserve fertility while addressing symptoms. The patient must be screened for all of this, educated about all of this, and the screening and education must be documented. If your price does not fund this level of clinical work, you will skip it. And if you skip it, the first patient with undiagnosed prostate cancer who receives six months of testosterone will become a malpractice case that ends your career.

Follow-up labs are where many testosterone practices fall apart. The standard of care requires repeat labs at intervals - typically six to twelve weeks after initiation, then every six months during stable therapy, or more frequently if problems arise. These labs must include testosterone to assess response, estradiol to assess aromatization, hematocrit to screen for polycythemia, and PSA when age-appropriate. If hematocrit rises above 54 percent, the patient needs therapeutic phlebotomy and a dose reduction. If PSA rises significantly, urology referral is indicated. If estradiol climbs too high, symptoms worsen and management is required. Every one of these follow-up lab sets requires staff time to order and track, physician time to review and interpret, documentation time to record the decision, and patient communication time to explain the results. This is continuous, ongoing, expensive clinical work. It is the heart of hormone therapy. And it must be fully funded by your program price.

Do not chase numbers without symptoms. This is one of the most common mistakes in testosterone practice and one of the most dangerous. A patient comes in with a total testosterone of 320 ng/dL and no symptoms. He read online that "optimal" testosterone is 800 ng/dL and he wants to get there. If you treat that number without symptoms, you are not practicing medicine. You are operating a hormone vending machine. The medical literature does not support treating asymptomatic men with low-normal testosterone levels. The risks -polycythemia, fertility suppression, potential cardiovascular effects, prostate concerns - are real, and they must be justified by symptomatic benefit. Your chart must show that symptoms drove the decision, not a number. If you prescribe because a patient asked and paid, you are one bad outcome away from an investigation.

Do not make anti-aging promises. This cannot be said loudly enough. Testosterone is not an anti-aging drug. It does not reverse aging. It does not restore youth. It treats hypogonadism. When a man with genuine hypogonadism receives appropriate testosterone therapy, he may experience improved energy, libido, mood, and body composition. These are real benefits for the right patient. But they are not anti-aging, and calling them anti-aging in your marketing, your consent, or your patient conversations creates regulatory and malpractice exposure that is entirely avoidable. The patient who expects to feel twenty-five again at age fifty-five will be disappointed, and disappointed patients in cash-pay practices complain to boards, file lawsuits, and post damaging reviews. Set realistic expectations from the first consultation, document those expectations, and charge enough that you can spend the time to manage them properly.

The pricing model for testosterone and hormone therapy should mirror the peptide model exactly. You charge a program fee that covers the medical supervision, not just the medication. That fee funds the intake, the baseline labs, the education, the follow-up visits, the follow-up labs, the refill reviews, the side-effect monitoring, and the documentation. Patients pay for the program monthly or quarterly. Medication may be an additional cost through the pharmacy, or it may be included depending on your model, but either way the program price must be sufficient to cover the clinical work. If you are including medication in a flat monthly fee, your price must account for pharmacy cost plus all the clinical overhead. A testosterone program at $150 a month including medication and labs is a losing proposition clinically and financially.

You will skip follow-up labs because you cannot afford them. You will ignore elevated hematocrits because addressing them requires time you do not have. You will auto-refill because reviewing each case takes thirty minutes and you have four hundred patients. This is not speculation. This is what happens when the math does not work.

A properly priced testosterone program in most markets runs between $250 and $500 per month depending on what is included, the local market, and the complexity of the patient population. Some concierge-style programs charge more and offer greater accessibility, more frequent follow-up, and additional services. The price should reflect what you are actually providing and what it actually costs to provide it safely. If your market cannot support a price that funds safe care, then your market cannot safely support a testosterone program. That is a hard truth, but it is better than the alternative of running an unsafe program that eventually gets shut down by the board.

The same documentation, consent, monitoring, and pricing standards that apply to peptides apply to hormones - and in some ways, the standard is higher. Testosterone is a known entity to regulators. They have seen the anti-aging clinics, the "Low T centers" that operated like drive-throughs, the physicians who prescribed to anyone with a pulse and a credit card. The board knows what bad testosterone practice looks like, and they are actively looking for it. Your charts need to be bulletproof. Your consent needs to explain polycythemia risk, fertility suppression, cardiovascular uncertainty, prostate monitoring, and the limits of what testosterone can realistically accomplish. Your follow-up needs to be systematic and documented. Your refill reviews need to be clinical, not automatic. Your pricing needs to signal that this is a medical program requiring genuine physician involvement, not a monthly subscription for a vial of cypionate.

One practical consideration unique to testosterone: the controlled substance aspect. Testosterone cypionate and enanthate are Schedule III controlled substances under the Anabolic Steroid Control Act. This means your prescriptions are tracked. Your prescribing patterns are visible to regulators. If you are writing for unusually high volumes, unusually high doses, or an unusually large number of patients relative to your practice type, flags may be raised. State prescription monitoring programs - PDMPs - capture every testosterone prescription you write. A physician with six hundred active testosterone patients, all on 200 mg per week, will show up on reports. That pattern, combined with a low program price, high patient volume, and thin charts, is practically an invitation for investigation. The way you avoid this is by prescribing appropriately, documenting thoroughly, and pricing in a way that demonstrates your program is clinical rather than commercial. A premium price with premium documentation looks like medicine. A discount price with thin charts looks like distribution.

The informed consent for testosterone needs to be exhaustive. It must cover the known risks: polycythemia and thrombosis, fertility suppression, acne and oily skin, fluid retention, gynecomastia from aromatization, potential cardiovascular effects, prostate effects including the uncertainty around prostate cancer risk, worsening of sleep apnea, mood changes including irritability and aggression, and the effects on lipid profiles. It must cover the unknowns: the long-term safety of testosterone therapy in men over sixty-five remains an area of active research and clinical uncertainty. It must cover the monitoring requirements: regular labs, symptom reporting, and the patient's duty to comply with follow-up. It must cover the limits of therapy: testosterone treats hypogonadism, it does not reverse aging, and individual results vary. And it must cover cost: what the patient is paying for, what is included, and what happens if they do not follow the program requirements. This level of consent takes time to explain and time to document. That time must be funded by your program price.

Patient selection for testosterone therapy follows the same principles as patient selection for peptides. When in doubt, say no. The patient with a borderline testosterone level and vague symptoms who demands therapy despite your recommendation against it is a patient who will eventually cause trouble. The patient who refuses baseline labs but wants a prescription anyway is a patient you should decline. The patient who has read online that testosterone cures everything from depression to diabetes and expects miraculous results is a patient whose expectations will not be met. Saying no is harder in a high-volume, low-price practice because every "no" represents lost revenue that the practice cannot afford to lose. In a properly priced practice, a "no" is just good medicine, and the revenue from patients who are appropriate makes up for the few you turn away. Financial pressure to prescribe inappropriately is one of the most dangerous forces in cash-pay medicine, and proper pricing is the antidote.

Let me talk about the practical structure of a hormone program price because physicians often ask how to present this to patients. I recommend a clear, itemized explanation that includes the following components. The program fee covers medical oversight and clinical consultation, including initial evaluation, screening, and treatment planning. It covers all required follow-up visits and check-ins, whether conducted in person, by phone, or through a telehealth platform. It covers all follow-up laboratory testing ordered by the physician as part of standard monitoring. It covers patient education and access to clinical staff for questions and concerns. It covers refill reviews conducted by a clinician before each prescription renewal. It covers documentation, compliance management, and quality assurance activities that ensure the program meets medical standards. Medication is either included in the program fee or billed separately through the pharmacy, and this is clearly explained at enrollment. Patients understand this. They may not like the price, but they understand what they are paying for, and that understanding prevents the confusion that leads to complaints.

One final point about testosterone pricing that many physicians overlook. The cost of managing complications must be built into your program price. When a patient develops polycythemia and needs therapeutic phlebotomy, that takes time and resources. When a patient has an aromatization problem and needs dose adjustment or adjunct therapy, that takes clinical management. When a patient's mood deteriorates and requires evaluation, that takes physician time. When a patient has a suspected cardiovascular event and you need to coordinate emergency care and document everything, that takes significant effort. These events are uncommon in well-managed patients, but they happen, and a practice priced at the margin cannot absorb them. The practice that charges enough to maintain clinical reserves - both financial and operational - can manage complications properly without cutting corners elsewhere. That is the difference between a sustainable program and a ticking time bomb.

Testosterone therapy, done correctly, is legitimate medicine that helps real patients with genuine hypogonadism. It improves quality of life, reduces symptoms, and when properly monitored, is generally safe. But it is not a cash machine, it is not an anti-aging fountain, and it is not something you can do well on the cheap. The same rules apply: diagnose properly, document thoroughly, consent completely, monitor systematically, and charge enough to fund every one of those activities. Your license depends on it. Your patients' safety depends on it. And your ability to sleep at night knowing you are practicing real medicine rather than running a hormone vending machine depends on it.

Let me also address a question I get constantly: how do you handle the patient who says they can get testosterone for half your price at the anti-aging clinic down the street? You handle it exactly the same way you handle the patient who says they can get semaglutide cheaper somewhere else. You do not argue price. You explain value. You ask the patient whether the other clinic includes systematic follow-up labs, whether a clinician reviews every refill, whether they have documented protocols for polycythemia management, whether they explained the fertility implications, and whether their charts would hold up if the board asked to see them. Most patients have not thought about any of this. They saw a number on a website and assumed all testosterone programs are the same. Your job is to educate them that they are not the same, that supervision matters, monitoring matters, documentation matters, and that the difference between a $150 program and a $400 program is the difference between medicine and merchandise. Some patients will still choose the cheaper option. That is their right. But the patients who choose you understand what they are paying for, and those patients - the informed, the thoughtful, the ones who value medical judgment over a bargain - are the patients who refer their friends, leave good reviews, and never file board complaints.

The "same model, same rules" framework also applies if you are running combined peptide and hormone programs. Many patients who come for testosterone also want sermorelin or CJC-1295. Patients on GLP-1 therapy may also benefit from testosterone evaluation. The stacking of these therapies increases clinical complexity and therefore increases the documentation burden, the monitoring requirements, and the price that must be charged to do the work safely. A combined program should not be priced as if it were a single therapy with a small add-on. It should be priced as a comprehensive medical supervision program that encompasses multiple therapies, multiple monitoring tracks, and the clinical judgment to manage their interaction. The physician who supervises a patient on testosterone, sermorelin, and semaglutide simultaneously is managing three distinct therapeutic areas with overlapping metabolic effects. That requires more time, more expertise, more documentation, and more money. Price accordingly.

There is a final war story I want to share, because it ties everything in this chapter together. A physician in Colorado ran a combined peptide and hormone practice. He charged $495 per month for a comprehensive program that included either a peptide or hormone therapy, all labs, all follow-up visits, refill reviews, and 24/7 messaging access to clinical staff. His competitor across town charged $179 for what appeared to be the same service. The competitor had fourteen hundred active patients. Our physician had three hundred. The competitor was investigated after six board complaints in eight months. Charts were pulled, and the investigator found systematic failures: no documented follow-up for hundreds of patients, automatic refills without review, no polycythemia monitoring despite elevated hematocrits in the records, consent forms that were two pages of incomprehensible legal language, and staff who were approving refills and giving dose advice without physician involvement. The board restricted the competitor's license and referred the case to the attorney general for possible criminal charges related to unlicensed practice by staff. Our physician, meanwhile, had zero complaints in three years. His patients were satisfied because they were well cared for. His charts were bulletproof because his price funded the time to make them bulletproof. When the board investigator, as a matter of routine, pulled his charts during the investigation of the competitor - because patients sometimes see multiple providers - he found complete documentation, systematic follow-up, clinician-reviewed refills, and informed consent that actually informed. The investigator closed the file on him in twenty minutes. That is what proper pricing buys you. It buys you the ability to practice medicine correctly. It buys you charts that defend your decisions. It buys you patient satisfaction that generates referrals instead of complaints. And it buys you peace of mind when the investigator comes calling -because they will come calling, for every peptide and hormone physician eventually, and when they come to your door, you want them to find a medical practice, not a fire sale.

So here is what I want you to remember from this entire chapter, not just this section. Your price is a clinical decision. It determines what you can afford to do, which determines how thoroughly you can care for patients, which determines what your charts look like, which determines what happens when someone asks to see them. Cheap prices attract patients you do not want, fund care you cannot provide, and create a profile regulators are actively hunting. Premium prices attract patients who value supervision, fund the infrastructure of safe care, and signal to every reviewer that you are practicing medicine rather than vending product. Charge for supervised medical care. Charge as much as the market will bear. Do not apologize for your price. Explain it. Own it. Let the patients who understand quality choose you, and let the price-shoppers become someone else's problem. Your license will thank you.

13 - The Peptides That Matter - A Practical Guide for Physicians

Each Peptide Profile: What It Is, How It Works, FDA Status, Why Consider It, Why Be Careful

Let me tell you something before you turn another page. This chapter is the one your patients think you already know inside and out. They have been on the internet. They have watched the podcasts. They have read the forums. They have seen the before-and-after photos. And now they are sitting in your exam room expecting you to be the expert on twenty-five different compounds, half of which did not exist in clinical conversation five years ago. That is the reality you are living in. So read this chapter carefully, because I am going to walk you through every major peptide that shows up in a cash-pay practice, tell you what the evidence actually says, what the FDA actually thinks, what your state board will care about, and what you need to document before you pull out your prescription pad.

Each profile in this chapter follows the same structure so you do not have to hunt around. I tell you what the compound is, in plain English, not in biochemistry jargon that impresses nobody. I tell you how it works, because you need to be able to explain that to a patient in thirty seconds. I tell you the FDA and regulatory status, because that determines your legal exposure before you ever write a dose. I tell you why a doctor might reasonably consider it, because I am not here to trash every peptide just to be contrarian. And I tell you why you should be careful, because being careful is what keeps your license on your wall. I also cover what patients usually experience, what you need to monitor, and what your chart needs to prove if a board reviewer reads it six months from now.

Do not skip around randomly. Read the profiles for the compounds you are actually considering prescribing. Read the ones your patients are already asking about. And definitely read the profiles for the compounds you have never heard of, because your next patient has.

Start with the Patient Problem, Not the Product Name

Here is the most common mistake I see in peptide practices, and it drives me nuts. The patient walks in and says "I want BPC-157 for my shoulder" or "I want semaglutide for weight loss"or "My buddy got CJC-1295 and says it changed his life." And the doctor, instead of starting with the clinical problem, starts with the product name. Bad move. Always a bad move. You are a physician, not a dispensing machine. The clinical problem comes first. The peptide, if any, comes second. If you cannot clearly articulate what medical problem you are treating, why that problem matters for this specific patient, what else has been tried or should be tried, and why this specific therapy is reasonable, then you are not practicing medicine. You are running a retail operation with a medical license attached.

For every patient, before you ever discuss a peptide name, document the following: What is the chief complaint? What is the relevant medical history? What has been tried already? What failed? What are the objective findings - labs, imaging, vitals, physical exam? What is the risk of doing nothing? What are the alternatives, including doing nothing? What is the patient's goal, and is it realistic? Only after you have answered those questions in writing should you even consider matching a peptide to the problem. This discipline protects you. It protects the patient. And it makes your chart bulletproof when someone asks why you prescribed what you prescribed.

Do Not Prescribe Because a Patient Saw It on a Podcast

Let me be direct about this. Podcasts are not CME. YouTube videos are not peer review. Instagram testimonials are not clinical evidence. The fact that a patient heard about a peptide from someone with a large following does not constitute medical indication. I have watched physicians get pulled into prescribing compounds they barely understand because the patient was persuasive, the clinic needed revenue, and nobody wanted to say no. That is a recipe for a board complaint.

When a patient comes in asking for a specific peptide, your job is to evaluate, not to comply. Ask why they want it. Ask what they expect. Ask where they heard about it. Ask what they have already tried. Document the answers. Then do your own assessment. If the peptide makes sense for the clinical problem, fine. Prescribe it with proper consent and monitoring. If it does not make sense, say no. Say no clearly, say it with a documented reason, and say it without apology. The easiest prescription to defend is the one you refused for the right reason. The hardest one to defend is the one you wrote because the patient wore you down.

Verify Every Status, Dose, and Pharmacy Pathway Before Prescribing

Regulatory status changes fast in peptide medicine. What was legal to compound last quarter may not be legal this quarter. What one pharmacy was willing to prepare last year, they may have stopped preparing. The FDA shortage list changes. State pharmacy boards change their posture. Compounding 503A versus 503B distinctions matter and they shift. Do not assume anything based on what you heard at a conference or read in a Facebook group.

Before you prescribe any peptide in this chapter, verify the following: Is the compound currently available through a lawful compounding pathway? Is the pharmacy you are using properly licensed, with current 503A or 503B status as appropriate? Is the FDA position on this compound current? Does the patient have an appropriate diagnosis documented in your chart? Have you obtained informed consent that covers the specific FDA status? Have you documented monitoring and stop criteria? If you cannot answer yes to every one of those questions, stop. Do not prescribe until you can. It is not worth your license to save a patient a phone call to another clinic.

Semaglutide: FDA-Approved, Real Medicine, Not a Vanity Shot -Monitoring and Cautions

Semaglutide is a long-acting GLP-1 receptor agonist. It mimics a naturally occurring gut hormone called glucagon-like peptide-1 that regulates appetite, gastric emptying, insulin secretion, and glucagon release. When a patient takes semaglutide, the drug binds to GLP-1 receptors in the pancreas, gut, and brain, creating a cascade of metabolic effects that reduce hunger, slow stomach emptying, improve post-meal glucose control, and promote weight loss. This is not a supplement. This is not a wellness hack. This is real pharmacology with real benefits and real risks. Treat it that way.

Semaglutide is FDA-approved under branded products for specific indications. Ozempic is approved for type 2 diabetes. Wegovy is approved for chronic weight management in adults with obesity or overweight with at least one weight-related comorbid condition. Rybelsus is the oral formulation for type 2 diabetes. These are not interchangeable products. The labels differ, the dosing differs, the indications differ, and the compounding pathways differ. The critical distinction every physician must understand is between branded FDA-approved medication and compounded products. When FDA-declared drug shortages exist, legitimate 503A compounding pharmacies may be able to prepare patient-specific semaglutide formulations. When those shortages end, that pathway narrows or closes. Do not build your practice around assumptions that shortages last forever. Verify the current status every time you prescribe.

A doctor might consider semaglutide for patients with obesity, overweight with weight-related risk factors, type 2 diabetes, or cardiometabolic risk reduction when it fits the patient's clinical picture and a legally defensible prescribing pathway exists. The drug is especially useful for patients who struggle with portion control, food noise, frequent snacking, and the appetite dysregulation that makes diet adherence nearly impossible. The STEP-1 trial showed an average weight reduction of roughly fifteen percent at sixty-eight weeks on 2.4 mg weekly, which is a genuinely impressive result for a pharmacologic intervention. The SELECT cardiovascular outcomes trial demonstrated reduced major adverse cardiovascular events in adults with overweight or obesity and established cardiovascular disease, which expanded the clinical rationale beyond pure weight management. This is evidence-grade medicine. The data are real.

But real medicine means real caution. Be extremely careful with any patient who has a personal or family history of medullary thyroid carcinoma or MEN-2 (multiple endocrine neoplasia type 2). Those are contraindications on the label for a reason. Pancreatitis history should give you serious pause - GLP-1 receptor agonists have been associated with pancreatitis in post-marketing surveillance. Gallbladder disease is another concern; rapid weight loss combined with delayed gastric emptying increases gallstone risk. Severe gastrointestinal disease, pregnancy or planned pregnancy, and active eating disorders are all reasons to decline or defer. Pay attention to patients on insulin or sulfonylureas because hypoglycemia risk is real when GLP-1 therapy is added. And for the love of your license, do not ignore lean-mass loss. Patients losing weight quickly on semaglutide lose muscle along with fat unless they are aggressively protecting it with protein intake and resistance training. Document that conversation. If you prescribe semaglutide and the patient loses twenty pounds of mixed lean and fat mass, you have not done your job.

Patients typically notice decreased appetite within the first one to two weeks. Early nausea, constipation, diarrhea, sulfur burps, reflux, fatigue, or food aversion are common during dose escalation. Some patients feel fantastic and wonder why they did not start sooner. Others feel nauseated at every dose increase and want to quit. Side effects often appear precisely when the dose goes up, which means your job as a physician is to prepare the patient before it happens. Set expectations. Explain the titration schedule. Tell them what to eat, how to hydrate, and when to call the office versus when to go to the emergency room. Refills should never be automatic. Before every refill, ask about nausea, vomiting, abdominal pain, hydration status, constipation severity, mood changes, dizziness, and whether they are actually eating enough protein to preserve lean mass. Your chart should show you asked.

Standard FDA-labeled dosing for Wegovy begins at 0.25 mg subcutaneous once weekly, then titrates every four weeks as tolerated to 0.5 mg, 1.0 mg, 1.7 mg, and 2.4 mg weekly. Ozempic for type 2 diabetes uses a similar titration to 2.0 mg maximum. In cash-pay clinical practice, many physicians use microdosing protocols for patients who cannot tolerate standard titration, who want slower weight loss, who are on maintenance after reaching goal, or who have significant GI sensitivity. Common compounded microdosing ranges are 0.05 to 0.15 mg subcutaneous once weekly, or 0.05 to 0.10 mg twice weekly. Some practices start even lower at 0.025 mg for patients with prior GLP-1 intolerance. Microdosing trades weight-loss speed for tolerability, and you must document why a sub-label dose was chosen, what the goal is, and what criteria trigger dose escalation, holding, or stopping. If the patient is on insulin or sulfonylureas, those doses need adjustment to avoid hypoglycemia. Verify compounded concentration per batch before any dose calculation. Do not guess.

Your chart must document baseline weight, BMI, vitals, medication list, diabetes medications, pregnancy status when relevant, thyroid and MEN-2 screening, pancreatitis and gallbladder history, GI tolerance, and a clear follow-up plan. The chart must show medical reasoning, not just a transaction. Write it for a skeptical board reviewer, because that is exactly who will read it if something goes wrong.

Tirzepatide: Dual Mechanism, Different Tolerability, Different Monitoring Problems

Tirzepatide is a dual GIP and GLP-1 receptor agonist. It is not just stronger semaglutide, and anybody who tells you that is oversimplifying to the point of being dangerous. Tirzepatide activates both the glucose-dependent insulinotropic polypeptide (GIP) receptor and the GLP-1 receptor, creating a broader incretin-based metabolic signal than GLP-1 agonism alone. The GIP component appears to enhance insulin sensitivity, modify appetite signaling in ways that differ from pure GLP-1 therapy, and potentially improve lipid metabolism beyond what GLP-1-only drugs achieve. Whether the dual mechanism produces meaningfully different long-term outcomes compared to optimized semaglutide dosing is still being studied, but the clinical reality is that many patients lose more weight on tirzepatide and tolerate it reasonably well.

Tirzepatide is FDA-approved under branded products. Mounjaro is approved for type 2 diabetes. Zepbound is approved for chronic weight management. Compounded tirzepatide must be evaluated against current FDA shortage status, compounding rules, pharmacy representations, and state law. Do not use last year's assumptions. Shortage-era compounding pathways change when FDA determines that supply is adequate. Check before every prescription.

A doctor may consider tirzepatide for patients who need more aggressive weight loss, have type 2 diabetes, have plateaued or failed on semaglutide, or need a stronger metabolic intervention. It can be very effective, which is precisely why you must not become casual about prescribing it. Greater efficacy means greater responsibility. The patient who loses twenty-five percent of their body weight has also lost significant lean mass unless aggressively protecting it, has altered their gallbladder dynamics, has changed their medication metabolism, and has shifted their nutritional status in ways that need monitoring.

The risk profile overlaps with GLP-1 therapy but has its own character. GI intolerance can be significant, sometimes more pronounced than semaglutide at equivalent weight-loss doses. Dehydration is a real concern, especially in patients who do not hydrate adequately and who reduce food intake dramatically. Gallbladder problems and pancreatitis concern remain class-level issues. Delayed gastric emptying means drug absorption changes for anything the patient takes orally. Hypoglycemia risk with insulin or sulfonylurea co-therapy is significant. The thyroid carcinoma and MEN-2 class cautions apply. Pregnancy concerns apply. And the greater expected weight loss means you absolutely must discuss lean mass preservation, protein targets, resistance training, and the difference between scale weight and body composition. Do not let patients celebrate a falling scale number while they are losing the muscle they need to stay functional.

Patients report major appetite suppression, smaller meals, dramatically reduced food noise, and progressive weight loss. Some feel great. Some feel nauseated, constipated, fatigued, or completely uninterested in food to the point where they are undernourished. A few cannot tolerate dose escalation at all. Your job is to set the right expectation: the goal is the lowest effective dose that the patient can tolerate, afford, and follow safely. Not the maximum dose on the label. The lowest effective dose. If a patient is losing well at 5 mg weekly, there is no clinical urgency to push to 15 mg. More is not always better. More often means more side effects, more cost, and more risk.

Standard FDA-labeled dosing for Zepbound begins at 2.5 mg subcutaneous once weekly, then titrates every four weeks as tolerated to 5 mg, 7.5 mg, 10 mg, 12.5 mg, and 15 mg weekly.

Mounjaro for type 2 diabetes follows the same titration ladder. Many patients reach their weight-loss target at 5 to 10 mg without needing the maximum. Tolerability, cost, weight-loss trajectory, and risk profile should drive the dose decision, not the label ceiling.

In compounded cash-pay practice, microdosing protocols are commonly used at 0.5 to 1.5 mg subcutaneous once weekly, or 0.5 to 1.0 mg twice weekly. Some practices begin at 0.25 mg weekly for patients with severe prior GLP-1 intolerance or for maintenance after higher-dose success. Microdosing is also useful when combining tirzepatide with other metabolic agents where lower doses reduce overlapping side-effect risk. The most common clinical complaints in this space come from over-titration into intolerance. If GI symptoms or dehydration risk are mounting, hold the dose, drop the dose, or pause for a couple weeks. Your patient will not die from a dose hold. They might leave your practice if you push them into relentless nausea.

Document baseline metabolic risk, current diabetes medications, weight history, prior GLP-1 exposure, all contraindications, dose plan, follow-up schedule, side-effect instructions, and stop rules. Before every refill, ask what dose the patient is actually taking, what vial strength they received, and how many units they are drawing up. Patients get confused. Compound concentrations vary. A confused patient with a high-concentration vial is an overdose waiting to happen. Verify, document, and monitor.

Retatrutide: Investigational, Promising, but Not Routine -Enhanced Consent Required

Retatrutide is a triple receptor agonist targeting GLP-1, GIP, and glucagon receptors. The addition of glucagon agonism is what separates this molecule from semaglutide and tirzepatide and is the theoretical basis for the dramatic weight-loss results seen in early trials. Glucagon activation increases energy expenditure through hepatic and possibly brown-adipose-tissue mechanisms, meaning retatrutide may help patients burn more calories in addition to eating less. That is genuinely interesting science. It is also genuinely investigational, and investigational means you document more, consent more, monitor more, and accept more liability.

Retatrutide is not FDA-approved as of this writing. It remains investigational. Legitimate access is primarily through clinical trials. Any compounded or grey-market retatrutide should be treated as high-risk from a regulatory, sourcing, and consent standpoint. Retatrutide is in Eli Lilly's Phase 3 development pipeline globally, under the TRIUMPH program. There is no approved retatrutide product anywhere in the world. Compounded or grey-market retatrutide is not a clinical trial product and should not be treated as if it has FDA blessing.

A doctor may consider discussing retatrutide only for patients with severe obesity or obesity-related risks who have not achieved adequate benefit with established options, and only after standard therapies, FDA-approved medications, and bariatric options have been considered or refused. The chart must explain, in specific patient-oriented language, why the risk-benefit discussion justifies considering an investigational agent over approved GLP-1 or dual-agonist therapy. General enthusiasm for new drugs is not a clinical rationale. The patient must understand that they are accepting unknown long-term risks that patients on approved drugs do not face.

Be careful because long-term human safety is still developing. GI side effects in Phase 2 trials were significant. A specific concern that emerged was dysesthesia - abnormal skin sensations, including tingling and burning, particularly at higher doses. This is not a typical GLP-1 side effect, and patients need to know about it before they start. Heart rate increases have been observed. Dehydration, pancreatitis and gallbladder class concerns, thyroid and MEN-2 class cautions, and product-source uncertainty all must be disclosed in exhaustive detail. This is not a drug where a one-page consent form is adequate.

Patients will likely expect dramatic weight loss because the Phase 2 data showed weight reductions exceeding twenty percent at the highest doses, which attracted enormous media attention. Reality check: appetite reduction and weight loss may indeed be substantial, but side effects can be stronger than patients expect, and the long-term safety profile is not yet written. Some patients may experience nausea, vomiting, constipation, diarrhea, fatigue, heart-rate changes, or those unusual tingling and burning skin sensations I mentioned. They need to know these are not surprises to hide from the office. They are expected possibilities that require reporting.

There is no FDA-approved dose for retatrutide. Any clinical use must be charted as investigational with rigorous consent, monitoring, and a clear rationale for choosing it over approved alternatives. Phase 2 obesity data titrated slowly over approximately twelve weeks from a starting dose near 0.5 mg subcutaneous weekly toward target doses of 4 mg, 8 mg, or

12 mg weekly. Dose-response weight loss was seen across that range. This is reference data, not a prescribing protocol.

In cash-pay practice, common compounded microdosing ranges are 0.5 to 2 mg subcutaneous once weekly with slow titration. Microdosing is typically used for patients who have failed or plateaued on semaglutide or tirzepatide, for cautious assessment of tolerability before going higher, or for patients who want the triple-agonist mechanism but cannot accept the unknown long-term risk of higher doses. Move slowly. Tolerability data on retatrutide outside the trial setting is still developing, and GI side effects can be more pronounced than with single- or dual-agonists at equivalent weight-loss outcomes. If a patient cannot tolerate retatrutide microdosing, do not escalate. Switch back to an approved agent. Your job is not to prove how cutting-edge your practice is. Your job is to help the patient safely.

Document failed or insufficient prior treatments, patient-specific urgency, FDA investigational status, evidence reviewed, alternatives considered, PCP involvement, monthly monitoring plan, emergency stop rules, and exact pharmacy source. A signed consent with an audit trail is not optional. Enhanced consent means the patient reads it, asks questions, has time to think, and then signs with a witness. This is not a quick signature at the front desk. If you are not willing to do all of this, do not prescribe retatrutide.

Sermorelin: Tells the Pituitary to Work, Does Not Replace GH Directly - Physiologic Approach

Sermorelin is a synthetic analog of growth hormone-releasing hormone (GHRH). It tells the pituitary gland to release the patient's own growth hormone in a pulsatile, physiologic pattern. This matters because the pituitary feedback system is still intact. When growth hormone rises, somatostatin feedback kicks in. IGF-1 production increases through the normal downstream pathway, but not in an uncontrolled surge. The body still regulates itself. That is the theoretical safety advantage of sermorelin over direct recombinant growth hormone injection, where IGF-1 can climb without the same endogenous restraint.

The original FDA-approved sermorelin product was withdrawn from the market for business reasons, not because of a classic safety withdrawal. Today sermorelin is generally discussed as a compounded prescription product, which makes pharmacy quality verification and documentation especially important. Do not assume that every pharmacy compounds sermorelin to the same standard. Ask about their testing, their source material, their sterility verification, and their stability data. Document the answers.

A doctor might consider sermorelin for carefully selected patients with symptoms and lab patterns suggesting growth-hormone-axis decline, poor sleep quality, impaired recovery, reduced exercise tolerance, or body-composition concerns where GH-axis support is clinically reasonable. It is most defensible when the goal is framed as physiologic stimulation rather than aggressive anti-aging transformation. The patient who expects to look twenty-five again at age fifty-five is going to be disappointed, and disappointment drives complaints. The patient who wants better sleep, gradual recovery improvement, and modest body-composition changes over months is more likely to be satisfied and less likely to file a board complaint when miracles do not occur.

Be careful with active cancer, recent cancer history, pituitary tumors or sellar masses, poorly controlled diabetes, edema-prone patients, and anyone expecting dramatic body transformation. The adult evidence base for sermorelin is thinner than patients assume. Most of the robust data comes from pediatric growth-hormone-deficiency testing and older adult pharmacology studies, not from large randomized outcome trials in middle-aged wellness patients. Compounded potency and sterility concerns are real - this is an injectable product from a 503A pharmacy, not a branded FDA-approved manufacturing line. Set expectations appropriately, monitor diligently, and document everything.

Patients commonly notice better sleep first, often within the first two to four weeks. That makes sense because growth-hormone pulsatility is tightly linked to slow-wave sleep. Energy and recovery may improve over subsequent weeks. Body-composition changes are modest and slower, usually measured in months rather than days. Patients chasing direct growth-hormone effects - dramatic muscle gain, fat melting away, skin tightening like a facelift - are often disappointed. Patients seeking sleep improvement, recovery support, and gradual enhancement tend to report more satisfaction. Match the therapy to realistic outcomes.

Your chart must document cancer history, pituitary history, diabetes status, baseline IGF-1 when appropriate, fasting glucose or HbA1c, edema symptoms, blood pressure, realistic expectations discussion, and follow-up plan. The chart should explicitly state that the goal is physiologic support, not a promise to reverse aging. Do not use anti-aging marketing language in medical records. It looks terrible when a board reviewer reads it.

Common dosing is subcutaneous at bedtime, often in the 200 to 500 mcg range, with individualized cycling or daily protocols. Some physicians prefer five-days-on, two-days-off schedules to preserve pituitary responsiveness. Dose should be guided by symptoms, IGF-1 response, adverse effects, and current pharmacy formulation. There is no one-size-fits-all protocol. If IGF-1 climbs above age-appropriate reference ranges, reduce the dose or stop. If glucose handling deteriorates, reassess. If the patient develops edema, carpal-tunnel-like symptoms, or joint stiffness, that is a signal to modify therapy.

Tesamorelin: The Legitimate FDA-Approved GHRH Analog -Narrow Label, Use Carefully

Tesamorelin is a stabilized GHRH analog that stimulates endogenous growth hormone release and raises IGF-1. Unlike sermorelin, tesamorelin carries an actual FDA-approved label, and that matters enormously for your legal defensibility. The approved indication is reduction of excess abdominal fat in HIV-infected adults with lipodystrophy. That is it. That is the label. It is not a general belly-fat drug for everyone who wants a smaller waist. It is not a weight-loss medication for the general population. It is a specific therapy for a specific metabolic complication of HIV treatment.

Tesamorelin is FDA-approved as Egrifta for HIV-associated lipodystrophy. Off-label use for non-HIV visceral adiposity, metabolic syndrome, liver fat reduction, or general body composition must be documented as off-label and patient-specific. The fact that it is FDA-approved gives you a stronger regulatory foundation than sermorelin, CJC-1295, or ipamorelin. But off-label use does not mean the label disappears. You still need to document why this specific patient, with this specific clinical picture, benefits from a therapy approved for a different condition.

A doctor might consider tesamorelin when visceral adiposity is the clear target - not scale weight, not cosmetic belly fat, but the metabolically dangerous fat around the organs that drives insulin resistance, inflammation, and cardiovascular risk. Waist circumference, metabolic syndrome markers, liver fat on imaging, or elevated cardiometabolic risk profiles are more defensible rationales than "patient wants to lose weight." Tesamorelin may be more defensible than other GH-axis peptides precisely because it has real Phase 3 evidence for its approved indication and a known safety profile from that program.

Be careful with active malignancy, pituitary disease, pregnancy, hypersensitivity reactions, glucose intolerance, diabetes risk, edema, and joint pain. The most common adverse effects in the pivotal trials were injection-site erythema, pruritus, rash, and flushing. Joint pain, edema, and glucose intolerance can occur. IGF-1 elevation is expected and must be monitored. Patients who expect dramatic total body weight loss may be disappointed because visceral-fat reduction does not always produce impressive scale numbers. The patient may lose dangerous internal fat while the bathroom scale moves modestly. You need to explain this distinction before they start, or they will think the therapy failed.

Patients may notice joint stiffness, mild edema, injection-site irritation, sleep or recovery changes, and gradual waist circumference changes. The measurable endpoint is often months, not days. Do not continue therapy indefinitely without reassessment. If there is no meaningful clinical benefit by twenty-six weeks, stop. There is no benefit in burning money and accumulating risk for a therapy that is not working.

The FDA-labeled dose for Egrifta is 2 mg subcutaneous daily for reduction of excess abdominal fat in HIV-infected adults with lipodystrophy. A common cash-pay protocol used outside the labeled indication is 0.5 mg subcutaneous on a five-days-on, two-days-off schedule, run for six to eight weeks, followed by four weeks off. Cycling is used to limit tachyphylaxis at the GH-axis and to give IGF-1 a chance to return toward baseline between cycles. Off-label or compounded dosing must be charted as such, with explicit consent, baseline and interval IGF-1 monitoring, and a documented rationale for choosing tesamorelin over the FDA-approved indication. Pharmacy concentration and reconstitution instructions must be verified before every dose calculation.

Your chart must document indication, on-label versus off-label status, waist or visceral-fat rationale, glucose and HbA1c, IGF-1, malignancy screen, pregnancy status when relevant, and a reassessment point around twenty-six weeks. If there is no meaningful benefit, do not continue because the patient likes the idea. Stop, reassess, and redirect.

CJC-1295/Ipamorelin: Popular GH Stack - Anti-Aging Language Outruns Evidence

CJC-1295 and ipamorelin are commonly combined as a growth-hormone-axis stimulation stack. CJC-1295 is a GHRH analog that stimulates the pituitary to release growth hormone. Ipamorelin is a growth hormone secretagogue - specifically a ghrelin-receptor agonist -that triggers a growth-hormone pulse with less cortisol and prolactin stimulation than older GHRP compounds like GHRP-2 or GHRP-6. The theoretical appeal of combining them is that CJC-1295 provides a sustained GHRH signal while ipamorelin provides a pulsatile ghrelin-driven GH release, producing a stronger overall GH signal while preserving a more physiologic pattern than direct growth hormone injection.

Neither CJC-1295 nor ipamorelin is FDA-approved for human use. Their compounding status has been the subject of FDA concern and active regulatory review. CJC-1295 comes in two forms that should not be treated as interchangeable: CJC-1295 with DAC (drug affinity complex) has a much longer half-life and produces more sustained GH exposure, while CJC-1295 without DAC (also called Mod GRF 1-29) has a shorter half-life and more closely mimics natural pulsatility. The DAC version produces higher average GH levels but may also increase the risk of GH overshoot and side effects. Most experienced peptide physicians prefer the no-DAC version for this reason, but whichever form you use, document it explicitly in the chart.

A doctor might consider this stack for selected patients seeking sleep improvement, recovery support, lean-mass preservation, and modest body-composition improvement when conventional causes have been assessed and the patient understands the evidence limits. The best clinical case is subtle physiologic support, not bodybuilding promises. The worst case is a fifty-year-old sedentary patient who expects to get ripped without changing diet or exercise. That patient will be disappointed, and disappointed patients who paid premium prices out of pocket are the ones who call the board.

Be careful with cancer history of any kind, pituitary disorders, diabetes or insulin resistance, edema, carpal-tunnel symptoms, active sleep apnea, and patients who want aggressive anabolic effects. Compounded quality matters enormously because you are relying on a 503A pharmacy to produce two separate peptides, potentially with DAC/no-DAC variation, at the right concentration, sterile, with verified identity and potency. Source matters. Frequency matters. The combination of two pituitary-active agents means more moving parts to monitor and more potential for axis dysregulation.

Patients usually report deeper sleep first, often within the first two weeks. Energy, recovery, skin texture changes, and body-composition shifts may follow over one to three months. Mild flushing, head rush, vivid dreams, edema, tingling, or injection-site irritation can occur. Dramatic muscle gain should not be promised. If a patient comes in expecting to look like they did at twenty-five, reset expectations immediately or decline to treat. The CJC/ipamorelin stack is subtle medicine for appropriate patients. It is not a time machine.

Your chart must document the exact form of CJC-1295 used, the rationale for with-DAC or without-DAC selection, baseline IGF-1, glucose and HbA1c, cancer history, edema and carpal tunnel symptoms assessment, expected timeline of benefits, and follow-up labs. The chart should say what you are monitoring, when you will reassess, and what criteria trigger dose reduction or stopping. Do not leave this vague. Vague charts look like vague medicine.

Common no-DAC protocols use CJC-1295 or Mod GRF 1-29 combined with ipamorelin at bedtime on an empty stomach. With-DAC protocols are typically less frequent - perhaps two to three times weekly - because of the prolonged half-life. Dosing must be pharmacy-specific and should never be copied from a gym forum or internet protocol. The evidence base for long-term clinical outcomes of this combination in healthy adults is limited. Both compounds work through physiologic pathways with feedback intact, which provides a reasonable mechanistic safety framework. But mechanistic safety is not the same as proven long-term safety, and your chart must acknowledge that distinction.

IGF-1 LR3: High-Risk, High-Exposure, Serious Legal and Clinical Problems - Avoid

Let me be as direct as I can possibly be about this compound. IGF-1 LR3 is a synthetic long-acting analog of insulin-like growth factor-1. Unlike sermorelin, tesamorelin, or CJC-1295/ ipamorelin, it does not stimulate the pituitary to produce a controlled downstream signal. It delivers an IGF-1-like anabolic signal directly, with reduced binding to IGF-binding proteins and dramatically longer systemic exposure. That means the body's normal regulatory mechanisms are bypassed. There is no feedback brake. There is no pulsatility. There is sustained, direct anabolic signaling at the tissue level. That is why bodybuilders love it. It is also why responsible physicians should think extremely hard before prescribing it.

IGF-1 LR3 is not FDA-approved for any human indication. It is not a routine lawful compounded medication. The only FDA-approved IGF-1-class therapy is mecasermin, which is unmodified recombinant IGF-1 approved for narrow pediatric indications of severe primary IGF-1 deficiency. IGF-1 LR3 should be treated as a restricted, high-risk research compound in U.S. practice. No country has approved IGF-1 LR3 as a finished human pharmaceutical. It is sold worldwide as a research-use-only reagent, which tells you everything you need to know about its clinical status.

The theoretical clinical attraction is direct anabolic signaling, muscle recovery, and anti-wasting interest. But for ordinary wellness, performance, or cosmetic goals, the risk-benefit profile is genuinely poor. The major concerns are severe. Hypoglycemia is a real and potentially dangerous risk because IGF-1 shares structural homology with insulin and can produce insulin-like effects at the receptor level. No pituitary feedback brake means sustained IGF-1 elevation without the body's normal regulatory shutoff. Cancer-promotion concerns are not theoretical - IGF-1 is a well-known growth factor for multiple tumor types, and sustained elevation is epidemiologically associated with increased cancer risk. Insulin resistance can develop with chronic exposure. Acromegalic soft-tissue effects - including joint pain, edema, organomegaly, and facial bone changes - can occur at high exposure. WADA prohibition means any athlete using it will fail drug testing. Grey-market sourcing means you have no reliable quality control. And there are no human clinical trials and no standardized monitoring framework.

If you are considering prescribing IGF-1 LR3, ask yourself a simple question: Can I explain this decision to a state medical board reviewer, under oath, in a way that sounds like responsible medical practice rather than performance enhancement? If the answer is anything other than an unhesitating yes, do not prescribe it.

For the physicians who still want to discuss it after all of those warnings, your chart must document that it is not FDA-approved, not legally routine, has no human trial base, and carries hypoglycemia and cancer concerns. Screen for cancer history, family cancer history, diabetes risk, glucose instability, and athletic drug-testing status. If you are not willing to do exhaustive documentation and accept the legal exposure that comes with prescribing a research-use-only compound, the defensible decision is simply not to prescribe it. Many experienced peptide physicians include IGF-1 LR3 on their "do not prescribe" list. I think that is the right call for most practices. There are safer ways to help patients with muscle wasting, recovery, and body composition.

Common cash-pay protocols reference 50 to 200 mcg subcutaneous on a five-days-on, two-days-off schedule, run for six to eight weeks, followed by four weeks off. Lower-end starting doses of 50 to 75 mcg are appropriate for first cycles. The cycling pattern is intended to limit sustained IGF-1 axis elevation and allow assessment of side effects between cycles. But cycling does not eliminate the fundamental risks. The mecasermin label catalogs hypoglycemia, intracranial hypertension, tonsillar hypertrophy, and lymphoid hyperplasia on a less aggressive, shorter-acting molecule. If mecasermin causes those problems, a longer-half-life unbound analog like LR3 cannot be assumed safer. Do not stack with insulin, growth hormone, or insulin secretagogues. Stop immediately if hypoglycemia, headache, visual changes, persistent joint or muscle pain, new masses, or pituitary or thyroid disturbances develop.

No formal human RCTs of IGF-1 LR3 have been published. None. The compound is a research-grade analog designed to extend half-life and bypass binding proteins. That is precisely why direct human use should be considered high-risk. If you prescribe this compound, you are flying without a net, and your chart is the only thing standing between you and serious regulatory consequences.

BPC-157: Popular Because Patients Are Injured and Desperate -Evidence Is Thin

BPC-157 is a synthetic 15-amino-acid peptide derived from a protective protein found in human gastric juice. It is marketed for tendon repair, ligament healing, muscle recovery, nerve regeneration, bone healing, gut mucosal repair, and wound healing. The proposed mechanisms include stimulation of angiogenesis, fibroblast migration, nitric oxide modulation, growth-factor signaling enhancement, and anti-inflammatory effects. Patients love it because they are in pain, they want to avoid surgery, and they have seen remarkable recovery stories online. Doctors should be cautious because the human evidence base does not match the marketing enthusiasm.

BPC-157 is not FDA-approved for human use. Its compounding status has been actively contested and remains under regulatory review. Some pharmacies continue to prepare it under varying interpretations of current rules. Others have stopped entirely. The regulatory landscape for BPC-157 can shift between quarters, which means you must verify current FDA, state board, and specific pharmacy status before every prescription. Do not assume that because a pharmacy filled it last month, they can fill it this month. And do not assume that your state's position matches the federal position. They often do not.

The evidence base for BPC-157 is overwhelmingly preclinical. The published literature consists almost entirely of animal studies, cell-culture work, and theoretical reviews, predominantly from Croatian and Japanese research laboratories. No controlled human efficacy trial in any indication has reached FDA approval status. One small human pharmacokinetic study has been published, which tells us something about absorption but nothing about whether the compound actually heals human tendons, repairs human gut lining, or regenerates human nerves. That is the honest state of the evidence. Any physician who tells patients otherwise is overselling.

A doctor might consider discussing BPC-157 for selected patients with stubborn soft-tissue injuries, tendon complaints that have not responded to standard conservative management, slow post-operative recovery, or gut-related inflammatory symptoms after standard evaluation has been completed. It is most defensible when the clinical goal is specific and measurable -a rotator cuff strain with documented MRI findings and failed physical therapy, for example, rather than vague "I want to feel better." The more specific your indication, the more defensible your chart.

Be careful because the evidence gap creates real clinical risk. Theoretical angiogenesis concerns matter in any patient with active cancer, recent cancer, or proliferative disease -stimulating blood vessel formation around an occult tumor is not something you want to explain to a board. Sterility and product quality are major concerns with compounded BPC-157. Do not let patients inject research-use-only vials they purchased online. That is not medical supervision. That is enabling self-experimentation, and if something goes wrong, the patient who bought the grey-market vial will still blame you for not stopping them.

Patients often expect pain relief, faster recovery, improved range of motion, or gut symptom improvement. Some report early reduction in inflammation or pain within one to three weeks. Others feel absolutely nothing. That variability is itself a clue that the effect size is modest at best. Set measurable goals: pain scale scores, range of motion measurements, functional assessments, repeat imaging when appropriate, or a structured symptom diary. Without measurable endpoints, you are selling hope without accountability. That is what gets doctors in trouble.

Your chart must document the specific injury or condition, prior evaluation by appropriate specialists, conventional care already attempted, specialist involvement when indicated, FDA status explained, evidence limitations disclosed, pharmacy source verified, dose and route specified, treatment duration defined, stop criteria established, and a cancer screen completed. For orthopedic complaints, do not skip diagnosis. A peptide is not a substitute for imaging when imaging is indicated. It is not a substitute for physical therapy. It is not a substitute for surgical evaluation when surgery is warranted. Prescribing BPC-157 instead of ordering an MRI for a patient who might have a complete tendon tear is malpractice, and no consent form fixes that.

Common protocols reference 250 to 500 mcg once or twice daily subcutaneously, often for four to six weeks, or oral use for gastrointestinal protocols. Injectable BPC-157 is typically administered near the injury site for localized effects or subcutaneously for systemic distribution. Oral formulations exist but have even less human evidence for systemic absorption. Any protocol must be adjusted to product concentration, route, patient risk profile, and current legal availability. Document why you chose the dose, route, and duration you chose. Do not copy dosing from internet forums.

TB-500 / Thymosin Beta-4: Do Not Confuse Full-Length with Fragment - Both Lack Human RCTs

Let me clear up a confusion that has tripped up many physicians. Thymosin beta-4 is a 43-amino-acid endogenous protein involved in actin regulation, cell migration, angiogenesis, and tissue remodeling. TB-500 is a shorter synthetic fragment associated with the active actin-binding region of the full-length molecule. Patients and clinics often use these terms interchangeably. You should not. They are related but distinct compounds with different evidence bases, different pharmacokinetics, and different regulatory considerations.

Neither thymosin beta-4 nor TB-500 is FDA-approved for human use. TB-500 in particular has been under FDA compounding review and its availability has been inconsistent. Full-length thymosin beta-4 has human research data in topical and ophthalmic wound-healing contexts from the RegeneRx Biopharmaceuticals program, but that evidence does not automatically validate injectable TB-500 fragment for systemic tissue repair. Both forms are on the World Anti-Doping Agency prohibited list at all times. Any athlete using either compound will fail drug testing. Document that warning clearly if you prescribe to anyone who participates in competitive sports.

A doctor might consider the thymosin beta-4 family in discussions of wound healing, soft-tissue injury, multi-site injury, or stacked repair protocols alongside BPC-157. The theoretical appeal is systemic cell migration support, actin-regulated tissue remodeling, and enhanced healing kinetics. For patients with multiple injury sites or chronic wound problems, the systemic distribution of an injectable compound makes more sense than trying to inject at each individual site.

Be careful because TB-500 itself lacks completed human randomized controlled trial evidence for the injectable indications patients usually request. The cancer and proliferation concern is not imaginary - pro-migratory and pro-angiogenic effects could theoretically support occult tumor growth or metastasis in a patient with undiagnosed malignancy. Product quality varies enormously. WADA status must be disclosed to any athlete. Regulatory uncertainty means the compound could become unavailable between your patient's first cycle and their refill. Do not promise results you cannot support with evidence.

Patients typically expect systemic healing benefits: less stiffness, better joint comfort, faster recovery from training or injury, improved flexibility. Effects, when reported, are usually gradual over several weeks. This is not a painkiller. It does not produce immediate relief like an anti-inflammatory. And it should absolutely not be sold as a way to avoid orthopedic evaluation, physical therapy, imaging, or surgery when those are indicated. I have seen practices prescribe TB-500 for months while a patient with a torn meniscus limped around avoiding the orthopedic surgeon. That is bad medicine, and the board will agree with me.

Your chart must document whether the discussion is about full-length thymosin beta-4 or TB-500 fragment, the evidence gap explicitly acknowledged, WADA status disclosed and documented, cancer history screened, injury-specific outcome measures established, specialist involvement noted, and a clear follow-up plan with stop criteria. For athletes, document the drug-testing warning prominently. Do not bury it in fine print.

Common TB-500 protocols reference 2 to 2.5 mg twice weekly during a loading phase, then weekly or every-other-week maintenance dosing. Doses vary widely in the literature. Verify pharmacy concentration and current legal availability before prescribing. Full-length thymosin beta-4 has human Phase 2 data in pressure ulcers and venous stasis ulcers from the RegeneRx program, which provides some human safety context, but applying that full-length safety data to the TB-500 fragment is an inference, not evidence. Treat TB-500 as a low-evidence preclinical compound and consent accordingly.

GHK-Cu: Route Matters - Topical and Injectable Are Completely Different Conversations

GHK-Cu is a naturally occurring tripeptide-copper complex found in human plasma, saliva, urine, and gastric juice. It is associated with collagen production stimulation, wound healing acceleration, antioxidant activity, copper ion delivery, skin remodeling, and hair-follicle support. Plasma levels decline substantially with age, which provides the theoretical rationale for therapeutic supplementation. This is a well-studied compound in certain contexts. But the context matters enormously, and route of administration is the single most important determinant of whether your prescribing conversation is reasonable or reckless.

Topical GHK-Cu has a relatively clear cosmetic and dermatologic use pathway. It is widely available in over-the-counter skincare products and professional dermatologic formulations. Cosmetic GHK-Cu serums and creams are permitted under U.S. FDA cosmetic regulations and analogous frameworks in the European Union and elsewhere. The safety record for topical use is favorable across decades of consumer and clinical use. When a patient wants GHK-Cu for skin texture improvement, photoaging, scar support, or hair-adjunct protocols, topical administration is the appropriate first-line approach.

Injectable GHK-Cu is a completely different conversation. Injectable copper peptide therapy has faced FDA compounding concerns and its status is more restricted. No country approves injectable GHK-Cu as a finished drug for anti-aging, tissue repair, or any systemic medical indication. When a patient asks for injectable GHK-Cu, your documentation burden increases substantially because you are now in investigational territory with an injectable product of uncertain regulatory status.

A doctor might consider topical or prescription topical GHK-Cu for skin texture, photoaging, scars, wound support, or hair-adjunct protocols where the patient has a specific dermatologic goal. Injectable use, if discussed at all, should be reserved for specific regenerative protocols with serious attention to regulatory status, source verification, and patient-specific rationale. For most skin indications, there is no clinical reason to jump to injections when topical use is safer, more established, and carries none of the compounding risks.

Be careful with Wilson's disease, copper metabolism disorders, metal allergy, active or recent cancer, pregnancy, and unverified injectable products. Copper is not benign in excess. Patients with Wilson's disease accumulate copper to toxic levels and GHK-Cu administration could be dangerous. Metal allergies can produce severe reactions. Cancer concerns exist because GHK-Cu promotes angiogenesis and tissue remodeling, which in the wrong patient could support tumor growth. For any patient with active or recent malignancy, think twice and document three times.

Patients using topical GHK-Cu may notice texture or firmness changes over several weeks, with hair-related effects taking months and usually requiring adjunctive therapy like minoxidil or finasteride depending on the cause of hair loss. Injectable users report skin, recovery, or joint comfort claims, but systemic evidence is much thinner than topical evidence. Mild irritation or redness can occur with topical use and usually resolves with frequency adjustment or formulation change.

Your chart must document route of administration prominently. That is the first defense. For topical use, document the skin goal, product instructions given, and expected timeline. For injectable discussion, document copper disorder screening, cancer history, pharmacy source, dose, route, monitoring plan, and explicit rationale for why topical therapy was insufficient. If you cannot articulate why injection is necessary for this specific patient, do not prescribe it.

Topical concentrations vary widely from commercial serums to compounded preparations. Injectable research protocols often mention 1 to 2 mg subcutaneously two to three times weekly in cycles, but injectable use must be treated as higher regulatory risk. Layering topical GHK-Cu with acidic products or high-concentration vitamin C can reduce tolerability or destabilize the peptide. Give patients clear product sequencing instructions. The decades of topical and dermatologic safety data are favorable, but they do not translate cleanly to subcutaneous or intravenous dosing. Keep the routes separate in your thinking and in your chart.

Thymosin Alpha-1: Strongest Non-GLP-1 Human Evidence -Immune Modulation, Not Wellness Booster

Thymosin Alpha-1, also known internationally as thymalfasin or by the brand name Zadaxin, is a 28-amino-acid immunomodulatory peptide. It acts through multiple immune signaling pathways including T-cell maturation, dendritic-cell function, natural killer cell activity, cytokine modulation, and Th1/Th2 balance. This is fundamentally different from tissue-repair peptides like BPC-157. It is different from metabolic peptides like the GLP-1 agonists. Thymosin Alpha-1 is an immune-modulating drug, and it should be prescribed with the same diagnostic specificity you would apply to any immunologically active therapy.

Thymosin Alpha-1 is approved in roughly 37 countries under the brand name Zadaxin, manufactured by SciClone Pharmaceuticals. Approved indications in those countries include chronic hepatitis B and C, selected cancer immunomodulation, and adjunctive therapy in severe sepsis. It is not FDA-approved as a finished drug in the United States. Its U.S. compounding status has been contested, and the FDA has raised specific concerns about immunogenicity and peptide impurities in compounded products. Verify current status before any use. The strongest non-GLP-1 human evidence base of any peptide in this chapter belongs to thymosin Alpha-1, but that evidence comes primarily from international trials, not from an FDA-approved U.S. label.

A doctor might consider thymosin Alpha-1 for carefully selected immune-related contexts: recurrent infections, immune dysregulation, chronic viral history, post-chemotherapy immune recovery, or other scenarios where immune modulation has a rational clinical basis. It should not be prescribed merely because a patient wants an "immune boost" or because the office wants to sell a wellness package. Immune stimulation is not always beneficial. In the wrong patient, it can be harmful. This is not vitamin C. This is a biologically active immunomodulator.

Be careful with autoimmune disease, organ transplant patients, pregnancy, severe allergic disease, and unclear immune diagnoses. Stimulating immune function in a patient with lupus, rheumatoid arthritis, or inflammatory bowel disease could trigger flares. Organ transplant patients on immunosuppression require specialist management - you do not adjust their immune regimen with a peptide. Vague marketing claims about immunity, cancer prevention, COVID protection, or longevity are dangerous territory. If your marketing or your chart makes thymosin Alpha-1 sound like a wellness booster rather than a targeted immunomodulator, you are asking for regulatory scrutiny.

Patients typically experience subtle effects. They may report fewer infections, better recovery from illness, improved resilience over weeks, not immediate dramatic changes. Side effects are usually mild - injection-site reactions or transient flu-like symptoms as the immune system activates. But immune activation symptoms should not be ignored. Fever, severe fatigue, joint pain, or worsening of autoimmune symptoms require immediate evaluation and discontinuation.

Your chart must document the specific immune indication, immune history including autoimmune screen, medication list, cancer or oncology context, baseline CBC with differential, liver function tests when relevant, risk discussion, and follow-up plan. The chart should make clear what immune problem is being addressed. "Patient wants immune boost" is not a clinical indication. "Patient with history of recurrent respiratory infections, three courses of antibiotics in six months, normal immunoglobulin workup, requesting immune modulation after standard evaluation" is a clinical indication. Write your chart for the skeptical reviewer.

International protocols commonly reference 1.6 mg subcutaneously twice weekly, but U.S. dosing must be evaluated against product source, legal pathway, and specific indication. Do not turn an international protocol into a casual domestic sales script. The evidence for thymosin Alpha-1 in hepatitis B, severe sepsis, and cancer adjunct settings comes from randomized trials. The evidence for general wellness use does not. Match your prescribing to the evidence or upgrade your consent and documentation to match the uncertainty.

AOD-9604: Not a Powerful Weight-Loss Drug - Modest Efficacy, Do Not Oversell

AOD-9604 is a synthetic fragment derived from the C-terminal region of human growth hormone, specifically amino acids 176 through 191. It was designed to preserve the lipolytic-fat-metabolizing - effects of growth hormone without the full growth-promoting, water-retaining, and diabetogenic effects that make GH therapy problematic for many patients.

Importantly, AOD-9604 does not meaningfully activate the GH axis or raise IGF-1 the way GH secretagogues do. That is both its theoretical advantage and its practical limitation.

AOD-9604 is not FDA-approved. It has an unfavorable regulatory history because its development as an obesity drug failed to demonstrate sufficient efficacy to justify approval, despite a relatively clean short-term safety profile. The compound received GRAS (Generally Recognized as Safe) self-affirmation status in 2014 for some food and cosmetic applications in Australia, but that is not drug approval. It is not approved as a drug for obesity or any clinical indication in any country. Its compounding status in the United States should be verified before any clinical use.

A doctor might consider AOD-9604 as an adjunct for selected patients who cannot tolerate GLP-1 receptor agonists, who want a low-burden fat-metabolism support agent, or who are combining it with lifestyle modification programs. It may also be discussed in investigational joint and cartilage contexts, though those claims are far from established clinical medicine. Think of AOD-9604 as a modest adjunct, not a primary therapy. If a patient needs significant weight loss, semaglutide or tirzepatide produces clinically meaningful results. AOD-9604 does not, and pretending otherwise creates the exact mismatch between expectation and outcome that generates complaints.

The main risk with AOD-9604 is overselling. The compound appears safe in many discussions-the human trial program included approximately 900 participants across multiple trials without serious safety signals - but controlled weight-loss efficacy was insufficient to support approval. Do not compare it to semaglutide, tirzepatide, or retatrutide. Do not promise dramatic fat loss. Do not tell patients they will melt away without diet changes. WADA status matters for athletes; AOD-9604 is prohibited. Document that warning.

Patients usually do not feel much when taking AOD-9604. No strong appetite suppression. No classic GLP-1 nausea. No stimulant energy rush. If it helps, the changes are usually subtle: gradual waist circumference improvement, modest body-composition shifts, or lipid marker changes over weeks to months. Many patients expecting a dramatic medication will be genuinely disappointed. That is why expectation management is everything with this compound. If the patient needs to feel something to believe it is working, AOD-9604 is the wrong choice.

Your chart must document realistic expectations discussion, weight history, why stronger approved options were not chosen or were not tolerated, baseline weight and waist measurements, body composition if available, lipid panel, glucose markers, and reassessment at 8 to 12 weeks. If there is no measurable benefit at reassessment, stop. Do not sell another cycle because the patient hopes next time will be different. Evidence-based medicine means being honest when the evidence says something does not work very well.

Common protocols reference 300 to 500 mcg subcutaneously daily, often in 8 to 12 week cycles. Oral or local joint protocols exist in discussion but are more speculative and should be documented as such. AOD-9604 is best positioned as an adjunct to diet, exercise, sleep, and stress management. It is not a standalone weight-loss solution and should not be priced or marketed as one.

MOTS-c: Interesting Mitochondrial Science - No Human Trials, Investigational

MOTS-c is a mitochondrial-derived peptide encoded by mitochondrial DNA. It appears to function as a retrograde signaling molecule - meaning it sends messages from the mitochondria back to the nucleus - and is associated with AMPK activation, improved glucose handling, enhanced insulin sensitivity, mitochondrial biogenesis, antioxidant pathway upregulation, and possibly bone metabolism regulation through osteoblast signaling. The science is genuinely interesting. The human clinical trial data is nonexistent. That gap between mechanism and evidence is what you need to manage with every patient conversation.

MOTS-c is not FDA-approved. It has been listed for FDA compounding review among peptides being considered for 503A bulk substance status. As of this writing, there are no completed human clinical trials of exogenous MOTS-c administration. None. Not Phase 1. Not a small pilot study. None. The available references are basic science characterizations from the original University of Southern California laboratory and subsequent academic groups. Animal data in mice show metabolic improvements and obesity resistance. Human data does not exist.

A doctor might consider MOTS-c conceptually for metabolic dysfunction, insulin resistance, early sarcopenia, osteopenia, or patients who cannot exercise adequately but are still willing to combine investigational therapy with lifestyle modification. It should be positioned as an adjunct, not a replacement for exercise, diet, sleep hygiene, and strength training. The patient who thinks MOTS-c is "exercise in a bottle" has been misled by marketing, and your job is to correct that misconception before prescribing, not after they have paid and feel cheated.

Be careful because the human interventional data gap is absolute. Dosing, pharmacokinetics, optimal route, long-term effects, ideal patient selection, drug interactions, and safety monitoring parameters are not established. Avoid big claims about longevity, fat loss, muscle growth, or osteoporosis reversal. The endogenous MOTS-c levels do correlate with metabolic status in observational human cohorts, and animal data support a plausible mechanism. But correlation plus mechanism does not equal treatment-grade efficacy or safety evidence. Do not pretend otherwise in your chart or your marketing.

Patients typically report subtle effects: modest energy improvement, slightly better exercise tolerance, perceived recovery changes, or metabolic shifts over weeks. Some feel nothing at all. It should not cause dramatic appetite suppression or rapid weight loss. Early fatigue, flushing, headache, or injection-site reactions may occur. Set the expectation that this is investigational, the effects are likely to be modest if present at all, and the main benefit may be simply participating in cutting-edge care with close monitoring.

Your chart must document the metabolic rationale, baseline glucose and HbA1c, insulin markers if used, lipid panel, body composition assessment, DEXA scan if bone goals are discussed, complete medication list including metformin or other AMPK-related therapies, and measurable endpoints. Reassess at the end of the cycle with objective data. If there is no measurable improvement, do not continue indefinitely. Investigational does not mean"prescribe forever and hope."

Common protocols discuss 5 to 10 mg subcutaneously two to three times weekly in 4 to 8 week cycles. Because human dosing is not established by any trial, the doctor must treat any dose as investigational and patient-specific. Start conservatively. Document why you chose the dose you chose. And be prepared to explain to a board reviewer why you prescribed a compound with no human trials to a patient who had other options.

KPV: Anti-Inflammatory Concept - Preclinical, Not a Cure for Inflammatory Bowel Disease

KPV is a tripeptide sequence derived from alpha-melanocyte-stimulating hormone. It is studied for anti-inflammatory effects, particularly in gut inflammation, mucosal healing, wound healing, and inflammatory signaling modulation. It is often discussed alongside BPC-157 in gut and tissue-repair protocols, and the combination is sometimes marketed as a comprehensive gastrointestinal healing stack. That marketing gets ahead of the evidence, and you need to know exactly how far.

KPV is not FDA-approved. It has been listed for FDA Pharmacy Compounding Advisory Committee review for potential 503A bulk-drug-substance consideration. Current availability depends on pharmacy interpretation of regulatory status, which means it can change without notice. There is no country with an approved finished KPV product. The alpha-MSH parent peptide has wider academic interest, but the KPV fragment specifically is preclinical in its evidence status.

A doctor might consider KPV where inflammation is the clear target: gut mucosal irritation, inflammatory skin conditions, wound contexts with significant inflammatory component, or as part of a broader anti-inflammatory plan. The more serious the underlying disease, the more important it is not to replace standard gastroenterology care with a peptide. A patient with active Crohn's disease, ulcerative colitis, or unexplained gastrointestinal bleeding needs colonoscopy, specialist evaluation, and standard therapy. KPV does not replace any of that.

Be careful with patients who have active inflammatory bowel disease, rectal bleeding, unexplained weight loss, fever, severe abdominal pain, immunosuppressive therapy, or cancer risk. Those patients need proper diagnosis and specialist involvement, not a peptide-only plan. The danger with KPV is that both patients and physicians can convince themselves that "natural anti-inflammatory" means "safe to try while we figure things out." That thinking leads to delayed diagnosis of serious pathology. If a patient has red-flag gastrointestinal symptoms, order the workup. Do not prescribe KPV and hope it resolves.

Patients may expect less gut irritation, reduced inflammation, improved food tolerance, or better mucosal comfort. Effects, if present, are usually gradual and symptom-based. They should be told explicitly to report blood in stool, severe pain, fever, dehydration, worsening diarrhea, or rapid weight loss immediately. Those are not side effects of KPV. Those are signs of underlying disease that KPV was never going to fix.

Your chart must document the specific inflammatory condition, conventional work-up completed, specialist involvement when appropriate, baseline symptoms quantified, current medications reviewed, red flags excluded, stop criteria established, and referral rules specified. For gut complaints, do not let KPV become an excuse to skip colonoscopy, labs, stool testing, or GI referral when indicated. Your chart should show you practiced medicine, not peptide retail.

Common protocols reference 200 to 500 mcg daily orally, subcutaneously, or topically depending on intended use. Route matters significantly because gut-local delivery is a different concept than systemic injection. Oral KPV is theorized to have mucosal contact effects as it passes through the gastrointestinal tract. Injectable KPV is theorized to have systemic anti-inflammatory effects. The evidence for either route in humans is preclinical. Document which route you chose and why.

PT-141/Bremelanotide: FDA-Approved for Narrow Indication -Off-Label Is Not a Free-For-All

PT-141, also known as bremelanotide, is a melanocortin receptor agonist. Unlike PDE5 inhibitors such as sildenafil or tadalafil, which primarily work by enhancing blood flow through nitric oxide pathways in vascular smooth muscle, bremelanotide works centrally through melanocortin pathways in the brain related to sexual desire and arousal. This is an important distinction because it means the mechanism is neuropsychological as well as physiological, and the patient selection is different. A patient with pure vascular erectile dysfunction may do fine with a PDE5 inhibitor. A patient with low desire, arousal disconnect, or central sexual motivation problems may not respond to blood-flow drugs at all. That is where PT-141 has its niche.

Bremelanotide is FDA-approved as Vyleesi for acquired, generalized hypoactive sexual desire disorder (HSDD) in premenopausal women. That is a very specific indication. Acquired means the desire problem is new - it was not always present. Generalized means it occurs across all situations and partners, not just specific contexts. HSDD means the lack of desire causes distress. And premenopausal women are the only population with an FDA-approved label. Use in men, postmenopausal women, or any sexual dysfunction context outside that narrow label is off-label and must be documented as such.

A doctor might consider PT-141 for appropriate HSDD patients who meet the label criteria, or for carefully selected off-label sexual-health cases where central desire or arousal dysfunction is the primary problem rather than purely vascular erectile dysfunction. In men with normal erectile function but low libido, or in postmenopausal women with desire changes that do not fit the label but have a clear clinical rationale after evaluation, off-label discussion may be reasonable. But off-label does not mean free-for-all. Each off-label prescription requires its own patient-specific justification in the chart.

Be careful with uncontrolled hypertension - bremelanotide can cause transient blood pressure increases and decreases that are clinically significant in patients with already-unstable cardiovascular status. Cardiovascular disease, severe nausea history, flushing disorders, headache disorders, and medication interactions all require review. It is not an aphrodisiac for every patient. It should not be used more frequently than labeled limits. The FDA-approved limit is no more than eight doses per month, and that limit exists for a reason. Do not let patients convince you that "just one extra" is fine. Document frequency and enforce limits.

Patients may experience flushing, nausea, warmth, headache, or increased sexual desire and arousal after administration. Some patients respond well and report meaningful improvement in desire and sexual satisfaction. Others feel the side effects without any benefit. The effect is not the same as sildenafil - it is not a blood-flow drug that produces a predictable erectile response. It is a centrally acting agent that modulates desire and arousal, and individual response varies significantly. Patients need to understand this distinction before they use it.

Your chart must document sexual-health history including relationship and psychological factors, cardiovascular status, blood pressure, indication, on-label versus off-label status with explicit documentation, dose limit explained, side effects reviewed, and emergency instructions given. Do not prescribe casually by text because a patient wants a weekend dose. Sexual-health prescribing without proper evaluation and documentation looks like recreational dispensing, and boards do not look kindly on that.

The FDA-approved Vyleesi dose is 1.75 mg subcutaneously as needed, at least 45 minutes before anticipated sexual activity, with limits on frequency. Compounded PT-141 protocols must be evaluated against current law and labeled safety principles. Patients should be counseled to avoid use within twenty-four hours of alcohol consumption because of the interaction risk. Nausea is the most common adverse effect and can be severe enough to limit utility. Focal hyperpigmentation has been reported with repeated use and should be discussed.

NAD+: Not a Peptide, IV Marketing Ahead of Evidence - Oral Precursors Have More Data

Let me get one thing straight right away. NAD+ is not a peptide. It is nicotinamide adenine dinucleotide, a coenzyme required for cellular energy metabolism, sirtuin activity, and DNA repair pathways. It is included in this chapter not because it structurally belongs with peptides, but because peptide and cash-pay clinics sell it next to peptides constantly. Patients come in asking for "NAD+ peptide therapy" and physicians need to understand what it actually is, what the evidence actually says, and how to manage the conversation without either dismissing a legitimate biochemical pathway or overselling an unproven intervention.

Injectable NAD+ is not FDA-approved for anti-aging, wellness, longevity, or performance indications. It may be available through certain compounding pathways depending on current regulatory interpretation. Oral precursors such as nicotinamide riboside (NR) and nicotinamide mononucleotide (NMN) are sold as dietary supplements, which puts them in a completely different regulatory category than prescription injectables. Supplements are not held to pharmaceutical manufacturing standards. The evidence base differs by route. The cost differs enormously. And the marketing enthusiasm far outpaces the clinical data for almost every route and indication.

A doctor might consider NAD+ discussions for fatigue, recovery support, metabolic stress, addiction-support contexts where IV NAD+ has been used clinically, or patients specifically interested in cellular-energy support. The strongest honest position is that the mechanisms are real - NAD+ is unquestionably essential for mitochondrial function, energy production, and sirtuin-mediated cellular maintenance - but clinical claims vary greatly by route and indication. The gap between mechanism and proven clinical benefit is where the trouble lives.

Be particularly careful with IV NAD+ anti-aging claims. The most marketed route - slow intravenous infusion over several hours - is also the route with the weakest outcomes evidence. IV infusions can be uncomfortable, expensive, time-consuming, and highly variable by clinic. Patients frequently report chest tightness, anxiety, cramping, nausea, flushing, palpitations, or a general sense of unease during the infusion, especially if the drip runs too fast. Compounding sterility matters because you are injecting a large volume over hours. Infusion rate matters because rapid administration produces more side effects. And cost matters because patients paying three hundred to a thousand dollars per infusion for unproven benefits are primed for disappointment and complaints.

Patients receiving IV NAD+ may feel that uncomfortable constellation of symptoms during infusion, followed by a variable sense of mental clarity or energy hours later. Some patients swear by it. Others feel nothing except lighter in the wallet. Oral precursors are slower, subtler, usually better tolerated, and have more published human data. The NADPARK study in Parkinson's disease showed that oral nicotinamide riboside raised brain NAD+ levels and was associated with some clinical signals. The NMN insulin-sensitivity trial in prediabetic women demonstrated improved muscle insulin sensitivity. These are legitimate studies on legitimate endpoints in defined populations. They do not translate to "IV NAD+ will make you young again," but they provide more scientific grounding than the infusion marketing.

Your chart must document route of administration, specific indication, cost discussion with the patient, infusion risks reviewed, cardiovascular history, cancer history, medication list, and measurable goals. Do not sell NAD+ as guaranteed cellular rejuvenation, anti-aging therapy, or longevity medicine. If you use those terms in your chart or your marketing, you are creating a record that will be used against you. Document what you are actually doing: supporting cellular energy metabolism in a patient with specific symptoms, with informed consent, with measurable endpoints, and with a plan to reassess and stop if no benefit is demonstrated.

Common IV doses are 250 to 500 mg infused over two to six hours. Intramuscular or subcutaneous protocols vary. Oral NR or NMN is typically dosed at 250 to 1000 mg daily. Route must be chosen based on the patient's goal, the available evidence for that route, cost considerations, and patient tolerance. If a patient wants NAD+ and the goal is general metabolic support, oral precursors with monitoring are more evidence-based and carry fewer risks than IV infusions. If the clinical context justifies IV administration - such as certain addiction-recovery protocols where IV NAD+ has established clinical use patterns -document that specific rationale.

Cerebrolysin, Selank, Semax, Epitalon: International Compounds with No US Pathway

This section covers a group of compounds that share one critical characteristic: they have substantial international use or research literature but no lawful U.S. clinical prescribing pathway. That is the first thing you need to understand. The second thing is that interesting international evidence does not create a domestic legal route. No matter how compelling the Russian or European literature, no matter how many patients swear by their effects, if you are practicing in the United States, these compounds present serious regulatory obstacles that you cannot hand-wave away with a consent form.

Cerebrolysin is a porcine brain-derived mixture of low-molecular-weight neuropeptides and amino acids manufactured by EVER Neuro Pharma in Austria. It is not a single defined peptide - it is a proprietary biologic mixture designed to mimic neurotrophic signaling and support neuronal survival, neuroplasticity, and recovery after brain injury. Cerebrolysin is registered or marketed in roughly fifty countries for neurological indications including acute ischemic stroke, traumatic brain injury, and Alzheimer-type dementia. It has decades of international clinical literature with mixed but substantive results. It is not FDA-approved in the United States. It cannot be legally compounded because it is a proprietary biologic mixture, not a simple peptide sequence that a 503A pharmacy can synthesize. Importation for clinical use is generally not lawful. For U.S. physicians, Cerebrolysin should be treated as a topic for patient education, not routine prescribing.

If a patient asks about Cerebrolysin, explain what it is, where it is used, why the U.S. pathway does not exist, and what alternatives are available. Document that conversation. Do not wink and suggest they import it themselves. Do not write a prescription knowing it will be filled from an grey-market overseas source. If you practice in a country where Cerebrolysin is approved, follow that country's guidelines for neurological indication, baseline assessment scales, renal function monitoring, allergy and porcine sensitivity screening, and follow-up neurological assessment. In the United States, the defensible posture is educational, not prescriptive.

Selank is a synthetic heptapeptide developed in Russia as a stabilized analog of tuftsin, an endogenous immunomodulator. It is registered in the Russian Federation as an anxiolytic and is described as reducing anxiety without the sedation, cognitive dulling, dependence, or withdrawal concerns associated with benzodiazepines. The principal published clinical literature is in Russian journals. Selank is not FDA-approved in the United States and has faced FDA compounding restrictions. There is no clear sanctioned U.S. prescribing pathway. Online intranasal products are overwhelmingly grey-market.

A doctor might discuss Selank scientifically in the context of mild-to-moderate anxiety, stress resilience, or fatigue-anxiety overlap. Clinically, the doctor must not use it to avoid proper psychiatric evaluation or standard therapy when indicated. Severe panic disorder, bipolar disorder, suicidality, PTSD, OCD, pregnancy, breastfeeding, autoimmune disease, and complex psychiatric medication regimens are all reasons to decline and refer. Psychiatric patients can destabilize quickly, and casually experimenting with mood-active peptides in unstable patients is dangerous medicine.

Patients may describe a calmer state without feeling drugged. Effects may appear within an hour or build over several days. Some report better sleep because anxiety is lower, not because Selank is a sedative. Nasal irritation or headache can occur. Document anxiety diagnosis, severity screening with PHQ-9 or GAD-7, suicidality screening, current psychiatric medications, standard alternatives discussed, regulatory status explained, and PCP or psychiatry involvement arranged.

Semax is a synthetic peptide derived from ACTH(4-10) with a Pro-Gly-Pro modification that extends activity. It is registered in Russia for cerebrovascular and cognitive indications including stroke, ischemia, cognitive disorders, and optic-nerve conditions. It is usually administered intranasally. Semax is not FDA-approved in the United States. The FDA has scheduled Semax-related substances for PCAC review for possible inclusion on the 503A bulk-drug-substances list. Until a final lawful pathway is clear, treat it as investigational and regulatory-sensitive.

A doctor might discuss Semax in the context of neuroprotection, post-stroke recovery support, or cognitive dysfunction, but it should not be sold as a productivity spray or casual focus enhancer for healthy people who want to perform better at work. Neurologic red flags, stroke or TIA symptoms, seizure history, psychiatric instability, hypertension, pregnancy, and pediatric use are all contraindications or strong cautions. Any acute neurologic symptom belongs in emergency or specialist care, not a peptide consult.

Patients may expect improved focus, mental stamina, or post-injury recovery support. Some notice clearer attention or reduced fatigue. Others feel nothing. Do not promise brain repair. Document neurologic indication, standard evaluation completed, specialist involvement, regulatory status disclosed, expectations set, symptom scales used, and adverse-effect instructions given.

Epitalon, also called Epithalon, is a synthetic tetrapeptide associated with pineal bioregulation, telomerase activation claims, circadian biology, and longevity marketing. Much of the literature comes from the Khavinson bioregulator research program at the St. Petersburg Institute of Bioregulation and Gerontology in Russia. It is not FDA-approved. The FDA has scheduled Epitalon-related substances for PCAC review. As with other longevity peptides, availability and legality can shift quickly.

Be particularly careful with the telomerase language. Telomerase activation sounds like anti-aging magic to patients. What they do not understand is that cancer biology is intimately tied to telomere maintenance - cancer cells activate telomerase to achieve immortality.

Stimulating telomerase in a patient with undiagnosed cancer or precancerous lesions is not necessarily beneficial. It may be harmful. Active or recent cancer, proliferative disorders, pregnancy, psychiatric instability, endocrine disorders, and patients seeking immortality medicine are all reasons to decline.

Patients may expect better sleep, circadian support, mood stability, or longevity effects. Realistic expectation should be modest: if anything occurs, it will likely be subtle and hard to separate from placebo, sleep hygiene improvements, and other concurrent interventions. Document that evidence is limited, FDA status disclosed, theoretical telomerase and cancer discussion completed, goals defined, measurable endpoints established, and stop rules specified. Do not use anti-aging marketing claims in the chart. They look reckless to a board reviewer.

Common Epitalon protocols discuss 5 to 10 mg daily for 10 to 20 day cycles, repeated a few times per year. This is not FDA-approved dosing and must be treated as investigational. For all four of these international compounds - Cerebrolysin, Selank, Semax, and Epitalon - the binding constraint for U.S. physicians is not absence of human evidence. It is absence of a legal U.S. prescribing pathway. Document that. Explain it to patients. And do not let enthusiasm for interesting science override regulatory reality.

Pinealon, PE-22-28, DSIP: Research Compounds - Interesting Science Is Not a Prescribing Pathway

This final section covers compounds that sit at the absolute frontier of peptide research. They are discussed in online communities, referenced in preclinical literature, and occasionally available through grey-market channels. For a U.S. physician in clinical practice, these compounds should be understood intellectually, discussed with patients who ask about them as educational topics, and generally not prescribed. If you choose to venture into this territory, your documentation burden is at its maximum and your legal exposure is at its highest.

Pinealon and PE-22-28 are unrelated neuroactive research compounds often discussed together in cognitive and mood peptide circles. Pinealon is a Russian bioregulator tripeptide associated with gene-expression modulation and neuroprotection claims. It is part of the Khavinson bioregulator program, with research and limited clinical use described in Russian literature. PE-22-28 is a spadin-derived peptide targeting TREK-1 potassium channels, studied preclinically for rapid antidepressant-like effects in animal models. Neither is FDA-approved. Neither has a clear U.S. clinical prescribing pathway. PE-22-28 has no approved form in any jurisdiction anywhere in the world. Pinealon has Russian and limited Eastern European use patterns but no FDA-standard pathway.

These compounds do not belong in an ordinary clinic menu. A doctor might discuss them only as educational examples of research frontiers: cognitive aging neuroscience, neuroprotection mechanisms, depression biology, and why mechanistic promise is insufficient for clinical adoption. They are not treatments for your Monday morning patient who wants better memory. PE-22-28's TREK-1 channel target raises theoretical cardiac electrophysiology questions that have not been studied in humans. That is not something a cash-pay wellness clinic should ignore.

Be careful with psychiatric instability, suicidality, bipolar disorder, cardiac disease, anesthesia interactions, and grey-market sourcing. Patients may expect memory improvement, mood enhancement, better focus, or sleep changes. Effects are uncertain at best. Pinealon effects, if any, are likely subtle and delayed over weeks or months. PE-22-28 is discussed as faster-acting in animal models, but human experience is entirely speculative. Document that these are research compounds, not routine therapies. For active psychiatric disease, referral to appropriate mental health care is the defensible and necessary step.

No standardized human dosing exists for PE-22-28. Pinealon protocols vary by Russian sources and research vendors. Do not present either as a standard clinical protocol. If you discuss these compounds with patients, document the educational nature of the conversation, the regulatory status, the absence of human trials, and the referral or standard care options offered.

DSIP, or delta sleep-inducing peptide, also known as emideltide, is a nonapeptide studied for sleep modulation, stress physiology, pain, withdrawal symptoms, and neuroendocrine effects. Unlike the newer frontier compounds, DSIP has a longer history - much of the published work came from European groups in the 1970s and 1980s, notably the Schoenenberger group at the University of Zurich. DSIP is not FDA-approved. It has been scheduled for FDA PCAC review for possible 503A bulk-drug-substance inclusion. Until final FDA action is clear, it remains regulatory-sensitive.

No country has an approved DSIP pharmaceutical product. It remains a research substance worldwide. A doctor might discuss DSIP in the context of refractory sleep problems or stress-related dysregulation after proper sleep evaluation and standard care have been considered. It should not replace evaluation for sleep apnea, medication-induced sleep disruption, psychiatric disease, pain, alcohol use, or stimulant use. Sleep complaints often hide serious issues, and masking them with an unproven peptide is not medicine.

Be careful with sedatives, alcohol, psychiatric medications, respiratory disease, untreated sleep apnea, and patients seeking peptide sedation instead of diagnosis. Patients may expect deeper sleep, fewer awakenings, improved recovery, or calmer stress response. Effects are highly variable across individuals. Some older studies suggested sleep architecture effects, but modern high-quality randomized trials are essentially absent. DSIP should be treated as a low-evidence sleep adjunct, not a primary therapy.

Your chart must document sleep history including apnea screening with STOP-BANG or equivalent, medication and substance review, mental health screening, prior treatments attempted, FDA status disclosed, and follow-up with sleep metrics. Use a sleep diary or standardized scales like the Pittsburgh Sleep Quality Index if possible. If there is no measurable improvement in sleep metrics after a defined trial period, stop. Investigational therapy does not mean indefinite therapy without accountability.

Protocols for DSIP vary widely and are not standardized. Treat any dosing as investigational and verify lawful product availability before any clinical discussion. The legacy human exposure from the 1980s literature suggests safety signals were not striking, but modern dosing standards, indication boundaries, comparator data, and long-term safety information are absent.

That is the honest framework: older work suggests DSIP was not acutely dangerous, but we do not have the evidence to treat it as a standard therapy.

For all the compounds in this section - Pinealon, PE-22-28, and DSIP - the principle is the same. Interesting science is not a prescribing pathway. Mechanistic plausibility is not clinical evidence. Preclinical data in animals is not human efficacy. And grey-market availability is not a justification for clinical use. If you are a researcher running an IRB-approved trial, that is a different conversation. If you are a clinician seeing patients in a cash-pay practice, the defensible posture is education, caution, and strong preference for established therapies with human evidence. When patients ask about these compounds, explain what is known, what is not known, why the legal pathway does not exist, and what evidence-based alternatives are available. Document that conversation thoroughly. And when in doubt, say no. No is the easiest prescription to defend when the alternative is an unproven compound with no regulatory status, no human trials, and no standardized monitoring framework.

Final Practical Notes on Every Peptide in This Chapter

Let me leave you with some hard-won wisdom that applies across every single profile you just read. The peptide does not matter as much as the physician's judgment, documentation, and willingness to say no when appropriate. A mediocre peptide prescribed with excellent screening, exhaustive consent, rigorous monitoring, and bulletproof charting is more defensible than the most evidence-based peptide prescribed casually with thin records and optimistic assumptions.

For every peptide you prescribe, verify the current regulatory status before the first prescription and re-verify before every refill. Pharmacy availability changes. FDA positions change. State board attitudes change. What was acceptable last quarter may not be acceptable this quarter. Build verification into your workflow, not as an afterthought.

For every patient you accept, start with the clinical problem, not the product name. Document the medical necessity. Document the alternatives considered. Document why this therapy, for this patient, at this time, is reasonable. Write your chart for a stranger who does not know you and does not like you, because that is exactly who reads it when things go wrong.

For every consent you obtain, make sure the patient actually understands what they are consenting to. FDA status, evidence limitations, known risks, unknown risks, no-guarantee language, cost, alternatives, and emergency instructions. A signature on a form the patient did not read is not consent. It is a piece of paper. Take the time to explain. Document the explanation. Your future self will thank you when the board letter arrives.

For every monitoring plan you create, set measurable endpoints and stop criteria. Do not prescribe indefinitely without reassessment. Do not continue therapy because the patient likes the idea when objective measures show no benefit. Do not ignore side effects because the patient is paying cash. Monitoring is not optional. It is the core of medical supervision.

And for every patient encounter, remember why you are doing this. Peptide medicine has the potential to help real patients with real problems that conventional medicine has failed to solve. That is why this field exists. That is why patients are willing to pay out of pocket. But that potential is realized only when physicians practice with discipline, integrity, and obsessive attention to documentation. When physicians get lazy, patients get hurt, and licenses get lost. Do not be the doctor who gives peptide medicine a bad name. Be the doctor who proves it can be practiced responsibly.

The peptides that matter are the ones you can prescribe with a clean conscience, a defensible chart, and a patient who understands exactly what they are getting into. Everything else is noise. Cut through the noise. Practice good medicine. Protect your license. Help your patients. In that order.

14 - Stacking, Dosing, and Not Getting Cute

Let me tell you something I have seen too many times. A young doctor, enthusiastic about peptides, opens a cash-pay practice. Learns a few things online. Gets a pharmacy relationship going. Starts with one or two peptides - simple, clean, defensible. Then a patient asks, "Can't we add this too?" Then another patient wants the "full protocol." Then the doctor starts seeing dollar signs in stack combinations. Six months later, the average patient is on five peptides, the chart has become a shopping receipt, and when someone develops a side effect, nobody can figure out which compound caused it. That is how good practices turn into board exhibits. This chapter exists to stop that from happening to you.

Stacking, dosing, and side-effect management are not glamorous topics. They will not get you featured on a podcast. They will not make patients excited during their consultation. But get these wrong, and nothing else in this book will save you. A perfect consent form cannot rescue a patient who overdosed because you confused milligrams with micrograms. A pristine marketing strategy cannot protect you when a patient lands in the emergency room dehydrated on a four-peptide stack and the board asks why you thought that combination was a good idea.

The workaday details of stacking logic, dose verification, and stop-rule discipline separate real medical practices from vial shops. This chapter is about those details.

A stack is not more scientific because it has more ingredients

The first thing you need to understand about stacking peptides is that patients and internet forums love complexity. The more compounds in a protocol, the more "advanced" it sounds. The more syringes in the kit, the more the patient feels they are getting their money's worth. This is nonsense, and you need to treat it as nonsense. A stack is not more scientific because it has more ingredients. In fact, the opposite is usually true. The more moving parts you add, the less scientific your protocol becomes, because you lose the ability to attribute effects - good or bad - to any single compound.

Let me be blunt about what I have observed in this field. The doctors who get in trouble are often the ones who got cute. They started reasonable, then added a peptide for sleep, then one for recovery, then one for "metabolic optimization," then something for cognitive enhancement. Before long, every patient was walking out with a bag of vials and a color-coded injection calendar that looked like a NASA launch schedule. You think the board cares that you meant well? You think they are impressed by your ambition? They are not. They look at the chart, see a kitchen-sink approach, and conclude that you were experimenting on patients without a coherent medical rationale.

Every compound you add to a stack must have its own specific reason for being there. Not a theoretical reason. Not a "synergy" claim you read on a forum. A patient-specific clinical reason that you can write in the chart and explain to a skeptical reviewer. If you cannot look at each component and say, "This patient needs this specific compound because of this specific clinical finding," then that component does not belong in the stack. Period.

Consider the difference between a defensible stack and an indefensible one. A patient comes in with a rotator cuff injury, has failed conservative management, imaging shows a partial tear, and they want to avoid surgery if possible. They have no contraindications, their PCP is aware, and they understand that peptides are adjunctive, not curative. You prescribe BPC-157 at a measured dose, with a specific duration, stop criteria, and follow-up plan. That is a clean, defensible decision. Now imagine the same patient, but you also add TB-500 because "it helps with healing," plus GHK-Cu because "collagen support," plus a growth-hormone secretagogue because "GH helps tissue repair," plus a gut peptide because "inflammation starts in the gut."

Suddenly you have gone from a targeted therapy to a philosophy project. The chart now reads like someone throwing spaghetti at the wall. And when this patient develops a reaction -edema, glucose changes, injection-site infection, who knows what - you will not be able to identify the culprit. Worse, neither will the emergency room doctor who has to sort it out at two in the morning.

The discipline of good stacking is the discipline of restraint. Start with the clinical problem, not the product catalog. Define what you are trying to accomplish in measurable terms. Pick the single compound with the best evidence and the cleanest risk profile for that specific goal. Give it a fair trial with appropriate monitoring. If it works, great. If it does not, reassess. Maybe add something. Maybe switch. But do not start with everything at once. That is not medicine. That is retail with delusions of grandeur.

Use stacks only when each component has a specific reason

Let me walk you through how stacking actually makes sense, because I am not opposed to combining peptides when the reasoning is sound. There are legitimate clinical scenarios where multiple peptides address different aspects of a complex problem, and in those cases, a thoughtful stack is appropriate. The key is that each component must address a distinct, identifiable need.

The healing stack is probably the most common defensible combination in peptide practice. A patient with a significant soft-tissue injury - a partial tendon tear, a stubborn ligament sprain, post-surgical recovery that is not progressing - may benefit from BPC-157 combined with TB-500. Here is the reasoning: BPC-157 has preclinical evidence for tendon-to-bone healing, angiogenesis, and fibroblast migration. TB-500, or the thymosin beta-4 fragment, has different mechanisms centered on actin regulation and cell migration. These address different phases and aspects of tissue repair. If you can document the injury, the failed conservative treatment, the imaging, the specialist involvement, and why each compound addresses a specific aspect of the healing problem, this is a defensible stack. But you still need to set duration limits, reassessment points, and clear stop criteria. You still need measurable endpoints like pain scale, range of motion, functional capacity, or repeat imaging.

The metabolic stack is another area where combinations appear, and it is also where doctors get themselves into the most trouble. Let me be direct: for most overweight patients with metabolic syndrome, a GLP-1 agonist like semaglutide or tirzepatide is the backbone of therapy. These are the most evidence-based, most monitored, best-understood medications in the entire peptide and incretin space. They have real FDA-approved products, real Phase 3 data, real cardiovascular outcomes trials. If a patient needs metabolic intervention, you start there. Not with a stack. Not with five different compounds. You start with the drug that has the strongest evidence and the clearest indication.

Where an adjunct might make sense is when the patient has a specific additional need that the GLP-1 does not address. Perhaps they have reached a weight-loss plateau on a GLP-1 and have significant visceral adiposity remaining. Discussing tesamorelin for visceral fat reduction might be reasonable, provided you document the rationale, monitor IGF-1 and glucose, and set a reassessment point. Perhaps the patient cannot tolerate GLP-1s at all due to severe GI sensitivity, and you are exploring AOD-9604 as an adjunct with appropriate expectation-setting. These are patient-specific decisions made one at a time, not boilerplate combinations handed to every patient who walks through the door.

The growth-hormone-axis stack - typically CJC-1295 combined with ipamorelin - is popular in anti-aging and wellness circles. I have reservations about this category because the evidence is thinner and the marketing is thicker, but when prescribed thoughtfully, it can be defensible. The rationale for combining a GHRH analog like CJC-1295 with a ghrelin agonist like ipamorelin is that they stimulate growth hormone release through complementary pathways. The combination aims for a more physiologic pulsatile GH pattern than either compound alone. If you document baseline IGF-1, set cycling parameters, monitor glucose and edema, and keep the goal modest - sleep improvement, recovery support, subtle body composition changes rather than dramatic transformation - this can be reasonable care. Where it becomes unreasonable is when you add sermorelin on top, plus maybe tesamorelin, plus maybe an IGF-1 analog, creating a GH-axis pile-on that no endocrinologist would recognize as standard care. The pituitary does not need five different signals. Your patient does not need to be a chemistry experiment.

What about immune and repair combinations? Thymosin alpha-1 for immune modulation might pair with a repair peptide when a patient has both recurrent infection issues and a healing problem. But you need to document both problems clearly, screen for autoimmune disease, monitor appropriately, and not pretend this is routine primary care. Selank for anxiety alongside a metabolic protocol? Only if the anxiety is well-characterized, psychiatric evaluation has been considered, and you are not using a peptide to avoid proper mental health care.

Here is my rule of thumb: if you cannot explain the stack to a skeptical board reviewer in under sixty seconds, with a clear one-sentence rationale for each component, it is too complicated. Simplify it. Your license is worth more than whatever revenue the extra vial generates.

Start with the fewest moving parts possible

The safest stack is the one-compound stack. I know that sounds obvious, but I see doctors skip right past the obvious because they are trying to impress patients or differentiate their practice. Differentiation should come from your clinical judgment, your thoroughness, your monitoring, and your patient communication. Not from your willingness to combine more compounds than the clinic down the street.

When you start a patient on a new peptide, begin with that peptide alone. Give it a fair trial at an appropriate dose with proper follow-up. This is not just good medicine - it is good risk management. If the patient improves, you know what worked. If the patient has a side effect, you know what caused it. If the patient does not respond, you have clean data for your next decision. You can document a clear trial and outcome. That chart reads like a physician's reasoning, not a guess.

This approach also protects you from the compounding problem. When a patient is on five peptides and develops nausea, which one caused it? The GLP-1? The MOTS-c? The NAD+? The combination? The injection technique? You will spend hours trying to untangle it. Meanwhile the patient is miserable, may stop everything on their own, and will likely blame you for the chaos. If you had started with one compound, you would know. The board would know too. Clean protocols produce clean charts. Clean charts produce defensible care.

There is a practical patient-management dimension here too. Patients on complex multi-vial protocols make mistakes. They mix up syringes. They forget which day to take which compound. They run out of one vial early and start improvising. They watch a YouTube video and decide to adjust their own doses. The more complicated you make the protocol, the more opportunities you create for patient error. And patient error becomes your problem when the chart shows you prescribed an unmanageable regimen.

Start simple. Document the reason for starting. Set a reassessment point. If you add something later, document why. Build the stack incrementally, with clinical reasoning at each step. That is how a physician practices medicine. That is how you keep your license.

If a patient has a side effect on a five-peptide stack, you won't know which caused it

I have been building toward this point throughout the section, and now I want to nail it down. The single biggest practical danger of complex stacking is diagnostic ambiguity when something goes wrong. And something will go wrong eventually. Every physician who prescribes long enough will see side effects, unexpected reactions, and patients who just do not respond the way the internet said they would. When that happens, your ability to identify the cause and respond quickly depends entirely on how clean your protocol was to begin with.

Imagine a patient on a five-peptide stack: semaglutide for weight, BPC-157 for a nagging shoulder injury, TB-500 for systemic healing support, CJC-1295 with ipamorelin for "recovery and sleep," and NAD+ injections for energy. This patient calls your office three weeks in reporting severe nausea, fatigue, dizziness, and a racing heartbeat. What do you do? You tell them to stop everything, of course - but now you have no idea what caused the problem. Was it the semaglutide dose titrated too fast? Was it the CJC-1295 causing fluid retention and blood pressure changes? Was it the NAD+ causing flushing and palpitations? Was it an interaction between the GLP-1 and the GH secretagogue affecting glucose? Was it the patient not eating enough because of the semaglutide nausea, then injecting TB-500 on an empty stomach? You cannot know. You have to stop everything, wait for resolution, and then maybe reintroduce compounds one by one if the patient even trusts you enough to try again.

Now compare that to a patient on semaglutide alone. Same nausea and dizziness. You know exactly what to do: hold the semaglutide, assess hydration, check the dose, review the titration, consider a lower dose or longer interval. Clean problem, clean solution, clean chart. The patient gets better, you adjust, and you move on. That is medicine. The other scenario is a guessing game that puts your patient at risk and your license on the line.

This diagnostic ambiguity extends to lab monitoring too. A patient on a complex stack shows elevated liver enzymes. Is it the BPC-157? The TB-500? The GHK-Cu? A supplement they did not disclose? Alcohol? Non-alcoholic fatty liver disease you did not screen for? The more compounds in the mix, the harder it is to interpret any abnormal result. Eventually you find yourself ordering more and more tests, referring to more and more specialists, and chasing your tail while the patient loses confidence in your care.

The board does not need to see a patient harmed to take action against you. They need to see that your practice looked sloppy. A five-peptide stack with no clear rationale for each component, no documented stop rules, and no structured follow-up looks sloppy. It looks like you were winging it. And maybe you were. Do not let that be you. Keep your stacks small, your reasoning clear, your documentation tight, and your patient management simple enough that when something goes wrong, you know exactly what to do.

Verify pharmacy-specific concentration before giving any instructions

If I had to pick one single cause of peptide-related patient harm, it would be dose confusion. Not the peptide itself. Not some rare allergic reaction. Good old-fashioned confusion about how much medicine the patient is actually injecting. Milligrams versus micrograms. Milliliters versus units. Concentration per vial that varies from one pharmacy to the next. This is where patients get hurt, and it is entirely preventable.

Let me tell you a story. A physician I consulted for prescribed what he thought was a standard dose of a compounded semaglutide product. The pharmacy shipped a vial at a different concentration than the physician expected - higher, as it turned out. The physician's instructions to the patient said "draw to the 10-unit mark on a U-100 insulin syringe." But the concentration was double what the physician had in his head. The patient followed the instructions exactly and injected twice the intended dose. Severe nausea, dehydration, a trip to the urgent care, and a very angry patient who later filed a board complaint. The physician's chart said "dosed per protocol." The board reviewer asked, "What protocol? Where is the concentration documented? Where is the calculation?" There was nothing. Just a vague assumption that led to a predictable error.

This happens more often than anyone admits. Pharmacies change concentrations. Different pharmacies compound differently. A 503A pharmacy may make a product at one strength while a 503B outsourcing facility makes it at another. The same pharmacy may change its standard concentration based on supply, batch size, or a pharmacist's clinical judgment. If you do not verify the exact concentration of the specific vial your patient will receive, you are practicing on autopilot. And autopilot kills people in medicine.

Here is what verification means in practice. Before you give any dosing instructions, you must know: the total milligrams of peptide in the vial; the volume of reconstitution or the total volume in the vial; the resulting concentration in mg per mL; how many units on the patient's syringe correspond to the intended dose; and the specific instructions written out in the patient's own words, not clinical shorthand.

Let me walk through an example. Your pharmacy ships semaglutide as a 2 mg/mL solution in a 2 mL vial. Total vial content: 4 mg. You want the patient to take 0.25 mg weekly. At 2 mg/mL,

The intended 0.25 mg dose equals 0.125 mL. On a standard U-100 insulin syringe, 0.125 mL is 12.5 units. So your instructions say: "Draw to the 12.5-unit mark on your U-100 insulin syringe. Inject subcutaneously once weekly." You document this in the chart. You document the pharmacy, the concentration, the calculation, and the patient's confirmation that they understand. Now if there is ever a question, you have a clear paper trail.

But what if the pharmacy changes and the next vial is 5 mg/mL? Same 12.5 units now delivers 0.625 mg - two and a half times the intended dose. If you do not verify each shipment, if you do not update your instructions when the product changes, this is exactly how overdoses happen. The patient trusts your instructions. They should be able to. Your job is to make sure those instructions match the vial in their refrigerator.

I want you to build a verification checklist into your workflow for every peptide prescription. Before any patient receives instructions: confirm the pharmacy's concentration for that specific product batch; calculate the dose in both milligrams and syringe units; write the instructions in plain language; have the patient repeat back their understanding; document everything in the chart. Do not skip any of these steps. Not for established patients. Not for "simple" doses. Not ever. The two minutes it takes to verify concentration could save you from a board investigation that consumes two years of your life.

Use mg, mcg, mL, and syringe units carefully - dose confusion hurts patients

The unit confusion problem deserves its own section because it is so persistent and so dangerous. Peptide dosing involves some of the smallest mass measurements in all of medicine. We are routinely working with micrograms - millionths of a gram - and patients are expected to measure these precisely at home using syringes designed for insulin. This is a recipe for error if you are not meticulous.

Let me be clear about the units. Milligrams (mg) are thousandths of a gram. Micrograms (mcg) are millionths of a gram. One milligram equals one thousand micrograms. This seems basic, and it is - until you are rushing through a busy clinic day and write "mg" when you meant "mcg," or a staff member transcribes your note incorrectly, or a patient misreads a decimal point. A semaglutide dose of 0.25 mg is 250 mcg. If someone writes 250 mg, that is a thousand-fold overdose. Sounds impossible? I have seen it happen. Not from malice. From haste.

Milliliters (mL) measure volume, not mass. The concentration of the product - how many milligrams or micrograms are in each milliliter - is what connects volume to dose. If you do not know the concentration, you cannot safely convert between volume and dose. Yet I see physicians write "inject 0.1 mL" without specifying the concentration, as if all vials are the same. They are not. A 0.1 mL injection from a 2 mg/mL vial delivers 0.2 mg. The same 0.1 mL from a 10 mg/mL vial delivers 1 mg. Five times the dose, same volume, same instructions. This is how patients get hurt while following directions perfectly.

Syringe units add another layer of confusion. U-100 insulin syringes are marked in units, where 100 units equals 1 mL. So 10 units equals 0.1 mL. But patients do not always use U-100 syringes. Some use U-40 syringes for other purposes. Some use tuberculin syringes marked differently. Some use whatever the pharmacy sent or whatever they had left over from a previous prescription. If your instructions say "draw to 10 units" and the patient uses a different syringe type, the actual volume - and therefore the dose - could be completely wrong.

The fix is straightforward but requires discipline. First, always specify the exact syringe type:"Use a U-100 insulin syringe with a 29-gauge, half-inch needle." Second, give the dose in multiple formats: milligrams, milliliters at the stated concentration, and syringe units. For example: "Inject 0.25 mg, which equals 0.125 mL, which equals 12.5 units on your U-100 syringe." Third, have the patient demonstrate their understanding. Ask them to show you on a syringe where they would draw to. If they cannot do it confidently, they are not ready to take the prescription home.

Staff training is critical here too. I have seen well-meaning nurses or medical assistants give patients verbal instructions that differ from what the physician wrote, or use shorthand that confuses the patient, or assume the patient knows more than they do. Every staff member who interacts with patients about dosing must follow a written protocol that includes: confirming the exact product and concentration; using only the written instructions from the physician; never improvising or adding personal interpretation; requiring patient demonstration of understanding; documenting the education in the chart. If your staff cannot follow this, they should not be giving dosing instructions.

Decimal points are another landmine. European-style notation uses commas where Americans use periods, and vice versa. A patient who grew up in another country may read 0.25 as 0,25 and vice versa. Handwritten notes are even worse - a sloppy decimal point can look like a smudge or disappear entirely. Typed instructions, verified before delivery, are the only safe approach. No handwritten dosing cards. No verbal-only instructions. No text messages with dose changes. Document everything formally, legibly, and in the chart.

I also want to address reconstitution because this is where patients make the most errors. Lyophilized peptides require the patient to add bacteriostatic water to the vial before use. The amount of water added determines the concentration. If the patient adds 1 mL of water to a 5 mg vial, the concentration is 5 mg/mL. If they add 2 mL, the concentration is 2.5 mg/mL. If they add the wrong amount, or use the wrong type of water, or contaminate the vial, every subsequent dose is wrong. Some practices have the pharmacy reconstitute before shipping. Some teach patients to do it. Either way, you must document the reconstitution instructions precisely, verify the patient understands, and confirm the resulting concentration before any dose calculation. Do not assume the pharmacy handles this perfectly every time. Verify it yourself.

Document route, frequency, titration, and cycle length every time

A dose is not just a number. It is a complete instruction set that includes the amount, the route of administration, the frequency, the titration plan if any, the cycle length, and the stop rules. Leave any of these out, and you have an incomplete prescription that invites patient error and board scrutiny.

Route matters because different routes have different absorption, different risks, and different evidence bases. Subcutaneous injection is the standard for most peptides, but intramuscular, intravenous, intranasal, oral, and topical routes all exist for various compounds. The route must match the evidence and the formulation. You do not give an oral formulation by injection or vice versa. You do not switch routes mid-cycle without documenting why. If a peptide has human evidence only for subcutaneous use, and you prescribe it intramuscularly because the patient prefers it, you need to document that rationale. The chart should show clinical reasoning, not convenience.

Frequency is where many protocols vary. Some peptides are dosed daily. Some are five days on, two days off. Some are once weekly. Some are twice weekly. The frequency must match the compound's half-life, the evidence base, the patient's goals, and their ability to comply. A patient who travels frequently may not manage a daily injection protocol. A patient who works odd hours may struggle with bedtime dosing. These are real-world considerations that belong in your clinical reasoning. But the frequency must still be evidence-based, not arbitrary. "As often as the patient wants" is not a frequency. "Follow the schedule we gave you" is not documentation. State the frequency explicitly in the chart: "Inject 0.25 mg subcutaneously once weekly, same day each week, preferably in the morning."

Titration is appropriate for some peptides and dangerous for others. GLP-1 agonists, for example, require slow titration because GI side effects are dose-dependent and patients need time to adapt. Starting a patient on 2.4 mg of semaglutide because they are eager for faster results is malpractice territory. The titration schedule must be written, not verbal. "Start at X, increase to Y after Z weeks if tolerated, hold if nausea exceeds level N, call the office before increasing." Every step documented. Every decision point clear.

For peptides that do not typically require titration - most repair peptides, many GH secretagogues, immune peptides - do not invent a titration schedule just to look thorough. A flat dose with clear stop criteria is often simpler and safer. If you do titrate, have a clinical reason: symptom response, lab value, tolerability, goal progression. Document that reason."Titrated up because the patient wanted more" is not a clinical reason. "Titrated up because the patient reports ongoing pain at 4/10 after 4 weeks at the lower dose, no side effects, and the goal is functional range of motion below 2/10" - that is a clinical reason.

Cycle length is particularly important for peptides used in time-limited courses. BPC-157 for tissue repair, tesamorelin for visceral fat, MOTS-c for metabolic support - these are typically not intended for indefinite use. A healing peptide should have an endpoint based on the injury timeline: "Six-week course, reassess at week 6 with repeat evaluation of pain and range of motion. Continue only if objective improvement documented and patient still has unmet goals." A GH-axis peptide should have cycling built in to limit tachyphylaxis: "Five days on, two days off, for 8 weeks, followed by 4 weeks off. Repeat IGF-1 and fasting glucose before any new cycle." These cycle parameters must be written in the chart, communicated to the patient, and enforced at follow-up. Indefinite continuation without reassessment looks like a subscription service, not medical care.

Let me also address what happens at the end of a cycle. Every cycle-based prescription needs a documented plan for what comes next. Does the patient stop entirely? Do they transition to maintenance dosing? Do they get a follow-up lab panel before deciding? Do they have a scheduled appointment to review outcomes? If you write a six-week course and then just auto-refill at week seven without any clinical contact, you are running a vial business. The chart must show that a physician reviewed the patient's status and made a conscious decision about continuation, modification, or discontinuation. Auto-refills without review are one of the fastest ways to attract board attention. Do not do it.

Do not copy dosing from online forums - that is not medicine

I cannot believe I need to say this, but the number of physicians I have encountered who base their dosing on Reddit threads, bodybuilding forums, or patient Facebook groups is staggering. Let me be as clear as I know how: online forum dosing is not a medical source. It is anecdote, often from anonymous users, frequently with financial motives, sometimes outright fabricated.

If you copy dosing from an internet forum into your prescription pad, you are not practicing medicine. You are crowdsourcing patient care to strangers on the internet. And when something goes wrong, that forum post will not defend you at a board hearing.

The forums are seductive because they feel like insider knowledge. "Dr. Smith never told me this, but the guys on the forum say..." Patients bring this information to you constantly. They will show you screenshots, links, YouTube videos, influencer protocols. Your job is not to be impressed by their research skills. Your job is to evaluate whether any of that information belongs in a medical decision. Usually it does not.

Here is the problem with forum dosing. First, there is no verification. Anyone can post anything. The person claiming to be a "biohacker with ten years of experience" could be a teenager in their parents' basement. The "protocol that worked for everyone" could be completely made up. There is no peer review, no quality control, no accountability. Second, forum dosing rarely accounts for individual variation. A dose that one person tolerated may cause severe side effects in another due to differences in body weight, metabolism, concurrent medications, genetics, or underlying conditions. Third, forum discussions do not document outcomes systematically. The person who reports amazing results may have also changed their diet, started exercising, took three other supplements, and experienced a placebo effect. The person who had a terrible reaction may never post about it. You are reading a self-selected, uncontrolled, unverified stream of anecdotes.

What about the dosing information in this book? This book gives you reference ranges, not prescriptions. It tells you what is commonly seen in practice, what the evidence suggests, and what the safety considerations are. It does not replace your clinical judgment, your patient-specific assessment, or your verification of the actual product your patient will use. Every dose in this book should be treated as a starting point for your own calculation, not a prescription to copy blindly. Verify the concentration. Adjust for the patient. Document your reasoning. That is medicine.

The same goes for dosing apps, online calculators, and third-party software. These can be helpful tools, but they are only as good as the data you put in and the judgment you apply to the output. An app that calculates units based on concentration still requires you to confirm the concentration is correct. A calculator that suggests a starting dose still requires you to assess whether that starting dose is appropriate for your specific patient. Never outsource clinical decision-making to a tool. Use tools to support your judgment, not replace it.

Finally, I want to address the patient who arrives with a stack already designed from online research. They have a list of five peptides, specific doses, a injection schedule, and a confident attitude. Your response should be polite but firm: "I appreciate that you have done research. I will evaluate your goals, your history, and your clinical needs, and I will recommend what I think is appropriate. I do not copy protocols from the internet." If the patient insists on their pre-designed stack, that is a red flag. Patients who dictate their own multi-compound protocols are often the same patients who file complaints when things do not go their way. They are not looking for a physician. They are looking for a prescription pad with a license attached. Say no when appropriate. Your license, your rules.

A side-effect plan must exist before the patient has a side effect

This section is the most important part of the most important chapter in the clinical section of this book. I do not say that lightly. If you remember nothing else from this entire manual, remember this: the side-effect conversation must happen before the patient starts therapy. Not when they call your office panicked. Not when they show up in the emergency room. Not when they write a bad review because they were scared and had no idea what to expect. Before. The first visit. While they are still calm, still thinking clearly, and still able to absorb information.

Why does this matter so much? Because patients who are surprised by side effects become patients who file complaints. It is that simple. A patient who was told "nausea is common for the first few weeks, here's what to do, and here's when to call us" will handle nausea very differently than a patient who was told "this is safe and natural" and then woke up vomiting. The first patient takes the anti-nausea measures you discussed, calls your office for guidance, and tolerates the adjustment period. The second patient panics, goes to the emergency room, tells the ER doctor they got "some injection from a wellness clinic," and starts down a road that leads to a board complaint, a negative review, and possibly worse.

Every patient who leaves your office with a peptide prescription must leave with four things written down: what common side effects to expect; what serious warning signs require immediate medical attention; what to do and who to call if they experience either category; and clear stop rules that tell them when to hold the dose and when to seek emergency care.

This is not just patient education. It is risk management. It is documentation. It is the difference between a patient who feels supported through an expected adjustment period and a patient who feels abandoned when something goes wrong. And feelings drive complaints. Happy patients refer friends. Unhappy patients file complaints. You have heard me say that before.

Side-effect preparation is one of the biggest determinants of which category your patient falls into.

The conversation should be specific to the peptide you prescribed, not generic. Telling a patient"some people have side effects, call us if anything bothers you" is worthless. It is so vague that it provides no actual guidance, and a board reviewer will see it as checking a box rather than real education. Instead, tell the GLP-1 patient exactly what to expect: nausea, constipation, possible sulfur burps, decreased appetite, possible fatigue in the first weeks. Tell them how to manage each: small meals, hydration, fiber, slower titration. Tell them the red flags: severe abdominal pain, persistent vomiting, jaundice, severe dehydration, confusion. Tell them to call your office for the common stuff and go to the emergency room for the red flags. Document that this conversation occurred. Document that they received written instructions. Document their questions and your answers.

For a GH-axis peptide, the conversation is different: possible fluid retention, joint stiffness, tingling in the hands, headaches, possible blood sugar changes. Tell them to monitor for swelling, report joint symptoms, and watch for signs of low blood sugar if they are diabetic or on glucose-lowering medications. For a repair peptide: injection-site reactions, possible redness or swelling at the site, signs of infection. For an immune peptide: flu-like symptoms, possible transient fatigue, any signs of allergic reaction. Each peptide category has its own pattern. Know the patterns. Teach the patterns. Document the teaching.

Stop rules must be crystal clear. "Stop the medication and call us immediately if you experience X." "Hold the dose and call us within 24 hours if you experience Y." "Continue and monitor if you experience Z, but call if it worsens or does not resolve in 48 hours." These categories - emergency stop, hold and call, continue and monitor - give patients actionable guidance. They know what level of response each symptom requires. Without this structure, every patient with a mild headache calls you in a panic, and every patient with a serious symptom waits too long because they do not want to bother you.

Distinguish annoying from dangerous - know which symptoms require immediate stop

Not every side effect requires stopping therapy. In fact, many of the most common peptide side effects are transient, manageable, and expected. Knowing the difference between annoying and dangerous is a core clinical skill that separates experienced prescribers from nervous ones. Patients need you to be calm, informed, and decisive. If you panic at every complaint, you will stop effective therapy unnecessarily and lose patient confidence. If you dismiss serious symptoms as "probably nothing," you will miss dangerous reactions and end up in a much worse position. The key is having a clear framework before the patient calls.

Let me lay out the categories as I see them. Manageable, expected effects that do not require stopping therapy include: mild injection-site redness or slight bruising that resolves within a day or two; mild nausea that responds to dietary changes; mild constipation that responds to hydration and fiber; mild headache in the first week of a new peptide; mild fatigue or sleepiness; mild flushing or warmth after injection; mild joint stiffness on GH-axis therapy that does not limit function. These should be discussed proactively, managed supportively, and monitored. The patient should know they are common, usually temporary, and not dangerous. They should also know to report them at follow-up and to call sooner if they worsen.

Hold-the-dose effects - symptoms that warrant pausing therapy and reassessing within 24-48 hours - include: moderate nausea or vomiting that does not improve with standard measures; diarrhea that raises dehydration concerns; moderate headache that does not resolve with over-the-counter measures; noticeable edema or swelling, especially in the hands, feet, or face; blood pressure changes that the patient can measure at home; moderate joint pain or stiffness; new or worsening fatigue that affects daily function; sleep disruption that is significant. For these, the rule is: hold the next dose, call the office, and a clinician will assess within one business day. Document the hold, the symptom, the assessment, and the decision to resume, modify, or discontinue.

Emergency stop effects - symptoms that require immediate discontinuation and urgent medical evaluation - include: severe or persistent abdominal pain, especially with vomiting; any signs of an allergic reaction including hives, swelling of the face or throat, difficulty breathing; jaundice or yellowing of the skin or eyes; severe shortness of breath; chest pain or severe palpitations; confusion, severe dizziness, or fainting; severe mood changes including suicidal thoughts; signs of infection at an injection site - spreading redness, warmth, pus, fever; severe headache with visual changes; any symptom the patient reasonably believes is an emergency. For these, the instruction must be: stop everything immediately and go to the nearest emergency room or call 911. Then call our office so we know where you are.

This three-tier system - continue and monitor, hold and call, stop and go to the ER - gives patients a decision tree they can use when they are symptomatic and anxious. It prevents unnecessary emergency room visits for mild nausea. It prevents dangerous delays when something is seriously wrong. And it demonstrates to any board reviewer that you had a real system, that you thought about safety before problems occurred, and that your patients were not left to guess.

One more point on this. When a patient calls with a symptom, your staff must have a protocol for how to triage. A receptionist or medical assistant who tells a patient "just keep taking it, the doctor will call you back next week" when the patient has severe abdominal pain is a liability. Staff must know which symptoms require immediate clinician notification, which can be scheduled for routine callback, and which require emergency referral. This should be written, trained, and reviewed regularly. Every person who answers your phone is part of your safety system. Make sure they know it.

Common side effects by category: GLP-1 GI effects, GH-axis edema and glucose changes, repair peptide injection reactions

Now let me get specific about the side effects you will actually see in practice, organized by the major peptide categories. This is not an exhaustive pharmacology reference. This is practical, war-room information about what your patients will experience and how you need to manage it.

GLP-1 and incretin therapies - semaglutide, tirzepatide, retatrutide - are where most of the volume is in peptide practice right now, and they are where most of the side-effect management happens. The GI effects dominate: nausea, vomiting, constipation, diarrhea, sulfur-tasting burps, reflux, and decreased appetite that can become pathologic under-eating. These are dose-dependent and titration-dependent. The faster you push the dose, the more GI side effects you will see. This is why slow titration is not just patient comfort - it is clinical risk management.

Nausea is the big one. It hits hardest during dose escalation and usually improves after the patient has been on a stable dose for a week or two. Management: smaller meals, avoid high-fat foods, stay hydrated, consider timing the injection to minimize disruption. Some patients do better with evening injections so they sleep through the worst nausea. Some do better with morning injections so any nausea resolves during the day. There is no universal answer -individualize based on your patient's schedule and response. Document what you recommend and why.

Constipation is nearly as common as nausea, especially on higher doses or when patients are under-eating. Management: aggressive hydration, fiber supplementation, stool softeners if needed, monitoring for obstipation. Severe constipation can lead to fecal impaction, bowel obstruction, and emergency surgery. Do not dismiss it. Ask about bowel habits at every follow-up.

Dehydration is the hidden danger. A patient who is nauseated, eating less, and possibly having diarrhea can become dehydrated quickly. Dehydration causes dizziness, orthostatic hypotension, confusion, kidney injury, and falls - especially dangerous in older patients. Ask about fluid intake. Ask about urine color and frequency. Tell patients to drink water even when they do not feel like eating. Dehydration is what sends GLP-1 patients to the emergency room more often than anything else. Prevent it.

Gallbladder symptoms are less common but serious. Right upper quadrant pain, fever, jaundice, severe nausea after fatty meals - these require immediate evaluation. GLP-1 therapy is associated with gallbladder disease in the label. Screen for gallbladder history before starting. Tell patients the warning signs. Do not let a gallbladder attack present for three days because the patient thought it was "just the medication."

Pancreatitis is rare but catastrophic. Severe, persistent abdominal pain radiating to the back, with vomiting - emergency room, stat. Every GLP-1 patient must know this symptom complex. Document that you told them.

GH-axis peptides - sermorelin, tesamorelin, CJC-1295, ipamorelin - have a different side-effect profile centered on fluid metabolism, glucose handling, and joint symptoms. Edema is the most common complaint. Patients notice puffiness in their hands, feet, or face. Rings feel tight. Shoes feel tight. This is usually dose-related and improves with dose reduction or cycling. Mild edema can be monitored. Moderate edema warrants holding the dose. Severe edema, especially with shortness of breath, requires immediate evaluation for cardiac or renal causes. Do not assume all edema is from the peptide - but do not ignore the possibility either.

Glucose changes are the metabolic concern. GH-axis stimulation can raise fasting glucose and worsen insulin resistance. Every patient starting a GH secretagogue needs a baseline fasting glucose or HbA1c, and repeat testing at 4-8 weeks. Diabetic patients need even closer monitoring and may require medication adjustment. Do not start GH-axis therapy in a poorly controlled diabetic without endocrine input. Document glucose screening, results, and monitoring plan.

Carpal-tunnel-type symptoms - tingling, numbness, pain in the hands, especially at night -are common enough that you should warn patients before they start. These usually respond to dose reduction, cycling changes, or simply stopping. Persistent symptoms warrant a real carpal tunnel evaluation. Do not let a patient suffer through months of hand numbness because you are committed to the peptide.

Headaches and joint stiffness round out the common GH-axis complaints. Usually mild, usually transient, usually manageable. But persistent headaches, especially with visual changes, could indicate intracranial hypertension - rare but reported with IGF-1 analogs. Any visual symptom on a GH-axis peptide requires immediate evaluation.

Repair peptides - BPC-157, TB-500, GHK-Cu - have a simpler side-effect profile because they are generally well-tolerated, but they carry their own risks. Injection-site reactions are the most common: redness, swelling, bruising, pain. These should be mild and localized. Spreading redness, warmth, increasing pain, or fever suggests infection and requires evaluation. Teach patients sterile technique. Inspect injection sites when they come in for follow-up. Ask about technique. Poor injection technique leads to infections, and infections lead to problems you do not want.

The bigger concern with repair peptides is what I call the masking problem. A patient with a significant injury - a partial tendon tear, a stress fracture, a joint derangement - may experience enough symptom relief from a repair peptide that they delay or avoid proper orthopedic evaluation. The peptide reduces inflammation and discomfort, so the patient feels better, resumes activity, and worsens the underlying injury. This is not a side effect of the peptide per se, but it is a clinical risk of using symptom-modifying therapy without addressing the structural problem. Document that you discussed this risk. Document any specialist referrals. Set imaging or re-evaluation milestones. Do not let a peptide become a substitute for proper diagnosis and management.

Theoretical concerns about angiogenesis and cancer promotion exist for repair peptides, particularly those with pro-angiogenic mechanisms. The preclinical evidence is suggestive but not conclusive. What you must do is screen for cancer history, document the discussion, and not use repair peptides in patients with active or recent malignancy where the theoretical risk is highest. This belongs in your informed consent. The patient must know that long-term human safety data are limited and that theoretical concerns exist.

Immune and metabolic peptides have their own patterns. Thymosin alpha-1 can cause transient flu-like symptoms, mild injection-site reactions, and in rare cases, immune-related symptoms depending on the patient's underlying condition. MOTS-c and AOD-9604 are generally well-tolerated but can cause mild GI upset, fatigue, or headache. NAD+ causes infusion-related symptoms when given IV - chest tightness, anxiety, flushing, nausea, palpitations - that are rate-dependent and usually resolve when the infusion is slowed. These are manageable when anticipated and dangerous when they surprise a patient.

When in doubt, hold the dose - document why and reassess

I want to close this chapter with the single most important operational rule in all of peptide prescribing. When you are uncertain about a patient's symptom, when the picture is unclear, when you cannot confidently say whether the reaction is benign or serious - hold the dose. Stop the medication. Document your reasoning. Reassess. This is not weakness. This is not indecision. This is the mark of a careful physician who puts patient safety ahead of protocol loyalty.

The most dangerous physicians in this field are not the ones who prescribe aggressively. They are the ones who cannot stop. They have a patient with persistent side effects, ambiguous labs, a confusing clinical picture, and they keep pushing forward because they are committed to the program, or because the patient is demanding, or because they do not want to admit uncertainty. These are the cases that end badly. The patient who should have been stopped at week three but was continued to week twelve because the doctor wanted to "give it more time." The patient who developed edema and glucose elevation but stayed on the GH secretagogue because the dose was "within range." The patient who had recurrent nausea but kept getting their GLP-1 refilled because the staff processed the refill without clinical review.

Holding the dose is a clinical tool. Use it freely. When a patient calls with a concerning symptom, and you are not sure whether it is related to the peptide, whether it is serious, whether it requires a workup - hold the dose. Tell the patient: "I want you to skip your next injection and come in for evaluation. We will figure out what is going on and decide whether to resume, change, or stop." Document this instruction. Document the patient's response. When they come in, evaluate, decide, and document the next step. Maybe you resume at the same dose. Maybe you lower the dose. Maybe you switch compounds. Maybe you stop entirely. Any of those is a valid outcome when supported by clinical reasoning in the chart.

What you must never do is tell a patient to "just keep going" when you have real uncertainty. Do not let patients talk you into continuing therapy that worries you. Do not let the revenue from a refill cloud your clinical judgment. Do not worry that holding the dose makes you look indecisive - it makes you look careful, and careful is exactly what a board reviewer wants to see. "I held the dose, evaluated the patient, and made a reasoned decision" is a defensible narrative. "I kept refilling while the patient got worse" is not.

Reassessment after a hold requires a plan. How long will you hold? What are you looking for? What criteria determine resumption versus discontinuation? These should be clear in your mind and in the chart. "Hold for one week. Reassess symptoms at follow-up call on day 5. If symptoms resolved, resume at 50% previous dose with plan to titrate slowly if tolerated. If symptoms persist, schedule in-person evaluation. If symptoms worsened, discontinue and refer to PCP for further workup." That is a plan. That is medicine.

I also want to address the patient who self-holds without telling you. This happens constantly in peptide practice. A patient feels a side effect, stops their injections, and does not call because they assume they are supposed to handle it themselves. Or they are afraid you will be annoyed. Or they plan to tell you at their next appointment, which might be weeks away. You need to tell patients explicitly: do not stop and hide it. Call us. We want to know. Even if you stopped on your own, tell us so we can document it and help you decide what to do next. Self-holding without communication creates gaps in the medical record that look bad later. Encourage communication. Reward it with responsive, non-judgmental follow-up.

Let me tell you something about how board investigations work. When a complaint comes in, the board does not start by assuming you are a bad doctor. They start by looking at the chart. If the chart shows a systematic approach - screening, consent, clear dosing, documented side-effect discussion, structured follow-up, appropriate holds and reassessments, reasonable decisions documented with clinical reasoning - they may close the file without further action. If the chart shows a mess - unclear dosing, no side-effect discussion, auto-refills without review, ignored symptoms, no documented decision-making - they dig deeper. The difference between those two outcomes is not dramatic. It is the boring, daily discipline of doing things right every single time.

That is what this chapter is about. Stacking with restraint and clear reasoning. Dosing with verification and meticulous unit management. Side-effect management with proactive planning, clear stop rules, and the humility to hold the dose when you are uncertain. None of this is exciting. None of it will make you famous. But it will keep you practicing medicine for the long haul, with your license intact and your conscience clear.

The peptide space attracts physicians who want to help patients in innovative ways, who are frustrated with the limitations of conventional medicine, who see the potential of these compounds to address problems that standard care does not solve well. That is a good impulse. But good impulses need good systems. A physician who prescribes peptides without rigorous dosing verification, without clear stop rules, without disciplined stacking logic, and without proactive side-effect management is not practicing innovative medicine. They are taking unnecessary risks with their patients and their license. Do not be that physician. Verify everything. Keep it simple. Plan for problems before they happen. And when in doubt, hold the dose and think.

15 - Marketing Without Drawing a Target on Your Back

Let me tell you something I have seen more times than I care to count. A good doctor - a smart, well-meaning physician who genuinely wants to help patients - builds a practice around peptide therapy. The medicine is sound, the protocols are careful, the pharmacy is legitimate, the charts are clean. And then this same doctor, this careful physician, puts up a website or a social media post that reads like a late-night infomercial. "Lose thirty pounds guaranteed!" "Reverse aging at the cellular level!" "Transform your body in ninety days!" And just like that, everything that doctor built becomes a target.

I am not exaggerating when I say this. I have watched state medical boards open investigations based on nothing more than a Facebook ad. I have seen assistant attorneys general print out Instagram posts and wave them around in administrative hearings like they were smoking guns. I have watched malpractice plaintiff's attorneys project website screenshots onto courtroom walls, turning a doctor's own enthusiastic marketing into the centerpiece of a negligence case. Your marketing is not separate from your medical practice. It is evidence. It is part of the record. And if you write it wrong, it will be used against you by people who do not care how good your intentions were.

This chapter is about staying alive in a world where everything you say to attract patients can also be used to destroy you. I am going to walk you through what marketing actually means for a peptide practice, what you can say without losing sleep, what you can never say under any circumstances, and how to build a patient acquisition system that runs on trust and referrals instead of hype and hope. If you follow what I lay out here, you will still attract patients. Plenty of them. But you will not hand your enemies the rope they need to hang you.

Assume every ad, post, and website statement will be read by someone who doesn't like you

Here is the mindset you need to adopt, and I want you to tattoo it on your brain: every single piece of marketing you put into the world - every website paragraph, every Instagram caption, every Google ad, every brochure, every radio spot, every email newsletter - assume it will be read by someone who wants to see you fail. Assume a disgruntled former patient will screenshot it and attach it to a board complaint. Assume a competitor will forward it to the state attorney general's office. Assume a plaintiff's lawyer will blow it up to poster size and show it to a jury. Assume a journalist doing a hit piece on peptide clinics will quote it out of context. Because I am here to tell you, all of those things happen. They happen regularly. And when they happen, the doctor who wrote the ad does not get to stand up and say, "But you don't understand what I meant."

The regulators do not care what you meant. The medical board investigator does not care that you were trying to help people. The assistant attorney general does not care that your patients love you. They care about what the words on the page actually say. And if those words promise results, guarantee outcomes, or imply that your compounded therapy is FDA-approved, then what the words say is that you are running a snake oil operation with a medical license attached.

Let me give you a real scenario. A physician in the Southwest - let us call him Dr. M - had a thriving hormone and peptide practice. Good training, careful protocols, legitimate pharmacy. He decided to run Facebook ads to bring in more patients. The ads said things like "Lose 20-30% of your body weight with physician-supervised peptide therapy" and "FDA-approved medications compounded for your individual needs." Now, the first problem is obvious: twenty to thirty percent weight loss is not a typical result, and stating it as if it were is a material misrepresentation. But the bigger problem was that second line - "FDA-approved medications compounded for your individual needs." Compounded medications are not FDA-approved. Period. That is not an opinion. That is a fact of federal law. The FDA does not review, approve, or verify compounded drug products for safety, efficacy, or quality. By saying his compounded products were "FDA-approved," Dr. M made a false statement that violated federal advertising regulations and state consumer protection laws.

A former patient - unhappy because she did not lose the promised twenty to thirty percent -filed a complaint with the state board. She attached the Facebook ads. The board opened an investigation. The state attorney general's office got involved because of the consumer protection angle. The pharmacy board took a look because of the compounding claims. Within six months, Dr. M was defending his license in an administrative hearing, spending thirty thousand dollars on legal fees, all because he let his marketing team write ad copy without running it past someone who understood what the words actually meant. His medicine was fine. His charts were fine. His pharmacy was fine. His marketing destroyed him.

You think the board cares that you meant well? You think the investigator takes your side against a patient who feels lied to? They do not. And here is what makes it worse: once the investigation starts, they do not stop at the marketing. They start pulling charts. They start calling patients. They start reviewing every prescription you wrote for the past two years. That one reckless ad becomes the key that unlocks your entire practice. You opened the door. You invited them in. And now they are going through your drawers.

So the first rule, the foundational rule, the rule from which every other rule flows, is this: write every piece of marketing as if your worst enemy is going to read it in front of a judge. Because someday, someone who does not like you will.

The ad should not promise what the consent later denies

Here is a mistake that seems obvious when I say it out loud but that doctors make constantly. Your marketing says one thing. Your informed consent says the opposite. Your website promises "dramatic weight loss results." Your consent form says "results vary and are not guaranteed." Your social media post shows a testimonial from a patient who "reversed their diabetes and got off all medications." Your consent form says "this therapy is not a cure and does not replace standard medical care." Do you see the problem? You have created a document trail that proves you are either lying to prospective patients or lying to your actual patients. Either your marketing is false, or your consent is false. Pick one, because a regulator will.

This is what trial lawyers call a "document contradiction," and it is one of the most powerful weapons in a plaintiff's attorney's arsenal. They do not need to prove you committed medical malpractice. They just need to prove you misled the patient. And when your website says"guaranteed weight loss" and your consent says "no guarantees," the contradiction proves itself. The patient believed the marketing - that is why they called your office - and then you handed them a consent form that admitted the marketing was not true. That patient now has a legitimate claim that they were induced to undergo medical treatment through false or misleading representations. You do not need to have harmed them clinically. The misrepresentation alone is enough to create liability.

I have seen this play out in deposition. The lawyer holds up the website printout in one hand and the signed consent in the other. "Doctor, your website told my client he would lose significant weight with your program. Is that correct?" The doctor squirms. "Well, we say results vary." The lawyer points to the bold text on the website: "Significant weight loss in just twelve weeks." Then he points to the consent: "No results are guaranteed. Individual results vary." The lawyer does not say anything. He just lets the documents sit there while the jury looks at them. It is devastating.

The fix is simple but it requires discipline. Your marketing language and your consent language must be consistent. They must tell the same story. If your consent says results vary, your marketing must say results vary. If your consent says not everyone qualifies, your marketing must say not everyone qualifies. If your consent says compounded medications are not FDA-approved, your marketing must not suggest they are. The marketing invites the patient in. The consent manages expectations and documents understanding. They are two parts of the same communication system. When they contradict each other, you look like you are either incompetent or dishonest. Neither one helps you keep your license.

Let me be even more specific. Go pull up your website right now. Read every page. Then pull up your informed consent form. Read every paragraph. Does your website use words like"transform," "revolutionize," "breakthrough," "guaranteed," or "clinically proven" in ways your consent would not support? Does your website suggest that peptide therapy is a well-established standard of care when your consent describes it as limited-evidence or investigational? Does your website imply that every patient gets medication when your consent says medication is only prescribed when clinically appropriate? If the answer to any of these is yes, you have a problem. Fix it today. Not tomorrow. Today. Because the contradiction sitting on your website is evidence, and it is evidence against you.

Reckless marketing creates exhibits for regulators

Let me explain how a regulatory investigation actually works, because understanding the mechanics will help you understand why your marketing matters so much. When a patient, competitor, payer, or anonymous tipster files a complaint against you, the first thing the medical board investigator does is gather publicly available information about your practice. And what is the most publicly available information there is? Your website. Your social media. Your Google ads. Your Yelp page. Your online reviews, which often quote your own marketing language back at you. Before the investigator ever pulls a chart, before they ever call a patient, before they ever look at a prescription, they have already read every word you have published about your practice. They have already formed an opinion about what kind of doctor you are.

If your marketing is conservative - if it emphasizes medical evaluation, individualized care, and appropriate monitoring - the investigator reads it and thinks, "This looks like a medical practice." If your marketing is aggressive - if it promises results, guarantees outcomes, and makes therapy sound like a consumer product - the investigator reads it and thinks, "This looks like a pill mill with better graphic design." That first impression shapes the entire investigation. A conservative marketing presence does not guarantee the board will go easy on you, but a reckless marketing presence virtually guarantees they will dig deeper, look harder, and assume the worst.

And once those marketing materials become part of the investigative file, they do not disappear. They get attached to the complaint. They get cited in the probable cause determination. They get referenced in the settlement negotiations. If the case goes to a hearing, they get entered as exhibits. I have sat in hearings where the board's attorney spent twenty minutes reading Google ad copy aloud while the physician sat there watching his own words being weaponized against him. "Lose weight fast with doctor-prescribed peptides.""Regenerate your metabolism." "Reverse the aging process." Every one of those phrases became an exhibit number. Every one of those exhibit numbers became part of the permanent record that any future employer, credentialing body, or licensing authority can look up.

Here is something most doctors do not realize: medical board investigations are public record in most states. Even if you win - even if the board finds no violation and closes the case -the complaint, the exhibits, and the marketing materials remain searchable. A patient who Googles your name five years from now can find the complaint. A hospital credentialing committee reviewing your application can find the complaint. A malpractice insurer running a background check can find the complaint. Your reckless marketing created the exhibit that started the investigation, and that exhibit lives forever on the internet even if the investigation went nowhere.

The pharmaceutical companies know this. That is why every drug advertisement you have ever seen is loaded with disclaimers, side effect warnings, and "talk to your doctor" language. They have armies of lawyers reviewing every word before it goes public. You do not have an army of lawyers. You have you, your marketing person, and hopefully enough common sense to know that if Pfizer needs three lawyers to approve a thirty-second television spot, you probably should not let your office manager write your Facebook ads without supervision.

Good marketing educates and invites evaluation - that's it

So if all of this danger is out there, if every word you publish is potential evidence, if regulators are watching and competitors are eager and patients are ready to feel misled, how do you actually market a peptide practice? You market it by doing the one thing that no regulator can criticize and no plaintiff's attorney can twist: you educate, and you invite evaluation. That is it. Two things. Education and invitation. If your marketing does those two things and nothing else, you are safe. Not boring - safe. And safety, in this business, is what lets you sleep through the night.

Educational marketing means you teach people something they did not know. You explain what peptides are in plain language. You describe how they work in the body. You discuss the difference between FDA-approved uses, off-label prescribing, compounded therapies, and investigational treatments. You talk about the importance of medical supervision, laboratory monitoring, and follow-up care. You explain why a proper evaluation is necessary before any medication decision. You share information about metabolism, hormone function, recovery, aging, weight management - real medical topics that real patients want to understand. When you educate, you demonstrate expertise. When you demonstrate expertise, you attract patients who want to be treated by an expert. That is marketing. It just does not look like the kind of marketing that gets doctors in trouble.

Invitational marketing means you create a clear path for interested people to become your patients. You tell them how to schedule a consultation. You explain what the initial evaluation includes. You describe what information they should bring, what the consultation will cost, and what they can expect from the first visit. You make it clear that not everyone qualifies, that medication is only prescribed when appropriate, and that the decision to treat is a medical one made by a physician after a thorough evaluation. You invite them to come in and be assessed. You do not promise them results. You do not guarantee them weight loss. You do not tell them they will be prescribed anything at all. You invite them to be evaluated by a physician. That is the offer. That is the call to action.

Think about what this approach accomplishes. The patient who calls your office after reading educational content has already been primed to understand that this is medical care, not a product purchase. They know peptides are serious therapies that require supervision. They know results vary. They know not everyone gets a prescription. When they show up for the consultation, their expectations are already aligned with reality. They are less likely to be disappointed, less likely to demand inappropriate treatment, less likely to file a complaint when results are not what they hoped. Your marketing has done pre-work that makes the rest of your practice easier.

Compare that to the patient who calls after seeing an ad that promised "lose thirty pounds in three months with our breakthrough peptide program." That patient walks in the door expecting thirty pounds of weight loss. If they lose fifteen - which would be a fantastic clinical result - they feel cheated. If they lose five - which is still meaningful for some patients - they are furious. They did not come to your office for medical care. They came for a guaranteed outcome that you advertised. When that outcome does not materialize, you become the problem. And that is when the complaints start.

Educational marketing attracts patients who want a doctor. Promotional marketing attracts patients who want a product. Patients who want a doctor will tolerate uncertainty, follow instructions, and accept that medicine is not guaranteed. Patients who want a product will write bad reviews, demand refunds, and file board complaints when the product does not perform as advertised. Which kind of patient do you want filling your waiting room? Because your marketing determines the answer.

Physician-supervised evaluation for appropriate candidates

Now let us get specific about language. I want to give you actual words and phrases that you can use safely in your marketing materials. Not vague guidance - specific sentences. Because I know what it is like to stare at a blank website page and wonder what the heck you are allowed to write without creating liability. So here is the first safe message, and it is the cornerstone of everything else: "We offer physician-supervised evaluation for appropriate candidates."

Read that sentence carefully. Every word matters. "Physician-supervised" establishes that this is medical care delivered by a licensed doctor, not a wellness coach, not a med spa technician, not an online vendor. It tells the reader that a real physician will be involved in their care."Evaluation" means assessment, not treatment. The patient is coming in to be evaluated. They are not coming in to buy a vial. The evaluation may or may not lead to treatment. That is a medical decision, and the marketing makes it clear that no treatment is promised. "Appropriate candidates" means not everyone qualifies. It sets the expectation that there are criteria for treatment, that the physician will apply clinical judgment, and that some people will be told this is not right for them.

That one sentence - "We offer physician-supervised evaluation for appropriate candidates" -communicates medical legitimacy, manages expectations, and implies appropriate patient selection without sounding defensive or negative. You can put that on your homepage. You can put it in your Google ad. You can put it on your brochure. No regulator is going to criticize you for offering physician-supervised evaluations. No plaintiff's attorney is going to wave that sentence around in court and claim it is misleading. It is a true, accurate, defensible statement of what your practice does.

Here are some variations that work equally well: "Our practice provides comprehensive medical evaluation for patients interested in peptide therapy." That emphasizes comprehensiveness and medical framing. Or: "Board-certified physician evaluates each patient individually to determine whether peptide therapy is clinically appropriate." That adds credentialing and individualization. Or: "New patients begin with a thorough medical assessment, including history review and laboratory evaluation when indicated." That describes the actual process and implies that testing may be required.

You can expand on this message in your website content. You can explain what the evaluation includes: detailed medical history, review of current medications, assessment of symptoms and goals, laboratory testing when clinically appropriate, discussion of treatment options including risks and benefits, and a collaborative decision about whether to proceed. You can describe the physician's qualifications, training, and experience with peptide therapy. You can explain your practice philosophy - that you believe in careful patient selection, conservative prescribing, and thorough monitoring. All of that is safe. All of that strengthens your position. All of that tells prospective patients that you are a serious medical practice, not a vial shop.

Individualized care with pharmacy-dispensed medication when appropriate

The second safe message is about the nature of the care you provide. Here is the core language:"We provide individualized care with pharmacy-dispensed medication when clinically appropriate." Again, every word is doing work. "Individualized care" means this is not one-size-fits-all. It means the treatment plan is tailored to the patient's specific needs, goals, medical history, and laboratory findings. It implies that different patients get different approaches, different doses, different monitoring schedules. That is a hallmark of legitimate medicine and a direct contrast to the assembly-line approach that regulators associate with questionable practices. "Pharmacy-dispensed medication" is a critical phrase. It tells the reader that medications come from a licensed pharmacy, not from the doctor's desk drawer, not from an online vendor, not from a compounding operation in someone's garage. It establishes legitimacy by connecting the practice to the formal pharmaceutical supply chain. If you use a 503A compounding pharmacy, you are still pharmacy-dispensed. If you use a 503B outsourcing facility, you are still pharmacy-dispensed. Either way, the medication is prepared by licensed pharmacists in a regulated facility. That matters. That is safe to say. "When clinically appropriate" is the qualifier that saves you. It means medication is not automatic. It means the physician makes a clinical judgment about whether prescribing is warranted. It means some patients will be evaluated and told that medication is not appropriate for them - because of contraindications, because of unrealistic expectations, because of incomplete information, because of clinical judgment. That phrase protects you from the implicit guarantee that everyone who walks in gets a prescription.

You can expand this message on your website. You can explain that treatment plans are developed based on individual assessment. You can describe how the practice works with licensed compounding pharmacies that meet quality and regulatory standards. You can explain that medication decisions are made after reviewing medical history, current symptoms, laboratory results, and treatment goals. You can note that the practice does not provide medication to patients who have not undergone a proper medical evaluation. All of that reinforces the message that this is medical care, not product sales.

Here is an example of how this might read on a services page: "Each patient receives an individualized treatment plan developed by our board-certified physician based on a comprehensive medical evaluation. When clinically appropriate, prescriptions are sent to licensed compounding pharmacies that meet strict quality standards. Medication is never dispensed without a thorough assessment of the patient's medical history, current health status, and treatment goals. Not every patient will be a candidate for peptide therapy, and our physician will discuss alternative approaches when treatment is not appropriate." That paragraph is bulletproof. A regulator reads it and thinks "proper medical practice." A patient reads it and understands that this is serious care. An attorney reads it and finds nothing to exploit. That is what good marketing looks like.

Follow-up and monitoring included - medical evaluation required

The third safe message addresses the ongoing nature of peptide therapy and the requirements for participation. Core language: "Follow-up care and monitoring are included. Medical evaluation and ongoing supervision are required." This message does two things simultaneously. It communicates value - follow-up and monitoring are included, which tells patients they are getting comprehensive care, not just a prescription and a goodbye. And it communicates requirements - medical evaluation and ongoing supervision are mandatory, which tells patients they cannot skip steps, ignore follow-up, or treat this like a one-time transaction.

Including follow-up in your marketing is strategically important because it distinguishes your practice from the online vendors and med spas that hand out prescriptions with no monitoring. Patients need to understand that peptide therapy requires ongoing supervision - lab work, symptom review, dose adjustments, side effect monitoring, refill assessments. When you advertise that follow-up is included, you are advertising medical thoroughness. That attracts patients who want proper care and repels patients who are looking for the easiest, fastest, cheapest path to a vial. The patients who want easy and cheap are the patients who cause problems later. Filter them out with your marketing.

The requirement language - "medical evaluation required," "ongoing supervision mandatory," "follow-up visits necessary for continued therapy" - establishes that participation in your program comes with obligations. Patients cannot skip their follow-up and expect refills. They cannot ignore lab orders and stay in the program. They cannot decide on their own that they do not need monitoring. These requirements are not barriers to care; they are the care. And stating them upfront in your marketing sets the right tone from the first interaction.

Here is how this might play out on a pricing or services page: "Our peptide therapy program includes comprehensive medical evaluation, individualized treatment planning, pharmacy coordination, and ongoing follow-up care. Patients are required to attend scheduled follow-up appointments and complete recommended laboratory monitoring. Continued participation in the program is contingent upon compliance with medical supervision requirements. Patients who do not complete required follow-up may be discontinued from therapy." That language is firm, clear, and protective. It tells patients exactly what is expected before they ever walk in the door.

You can also use this message to justify your pricing structure, which we covered in Chapter 29. When patients understand that the program price includes evaluation, monitoring, follow-up, pharmacy coordination, and staff time, they stop comparing your price to the cost of a vial online. They start comparing it to the value of supervised medical care. Your marketing frames the transaction properly: they are not buying medication; they are enrolling in a medical program that includes medication when appropriate. That framing protects you from price shoppers, helps patients understand what they are paying for, and reinforces the medical legitimacy of your practice.

Results vary, not everyone qualifies, no guarantees

The fourth safe message is the disclaimer language that should appear, in some form, on every piece of marketing you publish. Core phrases: "Individual results vary." "Not everyone is a candidate for treatment." "No results are guaranteed." "Outcomes depend on individual factors including adherence, lifestyle, and medical history." These are not just legal protections -they are true statements. And their truth is what makes them defensible.

Every doctor knows that medicine is not guaranteed. Two patients with identical diagnoses, identical prescriptions, and identical instructions can have completely different outcomes. One patient loses twenty pounds. The other loses three. One patient reports dramatic energy improvement. The other feels no change. One patient tolerates the medication perfectly. The other has side effects that require discontinuation. That is medicine. That is reality. And your marketing should reflect that reality, not pretend it away. "Individual results vary" is the most important four words in your marketing disclaimer. It is true, it is accurate, and it is legally protective. Put it on your website. Put it in your ad copy. Put it at the bottom of your brochures. Every patient who reads it understands, at some level, that their results might not match what they are hoping for. That does not stop them from calling -patients still want to be evaluated, still want treatment, still want help. But it does stop them from claiming later that you guaranteed an outcome. "Not everyone qualifies" or "not everyone is a candidate" is equally important. It tells prospective patients that your practice has standards. It filters out the patients who expect to walk in and walk out with a prescription regardless of their medical history. It creates a small but healthy barrier to entry that improves the quality of your patient population. And it protects you from accusations that you prescribe indiscriminately. "No results are guaranteed" should appear prominently in any marketing that discusses potential outcomes. If your website mentions that peptide therapy has been associated with weight loss, muscle preservation, improved recovery, or other effects - and it can, if worded carefully - then the very next sentence should be "no results are guaranteed." Not buried at the bottom of the page in six-point font. Right there in the same paragraph, in the same size text, where every reader will see it. Because a disclaimer that no one reads is not a disclaimer.

Here is how this might look in practice. Your website has a section titled "What to Expect." It reads: "Peptide therapy has been associated with improvements in body composition, recovery, energy levels, and metabolic function in some patients. However, individual results vary significantly based on factors including age, baseline health, adherence to treatment, lifestyle habits, and concurrent medical conditions. Not every patient who undergoes evaluation will be prescribed peptide therapy, and not every patient who is prescribed therapy will experience the desired results. No specific outcome is guaranteed. During your consultation, our physician will discuss realistic expectations based on your individual circumstances." That paragraph manages expectations, states the truth, and creates a record of appropriate communication. It is perfect.

No guaranteed weight loss, no cure claims, no reversal language

Now we get to the fun part. The part where I tell you what will get you investigated, sued, or stripped of your license if you put it in your marketing. And I want you to pay attention here, because the line between what you can say and what you cannot say is not blurry. It is bright red and it has flashing lights on it. Cross it at your peril.

First and forever: you cannot guarantee weight loss. You cannot say "lose twenty pounds in three months." You cannot say "patients typically lose fifteen to twenty-five percent of their body weight." You cannot say "guaranteed weight loss results." You cannot say "our patients lose an average of X pounds." You cannot even say "most patients lose significant weight"unless you have rigorous clinical data from your own practice to support that claim - and even then, you are walking into territory that requires statistical validation you probably do not have.

Here is why. Weight loss claims are among the most heavily regulated statements in all of health care advertising. The Federal Trade Commission has specific guidance on weight loss advertising that requires substantiation for any specific claim. State consumer protection laws treat unsubstantiated weight loss promises as deceptive trade practices. Medical boards view guaranteed weight loss claims as evidence of commercial motivation overriding clinical judgment. And plaintiff's attorneys treat them as the gift that keeps on giving - an admission by the physician that the program was sold on a promise that medicine cannot keep.

Let me tell you about a case I reviewed. A clinic in the Southeast ran ads saying "Lose 20-30 lbs in 12 weeks with our medical weight loss program." The ads included before-and-after photos and testimonials from patients who had achieved those results. One patient lost eight pounds in twelve weeks - which, for her body composition, was actually a good clinical outcome. But she had seen the ad promising twenty to thirty pounds. She felt defrauded. She filed a complaint with the state medical board, a complaint with the attorney general's consumer protection division, and a civil lawsuit for deceptive trade practices. The clinic's defense - that eight pounds was a medically appropriate result for that patient - was true but irrelevant. The ad had promised twenty to thirty. The clinic's own marketing proved the patient's case.

You also cannot use cure language. You cannot say peptide therapy "cures" obesity, diabetes, metabolic syndrome, aging, or any other condition. You cannot say it "reverses" diabetes,"reverses" aging, "reverses" metabolic damage, or "reverses" hormone decline. "Reverses" is just "cures" in a slightly fancier outfit, and regulators know it. You cannot say it "eliminates"any disease or condition. You cannot say it "restores" normal function in a way that implies permanent cure. You cannot say it "fixes" the underlying problem.

The only safe language around therapeutic effects is associative and cautious. "May help with." "Has been associated with." "Some patients experience." "Can be part of a comprehensive approach to." These phrases describe possibility, not certainty. They invite evaluation without promising outcomes. They educate without guaranteeing. They are the difference between medical communication and snake oil.

And let me address a specific temptation that gets doctors in trouble: percentage claims. You cannot say "our patients lose an average of twenty percent of their body weight" unless you have actual patient data, verified by appropriate methodology, covering a meaningful sample size, and you are prepared to produce that data when challenged. "Average" is a statistical claim. It requires statistical support. If you say it and you cannot prove it, you have made a false statement. If you can prove it but your methodology would not survive expert review, you have still made a problematic statement. Just do not go there. Do not use numbers you cannot defend with research-grade data.

No before/after photos without proper consent and disclaimers

Before-and-after photographs are one of the most powerful marketing tools in aesthetic and wellness medicine. They are also one of the most dangerous. A single before-and-after photo, used without proper consent, without proper disclaimers, and without proper context, can create more liability than a page of reckless text. And most doctors who use them do it wrong.

First, the consent issue. Every before-and-after photo used in marketing must have a signed, specific, detailed release from the patient depicted. Not a blanket consent buried in the intake paperwork. Not a verbal "sure, go ahead." A separate, standalone photograph release that specifically authorizes use in marketing materials, on websites, in social media, in advertising, and in any other medium the practice employs. The release should state exactly how the photo will be used, should note whether identifying features will be concealed, should specify the duration of authorization, and should include the patient's signature and date.

Why so detailed? Because patients change their minds. A patient who was thrilled to have their photo on your website in January may be horrified by it in June when their employer finds it. A patient who gave vague verbal permission may claim they never authorized marketing use. A patient who signed a blanket consent on page seventeen of a forty-page intake packet may argue they did not understand what they were signing. Specific, standalone, detailed photo releases protect you from all of these problems. They prove exactly what the patient authorized, exactly how the photo would be used, and exactly when the authorization was given.

But consent is only the first requirement. The second requirement is disclaimers. Every before-and-after photo must be accompanied by clear, prominent language stating that results vary, that the depicted result is not typical, that individual outcomes depend on multiple factors, and that no specific result is guaranteed. That disclaimer must appear with the photo - not on a separate page, not at the bottom of the website, not in the fine print. Right there, next to the image, where anyone viewing the photo will see it.

Why? Because before-and-after photos create an implicit promise. The viewer sees the transformation and thinks, "That could be me." That thought is the entire reason the photo is effective as marketing. But it is also the reason the photo is dangerous. If the viewer becomes a patient and does not achieve a similar transformation, they feel misled. They believed the photo was a representation of what the program would do for them. Your disclaimer is what breaks that implicit promise and replaces it with appropriate expectations.

The third requirement is context. The photo should tell a story that includes all relevant factors. How long was the treatment period? What medications were used? What was the patient's starting weight, age, and health status? What lifestyle changes did the patient make? What was the patient's adherence to the program? Were there any adverse effects? This context helps viewers understand that the result depicted was achieved in specific circumstances that may not apply to them. It also demonstrates your commitment to transparency and thoroughness.

Here is what I recommend: do not use before-and-after photos at all. They are more trouble than they are worth. If you must use them - and I understand that in some markets they are expected - then build a system around them that is bulletproof. Standalone photo releases. Prominent disclaimers on every image. Detailed context including treatment duration, medications, and patient-specific factors. Regular re-confirmation of consent. And a policy of immediately removing any photo if the patient requests it, no questions asked, no argument, no delay. That system will protect you. Anything less leaves you exposed.

And one more thing about photos: do not use stock photos or photos from other practices. Do not pull an image from the internet and put it on your website. Do not use a photo that your marketing person found on a stock photo site labeled "medical weight loss." Those photos are not your patients. They did not sign your consent. They did not use your program. Using someone else's before-and-after photo is fraudulent misrepresentation, plain and simple. If a regulator discovers it, you are done. If a competitor discovers it, they will report you. If a patient discovers it, they will never trust you again. Use only your own patients' photos, with proper consent, or use no photos at all.

No testimonials that promise results or imply medical endorsement

Patient testimonials are the Wild West of medical marketing. Every doctor wants them - they are persuasive, they are authentic, they build trust - and every regulator hates them - they are unverified, they are inherently promotional, and they create expectations that medicine cannot meet. The result is a regulatory minefield that very few practices navigate successfully.

The core problem with testimonials is that they are, by definition, atypical patient experiences presented as representative. A patient who lost fifty pounds and feels twenty years younger is thrilled and wants to tell the world. That patient gives a glowing video testimonial about how your peptide program changed their life. Prospective patients watch it and think, "I want that result." But that testimonial does not mention the patient's starting weight, their adherence to the program, their lifestyle changes, their genetic factors, or the fact that their result was exceptional rather than typical. It creates an expectation that most patients will not meet.

And here is where it gets legally dangerous. The Federal Trade Commission's Endorsement Guides specifically state that testimonials that represent atypical results must be accompanied by a clear disclosure of what results consumers can generally expect. In medical practice,"what consumers can generally expect" is nearly impossible to define because individual results vary so widely. So the typical testimonial - "I lost forty pounds and feel amazing!" -creates an obligation to provide a general results disclosure that most practices cannot substantiate.

Beyond the FTC issue, testimonials create medical board problems. A testimonial that describes specific results implies that those results are achievable for other patients. If they are not generally achievable, the testimonial is misleading. A testimonial that mentions specific medications or doses implies medical endorsement of those choices. If the board disagrees with those choices for the general population, the testimonial becomes evidence of inappropriate practice patterns. A testimonial that compares your care favorably to other doctors implies superiority claims that may violate professional advertising rules.

Here is what I tell every doctor: if you use testimonials, control them ruthlessly. Every testimonial must include a disclaimer that results vary, that the experience described is not typical, and that no specific result is guaranteed. That disclaimer must be visible and prominent- not a line of fine print that no one reads. Every testimonial must be truthful and must not have been edited in a way that creates a false impression. If you edit a thirty-minute interview down to thirty seconds, you must not have removed important context that changes the meaning. Every testimonial should avoid specific numbers - pounds lost, inches reduced, dosages used - because those specifics create the strongest and most dangerous expectations.

But honestly? The safest approach is to skip testimonials entirely. Replace them with something equally powerful but far less risky: patient satisfaction data. "Ninety-two percent of our patients report being satisfied with their care." That is a survey result, not a personal endorsement. It does not promise weight loss. It does not describe medical outcomes. It speaks to the quality of the patient experience, which is what testimonials are actually trying to communicate anyway. Patients do not need to hear that someone else lost weight. They need to hear that your practice provides good care. Satisfaction data says that without the liability.

If you absolutely must use testimonials, I recommend using them only in one context: in your office, during the consultation, after the patient has already been educated about realistic expectations. A testimonial video playing in your waiting room or consultation office, seen by patients who are already engaged in the evaluation process and who have already received appropriate expectation-setting, is far less risky than the same testimonial on your website where anyone in the world can see it without context. But even in-office testimonials need disclaimers. Even in-office testimonials need to be truthful. Even in-office testimonials create some level of expectation. Use them sparingly, use them carefully, and never let them replace your own educational marketing.

And under no circumstances should you ever write your own testimonials and attribute them to patients. I should not have to say this, but I have seen it done. I have seen practices create fake patient reviews for their Google Business profile. I have seen website testimonials attributed to"Sarah M., satisfied patient" that were written by the office manager. I have seen video testimonials featuring staff members' relatives pretending to be patients. If you do this, you are committing fraud. Not "unwise marketing." Not "a gray area." Fraud. When - not if, when -this is discovered, your license, your reputation, and your practice are finished. Do not even think about it.

No claims that compounded products are identical to FDA-approved brands

This one makes me angrier than almost anything else in peptide marketing, because it is not just reckless - it is factually wrong, and doctors who say it either know it is wrong or should know it is wrong. Compounded medications are not FDA-approved. They are not identical to FDA-approved brand products. They are not interchangeable with commercially available drugs. Any statement that suggests otherwise is false, misleading, and potentially illegal.

Let me explain why, because understanding the "why" will help you avoid this mistake completely. The FDA approval process involves rigorous review of safety, efficacy, manufacturing quality, labeling, and post-market surveillance. A drug that receives FDA approval has been through clinical trials, has established dosing guidelines, has verified manufacturing processes, and has a known adverse event profile. The FDA monitors that drug after approval for new safety signals and can take action if problems emerge.

Compounded medications undergo none of this. A 503A compounding pharmacy prepares medications pursuant to individual prescriptions, using active pharmaceutical ingredients that may or may not have FDA-approved source applications. The pharmacy is regulated by the state board of pharmacy, not by the FDA's drug approval process. The compounded product has not been through clinical trials for safety or efficacy. The FDA explicitly states that compounded drug products are not FDA-approved and that the FDA does not verify their safety, effectiveness, or quality.

When your marketing says "the same medication as the brand name, just compounded" or"FDA-approved ingredients compounded for you" or "identical to the FDA-approved version,"you are making a false statement. The ingredients may be the same chemical compound -though sometimes they are not even that - but the product itself is fundamentally different because it has not been through the FDA approval process. Saying it is "the same" ignores the entire regulatory and quality framework that makes FDA-approved drugs what they are.

And the regulators are watching this closely. The FDA has issued warning letters to compounding pharmacies and to physicians who make false or misleading claims about compounded products. State boards of pharmacy have taken action against pharmacies that imply their products are equivalent to FDA-approved versions. State medical boards have disciplined physicians whose marketing created the impression that compounded therapies carried FDA approval. This is not theoretical. This is happening, right now, to doctors who thought they were being clever with their wording.

So what can you say? You can say "compounded medications are prepared by licensed pharmacies pursuant to individual prescriptions." You can say "compounded therapies are not FDA-approved and have not been evaluated by the FDA for safety or efficacy." You can say"some patients choose compounded medications for reasons including dosing flexibility, ingredient customization, or cost." You can say "our practice works with licensed compounding pharmacies that meet applicable state and federal quality standards." All of those statements are true. None of them create false equivalencies. None of them invite regulatory action.

If a patient asks you directly whether a compounded product is "the same as" the FDA-approved brand, your answer should be clear and complete: "The active ingredient may be the same chemical compound, but the compounded product is not FDA-approved. It has not been through the FDA's review process for safety, efficacy, or manufacturing quality. It is prepared individually by a compounding pharmacy under different regulatory standards. I believe it is appropriate for your situation, but it is important that you understand the difference." That answer is honest, accurate, and protective. It respects the patient's right to understand what they are receiving. And it documents, in the conversation, that you provided appropriate education.

Your marketing must reflect that same honesty. If your website discusses compounded products, it should include clear language about their regulatory status. If your advertising mentions specific peptides, it should note whether they are FDA-approved, off-label, compounded, or investigational. If your staff speak with prospective patients about medications, they should use language that accurately describes the products without creating false impressions. Every communication channel must tell the same truthful story.

Referrals from happy patients are your best and safest marketing

Let me tell you the secret to building a peptide practice that thrives without creating regulatory exposure. It is not search engine optimization. It is not social media virality. It is not paid advertising on every platform. It is referrals from happy patients who trust you, respect you, and want their friends and family to receive the same quality of care they received. That is it. That is the whole formula. Everything else is icing. Referrals are the cake.

Why are referrals so much safer than every other form of marketing? Because a referral is not an advertisement you wrote. It is a conversation between two private individuals. When your patient tells their friend, "You should go see my doctor, she really takes the time to explain everything and the program has helped me," that is not commercial speech regulated by the FTC. That is a personal recommendation protected by the First Amendment. You did not write it. You did not approve it. You cannot control what the patient says. And because you cannot control it, you generally cannot be held liable for it - provided, of course, that you did not coach the patient to make false claims or offer incentives for specific types of endorsements.

Compare that to a Google ad you wrote that promises "medical weight loss with guaranteed results." You wrote that. You approved it. You published it. Every word in it is attributable to you. If it is false or misleading, you are responsible. But when Mrs. Johnson tells her book club that Dr. Smith helped her feel better than she has in years, Mrs. Johnson is exercising her right to free speech about her own experience. Even if she exaggerates - even if she says she lost more weight than she actually did, even if she attributes improvements to your care that had other causes - that exaggeration is not your advertisement. It is her personal story. And while you should certainly not encourage patients to make false claims, you are not generally responsible for what they say in private conversation.

The practical implication is this: your number one marketing priority should be creating patients who are so satisfied with their experience that they tell other people about it. Not satisfied because you overpromised and they got lucky. Satisfied because you managed their expectations, delivered quality care, communicated clearly, followed up consistently, and treated them with respect. Satisfied because the entire experience - from the first phone call to the ongoing monitoring - felt like real medicine delivered by people who cared. That satisfaction generates referrals. And referrals generate the safest, highest-quality patient acquisition you can achieve.

Let me be clear about what "happy patient" means in this context, because it is not what most doctors think. A happy patient is not necessarily a patient who achieved dramatic results. A happy patient is a patient who feels heard, respected, informed, and well-cared-for throughout the process. I have seen patients who lost five pounds and were thrilled because their doctor explained why five pounds was a meaningful outcome for their specific situation. I have seen patients who were not prescribed any medication at all and were grateful because their doctor took the time to explain why treatment was not appropriate and what alternatives might help. I have seen patients who experienced side effects and remained loyal to their physician because the side effects were managed promptly, communicated transparently, and addressed with genuine concern.

Those patients refer. They tell their friends. They leave positive reviews. They defend the practice when someone says something negative. They become ambassadors not because they got the best result, but because they had the best experience. And the experience is something you control completely - through your staff training, your communication protocols, your follow-up systems, your expectation management, and your genuine commitment to patient wellbeing.

Here is how you build a referral culture intentionally. First, you deliver care worth referring to. That is the foundation. No referral system can compensate for poor care. Second, you make it easy for satisfied patients to refer. Give them extra business cards. Send a follow-up email that includes a "share with a friend" option. Mention, at appropriate moments, that you are always happy to evaluate friends and family members. Third, you acknowledge and appreciate referrals. A simple "Thank you so much for recommending us to your sister" goes a long way. Fourth, you protect the referring patient's privacy by never discussing their care with the new patient. Fifth, you treat every referred patient with the same thoroughness you showed the original patient - never cut corners because "they're a referral" or "their friend said great things about us." Each patient gets a full evaluation, full consent, full documentation, and full follow-up. Every single time.

The practices I see that are thriving five years in are not the ones that spent the most on advertising. They are the ones that built a referral engine through exceptional patient care. Their marketing budget shrinks over time because their patient base does the marketing for them. And because that marketing happens in private conversation rather than public advertisement, it creates none of the regulatory exposure that paid advertising creates. That is the model. That is the goal.

Conservative digital presence: educational content, not promotional claims

In today's world, you need a digital presence. Patients will Google you before they call. They will check your website, read your reviews, look at your social media, and form an opinion before they ever speak to a human being in your office. Having no digital presence is almost as bad as having a reckless one - it suggests you are not a legitimate practice or that you have something to hide. So you need to be online. But you need to be online the right way.

The right way is educational content. Not promotional claims. Educational content teaches, informs, explains, and clarifies. It demonstrates expertise without promising outcomes. It attracts patients by showing them that you know what you are talking about, not by telling them you can solve all their problems.

Here is what educational content looks like in practice. A blog post titled "What Are Peptides and How Do They Work in the Body?" - that is educational. It explains the biology, discusses different types of peptides, describes how they interact with cellular processes, and notes that peptide therapy is an evolving field with varying levels of evidence. It does not promise weight loss. It does not guarantee muscle gain. It does not tell the reader that peptides will change their life. It educates. And at the end, it includes a call to action: "If you are interested in learning whether peptide therapy might be appropriate for your situation, contact our office to schedule a physician consultation." That is it. Education plus invitation. Perfect.

Compare that to a social media post that says "Struggling to lose weight? Our peptide program helps patients shed pounds fast! DM us to get started!" That is promotional. It promises weight loss - "shed pounds fast." It creates urgency - "DM us to get started." It does not mention medical evaluation, individualized care, or the fact that not everyone qualifies. It reads like an ad for a product, not an invitation to medical care. And if a regulator sees it, they will treat it exactly that way.

Your blog should focus on topics that prospective patients want to understand: how peptides differ from hormones, what the evidence says about specific peptides, how compounding works, what to expect from a medical evaluation, why monitoring matters, what the difference is between FDA-approved and investigational therapies. Each post should be thorough, accurate, and written in plain language that a non-medical reader can understand. You or someone on your staff can write these, or you can hire a medical writer who understands the compliance requirements. Either way, every post should be reviewed before publication by someone who knows what you can and cannot say.

Your social media should amplify your educational content without turning into a promotional channel. Share blog posts. Post short educational videos - sixty to ninety seconds - where you or your physician explains a concept, answers a common question, or discusses a topic of interest. Share practice updates: new staff, new services, community involvement. Respond to comments and questions in a way that is helpful but does not cross into medical advice for non-patients. Use social media to build familiarity and trust, not to make sales.

What you should not post: before-and-after photos without proper consent and disclaimers. Patient testimonials that promise results. Promotional language about discounts, specials, or limited-time offers. Claims about efficacy, cure, or guaranteed outcomes. Comparisons to other providers that suggest superiority. Anything that could be read as a specific medical recommendation for a general audience. If you would not want the state medical board to read it at a hearing, do not post it.

One specific recommendation about social media: disable comments if you cannot monitor them constantly. Patient comments on your posts can create liability if they make claims you do not correct, if they ask medical questions you answer inappropriately, or if they share personal health information in a public forum. If you keep comments enabled, you need a staff member checking them regularly and a clear protocol for what to do when problematic comments appear. Many practices find it easier to simply disable comments and use social media as a one-way educational channel. That is a perfectly reasonable approach.

Your website should be a comprehensive resource that answers every question a prospective patient might have. What peptides do you work with? What conditions do you evaluate? What does the initial consultation include? How much does it cost? What is your follow-up process? What are your requirements for participation? What should patients bring to their first visit? How do you handle prescriptions? What pharmacy do you use? The more information you provide upfront, the fewer questions your staff has to answer on the phone, and the more confident prospective patients feel about calling.

But every page of that website should be written with the compliance filter on. No promises. No guarantees. No cure language. No implicit FDA approval of compounded products. Clear disclaimers on every page. Consistent messaging that matches your informed consent documents. A prominent statement that this is medical care requiring physician evaluation, not a product available for purchase. If you have staff who update the website, they need training on what they can and cannot write. If you use an outside web designer or marketing agency, they need to understand the regulatory constraints or they will write copy that gets you in trouble.

Screenshots and approvals: save every marketing decision

Here is a practice habit that separates doctors who survive investigations from doctors who do not: documentation of marketing decisions. Every ad you run, every website update you make, every social media post you publish, every brochure you print - you save a record of it. You save the original content. You save the approval. You save the date it was published and the date it was taken down. You treat your marketing decisions with the same documentation rigor you treat your clinical decisions. Because when the investigator shows up - and I say when, not if, because in this line of work investigations are a matter of time, not luck - they are going to ask about your marketing. And your ability to produce organized records will determine whether you look like a careful physician or a careless operator.

Let me walk you through what this looks like in practice. Your practice decides to run a Google ad campaign. Before the ad goes live, the ad copy is reviewed by the physician - that is you - and by your compliance designee, which might be your office manager, your nurse, or your paralegal if you have one. The review checks for prohibited language: no guarantees, no cure claims, no FDA approval implications for compounded products, no atypical testimonials, no before-and-after photos without releases. The ad is approved or revised. The approval is documented - an email saying "approved" is sufficient, though a formal approval form is better. The approved ad is saved as a PDF or screenshot with the approval date. The ad runs. When the campaign ends, the final version is archived with end dates.

That record now exists forever. If a patient complains two years later that your ad promised something it should not have, you pull the archived ad and you show exactly what it said. If the ad was compliant - and it was, because you reviewed it - the complaint dies. If you have no record of what the ad said because you never archived it, you are now in a he-said-she-said situation where the patient produces a screenshot and you have nothing to counter it. That is a bad place to be. Archiving prevents it.

This applies to everything. Website pages should be archived whenever they are updated. Social media posts should be screenshotted before they go live. Email campaigns should be saved. Brochures should be saved as PDFs. Radio or television scripts should be archived. Any marketing material that represents your practice to the public should have a dated record in your files.

I recommend creating a simple marketing archive system. A shared drive folder or cloud storage location with subfolders by year and by channel: Website, Social Media, Google Ads, Print Materials, Radio, Email, etc. Every item gets a filename that includes the date and a brief description: "2026-01-15_GoogleAd_WeightLossEvaluation." The approval record - an email, a signed form, or a note in your compliance log - gets saved alongside the material. When the material is updated or retired, the new version is saved with a new date and the old version is moved to an archive subfolder. It takes five minutes per item. It saves you hundreds of hours if an investigation ever happens.

Why does this matter so much? Because investigations do not happen the week after you run an ad. They happen months or years later, when the ad has been changed, the website has been updated, the social media post has been deleted, and nobody remembers exactly what was published. The patient who files the complaint attaches the screenshot they saved. The investigator asks you to explain. If you have no record, you look disorganized at best and deceptive at worst - like a practice that changes its marketing to hide what it said. If you have a complete archive, you look like a practice that takes compliance seriously and documents its decisions. Which impression do you want the investigator to have?

And here is something that most doctors do not think about: your marketing archive also helps you identify patterns. If you review your archived materials every six months, you might notice that your messaging drifted over time - that what started as conservative educational content gradually became more promotional as someone on your staff got more confident with marketing. You might notice that your disclaimers got smaller or moved to less prominent locations. You might notice that testimonials started creeping in without proper approvals.

Catching that drift early, before a regulator catches it, is invaluable. Your archive is not just a defensive tool. It is a quality control tool.

One more thing: save your competitors' marketing too. Not to copy it - heaven forbid - but to distinguish yourself from it. If a regulator ever asks whether your marketing is typical for the industry, you want to be able to show that your materials are substantially more conservative than what else is out there. You want to demonstrate that you took a cautious, medical approach while others were making claims you never would. That comparison works in your favor. It shows judgment. And judgment is what regulators want to see.

Staff must never make medical claims or promise outcomes

I want to close this chapter with the single most important marketing control that most practices overlook: your staff. Every person who answers your phone, responds to your emails, manages your social media, greets patients at the front desk, or speaks with anyone outside the practice is a marketing representative. And if they say the wrong thing - if they promise results, guarantee outcomes, imply FDA approval, or make claims the physician cannot defend- those words become your words. The state medical board does not care that it was your receptionist, not you, who told the patient they would definitely lose weight. The receptionist works for you. The receptionist speaks for your practice. The receptionist's words are your words.

This is where staff training becomes a matter of license protection, not just customer service. Every staff member who interacts with patients or the public must understand what they can and cannot say about your peptide program. They must know that they cannot promise weight loss. They cannot guarantee results. They cannot discuss specific medications or doses unless that is within their scope and they are following a script approved by the physician. They cannot compare your practice to competitors in ways that suggest superiority. They cannot discuss other patients' results, even anonymously. They cannot provide medical advice, treatment recommendations, or clinical opinions.

What they can say is limited but sufficient. They can explain the process: call to schedule, complete the intake forms, meet with the physician for an evaluation, discuss whether treatment is appropriate. They can describe what is included in the program: medical evaluation, laboratory testing when indicated, individualized treatment planning, pharmacy coordination, follow-up visits, monitoring. They can discuss pricing and payment: the cost of the program, what forms of payment you accept, your policy on refunds or cancellations. They can answer scheduling questions: available appointment times, how long the initial visit takes, what the patient should bring. That is it. Process, logistics, and pricing. Nothing clinical. Nothing outcome-related. Nothing that could be construed as a promise.

I strongly recommend developing a staff script for common questions. Every question a prospective patient might ask should have a pre-approved response that staff can read verbatim. How much weight will I lose? "Results vary significantly from patient to patient. The physician will discuss realistic expectations during your consultation." Is this FDA-approved? "That depends on the specific medication and use. The physician will explain whether a prescribed therapy is FDA-approved, off-label, compounded, or investigational."How long until I see results? "Individual response times vary. The physician will discuss what to expect based on your specific situation during your evaluation." Will I definitely get a prescription? "Medication is only prescribed when the physician determines it is clinically appropriate after a thorough evaluation. Not every patient who comes in for a consultation will receive a prescription."

These scripts should be written down, distributed to every staff member, reviewed regularly, and updated as needed. New staff should be trained on them before they ever answer a patient call. Existing staff should be quizzed periodically to make sure they are using approved language. Phone calls should be spot-checked - listen to recordings if your system captures them, or have a supervisor periodically monitor live calls. Social media responses should be reviewed before posting if they come from staff rather than the physician. Email responses should follow templates that have been pre-approved.

The most dangerous staff member is the enthusiastic one who wants to help patients and thinks being encouraging means making promises. "Oh, you'll love Dr. Smith, his patients lose so much weight!" "Everyone does great on this program!" "You're going to feel amazing in just a few weeks!" That staff member thinks they are being helpful. They are actually creating liability with every encouraging word. They are making claims that the physician never authorized, that the practice cannot substantiate, and that will be attributed to the physician if there is ever a complaint. You must train that enthusiasm out of them or redirect it toward safe, supportive, non-clinical communication.

Social media is a particular staff danger zone. A well-meaning staff member managing your Instagram account might respond to a comment by saying "Most of our patients lose 20+ lbs!"or "Semaglutide works for almost everyone!" Those responses look informal. They look conversational. They look harmless. But they are marketing claims published by your practice, and they carry the same liability as a paid advertisement. If you let staff manage your social media, you need a clear policy about what they can and cannot say, and you need to review their activity regularly. Better yet, have all social media responses drafted by staff and approved by the physician or compliance designee before posting. It adds a step, but it prevents disasters.

The same applies to online reviews. When a patient leaves a positive review mentioning specific results, your staff should not respond by confirming or amplifying those results. "So glad you lost thirty pounds, Sarah!" sounds like a nice response, but it turns the review into a documented practice record acknowledging a specific outcome that other patients might expect. The safe response is: "Thank you for your kind words, Sarah. We appreciate the opportunity to be part of your care." Generic. Grateful. Non-specific. Safe.

And when a patient leaves a negative review - and eventually, someone will - your staff must be trained never to argue, never to disclose patient information in the response, never to contradict the patient's account in a public forum. "Actually, Sarah, we told you multiple times that results vary and you signed a consent form acknowledging that" - that response is a

HIPAA violation waiting to happen. It discloses that Sarah is a patient. It discusses the content of her care. It does all of this in public. The correct response to any negative review is: "We are committed to providing quality care to all our patients. We would welcome the opportunity to discuss your concerns directly. Please contact our office at [phone number]." That is it. Nothing more. Take the conversation offline where it belongs.

Let me leave you with this thought. Marketing is not separate from medicine. In a peptide practice, marketing is the front door through which every patient enters, and if that front door promises things the practice cannot deliver, the patients who walk through it will be disappointed, angry, and litigious. Your marketing sets the expectations that your clinical care must either meet or fall short of. If you set realistic expectations through conservative, educational marketing, your clinical care will exceed those expectations and your patients will be satisfied. If you set unrealistic expectations through promotional hype, your clinical care will fall short and your patients will complain, sue, or report you.

The choice is that simple. Educate and invite. That is all your marketing needs to do. Every word beyond that is a risk. Every promise is a potential exhibit. Every guarantee is a future complaint. Be the doctor who patients trust because your marketing told them the truth, not because it sold them a dream. The patients who come through your door knowing that medicine is uncertain, that results vary, and that their physician will give them an honest evaluation - those patients will stay, they will comply, they will refer their friends, and they will never file a complaint. Build your practice on that foundation. It is the only one that lasts.

16 - The Consultation - Educate, Don't Sell

BLUNT RULE: Pressure sells today and creates complaints tomorrow.

Let me tell you something I have watched destroy more peptide practices than bad pharmacy choices or sloppy charting combined. It is the consultation that goes wrong. Not because the physician did not know the medicine. Not because the patient was a bad candidate. It went wrong because the physician treated the consultation like a sales conversation instead of an education session. And when that patient later feels disappointed, embarrassed, or betrayed -maybe they did not lose the weight they expected, maybe they had a side effect they did not understand, maybe their spouse saw the credit card bill and started asking questions - that patient becomes a complaint. Not a refund request. A complaint. To the state medical board. Maybe to an attorney. And the board does not care that you thought you were being helpful. They care about what the chart says. They care about whether the patient felt pressured. They care about whether the patient actually understood what they were getting into.

This chapter is about the consultation as a protective tool. Done right, it is the moat around your castle. It is the documentation that saves your license when the disappointed patient files a complaint six months later. It is the moment when you separate candidates from non-candidates, set expectations that prevent future conflicts, and build the kind of patient relationship that generates referrals instead of chargebacks. The consultation is not a sales pitch. It is not a conversion funnel. It is a structured medical evaluation with a teaching component. Educate, don't sell. Let the patient decide. Then document everything.

The Consultation Structure

A good consultation does not happen by accident. It follows a structure, and that structure exists for two reasons. First, it ensures that every medically relevant topic gets covered -goals, history, contraindications, costs, alternatives, risks, follow-up, and the decision itself. Second, it creates a defensible record. When the board reviewer picks up your chart six months from now, they should see a methodical, thorough, patient-centered evaluation. Not a rushed phone call. Not a five-minute Zoom where the patient got a prescription before the video loaded.

I have seen physicians do consultations in twelve minutes. That is not a consultation. That is a transaction. Twelve minutes is barely enough to review a medication list, let alone discuss goals, explore history, explain risks, talk about costs, review alternatives, answer questions, and arrive at a mutual decision. If your consultation is under thirty minutes for a new patient evaluating peptide therapy, you are moving too fast. I do not care how efficient you think you are. Speed in this business is not a virtue. Thoroughness is.

Start with the patient's goals. Not with your treatment menu. Not with what you think they need. Ask them what brought them in. What have they tried before? What worked, what did not, and why do they think peptide therapy might be different? This is not small talk. This is clinical intelligence. The patient who says "I want to lose thirty pounds in six weeks because my daughter is getting married" is telling you something very different from the patient who says "I have been working with my endocrinologist for two years, I have tried metformin and lifestyle changes, my A1C is still creeping up, and I read about GLP-1 agonists and want to understand my options." The first patient has unrealistic expectations and an event-driven timeline. The second patient has a medical narrative, prior attempts, and a collaborative mindset. You need to hear the difference. The chart needs to show you heard it.

When you document goals, be specific. Do not write "patient wants weight loss." Write"patient reports goal of 30-pound weight reduction over 6 months, acknowledges this is ambitious, states prior attempts with commercial diet program resulted in 8-pound loss followed by regain, expresses interest in GLP-1 therapy after online research, understands that results vary and that medication is not a substitute for dietary change." That paragraph tells a story. It shows you assessed motivation, prior effort, and expectation level. It shows you did not just take an order.

Next, review the medical history exhaustively. And I mean exhaustively. The history is where landmines hide. The patient who forgot to mention they had pancreatitis five years ago. The patient who takes a supplement that interacts with what you are prescribing. The patient who had thyroid surgery and did not think it was relevant. The patient who is on an SSRI and wants PT-141 for sexual dysfunction without understanding the blood pressure interaction. Every one of these scenarios has ended up in a board complaint somewhere. Your job in the consultation is to dig until you are satisfied - not until the patient gets impatient.

Go through medications systematically. Prescription, over-the-counter, supplements, herbal products, and anything they bought online because an influencer recommended it. Ask about allergies - not just "are you allergic to anything?" but "have you ever had a reaction to an injection, a medication, a supplement, anything that made you feel strange or sick?" Ask about surgeries, hospitalizations, and why. A hysterectomy at forty-two is different from a hysterectomy at forty-two for endometrial cancer. The chart needs to show you knew the difference.

Review contraindications honestly and directly. If the patient's history reveals a condition that makes peptide therapy unsafe, say so. Do not hedge. Do not say "well, we could maybe try a low dose and see." That is how patients get hurt. The patient with a personal history of medullary thyroid carcinoma should not get a GLP-1 agonist. The patient with a recent DVT should not start growth hormone secretagogues without hematology clearance. The patient with uncontrolled hypertension should not get PT-141. These are not judgment calls. These are hard stops. Your consultation must identify them, document them, and either explain why the patient is not a candidate or document what additional clearance is needed before proceeding.

Discuss costs clearly and early. Nothing destroys a patient relationship faster than sticker shock. The patient who hears "$395 a month" for the first time when the invoice arrives is a patient who feels deceived. Even if you had a pricing page on your website. Even if your intake coordinator mentioned it. If the physician - the authority figure in the room - did not look the patient in the eye and say "this is what this costs, this is what is included, this is what is not included, and this is how long you should expect to pay," then the patient did not really hear it.

When you discuss costs, break it down. What does the program fee cover? What does the medication cost? Are labs included or separate? What about follow-up visits? Is there a refill fee? What happens if they need to pause - do they pay to restart? The patient who understands the full financial picture before they commit is a patient who does not later claim they were misled. Document that this discussion happened. Document that the patient had a chance to ask financial questions. Document that they acknowledged the cost before proceeding. The board reviewer who sees a detailed cost disclosure in your chart note knows you are running a medical practice, not a surprise-billing operation.

Review alternatives seriously. This is where a lot of physicians slip up. They know what they want to prescribe, and they subtly - sometimes unconsciously - frame the alternative as inferior. "Well, you could try diet and exercise, but most people find that difficult." That is not a neutral presentation of alternatives. That is a sales technique called objection handling. The board knows what it looks like. Your chart should show that you presented alternatives fairly, including continued care with their PCP, lifestyle modification, FDA-approved conventional therapies, and doing nothing at all. Some patients, after hearing the full picture, will choose not to proceed. That is fine. A patient who walks away informed is not a lost sale. They are a potential referral source who trusts you. A patient who proceeds because they felt cornered is a complaint waiting to happen.

Give patients real space to ask questions. This is not a throwaway line at the end of a thirty-minute data dump where you say "any questions?" while already reaching for the prescription pad. Questions are where learning happens. Questions are where you discover what the patient actually understood versus what they nodded along with. Questions are where you catch misunderstanding before it becomes noncompliance.

Pause after each major topic. "I just covered quite a bit about how this medication works and what the common side effects are. Before we move on, what questions do you have?" Then wait. Count to ten in your head. Most patients need seven to ten seconds of silence before they formulate a question. If you jump in to fill the silence, you have just robbed them of their chance to think. The patient who says "I think I understand" but cannot articulate a single risk factor back to you does not understand. The patient who asks "if I get nauseous, should I stop or just push through?" is engaged, thinking ahead, and giving you an opportunity to set clear instructions. That question deserves a thoughtful answer, not a dismissive "just call the office."

The patient should feel understood, not cornered. This is the heart of the consultation. The patient who feels understood trusts you. The patient who feels cornered resents you. And resentment is the fuel that powers complaints, bad reviews, chargebacks, and board letters. Think about the last time you felt sold to - a car dealership, a timeshare presentation, a pushy retail clerk. Remember that sense of pressure, that feeling that the person across from you cared more about closing the deal than about whether the product was right for you? That is exactly what you must avoid in a peptide consultation. The patient should leave the consultation feeling like they had a thorough medical evaluation with a physician who explained everything, answered their questions, and let them make their own decision. Not like they just sat through a pitch.

The way you achieve this is through pacing and tone. Speak at a speed the patient can follow. Check in. "Does this make sense so far?" "Is there anything I said that worries you?" "You look like you have something on your mind - what is it?" These small moments of invitation tell the patient that this is a dialogue, not a monologue. They also create documentation opportunities. When you write your note, you can document that the patient was given multiple opportunities to ask questions, that they asked specific questions about X and Y, and that their concerns were addressed. That is a powerful chart entry if the patient later claims nobody explained anything to them.

End every consultation with a clear decision. Ambiguity is your enemy. The patient who leaves the consultation not knowing whether they are starting therapy, waiting for labs, or declined entirely is a patient who will fill in the blanks with their own assumptions - and those assumptions will be wrong. Your job is to end with a documented decision in one of these categories: the patient is a candidate and we are proceeding; the patient is a candidate pending lab results; the patient needs PCP clearance or specialist clearance before we proceed; the patient is not a candidate at this time and we discussed alternatives; the patient needs time to consider and will follow up.

Each of these outcomes gets documented in the chart with the rationale behind it. "Patient is a candidate for semaglutide program pending CBC, CMP, TSH, and fasting lipid panel. Labs ordered today. Follow-up scheduled for two weeks to review results and initiate therapy if appropriate. Patient instructed not to start any new supplements or medications before follow-up." That is a complete thought. It shows what was decided, why, what the next steps are, and what the patient was told. Compare that to "patient interested in peptides, will follow up." That second note tells a board reviewer nothing. It suggests the physician was disengaged, the process was unstructured, and the patient was left hanging. Do not write notes like that.

The consultation structure exists to protect you. But it only works if you actually follow it. Every time. Not just when the patient seems complicated. Not just when you have extra time. Every single consultation should cover goals, history, contraindications, costs, alternatives, risks, and a clear decision. Skip a step because the patient seems eager and you are running behind schedule, and that is the patient who will surprise you six months later. I have seen it happen too many times.

Overexplaining Risk

If there is one thing I want you to take away from this entire chapter - hell, from this entire book - it is this: you cannot explain risk too much. There is no such thing as overexplaining risk to a patient. The physician who worries about "scaring the patient away" by being too thorough about side effects is the physician who ends up explaining their chart to an investigator. The patient who truly understands what could go wrong is a patient who does not file a complaint when something actually goes wrong. They knew. They consented. They chose to proceed anyway. That is the difference between an informed patient and a deceived patient, and the board knows the difference when they read your chart.

Let me be absolutely clear about what I mean by "overexplaining." I do not mean reciting a laundry list of adverse reactions from a pharmaceutical insert and calling it informed consent. That is not education. That is liability theater. I mean taking the time to explain, in plain language the patient can actually understand, what the real risks are for them specifically, why those risks matter, what they would feel like if they occurred, and what the patient should do if they happen. I mean slowing down. I mean asking the patient to repeat back their understanding. I mean documenting not just that risks were mentioned, but how they were explained and what the patient said in response.

Risk factors must be explained in exhaustive detail - more explanation, not less. Start with the common risks because those are what the patient is most likely to experience. If you are prescribing a GLP-1 agonist, you do not just say "nausea is common." You say "most patients on this medication experience some nausea, especially in the first two to four weeks. It typically feels like a full, unsettled stomach, sometimes with a sense of early fullness where you cannot finish a normal meal. For most people, this improves as the body adjusts. But for some, it persists. There are strategies we can use to minimize it - slow dose titration, timing of injections, dietary adjustments - but I need you to understand that nausea is not a side effect that happens to someone else. It is the side effect that happens to most people, and it may happen to you." That is overexplaining. And it is exactly what your chart should reflect you said.

Then move to the serious risks. Do not skip them because they are rare. Rare risks are the ones that generate lawsuits. The patient who develops pancreatitis on a GLP-1 agonist and was never told what pancreatitis feels like will credibly claim they had no idea what was happening. The patient who develops severe abdominal pain and does not know to seek emergency care because "nobody told me it could be serious" is a patient whose attorney will have a field day with your chart. Explain serious risks in concrete terms. "Pancreatitis is inflammation of the pancreas. It causes severe, persistent upper abdominal pain that may radiate to your back. It is accompanied by vomiting. It is a medical emergency. If you feel this, you do not call our office and wait for a callback. You go to the emergency room. And you tell them you are on this medication." That level of specificity might feel like too much. It is not. That is exactly what informed consent looks like when it is done right.

For every peptide or medication you discuss, the risk conversation should cover: common side effects and what they feel like; serious side effects and what to do if they occur; drug interactions with their current medications; contraindications specific to their medical history; risks related to their age, sex, and physiological status; unknown risks for compounded or investigational products; and what happens if they want to stop - withdrawal effects, rebound considerations, and the proper way to discontinue. Each of these categories gets addressed with the patient, not at them. You are not checking boxes. You are teaching.

Every patient must understand what could go wrong before anything goes right. This is a hard mindset shift for physicians who are used to focusing on benefits. In conventional medicine, you lead with the therapeutic goal. "We are prescribing this to lower your blood pressure." The risks get mentioned quickly, often in a hurried monologue while the patient is already thinking about stopping at the pharmacy. In peptide medicine, that approach does not work. These are not standard therapies. Many are off-label. Many are compounded. Many have limited long-term data. The patient's enthusiasm is already high - they sought you out. Your job is not to increase their enthusiasm. Your job is to balance it with a realistic understanding of what they are getting into.

Here is how I want you to think about it. The patient comes in hoping for a great outcome. You want them to have a great outcome too. But before you both get excited about what might go right, you need to spend serious time on what could go wrong. Not as a formality. Not as a legal checkbox. But as the central educational component of the consultation. The patient who understands the risks and still wants to proceed is the patient you want in your practice. The patient who blanches when they hear the real risks and decides to think about it is also a good outcome. They are making an informed decision. The patient who only wants to hear the benefits and gets impatient when you talk about risks? That patient is a red flag. That is the patient who will blame you when reality does not match their Instagram feed.

Document that risks were explained - the consent form is not enough. Let me repeat that because it is critically important. The consent form is not enough. A signed piece of paper that says "risks discussed" is a weak defense. Any attorney can argue that the patient signed without reading, or that the physician rushed through the form, or that the risks were mentioned but not explained. What holds up is your chart note. Your chart note should document, in your own clinical language, what risks you explained, how you explained them, and what the patient's response was.

Here is what a strong risk documentation looks like: "Risks of semaglutide therapy discussed in detail including common GI side effects (nausea, vomiting, diarrhea, constipation, early satiety), gallbladder disease, pancreatitis (patient instructed to seek emergency care for severe persistent abdominal pain radiating to back with vomiting), potential thyroid C-cell tumor risk (patient counseled that this is based on rodent data, relevance to humans unknown, but medication contraindicated in personal or family history of medullary thyroid carcinoma or MEN2), hypoglycemia risk when combined with other diabetes medications, and potential for weight regain upon discontinuation. Patient asked specific questions about gallbladder risk given remote history of cholelithiasis; patient counseled that prior gallbladder disease increases risk and that any new right upper quadrant pain should be reported promptly. Patient verbalized understanding, stated 'I know this is serious medicine and I need to pay attention to my body,'and confirmed desire to proceed with close monitoring." That paragraph tells a story. It shows depth, specificity, patient engagement, and clinical judgment. A board reviewer reads that and sees a physician who took the time to do this right.

Compare that to: "Risks discussed. Consent signed." That tells the reviewer nothing. Worse, it suggests the discussion was perfunctory. And when the patient later says "nobody told me about gallbladder problems," the reviewer has no evidence to the contrary. The consent form with a signature is not contemporaneous documentation of a conversation. It is a piece of paper. Your chart note is your voice, your record, your defense.

Patients who understand risk are less likely to complain when side effects occur. This is a simple truth that too many physicians do not appreciate. Complaints often arise not from the side effect itself, but from the feeling of betrayal. "If I had known this could happen, I never would have taken it." That sentence is the opening line of countless board complaints. And when the chart shows a two-minute consultation with a generic consent form, the patient has a credible case. But when the chart shows a thirty-minute risk discussion with specific examples, patient questions, documented understanding, and clear emergency instructions, that sentence loses its power. The patient was told. The patient understood. The patient chose to proceed. You cannot prevent every side effect, but you can prevent the surprise that turns a side effect into a complaint.

Here is the psychology behind it. When a patient experiences a side effect they were never warned about, they feel ambushed. The medication betrayed them, and by extension, the physician betrayed them. They start wondering what else they were not told. They get angry. Angry patients call lawyers. Angry patients post reviews. Angry patients file complaints. But when a patient experiences a side effect they were specifically warned about, the dynamic is completely different. "The doctor told me this might happen, and it did. I do not like it, but I was prepared." That patient calls your office, asks what to do, and works with you to manage it. They do not feel deceived. They feel like they are in a partnership. That is the difference that overexplaining risk makes.

Let me give you a practical framework for the risk discussion. I call it the Three Layers of Risk, and you should cover all three in every consultation. Layer One is the common, expected side effects - the things that happen to most patients. These are not emergencies, but they are uncomfortable, and the patient needs to know they are normal. Layer Two is the serious but uncommon risks - the things that require medical attention if they occur. These are your pancreatitis, your gallbladder disease, your severe allergic reactions, your cardiac events. The patient needs to know the warning signs and the action steps. Layer Three is the unknown -the risks we do not fully understand because the data is limited, the therapy is compounded, or the long-term studies have not been done. This is the hardest layer to discuss because there is no checklist. But it is also the most important, because it is where peptide therapy differs from prescribing a statin.

For Layer One, use specific, sensory language. Do not say "you might feel nauseous." Say"you might feel like you have eaten too much at a big meal, that heavy, queasy feeling in your upper stomach that makes you not want to eat anything else. It may last a few hours after your injection. It usually gets better after a couple of weeks." The patient who knows what to expect does not panic. The patient who panics calls the emergency room at 2 AM and tells them their peptide doctor poisoned them. Specificity prevents panic.

For Layer Two, use clear action language. "If you feel this, do this." Not "seek medical attention if severe" - that is vague and useless. Say "if you have severe abdominal pain that lasts more than an hour, especially if it goes through to your back, and especially if you are vomiting, you go to the emergency room. You do not call us first. You do not wait to see if it gets better. You go. And you tell them you are on semaglutide." That is a directive the patient can actually follow in a crisis.

For Layer Three, use honest uncertainty language. "This medication is compounded. It is not FDA-approved in the same way as the brand-name product. That does not mean it is unsafe, but it means the regulatory oversight is different. The long-term data for this specific use is limited. We are making a clinical judgment based on available evidence, your specific situation, and your informed consent to proceed with monitoring. If you are not comfortable with uncertainty, this may not be the right therapy for you." That level of honesty is disarming. Patients respect it. More importantly, it is accurate, and accuracy is your shield.

The patient who hears all three layers and still wants to proceed is your ideal patient. They are informed, realistic, and engaged. Document that you covered all three layers. Document the patient's reaction. Document their questions. Document their verbal confirmation that they understood and still wish to proceed. Then, and only then, do you write the prescription.

Setting Boundaries

Here is a truth that every physician running a peptide or hormone practice needs to internalize: your patient does not want you to be their everything. They think they do. They will act like they do. They will ask you about their blood pressure medication, their rash, their anxiety, their kid's asthma, and whether the back pain they have had for ten years might be related to their new peptide program. But what they actually need - what keeps you safe, what keeps them safe, and what makes your practice sustainable - is a clear boundary. You are a specialist. You do one thing, and you do it well. You are not their primary care doctor. You are not their urgent care. You are not their 24/7 medical hotline. And the sooner you make that clear, with warmth but with absolute firmness, the better your practice will run.

Your practice is specialized - you are not replacing their primary doctor. This is not a subtle point. This is a boundary that protects your license. Primary care physicians have a scope of practice, a training background, and a role in the healthcare system that you do not have and should not try to replicate. When you start managing a patient's hypertension, adjusting their statin, or treating their urinary tract infection because "it was easier than sending them back to their PCP," you have crossed a line. Not a small line. A line that state medical boards draw in bright red ink. You are now practicing primary care without a primary care relationship, and that is a fast path to a disciplinary inquiry.

Make this boundary explicit in the consultation. Say it out loud. "I want to be clear about my role. I specialize in peptide and metabolic therapy. I will manage your peptide program, monitor your response, adjust your dosing within this program, and coordinate with your primary care doctor when needed. But I am not replacing your PCP. Your blood pressure medication, your diabetes management, your annual screenings, your urgent medical issues -those stay with your primary care team. I will communicate with them, and I expect you to keep them in the loop, but those are not services I provide." Write that in your chart note. Have the patient acknowledge it. If they push back - "well, my PCP does not understand peptides"- your response is not to take over more of their care. Your response is: "That is exactly why communication between us and your PCP is so important. Let me help facilitate that."

The PCP involvement is your secret weapon. I have said this throughout this book and I will keep saying it until every physician who prescribes peptides gets it through their head. A PCP who knows about your peptide program, who has been consulted, who has given their input -that PCP is your ally if something goes wrong. They are a witness that you practiced collaboratively. They are a buffer between you and the isolation that makes peptide physicians vulnerable to board complaints. The patient who says "my PCP does not know I am doing this"is a patient who needs a serious conversation before you write any prescription. Either they involve their PCP, or you need a documented, thoughtful reason why PCP involvement is not appropriate in this specific case. "The patient does not have a PCP" is not an automatic green light. That patient needs a PCP, and your practice should help them find one.

In the consultation, ask about the PCP directly. Who is it? When did they last see them? Have they discussed peptide therapy? What was the PCP's reaction? Document all of this. If the PCP was supportive, document that. If the PCP was neutral, document that. If the PCP was opposed, document what the patient was told about that opposition and how the decision to proceed was still reached through informed consent and medical judgment. The chart note that shows PCP awareness and engagement is a chart note that demonstrates responsible, collaborative medicine. The chart note that pretends the PCP does not exist looks like corner-cutting to a board reviewer.

Other medical issues stay with the PCP or specialists. This sounds obvious, but in practice it is where physicians constantly drift. A patient on a GLP-1 agonist starts having diarrhea. They call your office. Your instinct - your good-doctor instinct - is to help. You want to be responsive. You want to be accessible. But diarrhea in a patient on a GLP-1 agonist could be a medication side effect, or it could be C. diff, or food poisoning, or inflammatory bowel disease, or a hundred other things. If you diagnose and treat it without a proper evaluation, you are now managing acute GI illness outside your scope. The right answer is: "I hear you, and I want to make sure this gets evaluated properly. Because this could be related to your medication or it could be something else entirely, I need you to see your PCP or go to urgent care for an evaluation. Once you know what is going on, have them send me the results and we will figure out whether any changes to your peptide program are needed."

That response does three things. First, it shows you are engaged and concerned - the patient feels heard. Second, it directs the patient to the appropriate level of care - you are not practicing outside your lane. Third, it creates a paper trail. The patient was told to see their PCP. The PCP evaluates and documents. You get the results and make any peptide-related adjustments based on that documentation. Everyone stays in their lane, and the patient gets comprehensive care. That is how medicine is supposed to work.

The temptation to drift is strongest with patients you know well. They have been in your program for eight months. They trust you. You trust them. They start asking you about their other medications, their other symptoms, their other concerns. And because you are a decent human being who wants to help, you answer. You adjust their levothyroxine because "it is just a small dose change." You prescribe an antibiotic for their sinus infection because "it is obvious what this is." Every one of those decisions is a board complaint waiting to happen. The patient who loves you today will not remember that you were "just being helpful" if something goes wrong tomorrow. They will remember that the specialist who was supposed to manage their peptides also managed their thyroid, and now they are in atrial fibrillation and someone has to answer for it. Do not be that physician.

The peptide program is one piece of care, not their entire healthcare system. This framing is important for the patient's mindset and for your documentation. When you describe your program as one component of a comprehensive health approach, you reinforce the boundary naturally. "Your peptide program is designed to support your metabolic health. It works best when it is part of a complete care plan that includes your primary care, your nutrition, your activity level, your sleep, and your stress management. I manage the peptide piece. Your PCP manages the whole picture. You manage your lifestyle. All three of us are needed for this to work." That is a framing the patient can understand and accept. It also happens to be true.

Set expectations for access: responsive but not on-call 24/7. This is where the user's instruction - that patients should always feel as though you are accessible - meets the hard reality of running a practice. Accessibility is an emotional quality, not a temporal one. The patient who feels accessible to their physician feels that way because their calls get returned promptly, their questions get answered thoroughly, and they never feel like they are being brushed off. They do not feel accessible because they have your cell phone number and can text you at midnight.

In the consultation, be explicit about how communication works. "Here is how you reach us. During business hours, you can call the office and expect a same-day response. For clinical questions that require my review, we aim to get back to you within one business day. After hours, if you have a medical emergency - chest pain, severe shortness of breath, signs of an allergic reaction, severe abdominal pain - you call 911 or go to the emergency room. You do not call this office and wait for a callback. If you have a non-urgent question after hours, leave a message or send a portal message and we will get back to you the next business day." Write this in your patient instructions. Have the patient acknowledge it. When they sign off on it, they have agreed to the boundaries.

The feeling of accessibility comes from quality of response, not quantity of availability. A patient who calls at 10 AM and gets a thoughtful, thorough callback at 2 PM from a clinician who knows their chart, answers their question, and asks a follow-up question feels incredibly well cared for. A patient who texts your personal phone at 9 PM and gets a one-word response at 11 PM feels like they are imposing, and they start to wonder if you are really the right doctor for them. Worse, the patient who has your cell phone and uses it for every little question becomes the patient who texts you a photo of their rash at 6 AM on a Sunday and expects a diagnosis. That is not accessibility. That is a boundary collapse, and it will burn you out and put your license at risk.

Here is how you create the feeling of accessibility without destroying your boundaries. First, invest in a good patient portal. Patients should be able to send secure messages, request refills, schedule appointments, and see their lab results. A portal that works well reduces phone calls, creates documentation automatically, and gives patients a sense of connection to your practice. Second, train your staff to triage appropriately. The patient who calls with "I have a question about my injection" should not always escalate to you. Your staff should be able to handle injection technique questions, scheduling questions, and billing questions within their scope. Only clinical questions - new symptoms, side effects, concerns about therapy - should come to you. Third, respond promptly to what does come to you. A same-day response to a clinical question, even if it is just "I received your message, I need to review your chart, and I will call you back by 3 PM with a detailed answer," is infinitely better than a two-day silence. The patient who knows their message was heard and is being handled feels accessible. The patient who sends a message into the void and wonders if anyone read it feels abandoned.

Let me also address the weekend and after-hours question because it comes up in every consultation. Patients want to know what happens if something goes wrong on a Saturday. Your answer should be: "For anything that cannot wait until Monday, you go to urgent care or the emergency room. Then have them send us the records and we will adjust your program accordingly." This is not dismissive. This is appropriate. You are not an emergency department. You are not on-call for acute care. If a patient has severe nausea and vomiting on a Saturday, they need IV fluids and evaluation, not a callback from you suggesting they try ginger tea. Direct them to the appropriate venue, coordinate after the fact, and document that you did so. That is responsible medicine.

The boundary conversation in the consultation should also cover refills. When do refills happen? What is the process? What if they miss a follow-up appointment? Patients need to know that refills are not automatic, that they require ongoing evaluation, and that running out of medication because they skipped their follow-up is their responsibility, not yours. "Refills are reviewed at each follow-up appointment. If you miss your follow-up, your refill may be delayed until we reconnect and confirm that therapy is still appropriate. This is not a punishment. This is how we make sure you are being monitored safely." Set that expectation in the consultation, and you will have far fewer angry phone calls six months later when someone assumes their prescription renews itself magically.

One more boundary that deserves its own paragraph: the boundary around dosing and self-adjustment. Patients will ask if they can adjust their dose. They read online that someone got better results by doubling their injection. They want to know if they can speed up their titration. Your answer is no. Not "I would prefer you don't." Not "technically the instructions say..." Just no. "The dose I prescribed is based on your specific evaluation. Do not change it. If you are having side effects, call us. If you think you need a higher dose, call us. But you do not adjust your own medication. If you do, we cannot continue to prescribe for you, because self-adjustment is not compatible with safe medical supervision." Document that you said this. Document the patient's acknowledgment. This is a hard boundary, and it needs to be hard. The patient who self-adjusts and then has an adverse event is the patient who will blame you -unless your chart clearly shows they were instructed not to and agreed not to.

Setting boundaries in the consultation is not cold. It is not unfriendly. It is the framework that makes a long-term, trusting physician-patient relationship possible. The patient who knows exactly what you do, exactly how to reach you, exactly what you expect, and exactly what happens if something goes wrong is a patient who feels safe. Safe patients do not file complaints. They refer their friends.

Documentation of the Consultation

If the consultation is the moat around your castle, the documentation is the drawbridge. Without it, the moat might as well not exist. Every conversation you have, every risk you explain, every boundary you set, every question the patient asks - if it is not in the chart, it did not happen. That is the standard by which board reviewers operate. They were not in the room. They did not hear your tone. They did not see the patient's nod of understanding. All they have is the chart. And if the chart is thin, generic, or missing, they will assume the worst. Not because they are malicious, but because they have seen too many charts that were written to cover up sloppy care rather than document good care. Your job is to make your chart so thorough, so detailed, so obviously authentic that a skeptical reviewer has no choice but to conclude that you did this right.

Document goals reviewed, history discussed, options explained. Let us start with the basics because too many physicians get these wrong. The chart note from a peptide consultation is not a progress note from a follow-up visit. It is not a quick "patient here for peptide consult, discussed options, will start semaglutide." That is a prescription pad, not a medical record. A consultation note for a new patient evaluating peptide therapy should read like a narrative that tells the complete story of how this patient arrived at your door, what you found when you evaluated them, what you discussed, what you decided, and what happens next.

Start with the patient's stated goals. Document them in the patient's own words whenever possible. "Patient states: 'I have been trying to lose weight for five years. I have done Weight Watchers, keto, intermittent fasting, and I work with a personal trainer twice a week. I lost 20 pounds twice and gained it back both times. My PCP says my labs are fine but I am 45 pounds overweight and I am pre-diabetic. I read about these new medications and I want to know if they could help me.'" That paragraph does extraordinary work. It shows the patient's motivation, their prior efforts, their medical context, and their entry point into peptide therapy. It shows they did not just walk in demanding a vial. They have a story. Your chart captures it.

Then document the history you reviewed. Medication list with dates, dosages, and prescribing physicians. Allergies with reactions specified. Surgical history with dates and indications. Hospitalizations with diagnoses. Family history relevant to the therapy being considered. Social history including occupation, exercise habits, dietary patterns, alcohol use, tobacco use, and substance use. Review of systems targeted to the therapy. "ROS positive for fatigue, early satiety when attempting dietary restriction, and difficulty with sleep onset. Negative for chest pain, shortness of breath, palpitations, GI bleeding, jaundice, or neurologic symptoms." This is standard clinical documentation, and there is no excuse for skipping it just because you are running a cash-pay practice.

Document the options you explained. Not just the peptide you ended up prescribing. All the options. "Discussed options including: 1) Continued lifestyle modification with PCP supervision and nutrition referral; 2) FDA-approved orlistat with PCP management; 3) Compounded semaglutide program through this practice with structured monitoring, dose titration, and follow-up; 4) Brand-name FDA-approved semaglutide or tirzepatide through patient's PCP if insurance coverage available; 5) No pharmacologic therapy at this time with reassessment in 6 months. Patient asked detailed questions about options 3 and 4, specifically regarding cost differential, efficacy data, and monitoring requirements. Patient states they will check with PCP on insurance coverage for option 4 but wishes to proceed with option 3 if coverage is denied or delayed." That level of detail shows you presented a balanced menu of alternatives. It shows the patient was an active participant in decision-making. It shows you did not have a predetermined outcome.

Document costs disclosed, no guarantees stated, follow-up explained. The financial documentation is where many charts fall apart. Physicians are uncomfortable talking about money, so they rush through it and document even less. This is a mistake. The cost discussion is a clinical event because affordability directly affects compliance, outcomes, and patient satisfaction. A patient who cannot afford therapy and takes it anyway is a patient who will eventually resent you. Document that you addressed this. "Cost of semaglutide program discussed in detail: initial consultation fee $XXX, monthly program fee of $XXX includes medication, supplies, and follow-up monitoring. Labs estimated at XXX-XXX depending on insurance coverage; patient understands labs may be out-of-pocket if not covered. Patient asked about pause policy; informed that program can be paused for up to 30 days without restart fee, longer pauses require re-evaluation. Patient asked about refund policy; informed that program fees are for clinical services rendered and are not refundable once medication is dispensed. Patient verbalized understanding, stated cost is manageable within their budget, and confirmed desire to proceed." That paragraph protects you from the "nobody told me it would cost this much" complaint that comes up constantly. The patient was told. They acknowledged. They proceeded. End of story.

The "no guarantees" discussion also needs explicit documentation. Every patient hopes for a dramatic result. Some will get it. Many will not. The patient who expects 50 pounds of weight loss and loses 12 is a disappointed patient unless they were explicitly told that 12 pounds might be their result. Document this. "Discussed that individual results vary significantly based on genetics, baseline metabolism, adherence to dietary and activity recommendations, prior medication history, and unknown factors. No guarantee of specific weight loss or body composition change was made. Patient counseled that medication is a tool, not a solution, and that optimal results require concurrent lifestyle modification. Patient stated understanding and confirmed they are committed to the behavioral components of the program."

Follow-up expectations need to be documented with specificity. "Follow-up plan: patient to return in 4 weeks for initial response assessment and side effect review. Labs to be drawn at 12 weeks including CBC, CMP, TSH, fasting lipid panel, and HbA1c. Patient instructed on how to report side effects through patient portal. Patient given written injection instructions and emergency contact guidelines. Next follow-up appointment scheduled for [date]." This shows a structured monitoring plan. It shows the patient was not just handed a vial and forgotten. It shows ongoing medical supervision, which is the whole justification for your program existing in the first place.

Document the decision and next steps. Every consultation note must end with a clear decision statement. Not implied. Not buried in the middle of a paragraph. Explicit. Here are the decision categories you should use, and you should use the same language every time so your charting is consistent and recognizable as a standard process. "DECISION: Candidate - proceed with therapy." Used when the patient is medically appropriate, informed consent is complete, labs are current or ordered, and all prerequisites are met or scheduled. "DECISION: Candidate pending." Used when the patient appears appropriate but labs, PCP clearance, or other prerequisites are still needed. Document exactly what is pending and what triggers the move from pending to active. "DECISION: Not a candidate at this time." Used when the patient has a contraindication, unrealistic expectations, inability to afford therapy, or any other factor that makes peptide therapy inappropriate currently. Document why, what alternatives were discussed, and whether re-evaluation is possible in the future. "DECISION: Needs different approach." Used when peptide therapy is not the right fit but the patient may benefit from a different therapy, a different specialty referral, or a modified plan. Document what was recommended instead.

Each of these decisions gets a paragraph in your chart note explaining the rationale. "Patient is a candidate for semaglutide therapy pending CBC, CMP, and TSH results. Labs ordered today, results expected within one week. Patient instructed to schedule follow-up once labs are available; medication will not be prescribed until labs reviewed. No contraindications identified based on history and physical. PCP Dr. Smith aware of referral and supportive of evaluation. Patient understands and agrees to above plan." That is a complete decision statement. It tells anyone reading the chart exactly where things stand and why.

If the patient is declined, document why and what alternatives were offered. This is the hardest documentation to write because it feels like a rejection, and physicians do not like rejecting patients. But a declined patient who is handled well is a safer patient than a marginally appropriate patient who is accepted because the physician did not want to say no. And the documentation of a decline is what protects you when that patient goes to another provider, gets into trouble, and later claims you were negligent for not treating them. Your chart shows exactly why you declined, what you offered instead, and what the patient was told.

Here is what a good decline documentation looks like: "DECISION: Not a candidate at this time. Rationale: patient reports personal history of acute pancreatitis requiring hospitalization in 2021, etiology thought to be gallstone-related with subsequent cholecystectomy. Patient currently asymptomatic with normal lipase at last check 3 months ago. However, GLP-1 receptor agonists carry a boxed warning regarding pancreatitis and are contraindicated in patients with prior pancreatitis per manufacturer labeling. Discussed with patient that risk of recurrent pancreatitis, while not precisely quantified, is unacceptably high given their history and the availability of alternative weight management approaches. Discussed alternatives including: structured lifestyle program with registered dietitian referral, referral to bariatric surgery evaluation given BMI of 42 and failed prior medical management, and follow-up with PCP for discussion of orlistat or other non-GLP-1 options.

Patient initially disappointed but acknowledged understanding of risk rationale after detailed discussion. Agreed to bariatric surgery referral and dietitian consultation. PCP notified of evaluation and recommendations via secure message. Patient may be re-evaluated for peptide therapy if future guidelines or patient-specific risk factors change; patient instructed to contact office if questions arise."

That note is thorough, compassionate, clinically sound, and completely defensible. It shows the patient was not just turned away. They were evaluated, educated about their specific risk, offered alternatives, connected to appropriate resources, and invited to return if circumstances change. A board reviewer reads that and sees a physician who made a hard decision for the right reasons and handled the patient with respect. The patient may still be disappointed, but they cannot credibly claim they were ignored or dismissed.

Here is another decline scenario that comes up frequently: the patient with unrealistic expectations. "Patient states goal of losing 60 pounds in 3 months for destination wedding. Educated that safe, sustainable weight loss averages 1-2 pounds per week, that GLP-1 therapy typically produces 10-15% body weight reduction over 6-12 months in responders, and that 60 pounds in 3 months would require an unsafe rate of loss inconsistent with medical supervision. Patient expressed frustration, stated they are 'willing to do whatever it takes.' Reinforced that this practice does not prescribe for event-driven timelines or unsafe weight loss goals. Discussed that medication is a tool for metabolic health improvement, not a rapid cosmetic intervention. Offered referral to registered dietitian for pre-wedding nutrition planning and exercise physiologist for optimized training program. Patient declined alternatives and stated they will 'find someone who will help.' Documented that patient was informed of risks of seeking unsupervised rapid weight loss and encouraged to involve their PCP in any decision. Patient left without prescription." That note protects you beautifully. It shows you had a hard conversation, set appropriate boundaries, offered alternatives, and the patient chose to leave. Their subsequent decisions are their own.

One more scenario: the patient who cannot afford therapy. "Patient expresses strong interest in CJC-1295/ipamorelin program for reported goals of improved recovery, body composition, and energy. Medical history reviewed, no contraindications identified. However, during cost discussion, patient disclosed current financial hardship including recent job loss and high-deductible health plan with no coverage for peptide therapy. Monthly program cost of $XXX discussed; patient stated this would require borrowing money or using credit they cannot afford to carry. Discussed that financial stress is a known barrier to compliance and that starting therapy that cannot be sustained is medically inadvisable. Recommended patient focus on foundational interventions including sleep optimization, stress management, and nutrition, which do not require out-of-pocket medication costs. Offered to re-evaluate in 6 months if patient's financial situation improves. Patient expressed appreciation for honesty and agreed to follow up when circumstances change." That is compassionate boundary-setting. You did not shame the patient. You did not pressure them into debt. You gave them a realistic assessment and a pathway back when they are ready.

Let me also address a documentation practice that I see far too often: the generic template note."Consultation completed. Risks discussed. Consent signed. Patient candidate. Start semaglutide." I know why physicians use templates. They are efficient. They save time. But a template that does not get individualized is worse than no note at all, because it signals to a reviewer that the physician goes through the motions without actually thinking about the patient. If you use templates - and many of you do, which is fine - you must customize every field. Fill in the patient's specific goals, their specific history, their specific questions, their specific risk discussion, and their specific decision. A template with blanks filled in thoughtfully is a time-saver. A template with the same text copied and pasted for every patient is evidence of assembly-line medicine. The board can tell the difference.

The documentation should also capture the patient's affect and engagement during the consultation. "Patient appeared engaged, took notes, asked three specific questions about dosing schedule, side effect management, and interaction with current metformin. All questions answered to patient's stated satisfaction." Or: "Patient appeared distracted, interrupted risk discussion twice to ask about cost, did not ask clinical questions when invited. Counselled patient to take time to consider and to review provided written materials before making decision. Patient scheduled follow-up call in 48 hours." These observations create a fuller picture of the consultation. They show you were paying attention to more than just checkboxes. They also document patients who seem disengaged or focused only on speed, which is relevant if those patients later claim they did not understand what they were getting into.

Finally, the consultation documentation must include a clear statement that informed consent was obtained. Not just "consent signed." Something like: "Informed consent obtained after detailed discussion of therapy nature, regulatory status, expected benefits, risks, alternatives, costs, follow-up requirements, and patient responsibilities. Patient given opportunity to ask questions, all questions answered to patient's stated satisfaction. Patient given copy of signed consent form, written injection instructions, emergency contact guidelines, and patient portal access instructions. Patient verbalized understanding and voluntarily agreed to proceed." That is a complete consent statement. It links the consent form to the conversation. It shows the form was not just shoved across a desk for a signature.

Your consultation note is the foundation of everything that follows in that patient's care. A strong consultation note makes every subsequent note easier to write because the rationale is already established. A weak consultation note leaves you scrambling to justify decisions later, trying to reconstruct from memory what you thought six months ago. Write it thoroughly. Write it the same day as the consultation while the conversation is fresh. Write it for the skeptical board reviewer who will read it with the assumption that something went wrong. If your note holds up under that assumption, you have done your job.

DOCTOR'S DEFENSE FILE - The Consultation

The following checklist represents what a defensible consultation record should contain. Use it as a quality check for your own charting. If any of these elements are missing from a new patient consultation note, add them before the patient leaves your office.

- Patient goals documented in patient's own words or with specific paraphrasing. - Complete medical history reviewed including medications, allergies, surgeries, hospitalizations, and family history. - Current medication list reviewed for interactions and documented. -Contraindications assessed and documented - either none identified or specific contraindications addressed with rationale for proceeding or declining. - All relevant therapy options discussed including non-pharmacologic alternatives, conventional FDA-approved options, and the peptide option being considered. - Risk discussion documented in detail -common side effects, serious risks, unknowns, and patient-specific risk factors explained. -Costs disclosed in detail including program fees, medication costs, lab costs, and what is and is not included. - No guarantees explicitly stated and documented. - Follow-up plan explained and documented including frequency, what is monitored, and what triggers changes or discontinuation. - Boundaries set and documented - scope of practice, PCP relationship, access expectations, and patient responsibilities. - PCP involvement discussed and documented- either PCP is aware and supportive, PCP clearance obtained, or a specific reason documented why PCP involvement was not pursued. - Clear decision statement documented using consistent language: candidate, candidate pending, not a candidate, or needs different approach. - Decision rationale explained in detail. - Alternatives offered and documented if patient was declined or deferred. - Informed consent documented as a process, not just a signature - discussion described, questions invited and answered, patient understanding confirmed, voluntary agreement stated. - Patient affect and engagement noted. - Next steps documented with specific appointments, lab orders, or follow-up actions.

The consultation is where your relationship with the patient begins. It is where expectations are set, risks are understood, boundaries are established, and decisions are made. Do it thoroughly. Document it completely. The chart you write today is the shield that protects your license tomorrow. Treat it with the respect it deserves.

PART IV: THE PEPTIDES

Patient problems, peptide choices, complaints, and the practical realities of handling this work without losing your mind.

17 - Refunds, Complaints, and Keeping Patients Happy

BLUNT RULE: A furious patient costs more than the money you're fighting over. Win the practice, not the argument.

A furious patient costs more than the money you're fighting over

Let me tell you something I've learned watching doctors lose their practices over the past three decades. It was never the clinical mistake that sank them. It was the patient who felt disrespected, ignored, cheated, or dismissed. That patient - the angry one, the one who felt hustled - that's the patient who picks up the phone and calls the state medical board. That's the patient who leaves the one-star review that never goes away. That's the patient who tells their sister, their coworker, their gym buddy, and their Facebook group never to go near your office. And here's the part that ought to keep you up at night: that patient probably started out believing in you. They walked through your door hoping you could help them. They paid cash- real money, out of their own pocket - because they trusted you more than the insurance-mills they'd been to before. And somewhere along the way, something went sideways. Maybe it was a misunderstanding about cost. Maybe it was a side effect they weren't prepared for. Maybe it was a staff member who was short with them on the phone. Maybe it was a refund request that got handled like a legal dispute instead of a human conversation. Whatever it was, that patient went from advocate to enemy. And enemies do damage that no amount of good clinical work can undo.

You think I'm being dramatic? I've sat in board hearings where the doctor's clinical care was impeccable. Labs ordered appropriately. Dosing conservative. Informed consent signed. Follow-up scheduled. The chart looked beautiful. But the patient told the board they were treated like a "cash transaction." They said the staff was rude. They said their refund request was ignored for three weeks. They said nobody called them back when they had a reaction. And you know what? The board listened. Because boards are made of humans, and humans believe stories. The story of the greedy peptide doctor who takes the money and runs - that's a story regulators are primed to believe. You're prescribing therapies the mainstream medical world side-eyes. You're taking cash outside the insurance system. You're working with compounded products the FDA would rather not think about. You are already operating in territory where the benefit of the doubt does not live. So when a patient complains, you don't get the presumption of good faith that the hospital-based internist gets. You get suspicion. You get scrutiny. You get investigated. And every hour you spend responding to a board inquiry, every dollar you spend on legal counsel, every night you spend staring at the ceiling wondering if your license is safe - all of that costs more than whatever refund the patient was asking for in the first place.

Let me put some rough numbers on this so you understand what we're really talking about. Say a patient paid $2,400 for a three-month peptide protocol. Two months in, they're not happy. Maybe they didn't lose the weight they expected. Maybe they had a reaction. Maybe their marriage is falling apart and they're looking for someone to blame. They call and ask for a refund of the final month - eight hundred dollars. Your staff says no, that's not the policy. The patient gets angry. They dispute the charge with their credit card company. Now you've got a chargeback on your hands. The merchant processor freezes a portion of your account.

You've got to spend two hours gathering documentation to fight the chargeback. Maybe you win, maybe you don't. But even if you win the chargeback, the patient is now posting on Reddit, on Facebook groups, on every forum they can find. They're telling anyone who will listen that Dr. So-and-So refused to stand behind their product. Other patients see it. Potential patients see it. Your reputation takes a hit that no amount of advertising dollars can repair. Meanwhile, you've spent staff time, your own time, and emotional energy fighting over eight hundred dollars. Was it worth it?

Here's the math that matters. In a well-run cash-pay practice, a single satisfied patient who refers friends might be worth ten, twenty, thirty thousand dollars in lifetime value. Not just their own ongoing care, but the patients they bring in. The friend from their CrossFit box. The cousin who saw their transformation. The coworker who asked what they've been doing differently. In a referral-driven practice, one happy patient is a marketing engine that works for free. But one furious patient is a demolition crew that works for free too. And the demolition crew works faster. One detailed negative review on the right forum can chase away five potential patients you never even knew were considering you. One board complaint - even one that gets dismissed - triggers a paper trail that follows you forever. Every license renewal, every credentialing application, every hospital privilege request, that complaint shows up and you get to explain it. Again and again. All because you wouldn't refund eight hundred dollars to someone who was genuinely unhappy.

Factor in chargebacks, bad reviews, staff time, complaints, and lost referrals

Let me walk you through what really happens when you fight with a patient over money, because most doctors don't think past the first move. They think: "If I give this refund, every patient will ask for one." They think: "I provided the service, I deserve to be paid." They think:"A refund is an admission that I did something wrong." Every one of those thoughts is understandable. Every one of them is wrong if it leads you into a war with a patient who has nothing to lose and you have everything to lose.

The chargeback is where it starts. When a patient disputes a credit card charge, the money gets pulled back from your account immediately. Your merchant processor - the company that handles your credit card transactions - now sees you as a risk. Too many chargebacks and your processing rate goes up. Your reserve requirements go up. In extreme cases, they drop you entirely. Good luck running a cash-pay practice when you can't take credit cards. And here's the thing about fighting chargebacks: you usually lose. The credit card companies are not on your side. They are on the cardholder's side. The burden of proof is on you, the merchant, to demonstrate that the charge was legitimate and that the patient received exactly what they paid for. In a peptide practice, that's a hard case to make. The patient says they didn't get results. They say they weren't told about the risks. They say the product caused side effects. The credit card company hears "I paid thousands for experimental drugs and got sick"and they reflexively side with the consumer. Even if you win the dispute and keep the money, the chargeback still counts against your merchant account. It still affects your risk rating. It still exists in the system as a black mark.

Then come the bad reviews. In peptide medicine, your reputation lives online. Patients find you through Google, through social media, through word-of-mouth forums. They check reviews before they call. They check reviews before they pay. A single one-star review with a detailed story - "Dr. X took $3,000, made me sick, and wouldn't even return my calls" - sits at the top of your search results like a dead skunk on a porch. You can't remove it. You can respond, but every response draws more attention to the complaint. The patient reads your careful, professional response and adds three more comments with additional grievances. Other patients pile on. I've seen practices where one detailed negative review spawned six more from other dissatisfied patients who saw that someone else had spoken up. It's like opening a pressure valve - once one person complains publicly, others feel permission to do the same. And potential patients reading these reviews don't know the full story. They don't know that the complaining patient refused follow-up labs, skipped their check-in calls, and mixed your peptides with who-knows-what they bought online. They just see a pattern of unhappy patients and they move on to the next doctor.

Staff time is the hidden cost that practice owners always underestimate. Your front desk person - who should be scheduling new patients, confirming appointments, and making your practice run smoothly - is now spending hours on the phone with an angry patient. Then with the patient's spouse. Then with the credit card company. Then drafting response letters. Then pulling chart records. Then consulting with you about what to do. Every hour your staff spends managing a dispute is an hour they're not generating revenue, not supporting other patients, not making your practice better. Multiply that by a few disputes a month and you've got the equivalent of a part-time employee whose entire job is cleaning up messes that a well-handled refund would have prevented.

Then there's the formal complaint - the one to the state medical board, or the attorney general's consumer protection division, or both. A patient who feels financially wronged will look for every lever of power they can pull. The board complaint is devastating even when it's baseless. You get a letter in the mail - certified, so you know it's serious - asking you to respond to allegations of unprofessional conduct, false advertising, or inappropriate prescribing. Now you need a lawyer. A good healthcare lawyer costs four to six hundred dollars an hour. The initial response alone might cost you five thousand dollars. If the board decides to investigate further, you're looking at tens of thousands. I've known doctors who spent thirty, forty, fifty thousand dollars defending against a board complaint that was ultimately dismissed. All because they wouldn't give back a thousand dollars to a patient who asked nicely before they got angry enough to escalate. The patient didn't get their money, but neither did the doctor - the lawyers got it all.

And finally, lost referrals - the cost that never shows up on a spreadsheet because you never see the patients who don't call. In a referral-driven practice, your new patient pipeline is your existing patients talking about you. When one of those patients is furious, they don't just stop referring - they actively warn people away. "Don't go to Dr. X. They'll take your money and good luck getting help when something goes wrong." That message travels through social circles, through gym communities, through online forums. Every potential patient who reads that message and chooses someone else is money you'll never see. Not just the initial consultation fee - the ongoing care, the refills, the protocol adjustments, the years of loyal patient relationship. In a peptide practice where patients stay for years when they're happy, losing one referrer might cost you fifty or a hundred thousand dollars over time. All because you stood on principle over a refund that amounted to pocket change in comparison.

You can win the refund argument and still lose the referral stream

This is the part that stubborn doctors never seem to understand. You can be right. You can be completely, legally, morally, clinically right - and still lose everything that matters. You can win the argument in your own mind, win it with your staff, win it with your lawyer, and lose it where it counts: in the minds of patients, potential patients, and the community that determines whether your practice thrives or struggles.

Let me give you a scenario I've seen play out more than once. A patient starts a peptide protocol for weight loss. The informed consent was thorough. The dosing was conservative. The labs were appropriate. The follow-up was scheduled. But the patient didn't lose as much weight as they hoped. They expected twenty pounds in three months and lost eight. Now they want a partial refund. They paid $3,600 and they want $1,200 back because, in their view, the treatment didn't work. Your staff points to the consent form where the patient acknowledged that results vary and no guarantees were made. You review the chart and confirm everything was done properly. You deny the refund. You're right. The consent form is clear. The care was appropriate. You have no obligation to refund. The patient gets angry. They leave a one-star review. They file a chargeback. They post in three Facebook groups about their experience. They tell everyone at their gym. Over the next six months, three people who were referred by that patient's friend choose a different practice instead. You never know about those lost patients. You just notice that referrals from that social circle dried up. You won the refund argument. You kept the $1,200. And you lost maybe $15,000 in future revenue from patients who never walked through your door because they heard a story about the doctor who wouldn't stand behind their work.

Here's what separates smart practice owners from stubborn ones. The smart ones understand that a refund is a marketing expense. When you give a refund to an unhappy patient - even a patient who's being unreasonable, even a patient whose expectations were unrealistic, even a patient who signed a consent form acknowledging exactly what happened - you're not admitting fault. You're buying peace. You're buying silence. You're buying the absence of a board complaint, the absence of a bad review, the absence of a warning to every potential patient that this doctor fights with patients over money. That purchase is almost always a bargain compared to the alternative.

Now, I'm not saying you refund every request from every patient who asks. We'll get into the strategy shortly. What I'm saying is that your reflex - your gut instinct - when a patient is unhappy and asking for their money back should not be "how do I say no?" It should be"what's the cost of saying yes versus the cost of saying no?" And when you run that calculation honestly, factoring in every downstream cost of a fight, the answer is almost always: give the refund, document it as a business decision, and move on with your life.

Sometimes the business decision and the legal decision are the same: keep them satisfied

There's a false dichotomy that doctors get stuck in. They think there's a tension between"doing what's right for the business" and "doing what's legally defensible." They think that giving a refund weakens their legal position, that it signals guilt, that it creates a precedent. Let me disabuse you of this notion. A goodwill refund - a refund given because it's cheaper than fighting, because it preserves the relationship, because it prevents a complaint - is not a legal admission of anything. It's a business decision. And business decisions are not evidence of malpractice. They're evidence that you're running a practice like a professional who understands that patient satisfaction is part of the equation.

The law understands this distinction. If a refund were an admission of fault, every department store that takes back a sweater would be admitting the sweater was defective. Every restaurant that comps a meal would be admitting the food was poisonous. That's not how refunds work. A refund is a settlement of a customer satisfaction issue. It has nothing to do with clinical quality unless you explicitly connect the two. And you never should. When you document a refund -and you will document it, because we document everything - the note says something like:"Patient expressed dissatisfaction with results. Goodwill credit issued per practice policy. No clinical concerns identified. Care provided in accordance with standards." That's it. You acknowledged the dissatisfaction. You resolved it with a credit. You noted that there were no clinical concerns. That's not an admission of fault. That's a record of sound business judgment.

The beautiful thing about operating a cash-pay practice outside the insurance system is that you have flexibility the institutional doctors don't have. A hospital clinic can't refund a copay because seventeen administrators would need to approve it and the patient would get a check in six months from the finance department. You can make a decision in thirty seconds. You can issue a credit today. You can turn an angry patient into a neutral one, or even a grateful one, with a single phone call and a few keystrokes. That flexibility is a massive competitive advantage - but only if you use it. If you take that flexibility and use it to be rigid and bureaucratic, you've turned your biggest asset into a liability. You're acting like an institution without any of the institutional protections. That's a losing strategy.

Let me be clear about something else. When I say "keep them satisfied," I don't mean "give every patient everything they want no matter how unreasonable." Some patients are genuinely unreasonable. Some patients want things no ethical doctor can provide. Some patients are looking for a fight and will escalate no matter what you do. We'll talk about those patients later. What I'm talking about here are the ordinary disputes - the patient who genuinely feels wronged, whose expectations weren't met, who experienced something they didn't expect, who feels like they paid premium prices and didn't get premium service. Those patients are not your enemy. They're your warning system. They're telling you something about your practice that you need to hear. Maybe your informed consent needs to be clearer about realistic outcomes. Maybe your follow-up process has a gap. Maybe your staff needs coaching on how to handle patient concerns. Every refund request is data. Smart practice owners collect that data and use it. Stubborn practice owners fight over the data and miss the lesson.

Have a written refund policy - clear, fair, and followed consistently

If you don't have a written refund policy, stop reading right now and write one. I'm serious. Before you see another patient, before you process another payment, before you have another conversation about money with anyone, you need a policy written down, reviewed by your lawyer, included in your patient paperwork, and posted where patients can see it. Not because the policy is there to prevent refunds - it's not. The policy is there so that everyone knows the rules. Your patients know the rules. Your staff knows the rules. And most importantly, you know the rules, which means when you make an exception - and you will make exceptions- you're doing it consciously and deliberately rather than haphazardly.

A good refund policy for a peptide practice has a few core elements. First, it states clearly that fees for clinical services - consultations, evaluations, lab reviews, time with the physician -are not refundable once the service is rendered. That should be obvious, but state it anyway. You're paying for the doctor's time and expertise, not for a guaranteed outcome. Second, it addresses product-related costs separately. If you dispense peptides directly or if patients pay for medication through your arrangement with a pharmacy, the policy should state the conditions under which product costs may or may not be refunded. Third, it addresses unused medication. If a patient has unopened, properly stored vials that are still within dating, will you take them back? Most practices won't, for safety and regulatory reasons, and your policy should say so. Fourth, it gives a timeframe. Refund requests must be made within a certain window - thirty days, sixty days, whatever makes sense for your practice. Fifth, it states the mechanism - who to contact, what information to provide, how the decision will be made, and how long it will take.

Here's a sample framework, not a legal document - have your lawyer review whatever you use:

Notice what's in that policy and what's not. What's in it: clarity about what's refundable and what's not. A process for requesting consideration. A timeline for response. An acknowledgment that outcomes aren't guaranteed. What's not in it: any language that sounds like you routinely refund medication costs. Any language that creates an expectation of refund. Any language that admits fault or suggests your products are risky. It's balanced. It's clear. It protects you while leaving room for the judgment calls that every practice has to make.

Now here's the part that most doctors miss: the policy has to be in the patient's hands before they pay. Not after they complain. Not in the fine print they sign on the way out. Before they hand over their credit card, they need to have seen and acknowledged the refund policy. This isn't just good business - it's consumer protection law in many states. If you take someone's money and only disclose the no-refund policy after they're unhappy, regulators and credit card companies will side with the patient every time. The policy needs to be part of your informed consent packet, part of your financial agreement, discussed by your staff as part of the new patient onboarding. "Just so you know, Dr. Smith's consultation fee covers the evaluation and personalized protocol. Medication costs are separate. We have a policy about credits and refunds that I'd like to walk you through." That sixty seconds of conversation prevents sixty hours of dispute later.

But having a policy isn't enough. Following it consistently is what matters. If your policy says consultation fees are non-refundable, you can't refund one patient's consultation because they're a friend of your nurse while telling the next patient that the policy is ironclad. Inconsistent application of your own policy is evidence of arbitrariness, and arbitrariness is what gets you in trouble with boards and consumer protection agencies. Every exception you make - and again, you'll make exceptions - needs to be documented with the rationale."Goodwill credit issued per practice policy, Section 4, discretion clause." That note goes in the business record, separate from the clinical chart. The patient gets the credit. The chart stays clean. And if anyone ever asks why this patient got a credit when the policy says fees are non-refundable, you have a written rationale.

Make exceptions quietly when judgment calls for it - that's running a practice

Let me tell you about Dr. K. I've changed the details to protect him, but the story is real. Dr. K ran a beautiful peptide practice in the Southwest. Excellent clinician. Meticulous documentation. Conservative dosing. Everything by the book. A patient came in - let's call her Margaret - a sixty-two-year-old woman with metabolic syndrome, prediabetes, and thirty pounds she couldn't lose. Dr. K put her on a GLP-1 protocol with supporting peptides. The informed consent was perfect. The labs were appropriate. Margaret paid $2,800 for the three-month protocol. Six weeks in, Margaret's husband was diagnosed with terminal cancer. She stopped everything - the peptides, the diet, the exercise - to care for him. She missed her follow-up. She called two months later, frazzled, grieving, and asked if she could get a credit for the medication she hadn't used. Dr. K's policy was clear: medication costs are non-refundable once dispensed. Margaret had opened the vials. She'd injected some of the medication. By the letter of the policy, there was no refund due.

Dr. K gave her a full credit anyway. Not because he had to. Not because Margaret threatened anything. Because it was the right thing to do, and because Dr. K understood something that took me years to learn: running a medical practice is not the same as enforcing a contract. A practice is a long-term relationship business. Margaret wasn't trying to take advantage. She was a patient whose life had fallen apart. The credit cost Dr. K maybe four hundred dollars in product cost. What did he gain? Margaret came back eight months later, after her husband passed, ready to restart her protocol. She stayed with him for three years. She referred four friends. One of those friends referred two more. That single four-hundred-dollar credit generated probably forty thousand dollars in lifetime patient value. And even if it hadn't -even if Margaret never came back - Dr. K still made the right call, because protecting his humanity is part of protecting his license. A doctor who treats patients like line items on a spreadsheet is a doctor who eventually makes decisions that attract board attention.

The key word in that story is quietly. Dr. K didn't announce to his staff that he was ignoring policy. He didn't put in the chart "exception made due to patient's personal circumstances." He documented a business decision: "Goodwill account credit issued." The clinical chart remained untouched. The refund was handled administratively, not clinically. Margaret felt cared for. The record stayed clean. That's how you make exceptions - with compassion, with discretion, and with separation between the business decision and the clinical record.

Now, let me be clear about the flip side. Making exceptions quietly does not mean making exceptions constantly. If you're issuing goodwill credits to every patient who asks, your policy is meaningless and your practice has a problem. Either your clinical outcomes aren't matching expectations, your informed consent isn't preparing patients adequately, your pricing is creating resentment, or you're attracting patients who aren't a good fit for cash-pay medicine. Exceptions should be rare - maybe one in twenty refund requests, maybe fewer. They should be made by you or a senior manager, not by front-line staff who want to make a problem go away. They should always be documented. And they should never, ever be connected to clinical documentation. The chart says what the chart says. The business record says what the business record says. The two do not meet.

Here's another scenario where the quiet exception makes sense. A patient has a genuine adverse reaction - nausea, injection site reaction, something real and documented. They call upset. They don't want to continue therapy. Your policy says medication costs are non-refundable once opened. But this patient didn't get what they paid for. They paid for a therapeutic benefit and got a side effect instead. Giving them a partial credit isn't weakness. It's acknowledging reality. It's saying, "You trusted us with your health and your money, and this didn't work out the way either of us hoped." That's not an admission of clinical fault. The side effect might be well-documented in the literature, disclosed in the consent, and not anyone's fault. But it's still not what the patient wanted when they wrote that check. A partial credit preserves the relationship, demonstrates good faith, and makes it very hard for that patient to later claim you didn't care about their experience.

The patients you make exceptions for remember it. They remember that when things went sideways, you did the right thing. And the patients you refuse - they remember that too. They remember that when they were struggling, you hid behind a policy. They remember that your staff treated them like a delinquent account instead of a human being. They remember that you took their money and disappeared when they needed support. Which memory do you want patients carrying out of your practice?

Do not admit fault casually - refund decisions are business, not admissions

This is the part where I have to shift from the warm and fuzzy to the cold and practical. Because as much as I believe in taking care of patients and being generous with credits, I also believe in protecting your license, and nothing jeopardizes a license faster than a casual admission of fault that gets documented and later used against you.

When you issue a refund - whether it's a routine policy refund, a goodwill exception, or a response to a genuine problem - the language you use matters enormously. What you say to the patient. What you write in the administrative record. What your staff says in emails. Every word is a potential exhibit. And if you're the kind of person who apologizes reflexively, who says "I'm sorry this happened" as a figure of speech, who writes "we made a mistake" in an email without thinking about what that means - you are creating evidence that may be used against you someday.

Let me be very specific about what I mean. If a patient has an adverse reaction to a peptide and you write in an email, "I'm sorry our medication caused this problem," you have just admitted causation. You have just accepted responsibility for an adverse event. That email can be subpoenaed. It can be shown to a board. It can be used to support a malpractice claim. Even if your clinical care was perfect, even if the reaction was a known risk disclosed in the consent, even if no malpractice occurred - your own words now create a problem that your lawyer has to explain away. "Your honor, my client didn't mean it literally when he said his medication caused the problem." Good luck with that.

The right language is deliberate and careful. "I'm sorry you're experiencing this." That's empathy. That's human. That's not an admission of anything. "I understand this is frustrating and not what you expected." That's acknowledgment. That's good communication. "Let's make sure you're safe and discuss how we move forward." That's clinical judgment. "I'm issuing a credit to your account as a goodwill gesture." That's business. None of those sentences admits fault. None of them creates liability. All of them demonstrate that you're a doctor who cares about your patient's experience while also protecting yourself.

Your staff needs to be trained on this. Every person who answers your phone, every person who responds to emails, every person who talks to patients about concerns needs to understand that refund language and clinical language are separate languages. Staff should never, ever say things like "the medication caused your problem" or "the doctor shouldn't have prescribed that" or "we made an error." Those are clinical determinations that only the physician makes, and even the physician should make them carefully, in the chart, with appropriate context. What staff can say: "I'm sorry this has been difficult for you. Let me get Dr. Smith involved right away." What staff can write: "Patient reports concern. Escalated to clinician for review." That's it. The concern gets documented. The clinician reviews it. The response - whether clinical or financial or both - comes from the physician with appropriate thought and documentation.

I know this sounds paranoid. I know it sounds like I'm telling you not to be human with your patients. I'm not. I'm telling you to be human in ways that don't create legal problems. You can express enormous empathy, enormous compassion, enormous generosity - all without ever saying "it's our fault." Because here's the truth: most of the time, it's not your fault. The patient had a known side effect. The patient didn't follow instructions. The patient's expectations were unrealistic. The patient's life circumstances changed. None of that is your fault. And you don't need to pretend it is in order to be kind and generous. You can say, "This didn't work out the way we hoped, and I want to make sure you're treated fairly." That's generous. That's kind. That's not an admission of anything.

The documentation of the refund decision needs to follow the same principle. In the business record - not the clinical chart - the note says: "Patient expressed dissatisfaction. Goodwill credit issued per practice discretion policy. No clinical deficiency identified." That's the template. Every time. Variation creates inconsistency, and inconsistency creates vulnerability. If one refund note says "patient unhappy, credit given" and another says "medication caused adverse reaction, full refund issued," a lawyer or board reviewer will notice the difference. The second note sounds like an admission. Don't write it that way. All refunds are goodwill decisions. All refunds are business decisions. All refunds are separate from clinical care. That's your framework. Stick to it.

Document every refund decision separately from clinical care

I want to hammer this point home because I've seen too many doctors blur the lines between clinical documentation and business decisions, and it always causes problems. The clinical chart is the medical record. It contains the history, physical, labs, diagnoses, prescriptions, informed consent, follow-up notes, and all clinical communication. The business record is the administrative file. It contains payment records, refund decisions, credit notes, and non-clinical correspondence. These two records live in separate worlds, and they should never be confused.

When you issue a refund, the note goes in the business record. Period. Not in the clinical chart. Not as an addendum to your last progress note. Not in the patient's medical record at all. The clinical chart should reflect the clinical reality: what was prescribed, what the patient reported, what you recommended, what the plan is. If the refund is related to a clinical event - say, a side effect that led the patient to discontinue - the clinical chart documents the clinical event appropriately. "Patient reported nausea after second injection. Advised to discontinue. Alternative protocol discussed." That's the clinical note. The business record gets a separate note: "Patient discontinued due to intolerance. Partial credit issued per policy." Two separate records. Two separate purposes. Two separate locations.

Why does this matter? Because when a board complaint or malpractice claim comes in, the first thing your lawyer does is review the clinical chart. Your lawyer wants a clean, coherent, clinically sound story. If the clinical chart is cluttered with refund discussions, credit decisions, and administrative notes, that story gets muddied. Worse, if the refund note contains language that sounds like an admission of fault - and it will, if you weren't careful - your lawyer now has to explain why the doctor's own chart includes self-incriminating language. A clean chart is a defensible chart. A chart mixed with business decisions is a liability.

Conversely, when a consumer protection inquiry or credit card dispute comes in, they look at the business record. They want to see payment history, refund policy, refund decisions, and the rationale. If your business record is clean and consistent - "Goodwill credit, policy Section 4, discretion clause" - you have a defensible position. If your business record contains clinical details, medical reasoning, or patient health information that the business office shouldn't have access to, you've created a HIPAA problem on top of everything else. Separate records. Separate access. Separate purposes.

Train your staff on this relentlessly. The clinical team accesses the clinical chart. The administrative team accesses the business record. When a refund request comes in, the administrative staff flags it for the physician's review. The physician reviews the clinical chart if needed, makes a decision, and communicates it to administrative staff. The administrative staff documents the decision in the business record. The clinical chart may get a note about the clinical aspects - "patient reports ongoing concern with [symptom], follow-up scheduled" - but the financial decision itself is administrative, not clinical. This sounds like overkill until the first time a lawyer asks for both records and you realize how much cleaner your position is when they're separated.

Here's a practical tip: use different systems if you can. Your EHR for clinical records. Your practice management system for business records. If they're in the same system, use clearly separated sections with different access permissions. When in doubt, ask yourself: "If a board reviewer read this note, would they see sound clinical judgment, or would they see a doctor arguing about money with a patient?" If it's the latter, that note is in the wrong place. Move it to the business record. Keep the clinical chart sacred. It's the story of your medical care, and it should be nothing but that.

Handle complaints calmly - do not argue every dispute to the death

If there's one personality trait that will destroy a peptide practice faster than bad medicine, it's the doctor who has to win every argument. The doctor who can't let a patient complaint go. The doctor who takes every criticism personally, who sees every refund request as a challenge to their integrity, who would rather spend ten thousand dollars on legal fees than give back five hundred dollars to a patient they believe is wrong. I've watched these doctors destroy themselves. They're usually smart. Usually excellent clinicians. Usually well-intentioned. And they always, always lose in the end because they cannot accept that being right is sometimes less important than being wise.

Let me be blunt about what a complaint actually is. A complaint is a patient saying, "This isn't what I expected, and I'm unhappy about it." That's it. It's not necessarily an accusation of malpractice. It's not necessarily a threat to your license. It's not necessarily a prelude to a board complaint, a lawsuit, or a bad review. It's a person who paid you money and feels like they didn't get what they bargained for. Your response to that complaint - your tone, your speed, your willingness to listen, your emotional posture - determines which path the complaint takes. A complaint that gets handled well disappears. A complaint that gets handled badly metastasizes.

The first principle of complaint handling is speed. The faster you respond to a complaint, the less damage it does. A patient who calls on Monday and gets a return call from the physician on Monday afternoon feels heard. That same patient who calls on Monday and gets no response until Thursday feels ignored. By Thursday, they've told their spouse, their friends, and possibly an online community about their experience. They've had three days to marinate in their frustration. They've mentally escalated from "I have a concern" to "this practice doesn't care about patients." Speed is your friend. Not speed in making decisions - you should never rush a clinical decision - but speed in acknowledging the complaint and getting the right person involved.

The second principle is elevation. Front-line staff should never be arguing with patients about clinical care, about refunds, or about the quality of their experience. When a patient expresses dissatisfaction, the staff member's job is to listen, acknowledge, and escalate. "I'm sorry you're frustrated, Mrs. Chen. I want to make sure Dr. Rodriguez hears about this directly. Can I have him call you this afternoon?" That's the script. It's not the staff member's job to defend the practice, to explain the doctor's decisions, or to negotiate over the phone. Those are physician-level conversations. When you let your staff argue with patients - even friendly, well-meaning argument - you put unlicensed people in the position of defending clinical decisions they didn't make. That's a scope-of-practice violation waiting to happen, and it's also terrible customer service.

The third principle is presence. When you call a complaining patient back, you are not a harried doctor squeezing in a difficult conversation between two other appointments. You are a physician taking seriously the concerns of someone who trusted you with their health and their money. Give the conversation your full attention. Close your office door. Sit down. Listen without interrupting for at least the first two minutes. Let the patient say everything they need to say. Don't defend. Don't explain. Don't justify. Just listen. Most patients - not all, but most- will de-escalate dramatically if they feel genuinely heard. The anger often isn't about the money or the outcome. It's about feeling dismissed. Give them the opposite of dismissal.

Give them your full, undivided, unhurried attention for ten minutes. It costs you nothing and pays enormous dividends.

After you've listened, you move to resolution. This is where you offer a path forward. Not necessarily a refund - we'll get to that - but a plan. "Mrs. Chen, I hear what you're saying. You expected more significant results by now, and you're concerned about the side effects. Here's what I'd like to do. First, I want to see you in the office this week so we can review your labs and adjust your protocol. Second, I'm going to have my nurse walk you through the injection technique to make sure we're doing everything right. Third, I understand that the past month has been frustrating, and I want to make sure you feel this practice is supporting you. Let me review your account and see what adjustments make sense." Notice what just happened. You acknowledged the concern. You offered concrete clinical steps. You demonstrated ongoing commitment. And you opened the door to a financial resolution without committing to one on the spot. That's professional. That's calm. That's how you turn a complainer back into a patient.

Now, some patients cannot be satisfied. Some patients are angry about things you cannot fix. Some patients are projecting life problems onto their medical care. Some patients are simply unreasonable - the kind of person who would complain about a free massage. You cannot let these patients consume your practice. But here's the thing: you don't know which patient is which until you listen. The patient who sounds unreasonable in the first thirty seconds might have a legitimate concern buried under their frustration. The patient who starts polite might be building a meticulous legal case against you. You can't tell from the initial tone. You have to engage, listen, and then make a judgment about what kind of patient you're dealing with. Only after that assessment do you decide whether resolution is possible or whether you need to protect the practice by disengaging carefully and documenting thoroughly.

A patient who feels heard refers; a patient who feels hustled complains to the board

This distinction - heard versus hustled - is the single most important concept in this entire chapter. Write it on a sticky note and put it on your monitor. A patient who feels heard walks away from a negative experience still respecting you. They might not get the outcome they wanted, but they got your attention, your empathy, and your best effort. That patient will often stay with your practice. They'll often tell their friends, "I had some issues but Dr. Smith really worked with me to figure it out." They're an advocate, even if the medicine didn't work perfectly. A patient who feels hustled - rushed, dismissed, treated like a revenue source, nickel-and-dimed, ignored when things went wrong - that patient becomes a weapon aimed at your license.

The difference between heard and hustled rarely comes down to clinical outcomes. It comes down to how the patient felt they were treated when things weren't going well. Every doctor has patients who don't respond to therapy. Every doctor has patients with side effects. Every doctor has patients whose expectations were unrealistic. The doctors who survive and thrive are the ones who handle those situations with grace, patience, and generosity. The doctors who end up in board hearings are the ones who handled them with defensiveness, dismissal, and a refusal to engage.

Let me give you a concrete example. Patient A and Patient B both start the same peptide protocol for similar reasons. Both pay $3,000. Both have suboptimal results after two months.

Patient A calls the office, expresses concern, and gets a return call from the physician within twenty-four hours. The physician listens for fifteen minutes. Acknowledges the frustration. Reviews the chart. Adjusts the protocol. Offers a partial credit toward the next cycle as a goodwill gesture. Patient A doesn't get the result she wanted, but she feels cared for. She stays with the practice. She tells her friend, "The first round didn't work great, but Dr. Smith is really attentive and we're trying something different." Patient B calls the office, leaves a message, and gets a call back three days later from a staff member who says, "Dr. Johnson reviewed your chart and the protocol was appropriate. You signed a consent form saying results vary. There's really nothing else we can do." Patient B feels dismissed. She hangs up furious. She leaves a one-star review. She files a chargeback. She posts in an online forum. She calls the state medical board and alleges that Dr. Johnson "takes thousands of dollars and doesn't care if it works." Both doctors provided clinically appropriate care. One patient felt heard. The other felt hustled. Only one of these stories ends with a board complaint.

The feeling of being heard is created through specific, concrete behaviors. Timely response -not hours, not days, but prompt acknowledgment. Undivided attention - not a call while you're driving, not a conversation while checking your email, but focused presence. Empathetic language - "I understand how frustrating this must be" rather than "The consent form you signed clearly states." Concrete action - specific next steps, specific follow-up, specific timeline rather than vague assurances. Generosity where possible - a credit, an extra visit at no charge, a protocol adjustment that shows you're invested in their success even when it's not generating new revenue. These behaviors are not weakness. They are not indulgence. They are the operational practices of a successful cash-pay medical practice that depends on patient satisfaction for its survival.

The feeling of being hustled, conversely, comes from its own set of behaviors. Slow or nonexistent response to concerns. Delegation to staff who can't address clinical questions and sound like they're reading from a script. Hiding behind forms - "you signed the consent" used as a shield against conversation. No flexibility - every request met with a policy citation instead of a human response. Upselling in the moment of dissatisfaction -"the reason you're not seeing results is you didn't add the premium support package." Nothing creates the feeling of being hustled faster than a patient who feels like their concern is being used as a sales opportunity. When a patient is unhappy, the last thing they want to hear is that the solution requires them to spend more money. That may be clinically true - maybe they do need additional testing or a different protocol - but the timing and framing matter enormously. First, listen. First, acknowledge. First, demonstrate that you care about their experience independent of their wallet. Then, if appropriate, discuss next steps that may involve cost.

The board complaint that comes from a hustled patient follows a predictable pattern. The patient describes paying significant cash for therapy. They describe experiencing a problem -side effects, lack of results, confusion. They describe calling the office and getting nowhere. They describe feeling dismissed, ignored, or treated like a number. They allege that the doctor was more interested in payment than in their wellbeing. The board reads this and sees a narrative they recognize: the greedy cash-pay doctor who exploits patients desperate for help. Is it fair? Often, no. The doctor may have provided excellent care. But the patient's perception is what drives the complaint, and the patient's perception is formed by how they were treated when they had a concern. You cannot control whether a patient has a side effect. You can absolutely control whether that patient feels heard when they report it.

Do not let angry patients become preventable board complaints

This subsection is about the practical mechanics of de-escalation. Most board complaints from patients are preventable. Not all - some patients are going to complain no matter what you do-but most. The preventable ones follow a trajectory that you can recognize and interrupt if you're paying attention. The trajectory looks like this: dissatisfaction → expression of concern→ inadequate response → escalation → formal complaint. Your goal is to catch it at stage two or three, before it gets to stage five.

Stage one: Dissatisfaction. The patient is unhappy but hasn't said anything yet. They're sitting at home, feeling frustrated, thinking about whether to call. Maybe they mentioned something briefly at their last visit and your response seemed dismissive. Maybe they had a side effect and didn't know if it was normal. This stage is invisible to you unless you have systems in place to detect it. Those systems are simple: follow-up calls after starting therapy, check-in emails or texts, surveys after visits. "Hi Mrs. Garcia, it's been two weeks since you started your protocol. How are you feeling? Any questions or concerns?" That simple outreach-automated, low-cost, routine - catches problems before they fester. A patient who gets a check-in call and mentions a concern gets immediate attention. A patient who never hears from you until their three-month follow-up has two months to stew in their dissatisfaction.

Stage two: Expression of concern. The patient calls or emails with a complaint or question. This is your make-or-break moment. The speed and quality of your response here determines everything that follows. If the patient gets a prompt, empathetic, physician-level response, the concern usually resolves. If they get voicemail, delays, staff deflection, or a dismissive tone, they move to stage three. Your practice needs protocols for this stage. Who screens complaints? Who escalates to the physician? What's the maximum response time? What language do staff use? These aren't suggestions - they're operational requirements. Train your staff. Role-play scenarios. Have scripts ready. The thirty seconds after a patient expresses dissatisfaction determines whether you have a minor issue or a major problem.

Stage three: Escalation. The patient didn't get satisfaction from their initial complaint, so they're getting louder. They're calling more frequently. They're copying their spouse on emails. They're mentioning lawyers or boards or reviews. This is where many doctors make their biggest mistake: they get defensive. They start treating the patient like an adversary. They slow down their responses, hoping the patient will go away. They consult their lawyer and let the lawyer's caution dictate their communication style, which now sounds stiff, legalistic, and hostile. This is exactly the wrong response. A patient at stage three is still reachable, but only if you engage with humanity and generosity. This is the stage where a physician call - personal, unhurried, empathetic - can still turn things around. "Mr. Thompson, I understand we've let you down in our communication. I want to hear everything, and I want to make this right." That sentence, delivered sincerely by the physician, prevents more board complaints than any legal strategy ever devised.

But let's be realistic. Some patients at stage three are past de-escalation. They've decided you're the enemy. They've already drafted their board complaint or posted their review. With these patients, your goal shifts from resolution to documentation. You engage carefully, professionally, and thoroughly document every interaction. You do not argue. You do not escalate emotionally. You offer reasonable resolution - a follow-up visit, a protocol review, a goodwill credit - and you document that you offered it. If the patient refuses reasonable resolution and continues escalating, your documentation now shows a practice that tried in good faith to address the concern. That documentation is your defense when the board complaint arrives.

Stage four: Formal complaint. The patient has filed a complaint with the board, left a public review, initiated a chargeback, or contacted a lawyer. At this stage, your lawyer is involved and your communication strategy changes. You do not contact the patient directly without legal guidance. You do not try to resolve the complaint informally if it could be construed as tampering or intimidation. You follow your lawyer's advice precisely. But here's what you can still do: you can review your documentation to make sure it's complete. You can review the chart to confirm your clinical care was sound. You can identify any gaps - any missing informed consent element, any undocumented phone call, any note that could be clearer - and address them going forward. Not by altering records, which is a felony, but by understanding where your documentation could have been stronger and making sure future charts are bulletproof.

The key insight about preventable complaints is that prevention happens at the front end, not the back end. By the time a patient is at stage four, you're in damage control. The real work of prevention happens in your daily operations: the follow-up calls, the responsive communication, the empathetic staff, the generous resolution of minor disputes. A practice that does the front-end work well rarely sees stage four. A practice that neglects the front-end work lives in a constant state of crisis management. Which practice do you want to run?

Use complaint patterns to improve your systems

Every complaint is data. Not just a problem to be managed, but information about your practice that you can use to get better. Smart practice owners track complaints - not just to handle them individually, but to identify patterns that reveal systemic problems. Because here's the truth: one complaint about a specific issue might be an outlier. Three complaints about the same issue is a pattern. And patterns tell you something is broken in your system.

Track your complaints formally. A simple spreadsheet will do. Date. Patient name. Nature of complaint. Department or process involved. Resolution. Time to resolution. Outcome. Review this spreadsheet monthly. Look for clusters. Are most complaints about communication delays? That's a staffing or workflow problem. Are most complaints about side effects that weren't adequately discussed? That's an informed consent problem. Are most complaints about cost surprises? That's a pricing transparency problem. Are most complaints about injection technique or delivery issues? That's a patient education problem. Each pattern points to a fixable system issue. And each system fix prevents future complaints.

Let me give you some examples of patterns I've seen and what they revealed. A practice I consulted for had four complaints in three months about patients not getting their medication on time. The pharmacy was slow. The shipping was inconsistent. Patients would pay and then wait a week or more for their vials. Each individual complaint was handled with an apology and a credit. But the pattern revealed a vendor problem. The practice switched to a more reliable pharmacy and the complaints stopped. Another practice noticed that multiple complaints came from patients three to four weeks into their first cycle, all expressing surprise about injection discomfort. The informed consent mentioned injection site reactions, but it didn't prepare patients for the reality of daily self-injection. The practice added a more detailed patient education session before starting therapy - including a demonstration with a practice injector - and those complaints dropped to zero. Pattern recognition turned individual problems into systematic improvements.

Sometimes the pattern reveals a people problem. If multiple patients complain about the same staff member's tone, responsiveness, or attitude, you have a training or personnel issue that needs addressing. Don't ignore it because the staff member is competent at their technical job. Patient-facing skills are non-negotiable in a cash-pay practice. One rude staff member can generate more board complaints than a year of mediocre clinical outcomes. Address it directly, train thoroughly, and if improvement doesn't happen, make a change. Your license is more important than any individual staff member's comfort.

Other times the pattern reveals a you problem - something in your own communication style, your approach to informed consent, your follow-up habits, that is generating patient dissatisfaction. This is harder to see and harder to hear, but it's the most valuable feedback you'll ever get. If multiple patients say you seem rushed, you seem rushed. If multiple patients say they didn't understand the cost structure, your cost explanation needs work. If multiple patients say they felt dismissed when they raised concerns, you need to examine your own defensive reflexes. The complaint pattern is a mirror. Look into it honestly.

Use your complaint data to drive quarterly reviews. Sit down with your key staff and review the complaint log. What's trending up? What's resolved? What systemic changes should we make? This isn't a blame session. It's a quality improvement process. The goal isn't to punish whoever handled a complaint poorly. The goal is to build a practice that generates fewer complaints because it operates better. Every complaint prevented is time you can spend on patient care instead of crisis management. Every complaint prevented is a board complaint that never gets filed. Every complaint prevented is a patient who stays satisfied and refers their friends. The return on investment for systematic complaint prevention is enormous.

A practice that gets most new patients from existing patients has earned trust

Let me tell you the most important business fact about a successful peptide practice: your best marketing is a happy patient telling their friend, "You have to go see my doctor." Not an Instagram ad. Not a Google search result. Not a billboard or a podcast sponsorship. A human being who trusted you with their health and their money, who got results and felt cared for, who voluntarily becomes your ambassador to everyone they know. That patient is worth more than any marketing budget. That patient is the foundation of a practice that doesn't just survive but thrives.

A referral culture is a practice environment where patient referrals are the primary source of new patients - not because you ask for them aggressively, but because patients want to give them. They want to share their experience. They want their friends to feel as good as they feel. They want to be the person who discovered the amazing doctor who finally helped them.

Referrals given freely, without prompting, are the highest form of trust a patient can show you. They're also the safest form of practice growth, because referred patients arrive with pre-established trust. They've heard the story. They know what to expect. They're not skeptical first-time callers scanning for red flags. They're warm leads who already believe you can help them.

Compare that to a practice that lives on cold marketing. Every new patient from an ad is a patient who doesn't know you, who found you through a search or a social media post, who is evaluating you with a skeptical eye from the first phone call. These patients are harder to convert, harder to satisfy, and harder to retain. They have no relationship capital. If something goes slightly wrong, they have no reason to give you the benefit of the doubt. They just leave and find the next doctor on their search results. A practice built on cold marketing has to keep spending money to keep the pipeline full. A practice built on referrals grows organically, sustainably, and profitably.

But referrals don't happen by accident. They happen because you create an experience so positive that patients can't help but talk about it. That experience has three components: clinical results, emotional connection, and operational excellence. Clinical results are obvious - the medicine has to work, or at least the patient has to perceive that it's working. You can't refer a friend to a doctor who didn't help you. Emotional connection is the feeling of being cared for, being heard, being treated like a human being rather than a chart number. Operational excellence is the smoothness of the entire experience - easy scheduling, responsive communication, clear pricing, no surprises, no hassles, no friction. All three components have to be present for the referral engine to run at full power. Two out of three gets you patients who stay but don't talk. One out of three gets you patients who leave. Zero out of three gets you a closed practice.

The trust that generates referrals is earned, not requested. I see doctors who put "We love referrals!" on their website and think that's a referral strategy. It's not. Patients don't refer because you asked them to. They refer because they had an experience worth sharing. Your job is to create that experience, consistently, with every patient, every visit, every phone call, every interaction. When you do that, the referrals happen naturally. When you don't, no amount of asking will make up for it. In fact, asking for referrals from patients who aren't fully satisfied is counterproductive - it feels pushy and transactional, which undermines the trust you're trying to build.

The math of a referral-driven practice is compelling. Let's say you have a hundred active patients. If each of those patients refers one new patient per year, you have a hundred new patients with zero marketing spend. At an average initial consultation fee of $500 and first-cycle protocol of $2,500, that's $300,000 in new patient revenue generated by word of mouth. Now let's say your retention rate is strong - eighty percent of patients stay year over year -so you're also maintaining your existing revenue base. Your practice grows by twenty percent annually without a single advertisement. That's the power of referral culture. It's not magic. It's the natural result of doing everything else right.

But the opposite math is worth contemplating too. Let's say you have a hundred patients and ten percent of them are unhappy enough to actively discourage others from coming to you. That's ten people out in the world telling their networks to avoid your practice. If each of them has a social circle of fifty people, that's five hundred people who've heard a negative story about you. Some of those five hundred were considering calling your office. Now they won't. The damage from unhappy patients is geometric, not arithmetic. One furious patient can undo the referrals from ten happy ones. That's why the first rule of referral culture is not "get more referrals." It's prevent negative word of mouth. Because negative word of mouth spreads faster and cuts deeper than positive word of mouth ever will.

Overdeliver on access, communication, and follow-up

If you want patients to refer their friends, you have to give them something to talk about. And the things patients talk about are rarely clinical. They don't go to their gym and say, "My doctor really understands the mechanism of action for GLP-1 receptor agonists." They say,"My doctor answers my texts." They say, "I had a question on Saturday and Dr. Martinez called me back within an hour." They say, "They checked on me three days after I started to make sure I was doing okay." Access, communication, and follow-up - these are the operational details that create the stories patients tell. Overdeliver on these, and your patients become a marketing department that works for free.

Access means patients can reach you when they need you. Not just during office hours. Not just through a phone tree that dumps them into voicemail. Real access - direct text to the office, email that gets answered, phone calls that get returned the same day, telehealth slots for quick questions that don't require a full visit. I'm not saying you need to be on call 24/7 like an emergency physician. But in a cash-pay practice where patients are paying premium prices, they expect premium access. A patient who's paying $300 a month for a peptide protocol doesn't want to hear "Dr. Johnson will call you back in three to five business days" when they have a question about their injection site. They want a response today. Build systems that make that possible - a nurse triage line, a secure messaging platform, designated same-day callback slots. Whatever it takes. Access is the currency of trust in a cash-pay practice.

Communication means patients always know what's happening, what's next, and what to expect. No surprises. No mysteries. No "we'll call you when the labs are in" followed by radio silence. Proactive communication is the standard. "Your labs look good. Continue your current protocol. See you in six weeks." "Your medication has shipped. Expected delivery Thursday.""Just checking in - it's been two weeks since your dose adjustment. How are you feeling?"These communications take seconds to send and create an impression of attentiveness that patients remember. The doctor who communicates proactively is the doctor patients refer to. The doctor who makes patients chase them for information is the doctor patients complain about.

The quality of communication matters too. Do you explain things in plain English or medical jargon? Do you check for understanding or assume they got it? Do you invite questions or rush to the next patient? A patient who leaves a consultation confused is a patient who won't follow the protocol correctly, won't get results, and won't refer anyone. A patient who leaves feeling educated and empowered is a patient who will execute the plan and tell their friends how knowledgeable their doctor is. Communication quality is clinical quality. Don't separate them.

Follow-up is where most practices fall down, and it's where the biggest referral opportunities live. The follow-up call three days after starting therapy. The check-in email two weeks into a new protocol. The personal note after labs come back showing improvement. These touchpoints demonstrate that your care doesn't end when the patient walks out the door. They show continuity. They show investment. They create the emotional connection that drives referrals.

Let me be specific about what overdelivering on follow-up looks like in practice. When a patient starts their first peptide protocol, someone from your office - a nurse, a care coordinator, ideally a human being, not an automated system - calls them within 72 hours."Hi, this is Maria from Dr. Chen's office. I wanted to check in and see how your first few injections went. Any questions? Any concerns? Anything feeling different?" That call takes five minutes. It catches problems early. It makes the patient feel supported. It generates enormous goodwill. Do that for every new patient, every new protocol, every dose adjustment, and you will have a practice full of patients who feel genuinely cared for.

After the initial check-in, schedule systematic follow-up touchpoints. Week one: how are they tolerating the medication? Week two: any side effects? Week four: preliminary check on results and adherence. Week eight: lab review and protocol adjustment if needed. Week twelve: comprehensive review and next-cycle planning. This isn't excessive hand-holding. This is good clinical care that also happens to generate referrals. Every touchpoint is an opportunity to demonstrate competence, empathy, and investment in the patient's success.

The practices that overdeliver on follow-up stand out dramatically from the competition. Most medical practices - even concierge practices - are follow-up failures. They see the patient, collect the fee, and disappear until the next scheduled visit. The patient is on their own in between. If they have a problem, they have to initiate contact. If they're confused, they have to figure it out. If they're struggling, nobody knows until the next appointment, which might be months away. A practice that breaks this pattern - that reaches out proactively, that checks in systematically, that makes the patient feel continuously supported - is a practice that patients talk about. Because it's rare. Because it's memorable. Because it feels like care instead of commerce.

Make every patient feel like they can reach you - accessibility builds loyalty

There's a difference between access and accessibility, and understanding that difference is crucial for building a referral culture. Access is the structural availability of your services -appointment slots, phone lines, messaging platforms. Accessibility is the patient's feeling that they can reach you, that you're available to them, that they matter enough to warrant your attention. A practice can have great access systems - online booking, telehealth, 24-hour voicemail - and still feel inaccessible if the patient never actually connects with a human being who knows their name and their situation.

Accessibility is created through specific behaviors that signal availability and attentiveness. Return calls personally. When a patient calls with a concern, the best response is often the physician calling back directly, not a staff member relaying a message. "Hi John, it's Dr. Smith. I got your message about the fatigue you've been feeling. Talk to me about it." That single behavior - the doctor taking time to call personally - creates a loyalty that no marketing campaign can replicate. It says, "You matter enough for me to pick up the phone." It transforms a transactional relationship into a personal one.

Remember details. When you see a patient for follow-up, reference something from their last visit. "How was that vacation you were planning?" "Did your daughter's soccer season start?""How's that new job working out?" These aren't clinical questions. They're human questions. They show that you see the patient as a person, not a case. Patients are astounded when doctors remember personal details because it's so rare. In a world of seven-minute visits and doctors who can't remember why they ordered a test, a physician who remembers that you're worried about your mother's health stands out like a lighthouse. That astonishment translates directly to referrals. "You won't believe it - Dr. Lee remembered to ask about my son's college applications." That's the story that gets told. That's what drives the phone call to a friend saying, "You have to meet my doctor."

Be present in the visit. This sounds obvious but it's vanishingly rare. When you're with a patient, be with them. Not checking your phone. Not thinking about the next patient. Not typing into the computer while half-listening. Eye contact. Active listening. Pausing before you respond. Asking "what else?" before you conclude. These behaviors create the felt sense of being truly heard, and that feeling is what patients carry with them out of your office. They don't know if your dosing was evidence-based. They don't know if your diagnosis was correct. But they know how they felt when they were with you. Make sure that feeling is one of being valued, respected, and genuinely cared for.

Create connection points beyond the clinical visit. A newsletter with useful health information - not promotional fluff, but genuinely valuable content. A text message on their birthday. A congratulatory note when they hit a milestone - fifty pounds lost, six months of consistent therapy, improved lab values. These small touchpoints keep the relationship warm between visits. They remind the patient that you're thinking about them even when they're not in your office. They create the ongoing sense of connection that makes a patient feel like they have a relationship with you, not just a business arrangement.

Accessibility also means being reachable in moments of need. When a patient has an unexpected side effect at 7 PM on a Friday, what happens? Do they get a recording telling them to go to the emergency room? Do they get an answering service that takes a message for Monday? Or do they get a physician or nurse who can talk them through it, assess severity, and direct them appropriately? I'm not saying you need to be on call around the clock for every patient. But I am saying that the practices with the strongest referral cultures have figured out how to provide real responsiveness for urgent concerns. That might mean a nurse triage line. It might mean a rotating on-call schedule. It might mean a secure messaging platform with evening coverage. Whatever the mechanism, the message to patients is: "When you need us, we're here." That message builds loyalty that outlasts any temporary clinical setback.

The practical reality is that accessibility is mostly about attention and systems, not about working eighty hours a week. A physician who checks and responds to patient messages for twenty minutes in the morning and twenty minutes in the evening is dramatically more accessible than one who reviews messages once every two days. A practice that schedules same-day phone slots for patient questions is more accessible than one that requires a full office visit for every concern. Small operational choices create outsized impressions of availability. Choose them deliberately.

And here's a counterintuitive truth: limiting your patient panel increases accessibility, which increases referrals. A doctor with three hundred active patients can know each one personally, respond to each one promptly, and create genuine relationships. A doctor with three thousand patients cannot. The cash-pay peptide model works best at scale where the physician can still be accessible. If you grow beyond your capacity to provide personal attention, your accessibility collapses, your referral culture dies, and you're back to buying ads to replace the patients who leave because they never felt connected to you. Grow carefully. Preserve accessibility. It's your most valuable asset.

Unhappy patients tell everyone - happy patients tell everyone who matters

This final section is about the asymmetric nature of word of mouth, and it's the hardest lesson for doctors to internalize. Negative experiences travel farther, faster, and to more people than positive experiences. An unhappy patient doesn't just tell one friend - they tell everyone. They post in public forums. They leave detailed one-star reviews. They tell their story to anyone who will listen. A happy patient, by contrast, tells the people who matter to them - a few close friends, a family member, maybe a colleague. The unhappy patient's message reaches a hundred people. The happy patient's message reaches five. But those five are the right people - warm leads who trust the referrer and are genuinely interested. So you need both strategies: minimizing negative word of mouth while maximizing positive word of mouth. They're not the same thing, and they require different tactics.

Minimizing negative word of mouth is everything we covered in sections 17.1 through 17.3. It's the refund strategy that prevents disputes from festering. It's the complaint handling that de-escalates before it reaches the board. It's the follow-up systems that catch problems early. It's the accessibility that gives patients a direct line to you instead of a public forum to vent. Every unhappy patient who gets their concern resolved privately is a patient who doesn't post a negative review. Every angry patient who gets a goodwill refund is a patient who doesn't file a board complaint. Every frustrated patient who gets a callback from the physician is a patient who doesn't tell their Facebook group to avoid your practice. Prevention is the name of this game. You cannot un-ring the bell of a public complaint. Your only option is to prevent it from going public in the first place.

But even with the best systems, some patients will be unhappy. Some patients cannot be satisfied. Some patients have expectations that no doctor could meet. When those patients go public - the one-star review, the forum post, the social media rant - how you respond matters enormously. Never argue publicly with a patient. Never. Not even if they're factually wrong. Not even if they're being unfair. Not even if their review violates the platform's terms of service. A public argument between a doctor and a patient always makes the doctor look worse, no matter who started it. The doctor has the power, the credentials, the institutional position. The patient is the vulnerable party who paid money and feels wronged. Public sympathy will always side with the patient, and your defensive response will be screenshot and shared as evidence of your arrogance.

The right public response to a negative review is short, professional, and non-clinical. "Thank you for your feedback. Patient care is our top priority, and we take all concerns seriously. We would welcome the opportunity to discuss this directly. Please contact our office at [number]." That's it. No details. No defense. No clinical information. Nothing that could violate HIPAA or escalate the dispute. Every reader of that review sees a practice that responds professionally and invites private resolution. Meanwhile, you work the back channel - call the patient directly, address their concern, offer resolution. Many patients who leave negative reviews will revise or remove them if they feel their concern was finally taken seriously. The ones who won't - let them be. One angry review amid twenty positive ones is context. A public argument with that one angry review becomes a story in itself.

Maximizing positive word of mouth is about creating the conditions where happy patients naturally want to share their experience. The first condition is results. Patients who feel better, look better, perform better - they want to talk about it. "What have you been doing?" is the question every peptide patient hopes to hear. When someone at their gym asks why they're suddenly making gains, or a coworker asks how they lost twenty pounds, or a friend says they look ten years younger - that's the referral moment. Your patient becomes your ambassador. But only if they feel confident recommending you. Only if their experience was smooth enough that they're proud to associate themselves with your practice. If their experience had friction - hard to reach, confusing process, cost surprises - they won't refer even if the results were good. Because referring someone to a frustrating experience reflects poorly on them. They want to refer a practice they can brag about.

The second condition for positive word of mouth is making it easy. Patients who want to refer should know exactly how to do it. Your website should have a simple "Refer a Friend" page. Your office should have referral cards - yes, actual physical cards - that patients can hand to friends. "Give this to someone who might benefit from a conversation with Dr. Smith. They'll get a complimentary initial consultation." That card costs you maybe a hundred dollars to print and a free consultation - let's say five hundred dollars in your time - but it might generate a new patient worth three thousand dollars in first-year revenue. The math is absurdly favorable. Make referral cards. Put them at the front desk. Hand them to patients at their three-month follow-up when they're feeling great and raving about their results. "I'm so glad you're happy, Mrs. Johnson. If you know anyone else who might benefit from this kind of care, we'd love to meet them. Here are a few cards - feel free to pass them along." That's it. No pressure. No hard sell. Just making it easy for someone who's already inclined to refer.

The third condition is recognition. Patients who refer should feel appreciated. A handwritten thank-you note. A small credit on their account. A phone call from the physician: "I just wanted to thank you personally for sending your friend David to us. That means a lot." Recognition doesn't have to be elaborate or expensive. It just has to be genuine. When patients feel that their referrals are noticed and valued, they refer more. It's human nature. We repeat behaviors that get acknowledged. A practice that systematically thanks referring patients will get more referrals than one that treats them like a number on a spreadsheet.

Now let me address something that makes doctors uncomfortable: should you incentivize referrals? Should you offer a financial reward - a hundred dollars credit, a free month of therapy, whatever - for every referred patient who becomes a paying customer? My answer is a qualified yes, but with important caveats. First, check your state laws. Some states have restrictions on fee-splitting or patient inducements that could make referral incentives problematic. Have your lawyer review anything you do. Second, keep it modest. You're not buying referrals. You're acknowledging and encouraging them. A small credit or a free follow-up visit is appropriate. A cash payment starts to feel transactional and potentially coercive. Third, be transparent. If you have a referral program, disclose it clearly. "We appreciate referrals from our patients. As a thank you, both you and your referred friend will receive a [credit] toward future care." Simple, clear, above-board.

Some practices take a different approach and don't incentivize referrals at all. They rely entirely on organic word of mouth, believing that financial incentives taint the authenticity of the referral. I understand that perspective, and if your practice generates enough organic referrals without incentives, that's a fine position. But in the early stages of building a peptide practice - when every new patient matters enormously - a modest incentive can help get the flywheel turning. Once you have a critical mass of happy patients and a steady referral stream, you can dial back or eliminate the incentive. The key is being intentional about your strategy rather than leaving referrals to chance.

The ultimate measure of a referral culture is this: what percentage of your new patients come from existing patient referrals? In a mature, well-run peptide practice, that number should be sixty percent or higher. If it's under forty percent, you have a satisfaction problem, a communication problem, or an operational problem - or all three. Track this number monthly. When it drops, investigate why. When it rises, understand what's working. Your referral rate is the single best indicator of practice health because it's the sum total of everything else you do. Clinical quality. Communication quality. Operational quality. Emotional connection. Accessibility. Generosity. All of it gets captured in that one number: are your patients so satisfied that they voluntarily bring you their friends?

Let me close this chapter with a story that sums up everything I've been trying to say. Dr. M -again, details changed - ran a peptide practice in Florida. Good doctor. Caring. Smart. But he had a blind spot: he couldn't stand it when patients questioned him. Any complaint, any request for a refund, any expression of dissatisfaction - he took it as a personal attack. He'd argue. He'd defend. He'd point to the consent form and the medical literature and his credentials. He won every argument. And he lost his practice. Over three years, he accumulated fourteen negative online reviews, four board complaints (two of which resulted in investigations that cost him fifty thousand dollars in legal fees), and a reputation in his local market as "the peptide doctor who fights with his patients." His referral stream dried up completely. He was spending twenty thousand dollars a month on advertising just to maintain a patient load that should have been growing organically. Eventually, he sold the practice for a fraction of what it was worth and went to work as an employee for a hospital system.

Down the street, Dr. N ran a similar practice. She wasn't a better clinician than Dr. M. Her protocols were comparable. Her outcomes were similar. But Dr. N had a different reflex when patients complained. She listened. She empathized. She made exceptions to her policy when judgment called for it. She called unhappy patients personally. She gave refunds that her accountant thought were unnecessary. She spent time on follow-up calls that her scheduler said she couldn't afford. And her practice? It grew by twenty-five percent a year, almost entirely from referrals. Her patients weren't just satisfied. They were evangelists. They brought their friends, their families, their coworkers. Her marketing budget was minimal. Her reputation was sterling. When a rare negative review appeared, it was drowned out by dozens of positive ones from genuine patients who had genuinely great experiences.

The difference between Dr. M and Dr. N wasn't clinical skill. It wasn't medical knowledge. It wasn't even business acumen in the traditional sense. It was emotional intelligence - the ability to prioritize the long-term relationship over the short-term transaction, to see the patient as a whole human being rather than an opponent in a dispute, to understand that winning the argument and losing the patient is a catastrophic trade. Dr. N understood the central truth of this chapter: a furious patient costs more than any refund. Dr. M never learned it.

You have a choice, every day, with every patient interaction. You can be right, or you can be successful. You can enforce your policy to the letter, or you can preserve a relationship that generates twenty thousand dollars in referrals. You can win the argument about why the side effect wasn't your fault, or you can win the patient's trust by helping them through it. You can be the doctor who patients fear calling when something goes wrong, or you can be the doctor who patients call first because they know you'll take care of them. The choice is yours. But make it with your eyes open, because the consequences - good and bad - compound over time. One generous refund creates a referrer. One petty argument creates a board complaint. Multiply either by a few hundred patients over a few years, and you have either a thriving practice built on trust or a burned-out doctor fighting for their license.

Cash-pay peptide medicine is a relationship business. It runs on trust, referrals, and reputation. Protect those assets the way you'd protect your license - because in the end, they are your license. A patient who feels heard refers. A patient who feels hustled complains to the board. Every interaction is a fork in the road. Choose the path that leads to patients who love you enough to bring their friends. Everything else flows from there.

18 - When Patients Test Your Character - And Your Chart

Let me tell you something I have learned the hard way, across four decades of watching physicians navigate the treacherous waters between patient care and regulatory survival. The patient who sends you a Christmas card this year can be the same patient who writes a complaint letter to the state medical board next year. I am not being cynical. I am being accurate. And if you want to keep your license, your practice, and your sanity, you need to understand that patient relationships in cash-pay medicine are not friendships. They are professional arrangements with human beings who have emotions, expectations, families, financial pressures, and memories that change depending on how they feel in the moment.

This chapter is about the daily pressure that will test your character, your systems, your staff, and ultimately your chart. Every single day you practice peptide medicine, someone will ask you for an exception. They will ask you to bend a rule, skip a step, make a special accommodation, look the other way, or just "this one time" approve something that your protocol says should not be approved. How you respond in that moment - and what you document about how you responded - will determine whether you are still practicing medicine five years from now.

I have watched too many good doctors, smart doctors, well-intentioned doctors get hung out to dry by medical boards because they made an exception for a patient they liked, or because their staff bent a rule to be helpful, or because the chart was silent at the exact moment it needed to speak. The board does not care that you meant well. The board does not care that the patient was your friend. The board does not care that your staff was just trying to be nice. The board cares about what you documented, what your protocol required, and whether you followed your own rules. Period.

So read this chapter carefully. Not because it is pleasant reading, but because it might save your career.

That is not cynicism - that is medicine

I want to be very clear about something right up front because I have seen too many physicians dismiss this advice as the ramblings of a cynical old man who does not understand patient care. Nothing could be further from the truth. I became a registered nurse because I care about patients. I have spent my entire adult life in healthcare because I believe in what good medicine can do for people. But I also spent eleven years in investment banking learning how relationships turn, and forty years as a paralegal watching civil cases unfold, and I can tell you with absolute certainty that the patient relationship is the most volatile professional relationship in all of medicine.

Think about it. A patient comes to you because they have heard about peptides. Maybe they read something online. Maybe a friend lost thirty pounds. Maybe they are desperate because nothing else has worked. They pay cash out of pocket - sometimes a significant amount of cash - and they come in with hope. Real, genuine, emotional hope. They are not just buying a medical service. They are buying possibility. They are buying a chance to feel better, look better, sleep better, recover faster, age slower. That hope is powerful, and when it works, when the patient starts feeling better, you become a hero in their eyes. They love you. They tell their friends about you. They send you thank-you notes. They become your best marketing.

But here is what too many doctors forget. That hope is a double-edged sword. The same emotional intensity that makes a grateful patient your biggest advocate can make a disappointed patient your most dangerous enemy. And disappointment does not always come from failure. Sometimes it comes from side effects the patient did not expect. Sometimes it comes from cost that turned out to be higher than they understood. Sometimes it comes from a spouse who thinks the whole thing was a waste of money. Sometimes it comes from another doctor - a primary care physician, an endocrinologist, a concerned family member with an MD - who tells the patient that peptide therapy is experimental nonsense and that you took advantage of them.

Let me give you a real scenario. I know a physician in Texas - let us call him Dr. Miller -who built a beautiful peptide practice. He was careful. He had good protocols. He used quality pharmacies. He had proper consent forms. And he had a patient, a successful businesswoman in her fifties, who came in for weight management and anti-aging support. She did wonderfully. Lost weight, had more energy, felt better than she had in years. She referred four friends. She sent Dr. Miller a gift basket at Christmas. She was, by every measure, a dream patient.

Then her husband left her. It had nothing to do with the peptide therapy. The marriage had been deteriorating for years. But in the emotional chaos of the divorce, she needed to blame someone for something, and she turned on Dr. Miller. She claimed he never told her the therapy was experimental. She claimed he pressured her into treatment. She claimed she had side effects she never reported and he never asked about. Every single one of her claims was false, but her chart had gaps. The consent form was signed, but the clinical note did not specifically document that the experimental nature of the therapy was discussed in plain language. The follow-up notes were thin. The refill approvals showed timestamps that suggested staff may have processed them without explicit physician review each time. None of this meant Dr. Miller did anything clinically wrong. But the board got the complaint, and Dr. Miller spent eighteen months and forty thousand dollars defending himself against a patient who had once sent him a gift basket.

That is not cynicism. That is the reality of cash-pay medicine. The patient relationship exists at the intersection of hope, money, emotion, and expectation - and when any one of those factors shifts, the entire relationship can turn on a dime. Your job is not to predict which patients will turn. Your job is to build a practice that is bulletproof regardless of which patient files the complaint.

The exception feels kind in the moment, then becomes Exhibit A

Here is where good doctors get into trouble. They make exceptions for patients they like, or patients they feel sorry for, or patients who seem trustworthy, or patients who promise they will never cause problems. The exception feels like the right thing to do in the moment. The exception feels flexible. The exception feels like customer service. Then the relationship changes and the exception becomes Exhibit A.

A medical practice cannot run on who seems nice, who is a friend, who knows the doctor, who paid cash, or who promises not to complain. That is how good intentions become bad charts. You think you are being a good doctor. You think you are building loyalty. You think you are practicing patient-centered care. What you are actually doing is building a paper trail of inconsistent decision-making that will be used against you by people who do not care about context.

Let me explain how this works because I have read enough board transcripts to know the pattern cold. The complaint gets filed. The investigator requests the chart. The chart gets reviewed by a physician consultant hired by the board - usually a retired academic who has never run a cash-pay practice in his life and views any deviation from textbook protocol with suspicion. That consultant looks at your chart and asks a simple question: "Why did the physician deviate from the standard protocol in this case?" And if your answer is "because the patient asked me to" or "because the patient seemed like a good person" or "because I was trying to be helpful," you have already lost.

The board does not evaluate your intentions. The board evaluates your documentation and your consistency. When you make an exception for Patient A, you are not just accommodating Patient A. You are creating a documented precedent that says your protocol is optional. And when Patient B files a complaint - maybe a completely different patient, maybe months or years later - that consultant will look at Patient B's chart and ask why they did not get the same accommodation Patient A got. Was Patient A special? Was Patient A favored? Did Patient A pay more? Did Patient A know the doctor personally? These questions lead to dark places, and they lead there fast.

I knew a physician in Florida who made what seemed like a minor exception. A long-term patient, a retired police officer, called the office on a Friday afternoon. He was going on a two-week cruise, had forgotten to request his refill, and his medication was going to run out on Sunday. The patient had been stable for eight months. His last labs were clean. He had never missed a follow-up. The physician authorized a seven-day early refill and told him to come in for labs when he got back. The patient was grateful. He sent a nice email thanking the doctor for being accessible. Two months later, that same patient had a cardiac event completely unrelated to the peptide therapy - he had underlying coronary disease that had never been diagnosed - and his family sued everyone involved in his medical care. The plaintiff's attorney found the early refill in the pharmacy records and used it to paint a picture of a doctor who was loose with prescriptions, who authorized medication without proper review, who let patient convenience override medical protocol. The early refill had nothing to do with the cardiac event. But it became Exhibit A in a narrative about a careless physician. That seven-day exception cost the doctor six figures in legal fees before the case was eventually dismissed.

The exception feels kind. The exception feels human. The exception feels like good medicine. And the exception will be used against you by people who do not care about your intentions. Every single time you consider making an exception, I want you to picture a lawyer standing in front of a jury holding your chart and asking you to explain why Patient A got something that your own protocol says no patient should get. If you cannot answer that question with a documented clinical rationale, do not make the exception.

Never make undocumented exceptions - never

I am going to say this as plainly as I can because it is the single most important rule in this entire chapter. Never make an exception that is not documented in the chart with the full clinical rationale explaining why the exception was medically appropriate and why it was in the patient's best interest. Never. Not once. Not for your mother. Not for your best friend. Not for the patient who has been with you since day one. Not for the patient who is crying on the phone. Not for the patient who threatens a bad review. Not for the patient who promises they will never tell anyone.

If you cannot document it, you cannot do it. That is the rule. It is not negotiable. It is not flexible. It is not something you apply when it is convenient and ignore when it is not. It is the bedrock principle that separates physicians who survive board complaints from physicians who lose their licenses.

Now, let me be clear about something because I know what some of you are thinking. I am not saying you can never deviate from your protocol. Medicine is art as well as science, and there are legitimate clinical reasons to adjust a plan for an individual patient. What I am saying is that any deviation must be documented with the same care and detail you would put into documenting a complex diagnosis. If you authorize an early refill, the chart needs a note explaining why - patient traveling, stable on therapy for X months, last labs within normal limits on date, no contraindications, authorized X-day early refill with explicit instruction to complete follow-up labs by date. If you adjust a dose based on patient response, the chart needs a note documenting the clinical reasoning - patient reported Y symptom at follow-up on date, assessment supports dose adjustment from A to B, patient counseled on expected effects and monitoring, follow-up scheduled for date with labs.

The documented exception is a clinical decision. The undocumented exception is a liability time bomb.

And here is something else you need to understand. When you document an exception, you are not just protecting yourself. You are protecting the patient. A well-documented exception shows that you thought about the decision, considered the risks, evaluated the patient's history, and made a deliberate clinical judgment. That is good medicine. An undocumented exception shows that you were winging it, and winging it is never defensible.

Let me tell you about a case that still makes me angry. A physician in Arizona - we will call her Dr. Chen - had a patient with a complex medical history who was doing well on a growth hormone secretagogue protocol. The patient developed a temporary financial hardship due to a job loss and asked if she could extend her current vial by drawing smaller doses to make it last longer. Dr. Chen, being compassionate, told her that would be fine for a month until she got back on her feet. The patient misunderstood the instructions, drew doses that were roughly half of what was prescribed, and when her symptoms returned she panicked, went to the emergency room, and told the ER physician that her "peptide doctor told her to cut her doses in half because she could not afford the medication." The ER doctor filed a complaint with the board suggesting that Dr. Chen was providing inadequate supervision and allowing patients to self-adjust medication based on cost. Dr. Chen's chart had no note about the conversation. No documentation of the temporary accommodation. No record of the specific instructions given. Just a silent chart that made it look like the patient was telling the truth. Dr. Chen eventually prevailed, but it took two years, cost her seventy thousand dollars, and left her with a board record that every credentialing organization and hospital privileges committee can see for the rest of her career.

All because she wanted to help a patient and did not document the decision.

Apply the same rules to every patient, every time

Consistency is your armor. Inconsistent application of your own rules is the easiest way to make yourself vulnerable to a board complaint, and it is the hardest problem to defend because it suggests that your clinical judgment is arbitrary rather than evidence-based.

Think about it from the board's perspective. They get a complaint from a patient who says you were negligent, careless, or exploitative. They pull your records. And what they find determines everything that happens next. If they find that every patient goes through the same intake process, the same consent process, the same lab requirements, the same follow-up schedule, the same documentation standards - regardless of who the patient is, how much they pay, whether they were referred by a friend, or how long they have been with you - then you have a defensible practice. You can stand in front of that board and say, "This is what we do for every patient. Here is the protocol. Here are the records showing we followed it." That is a powerful defense because it demonstrates that your medical decisions are systematic, not personal.

But if they find that some patients get special treatment, that rules get bent for people the doctor likes, that intake steps get skipped for friends of existing patients, that lab requirements get waived for patients who complain loudly enough, that consent forms get signed after the medication ships - now the board has a very different picture. Now the board sees a physician who plays favorites, who lacks discipline, whose clinical standards depend on who is asking. And that picture is nearly impossible to defend because the board can simply ask: "If the rules did not matter for Patient A, why should we believe they mattered for Patient B?"

I am not saying you cannot have discretion as a physician. Of course you can. Clinical judgment is the foundation of medical practice. What I am saying is that your discretion must be exercised within a consistent framework and documented with the same rigor whether you are treating a VIP or a first-time patient. The intake form is the same. The consent process is the same. The lab requirements are the same. The follow-up schedule is the same. The documentation standards are the same. If you deviate, the deviation is documented with clinical rationale. Every single time.

This is not just about board defense. It is also about staff sanity. When your staff knows that the rules are the rules and there are no secret exceptions for special patients, they can do their jobs without ambiguity. They do not have to guess whether this patient is important enough to warrant special handling. They do not have to navigate the awkward situation of explaining to Patient B why Patient A got something they did not. They can simply say, "Our protocol is the same for every patient, and we follow it consistently because that is how we ensure safe care." That is a sentence that protects your staff, your patients, and your license.

The hardest moment for consistency is when you have a long-term patient who has been with you for years, who has never caused a problem, who you genuinely like as a person, and who asks for something that falls just outside your protocol. That is the moment that tests your character. That is the moment when the easy thing is to say yes and the right thing is to say,

"I would love to accommodate you, and here is what I can do within our medical protocol," and then document the conversation thoroughly. It feels small in the moment. It feels like you are being rigid, unreasonable, maybe even cold. But years later, when that patient relationship has turned - and some of them will turn - that documented consistency will be the wall that keeps the board complaint from becoming a career-ending event.

I have been doing this a long time. I have watched physicians lose everything over exceptions that seemed tiny when they made them. I have read board transcripts where a doctor's own chart became the prosecution's best evidence. I have seen good practitioners hung out to dry by medical boards that had no interest in context, no patience for explanations, and no sympathy for good intentions. And the one thing that every one of those cases had in common was this: somewhere along the line, the doctor made an exception and did not document it. That is the thread that runs through every story of a physician who thought it could not happen to them.

It can happen to you. The question is whether your chart will save you or hang you.

Faster refills, higher doses, skipped labs, medication shipped before review

Now let us get practical. You are running a peptide practice. Patients are coming through your door - or your telehealth portal - every day, and every one of them is going to test your boundaries in ways that seem small, reasonable, and entirely predictable. The key is recognizing these tests for what they are and having a system that handles them without requiring you to make a fresh moral decision every single time.

Let us start with the refill request that comes in early. This is probably the most common boundary test in peptide medicine. The patient has been on therapy for three months. They are doing well. Their labs from last month looked fine. And now they call the office two weeks before their scheduled follow-up because they are going out of town, or they miscalculated their remaining supply, or they "just want to make sure they do not run out." The request seems trivial. Two weeks early on a stable patient - what is the harm?

The harm is that you are now establishing a pattern where refill timing is negotiable. And once refill timing is negotiable, every patient who hears about it - and patients talk to each other, especially in the peptide and hormone space - will expect the same flexibility. More importantly, the patient who gets an early refill today may be the patient who files a complaint tomorrow, and when the board reviews your pharmacy records and sees a pattern of early refills without documented clinical justification, they will not see flexibility. They will see sloppiness.

Your protocol needs a hard rule: refills are approved at or after the scheduled follow-up, following clinician review of current status, labs if required, and patient-reported symptoms. Not before. Not because the patient asked nicely. Not because the office wants to be helpful. The only exception - and it must be documented - is a genuine clinical or logistical circumstance that the physician evaluates and approves with a note in the chart explaining the medical rationale. Vacation travel is not automatically a rationale. "Patient has been stable" is not automatically a rationale. The rationale needs to be specific: patient traveling dates X to Y, stable on current dose for Z months, last labs date within parameters, no reported adverse effects, approved one-time early refill of A units to cover through return date, follow-up rescheduled for date.

Then there is the dose escalation request. This one is particularly dangerous in peptide and hormone practices because patients talk to each other online, in gyms, in Facebook groups, and at dinner parties. They hear that someone got better results on a higher dose. They read a forum post where someone says they doubled their dose and felt amazing. They come to your office with a specific number in mind, and they frame it as a question: "Could we try a little more?"or "My friend is on X amount and it really worked for him." What they are really doing is asking you to practice crowd-sourced medicine, and if you say yes without your own clinical assessment, you are agreeing to it.

Dose changes require the same clinical rigor as initial prescribing. What is the patient's current response? What do their labs show? Are there any emerging contraindications? What does the literature say about the dose-response relationship at the level the patient is requesting? What are the risks of going higher? Is there a ceiling to the benefit that makes more medication counterproductive? These are medical questions, and they require medical evaluation. If a patient wants a dose adjustment, the answer is: "Let us review your current status, your labs, and your goals at your next follow-up, and I will make a clinical decision based on what makes medical sense for you." Not "sure, we can bump it up." Not "I guess a little more would not hurt." Those answers are how you end up with a patient on a dose that exceeds anything supported by literature, with a chart that cannot explain why, and a board consultant who views the whole thing as reckless prescribing.

Skipped labs are another boundary test that starts small and ends big. The patient calls and says they cannot get to the lab this month because they are busy, or their insurance changed and the lab they used to go to is not in network anymore, or they just do not like needles and would rather skip it this time. And because the patient has been stable, and because you have a hundred other things to do, and because it feels like a small accommodation, you say okay. One month becomes two. Two months becomes three. And now you are prescribing medication without monitoring, which is exactly the narrative that board consultants love to tear apart.

Your lab protocol needs to be non-negotiable. The chart must show that therapy continuation is contingent on timely lab completion, and if a patient cannot or will not complete required labs, the correct response is not accommodation - it is holding or discontinuing therapy until compliance is restored. That needs to be written into your informed consent from day one, it needs to be reinforced at every follow-up, and it needs to be enforced without exception. A patient who will not complete labs is a patient who cannot be safely monitored, and a patient who cannot be safely monitored should not be on therapy. That is not harsh. That is medicine.

Finally, there is the request to ship medication before clinical review is complete. This one usually comes in telehealth practices where the patient has completed intake forms but has not yet had their live consultation, or where labs are pending but the patient is anxious to start. The pressure is real - the patient has paid money, they are excited, they do not want to wait - and the business side of your brain is saying that faster starts mean happier patients and better cash flow. But the medical side of your brain, the side that wants to keep your license, needs to say no every single time.

Medication ships only after clinician review of the complete intake, required labs, informed consent, and a determination that therapy is medically appropriate for this patient at this time. Not before. Not because the patient is impatient. Not because the office wants to show good customer service. If the patient has not been clinically reviewed, medication does not ship. If labs are pending, medication does not ship. If the consent form has not been signed and discussed, medication does not ship. These are not business policies. They are clinical guardrails, and every time you drive through one because a patient asked you to, you are taking an unnecessary risk with your license.

Staff asked questions requiring a license - don't let helpfulness become medical advice

This is one of the most dangerous areas in peptide practice, and it is dangerous precisely because it feels so innocent. Your staff wants to be helpful. They want patients to have a good experience. They want to answer questions, solve problems, and make people feel taken care of. That is what makes them good at their jobs. It is also what can destroy your practice if you do not put hard boundaries around what they are allowed to say and do.

Here is how it happens. The patient calls the office with a question. Maybe they are experiencing a side effect and want to know if it is normal. Maybe they want to know if they can take their peptide injection at a different time of day. Maybe they want to know if it is okay to skip a dose because they are not feeling well. The patient is not asking to speak to the doctor- they just want a quick answer. Your front desk staff member, or your medical assistant, or your office manager, who has been working in the practice for two years and has heard the doctor answer these questions a thousand times, picks up the phone and says something that sounds perfectly reasonable. "Oh, that is normal, do not worry about it." Or "Yes, you can take it in the evening instead." Or "Go ahead and skip tonight if you are not feeling well."

And just like that, your unlicensed staff member has practiced medicine.

Let me be very clear about what the law says here, because this is not a gray area and it is not something you can be cute about. Interpreting symptoms, recommending dose changes, advising on medication timing, evaluating whether a side effect is concerning - these are clinical activities that require a medical license. When your staff does them, they are practicing medicine without a license. When your staff does them under your supervision, in your office, on behalf of your patients, you are potentially liable for allowing unlicensed practice. And when a patient has a bad outcome based on something your staff told them, the complaint will name you, not the staff member who gave the advice.

I have seen this play out in devastating ways. A practice in Georgia had a medical assistant who had worked with the physician for four years. She was experienced, well-liked, and genuinely knew the practice inside and out. A patient called asking whether he should be concerned about some redness at his injection site. The medical assistant, trying to be helpful and drawing on her experience, told him it sounded normal and he should just watch it. The patient actually had a developing cellulitis that required antibiotic treatment, and by the time he sought in-person care, the infection had progressed significantly. The patient recovered fully, but he filed a complaint alleging that the practice failed to properly triage his symptoms and that an unlicensed staff member provided medical advice that delayed appropriate care. The board investigation did not focus on the medical assistant. It focused on the physician's supervision systems - or lack thereof - that allowed an unlicensed employee to make clinical assessments. The physician ended up with a formal reprimand and a mandatory supervision plan that cost thousands of dollars to implement.

Your staff needs written, explicit boundaries that are reviewed regularly, signed off on, and enforced. They can gather information. They can schedule appointments. They can send forms. They can explain office processes like how to submit a refill request or how to access lab results. They can take messages and route them to the appropriate clinical staff. They can document patient-reported information verbatim - "Patient reports redness at injection site, message routed to clinician for review."

What they cannot do is interpret that information. They cannot say whether something is normal or concerning. They cannot recommend dose adjustments, timing changes, or medication holds. They cannot tell a patient whether they should continue therapy, stop therapy, or seek emergency care. They cannot provide reassurance that a symptom is nothing to worry about. They cannot offer any statement that a reasonable person would interpret as clinical advice or a clinical assessment.

The script for your staff needs to be simple and consistent: "That is a clinical question that needs to be reviewed by the clinician. Let me take the details and make sure they get back to you." No exceptions. No matter how simple the question seems. No matter how many times they have heard the doctor answer it. If it requires a license to answer, it requires a license to answer, and your staff does not have one.

Discounts, credits, exceptions, favors, shortcuts

Let me talk about something that does not get enough attention in compliance discussions: the business-side boundary tests. Patients will ask you for financial accommodations that seem unrelated to clinical care but can create exactly the same problems as clinical exceptions. They will ask for discounts because they referred a friend. They will ask for credit because they had a bad month. They will ask you to waive the follow-up fee because they cannot afford it. They will ask for a free month because they have been loyal. And every one of these requests, if handled inconsistently, creates a record of arbitrary decision-making that can be used against you.

Here is the thing about discounts in a cash-pay practice: they are not illegal, they are not unethical, and they can be a legitimate business tool. But they need to be structured, documented, and applied consistently. If you give Patient A a 20% discount because they referred three friends, and Patient B finds out and files a complaint, the question becomes: what is your discount policy? If you do not have one - a written, explicit policy that defines who qualifies for discounts, under what circumstances, in what amount - then your discounts look like favoritism. And favoritism in a medical practice is a dangerous narrative because it suggests that clinical decisions might also be influenced by personal relationships rather than medical judgment.

The same applies to credits, refunds, fee waivers, and any other financial accommodation. You need a written policy. The policy needs to define what accommodations are available, under what circumstances, and how they are approved. Staff should never have discretion to offer financial accommodations on their own - that should require physician or practice manager approval every time. And every accommodation should be documented with the rationale: patient referred three new patients per referral program, 15% discount applied per policy section X; patient experienced unexpected job loss, one-time payment deferral approved per hardship policy. When the discount is part of a structured program and documented accordingly, it is a business decision. When the discount is an off-the-cuff favor for a patient the doctor likes, it is a liability.

Shortcuts are the most insidious category because they masquerade as efficiency. The patient has been through intake before at another practice, so can we skip some of the history questions? The patient signed a consent form at their last doctor's office, so do they really need to sign ours? The patient is a healthcare professional themselves, so they understand the risks and we do not need to explain as much. The patient is in a hurry and asks if we can just start the medication and catch up on paperwork later. Each of these shortcuts saves five minutes today and costs you five months of legal defense tomorrow.

Your intake is your intake. Every patient completes it. Your consent is your consent. Every patient signs it after a thorough discussion. Your documentation standards are your documentation standards. Every patient encounter gets the same level of clinical note. There are no shortcuts because shortcuts are how you end up with a chart that cannot explain what you did or why. And a chart that cannot explain what you did is a chart that cannot protect you.

Some are sincere, some are desperate, some are manipulative - the rule is the same

I want to say something about patient motivation because it matters for how you think about these boundary tests. Some patients who ask for exceptions are sincere. They really are traveling. They really did have a hard month financially. They really are confused about the instructions and just want clarification. These patients are not trying to game the system. They are human beings navigating a complicated medical world, and they deserve compassion and clear communication.

Some patients are desperate. They have been struggling with their health for years. They have tried everything. They have pinned their last hopes on your peptide program, and every delay, every requirement, every additional cost feels like another barrier between them and the relief they have been seeking. These patients pull at your heartstrings because their suffering is real, and you became a doctor to help people who are suffering. The desire to accommodate them

- to remove barriers, to speed things up, to make the process easier - comes from the best part of your character.

And some patients are manipulative. They know exactly what they are doing. They have learned that charm gets them what they want. They have learned that persistence wears people down. They have learned that guilt is a powerful tool - "I guess I will just have to go somewhere else" or "I thought you cared about your patients" or "The other doctor I talked to did not make me jump through all these hoops." These patients test your boundaries deliberately, systematically, and without any intention of following your protocol once they get what they want.

Here is the critical insight: it does not matter which category the patient falls into. The rule is the same. Your protocol is the same. Your documentation standards are the same. Your staff boundaries are the same. Because you cannot reliably distinguish between the sincere patient who will never complain and the manipulative patient who is setting you up for a problem six months from now. And even if you could, the board does not care about your patient psychology assessment. The board cares about whether you followed your own procedures consistently.

Be kind to every patient. Be compassionate to every patient. Communicate clearly with every patient. And apply your rules with absolute consistency to every patient. That is how you help the sincere ones, protect the desperate ones, and defend against the manipulative ones. Kindness without boundaries is not kindness - it is negligence dressed up as compassion. And it will be used against you by people who have no interest in your good intentions.

Staff scope: gather information, schedule, send forms, explain office process

Your staff is the front line of your practice, and in many ways they are more important to your regulatory survival than you are. You see patients for fifteen or thirty minutes at a time. Your staff talks to them every day. They field the calls, answer the emails, process the refill requests, handle the complaints, and manage the thousand small interactions that make up the patient experience. If your staff does not understand their role boundaries - if they drift into clinical territory because they want to be helpful, because they have picked up medical knowledge by osmosis, or because no one ever told them where the line is - your practice is sitting on a regulatory time bomb.

Let me be very specific about what your support staff can do because clarity here protects everyone. Support staff can collect information from patients - demographic data, insurance information if you collect it for any reason, medical history through structured forms, symptom descriptions taken verbatim without interpretation. They can schedule appointments, send forms and instructions, explain office processes like how to submit a refill request or how to access lab results, and route questions to the appropriate clinical personnel. They can verify that required documentation has been received - intake forms signed, consent forms completed, lab orders drawn. They can handle administrative tasks like payment processing, appointment reminders, and supply ordering. These are valuable functions, and a good support staff makes your practice run smoothly.

But the boundaries need to be as clear as a brick wall. When a patient asks a question that requires clinical judgment - Is this side effect normal? Should I change my dose? Can I take this with my other medications? Should I stop if I am feeling sick? - your staff's job is not to answer. Their job is to collect the information and route it to someone with a license. Period. No exceptions. No "I have heard the doctor answer this before." No "it is probably fine." No"just watch it and call back if it gets worse." Those phrases, spoken by unlicensed staff, are the opening paragraphs of board complaints.

I want you to think about your office from the perspective of a state investigator who walks in unannounced. This is not theoretical - it happens. An investigator shows up at your office, flashes a badge, and starts asking questions. They talk to your staff. They ask your medical assistant what she tells patients when they call with questions about side effects. They ask your front desk person how refill requests are processed. They ask your office manager who approves dose changes. If your staff gives answers that suggest they are making clinical assessments, providing medical advice, or exercising discretion over prescription decisions, you now have a problem that goes far beyond one patient's complaint.

The only way to prevent this is through written protocols that are specific, explicit, and reviewed regularly. Every staff member should have a job description that clearly defines their role boundaries. They should sign an acknowledgment that they understand what they can and cannot do. They should receive training on scope of practice during onboarding and refresher training at least annually. And there should be consequences - documented in your personnel policies - for staff who violate these boundaries, because one staff member who decides they know enough to answer clinical questions can undo every protection you have built.

Staff cannot: diagnose, approve therapy, interpret symptoms, recommend dose changes

Let me drill down on the specific activities that are absolutely off-limits for unlicensed staff because these are the ones that come up most often and cause the most trouble. These prohibitions need to be in writing, signed by every staff member, posted in areas where staff can see them, and enforced without exception.

Staff cannot diagnose. This seems obvious, but it happens in subtle ways. A patient calls and describes symptoms, and the staff member says, "That sounds like a common reaction, it usually goes away in a few days." That is a diagnostic statement - it classifies the patient's symptoms into a category and offers a prognosis. It is also medical advice, and it is illegal for unlicensed personnel to provide. The correct response is: "I will document what you are experiencing and make sure the clinician reviews it today."

Staff cannot approve therapy. No staff member should ever tell a patient they are "approved" to start treatment, "cleared" for a particular medication, or "good to go" on a new protocol. Therapy approval is a clinical decision that requires physician evaluation of the patient's history, labs, contraindications, and goals. When staff pre-approves patients - even informally, even just to be encouraging - they create an expectation that may not align with the clinical decision, and they create documentation problems when the chart shows staff interactions that look like clinical gatekeeping.

Staff cannot interpret symptoms. This is the big one because it comes up constantly. Patient calls with a question. Staff member listens, draws on their experience, and offers an interpretation: "That does not sound serious." Or "You should probably go to the ER." Or "I have heard other patients say the same thing and it was nothing." Every one of those statements is symptom interpretation by an unlicensed person, and every one of them can create liability if the patient has a bad outcome. The staff member's job is to collect the symptom description verbatim, document it, and route it to a clinician for evaluation. Not to interpret. Not to triage. Not to reassure. Collect, document, route. That is the entire job.

Staff cannot recommend dose changes. This includes suggesting patients take more, take less, skip a dose, double up, split doses, or modify their protocol in any way. Dose decisions belong to the prescriber and the prescriber alone. Even if a patient says, "I think I need more, can you ask the doctor?" the staff member's role is to relay the request, not to validate it, not to suggest the doctor will probably agree, not to offer any opinion about whether the dose should change. Relay the request and document that it was relayed.

I know this sounds rigid. I know it sounds like I do not trust your staff. That is not it at all. I have worked with extraordinary medical assistants, office managers, and front desk staff who are the backbone of successful practices. The issue is not trust. The issue is that the law does not care how trustworthy your staff is. The law cares whether clinical activities are performed by licensed personnel. And when your staff crosses into clinical territory - even with the best intentions, even with genuine knowledge, even under your general supervision - you are allowing unlicensed practice, and that is one of the fastest ways to attract regulatory attention.

Let me give you a war story that illustrates how fast this can go wrong. A physician in Colorado had a practice manager who had been with him for six years. She was capable, loyal, and genuinely indispensable to the practice's operations. She handled everything from scheduling to billing to inventory. And because she had been there so long and heard so many clinical conversations, she gradually started answering patient questions directly. A patient would call about a mild side effect, and she would say, "Oh, that is very common, most patients experience that in the first week, just give it a few days." She was almost always right. But then a patient called about chest tightness, and the practice manager - drawing on her experience - told the patient it was "probably just anxiety from the new medication" and to"try to relax and see how it feels tomorrow." The patient actually had a cardiac issue that required immediate attention. The delay in appropriate triage was documented in the subsequent lawsuit, and while the patient was ultimately fine, the board investigation focused on the practice's systems for preventing unlicensed staff from making clinical assessments. The practice manager was not malicious. She was not incompetent. She was trying to be helpful in a system that never drew a clear enough line. The physician ended up with a consent order, mandatory staff retraining, and a board monitor in his practice for two years.

That is what happens when helpfulness becomes medical advice. Draw the line clearly. Enforce it consistently. Review it regularly. Your staff will thank you for the clarity, and your license will survive another day.

Nursing staff: valuable but not a substitute for the prescriber

Licensed nursing staff occupy a special middle ground in peptide practice, and that middle ground requires special attention. Nurses are licensed professionals with training, expertise, and scope of practice that unlicensed staff do not have. They can do more. They can take more detailed health histories, perform certain assessments within their scope, administer injections if that is part of your practice model, and provide patient education on medication administration and side effect monitoring. They are enormously valuable, and a good nurse makes your practice better in every measurable way.

But here is what too many physicians forget: a nurse is not a substitute for the prescriber. Licensed practical nurses and registered nurses have their own scope of practice, their own licensing board, and their own standards of care. When a physician delegates clinical tasks to a nurse, the delegation must be appropriate to the nurse's training, licensure, and the state's nurse practice act. And when a physician allows a nurse to function as a de facto prescriber -making decisions about therapy initiation, dose adjustments, therapy holds, or patient selection- the physician is creating a regulatory problem that can affect both licenses.

You need written protocols that define exactly what your nursing staff may do without direct physician oversight, what they may do with physician oversight or cosignature, and what requires physician assessment before any action is taken. These protocols need to be specific, not general. "Nurses may provide patient education" is too vague. "Nurses may educate patients on injection technique, storage requirements, and the importance of reporting specific side effects as listed in Protocol Appendix A" is specific. "Nurses may triage patient calls" is too vague. "Nurses may collect patient-reported symptoms verbatim, document them in the chart, and route them to the physician for clinical assessment; nurses may not offer clinical assessments, diagnostic impressions, or treatment recommendations" is specific.

Refill review is a particular danger zone for nursing scope creep. A nurse who has been with your practice for a while can easily start functioning as a refill gatekeeper - reviewing pending refills, checking whether labs are current, and even flagging refills for approval or denial based on protocol compliance. There is nothing wrong with a nurse gathering the information needed for a refill review. There is everything wrong with a nurse making the refill decision. That is prescribing, and prescribing belongs to the prescriber. Even if the nurse is following a protocol, even if the decision seems automatic based on lab dates, the final clinical judgment about whether a refill is appropriate must be documented as a physician decision. If your refill process does not include explicit physician review and documentation of that review, you have a hole in your system.

Dose escalation decisions, contraindication evaluations, and adverse event triage are the same. A nurse can document the information. A nurse can alert the physician. A nurse can follow protocols for emergency situations where immediate action is needed and physician contact is being attempted. But the clinical assessment - the medical reasoning that says this patient can safely continue on this dose, or this patient needs to hold therapy, or this patient needs emergency evaluation - that belongs to the physician. When nursing staff drift into that territory because the office is busy, because the physician trusts them, or because it seems efficient, the practice is skating on thin ice.

I want to emphasize something here because I have seen physicians get defensive about this. I am not saying you should not trust your nursing staff. I am not saying nurses are not capable professionals. I am saying that every licensed professional has a scope, and when scopes overlap, the documentation needs to be crystal clear about who did what, who decided what, and whose clinical judgment governed the outcome. A nurse who documents a thorough assessment and routes it to the physician for decision is practicing good nursing. A nurse who documents a decision and has the physician rubber-stamp it afterward is practicing delegated medicine, and that is not the same thing.

Electronic prescribing: if it leaves under your name, you own it

Let us talk about electronic prescribing because this is one of the most dangerous areas in modern practice, and it is especially dangerous in peptide medicine where the medications are already under heightened scrutiny. If a prescription leaves your electronic system under your name, you own it. That is the rule. It does not matter who clicked the button. It does not matter who gathered the information. It does not matter whether you were in the office or on vacation. If the prescription carries your name and your DEA or NPI identifier, it is your prescription, and you are responsible for every clinical decision it represents.

This matters because many electronic health record and e-prescribing systems have features that can create the illusion of physician oversight without the reality of physician oversight. Refill queues that staff can process. Standing orders that renew automatically. Prescription templates that prepopulate doses and pharmacies. Protocol-driven prescribing pathways that suggest medication orders based on intake data. These features are designed to make practices more efficient, and in a conventional primary care setting with well-established medications and standard protocols, they may be entirely appropriate. In peptide medicine, where every prescription is already being viewed with skepticism by potential reviewers, they are a license to create problems.

You need hard controls around your e-prescribing system, and they need to be documented in writing. Your credentials should not be shared with staff. Not your password, not your token, not your biometric login, not your digital signature. If staff need to prepare prescription drafts for your review, they should do so in a way that requires your explicit approval before the prescription transmits to the pharmacy. If your EHR has a refill authorization workflow, it should be configured so that staff can flag refills for review but cannot transmit them without your documented approval. If your system has standing order or protocol-driven features, they should be disabled or severely restricted for peptide and hormone medications unless you have specifically reviewed and approved the protocol in writing.

Let me be blunt about something. If your medical assistant can log into the e-prescribing system under your credentials and send a prescription to the pharmacy without you reviewing it, you are practicing recklessly. It does not matter how good your assistant is. It does not matter how long they have worked for you. It does not matter that they have never made a mistake. The moment a prescription leaves under your name without your knowledge and review, you have committed a prescribing act that you cannot defend. And if that prescription ever becomes part of a board complaint, a malpractice case, or a criminal investigation, your only explanation will be "my staff sent it" - which is not a defense, it is a confession.

I know a physician in Nevada who learned this lesson the hard way. He had a trusted office manager who had been with him for a decade. She had his e-prescribing login because the system required it for certain administrative functions. Over time, she started processing refill requests directly - she would review the patient's chart, check that labs were current, and send the refill. The physician knew about it and considered it a reasonable delegation of administrative work. Then a refill went out for a patient who had an abnormal lab result in the chart - an elevated marker that should have triggered physician review before any refill. The office manager missed it. The refill went out. The patient had an adverse event that was probably unrelated to the medication but was blamed on it in the subsequent lawsuit. And when the pharmacy records showed that the prescription was transmitted by the office manager using the physician's credentials, the case shifted from a clinical question to a prescribing control question. The physician's insurance company settled because the facts around e-prescribing access were indefensible.

If a prescription leaves under your name, you own it. That means you review it. You approve it. You document that review and approval. There are no shortcuts to this. There are no trusted staff exceptions. There are no "the system makes us do it this way" workarounds. You are the prescriber. The prescription is yours. Act like it.

A dirty office tells a regulator you're careless before they read the chart

I want to shift gears now and talk about something that sounds superficial but is actually deeply important: the physical environment of your practice. I have been in hundreds of medical offices over my career - primary care clinics, specialty practices, urgent care centers, concierge medicine suites, telehealth offices that serve as administrative hubs. And I can tell you with absolute certainty that regulators form an opinion about your practice before they ever open a chart. They form it when they walk through your door. They form it when they look at your waiting room. They form it when they see your exam rooms, your storage areas, your medication handling, your sharps disposal, your record-keeping systems. They form it in the first thirty seconds, and that first impression colors everything they find afterward.

A dirty office tells a regulator you are careless. I am not talking about whether your decor is modern or your furniture is expensive. I am talking about basic cleanliness, organization, and control. Needles in an unlocked drawer. Medication vials stored at room temperature when they require refrigeration. Sharps containers that are overfull. Paper charts stacked in open boxes in a hallway. Expired supplies still on shelves. Bathrooms that have not been cleaned. Dust on surfaces. Clutter everywhere. These things do not just violate basic infection control standards - they signal to an investigator that this is a practice where details do not matter, where protocols are not followed, where the basic standards of medical practice are treated as optional.

And here is the thing: that first impression is almost impossible to undo. Once an investigator has seen your messy back room, they will read your charts looking for confirmation that your clinical care is as sloppy as your housekeeping. Every thin note becomes evidence of sloppiness. Every missing lab becomes evidence of negligence. Every unsigned document becomes evidence of carelessness. The narrative writes itself: "This physician does not pay attention to details." And in peptide medicine, where the board already views you with skepticism, that narrative is fatal.

Your office does not need to be fancy. It needs to be clean. It needs to be organized. It needs to demonstrate that you run a controlled medical environment where medications are stored properly, sharps are disposed of safely, supplies are current, surfaces are sanitized, records are secured, and access is controlled. These are not luxury amenities. They are basic requirements of medical practice, and they matter more in peptide medicine than in conventional practice because you are already under a microscope.

Let me be specific about what this looks like in practice. Medications, whether you dispense in-office or receive shipments from a pharmacy, need proper storage - temperature-controlled if required, secured if controlled or valuable, organized so that you can account for every vial. Sharps containers need to be current, properly sized, not overfilled, and disposed of through an approved medical waste vendor with documentation. Exam rooms, if you have them, need to be clean, equipped, and maintained. Waiting areas need to be professional. Administrative areas need to be organized - patient records secured, financial records maintained, personnel files confidential. If you have a laboratory area for point-of-care testing, it needs to meet applicable standards. If you have an injection room, it needs to meet applicable standards.

And if you run a telehealth-only practice, do not think this section does not apply to you. You still have an office. You still receive shipments. You still handle patient information. You still have staff who work in a physical space. An investigator can still walk into your administrative office and draw conclusions about your practice based on what they see. Clean, organized, controlled - these are non-negotiable regardless of your practice model.

Regulators trust boring, clean, documented systems

I want you to internalize a truth that took me decades to fully appreciate: regulators do not trust excitement. They do not trust innovation. They do not trust practices that look cutting-edge, revolutionary, or ahead of the curve. They trust boring. They trust predictable. They trust systems that look exactly like what they expect a medical practice to look like, because predictable systems are auditable systems, and auditable systems are defensible systems.

This is a hard truth for peptide physicians because peptide medicine, by its nature, looks unconventional. You are prescribing medications that many regulators have never heard of, using compounds that are not FDA-approved in the conventional sense, in cash-pay models that operate outside the insurance infrastructure they understand. You are already unusual. You are already suspicious. Your job is to make everything else about your practice so boring, so clean, so documented, so by-the-book that the unusual nature of your clinical work gets evaluated on its own merits rather than being amplified by sloppy systems.

What does a boring, trusted system look like? It looks like a protocol manual that sits on a shelf - or better yet, in a digital document repository - and defines exactly how every clinical and administrative process works. Patient intake follows Protocol A. Informed consent follows Protocol B. Refill authorization follows Protocol C. Lab monitoring follows Protocol D. Staff scope boundaries are defined in Policy E. E-prescribing controls are defined in Policy F. Complaint handling follows Policy G. Every process has a written standard. Every standard is reviewed regularly. Every review is documented. It is not sexy. It is not innovative. It is boring as watching paint dry, and that is exactly the point.

Your chart documentation should be the same - thorough, consistent, predictable. Every chart note follows the same structure. Every patient encounter includes the same elements. Every decision is documented with the same level of clinical rationale. A board reviewer should be able to pick up any chart in your practice and find the same standard of documentation, the same attention to detail, the same evidence of physician review and clinical reasoning. When your charting is consistent across patients, it demonstrates that your clinical process is systematic, not arbitrary. When your charting varies wildly - some patients have comprehensive notes, others have one-line entries - it suggests that your attention to clinical detail is inconsistent, and inconsistent attention means some patients are getting less care than others.

I have seen practices that blew investigators away not because their medicine was extraordinary but because their systems were bulletproof. The investigator asked to see the protocol manual, and there it was - comprehensive, current, signed off on by every staff member. The investigator asked how staff were trained on scope of practice, and the practice produced training records, signed acknowledgments, and dated refresher sessions. The investigator asked about a specific patient's care, and the chart showed clear documentation at every step - intake, consent, labs, prescribing, follow-up, refill review, ongoing monitoring. The investigator could not find a gap because there was no gap to find. That practice passed its investigation not because the medicine was glamorous but because the systems were boring, and boring is exactly what regulators trust.

Your chart is the story your lawyer will need if the relationship turns ugly

I want you to think about your chart differently than you probably do now. Most physicians view the chart as a clinical tool - a way to track patient status, document encounters, and support continuity of care. And it is all of those things. But in peptide medicine, your chart is something else too. It is the story your lawyer will need to tell if the patient relationship ever turns ugly. It is the narrative that will either save you or hang you when a complaint lands on a regulator's desk. And that means you need to write it not just for yourself, not just for the next clinician who sees the patient, but for a skeptical stranger who has never met you and has every reason to assume you did something wrong.

That skeptical stranger - the board investigator, the physician consultant, the administrative law judge - does not know you. They do not know your training, your experience, your reputation, your good intentions. They know only what is in the chart. And if the chart is thin, if it has gaps, if it assumes knowledge that the reader does not have, if it uses abbreviations without explanation, if it references decisions without rationale - then the skeptical stranger fills in those gaps with the worst possible interpretation. That is human nature. When you are tasked with evaluating whether a physician did something wrong, and the documentation does not clearly show what the physician did or why, the default assumption is that something was missed.

Every chart note you write needs to answer three questions that a lawyer or investigator will ask. First, what did you do? This means your note needs to clearly describe the encounter - what was discussed, what was assessed, what was decided, what was ordered, what was prescribed. Not "saw patient, doing well, continue current plan." That tells the reader nothing. A proper note says: "Patient reports improved energy and sleep quality since initiating therapy eight weeks ago. No adverse effects reported. Weight decreased 4 lbs from baseline. Reviewed home blood pressure log - readings stable within normal range. Physical exam unremarkable. Labs from date reviewed - all parameters within acceptable ranges per protocol. Assessment: patient tolerating therapy well, clinically appropriate to continue. Plan: continue current dose, repeat labs in 8 weeks, follow-up appointment scheduled date, patient instructed to call office immediately if new symptoms develop."

Second, why did you do it? This is the clinical rationale, and it is where most chart notes fall short. You need to document not just what you decided but the reasoning behind the decision."Continue current dose because patient is responding appropriately, labs are stable, no contraindications identified, and benefit-risk assessment supports ongoing therapy at this level." That sentence transforms a routine note into a defensible record of clinical judgment. It shows that you thought about the decision, evaluated the relevant factors, and made a deliberate medical choice. Without that rationale, your note just says what happened. With the rationale, your note says why it was medically appropriate.

Third, what did the patient understand? This is the consent and communication component, and it is especially critical in peptide medicine where patients are paying cash for therapies that are not conventionally FDA-approved. Your note needs to reflect not just that you discussed risks and alternatives but that the patient had an opportunity to ask questions, demonstrated understanding, and agreed to the plan voluntarily. "Discussed risks including [specific risks], benefits, alternatives including [specific alternatives], compounded status, no guarantees, cost, follow-up requirements, and stop criteria. Patient asked questions about [specific topics], questions answered to patient's satisfaction. Patient verbalized understanding and agreed to continue therapy. Consent form signed and scanned to chart." That level of detail makes it very hard for a patient to later claim that nobody explained anything to them.

I want to stress something that many physicians resist because it feels like extra work: a good chart note takes longer to write than a bad one. There is no way around that. The five-minute note saves time today and costs you everything tomorrow. The fifteen-minute note feels like a burden in the moment and becomes your lifeline when you need it. If you are finding that you do not have time to document properly, the answer is not to document less - it is to see fewer patients, improve your systems, hire support staff for administrative tasks, or restructure your practice so that documentation gets the time it deserves. Because when the relationship turns ugly - and eventually, for some patient, it will - your chart is the only witness who never forgets, never lies, and never changes their story. Make sure it tells the right one.

Character is tested when the patient wants the shortcut and you want to avoid conflict- that's when the rules matter most

I want to close this chapter by coming back to where we started - the question of character. Character is not tested when things are easy. Character is not tested when the patient is grateful, the staff is compliant, the systems are working, and the money is flowing. Character is tested when the patient wants the shortcut and you want to avoid conflict. That is the moment- that exact moment - when the rules matter more than they ever have before.

Think about it. A long-term patient calls. They have been with you for a year. They have referred friends. They have always been pleasant. And now they are asking you to ship their refill before their labs come back because they are going on vacation and they do not want to run out. Just this once. They promise it will be fine. They remind you how loyal they have been. They appeal to your relationship. And you feel the pressure - not just from them, but from the part of you that does not want an awkward conversation, that does not want to seem rigid, that wants to be the good guy who takes care of his patients.

That is the moment that tests your character. Because the easy thing - the path of least resistance - is to say yes, ship the refill, deal with the labs when they get back. It takes five seconds. It avoids conflict. It preserves the relationship. And it creates a gap in your protocol that a plaintiff's attorney or board investigator will drive a truck through if that patient ever has a problem.

The hard thing - the thing that takes character - is to say no, kindly but firmly, and to document why. "Patient requested early refill prior to lab review due to travel. Per practice protocol, refills require current labs and clinician review. Explained rationale to patient - labs ensure safe continuation of therapy. Patient may experience brief gap in medication during travel; discussed options including scheduling labs prior to departure or resuming therapy upon return with lab clearance. Patient initially frustrated but ultimately agreed to schedule pre-travel lab draw." That note took two minutes to write. It avoided an exception. It enforced the protocol. It demonstrated to any future reviewer that you applied your rules consistently even when it was uncomfortable. And it protected both you and the patient.

The same test applies to your staff. Your medical assistant comes to you and says a patient called with what sounds like a minor side effect, and the assistant told them it was probably nothing to worry about but wanted to let you know. Do you say "thanks for handling it" because the assistant saved you time and the patient seemed fine? Or do you say "I appreciate you trying to help, but we need to document this properly and you cannot offer clinical assessments - let us review together what the patient reported and I will do the clinical evaluation"? One answer takes five seconds and trains your staff that bending the rules is okay. The other answer takes five minutes and reinforces the boundary that keeps your practice safe.

The same test applies to your documentation. You are exhausted at the end of a long day. You have seen twelve patients. You have fifteen notes to write. And you are tempted to cut corners- copy-paste from the last visit, use a template without customizing it, write "no changes, continue plan" instead of a substantive note. Do you take the shortcut because nobody will know the difference? Or do you write the full note because you understand that the chart is your only defense if any of those twelve patients ever files a complaint? One choice saves fifteen minutes tonight. The other choice might save your career in three years.

Character in medicine is not about being a saint. It is not about never feeling tempted to bend a rule, never wanting to avoid an awkward conversation, never wishing you could just take the easy path. It is about doing the right thing anyway, even when it is inconvenient, even when it is uncomfortable, even when nobody would know if you did not. Because in peptide medicine, the day will come when someone does know. The board investigator will know. The plaintiff's attorney will know. The medical expert reviewing your chart will know. And when that day comes, your character will be measured not by your intentions but by your documentation, your consistency, and your willingness to follow your own rules when following them was hardest.

I have spent my career watching physicians navigate these waters. The ones who survive -the ones who keep their licenses, their practices, and their peace of mind - are not the smartest or the most charismatic or the most clinically brilliant. They are the ones who built boring systems, followed them consistently, documented everything thoroughly, and had the character to say no when saying yes would have been easier. They are the ones who understood that the patient who loves them today really might hate them tomorrow, and they prepared for that possibility every single day.

You think the board cares that you meant well? They do not. You think the plaintiff's attorney cares that the patient was your friend? They do not. You think the investigator cares that your staff was just trying to be helpful? They do not. They care about what is in the chart. They care about whether you followed your own rules. They care about whether your practice looks like a medical practice or a business that happens to employ someone with an MD.

The clean office tells them you are careful before they read a word. The clean chart tells them you are thorough as they review every page. The clean conscience - the knowledge that you did the right thing even when it was hard - tells them you are a physician who takes the responsibility seriously. That is how you survive in this field. That is how you keep your license. That is how you look yourself in the mirror every morning and know that whatever comes, your chart will save you, not hang you.

Never make the undocumented exception. Never let staff drift into licensed work. Never let a cash-pay transaction outrun medical judgment. Never let the desire to avoid conflict override the duty to follow your protocol. The patient who loves you today can hate you tomorrow. Your systems do not have feelings. Your chart does not have friends. Your protocol does not play favorites. Build them clean. Run them clean. Keep them clean. That is the only armor you have, and it is enough if you use it every single day.

19 - Real-World Scenarios: What Actually Happens

Let me tell you something about textbook medicine. It is clean, organized, and makes sense on paper. Then the patient walks in, and everything gets dirty. Real patients do not follow algorithms. They skip doses, they lie about their bowel habits, they buy chemicals from websites with no phone number, and they expect you to fix their problem while they ignore every instruction you give them. This chapter is not theory. These are the situations you will face next week, probably next Tuesday, if you are running a real practice. Each scenario in this chapter is drawn from what actually happens when you put a peptide program into the world. I have seen every one of these situations multiple times, and I have seen good doctors handle them badly - and bad doctors handle them well. The difference is never about brilliance. It is about having a system, following it, documenting everything, and keeping your head when the patient is unreasonable. Read these scenarios carefully. They are your playbook.

The Patient with Constipation

Here is a phone call you will get a hundred times if you prescribe GLP-1 medications. The patient has been on semaglutide for three weeks. They started at the standard low dose. They tolerated the first week fine - a little nausea, nothing dramatic. Week two they noticed they were not going to the bathroom as often. Now it is week three, and they have not had a bowel movement in four days. They are uncomfortable, a little bloated, and starting to panic. Your staff gets the message, or the patient sends a portal note, or worse, they mention it casually at the front desk while checking out from a follow-up visit.

Let me be very clear about what not to do. Do not blow this off. Do not tell the patient constipation is normal and send them on their way. Do not have your receptionist say, "Oh yeah, that happens to everyone." Constipation on GLP-1 therapy is common - the drug slows gastric emptying, reduces gut motility, and many patients are also eating significantly less fiber because their appetite is suppressed. But common does not mean harmless. Severe constipation can lead to fecal impaction, bowel obstruction, dehydration, and significant abdominal pain. A patient who cannot move their bowels for a week and a half is not having a minor inconvenience. They are having a medical problem.

What you do is this: you assess. You ask specific questions. When was the last bowel movement? What was the consistency? Any abdominal pain - and if so, where, how severe, constant or intermittent? Any vomiting? Any blood in the stool? Any fever? How much fluid are they drinking daily? What does their diet look like now compared to before starting the medication? Are they taking any other medications that constipate - anticholinergics, opioids, certain antidepressants, iron supplements? Do they have a history of bowel disease, IBS, diverticulitis, prior obstructions?

The documentation in the chart needs to show that this assessment happened. Write it down:"Patient reports no bowel movement in four days. Denies severe abdominal pain, vomiting, fever, hematochezia. Hydration status reviewed. Dietary fiber intake assessed and found inadequate." Then document your instructions. Increase fluid intake to at least sixty-four ounces daily. Add a fiber supplement - psyllium or similar. Consider an over-the-counter stool softener or gentle osmotic laxative like polyethylene glycol. Explain that if they develop severe abdominal pain, vomiting, inability to pass gas, or go another seventy-two hours without a bowel movement, they need to stop the medication and seek urgent care or go to the emergency department.

The escalation pathway matters. Most cases of GLP-1-related constipation are manageable with conservative measures and resolve or improve as the patient adjusts. But you need a threshold for when this becomes an emergency. Severe or worsening abdominal pain, vomiting, fever, rectal bleeding, or a complete inability to pass stool despite laxatives - any of these means the patient stops the medication and gets evaluated urgently. Document that you gave these instructions. Document that the patient acknowledged them.

Why does this matter for board defense? Because a patient with untreated severe constipation who ends up in the hospital with an impaction or obstruction becomes a complaint. And if your chart shows no discussion of constipation, no monitoring instructions, no escalation criteria -you look sloppy. You look like someone who shipped a vial and stopped caring. The board does not need to prove malpractice. They only need to decide your care was below standard. A chart that shows you assessed, instructed, monitored, and gave clear stop rules is a chart that defends you. The patient may still have a problem - but you did not cause it by negligence.

The Patient Vomiting After Dose Increase

This scenario is even more serious than constipation because vomiting on GLP-1 therapy raises the specter of pancreatitis, gallbladder disease, and severe dehydration. The patient was doing fine on 0.5 milligrams weekly. They bumped up to 1 milligram as planned, and two days later they are vomiting. Maybe they vomited once. Maybe they cannot keep anything down. Maybe they have abdominal pain along with it. Your response needs to be swift, methodical, and thoroughly documented.

First, you hold the dose. Do not continue a medication that is making the patient vomit. If they cannot tolerate the current dose, escalating or maintaining at that level is not reasonable. Tell the patient to stop injecting until they speak with you. If they are actively vomiting, the medication is held immediately - no debate, no "see how it goes."

Second, you assess for seriousness. Is there abdominal pain? Where is it located? Epigastric pain radiating to the back is a pancreatitis red flag. Right upper quadrant pain after meals suggests gallbladder involvement - and GLP-1 drugs are associated with gallbladder disease. Is the pain severe? Is it constant? Any fever? Any jaundice? Can they keep fluids down? How many times have they vomited? When did it start relative to the dose? Did they eat a large meal or a high-fat meal before the episode? Any history of gallstones, prior pancreatitis, or heavy alcohol use?

Third, you think about dehydration. A patient who has vomited multiple times over twenty-four to forty-eight hours is losing fluid and electrolytes. GLP-1 patients are often already drinking less because their appetite is suppressed. Dehydration can cause dizziness, orthostatic hypotension, kidney injury, and worsening nausea. Ask about urine output - when did they last urinate, and what color was it? Are they dizzy when standing? Are their lips dry? These are basic questions that belong in your note.

If the vomiting is mild, the patient has no severe pain, no fever, no jaundice, and they can sip fluids, your plan may be to hold the medication, push oral rehydration, advance diet slowly as tolerated, and consider restarting at the prior tolerated dose after a week of normal eating and drinking. But this decision belongs in the chart, not in a text message from your staff. Document the symptom assessment, the hold decision, the differential considerations, and the follow-up plan.

If the vomiting is severe, persistent, or accompanied by significant abdominal pain, the patient needs urgent evaluation - urgent care at minimum, emergency department if symptoms are serious. You do not diagnose pancreatitis over the phone. You do not rule out gallbladder disease by text. You send them for assessment. Document that you advised urgent evaluation, document the symptoms that triggered that recommendation, and document whether the patient followed your advice.

The board risk here is significant if handled poorly. A patient with early pancreatitis whose doctor told them to "push through the nausea" is a patient who may end up hospitalized - and whose attorney will have a field day with your chart. A patient with gallbladder disease that was missed because vomiting was dismissed as "just a side effect" is a lawsuit waiting to happen. Your defense is your documentation of careful assessment, appropriate escalation, and a hold decision that protected the patient from continued exposure to a drug that was clearly not tolerable at that dose.

One more thing about vomiting patients: your staff needs a protocol for these calls. A patient who calls the front desk and says they are vomiting after their injection should not be told "the nurse will call you back tomorrow." That call gets escalated the same day, to a clinician, with documentation of the symptoms, the advice given, and the follow-up plan. Your staff should know the red-flag questions: are you having severe abdominal pain? Can you keep fluids down? Any fever? Any yellowing of the skin or eyes? If any answer raises concern, the staff member transfers immediately to clinical personnel. Do not let a non-clinical staff member triage what might be pancreatitis. That is practicing medicine without a license, and it is dangerous for the patient and for your practice.

The Patient Who Wants to Skip the Starting Dose

This patient has done their research - or so they think. They have been on Reddit. They have talked to a friend who has been on semaglutide for six months. They read that the starting dose is "just to get your body used to it" and they do not want to waste four weeks on a dose that will not make them lose weight. They want to start at 1 milligram, or even higher. They make this request sound reasonable. They frame it as saving time and money. They may even imply that another clinic would let them do it.

Your answer is no. Not a tentative no, not a maybe, not a "well, we usually start lower but let me think about it." No. The starting dose exists for a reason. GLP-1 receptor agonists cause dose-dependent gastrointestinal side effects - nausea, vomiting, diarrhea, constipation, reflux. The gastrointestinal system needs time to adapt to the medication. Starting too high does not accelerate weight loss. It accelerates side effects, discontinuation, dehydration, and emergency department visits. The drug labeling - yes, even the FDA-approved labeling that you should know - includes titration schedules precisely because this class of medication is not well tolerated when started at therapeutic doses.

What you say to the patient matters. You do not say, "Sorry, it is just our policy." That makes you sound like a bureaucracy, not a doctor. You say: "The starting dose is not about being cautious for caution's sake. It is about keeping you on the medication. Patients who start too high often feel so sick that they quit entirely. Then they have spent money, lost no weight, and feel terrible. The slow start keeps patients in the program. That is why we do it this way." You explain that you are not just following a cookbook - you are following a principle of maintaining tolerability so the patient can achieve sustained benefit.

You also explain the practical risk. Severe nausea and vomiting lead to dehydration. Dehydration leads to dizziness, orthostatic falls, acute kidney injury, and electrolyte disturbances. A patient who vomits repeatedly after an oversized first dose may end up in urgent care or the ER. That is not good patient care, and it is not good practice economics either.

Document this conversation thoroughly. The chart note should read: "Patient requested starting dose higher than standard. Patient counseled that titration schedule exists to maintain tolerability and prevent GI side effects that commonly lead to discontinuation. Patient educated on risks of nausea, vomiting, dehydration with rapid dose escalation. Patient instructed to follow prescribed titration schedule and not to self-escalate. Patient acknowledged understanding." If the patient pushes back, document their response and your reiteration of the plan. If the patient is unhappy and threatens to go elsewhere, document that too - calmly, professionally, without defensiveness. "Patient expressed dissatisfaction with titration plan. Risks re-explained. Patient declined to proceed with recommended plan at this time." This chart note protects you if the patient later claims you were inflexible or that nobody explained why the low dose mattered. The explanation is right there.

The board loves to see a doctor who stood firm for medical reasons, not arbitrary ones. A note that explains the clinical rationale for titration - tolerability, adherence, safety - is a note that defends the doctor. A note that says nothing because the argument happened verbally and was never recorded is a note that leaves you exposed.

The Patient Who Loses Too Much Appetite

This scenario sneaks up on practices because it sounds like success. The patient is losing weight. They are not hungry. They are hitting their goals. What is the problem? The problem is when appetite suppression becomes pathological - when a patient is eating eight hundred calories a day, losing muscle mass, becoming nutritionally deficient, dehydrated, and too weak to function. The GLP-1 medications are powerful. In some patients, they are too powerful. And if your practice celebrates every pound lost without asking how it is being lost, you are practicing bad medicine.

The patient comes in - or sends a message - saying they feel weak, tired, dizzy, or that food has become repulsive. They may have lost twenty pounds in six weeks. That is a lot of weight. It may be too fast. Ask about intake: what are they eating in a typical day? How many meals? How much protein? Are they drinking enough? Are they able to meet their nutritional needs, or has food become aversive? Are they experiencing hair loss, brittle nails, cold intolerance -signs of nutritional deficiency? Are they able to exercise, or are they too fatigued? Are they losing weight from fat, or are they losing muscle?

This assessment is critical because the chart needs to show you were not just cheering the weight loss. The chart needs to show you monitored for safety. Document the patient's reported intake. Document their weight loss trajectory. Document any symptoms of undernutrition - weakness, dizziness, fatigue, hair loss, poor wound healing. Ask about protein intake specifically; GLP-1 patients often reduce food volume dramatically and do not compensate with protein-rich foods, leading to loss of lean body mass.

Your response depends on severity. If the patient is mildly under-eating but still functional, you counsel on nutrition - protein targets, meal timing, nutrient-dense foods, hydration. You may hold the dose increase or even reduce the current dose if appetite suppression is excessive. If the patient is severely under-eating, losing weight too rapidly, or showing signs of nutritional deficiency, you reduce the dose, provide specific nutritional guidance, and consider whether the medication should be held entirely until eating patterns normalize. You also consider whether a referral to a registered dietitian is appropriate.

For patients losing weight rapidly, you must discuss the risk of gallbladder disease. Rapid weight loss is a known risk factor for gallstone formation. Combine that with GLP-1 therapy, which already carries a gallbladder warning, and you have a patient who needs monitoring. Ask about right upper quadrant pain, fatty food intolerance, nausea after meals. Document these questions and the patient's answers.

The board risk is nuanced here. A board reviewer looking at your chart will see weight loss numbers and may initially think the patient was doing well. But if your notes show no discussion of nutrition, no monitoring of intake, no assessment of whether the weight loss was safe - that looks like a weight-loss mill, not a medical practice. The defense note shows you asked about intake, you identified excessive appetite suppression, you adjusted the plan, and you monitored for nutritional safety. The chart proves you cared about the patient's health, not just the number on the scale.

The Patient with Thyroid Cancer Family History

This is one of the most important contraindication conversations you will have in GLP-1 prescribing, and it is also one of the most frequently botched. The patient checks the box for"family history of thyroid cancer" on their intake form. Your staff sees it. You see it. And if you are like too many doctors, you think, "Well, it is a family history, not a personal history. The labeling says personal or family history of medullary thyroid carcinoma or MEN2. Let me ask a quick question and move on." That is lazy medicine, and it can cost you.

The GLP-1 receptor agonist class carries a boxed warning - the most serious warning the FDA issues - for risk of thyroid C-cell tumors. The evidence comes from rodent studies. In humans, the data are limited, but the risk cannot be dismissed. The warning specifically applies to patients with a personal or family history of medullary thyroid carcinoma and patients with Multiple Endocrine Neoplasia syndrome type 2. Not all thyroid cancers are medullary thyroid carcinoma. Papillary thyroid cancer, follicular thyroid cancer, anaplastic thyroid cancer -these are different diseases with different genetics and different risk profiles. The GLP-1 warning is about medullary thyroid carcinoma specifically.

So when your patient checks the family history box, you do not give vague reassurance. You ask precise questions. What family member had thyroid cancer? What type of thyroid cancer was it? Was it medullary thyroid carcinoma specifically? Was it another type? Has the patient ever been evaluated for MEN2? Does the patient have a known RET proto-oncogene mutation? Has the patient themselves ever had thyroid nodules, thyroid cancer, or thyroid surgery? When was their last thyroid evaluation? Have they had thyroid function tests? Have they had a neck ultrasound?

If the family member had papillary thyroid cancer - the most common type - that is not a GLP-1 contraindication. If the family member had medullary thyroid carcinoma, it may be. If the patient has a personal history of any thyroid cancer, or MEN2, or a known RET mutation, you do not prescribe GLP-1 therapy. Period. The risk is not justified for weight loss. Document the reasoning. Document the referral to endocrinology if appropriate.

The chart note for this conversation needs to be detailed. Do not write: "Family history of thyroid cancer discussed. Risk reviewed. Patient cleared." That is worthless. Write: "Patient reports paternal aunt with papillary thyroid cancer diagnosed at age 62. Patient counseled that GLP-1 boxed warning applies specifically to medullary thyroid carcinoma and MEN2, not to papillary thyroid cancer. Patient denies personal history of thyroid nodules, thyroid cancer, or MEN2. Patient denies known RET mutation. No contraindication to GLP-1 therapy identified based on available history. Patient counseled to report any neck mass, hoarseness, dysphagia, or persistent throat symptoms. Patient advised to maintain routine thyroid monitoring with PCP." That note tells a story. It shows precision. It shows you know the difference between cancer types. It shows you did not just wave the concern away.

If the history is unclear - the patient does not know what type of thyroid cancer their relative had - you have a decision to make. If the information is obtainable, you ask the patient to find out, or you request records, or you defer prescribing until the question is answered. If the information is not obtainable and the family history is concerning, you err on the side of caution. You decline to prescribe GLP-1 therapy and you document why. You consider a non-GLP-1 weight loss approach. The board will never criticize you for being too careful with a boxed warning. They will criticize you for being sloppy.

The Patient with Gallbladder Symptoms

Upper abdominal pain in a patient on GLP-1 therapy is not a symptom to manage over the phone. It is a symptom to take seriously, evaluate properly, and document thoroughly. The patient calls your office and says they have pain in the upper right side of their abdomen. It started a few days ago. It gets worse after they eat, especially after fatty meals. Maybe they feel nauseated. Maybe they have had a low-grade fever. Maybe their stools look different -clay-colored or unusually pale.

Here is what gallbladder disease on GLP-1 therapy can look like: biliary colic from gallstones, cholecystitis, cholelithiasis precipitated by rapid weight loss, or pancreatitis from a common bile duct stone. All of these are potentially serious. GLP-1 medications slow gallbladder emptying and are associated with an increased risk of gallbladder disease, including cholecystitis and gallstone formation. The drug labeling says so. You cannot claim you did not know.

When this patient calls, your staff needs to route the call to a clinician immediately. This is not a "we will get back to you tomorrow" situation. You assess the character of the pain -location, radiation, severity, timing relative to meals, constant or colicky. You ask about fever, chills, jaundice, dark urine, pale stools, vomiting, and whether they can keep fluids down. You ask about prior gallbladder disease, known gallstones, prior gallbladder removal. You ask when they started the GLP-1, what dose they are on, how much weight they have lost, and how fast.

If the symptoms are mild and suggestive of biliary colic without red flags - no fever, no jaundice, tolerable pain, no vomiting - you still hold the GLP-1 dose. You tell the patient to eat a low-fat diet temporarily. You arrange imaging - a right upper quadrant ultrasound -and you refer them to their primary care physician or a gastroenterologist for evaluation. You do not restart the GLP-1 until gallbladder disease has been ruled out or addressed.

If the symptoms include fever, jaundice, severe or worsening pain, persistent vomiting, or signs of systemic illness, you send the patient to the emergency department. Now. Not later today. Now. You document the symptoms, your assessment, your instructions, and the time of communication. You follow up to confirm the patient went.

The chart note is critical. You write: "Patient reports RUQ abdominal pain x 3 days, worse postprandially, associated with nausea. No fever reported. No jaundice. GLP-1 held. Patient instructed to follow low-fat diet. RUQ ultrasound ordered. Referral to PCP for gallbladder evaluation. Patient instructed to seek emergency care if fever, jaundice, severe pain, or vomiting develop." If red flags were present, you document those and your emergency referral. If the patient refused to go, you document that too, along with your warning about the risks of delaying care.

The board will ask a simple question if this patient ends up with a perforated gallbladder or pancreatitis: did the doctor take the symptom seriously, or did they manage it like an inconvenience? A chart that shows immediate evaluation, appropriate holding of the medication, and proper referral tells the story of a careful physician. A chart that says "Patient complained of stomach pain. Advised to take antacids" is the chart of a doctor who will be explaining themselves to the board.

The Patient with Uncontrolled Blood Pressure

A patient comes to you for weight loss. They want semaglutide or tirzepatide. They are forty pounds overweight, and they are motivated. But when you check their vital signs - and you do check vital signs, because that is basic medicine - their blood pressure is 178 over 104. They are not on blood pressure medication. Or they are on a low-dose ACE inhibitor they have not taken regularly in months. Their last primary care visit was three years ago.

This is not a patient who should start GLP-1 therapy today. This is a patient who needs blood pressure management first. Now, it is true that GLP-1 medications, particularly semaglutide and tirzepatide, can lower blood pressure as part of their metabolic effects. Some weight loss itself lowers blood pressure. But uncontrolled hypertension is a cardiovascular risk factor. It suggests the patient is not under appropriate medical care. It may indicate renal disease, vascular disease, sleep apnea, or medication noncompliance. Starting a weight-loss medication in a patient with stage 2 hypertension who is not being followed for that hypertension is poor medical judgment.

Your approach is direct and non-negotiable. You tell the patient: "We cannot start weight-loss medication today because your blood pressure is dangerously high. This needs to be addressed first." You explain that uncontrolled hypertension increases the risk of stroke, heart attack, kidney damage, and other serious complications. You explain that weight-loss therapy requires medical monitoring, and that monitoring starts with making sure basic health risks are controlled. You refer the patient to their primary care physician or, if they do not have one, to an urgent care or primary care clinic for blood pressure evaluation and management.

You document everything. The vital signs. The blood pressure reading. Your concern. Your counseling. Your referral. Your explanation that weight-loss therapy will be reconsidered once blood pressure is controlled and the patient is under primary care supervision. You set a follow-up plan: the patient returns in six to eight weeks with documentation of blood pressure management from their PCP, or with updated vitals showing controlled hypertension.

Some patients will push back. They will say they feel fine - and many hypertensive patients do. They will say the blood pressure is just from stress or "white coat syndrome." You acknowledge that white coat hypertension exists. You also say that a reading of 178 over 104 cannot be assumed to be entirely white coat. You offer to recheck the pressure at the end of the visit. You offer to have them sit quietly for fifteen minutes and recheck. But if the pressure remains elevated, the answer does not change. The risk of ignoring severe hypertension is greater than the risk of delaying weight-loss therapy by a few weeks.

Document the pushback too. "Patient expressed frustration with delay in starting therapy. Patient counseled that uncontrolled hypertension is a contraindication to initiating GLP-1 therapy in this practice. Patient instructed to follow up with PCP for blood pressure management and to return with controlled BP and PCP clearance." This note shows you were not being arbitrary. You were being careful. And careful doctors keep their licenses.

The Patient with Prior Pancreatitis Who Wants GLP-1 Anyway

This scenario tests your backbone more than almost any other. The patient had pancreatitis two years ago. They were hospitalized. They recovered. Now they want to lose weight, they have heard about semaglutide, and they want it. They may downplay the pancreatitis - "It was just a little inflammation, I was fine after a few days." They may argue that their pancreatitis was from gallstones, not from a medication, so the risk does not apply. They may bring you articles or social media posts saying GLP-1s are safe in patients with prior pancreatitis. They may get emotional. They may plead.

Your job is to be a doctor, not a friend. The GLP-1 class carries a warning for pancreatitis. The evidence is not as robust as the thyroid cancer warning - it is based on post-marketing surveillance and clinical trial data showing a signal. But pancreatitis is a serious, potentially life-threatening condition. Acute pancreatitis can progress to necrotizing pancreatitis, organ failure, and death. Recurrent pancreatitis can lead to chronic pancreatitis, exocrine and endocrine insufficiency, and a lifetime of medical problems. This is not a remote theoretical risk. This is real.

When a patient with prior pancreatitis asks for GLP-1 therapy, you start with a detailed history. What caused the prior pancreatitis? Was it gallstone-related? Alcohol-related? Medication-related? Idiopathic? Hypertriglyceridemia? How severe was it? Was there necrosis? How long were they hospitalized? Did they have any recurrence? Have they had their gallbladder removed? What is their current triglyceride level? What is their alcohol use? Are they on any medications that can cause pancreatitis?

If the pancreatitis was severe, recurrent, or from an unclear cause, the answer is no. Not maybe. No. GLP-1 therapy is not appropriate. Document the reasoning: "Patient with history of severe acute pancreatitis requiring hospitalization. GLP-1 class carries pancreatitis warning. Risk of recurrence exceeds potential benefit of weight-loss therapy. Patient declined for GLP-1 therapy. Alternative weight-loss strategies discussed, including dietary counseling, other medication classes with different risk profiles, and referral to bariatric medicine."

If the pancreatitis was mild, clearly gallstone-related, the gallbladder has been removed, triglycerides are normal, alcohol use is minimal, and the patient has had no recurrence - you may consider GLP-1 therapy with enhanced consent and close monitoring. But enhanced consent means you document extensively. Close monitoring means you see the patient more frequently, you ask about abdominal pain at every visit, you check lipase or amylase if symptoms develop, and you have a very low threshold for stopping the medication and referring for evaluation. This is not standard prescribing. This is high-risk prescribing with extra precautions.

The patient who argues with your decision needs to be handled firmly and professionally. You do not debate social media posts. You say: "I understand you have done research, and I respect that. My job is to evaluate the risks based on your specific history. In my clinical judgment, the risk of triggering another episode of pancreatitis is not justified for weight loss. There are other ways to lose weight, and I am happy to discuss those with you." If the patient insists, you document their insistence and your continued refusal. If the patient becomes threatening or abusive, you terminate the encounter and document that too.

The board will look at whether your decision was defensible. A chart that shows a thorough history of the prior pancreatitis, an understanding of the drug warning, a risk-benefit analysis, and a clear decision - whether yes with precautions or no with rationale - is defensible. A chart that shows a prescription for semaglutide in a patient with prior pancreatitis with no discussion of the risk is indefensible. The patient does not get to consent you into bad medicine.

The Patient Using Another Clinic Simultaneously

This is a situation that should make every hair on the back of your neck stand up. You review your follow-up list and see that Mrs. Henderson is due for her refill. She has been on your program for three months, doing reasonably well. You check your notes from her last visit. Then your staff mentions they saw a charge on her credit card from another weight-loss clinic across town. Or maybe she casually mentions during a check-in that she got "a little extra"from another doctor because she wanted to try a different dose. Or worst of all, you get a pharmacy callback about a drug interaction and discover she is on two GLP-1 medications from two different prescribers.

Duplicate prescribing is not a minor administrative issue. It is a serious medical and legal problem. When a patient is on two GLP-1 receptor agonists simultaneously - say, semaglutide from you and tirzepatide from another clinic - they are getting additive or synergistic effects on appetite suppression, gastric emptying, and glucose metabolism. The risk of severe nausea, vomiting, dehydration, gallbladder disease, and pancreatitis increases dramatically. If something goes wrong - and with dual GLP-1 therapy, eventually something often does - both prescribers will be named in the complaint. And you will have a very hard time explaining why you did not know your patient was seeing another prescriber.

Your intake process should include a direct question: "Are you currently receiving weight-loss medication, hormone therapy, peptide therapy, or any similar treatment from any other provider, clinic, or telehealth service?" The question needs to be specific, because patients do not always think of telehealth or med spas as "real" medical care. Ask about online clinics, med spas, hormone clinics, wellness centers, anti-aging practices - anywhere that might be prescribing overlapping medication.

If you discover duplicate prescribing, you act immediately. You call the patient and ask directly what they are taking, from whom, at what doses, and for how long. You ask them to bring in the vials, labels, or pharmacy records so you can see exactly what they have. Then you make a clinical decision: does the patient's regimen need to be consolidated under one prescriber? Should therapy be paused while the situation is sorted out? Is the duplicate prescribing dangerous enough that the patient needs to stop everything and start over with clear monitoring?

Document this thoroughly. "Patient found to be receiving tirzepatide from outside telehealth clinic simultaneously with semaglutide prescribed by this practice. Patient counseled on risks of concurrent GLP-1 receptor agonist use including severe GI side effects, dehydration, gallbladder disease, and pancreatitis. Patient instructed to discontinue outside medication immediately. Patient instructed to bring all vials and labels to next appointment. Plan consolidated under single prescriber with clear dosing plan. Patient acknowledged risks and agreed to single-provider plan. Refill held pending confirmation that outside medication has been discontinued."

The board risk here is about duty and oversight. A prescribing physician has a duty to know what their patient is taking - or at least to ask. If your chart shows no question about other prescribers, no policy about single-provider care, and no documentation when duplicate prescribing was discovered, you look negligent. If your chart shows a systematic screening question, a documented discovery, an immediate clinical response, and a clear plan to consolidate care, you look responsible. The difference is in the documentation.

The Patient Using Research Chemicals

This patient walks in - or calls, or sends a message - already using peptides they bought online. They have a vial of something labeled "research use only" that they reconstituted themselves. They found a dosing protocol on a forum. Their friend has been using the same product and "feels amazing." They want you to take over their care, or they want your blessing for what they are doing, or they want you to prescribe something to stack on top of their internet vials.

Your first job is not to moralize. Your first job is to assess risk and document your warning. This patient is self-experimenting with an injectable compound of unknown identity, purity, sterility, and concentration. The certificate of analysis they proudly show you on their phone means nothing about sterility - it only speaks to chemical identity. The vial could contain the labeled compound at the labeled concentration. It could contain half the labeled dose. It could contain a completely different peptide. It could contain endotoxin, bacterial contamination, heavy metals, or synthetic byproducts. The patient has no idea, and neither do you.

You ask specific questions. What exact product did they buy? From what website or vendor? What is the lot number? What dose are they using? How did they reconstitute it - what diluent, what volume, what technique? How are they storing it? How are they injecting it -what needles, what sites, what rotation, what sterile technique? When did they start? What effects have they noticed? Any side effects? Any injection-site reactions, fevers, chills, or unusual symptoms?

Then you give a clear, documented warning. Tell the patient that research-use-only products are not manufactured or tested for human use. They have not been through FDA review, sterility testing appropriate for injectable medications, or quality controls required for pharmaceutical products. The vendor has no medical liability if the product is contaminated or mislabeled. The patient is assuming all risk. You do not incorporate the research chemical into their treatment plan. You do not endorse it. You do not calculate doses based on it. You treat it as an unverified, potentially dangerous substance.

If the patient wants to transition to legitimate therapy, you explain the pathway: stop the research chemical, complete your intake process, get appropriate labs if indicated, and you will evaluate whether a legitimate, pharmacy-compounded or FDA-approved option is appropriate. You do not prescribe over the research chemical. You do not "take over" the dosing. The patient starts over with you, cleanly, under your monitoring, with your pharmacy.

The chart note must capture the warning. Use the grey-market counseling template: "Patient reports use of online peptide product labeled for research use only. Patient counseled that research-use-only products are not legitimate clinical medication sources and carry risks of contamination, mislabeling, dosing error, sterility failure, endotoxin exposure, and unknown safety. Patient advised to discontinue unverified product and to use legitimate medical/pharmacy channels. Risks of continued self-injection with unverified product explained.

Patient's understanding and response documented." This note is evidence that you did your duty. You did not ignore the behavior. You did not endorse it. You warned the patient and offered a safer alternative.

The Patient Who Misses Follow-Up but Wants More Medication

This scenario is deceptively common and deeply annoying. The patient signs up for your program. They get their initial evaluation, their prescription, their medication. They are supposed to check in at week four, then week eight, then week twelve. But week four comes and goes - no response to your texts, no portal check-in, no answer to your calls. Week eight, same thing. Week twelve, the patient suddenly appears and wants their refill. They have been injecting for three months with zero medical oversight. Now they want more.

Your answer should be: not yet. Not automatically. Not because they showed up with money in hand. A medical program requires monitoring. If the patient has been absent for three months, you do not know their weight trend, their side effects, their nutritional status, their blood pressure, or whether they have developed any of the warning signs that would require stopping therapy. You are not a vending machine. You are a medical practice. And medical practices have rules.

What you do is this: you welcome the patient back without scolding them. You explain that their therapy was on hold because required follow-up was not completed. You tell them that before any refill is issued, you need to do a comprehensive re-evaluation - current weight, vital signs, symptom review, assessment of tolerance, and review of any interim medical issues. You may need updated labs depending on the therapy and the duration of missed follow-up. You schedule the appointment. You do not issue an emergency refill to tide them over while they wait.

If the patient becomes angry or entitled - and some will - you remain calm and consistent."I want to help you, and I understand you have been busy. But my responsibility is to make sure this therapy is safe for you. I cannot do that without checking in. The follow-up visits are part of the program, not an optional add-on." If the patient insists on an immediate refill and threatens to go elsewhere, you document the interaction professionally. You do not argue. You do not get defensive. You state your policy, document it, and let the patient make their decision.

The chart note captures the noncompliance and your response: "Patient missed required follow-up appointments at weeks 4, 8, and 12. No symptom check-ins or weight reports received during this period. Patient contacted practice requesting refill. Patient counseled that missed follow-up places therapy on hold pending re-evaluation. Patient scheduled for comprehensive reassessment including vitals, weight, symptom review, and lab review. Refill declined pending completion of required follow-up. Patient informed of safety rationale. Patient [acknowledged / expressed frustration / declined reassessment]." If the patient does not return for reassessment and you never hear from them again, that note sits in the chart as evidence that you maintained your standard of care. If the patient went elsewhere, got into trouble, and tried to blame you - that note protects you. You did not abandon them. They abandoned the monitoring plan, and you enforced your safety protocols.

The Patient Who Is Angry About Side Effects

This phone call or visit is emotionally charged, and it tests your composure. The patient is furious. They were told the medication was safe. They paid good money. Now they feel nauseated, or they are constipated, or they have sulfur burps, or they feel tired and weak - and they believe someone should have warned them better. They may accuse you of overselling the benefits and minimizing the risks. They may demand a refund. They may threaten a bad review, a complaint to the board, or a lawsuit. They are angry, and anger makes doctors defensive.

Do not get defensive. Do not argue. Do not tell the patient they were warned - even if they were. Do not dismiss their experience as "just side effects" or imply they should have known better. None of that helps, and all of it creates chart and legal problems. What you do is this: you listen. You acknowledge. You review. And you act clinically.

Start by acknowledging the patient's distress. "I hear you. Feeling sick from a medication is frustrating, especially when you were hoping to feel better. Let me review what is happening and see what we can do to help." This is not admitting fault. This is being a decent physician. Then you ask systematic questions about the side effects - what they are, when they started, how severe they are, whether they have worsened or improved, what the patient has tried, and whether any red-flag symptoms are present.

Next, you review the consent. Not to wave it in the patient's face - that will escalate the conflict - but to ground your own documentation and to refresh your memory about what was discussed. You documented the side effect discussion at the initial visit, right? You documented that nausea, constipation, vomiting, fatigue, and other GI symptoms were explained. You documented that the patient signed the consent form. If all of that is in the chart, you have a solid foundation. But you still do not lead with "You signed the form." You lead with clinical care.

Based on the severity and nature of the side effects, you make a clinical decision. Mild nausea that started with dose escalation and is improving? You may counsel on management techniques and continue at the current dose with close follow-up. Severe persistent vomiting? You hold the dose, assess for dehydration and pancreatitis, and do not restart until the patient is evaluated. Intolerable side effects at any dose? You discuss discontinuation, transition to a different agent, or alternative approaches. The patient's experience matters clinically. If they cannot tolerate the medication, continuing it is not good medicine regardless of what the consent says.

Document the encounter carefully. Record the patient's reported symptoms in their own words. Record your assessment. Record the review of consent and prior warnings. Record your clinical recommendation. Record the patient's response. If the patient remains angry and leaves dissatisfied, document that too - without editorializing. "Patient expressed significant frustration regarding nausea and fatigue. Reported symptoms reviewed. Consent and prior side-effect counseling discussed with patient. Dose held pending evaluation. Patient offered appointment for reassessment. Patient declined and stated intent to discontinue therapy. Patient advised to follow up with PCP for ongoing symptoms. Risks of abrupt discontinuation reviewed." This note shows you responded clinically, you did not argue, you offered appropriate care, and you documented thoroughly. It is your defense if the complaint comes.

The Patient Who Wants Therapy for a Child

This is a hard no, and it needs to be a hard no with clear documentation. A parent or guardian contacts your practice asking about semaglutide, or growth hormone-releasing peptides, or any other peptide therapy for their child. The child is twelve, or fourteen, or sixteen. Maybe they are overweight. Maybe the parent read online that certain peptides can help with growth, or athletic performance, or focus, or whatever the latest wellness trend claims. The parent is asking you to prescribe an injectable medication for a minor based on internet research.

You do not do this. Not because you do not care about the child. Precisely because you care about the child. Pediatric patients are not small adults. Their physiology is different. Their risk profiles are different. Their ability to consent, to self-administer, to report symptoms, and to comply with monitoring is different. GLP-1 receptor agonists, for example, have specific pediatric approvals for certain ages in certain formulations - but those approvals exist within a framework of specialized evaluation, endocrinology involvement, growth monitoring, and longitudinal follow-up that a cash-pay wellness clinic is not equipped to provide. Other peptides have no pediatric data at all. None. Zero clinical trials in children. Giving an injectable peptide to a child based on adult data and parental enthusiasm is reckless.

Your response is firm, kind, and documented. You explain that your practice does not provide peptide therapy to pediatric patients. You explain that children with weight concerns should be evaluated by a pediatrician, and if there is a medical indication for pharmacological intervention, that should be managed by a pediatric endocrinologist or other appropriate specialist. You offer to provide the parent with information about pediatric weight management resources. You do not hedge. You do not say "let me think about it" or "maybe if we get special consent." You say no, explain why, refer appropriately, and document.

The chart note for an inquiry - even if the child was never seen - should be documented:"Parent/guardian of [age]-year-old patient inquired about [specific peptide] therapy for child. Practice policy: peptide therapy is not provided to pediatric patients. Parent counseled that pediatric weight management requires evaluation by pediatrician or pediatric endocrinologist. Referral information provided. No prescription issued. No evaluation performed. Parent's response documented." If the parent becomes pushy or tries to argue, you stay firm. If they threaten to go elsewhere, you wish them well. You do not compromise on pediatric safety to avoid losing a case.

The board risk of treating a child inappropriately is enormous. State medical boards view pediatric patients as a vulnerable population. Prescribing to a minor without appropriate specialty involvement, without pediatric-specific indications, and without a system for pediatric monitoring is the kind of decision that ends careers. The complaint may come from the other parent, from a school nurse, from a pediatrician the child sees later, or from the child themselves when they turn eighteen and wonder why a wellness clinic gave them injections at age thirteen. Your hard no, documented clearly, is your protection.

The Patient Who Wants Therapy for a Spouse Without Evaluation

This scenario comes in several varieties, and all of them end the same way. A patient has been in your program for six months and loves the results. Their spouse is struggling with similar issues. The spouse does not want to come in for a full evaluation - they are busy, they are skeptical, they do not like doctors, they are sure they are "just like" their partner and need the exact same thing. The existing patient asks if you can just "add them to the order" or "send them the same medication" or "write a quick prescription without all the paperwork."

No. A thousand times no. Every patient needs their own evaluation. Every patient needs their own history, their own vital signs, their own contraindication screen, their own consent, their own assessment of whether therapy is appropriate. There are no exceptions. Not for spouses. Not for family members. Not for "they are exactly the same as me." They are not the same. They have different medical histories, different medications, different allergies, different blood pressure, different organ function, different risk factors, and different contraindications. A medication that is appropriate and safe for one person can be dangerous or fatal for another.

The husband on semaglutide may have no thyroid history and a normal gallbladder. The wife may have a family history of medullary thyroid carcinoma she has never mentioned because nobody ever asked her - because nobody ever evaluated her. The wife may have a history of pancreatitis from prior gallstones that the husband does not know about. The wife may be on medications that interact with the peptide. The wife may have uncontrolled hypertension, or an eating disorder, or be planning pregnancy. You do not know any of this because you have never evaluated her. And you cannot know it from a secondhand report from her husband.

Your response to the patient is polite but absolute: "I am glad the program has worked well for you. I cannot prescribe for your spouse without evaluating them personally. Every patient needs their own medical assessment, and that is a legal and safety requirement we cannot waive. If your spouse is interested, they are welcome to schedule a new patient evaluation, and we will be happy to see if the program is appropriate for them." If the patient pushes back, you do not negotiate. You repeat the boundary. If the patient implies that another clinic would do it, you say: "That may be, but our standard is individual evaluation for every patient. That is how we practice medicine."

Document the request and your response. "Patient requested prescription for spouse [name] without evaluation. Practice policy explained: every patient requires individual medical assessment, history, vitals, contraindication screening, and informed consent. Patient informed that no exceptions are made for family members. Spouse invited to schedule new patient evaluation if interested. Patient [acknowledged / expressed frustration]. No prescription issued." This note is your shield if the patient later claims you were unhelpful, or if the spouse goes to another clinic, has a problem, and someone asks whether your practice was involved.

Prescribing without evaluation is called practicing medicine without a standard of care. The board calls it unprofessional conduct. A plaintiff's attorney calls it negligence. You call it unacceptable. Every patient, every time, no exceptions.

Here is a practical safeguard you should build into your intake process: ask every new patient whether they have a spouse, family member, or friend who is currently in your program or who encouraged them to come in. This simple question flags the relationship dynamic early. It lets your staff know that this patient may have expectations shaped by someone else's experience, and it reminds your clinical team to evaluate this patient as a unique individual with their own history, risk factors, and contraindications. If the spouse calls later asking for a favor, your chart already shows that you identified the relationship at intake and applied your standard evaluation protocol. That is the kind of documentation that ends conversations before they become complaints.

The Patient Threatening a Bad Review

This is a situation that makes practice owners sweat. The patient is unhappy. Maybe they had side effects. Maybe they did not lose as much weight as they expected. Maybe they want a refund and you said no because they signed a policy acknowledging that results are not guaranteed and fees are not refundable after medication has been dispensed. Now the patient says: "If you don't give me what I want, I am going to post a terrible review on every platform.

I am going to tell everyone this practice is a scam. I am going to ruin your reputation."

Your first instinct may be to panic. Do not panic. Your second instinct may be to give them a refund just to make the problem go away. Do not do that either. Your third instinct may be to argue with them online or call them back and try to reason with them. Do not do any of these things. Here is what you do instead.

First, you do not negotiate under threat. The moment you change a clinical or business decision because a patient threatened you, you have opened a door that never closes. Every future dissatisfied patient will learn that threats work. Your practice becomes hostage to anyone with a Yelp account. You maintain your policy, whatever it is, because the policy exists for reasons- clinical, legal, and financial. If the policy says no refunds after medication ships, you stand by it. If the clinical decision was sound, you stand by it.

Second, you do not engage in a public argument. If a bad review appears, you do not respond online in detail. You do not defend the case in public. You do not disclose any protected health information - even confirming that the person was a patient can be a HIPAA violation in some circumstances. If you respond to reviews at all, your response is a generic, professional statement: "We take patient feedback seriously. Please contact our office directly so we can address your concerns." That is it. Nothing more. The public argument is a trap that catches more doctors than the original complaint.

Third, you document the threat. You write a chart note: "Patient expressed dissatisfaction with [specific issue]. Patient requested [refund / dose change / exception to policy]. Request reviewed and declined per practice policy [or clinical rationale explained]. Patient stated intent to post negative online review if request not granted. Patient counseled on policy and clinical rationale. No PHI disclosed. Patient's statement and practice response documented." If the threat escalates - if the patient becomes abusive, makes threats of violence, or engages in harassment - you document that and you consider terminating the patient from the practice with appropriate notice.

Fourth, you consider whether a board complaint may follow. Patients who threaten bad reviews sometimes follow through with complaints to the state medical board. A well-documented chart is your best preparation. If you have followed your protocols, documented your care, obtained proper consent, and maintained professional boundaries, a board complaint founded on nothing more than patient unhappiness will typically go nowhere. The board sees these constantly. They distinguish between complaints based on poor care and complaints based on unmet expectations. Your chart proves which category yours falls into.

Fifth, you accept that you cannot please everyone. A peptide and weight-loss practice will have dissatisfied patients. Some will not lose weight despite adherence. Some will have side effects despite proper screening. Some will have unrealistic expectations that no amount of counseling can correct. A bad review from a dissatisfied patient is not a catastrophe. A pattern of bad reviews suggesting systemic problems would be. One or two angry reviews in the context of hundreds of satisfied patients is normal business. Do not let a threatened review change your clinical judgment or your policies.

The Patient Whose Insurance Asks Questions

Cash-pay medicine and insurance are oil and water. They do not mix, and when they collide, the result is usually trouble for the physician. This scenario usually goes something like this: your patient paid cash for their peptide program. They have health insurance through their employer. They submitted their receipt to their insurance company hoping for out-of-network reimbursement. The insurance company denied the claim - because your service is not covered, or because the coding on the receipt does not match their requirements, or because they simply do not reimburse for peptide therapy. Now the patient is upset and wants you to fix it. They want you to provide different documentation. They want you to submit a claim on their behalf. They want you to change the date of service or the description of the service so it will be covered. Or worse - the insurance company sends you a letter asking for medical records, or copies of your superbills, or an explanation of the services provided.

Here is your position, and it must be absolute: you do not file insurance claims. You do not change your documentation to satisfy an insurance company's billing requirements. You do not provide medical records to an insurance company without proper patient authorization and without understanding exactly why they are requesting them. Your practice operates on a cash-pay model, and that model means the financial relationship is between you and the patient. The insurance company is the patient's problem, not yours.

When a patient asks you to help with insurance reimbursement, your answer is straightforward:"Our practice operates on a cash-pay basis and does not file insurance claims. We can provide you with a receipt for services rendered, which you are welcome to submit to your insurance company on your own. We cannot guarantee reimbursement, and we cannot modify our documentation to meet insurance billing requirements." If the patient wants a receipt with specific codes, you provide a receipt that accurately describes what was done - not what the patient wishes was done so their insurer will pay.

When an insurance company contacts you directly, you proceed carefully. Do not automatically send records. Determine what they are asking for and why. Are they conducting a routine claim review? Are they investigating fraud allegations? Are they responding to a patient complaint? Each scenario requires a different response, and your malpractice attorney or healthcare counsel should guide you. A blanket response of sending everything they ask for can create more problems than it solves. You need to verify that the patient has authorized the release. You need to understand whether the request is appropriate. And you need to recognize that some insurance companies use record requests as fishing expeditions to find documentation problems they can exploit.

The Medicare situation requires special attention. If your patient is a Medicare beneficiary, you must be extremely careful about how services are presented. Medicare has specific rules about non-covered services. You cannot bill Medicare for peptide therapy in a way that implies it is covered. You cannot accept assignment from Medicare for non-covered services in certain circumstances. The rules are complex, vary by service type, and change. If you see Medicare patients in your cash-pay practice, you need specific legal guidance on how to structure that relationship. This is not optional. Medicare violations carry penalties that make state board discipline look gentle.

Document your insurance policy clearly in your patient materials and in the chart. The patient acknowledgment form should state: "This practice does not participate with insurance plans, does not file insurance claims, and does not guarantee reimbursement. The patient is responsible for payment at the time of service. Receipts are provided for the patient's personal use in seeking reimbursement, if any, from their insurer." When a patient asks you to get involved with their insurance, document the request and your response. When an insurance company contacts you, document the contact, what was requested, what you provided, and any legal counsel you consulted.

The board risk of insurance involvement is real and underestimated. Insurance companies that deny claims sometimes file complaints with state medical boards as leverage. They may allege that your coding was improper, your documentation insufficient, or your services not medically necessary - not because they care about medical quality, but because they want to avoid paying and want pressure on you to stop billing their members. A cash-pay model insulates you from much of this, but only if you truly operate as cash-pay. The moment you start filing claims, accepting assignment, or modifying documentation for insurers, you have invited the wolf into your house. Keep the boundary clean. Cash pay means cash pay. The patient's insurance is their business, not yours.

Let me close this chapter with a final thought that runs through every scenario above. Medicine practiced well is mostly boring. The same questions every time. The same documentation every time. The same policies applied to every patient regardless of charm, wealth, persistence, or threat. Boring medicine keeps licenses safe. Exciting medicine - the fast exceptions, the verbal agreements, the "just this once" decisions, the undocumented phone calls - is what ends careers. Every scenario in this chapter is a test of whether you will follow your system when it is inconvenient, when the patient is unhappy, when money is on the line, or when your compassion tempts you to bend a rule. Follow the system. Document your reasoning. Protect your patient, and in doing so, protect yourself. The board will not ask whether you were popular. They will ask whether your chart proves you were careful. Make sure it does.

Think of this chapter as your field manual. When one of these scenarios walks through your door - and they will, I promise you - you will not have time to look up the perfect response. You will be in the moment, with a patient staring at you, expecting an answer, maybe pushing back, maybe threatening, maybe pleading. That is when your preparation shows. If you have read these scenarios, internalized the principles, and built your protocols accordingly, the right response will come naturally. You will know to hold the dose, to ask the hard questions, to document thoroughly, and to say no when no is the only safe answer. The doctors who get in trouble are the ones who wing it. The doctors who thrive are the ones who have a playbook and follow it. This is your playbook. Use it.

One last piece of advice that applies to every single scenario in this chapter: when you are uncertain, slow down. Uncertainty is not weakness. It is clinical wisdom recognizing that more information is needed. A patient with an unclear history, an ambiguous symptom, a questionable request, or a complicated risk profile deserves your careful deliberation, not your rushed decision. Pause. Gather more data. Consult a colleague. Refer to a specialist. Sleep on it if the situation allows. The patient who pressures you for an immediate answer when you are uncomfortable is exactly the patient who will file a complaint when that rushed decision turns out badly. Slow medicine is safe medicine. Documented medicine is defensible medicine. That combination is how you practice peptide therapy for decades without ever hearing your name mentioned at a board hearing.

PART V: PATIENTS, MARKETING, AND KEEPING YOUR SANITY

How to say no, avoid bad-fit patients, and run a cleaner practice.

The human side: consultations, complaints, and character.

20 - When to Say No - And Mean It

Saying No Is Part of Medicine and Part of Business

Let me tell you something I have learned watching doctors come and go over thirty-plus years in this business. The ones who last - the ones who keep their licenses, their money, and their sleep at night - are not the doctors who never say no. They are the doctors who say no early, say it often, and say it without losing a minute of sleep afterward. The doctors who end up in front of a board, or worse, in a courtroom, are almost always the ones who knew better but said yes anyway. They said yes because the patient pushed. They said yes because the sale was tempting. They said yes because they did not want a bad review. They said yes because they told themselves it would probably be fine. And it was not fine.

Saying no is not some philosophical posture. It is not about being difficult or elitist or turning patients away for sport. It is a clinical tool, the same as your stethoscope or your prescription pad, and it is every bit as essential to good medicine. In fact, in the world of peptide prescribing - where you are already operating at the edge of mainstream acceptance, where the compounds are compounded and not FDA-approved for most indications, where the board is watching and the plaintiff's bar is circling - your ability to say no may be the single most important clinical skill you possess. More important than your knowledge of dosing protocols. More important than your compounding pharmacy relationships. More important than your marketing or your pricing or your patient volume. Because none of that matters if you lose your license.

Let me be crystal clear about something. When you refuse a patient for the right clinical reasons, you are not declining a sale. You are making a medical decision. You are exercising physician judgment in exactly the way the board expects you to. The board does not want to see a practice where every single person who walks through the door or fills out an online questionnaire gets a prescription. The board knows what that looks like. They have seen those practices. They call them pill mills, or vial shops, or whatever pejorative is in fashion that year. And they shut them down. Hard.

What the board respects - what any reasonable reviewer respects - is a physician who demonstrates pattern recognition, risk assessment, and clinical judgment. A physician who looks at a patient and says, "You know what? This does not make sense for you right now. Let me explain why." That is not a physician being difficult. That is a physician being a physician. And when the chart reflects that thought process, when the documentation shows a clear clinical rationale, an explanation to the patient, alternatives offered, and a plan going forward- that chart is a shield. That chart says, "I am a careful doctor who takes this seriously." That chart wins cases.

I want you to think about this from the board's perspective for a moment, because most doctors never do until they are sitting in a hearing room staring at a panel of strangers who hold their career in their hands. The board sees hundreds, maybe thousands, of charts a year. They know what a legitimate medical practice looks like. They also know what a prescription factory looks like. The prescription factory has thin charts, missing histories, no follow-up plans, no documented refusals, and a hundred-percent approval rate. Every patient gets something. Nobody gets turned away. That is not a medical practice. That is retail with a DEA number. And the board crushes those operations because they are dangerous to the public and an embarrassment to the profession.

Your chart, by contrast, should tell a different story. Your chart should show that you assessed each patient individually. That you considered risks and benefits. That you documented your reasoning. And critically - that you said no when the situation warranted it. A pattern of thoughtful, well-documented refusals does not make you look stingy or difficult. It makes you look careful. It makes you look like a physician who puts patient safety ahead of revenue. And that, believe it or not, is exactly what the board wants to see. They may not love peptide therapy as a category, but they will respect a physician who practices it conservatively and defensibly.

Now let me address the business side, because I know what some of you are thinking. You are thinking, "Jim, every refusal is lost revenue. I have overhead. I have staff. I have a mortgage."

And you are right. Every refusal does represent a lost sale in the short term. But here is what thirty years of watching this industry has taught me: the revenue you lose from saying no to the wrong patient is the cheapest insurance policy you will ever buy. It is far cheaper than the attorney you will hire when that patient files a complaint. It is cheaper than the lost income during a board investigation that takes eighteen months to resolve. It is cheaper than the settlement or judgment when that patient has a bad outcome and sues. It is cheaper than the reputational damage when word gets around that you prescribed recklessly. It is infinitely cheaper than losing your license entirely and having to figure out how to feed your family with a medical degree you can no longer use.

I have seen doctors lose everything over a single bad prescription. One. A physician in Texas-experienced, well-trained, had been practicing for fifteen years - prescribed a growth hormone secretagogue to a patient who had an uncontrolled medical condition that should have been an automatic disqualifier. The patient did not disclose it on the intake form. The doctor did not verify it. The patient had a serious adverse event, ended up in the hospital, and the board came calling. That doctor's chart showed no discussion of contraindications, no refusal documentation, no follow-up plan - just a prescription and a billing code. The board did not care that the patient had lied on the form. They cared that the doctor had not done the work. That doctor's license was restricted for two years, during which time his practice income dropped by seventy percent. He told me later that the twenty-five hundred dollars he would have lost by refusing that patient would have been the best money he never spent.

That is the math, folks. And it is not hard math. Every refusal is a deposit in the bank account that matters most: your defensibility account. You want a thick file of documented, well-reasoned refusals. You want the board to see that you say no regularly, consistently, and clinically. Because that pattern protects you more than any consent form, any hold-harmless clause, or any fancy arbitration agreement ever will.

The Patient May Be Angry, the Practice May Lose a Sale - That's Cheaper Than Losing a License

Here is something they do not teach you in medical school, and they sure as hell do not teach it in business school: an angry patient who walks out of your office without a prescription is a gift. I know that sounds counterintuitive. I know it stings in the moment. I know your staff does not love dealing with someone who is frustrated and vocal about it. But that angry patient is a gift because they are no longer your problem. They are someone else's problem. And that someone else can deal with the headache, the liability, and the board complaint that may follow.

The patient who gets angry when you refuse them is often exactly the patient you should have refused. Think about it. The patient who storms out because you will not prescribe a growth hormone secretagogue without current labs and PCP clearance - that patient just proved your point. They demonstrated impulsivity, poor tolerance for boundaries, and an unwillingness to follow medical recommendations before they even started therapy. Those are the patients who self-adjust doses, who buy black market product on the side, who ignore side effects until they land in the ER, and who file complaints when things do not go their way. You just dodged a bullet. Say thank you and move on.

I am not saying you should enjoy making patients unhappy. I am a nurse. I got into this field because I care about people. But caring about people does not mean giving them everything they ask for. Sometimes the most caring thing you can do is say no. Sometimes protecting a patient from their own poor judgment - and protecting yourself in the process - is the best medicine you can practice that day.

Let me tell you about a call I got from a physician in Florida a few years back. This doctor had built a beautiful peptide practice, high-end, cash-pay, everything done right. One day a patient came in demanding a specific peptide protocol he had read about on a bodybuilding forum. The patient had no relevant medical indication for this protocol, was not willing to provide lab work, refused to involve a primary care physician, and became verbally aggressive when the doctor explained why that was not possible. The doctor stood his ground. The patient left a one-star review on three different platforms, posted on social media that the practice was "a scam," and threatened to file a board complaint. The doctor called me in a panic, worried that his reputation was ruined and that the board was going to come after him.

I asked him one question: "Did you document the interaction?" He had. Beautiful documentation. The chart showed the patient's request, the clinical reasoning for refusal, the explanation given, the alternatives offered, the patient's reaction, and the physician's decision to decline care. I told him to sleep well that night. The one-star reviews stung his Google rating, sure. But here is what happened next. The board did get a complaint - from the patient. The investigator requested the chart. The doctor's attorney sent over the documentation. The investigator closed the file in six weeks with no finding of wrongdoing. Meanwhile, the patient had gone to a less careful practitioner, gotten exactly what he demanded, and ended up in the hospital with a complication related to an undisclosed preexisting condition. That other practitioner? He is still under board investigation, two years later.

The lesson is simple: the patient may be angry, and the practice may lose a sale, and your Google rating may take a hit. All of that is temporary. A board finding against you is permanent. A lawsuit judgment is permanent. A lost license is permanent. You do the math.

And here is something else worth considering. The patients who respect your clinical judgment, who appreciate that you are careful and conservative, who see that you put their safety first - those patients become your best marketing. They tell their friends, "This doctor would not just give me what I asked for. He made sure it was safe for me first." That kind of referral is worth ten times more than the patient who got a prescription after a five-minute phone call. Because the referred patient trusts you before they even walk in the door. They know you are the real deal. And they are far less likely to cause problems down the road.

The patients who want fast, cheap, no-questions-asked prescribing are not your patients. Let them go. Let them find the vial shop down the street that will give them whatever they want with a credit card and a smile. That place will not be in business three years from now, or if it is, it will be under investigation, understaffed, and fighting for its life. You, meanwhile, will be sleeping soundly, practicing good medicine, and building a defensible practice that lasts.

A Patient Cannot Consent You Into Bad Medicine

This is a point I cannot emphasize enough, and it is one that physicians constantly get wrong. I hear it all the time. "But the patient signed the consent form." "But the patient acknowledged the risks." "But the patient said they understood and still wanted to proceed." Let me be as clear as I possibly can about this: a patient signature on a consent form does not transform bad medicine into good medicine. A patient cannot consent you into a clinical decision that was reckless, contraindicated, or below the standard of care. Period. Full stop. End of story.

Informed consent is not a magic spell. It does not erase your clinical obligation to exercise good judgment. If you prescribe a peptide to a patient who has a clear contraindication, and that patient signs twenty consent forms acknowledging every possible risk, and then has a catastrophic outcome - the consent forms will not save you. The board will look at the prescription decision and ask one simple question: "Doctor, why did you prescribe this to a patient for whom it was clearly inappropriate?" And your answer - "Because the patient really wanted it and signed all the forms" - will not be good enough. It will not even be close to good enough.

Let me put this in terms that might resonate. If a patient walked into your office and asked you to amputate a healthy limb because they read online that it would improve their athletic performance, would you do it? Of course not. And if they signed a consent form saying they understood all the risks of amputation and wanted to proceed anyway, would that change your answer? Of course not. Because the procedure is inappropriate regardless of consent. The same principle applies to peptide prescribing, even if the stakes feel less dramatic. An inappropriate prescription is an inappropriate prescription. The patient's enthusiasm does not make it appropriate. Their signature does not make it appropriate. Your job is not to give patients what they want. Your job is to give patients what is medically appropriate, explain the alternatives, and let them make an informed choice among appropriate options.

I have sat in on board hearings where physicians genuinely believed that robust informed consent documentation would protect them from allegations of poor prescribing. They brought stacks of paper. Multi-page consent forms. Video recordings of the consent discussion. Pages of risk disclosure. And the board looked at all of it, nodded politely, and then asked: "Doctor, what was the medical indication for this therapy in this patient?" And when the answer was weak, or missing, or contradicted by the patient's own history - the consent forms became irrelevant. They became evidence not of careful practice, but of a physician who knew the decision was questionable and tried to paper over it with documentation.

That is the worst possible position to be in. Because now you do not just look careless. You look like you knew better and did it anyway. The board hates that. Judges hate that. Juries hate that. And they should, because that is exactly what happened. You knew the patient was not a good candidate. You knew the risks outweighed the potential benefits. You knew the chart would look bad if anyone ever reviewed it. But you prescribed anyway, and then you layered on documentation to try to protect yourself. That is not defensible practice. That is self-aware recklessness, and it is the fastest route to a severe sanction that I know of.

The correct approach is the opposite. Make the right clinical decision first. Prescribe when it is appropriate. Refuse when it is not. Then document the reasoning, the discussion, the consent, and the plan. When you do it in that order - good medicine first, documentation second -your chart is naturally defensible. You do not need twenty-page consent forms because the clinical decision itself makes sense. The consent becomes the cherry on top, not the armor you are hiding behind.

Let me give you a concrete example. A patient comes to you wanting CJC-1295 with ipamorelin for general anti-aging. They are seventy-two years old, have uncontrolled atrial fibrillation, are on multiple cardiac medications, have not seen a cardiologist in three years, and refuse to get cardiac clearance before starting therapy. Their argument is: "I read online this is safe. I understand the risks. I will sign whatever you want. Just give me the prescription."

If you prescribe, you have made a terrible clinical decision. Growth hormone secretagogues can affect fluid balance, cardiac function, and metabolic parameters in ways that matter enormously in uncontrolled atrial fibrillation. No amount of consent documentation fixes that. The correct response is to refuse, explain why cardiac stability must come first, offer to reassess after cardiology clearance, document everything, and move on. The patient may be furious. They may go to another practitioner who says yes. That practitioner now owns the liability. You have protected yourself, protected the patient from a potentially dangerous intervention, and demonstrated clinical judgment that the board would respect.

That is the standard you should hold yourself to. Every single time. Not "Did they consent?"but "Was this the right medical decision?" If the answer to the second question is no, then the answer to the first question does not matter.

No Is a Complete Sentence - Document the Reason and Move On

I want to leave you with one final thought before we move into the specifics of when and how to say no. And it is this: no is a complete sentence. You do not owe patients elaborate justifications that they can debate and pick apart. You do not need to negotiate with them like you are haggling over a used car. You do not need to apologize for exercising clinical judgment. You explain your reasoning clearly, kindly, and firmly. You document it thoroughly. And then you move on.

The physicians who get into trouble with refusals are the ones who turn every no into a conversation that never ends. They explain their reasoning, the patient challenges it, they explain more, the patient brings in something they read online, they counter that, the patient gets emotional, they soften their position, and before they know it they have talked themselves into a prescription they never should have written. Do not do this. Your no should be as clean and definitive as your yes. The patient deserves an explanation, but they do not deserve an argument.

Document the refusal with the same care you would document a prescription. Actually, document it with more care, because this is the chart entry that may save your license one day. Include the patient's request, your clinical assessment, the specific reason for refusal, the explanation you provided, the alternatives you offered (referral, specialist consultation, lifestyle modifications, reassessment at a later date), and the patient's response. Sign it. Date it. Move on to the next patient who actually needs your help.

The beauty of a well-documented refusal is that it is done. There is no follow-up lab to review. No side effect to manage. No middle-of-the-night phone call from an ER physician asking what you prescribed and why. The case is closed. You have exercised good judgment, protected a patient from potential harm, and created a chart entry that demonstrates exactly the kind of conservative, thoughtful practice the board wants to see. That is a win in every possible way. Treat it like one, and move on to the next patient.

When to Say No

Now let us get specific. In the previous section, I talked about the philosophy of saying no -why it matters, why it protects you, why it is good medicine. That is all well and good, but philosophy does not help you when you have a patient sitting across from you - or on the other end of a telehealth screen - and you need to make a decision in real time. So in this section, I am going to walk you through the concrete situations where no is the only appropriate answer. These are not suggestions. These are not "use your judgment" gray areas where reasonable physicians might disagree. These are the situations where every experienced practitioner I know - every one - says the same thing: not this patient, not now, not under these circumstances. Learn to recognize them, learn to act on them, and learn to document them.

Missing or Unreliable History - No Chart, No Prescription

The most common mistake I see in peptide practices - and I see it constantly - is prescribing without adequate history. And I do not mean history that is thin or incomplete. I mean history that is essentially nonexistent. A patient fills out an online questionnaire with one-word answers. They skip the medication section. They leave the family history blank. They write"none" for allergies without any elaboration. They provide no primary care physician information. They have not had labs in five years. And somehow, somewhere in the process, a prescription gets written.

Let me be absolutely clear about this. If you do not have a reliable, comprehensive medical history on a patient, you do not prescribe. Period. It does not matter how healthy they claim to be. It does not matter how insistent they are. It does not matter that they "just want to try it" or that they "read it is safe" or that they "had it before from another doctor and it was fine." If you cannot document a thorough history, you cannot assess risk. And if you cannot assess risk, you cannot prescribe safely. This is not optional. This is foundational.

The history is the foundation upon which every clinical decision rests. Without it, you are prescribing blind. You do not know what medications they are on that might interact. You do not know what conditions they have that might contraindicate therapy. You do not know what their family history suggests about future risk. You do not know whether their prior doctor stopped therapy for a reason. You are flying in fog with no instruments, and eventually you are going to hit something.

I consulted on a case in Arizona where a physician prescribed a GLP-1 receptor agonist peptide to a patient based on a fifteen-minute telehealth consultation. The patient's intake form listed no medications and no medical conditions. What the patient had not disclosed - because the form did not specifically ask in the right way, and nobody followed up - was that she was already on metformin, a sulfonylurea, and a DPP-4 inhibitor through her endocrinologist for type 2 diabetes. She had been stable on that regimen for years. The addition of a GLP-1 agonist sent her into severe hypoglycemia that landed her in the ICU for three days. The board's review focused on one fact above all others: the prescribing physician had never obtained records from the patient's endocrinologist, had never verified her medication list, and had prescribed based on an intake form that was functionally useless.

The physician's defense - that the patient had failed to disclose her medications - went nowhere. The board's position was unambiguous: it is the physician's responsibility to verify the history, not the patient's responsibility to volunteer it. That doctor received a public reprimand, mandatory continuing education, and a restriction on his ability to prescribe through telehealth for eighteen months. All because he said yes to a patient with no verifiable history.

Here is what you do instead. Every patient completes a comprehensive intake form. Every field is required. If they skip a section, staff flags it and the patient is contacted to complete it before the consultation. For any patient with a significant medical history - which, in a peptide practice, is most of them - you request records from their primary care physician. If they do not have a PCP, that is a red flag that requires discussion. If they refuse to provide records or contact information for their other providers, you decline to prescribe until they do. Not because you are being difficult, but because you cannot practice safe medicine without information.

For medication reconciliation specifically, I recommend requiring patients to bring in their actual medication bottles or a pharmacy printout for the initial consultation. Self-reported medication lists are notoriously inaccurate. Studies have shown that patients forget to list up to half of the medications they are actually taking, especially over-the-counter products, supplements, and medications prescribed by specialists they see infrequently. A pharmacy printout does not lie. Use it.

And when a patient says, "Oh, I do not really have a PCP, I never go to the doctor, I am totally healthy" - that should make you more cautious, not less. The patient who has not seen a physician in ten years and claims to be perfectly healthy is the patient who has ten years of undiagnosed hypertension, pre-diabetes, subclinical thyroid dysfunction, or early cardiac disease lurking under the surface. They are not healthy. They are undiagnosed. There is a difference, and that difference matters enormously when you are considering peptide therapy.

When a patient presents with missing or unreliable history, your response is straightforward: "I cannot prescribe for you today because I do not have adequate information to assess whether this therapy is safe for you. Here is what I need you to do before we can proceed." Then list the requirements. PCP records. Current labs. Completed intake form. Specialist clearance if indicated. Document the conversation, document the requirements, document the patient's response, and schedule a follow-up. If the patient comes back with the information, great. You can proceed with confidence. If they do not, you have a documented refusal based on inadequate history, and that chart entry protects you forever.

Pregnancy or Breastfeeding Risk - Not Worth It

Let me make this as simple as I possibly can. If a patient is pregnant, might be pregnant, is trying to become pregnant, or is breastfeeding, you do not prescribe peptides. Full stop. There is no peptide in this book for which human pregnancy safety data exists. None. Zero. Every single one of these compounds falls into the category of "insufficient data to establish safety in pregnancy" or, more commonly, "no human pregnancy data available." And in the absence of safety data, the only defensible clinical decision is to decline.

I know this sounds obvious, but you would be amazed how many physicians try to talk themselves around this one. "Well, the patient says she is not planning to get pregnant." "She is on birth control." "She says her husband had a vasectomy." "The peptide is just a fragment, it probably does not cross the placenta." "Animal studies showed no teratogenicity." I have heard every rationalization in the book, and every single one of them is a fast track to a board sanction or a malpractice judgment if something goes wrong.

Here is the reality. Peptide therapies affect growth factors, hormonal pathways, metabolic function, tissue repair mechanisms, and immune modulation. These are exactly the biological processes that matter most during fetal development. The idea that a compound which manipulates growth hormone secretion, or IGF-1 signaling, or angiogenesis, or immune function could somehow have no effect on a developing pregnancy is biologically implausible at best and dangerously naive at worst. And because there are no controlled human pregnancy studies for any of these compounds, you are prescribing in a complete evidence vacuum. No board in the country will accept that as reasonable medical practice.

Let me tell you about the case that keeps me up at night. A physician in the Midwest prescribed a growth hormone-releasing peptide to a thirty-four-year-old woman for weight management and "anti-aging." The intake form indicated she was not pregnant. She was on oral contraceptives. The physician prescribed without obtaining a pregnancy test. The patient was, in fact, in the very early weeks of an unplanned pregnancy - the contraceptive had failed. She continued the peptide therapy for the first eight weeks of gestation before realizing she was pregnant. She subsequently miscarried. The miscarriage was almost certainly unrelated to the peptide therapy - first-trimester miscarriages are tragically common - but the patient believed it was related. She filed a board complaint. She filed a malpractice lawsuit. The board found that the physician had prescribed a compound with no pregnancy safety data without confirming pregnancy status, and issued a public reprimand with required education. The malpractice case settled for a mid-six-figure amount because the insurer did not want to take it to trial. That physician's career never fully recovered.

Was the peptide responsible for the miscarriage? Almost certainly not. But that is not the point. The point is that the physician created a situation where the question could even be asked. The physician created a situation where a reasonable person could look at the chart and say, "Why would you prescribe this to a woman of childbearing age without even checking if she was pregnant?" And there is no good answer to that question. None.

Here is what you do. For every female patient of childbearing potential, pregnancy status is confirmed before the initial prescription and documented in the chart. If there is any possibility of pregnancy, a serum or urine pregnancy test is obtained. If the patient is breastfeeding, peptide therapy is deferred until breastfeeding is complete. These are not negotiable clinical decisions. They are standard of care for any medication without established pregnancy safety data, and peptides fall squarely in that category.

Some physicians worry that requiring pregnancy testing will offend patients or that it adds unnecessary cost. Let me address both concerns. Patients are not offended by pregnancy testing when you explain why it is necessary: "I need to confirm that you are not pregnant before prescribing this therapy because there is no safety data for this compound during pregnancy. This is standard practice for any medication where pregnancy safety has not been established."Every patient I have ever seen has understood that explanation immediately. As for cost, a urine pregnancy test costs less than a latte. A serum beta-hCG costs maybe fifty dollars. Compare that to the cost of a board complaint, a malpractice claim, or the professional damage from being the physician who prescribed a peptide to a pregnant patient. The math is not even close.

For male patients, pregnancy risk obviously does not apply directly, but family planning should still be discussed. Some peptide therapies could theoretically affect spermatogenesis or fertility. Document the discussion. If a male patient's partner is pregnant or trying to conceive, that is worth noting in the chart as part of the overall risk assessment.

When it comes to pregnancy and breastfeeding, the rule is simple: not worth it. Not worth the risk to the patient. Not worth the risk to a potential pregnancy. Not worth the risk to your license. Decline, explain, document, and move on. There will be other patients. There will be other opportunities. There is no peptide indication that is urgent enough to override the absolute requirement for pregnancy safety. None.

Unstable Medical Condition - Stabilize First, Peptides Later

This is where I see experienced, well-intentioned physicians get themselves into the most trouble. They have a patient with a genuine medical indication for peptide therapy. The patient is motivated. The patient has read the literature. The patient has realistic expectations. Everything looks good - except the patient has an uncontrolled or unstable medical condition that makes peptide therapy unsafe or, at minimum, inadvisable at this time. And the physician, wanting to help, wanting to be therapeutic, wanting to keep a promising patient in the pipeline, says yes anyway.

Do not do this. An unstable medical condition is an automatic no until it is stable. I do not care how motivated the patient is. I do not care how much revenue they represent. I do not care that they promise to follow up with their specialist "next week." If the condition is unstable now, the peptide prescription waits until it is stable. Period.

Let me give you the most common examples I see, because these are the landmines that blow up practices. Uncontrolled hypertension - blood pressure consistently above 160 over 100 on multiple readings, or a patient who admits they stopped taking their antihypertensives because they "did not like the side effects." You do not prescribe growth hormone secretagogues to this patient. You do not prescribe any peptide that affects fluid balance, vascular tone, or metabolic parameters. What you do is send the patient back to their PCP or cardiologist, get the blood pressure controlled, and then reassess. That is not a refusal forever. That is a refusal until the condition is addressed. Big difference.

Uncontrolled diabetes - HbA1c above nine percent, wildly fluctuating glucose readings, frequent hypoglycemic episodes, or a patient who is supposed to be on insulin but is not taking it consistently. Any peptide that affects glucose metabolism, insulin sensitivity, or appetite regulation is contraindicated in this setting. GLP-1 agonist peptides, which are actually used for diabetes management in their FDA-approved forms, are no exception when the prescribing physician is not the physician managing the diabetes. If you are not the endocrinologist or primary care physician responsible for this patient's glycemic control, you do not add a glucose-active peptide to an unstable diabetic regimen. That is a recipe for disaster, and when the disaster happens - a hypoglycemic event, a hyperosmolar crisis, diabetic ketoacidosis -the board will ask why you thought it was appropriate to prescribe an adjunct therapy when the primary condition was uncontrolled.

Uncontrolled thyroid disease - whether hyper or hypo. Thyroid function affects everything: metabolism, cardiac function, mood, energy, weight, sleep. Peptide therapies that influence metabolic rate, growth hormone axis, or tissue repair can have unpredictable effects in the setting of unstable thyroid function. The patient needs to be euthyroid, or at least on a stable regimen with consistent follow-up, before you add peptide therapy into the mix. This is especially important for any patient with a history of thyroid cancer, because growth hormone and IGF-1 activity is theoretically concerning in that population, even when they are disease-free.

Active cardiac disease - recent myocardial infarction, unstable angina, uncontrolled arrhythmia, newly diagnosed heart failure, significant valvular disease awaiting intervention. I should not have to explain why growth hormone secretagogues, which affect fluid balance, cardiac remodeling, and metabolic demand, are contraindicated in this population. But I do have to explain it, because I have seen it happen. A patient had a stent placed six weeks ago, is on dual antiplatelet therapy, has an ejection fraction of thirty-five percent, and some physician somewhere prescribed CJC-1295 with ipamorelin because the patient wanted to lose weight and "feel better." That physician is now defending a board complaint. And he will lose. He should lose.

Active cancer or recent cancer treatment. This one should be obvious, but it is not, because patients who have been through cancer treatment are often desperate to feel like themselves again. They want energy. They want body composition improvement. They want to recover from the ravages of chemotherapy. And they read online that certain peptides can help. But any peptide that affects growth factors, angiogenesis, or immune modulation must be approached with extreme caution in patients with active cancer or recent cancer history. In many cases, the appropriate response is simply no - not now, not until oncology clears the patient, not until there is adequate disease-free interval, not until the oncologist weighs in on whether the theoretical risks are acceptable. If you are not the oncologist, you do not make that call alone.

And here is the key point for all of these scenarios: saying no to an unstable patient does not mean saying no forever. One of the most powerful tools in your clinical arsenal is the phrase,"Not now, but let us reassess once this is controlled." That phrase transforms a refusal from a permanent rejection into a clinically appropriate deferral. It shows the patient that you are not dismissing them. It shows the board that your refusal was measured and conditional, not arbitrary. It keeps the door open for future treatment while protecting everyone in the present moment.

The documentation for these refusals should include the specific condition that is unstable, the relevant clinical parameters (blood pressure readings, HbA1c, thyroid levels, cardiac imaging, oncologist status), the reason the unstable condition makes peptide therapy inadvisable, the referral made to the appropriate specialist or PCP for stabilization, the plan for reassessment once the condition is controlled, and the patient's understanding and response. That is a complete refusal note. It tells a story of careful medical judgment, and it is bulletproof.

Active Psychiatric Condition or Substance Abuse - Refer, Don't Prescribe

This is the section where I am going to be very direct, and some of you may not like what I have to say. So be it. If a patient has an active, uncontrolled psychiatric condition, you do not prescribe peptides. If a patient has a substance use disorder that is active or in very early recovery, you do not prescribe peptides. If a patient is on a psychiatric medication regimen that is in flux - new antidepressant started last week, antipsychotic dose just changed, lithium level not yet checked - you do not prescribe peptides until things are stable. This is not because I lack compassion for patients with mental health conditions or addiction histories. It is precisely because I have compassion for them that I am telling you this. These are vulnerable patients, and peptide therapy is not the right intervention when their psychiatric stability is in question.

Let me explain the clinical reasoning, because it is important. Peptide therapies affect neurotransmitters, stress hormones, sleep architecture, energy levels, appetite, body composition, and self-perception. These are exactly the domains that are already disrupted in patients with active psychiatric conditions. Adding a biological intervention that affects growth hormone, cortisol, leptin, ghrelin, or inflammatory markers to a patient whose neurochemistry is already unstable is like throwing a rock into a pond that is already churning. You have no idea what the ripple effects will be, and neither does anyone else, because there is no research on peptide therapy in patients with active major depression, bipolar disorder, schizophrenia, borderline personality disorder, eating disorders, or substance use disorders.

The patient with active major depression who starts a growth hormone secretagogue and then experiences a mood worsening - is that from the peptide? Is it from the depression itself? Is it from a medication interaction? Is it from the insomnia that sometimes accompanies GH secretagogue initiation? You cannot answer those questions, and neither can the patient's psychiatrist, because there is no data. So what you have created is a clinical muddle where no one knows what is causing what, the patient's psychiatric condition may be destabilized, and you are the prescriber who introduced an uncontrolled variable into an already unstable system.

Even more concerning is the patient who wants peptide therapy for body composition changes and has an active eating disorder. This is a disaster waiting to happen. Patients with anorexia nervosa, bulimia nervosa, or binge eating disorder are often preoccupied with body image, weight, and control. Offering them a pharmacological intervention that promises fat loss, muscle gain, or body recomposition is pouring gasoline on a fire. I have seen physicians prescribe semaglutide-related peptides to patients with eating disorders because the patient presented with obesity and the physician did not screen adequately for the underlying eating pathology. The result in several cases was a worsening of the eating disorder, dangerous caloric restriction, and in one tragic case, a hospitalization for refeeding syndrome that nearly killed the patient.

Substance use disorders present a different but equally serious set of concerns. Patients in active addiction will use anything they can get their hands on to alter how they feel. Peptide vials are just another substance. More concerning is the risk that a patient in early recovery -that vulnerable first six to twelve months - will experience side effects, cravings, or mood changes from peptide therapy that trigger a relapse. We know that sleep disruption, which can occur with some peptide protocols, is a significant relapse trigger for both alcohol and opioid use disorders. We know that body dysmorphia is common in patients with stimulant use disorders, and that offering body-composition-enhancing peptides to this population feeds into the same dysmorphic thought patterns that drove their drug use in the first place.

Even for patients in stable recovery, with good support systems and documented psychiatric stability, I proceed with extreme caution. I require clearance from their psychiatrist or addiction medicine physician before initiating therapy. I require that psychiatric medications be on stable doses for at least three months. I require documented follow-up with their mental health provider throughout the peptide therapy. And I have a low threshold for stopping therapy if any psychiatric symptoms emerge or worsen.

But for the patient who is actively symptomatic, actively using, or in early and unstable recovery - the answer is no. Not maybe. Not let us try a low dose. Not let us see how it goes. No. With a referral to the appropriate psychiatric or addiction specialist. With documentation of the concern. With a plan to reassess once stability is achieved. And with the understanding that some patients may never be appropriate candidates for peptide therapy, and that is okay. Your practice will not fail because you declined to treat patients who need psychiatric care more than they need growth hormone optimization.

Unrealistic Expectations - These Patients Complain No Matter What

This is the category of refusal that makes physicians the most uncomfortable, because it does not feel medical. It feels subjective. It feels like you are judging the patient. And to some extent, you are - because unrealistic expectations are a clinical risk factor every bit as real as hypertension or diabetes. A patient who expects miracles will be disappointed by reality. A disappointed patient complains. A complaining patient files board complaints, posts negative reviews, initiates chargebacks, and tells everyone they know that your practice is a fraud. These patients are poison to your practice, and learning to identify them during the initial consultation - and decline them before they ever become patients - is one of the most valuable skills you can develop.

What do unrealistic expectations look like in a peptide practice? They look like the patient who wants to lose forty pounds in eight weeks without changing their diet or exercise habits. They look like the patient who expects to gain twenty pounds of muscle in a month with a peptide and no training program. They look like the patient who believes a peptide will reverse their twenty years of sun damage and make them look twenty-five again. They look like the patient who read online that BPC-157 will heal a ten-year-old rotator cuff tear without surgery. They look like the patient who wants to stack four different peptides and expects synergistic results that exceed what any of them can do individually. They look like the patient who says, "Money is no object, just give me whatever works best."

These patients do not understand, or do not want to understand, that peptide therapy is incremental, individual, and uncertain. Results vary. Some patients respond robustly. Some patients respond modestly. Some patients do not respond at all. The factors that determine response - genetics, baseline hormone levels, adherence, lifestyle, sleep quality, stress, nutrition, training - are complex and largely outside your control. You cannot guarantee results. You can only offer a reasonable possibility of improvement based on the available evidence and the patient's individual profile. A patient who cannot accept that framework is a patient who will be dissatisfied no matter what outcome they achieve.

I know a physician in California who learned this lesson the hard way. She had a patient who came in wanting weight loss peptides and was explicit that she expected to lose thirty pounds in three months. The physician explained that results vary, that lifestyle modification is essential, that the average weight loss with these therapies is typically more modest. The patient nodded along, signed the consent forms, and started therapy. Over three months, she lost twelve pounds - which is actually a very good result for peptide-assisted weight loss. But it was not thirty pounds. The patient was furious. She demanded a refund. She posted online that the practice was a "scam" and that the peptides "do not work." She filed a board complaint alleging false advertising. She initiated a credit card chargeback. The board complaint was ultimately dismissed because the physician's documentation was excellent, but the chargeback stuck, the online reviews cost the practice an estimated fifteen thousand dollars in lost new patient inquiries, and the physician spent forty hours dealing with the fallout. All because she said yes to a patient whose expectations were never aligned with reality.

Here is what I recommend. During every initial consultation, before you ever discuss specific peptides or dosing, you have a frank conversation about expectations. What does the patient hope to achieve? What is their understanding of how peptide therapy works? What are they willing to do in terms of lifestyle modification, monitoring, and follow-up? If their stated goals are wildly inconsistent with what the evidence supports, that is a red flag. If they push back when you explain realistic outcomes, that is a bigger red flag. If they say things like "I do not care about the risks, I just want results" or "I have tried everything else and nothing works, so this has to work" - those are automatic nos.

The phrase I use is this: "I want to be honest with you about what peptide therapy can and cannot do. The research is promising but limited. Individual results vary significantly. I cannot guarantee that you will achieve the outcomes you are hoping for, and if that is not acceptable to you, then I am not the right physician for your care." That statement is honest, it is kind, and it is a built-in filter. Patients who hear that and say, "I understand, I want to proceed with realistic expectations" - those are your patients. Patients who hear that and say, "Well I need to lose thirty pounds or this is a waste of time" - those are not your patients. Decline them. Document the conversation. Move on. You have just saved yourself months of headache and potential liability.

Refusal of Monitoring - If They Won't Follow Up, They Can't Be Treated

This is the final category of automatic refusal, and it is the one that physicians most often rationalize their way around. A patient refuses to get labs. A patient refuses to follow up at three months. A patient refuses to see their PCP for clearance. A patient says, "Just give me the prescription, I will handle the rest." And the physician, not wanting to lose the sale, not wanting to seem demanding, not wanting to inconvenience the patient, says okay.

That is malpractice waiting to happen. Not metaphorically. Literally. Monitoring is not optional in peptide therapy. It is an integral part of the therapeutic protocol. The labs tell you whether the therapy is working. They tell you whether it is safe. They tell you whether the patient is having adverse effects they have not reported. They tell you whether dosing adjustments are needed. Without monitoring, you are prescribing blind, and prescribing blind is not medicine. It is gambling with someone's biology, and eventually the house wins.

Every peptide therapy in your practice should have a defined monitoring protocol. Baseline labs before initiation. Follow-up labs at defined intervals - typically four to six weeks after initiation, then every three months during the first year, then every six months if the patient is stable. Specific labs tailored to the peptide: IGF-1 and fasting glucose for growth hormone secretagogues, inflammatory markers for BPC-157, thyroid function for anything that might affect metabolism, comprehensive metabolic panel and CBC for almost everything. If a patient refuses to get these labs, you stop prescribing. It is that simple.

I want to be clear about something, because I know the objection that is forming in some of your minds. You are thinking, "What about the patient who says they cannot afford labs? What about the patient who lives two hours from the nearest lab? What about the patient who is afraid of needles?" These are legitimate concerns, and they deserve legitimate responses. For the patient who cannot afford labs, you can discuss payment plans, cash pricing at independent labs, or whether their PCP can order the labs through insurance. For the patient who lives far from a lab, you can discuss home phlebotomy services or telehealth lab partnerships. For the patient who is afraid of needles, you can discuss their concerns, provide reassurance, and work with them on coping strategies. What you cannot do is say, "Oh well, labs are not that important anyway, let us skip them this time." That is a clinical decision that no board in the country will support.

If a patient absolutely refuses monitoring after you have discussed the importance, explained the options, and addressed their concerns, your response is a refusal to continue or initiate therapy. Document the conversation. Document that you explained why monitoring is medically necessary. Document the alternatives you offered. Document the patient's refusal. Document your decision that peptide therapy is not appropriate without monitoring. That chart entry is clean, it is defensible, and it shows that you take patient safety seriously.

The patient who refuses monitoring is telling you something important about themselves. They are telling you that they do not take medical recommendations seriously. They are telling you that they are willing to cut corners on their own safety. They are telling you that convenience matters more to them than appropriate care. These are exactly the patients who will self-adjust doses, who will buy additional product online, who will ignore side effects, and who will blame you when things go wrong. By refusing to treat them without monitoring, you are not just protecting yourself. You are protecting every other patient in your practice by demonstrating that your standards are non-negotiable.

How to Say No

Knowing when to say no is essential, but it is only half the battle. The other half is knowing how to say no - how to deliver the refusal in a way that is clear, professional, defensible, and does not create more problems than it solves. I have seen physicians who knew perfectly well that they should decline a patient but botched the delivery so badly that the patient left angry, filed a complaint, and created a headache that lasted for months. Saying no the right way is a skill, and like any skill, it gets better with practice. This section will give you the framework.

Explain the Reason Without Arguing - Be Kind, Be Clear, Be Firm

The golden rule of refusing a patient is this: you owe them an explanation, but you do not owe them a debate. A good refusal has three components - kindness, clarity, and firmness - and you need all three. Kindness without firmness leads to patients talking you into reversing your decision. Firmness without kindness leads to patients feeling dismissed and disrespected, which drives complaints. Clarity without either kindness or firmness leads to confusion and misunderstanding. Let me walk you through each component.

Kindness means acknowledging the patient's goals and validating their desire to improve their health. It means looking them in the eye - or at the camera, for telehealth - and speaking with genuine compassion. It means using language that respects their intelligence and their autonomy. Here is an example of a kind refusal: "I can see how much thought you have put into this, and I genuinely appreciate that you are taking an active role in your health. I can tell you have done your research, and I respect that." That takes ten seconds to say, and it transforms the dynamic from adversarial to collaborative. The patient feels heard. They feel respected. They are far more likely to accept your decision gracefully.

Clarity means explaining the clinical reasoning in plain English that the patient can understand. Not medical jargon that goes over their head. Not legalistic language that sounds like you are covering yourself. Not vague generalities that leave them wondering what you really meant. Plain, specific, understandable English. Here is an example: "The reason I am not comfortable prescribing this for you right now is that your blood pressure has been running very high, and this medication can raise blood pressure further. I am concerned that the combination could put you at risk for a serious cardiovascular event. My job is to make sure anything I prescribe is safe for you, and in this case, I cannot do that until your blood pressure is better controlled." That explanation takes thirty seconds. It tells the patient exactly what the problem is, exactly why it matters, and exactly what would need to change for the decision to be different.

Firmness means that once you have explained your reasoning, you do not negotiate. You do not engage in back-and-forth. You do not soften your position because the patient pushes back. You do not offer compromises that undermine your clinical judgment. The patient's response to a well-reasoned refusal might be disappointment, frustration, or even anger. All of those are acceptable. What is not acceptable is you reversing a clinical decision because a patient made you uncomfortable. That is not patient-centered care. That is pressure-driven prescribing, and it is dangerous.

Here is a practical tip that I have seen work beautifully in practice. After you explain your reasoning and deliver the refusal, pause. Let there be silence. Physicians are uncomfortable with silence and tend to fill it - often by backtracking, offering qualifications, or opening the door to negotiation. Do not do this. State your position clearly. Pause. Let the patient process. If they ask a clarifying question, answer it. If they challenge your reasoning, restate your position once more, kindly and firmly. If they continue to push, you say: "I understand this is not the answer you were hoping for. I have explained my clinical reasoning, and my decision stands. I am happy to discuss alternatives or a plan for moving forward, but I will not be prescribing this therapy for you today." Then you move on.

Some patients will escalate. They will threaten to go elsewhere. They will threaten to file complaints. They will threaten to post negative reviews. Let them. A patient who threatens you to try to get a prescription they are not medically appropriate for is confirming that your refusal was correct. Document the threat calmly and professionally. Do not engage emotionally. Do not threaten back. Do not get defensive. Document and move on.

Let me address the telehealth dimension briefly, because so much peptide prescribing happens through virtual consultations. Refusing a patient over video requires the same three components - kindness, clarity, firmness - but with extra attention to tone and presence. On video, you do not have physical presence to convey compassion. Your tone of voice, your facial expressions, and your eye contact become even more important. Look at the camera, not at the patient's image on your screen - that creates the illusion of eye contact. Speak slightly more slowly than you would in person. Use the patient's name. These small adjustments make a significant difference in how your refusal lands.

One more thing about delivery. Do not delegate the refusal to staff. I have seen practices where the physician makes the clinical decision to decline but has the front desk or a medical assistant call the patient to deliver the news. That is a mistake. The refusal should come from the physician who made the clinical decision. It demonstrates accountability, it allows the patient to ask questions of the person who actually evaluated them, and it creates a direct physician-patient communication that is documented as part of the clinical record. Staff can handle scheduling, referrals, and administrative follow-up, but the clinical conversation belongs to the clinician.

Offer Alternatives: PCP Referral, Specialist Referral, Lifestyle Approaches, Reassessment Later

A refusal without alternatives feels like a dead end. It leaves the patient frustrated, with nowhere to go and nothing to do. A refusal with alternatives feels like a roadmap. It shows the patient that while this particular therapy is not appropriate right now, there are still paths forward. Offering alternatives is not just good patient care - it is also excellent risk management, because it demonstrates in the chart that your refusal was not arbitrary. It was part of a comprehensive clinical plan.

The alternatives you offer will depend on the reason for the refusal, but here are the categories I use most often.

Primary Care Physician Referral. For the patient with an uncontrolled medical condition, the PCP referral is your first and best alternative. "I want you to see your primary care doctor about getting your blood pressure under control. Once it is consistently below 140 over 90 for at least three months, come back and see me. We can reassess at that point, and I am optimistic we will be able to move forward." This does two things. It addresses the medical issue that made peptide therapy unsafe, and it brings the patient's PCP into the loop. That PCP involvement is gold from a defensibility perspective. It shows that you are not practicing in isolation, that you are coordinating care with the patient's established medical team, and that you deferred to the appropriate specialist for the primary management.

Specialist Referral. For patients with complex or specific conditions, a specialist referral is appropriate. Endocrinology for uncontrolled diabetes or thyroid disease. Cardiology for uncontrolled hypertension or cardiac disease. Psychiatry for active mental health conditions. Oncology for recent cancer history. Gastroenterology for inflammatory bowel disease or other GI conditions that might interact with peptide therapy. The specialist referral does two things clinically: it ensures the underlying condition is managed by the expert best equipped to handle it, and it provides you with specialist input on whether peptide therapy is appropriate once the condition is stable.

Lifestyle Approaches. For patients whose expectations are unrealistic or whose clinical picture suggests that lifestyle modification should come first, offering concrete lifestyle guidance is an excellent alternative. "Before we consider peptide therapy, I would like you to work with a nutritionist for three months and establish a consistent exercise routine. Peptides work best when the foundation is solid, and I want to set you up for success. Let us reassess in ninety days and see where we are." This is not a brush-off. It is a legitimate clinical recommendation, and for many patients, the lifestyle changes alone will produce results that make peptide therapy unnecessary or at least more effective when it is eventually initiated.

Reassessment Later. This is the most underutilized tool in the refusal toolkit. Not now does not mean not ever. A patient who is inappropriate today may be perfectly appropriate in six months. The patient who needs to get their blood pressure controlled, the patient who needs to establish care with a PCP, the patient who needs to complete their psychiatric medication adjustment, the patient who needs to finish breastfeeding - all of these patients can be invited back for reassessment once their situation changes. "I cannot prescribe for you today because you are pregnant, and there is no safety data for these compounds during pregnancy. Once you have delivered and finished breastfeeding, please come back. We will reassess at that time, and there is a good chance you will be an excellent candidate." That is not a rejection. That is a clinical plan with a timeline.

Document every alternative you offer. If you referred to a PCP, document the PCP's name and contact information, the information you sent, and the reason for the referral. If you recommended lifestyle modifications, document specifically what you recommended and the timeframe for reassessment. If you referred to a specialist, document the specialty, the reason, and the information the specialist will need. This documentation transforms a simple refusal into a comprehensive clinical encounter that demonstrates your thoroughness and commitment to the patient's overall care.

Document the Refusal, the Education Given, and the Alternatives Offered

I have said it before and I will say it again: documentation is everything. The chart proves your case. A verbal refusal that is not documented might as well not have happened. When the board investigator asks, "Doctor, why did you not prescribe to this patient?" and you say, "Oh, I explained it to them and they understood," without documentation to support that claim, you are in a weak position. When you can produce a chart note that details the patient's request, your clinical assessment, your specific reasoning for refusal, the explanation provided, the education given, the alternatives offered, and the patient's response - you are in an unassailable position.

Here is what a proper refusal note should contain. I am going to lay this out in detail because getting this right is one of the most important things you can do for your professional protection.

Patient's Request. Document exactly what the patient asked for. "Patient requests initiation of CJC-1295 with ipamorelin for weight loss and body composition improvement." Be specific. If they asked for a particular dose or protocol, document that too. This establishes what the patient wanted and frames your response in context.

Clinical Assessment. Document the relevant findings that informed your decision. "Blood pressure today 168/104. Patient reports she stopped taking her lisinopril two months ago due to dizziness. No current PCP. Last labs from 2021." This is the factual foundation of your refusal. These are the objective clinical parameters that made the decision clear.

Specific Reason for Refusal. State the refusal and the reasoning clearly and directly. "I declined to prescribe CJC-1295/ipamorelin due to uncontrolled hypertension (BP 168/104) and lack of current labs or PCP involvement. Growth hormone secretagogues can affect fluid balance and cardiovascular parameters. Initiating therapy in the setting of uncontrolled hypertension carries unacceptable risk." That is a complete clinical rationale in three sentences. Any board reviewer can read that and understand exactly why the decision was made.

Explanation Provided to Patient. Document what you told the patient. "Explained to patient that her blood pressure is dangerously elevated and must be controlled before any peptide therapy can be considered. Explained that GH secretagogues can affect blood pressure and that prescribing in this setting would be unsafe. Patient initially frustrated but appeared to understand after discussion." This shows that the patient was not blindsided - they received an explanation that they could understand.

Education Given. Document any additional education you provided. "Provided patient with educational materials on hypertension management. Discussed importance of medication adherence. Explained that uncontrolled hypertension increases risk of stroke, heart attack, and kidney failure." Education documentation demonstrates that your refusal was not just a denial but part of a broader clinical encounter focused on the patient's wellbeing.

Alternatives Offered. Document every alternative. "Referred patient to Dr. Smith, internal medicine, for blood pressure management - patient given contact information and appointment scheduled for next week. Recommended daily home blood pressure monitoring and medication compliance. Patient may return for reassessment of peptide candidacy once

BP consistently below 140/90 for three months with PCP documentation." This shows that you did not just close the door - you pointed the patient toward a path that could eventually lead to them getting what they want, safely.

Patient's Response. Document how the patient reacted. "Patient expressed disappointment but agreed to pursue PCP referral. Verbalized understanding that safety must come first. No hostility or threats observed." If the patient did become hostile or threatening, document that factually and without editorializing: "Patient became angry, stated she would find another doctor, threatened to post negative review. Remained calm, restated clinical rationale, ended encounter professionally." This kind of documentation protects you if the patient follows through on threats, because it shows the pattern of behavior that prompted your refusal.

Follow-Up Plan. Document what happens next. "Will reassess peptide candidacy after PCP stabilization and documentation of controlled BP for minimum three months. Patient aware she may schedule follow-up at that time." This closes the clinical loop and shows that your refusal was a deferral, not a permanent rejection.

A note containing all of these elements is bulletproof. It tells a complete clinical story. It demonstrates thoughtful medical judgment. It shows patient education and shared decision-making. And it makes any allegation of arbitrary refusal look absurd. Take the time to write these notes properly. They are among the most important documentation you will ever create.

Do Not Let the Patient Talk You Into Reversing a Well-Reasoned Refusal

This is the hardest part, and it is where even experienced physicians falter. You have done everything right. You have assessed the patient. You have identified a clear contraindication. You have explained your reasoning kindly and clearly. You have documented everything. And then the patient starts to push. They pull out their phone and show you a forum post. They cite another doctor who prescribed it for them before. They appeal to your compassion. They offer to sign any waiver you want. They escalate to anger, then soften to pleading, then appeal to your sense of fairness. And somewhere in that emotional rollercoaster, you start to waver. Maybe you were being too conservative. Maybe the risk really is minimal. Maybe just this once, with extra monitoring... Stop. The moment you feel yourself wavering is the moment you need to be most firm. Because here is the truth: the patient who talks you into reversing a well-reasoned refusal is the patient who will blame you when the predictable outcome occurs. The patient who wore down your resistance and then had an adverse event is the patient who will tell the board, "He did not want to prescribe it at first, but I convinced him." And they will be telling the truth. And the board will ask you: "Doctor, if you believed it was unsafe enough to refuse initially, what changed your mind?" And if your answer is "The patient pressured me," you have just admitted that your clinical judgment is for sale to the highest bidder. That is not a position you want to be in.

I am going to give you some practical strategies for maintaining your position when a patient pushes back, because this is a real challenge and platitudes about "being firm" are not enough.

First, remember your decision-making process. Before you deliver the refusal, take thirty seconds to review in your own mind why the answer is no. What is the specific clinical concern? What is the specific risk? What would need to change for the answer to be different? Having this clear in your own mind before the conversation starts makes you far less likely to be swayed by emotional appeals. You are not refusing arbitrarily. You are refusing for specific, defensible, clinical reasons. Hold onto those reasons.

Second, do not get drawn into evidence debates with patients. I have seen physicians spend forty-five minutes going back and forth with a patient about study methodology, online forum anecdotes, and YouTube videos. Do not do this. It is a trap. The patient has infinite time to research cherry-picked information and zero obligation to evaluate it critically. You will not win an evidence debate with a motivated patient who has spent forty hours on the internet. Your response to "But I read that..." should be: "I understand you have done a lot of research.

I have reviewed the same literature, and I have also evaluated your specific clinical situation. Based on your individual medical profile, this is not safe for you at this time. My decision stands." Then redirect to alternatives.

Third, recognize emotional manipulation for what it is. When a patient says, "You are my last hope," or "If you do not help me, I do not know what I will do," or "I thought you were different from other doctors" - those are emotional appeals designed to bypass your clinical judgment. They may be genuine expressions of the patient's distress, and you can respond to them with compassion without changing your clinical decision. "I hear how important this is to you, and I wish I could say yes. But my responsibility is to keep you safe, and prescribing this for you today would not be safe. I know that is hard to hear. Let us focus on what we can do to get you to a place where this might be possible." Compassion and firmness are not mutually exclusive.

Fourth, have a prepared phrase for when the patient will not let go. I keep a few in my back pocket for just this situation. "I have explained my clinical reasoning, and my decision is final." "I am not going to debate this further. My job is to make safe prescribing decisions, and this is not a safe prescription for you." "I understand you disagree, and you are entitled to seek another opinion. But I will not be prescribing this." Deliver these phrases calmly, without anger, without defensiveness. Then move to closing the encounter. If the patient continues to escalate, you may need to end the consultation. "I can see we are not going to agree on this today. I am going to step out now. My staff will provide you with the information we discussed, and you are welcome to schedule a follow-up once the situation I described has been addressed." Then leave.

Finally, and this is critical, debrief after difficult refusals. If you had a challenging conversation with a patient who pushed back hard, take five minutes before your next encounter to process it. Talk to a colleague. Review the chart note. Remind yourself why you made the decision you made. The emotional residue of a difficult refusal can linger and affect your next patient encounter or your confidence going forward. Do not let it. You made the right call. The chart proves it. Move on.

The Refusal as Your Strongest Defense

We have talked about when to say no and how to say no. Now I want to talk about why your refusals are, counterintuitive as it may seem, among the most powerful protective tools in your entire practice. Every refusal you document is a brick in the wall that separates you from the physicians who end up in front of the board. Every well-reasoned, well-documented refusal tells a story about you as a clinician - a story of judgment, caution, and patient-centered decision-making. When the investigator comes calling, and eventually they will for every peptide-prescribing physician in this country, the physicians who weather that storm are the ones who can point to a pattern of careful, conservative practice. And there is nothing that demonstrates careful, conservative practice better than a file full of thoughtful refusals.

A Documented Refusal Shows Clinical Judgment - The Board Respects This

Here is something that surprises a lot of physicians: state medical boards are not out to get you. I know it feels that way. I know the investigators can seem adversarial. I know the process is stressful, expensive, and time-consuming. But fundamentally, the board's job is to protect the public from unsafe practitioners. And one of the primary ways they identify unsafe practitioners is by looking for patterns of inappropriate prescribing - physicians who say yes to everyone, who ignore contraindications, who prescribe without adequate assessment, who never document a refusal. Those are the physicians the board worries about. Those are the physicians who get sanctioned.

When a board investigator reviews your charts, they are looking for evidence of clinical judgment. They want to see that you assessed each patient individually. They want to see that you considered risks and benefits. They want to see that you made decisions based on the patient's specific clinical picture, not on their ability to pay or their persistence in asking. And nothing demonstrates individual clinical assessment better than a documented refusal.

Think about it from the investigator's perspective. They pull twenty charts at random from your practice. In fifteen of them, they see appropriate prescriptions with good documentation, informed consent, monitoring plans, and follow-up. Solid. In three of them, they see documented refusals - a patient with uncontrolled hypertension, a pregnant patient, a patient with active psychiatric symptoms. Each refusal note is thorough: clinical rationale, patient education, alternatives offered, follow-up plan. What does that investigator think? They think:"This physician is careful. This physician says no when the situation warrants it. This physician exercises independent clinical judgment." That is exactly what you want them to think.

Contrast that with the physician whose twenty charts show twenty prescriptions and zero refusals. Every patient got something. No one was ever declined. There is no evidence of clinical judgment because there is no evidence of clinical decision-making. Every patient was a yes. That is not medicine. That is a fulfillment center. And the board knows it.

I consulted on a board investigation in Georgia where the investigator's report specifically cited the presence of documented refusals as evidence that the physician was practicing responsibly. The investigator wrote - and I am paraphrasing from memory - "The respondent's chart documentation includes multiple instances of appropriately declined therapy, with clear clinical rationale and referral for alternative care. This pattern is consistent with conservative, patient-centered medical practice and weighs against a finding of inappropriate prescribing." That physician received a private letter of concern on a minor documentation issue and no sanctions on the prescribing allegations. The refusals saved him.

I want you to internalize this. A documented refusal is not a negative mark on your record. It is a positive mark. It is evidence of good medicine. The board may not love peptide therapy, but they respect physicians who exercise caution within it. Your refusal notes are proof that you are one of those physicians. Treat them with the same care you would treat any other critical chart entry, because that is exactly what they are.

The Patient Who Was Declined and Later Harmed Themselves Elsewhere Is Not Your Patient

This is the part of refusal practice that physicians worry about most, and it is also the part where the law and the board are most clearly on your side. You declined a patient for appropriate clinical reasons. You documented the refusal thoroughly. You offered alternatives and referrals. The patient left your office angry, found another practitioner who said yes, and subsequently experienced a bad outcome. Are you liable? Are you responsible? Can the board come after you for the patient's harm?

In almost every case, the answer is no. And the reason is simple: that patient was not your patient. You established a clear clinical boundary. You declined to enter into a physician-patient treatment relationship for the specific therapy requested. You documented that decision and the reasoning behind it. The patient then made an independent decision to seek care elsewhere. Whatever happened next is the responsibility of the practitioner who chose to treat them, not of the practitioner who appropriately declined.

Now, let me qualify this slightly, because I am not a lawyer and this is not legal advice -consult your own counsel for your specific jurisdiction. There are theoretical scenarios where a board might question whether your refusal was adequate. Did you explain the risk clearly enough that the patient understood why you were saying no? Did you provide appropriate emergency instructions if there was an imminent risk? Did you document the encounter sufficiently? These are the questions that matter. But if your documentation is solid - if you documented the refusal, the rationale, the education, the alternatives, and the patient's response- then you have done everything required of you. The patient's subsequent decision to find a less careful practitioner is not your responsibility.

Let me give you a real-world example. A physician in Colorado appropriately declined to prescribe growth hormone secretagogues to a patient with a recent history of pituitary adenoma. This is a clear contraindication - stimulating growth hormone secretion in a patient with a history of pituitary tumor is dangerous. The physician documented the refusal thoroughly, explained the rationale, referred the patient back to their endocrinologist, and offered to reassess after endocrinology clearance. The patient went to three other peptide practitioners before finding one who would prescribe without asking about pituitary history. Six months later, the patient developed symptoms consistent with tumor recurrence and required surgery.

The patient filed a complaint against the original physician, alleging that the physician had"wasted time" with the refusal and that earlier treatment might have prevented the recurrence. The board reviewed the chart, reviewed the documentation, and dismissed the complaint in eight weeks. The investigator's note specifically referenced the "exemplary documentation of appropriate clinical refusal" as the basis for dismissal. The physician who eventually prescribed without adequate history assessment? He received a letter of concern and a mandatory chart review. Two different outcomes for two different approaches to the same patient. One physician said no and documented it. The other said yes without doing the work. You tell me which one you want to be.

The legal concept here is called the "independent intervening cause" - the patient's decision to seek treatment from another provider breaks the chain of responsibility that might otherwise connect your actions to their outcome. When you appropriately decline care and document that decline, you have fulfilled your duty. What the patient does after that is on them and on the subsequent provider. You are not responsible for the medical decisions of every other practitioner in your city. You are responsible for your own decisions. Make them good ones, document them well, and move on.

Pattern of Thoughtful Refusals Demonstrates Conservative, Careful Practice

One refusal note is good. Five refusal notes are better. Twenty refusal notes, spread across your practice charts over months or years, tell a story that no single chart entry can tell. They tell the story of a physician who practices at a consistent standard. Who applies clinical criteria evenly. Who does not make exceptions for charming patients, wealthy patients, or persistent patients.

Who treats every patient by the same medical standards, regardless of how much revenue they represent or how much pressure they apply.

That pattern is incredibly powerful. When a board investigator or a plaintiff's attorney reviews your charts, they are not just looking at individual encounters - they are looking for patterns. Patterns of carelessness. Patterns of cutting corners. Patterns of prescribing without adequate assessment. Or, on the flip side, patterns of thoroughness. Patterns of caution. Patterns of consistent clinical judgment. A steady drumbeat of well-documented refusals creates a pattern that screams "this physician takes patient safety seriously." And that pattern protects you in ways that no individual chart entry ever could.

Think of it like this. If you are a board investigator reviewing charts from a physician who has been accused of inappropriate prescribing, and you see one refusal note, you think: "Okay, this physician declined one patient. That is something." If you see five refusal notes, you think:"This physician regularly declines patients who are not appropriate candidates. That is a pattern of careful practice." If you see twenty refusal notes, you think: "This physician is conservative and cautious. The prescribing decisions that are being questioned need to be evaluated in the context of a physician who regularly says no when the clinical picture warrants it." That is the narrative you want the investigator to have in their head when they review the rest of your charts. That context matters enormously.

I have seen board investigations where the investigator's final report specifically highlighted the pattern of refusals as mitigating evidence. In one case, the investigator wrote: "While the respondent's prescribing of [specific peptide] in two specific cases raised concerns, the overall pattern of practice demonstrates consistent clinical judgment. The respondent's charts include numerous documented refusals with appropriate clinical rationale, suggesting a conservative prescribing posture rather than an indiscriminate one." That language - "conservative prescribing posture" - is gold. It is exactly what you want in a board investigator's report. And you earn it one refusal at a time.

Building this pattern requires discipline. It requires that you apply your clinical criteria evenly, even when it is inconvenient. Even when the patient is a referral from a good source. Even when the patient is willing to pay cash upfront. Even when you have had a slow month and the revenue would help. Every time you make an exception - every time you say "well, just this once" - you are not just endangering that patient. You are eroding the pattern of careful practice that protects your entire career. Do not do it. The standard is the standard. Apply it evenly. Document your refusals. Build the pattern. Let it protect you.

Every Time You Say No to a Bad Candidate, You Protect Every Other Patient in Your Practice

This is the final point I want to make in this chapter, and it is perhaps the most important one. When you say no to a patient who is not a good candidate for peptide therapy, you are not just protecting yourself and that individual patient. You are protecting every other patient in your practice. You are protecting the integrity of your clinical standards. You are protecting the reputation of your practice. You are protecting the trust that your good patients have placed in you. And you are protecting the future of peptide medicine itself, because every bad outcome from a poorly chosen candidate becomes ammunition for the people who want to shut this field down entirely.

Let me explain what I mean. We operate in a hostile environment. I do not think that is an exaggeration. The FDA does not love compounded peptides. State medical boards view peptide-prescribing physicians with skepticism. Mainstream endocrinology and internal medicine often see us as quacks or cowboys. The media loves a good "dangerous alternative medicine" story. Plaintiff attorneys know that physicians prescribing non-FDA-approved compounds make attractive targets. And Big Pharma has a vested interest in seeing this field constrained or eliminated entirely, because every patient treated with a compounded peptide is a patient not buying their branded products.

In that environment, every bad outcome matters. Every patient who experiences a serious adverse event from inappropriate peptide prescribing becomes a data point for the opponents of this field. Every board complaint becomes a case study in why peptide prescribing should be restricted. Every lawsuit becomes a headline. Every scandal at one practice becomes a reason for legislators to consider new restrictions on all practices. We are not isolated practitioners operating in our own little bubbles. We are part of a field, and the actions of the least careful among us affect all of us.

When you say no to the patient with uncontrolled hypertension, you are preventing a potential cardiovascular event that could become a news story about "dangerous peptide therapy." When you say no to the pregnant patient, you are preventing a potential fetal exposure that could become a board case study. When you say no to the patient with unrealistic expectations, you are preventing a dissatisfied patient who will tell everyone that "peptides do not work." When you say no to the patient who refuses monitoring, you are preventing the adverse event that would have been caught and managed if labs had been done. Each refusal is not just a clinical decision. It is a vote for the continued viability of responsible peptide medicine.

And on the positive side, every time you say no appropriately, you reinforce the standards that make this field defensible. You demonstrate that peptide prescribing is not indiscriminate. You show that there are physicians who take patient safety seriously, who apply clinical criteria rigorously, who document thoroughly, and who put medicine ahead of revenue. That is the narrative we need. That is the narrative that will keep this field alive and accessible for the patients who genuinely benefit from it. You are not just protecting yourself when you say no. You are protecting the entire ecosystem of responsible peptide practice.

Let me close with a story. I know a physician - let us call her Dr. Chen - who has been prescribing peptides for twelve years. In that time, she has built a thriving practice, helped thousands of patients, and never had a serious board complaint or malpractice claim. When I asked her what her secret was, she did not talk about her clinical knowledge or her pharmacy relationships or her marketing. She said: "I say no to at least thirty percent of the people who want to be my patients. And I document every single refusal like my license depends on it. Because it does."

Thirty percent. Think about that. One in three people who walk through her door or fill out her intake form gets declined. Not because she is difficult or elitist, but because she has clear clinical criteria and she applies them evenly. Her chart documentation includes hundreds of refusal notes, each one thorough, each one compassionate, each one bulletproof. When the board came calling once - as they eventually do for every physician in this space - she handed over her charts with confidence. The investigator spent three months reviewing her files and closed the case with a one-paragraph finding of no wrongdoing. Dr. Chen told me the thirty percent of patients she declined over twelve years represented maybe a million dollars in lost revenue. And she said it was the best million dollars she never made.

That is the standard. That is the physician you want to be. The one who sleeps soundly at night. The one who hands over charts to an investigator without breaking a sweat. The one who knows that every well-reasoned refusal is an investment in her career, her patients, and the field she practices in. The one who understands that the easiest prescription to defend is the one she refused to write.

You have made it through twenty chapters of this book. You have learned about the regulatory landscape, the clinical protocols, the documentation requirements, the consent processes, the pharmacy relationships, the business structures, and the real-world scenarios that define this field. But if there is one thing I want you to take away from all of it - one principle that matters more than any dosing chart, any consent form, any marketing strategy - it is this: have the courage to say no. Say it early. Say it often. Say it with kindness and clarity and firmness. Document it thoroughly. And never, ever let a patient talk you into a prescription that your clinical judgment tells you is wrong.

That is the art of peptide medicine. Everything else is just details. Now go practice it well.

Appendix A: The Master Informed Consent Form

A.1 Universal Peptide and Wellness Therapy Informed

Consent

A Note from the Author Before You Use This Thing

Listen. The last edition of this book had twenty-plus individual consent forms spanning one hundred and fourteen pages. Semaglutide got its own form. Tirzepatide got its own form. Sermorelin, tesamorelin, CJC-1295, ipamorelin, BPC-157, TB-500, melanotan, oxytocin, kisspeptin, PT-141, every single peptide and wellness medication profiled in this book had a separate form. You were supposed to print a different consent for every patient, for every medication, and somehow keep them all organized in your practice. It was ridiculous. It was wasteful. And most physicians using this book told me the same thing: "The forms are good, but I don't use half of them because I can't manage twenty different templates."

Well, here is the fix. One universal consent form. One document that covers every peptide, every wellness therapy, every hormone adjunct, every compounded medication, every off-label use, every investigational discussion, and every reasonable clinical scenario you will encounter in a peptide and wellness practice. You print one form. You fill in the medication-specific details on the Medication-Specific Addendum at the end. You counsel the patient properly. You sign it. You scan it into the chart. Done.

BLUNT RULE: If your consent process requires a filing cabinet, you are doing it wrong. Consent is a conversation documented on paper, not a paper mill that buries the conversation.

Why One Form Instead of Twenty

The regulators at the state medical board do not care how many different consent templates you own. They care about whether the patient understood what they were getting into. Whether the risks were disclosed. Whether alternatives were discussed. Whether the patient had capacity. Whether the chart shows a real medical conversation, not a signature hunt.

Every single peptide consent form in the old Appendix K contained the same twelve sections. Nature of treatment. Regulatory status. Benefits. Risks. Contraindications. Symptoms to report. Alternatives. Monitoring. No guarantee. Costs. Voluntary participation. PCP certification. The only parts that changed from form to form were the peptide-specific risks in section four, the peptide-specific contraindications in section five, the peptide-specific symptoms in section six, and a few lines in the benefits section. Everything else was identical. Cut. Paste. Next form. One hundred and fourteen pages of mostly the same language.

So here is what changed. The universal form below contains every common element that applies to every peptide and wellness therapy. The Medication-Specific Addendum at the end contains the customizable sections for each therapy category. You complete the universal form once per patient encounter, attach the relevant addendum section for the specific medication being prescribed, and you have a complete, thorough, defensible consent document that would make a lawyer proud and a medical board reviewer satisfied.

How to Use This Form

1. Print the universal consent form. It does not change.

2. Print or attach the relevant Medication-Specific Addendum section for the therapy being prescribed. Each addendum section is labeled by therapy category.

3. Fill in all patient information blanks at the top of the universal form.

4. Fill in the medication-specific blanks on the addendum: dose, route, frequency, pharmacy, monitoring schedule, and costs.

5. Review the entire form with the patient. Not a staff member. Not a coordinator. The clinician. If that means blocking fifteen minutes for consent review, then block fifteen minutes.

6. Check the applicable boxes together with the patient. Do not pre-check boxes. The patient checks the box while you watch. This proves participation.

7. Answer every question the patient asks. Document any significant questions and your answers in the clinician notes section.

8. Both parties sign and date. Both copies get filed: original in the chart, copy to the patient if requested.

9. If you are prescribing multiple peptides, attach multiple addendum sections. The universal form stays the same.

> **BLUNT RULE: A pre-checked consent form is evidence of a pre-fabricated consent process. Let the patient check the boxes while you watch. It takes thirty seconds and it proves the conversation happened.**

Legal Review Disclaimer

This form is an educational template. It is not legal advice, medical advice, a prescribing protocol, or a substitute for qualified healthcare counsel. Before you put this form in front of any patient, have it reviewed by healthcare counsel licensed in your state, by your malpractice carrier or counsel, and by any pharmacy counsel you rely on. State law varies. Medical board expectations vary. Compounding rules change. FDA policy changes. Telemedicine rules vary by state. What passes in one jurisdiction may need modification in another.

Your counsel should review: (1) the regulatory status language for accuracy in your state; (2) the arbitration and dispute-resolution references for enforceability; (3) the patient certification language for consistency with your state's consumer protection and medical practice laws; (4) the scope-of-practice references if midlevel providers will be using this form; and (5) any therapy-specific risks that require additional disclosure beyond what this template contains.

Do not skip this step. I have been doing this for thirty years. The physicians who get in trouble are not the ones who used a template. They are the ones who used a template without making sure it fit their state, their specialty, their patient population, and their risk profile.

Universal Informed Consent for Peptide and Wellness Therapy

Patient Name: ____

Date of Birth: ____

Medical Record Number:

____

____

Prescribing Clinician:

____

____

Practice / Clinic Name:

____

Clinic Address: ____________________________________ Clinic Phone:

____

____________________________________ Medication(s) Prescribed: (check all that apply; attach relevant Medication-Specific Addendum for each) - Semaglutide / GLP-1 receptor agonist - Tirzepatide / GIP-GLP-1 receptor agonist - Retatrutide / Triple agonist (investigational) - Sermorelin / GHRH analog - Tesamorelin / Stabilized GHRH analog - CJC-1295 / Ipamorelin / GH secretagogue combination - Growth hormone-releasing peptide (GHRP-2, GHRP-6, or related) - BPC-157 / Body protection compound - TB-500 / Thymosin beta-4 - Melanotan II / Melanocortin agonist - PT-141 / Bremelanotide - Oxytocin - Kisspeptin - Human chorionic gonadotropin (hCG) - Testosterone / hormone replacement therapy - Estrogen / progesterone / hormone replacement therapy - Thyroid hormone / T3 / T4 / combination - NAD+ (intravenous, subcutaneous, or other route) - Other:

____

Dose Prescribed: ____

Frequency: ____

Route of Administration:

____

____

Pharmacy Phone: ____

Expected Start Date:

____

____

Monitoring Schedule:

____

____

Section 1: Nature of the Treatment

I am being offered or prescribed one or more peptide and/or wellness therapies as part of a physician-supervised treatment plan. The specific medication(s), dose(s), frequency, route, and duration are documented above and/or in my medical record. I understand that I must not change my dose, frequency, route, schedule, or pharmacy source unless my prescribing clinician specifically instructs me to do so in writing or through direct clinical communication.

I understand that peptide and wellness therapies are part of an emerging field of medicine. Some therapies are well-established with strong evidence. Others have moderate, limited, preclinical, or insufficient evidence. My clinician has discussed where my specific therapy falls on this evidence spectrum.

I understand that most peptide therapies are administered by subcutaneous injection that I will perform at home after receiving proper training and instructions from the pharmacy and/or my clinician. I understand that proper sterile technique, storage, reconstitution (if required), and safe disposal of sharps are my responsibility. I understand that injection-site technique, hand washing, alcohol swab use, needle safety, and sharps container disposal are essential to my safety.

- I understand the nature of the treatment being prescribed, including the medication name, dose, frequency, route, and expected duration as documented above.
- I understand that I must follow administration instructions exactly and must not deviate without clinician approval.
- I have received or will receive adequate instruction on how to prepare, store, and administer this medication safely.

Section 2: Regulatory Status and Disclosure

I understand that peptide and wellness medications exist in multiple regulatory categories, and that my clinician has disclosed which category applies to each medication I am receiving.

These categories include but are not limited to:

FDA-approved for labeled indication: The medication has FDA approval for a specific use, dose, and population. My use may or may not match that exact label.

FDA-approved medication used off-label: The medication is FDA-approved for some indication, but I may be receiving it for a different indication, at a different dose, by a different route, or in a different population than the label specifies. Off-label use is common in medical practice but requires additional disclosure.

Compounded medication: The medication is prepared by a licensed compounding pharmacy specifically for me. Compounded medications are not FDA-approved in the same manner as branded commercial medications. Quality, sterility, purity, potency, and availability depend on the specific pharmacy and may vary.

Investigational medication: The medication is not FDA-approved and is still being studied in clinical trials. Use outside a clinical trial requires additional justification, stronger consent, and close monitoring.

Research-use-only product: Products labeled “research use only,” “not for human consumption,” or similar are NOT legitimate clinical medication sources. I have been warned not to use these products.

- I understand the regulatory status of each medication I am receiving, and my clinician has explained which category applies to each medication listed above.
- I understand that compounded medications are not FDA-approved in the same manner as branded, commercially available FDA-approved drugs, and that quality, sterility, purity, and availability may vary by pharmacy and may change over time.
- I understand that investigational therapies have unknown long-term safety profiles and that my use is based on limited evidence, clinical judgment, and my specific risk-benefit situation.- I understand that I should not use research-use-only, grey-market, or internet-sourced peptides unless specifically reviewed and documented by my clinician, and that legitimate pharmacy sourcing is the safer approach when legally available.
- I understand that FDA policy, compounding rules, and pharmacy availability can change, and that a medication available today may become restricted, unavailable, or legally complicated tomorrow.

Section 3: Potential Benefits and Goals of Therapy

The potential benefits and goals of my specific therapy have been discussed with me and are documented below or in my medical record. These may include one or more of the following, depending on the specific medication and my clinical situation: - Appetite reduction and improved portion control - Weight management or weight-loss support - Improved glycemic control or metabolic markers - Cardiometabolic risk reduction - Growth-hormone-axis support - Improved sleep quality - Recovery support after exercise, injury, or surgery - Body-composition support (maintenance of lean mass, reduction of adiposity) - Energy and vitality improvement - Sexual function support - Cognitive or mood support

- Tissue healing, repair, or recovery support
- Anti-inflammatory or immune-modulating effects
- Hormonal optimization or support

- Other goals discussed:

____

- I understand that the benefits listed above are potential goals, not promises. My individual results may be mild, delayed, absent, or different than expected. No specific outcome has been guaranteed.
- I understand that peptide and wellness therapies work best when combined with appropriate lifestyle measures including nutrition, physical activity, adequate protein intake, resistance training, sleep optimization, stress management, and follow-up monitoring.

Section 4: Risks, Side Effects, and Uncertainties

I understand that all medications carry risks, and that peptide and wellness therapies are no exception. The following risks apply broadly to all injectable peptide and wellness therapies. Additional medication-specific risks are detailed in the Medication-Specific Addendum attached to this consent.

Universal Risks (Apply to All Peptide and Wellness Therapies)

-Injection-site reactions: Pain, redness, bruising, itching, swelling, infection, bleeding, scarring, skin discoloration, nodules, lipodystrophy, or irritation at or near the injection site. These are common with repeated subcutaneous injections.

-Allergic reactions: Rash, hives, itching, flushing, swelling of face/lips/tongue/throat, shortness of breath, wheezing, dizziness, lightheadedness, or anaphylaxis requiring emergency medical treatment with epinephrine and/or hospitalization.

-General systemic effects: Headache, fatigue, nausea, flushing, warmth, dizziness, lightheadedness, mood changes, sleep disturbance or insomnia, anxiety, irritability, or temporary worsening of symptoms.

-Unknown long-term risks: Especially with compounded, off-label, investigational, or limited-evidence therapies, the long-term safety profile may not be fully established. Unknown risks may emerge with extended use or in specific populations.

-Product quality risks: Product concentration, sterility, purity, endotoxin levels, potency, and availability can vary. Compounded medications are not FDA-approved in the same manner as branded medications. Even pharmacy-compounded products carry a small but real risk of contamination, potency variation, or quality issues.

-Interaction risks: Risk may increase if I use other medications, supplements, herbs, hormones, alcohol, recreational drugs, online products, or research-use-only peptides that I have not fully disclosed to my clinician. I must disclose everything.

-Regulatory and access uncertainty: Availability of compounded peptides can change based on FDA enforcement discretion, drug shortage designations, state pharmacy board actions, and other regulatory factors. My medication may become unavailable without warning.

-Reconstitution and administration errors: If I am required to reconstitute (mix) my medication, errors in adding diluent, calculation of dose, sterile technique, or storage can lead to underdosing, overdosing, infection, or product degradation.

-Needle-related injury: Needle sticks, sharps injury, improper disposal, reuse of needles, sharing of needles, or accidental injection into incorrect tissue planes.

-Psychological effects: Unrealistic expectations, disappointment with results, body-image concerns, dependency concerns, or anxiety about self-injection.

-Cost and financial risk: I am responsible for costs regardless of outcome. My insurance may not cover these therapies. I may not achieve the benefits I hope for despite paying out of pocket.

Additional Medication-Specific Risks

See the Medication-Specific Addendum attached to this consent for peptide-specific and therapy-specific risks that apply to the medication(s) I am receiving. I acknowledge that I have reviewed and understand those additional risks.

- I have read, understood, and discussed all risks above and in the attached addendum with my clinician.

Section 5: Contraindication and Caution Screening

I have been asked to disclose whether any of the following apply to me. I understand that checking a box does not automatically mean I cannot receive treatment, but it requires clinician review and may require additional evaluation, specialist clearance, or a decision not to proceed before treatment begins.

Cancer and Tumor History - Personal or family history of medullary thyroid carcinoma - Personal or family history of Multiple Endocrine Neoplasia syndrome type 2 (MEN2)- Active cancer or currently receiving oncology treatment - Recent cancer diagnosis (within past 5 years) without oncology clearance - Concerning unexplained mass, lump, or abnormal imaging - Pituitary tumor, pituitary adenoma, or history of pituitary surgery/radiation Gastrointestinal Conditions - History of pancreatitis (acute or chronic) - History of gallbladder disease, gallstones, or cholecystectomy - Severe gastroparesis, delayed gastric emptying, or severe reflux disease - Inflammatory bowel disease, Crohn's disease, or ulcerative colitis - Chronic severe constipation or bowel obstruction history - Active eating disorder (anorexia, bulimia, binge eating disorder) Endocrine and Metabolic Conditions - Diabetes (Type 1 or Type 2) or prediabetes - Use of insulin, sulfonylureas, or other diabetes medications - History of hypoglycemia or hypoglycemia unawareness - Thyroid disease (hypothyroidism, hyperthyroidism, thyroid nodules, thyroid cancer)- Adrenal insufficiency or Addison's disease

- Cushing's syndrome or disease - Uncontrolled hypertension - Significant cardiovascular disease, arrhythmia, or heart failure Pregnancy and Reproductive Status - Currently pregnant - Planning pregnancy in the next 12 months - Currently breastfeeding - Women of childbearing potential not using reliable contraception Neurologic and Psychiatric Conditions - History of suicidal ideation or suicide attempt - Active severe depression, bipolar disorder, or psychotic disorder - History of stroke or transient ischemic attack - History of seizure disorder - Migraine with aura - Cognitive impairment or dementia Other Significant Medical Conditions - Chronic kidney disease or renal impairment - Liver disease, hepatitis, cirrhosis, or abnormal liver function - Severe sleep apnea or use of CPAP/BiPAP - History of blood clots (DVT, PE), thrombophilia, or hypercoagulable state- Bleeding disorder or use of anticoagulants - HIV/AIDS or immunocompromise - Severe allergies or history of anaphylaxis to medications Medication and Substance Disclosure
- Current prescription medications not yet disclosed - Current over-the-counter medications or supplements not yet disclosed - Current hormone therapies (testosterone, estrogen, progesterone, thyroid, growth hormone, etc.) - Use of anabolic steroids, SARMs, or performance-enhancing substances (current or past)- Use of recreational drugs or substances - Heavy alcohol use (more than 14 drinks per week for men, more than 7 for women) Treatment Readiness and Prior Care - Unwillingness or inability to complete baseline or follow-up laboratory testing - Unwillingness or inability to attend scheduled follow-up appointments - No established primary care physician - Current management by

a specialist for a condition related to this treatment (cardiology, endocrinology, oncology, nephrology, hepatology, psychiatry, etc.) - Prior serious reaction to an injectable medication, vaccine, or biologic - Prior peptide therapy with significant adverse reaction I certify that I have answered all questions truthfully and completely. I understand that withholding information could result in serious harm.

- I certify that my answers above are truthful and complete to the best of my knowledge.

Section 6: Symptoms I Agree to Report Immediately

I agree to contact my prescribing clinician immediately or seek emergency/urgent medical care (including calling 911 or going to the nearest emergency department) if I experience any of the following symptoms. I understand that delaying care could result in serious injury or death.

Cardiovascular and Respiratory Emergencies - Chest pain, pressure, tightness, or discomfort - Shortness of breath, difficulty breathing, or feeling unable to catch my breath

- Fainting, near-fainting, or loss of consciousness - Severe or rapid heartbeat, palpitations, or irregular heartbeat - Severe dizziness or lightheadedness not resolving with rest and hydration Severe Allergic Reactions - Swelling of face, lips, tongue, or throat - Difficulty swallowing or speaking - Widespread hives, severe rash, or blistering - Wheezing or severe coughing - Feeling of impending doom or severe anxiety with physical symptoms Gastrointestinal Emergencies - Severe or persistent abdominal pain, especially with vomiting - Repeated vomiting or inability to keep fluids down for more than 12 hours - Vomiting blood or coffee-ground material - Black tarry stools or blood in stool - Severe constipation with abdominal swelling and inability to pass gas - Yellowing of skin or eyes (jaundice), dark urine, or clay-colored stools - Severe right upper abdominal pain, especially with fever Metabolic and Endocrine Emergencies - Symptoms of severe low blood sugar: confusion, sweating, shaking, severe weakness, rapid heartbeat, irritability, hunger that doesn't resolve with eating - Severe thirst with excessive urination and confusion (possible severe hyperglycemia)- Severe headache with vision changes, especially with high blood pressure Neurologic Emergencies - Severe headache unlike any I have had before - Sudden vision loss, double vision, or severe vision changes
- Weakness or numbness on one side of the body - Difficulty speaking, slurred speech, or confusion - Severe neck stiffness with fever Infection and General Emergencies - Signs of severe infection at injection site: spreading redness, warmth, pus, red streaks, fever- Fever higher than 101.5 degrees Fahrenheit (38.6 Celsius) - Severe dehydration: very dark urine, minimal urination, severe weakness, confusion, dry mouth, sunken eyes - Rapidly worsening symptoms of any kind - Any symptom that feels severe, unusual, or frightening to me - I understand that when in doubt, I should seek emergency care. It is better to be evaluated and told I am okay than to delay care and suffer a preventable complication.

Section 7: Alternatives Discussed

My clinician has discussed the following alternatives to peptide and wellness therapy with me, including the option of doing nothing: -Lifestyle modification: Improved nutrition, calorie management, increased physical activity, resistance training, adequate protein intake, sleep optimization, stress reduction, and behavioral modification.

-Standard medical care: Evaluation and treatment by my primary care physician or appropriate specialist (endocrinology, cardiology, gastroenterology, bariatric medicine, sleep medicine, psychiatry, etc.).

-FDA-approved medications: For my specific condition or goal, FDA-approved pharmaceutical options exist and have been discussed.

-Surgical options: Bariatric surgery, metabolic surgery, or other surgical interventions have been discussed when clinically relevant.

-Behavioral and psychological support: Counseling, cognitive behavioral therapy, support groups, eating disorder treatment, addiction treatment, or other mental health services.

-Complementary and integrative approaches: Physical therapy, acupuncture, massage, meditation, or other non-pharmacologic interventions.

-No medication or intervention: The option of continuing my current approach without adding peptide or wellness therapy is a valid alternative.

- I understand that doing nothing is an alternative, and that I may choose conventional or FDA-approved treatments at any time, even if I have already started peptide therapy.
- I have had the opportunity to discuss alternatives, including their benefits, risks, costs, and the option of involving my primary care physician or specialist, before making my decision.

Section 8: Monitoring and Follow-Up Requirements

I understand that peptide and wellness therapy requires ongoing medical supervision and that my participation in monitoring is a condition of continuing treatment.

- I agree to complete all scheduled follow-up visits, symptom check-ins, vital sign measurements, laboratory testing, and other monitoring requested by my clinician. The specific monitoring schedule for my therapy is documented above and/or in my medical record.
- I understand that common monitoring may include: body weight, vital signs (blood pressure, heart rate), fasting glucose or HbA1c, lipid panel, liver function tests, kidney function tests, thyroid function tests, IGF-1, complete blood count, inflammatory markers, pregnancy testing when applicable, and other labs as clinically indicated.
- I understand that refills may be denied, delayed, stopped, or changed if I miss follow-up appointments, do not report side effects as instructed, do not complete required laboratory testing, fail to respond to check-in requests, or if my clinician determines that treatment no longer appears medically appropriate or safe.
- I agree not to share my medication with anyone else under any circumstances, and not to use medication prescribed to another person.
- I agree to inform my prescribing practice promptly of any hospitalizations, emergency department visits, urgent care visits, new medical diagnoses, planned surgeries, new medications started by other providers, pregnancy, or any major change in my health status.
- I agree to inform all of my other healthcare providers (primary care physician, specialists, dentists, surgeons) that I am taking peptide and/or wellness medications.

- I agree to maintain an adequate supply of medication and not to allow myself to run out without contacting the practice in advance. I understand that abrupt discontinuation of some therapies may have consequences.
- I agree to store my medication properly (refrigeration if required, protection from light, out of reach of children and pets) and to check expiration dates before use.

Section 9: No Guarantee of Results

No clinician, staff member, pharmacy, website, advertisement, social media post, influencer, online forum, podcast, or educational material associated with this practice has guaranteed me any specific result, amount of weight loss, degree of symptom relief, cosmetic change, healing response, laboratory improvement, sexual response, cognitive effect, sleep effect, anti-aging effect, muscle gain, fat loss, energy level, mood improvement, or freedom from side effects.

Medicine involves uncertainty. Individual responses to therapy vary based on genetics, adherence, lifestyle, underlying medical conditions, concurrent medications, age, sex, hormone status, and factors that may not be fully understood.

The goal of therapy is to improve my health and well-being within a reasonable medical framework. Improvement is hoped for but not guaranteed. Some patients experience significant benefit. Some experience modest benefit. Some experience no perceptible benefit. Some experience side effects that require stopping therapy. I understand and accept this uncertainty.

- I understand that no results have been guaranteed and that my individual response cannot be predicted with certainty.

Section 10: Costs and Financial Understanding

- I understand that costs for my therapy were provided to me separately or will be provided to me in writing before I purchase or begin treatment. I have had or will have the opportunity to ask questions about costs before agreeing to treatment.
- I understand which services and items are included in my fees and which are billed separately, including: initial consultation, follow-up visits, medication, supplies (syringes, alcohol swabs, sharps container), laboratory testing, shipping costs, and refill fees.
- I understand that my insurance may not cover peptide therapy, compounded medications, off-label use, or wellness services, and that I am responsible for payment regardless of insurance coverage or reimbursement.
- I understand that I am responsible for all costs incurred, including those related to follow-up visits, lab testing, and monitoring that may be required for safe continuation of therapy.
- I understand that my ability to pay for therapy does not, by itself, make the therapy medically appropriate. My clinician may stop treatment at any time if the risks outweigh the benefits, even if I am willing and able to continue paying.
- I understand the practice's refund policy, which has been provided to me separately or is available upon request.

- I understand that medication shipped by the pharmacy may not be returnable or refundable, and that I am responsible for understanding the pharmacy's specific policies.

Section 11: Voluntary Participation and Decisional Capacity

- I am signing this consent form voluntarily, without coercion, duress, pressure, undue influence, or guarantee of outcome. No one has threatened me or offered me anything of value in exchange for signing.
- I believe I have the mental capacity to understand the information in this consent form, to appreciate the risks and benefits of the proposed treatment, to consider alternatives, and to make an informed decision. I am not under the influence of alcohol, recreational drugs, or sedating medications that would impair my judgment at the time of signing.
- I was given adequate time to read this consent form, to ask questions, and to consider my decision before signing. I was encouraged to take the form home, discuss it with family members or advisors, and return with questions if needed.
- I was given the opportunity to consult another clinician, an attorney, a family member, a trusted advisor, or my primary care physician before signing, and I either did so or chose not to.
- I understand that I can decline treatment or withdraw my consent and stop treatment at any time, for any reason or no reason, without penalty. If I choose to stop, I must notify the practice and follow any medical instructions for safe discontinuation.
- I understand that my primary care physician's awareness of and comfort with my treatment is important, and I have been encouraged to involve my PCP in my care decisions.

Section 12: Patient Independent Decision, Primary Care Physician Certification, and Prior Treatment History

This section certifies that I have approached this treatment decision as an informed adult, have involved my primary care medical team appropriately, and have a genuine clinical basis for considering peptide or wellness therapy.

-Independent Decision: With all information available to me, I have independently decided to proceed with the treatment documented above, regardless of cost, inconvenience, time commitment, uncertainty, and known or unknown risk factors. I understand that my decision to proceed does not require my clinician to prescribe, continue, refill, increase, or repeat this treatment if my clinician believes that risks outweigh benefits, if monitoring is incomplete, if I develop contraindications, or if I fail to comply with the treatment plan.

-PCP Discussion: I have discussed the use of the specific peptide and/or wellness medication(s) named in this consent with my primary care physician or appropriate treating specialist. I have informed them of my intention to proceed, shared information about the therapy, and discussed monitoring requirements, potential interactions with my existing conditions and medications, and any concerns they may have. My primary care physician or specialist knows I am pursuing this treatment and has not objected based on the information available to them, OR I have chosen to proceed despite their concerns, which I have documented with my clinician.

My Primary Care Physician Information:

PCP Name: ____

PCP Practice: ____

PCP Phone: ____

Date of Discussion:

____

- I do not have a current PCP. I understand I have been advised to establish care with one. Date discussed: __________

-Prior Treatment Attempts: I have attempted, for a clinically reasonable period documented in my medical record (typically at least several months to years depending on the condition), to address my symptoms or goals through traditional and conventional approaches including one or more of the following: FDA-approved medications, lifestyle changes, nutrition counseling, exercise programs, sleep improvement, behavioral modification, physical therapy, specialist care, mental health services, standard medical treatments, or other conventional approaches. These efforts did not provide adequate relief or acceptable results, OR they were not appropriate for my specific situation, OR they were refused due to contraindications or intolerance. This history is documented in my medical record.

-Independent Research: I have independently researched the specific peptide and/or wellness medication(s) named in this consent, including their possible benefits, limits, risks, side effects, regulatory status, off-label or compounded status when applicable, and available alternatives. I am not relying solely or primarily on advertisements, social media posts, influencer recommendations, internet forums, podcast discussions, discount codes, or statements from clinic staff in making my decision. I have sought independent information from medical literature, reputable sources, or professional consultation.

-Voluntary and Informed: I certify that all of the above statements are true to the best of my knowledge. I have read this entire consent form (or had it read to me), I understand its contents, my questions have been answered to my satisfaction, and I voluntarily choose to proceed with treatment.

Patient Certification and Signature Block

- I certify that I have read this entire consent form, that the information I have provided is truthful and complete, and that all of my questions have been answered to my satisfaction.
- I understand that I may stop treatment or withdraw my consent at any time, but that I must notify the practice and follow any medical instructions for safe discontinuation.
- I have received a copy of this signed consent form (or I decline a copy, noted below).
- I consent to the practice communicating with me via the methods I have authorized (phone, text, email, patient portal) for treatment-related purposes.

Patient Name (Print):

____

Date of Birth: ____

Patient Signature: ____________________________________ Date: ____________________________________ Time: ____________________________________ Witness Name (Print): ____________________________________ Witness Signature: ____________________________________ Date: ____________________________________

Clinician Certification and Signature Block

I certify that I have personally reviewed this consent form with the patient, answered their questions, discussed risks, benefits, alternatives, costs, monitoring requirements, and emergency instructions, and that the patient appears to understand the contents and voluntarily consents to treatment.

Clinician Name (Print): ____________________________________ Credentials (MD/DO/NP/PA): ____________________________________ License Number: ____________________________________ Clinician Signature: ____________________________________ Date: ____________________________________ Time: ____________________________________

Clinician Notes, Exceptions, and Patient-Specific Risk Documentation

Use this section to document any patient-specific risks, exceptions, modifications to standard consent, additional disclosures, significant patient questions and answers, or other clinically relevant notes that should be part of the permanent record.

Medication-Specific Addendum

Instructions for the Prescribing Clinician

This addendum contains therapy-specific risk disclosures, contraindication additions, symptom-reporting additions, and monitoring requirements for each major peptide and wellness therapy category. Print and attach the relevant section(s) to the universal consent form above. If prescribing multiple medications, attach multiple addendum sections. Each addendum section is labeled and corresponds to a checkbox option on the universal form. Fill in the blanks for dose, route, frequency, pharmacy, monitoring schedule, and costs before the patient signs. The patient must initial the bottom of each attached addendum section to confirm they reviewed it.

Addendum A: GLP-1 Receptor Agonists (Semaglutide and Related)

Medication name: ______________________ Specific dose and frequency: ______________________ Additional risks specific to this medication category: - Nausea, vomiting, diarrhea, constipation, abdominal pain, bloating, sulfur burps, reflux/ heartburn, delayed gastric emptying - Decreased appetite that may be excessive, leading to inadequate nutrition, dehydration, or protein deficiency - Dehydration, especially if GI side effects are significant; dehydration can worsen kidney function - Possible gallbladder disease or worsening of existing gallbladder disease - Pancreatitis: severe abdominal pain with vomiting requires immediate emergency evaluation- Possible risk of thyroid C-cell tumors; contraindicated in personal/family history of medullary thyroid carcinoma or MEN2

- Hypoglycemia when combined with insulin or sulfonylureas - Possible worsening of diabetic retinopathy in patients with pre-existing retinopathy - Injection-site reactions; rotate sites to prevent lipodystrophy - Hair shedding during rapid weight loss; usually temporary but distressing - Loss of lean muscle mass during rapid weight loss without adequate protein and resistance training - Possible allergic reaction including anaphylaxis Additional symptoms to report immediately: - Severe or persistent abdominal pain, especially radiating to the back, with or without vomiting - Repeated vomiting with inability to keep fluids down - Signs of dehydration: very dark urine, minimal urination, dizziness, dry mouth, confusion- Yellowing of skin or eyes, dark urine, pale stools, severe right upper abdominal pain- Severe constipation with abdominal swelling and inability to pass gas (possible ileus)- Severe or repeated hypoglycemia symptoms if on diabetes medications - New neck mass, hoarseness, difficulty swallowing, or shortness of breath - Worsening vision in patients with diabetic retinopathy Monitoring requirements: - Baseline weight, blood pressure, heart rate - Baseline metabolic panel (glucose, HbA1c when indicated, lipids, liver enzymes, kidney function) - Follow-up weight and vital signs at [frequency: typically every 2-4 weeks initially] - Follow-up labs at [frequency: typically every 3 months initially] - Pregnancy test before starting and ongoing pregnancy monitoring when applicable Patient initial: __________ Date: __________

Addendum B: Dual GIP-GLP-1 Receptor Agonists (Tirzepatide and Related)

Medication name: ______________________ Specific dose and frequency: ______________________ Additional risks specific to this medication category: - Nausea, vomiting, diarrhea, constipation, abdominal pain, bloating, reflux, delayed gastric emptying - Decreased appetite and food aversion that may be stronger than with single GLP-1 agonists- Dehydration with greater intensity than some older therapies - Possible gallbladder disease or pancreatitis - Pancreatitis risk; severe abdominal pain with vomiting requires emergency evaluation- Possible risk of thyroid C-cell tumors; contraindicated in personal/family history of medullary thyroid carcinoma or MEN2 - Hypoglycemia when combined with insulin or sulfonylureas - Injection-site reactions - Hair shedding during rapid weight loss - Loss of lean muscle mass if protein intake and resistance training are inadequate - Rapid weight loss may cause weakness, fatigue, or nutritional deficiency - Dysphagia or esophageal symptoms related to delayed gastric emptying Additional symptoms to report immediately: - Severe abdominal pain, especially with vomiting - Repeated vomiting with signs of dehydration - Severe constipation with abdominal swelling - Yellowing of skin or eyes, severe right upper abdominal pain - Signs of hypoglycemia if on diabetes medications

- Severe or persistent reflux, difficulty swallowing, or chest pain after eating - New neck mass, hoarseness, or trouble swallowing Monitoring requirements: - Baseline weight, blood pressure, heart rate - Baseline metabolic panel (glucose, HbA1c when indicated, lipids, liver enzymes, kidney function) - Follow-up weight and vitals at [frequency: _________] - Follow-up labs at [frequency: _________] - Pregnancy monitoring when applicable Patient initial: _________ Date: _________

Addendum C: Investigational Triple Agonists (Retatrutide and Related)

Medication name: ______________________ Specific dose and frequency: ______________________ Additional risks specific to this investigational medication: - This medication is investigational and NOT FDA-approved - All risks associated with GLP-1, GIP, and glucagon receptor activation apply - Glucagon agonism may increase heart rate and energy expenditure; cardiac rhythm effects are not fully characterized - Abnormal skin sensations (dysesthesia, burning, tingling, numbness) reported in trials, possibly more common at higher doses - GI side effects may be more pronounced than with dual agonists - Unknown long-term safety; limited human data beyond clinical trials - Legal availability uncertain; sourcing requires careful verification

- Sourcing risk: compounded or grey-market retatrutide is not clinical trial product and should be treated with additional caution - Dehydration, gallbladder disease, pancreatitis risks as with other incretin-class therapies- Thyroid C-cell tumor risk as a class concern Additional symptoms to report immediately: - All emergency symptoms listed in the universal form - Persistent or severe skin sensations: burning, tingling, numbness, dysesthesia - Rapid or irregular heartbeat, palpitations, or chest discomfort - Any symptom that feels new, unusual, or concerning, even if not on standard lists Monitoring requirements: - Enhanced monitoring due to investigational status: [frequency: typically every 2-4 weeks]- Baseline comprehensive metabolic panel, ECG if clinically indicated - Weight, blood pressure, heart rate at every follow-up - Interval labs every 4-8 weeks initially - Close documentation of any new or unusual symptoms - Patient must understand that stopping rules may be applied more strictly due to limited safety data Patient initial: _________ Date: _________

Addendum D: Growth Hormone-Releasing Hormone Analogs (Sermorelin, Tesamorelin, and Related) Medication name: ______________________ Specific dose, frequency, and cycling protocol: ______________________ Additional risks specific to this medication category: - Increased IGF-1 levels; requires monitoring to avoid excessively high levels

- Edema (fluid retention), swelling of hands or feet - Joint pain, stiffness, or aching - Carpal tunnel syndrome symptoms: numbness, tingling, weakness in hands - Headache, flushing, warmth after injection - Possible glucose intolerance or worsening of blood sugar control - Possible worsening of sleep apnea - Vivid dreams or sleep disturbance - Theoretical concern in active malignancy, recent malignancy, or unexplained masses (GH/ IGF-1 axis may stimulate certain tumor types) - Hypersensitivity reactions - Tesamorelin specifically: possible rash, itching, injection-site reactions; off-label use requires additional disclosure - Cycling may be recommended; I understand my specific cycling protocol Additional symptoms to report immediately: - Significant swelling of hands, feet, or face - Numbness, tingling, or weakness in hands (possible carpal tunnel) - Severe joint pain or stiffness - Rapid weight gain from fluid retention - Severe headache, vision changes, or confusion - New lump, unexplained bleeding, night sweats, or unexplained weight loss - Worsening snoring or sleep apnea symptoms - Signs of high blood sugar: excessive thirst, frequent urination, blurry vision - Severe allergic reaction Monitoring requirements: - Baseline IGF-1, fasting glucose or HbA1c
- Follow-up IGF-1 at [frequency: typically every 3 months] - Follow-up glucose/HbA1c at [frequency: _________] - Blood pressure monitoring - Assessment of edema, joint symptoms, carpal tunnel symptoms at each follow-up- Cancer screening current (age-appropriate); specialist clearance if cancer history Patient initial: _________ Date: _________

Addendum E: CJC-1295 / Ipamorelin and Growth Hormone Secretagogue Combinations

Medication name(s): ______________________ Specific dose, frequency, and protocol: ______________________ DAC or no-DAC specification: ______________________ Additional risks specific to this medication category: - Flushing, warmth, redness after injection (common, usually transient) - Head rush or lightheadedness after injection - Increased appetite (ipamorelin may increase ghrelin signaling in some patients) - Vivid dreams or sleep changes - Increased IGF-1 with chronic use; requires monitoring - Edema, fluid retention - Joint discomfort or carpal-tunnel-type symptoms at higher exposures - Possible glucose changes - Theoretical cancer concern as with all GH-axis therapies - DAC (drug affinity complex) versus no-DAC matters: different half-life, different exposure patterns, different monitoring needs - Neither CJC-1295 nor ipamorelin is FDA-approved; compounded quality is critical

- Headache, dizziness, fatigue Additional symptoms to report immediately: - Severe or persistent flushing with other symptoms - Severe headache, vision changes - Significant swelling or fluid retention - New neurologic symptoms - Signs of high blood sugar - New or unexplained symptoms Monitoring requirements: - Baseline IGF-1, fasting glucose or HbA1c - Follow-up IGF-1 at [frequency: typically every 3 months initially]- Assessment of sleep, energy, side effects at each follow-up - Clear documentation of DAC versus no-DAC in the record Patient initial: _________ Date: _________

Addendum F: BPC-157 and Tissue Repair Peptides

Medication name: ______________________ Specific dose, frequency, route, and duration: ______________________ Additional risks specific to this medication category: - BPC-157 is NOT FDA-approved for any human indication - Evidence in humans is limited; most data comes from animal studies - Regulatory status is uncertain and may change; availability is not guaranteed- Unknown long-term safety in humans - Sourcing risk: many BPC-157 products on the market are of uncertain quality

- Injection-site reactions - Possible effects on blood vessel formation (angiogenesis); theoretical concern in active cancer - Possible effects on blood pressure (may lower blood pressure in some reports) - Possible effects on wound healing that could theoretically affect surgical planning - Interaction with other medications not well studied - Oral, subcutaneous, and other routes have different absorption and different evidence bases Additional symptoms to report immediately: - Any signs of infection at intended or unintended injection sites - Severe dizziness or low blood pressure symptoms - Unusual bleeding or bruising - Any new or worsening symptoms Monitoring requirements: - Documentation of the specific clinical problem being treated - Photographic documentation when appropriate (wounds, injury sites) - Assessment of response at follow-up visits - Clear stop criteria if no benefit by specified reassessment date - Blood pressure monitoring if hypotension concern Patient initial: _________ Date: _________

Addendum G: Melanocortin Agonists (Melanotan II, PT-141 / Bremelanotide)

Medication name: ______________________ Specific dose, frequency, route, and duration: ______________________ Additional risks specific to this medication category:

- Nausea and flushing (very common, especially with initial doses) - Darkening of skin, moles, freckles, or areas of previous pigmentation - New moles or changes in existing moles - Yawning, stretching, or fatigue after administration - Increased libido or sexual desire (intended effect but may be distressing if unexpected)- Transient increase in blood pressure - Possible effects on appetite - PT-141 (bremelanotide) is FDA-approved for hypoactive sexual desire disorder in premenopausal women; other uses are off-label - Melanotan II is NOT FDA-approved and has significant regulatory and safety concerns- Melanotan II carries risk of uncontrolled pigmentation, mole changes, and unknown long-term dermatologic effects - Both medications require discussion of blood pressure effects Additional symptoms to report immediately: - Severe nausea with vomiting - Severe headache, chest pain, or severe increase in blood pressure - Changes in moles: asymmetry, border changes, color changes, diameter increase, evolution (ABCDE criteria) - New moles appearing - Severe allergic reaction - Any symptom of stroke: sudden weakness, numbness, vision loss, confusion, severe headache Monitoring requirements: - Baseline blood pressure - Skin examination or dermatology clearance if personal/family history of melanoma or significant moles
- Blood pressure check after initial dose when clinically appropriate- Ongoing monitoring of skin changes - Photographic documentation of skin baseline when appropriate Patient initial: _________ Date: _________

Addendum H: Oxytocin and Related Peptides

Medication name: ______________________ Specific dose, frequency, route, and duration: ______________________ Additional risks specific to this medication category: - Oxytocin has FDA-approved uses in obstetrics; other uses are off-label or limited-evidence- Hypotension (low blood pressure), especially with higher doses - Nausea, vomiting - Flushing, warmth - Headache - Changes in mood, emotional sensitivity, or social behavior - Uterine contraction effects in women of childbearing potential - Water intoxication (hyponatremia) with high doses; headache, confusion, seizures in severe cases - Interaction with antihypertensive medications - Limited evidence for many off-label uses Additional symptoms to report immediately: - Severe dizziness, fainting, or signs of very low blood pressure - Severe headache with confusion or altered mental status - Severe nausea and vomiting - Signs of pregnancy when applicable (oxytocin has uterine effects)

- Severe mood changes Monitoring requirements: - Baseline blood pressure - Blood pressure monitoring after initial doses - Assessment of mood and emotional effects at follow-up- Monitoring for fluid retention or hyponatremia symptoms Patient initial: _________ Date: _________

Addendum I: Testosterone and Hormone Replacement Therapy

Medication name: ______________________ Specific dose, frequency, route, and protocol: ______________________ Additional risks specific to this medication category: - Testosterone is a controlled substance (Schedule III); additional prescribing rules apply- Polycythemia (increased red blood cell count); requires regular hematocrit/hemoglobin monitoring - Elevated hematocrit increases risk of blood clots, stroke, heart attack - Acne, oily skin, increased body hair - Male pattern baldness or hair thinning in genetically susceptible individuals - Testicular atrophy or shrinkage - Infertility or decreased fertility; suppression of sperm production - Gynecomastia (breast tissue enlargement in men) - Mood changes, irritability, aggression, or emotional lability - Sleep apnea worsening - Fluid retention, edema

- Elevation of liver enzymes (with oral formulations especially) - Prostate effects: urinary symptoms, theoretical concern for prostate cancer acceleration (controversial but requires disclosure) - Cardiovascular risk remains debated; requires patient-specific risk assessment - In women: virilization (deepening voice, facial hair, clitoral enlargement) which may be irreversible - Transfer risk: skin-to-skin transfer of topical testosterone to children, partners, or pets- Proper disposal of used patches, syringes, and vials Additional symptoms to report immediately: - Chest pain, shortness of breath, leg swelling or pain (possible blood clot) - Severe headache, vision changes, weakness, numbness, confusion (possible stroke) - Severe mood changes, suicidal thoughts, or violent ideation - Severe urinary symptoms - Signs of severe polycythemia: severe headache, dizziness, blurred vision, flushed skin- Signs of liver problems: jaundice, dark urine, severe right upper abdominal pain - In women: any signs of virilization Monitoring requirements: - Baseline testosterone (total and free), estradiol, CBC, hematocrit/hemoglobin, PSA (age-appropriate), liver function, lipid panel - Follow-up testosterone, estradiol, hematocrit at [frequency: typically every 3-6 months]- PSA monitoring per standard guidelines for men - Assessment of acne, hair loss, mood, urinary symptoms, edema at each follow-up - Fertility discussion documented; sperm preservation offered if fertility desired - Clear stop rules if hematocrit exceeds practice threshold (commonly 54%) Patient initial: _________ Date: _________

Addendum J: NAD+ Therapy

Medication name: ______________________ Specific dose, route, frequency, and protocol: ______________________ Additional risks specific to this medication category: - NAD+ is NOT FDA-approved for the conditions commonly treated in wellness practice- Evidence for most wellness claims is limited, preclinical, or theoretical - Flushing, warmth, chest tightness, or discomfort during intravenous infusion (very common)- Nausea, abdominal cramping - Headache, dizziness, lightheadedness - Hypotension during or after infusion - Anxiety, restlessness, or agitation during infusion - Taste perversion (unusual or metallic taste in mouth during infusion) - Risk of infection with any intravenous access - Vein irritation, phlebitis, or infiltration at IV site - Cost is typically high and not covered by insurance - Oral and subcutaneous routes have different absorption and different risk profiles than IV Additional symptoms to report immediately: - Severe chest pain, chest tightness, or difficulty breathing during or after infusion - Severe allergic reaction - Fainting or near-fainting - Signs of infection at IV site: redness, warmth, pus, fever, red streaks - Severe or persistent nausea Monitoring requirements: - Baseline vital signs

- Vital signs during IV infusion at protocol-specific intervals - Assessment of tolerance after initial dose before escalating - Observation period after infusion per practice protocol - Patient should not drive if experiencing significant dizziness or lightheadedness Patient initial: _________ Date: _________

Addendum K: Other Peptide or Wellness Therapy

Use this blank addendum for any therapy not covered above. The clinician must document: Medication name: ______________________ Regulatory status: ______________________ Evidence level: ______________________ Specific dose, route, frequency: ______________________ Therapy-specific risks (clinician must document all known risks): - ____ - ____ - ____ - ____ - ____ - ____ - ____ - ____ Additional symptoms to report immediately: - ____ - ____

- ____ - ____ Monitoring requirements: - ____ - ____ - ____ Patient initial: _________ Date: _________

General Emergency Instructions

Seek emergency care immediately (call 911 or go to the nearest emergency department) for: - Severe allergic reaction (difficulty breathing, swelling of throat, severe rash, fainting) - Chest pain or pressure - Severe shortness of breath - Signs of stroke (sudden weakness, numbness, vision loss, confusion, severe headache) - Severe abdominal pain with vomiting - Fainting or loss of consciousness - Severe bleeding that won't stop - Suicidal thoughts or intent to harm yourself or others - Any symptom that feels life-threatening or rapidly worsening After-hours clinic phone: ______________________ After-hours clinician pager/messaging: ______________________ My primary care physician: ______________________ My PCP after-hours line: ______________________ Nearest emergency department: ______________________ Emergency department address: ______________________ Emergency department phone: ______________________ This form and all attached addenda have been reviewed with me. I understand the contents. My questions have been answered. I voluntarily consent to treatment.

Patient initials (confirming all addenda reviewed): __________ Date: __________

Clinician initials: __________ Date: __________

Template Version: June 2026 Edition. This is an educational template only. Have healthcare counsel in your state review before use in clinical practice. Adapt with malpractice counsel, pharmacy counsel, and the responsible clinician before any patient signs.

Appendix B: Dosing Reference Tables

Look, I have been around long enough to watch physicians get burned by cookbook medicine. Some regulator, some board reviewer, some plaintiff attorney will hold up this very table and ask why you prescribed exactly what it says without considering the patient in front of you. So let me be painfully clear: these tables are starting points, clinical shorthand, memory aids. They are not protocols. They are not orders. They are not a defense if you prescribed blindly.

Every dose must be individualized by the treating clinician and verified against current pharmacy concentration, product availability, patient-specific risk, renal and hepatic function, concurrent medications, and current evidence. Regulatory status changes. Shortages end. Compounding rules shift. The FDA publishes new guidance. The board changes its posture. Verify everything before the patient touches a vial.

The tables below are organized by clinical category, not alphabetically. Why? Because when you are staring at a patient chart, you should be thinking about the clinical problem first and the product name second. If your brain works the other way around, you are doing retail, not medicine.

UNIVERSAL DISCLAIMER - READ THIS FIRST

B.1 Quick Reference by Peptide Category B.1.1 GLP-1 / GIP / Triple-Agonist Table: Incretin-Based Metabolic Therapy Category-Specific Administration Notes: - All GLP-1-class drugs: Verify compounded concentration before every patient instruction. Patients confuse mg, mcg, mL, and “units”constantly. Document the exact strength of the vial the pharmacy will ship. - Titration: Slow titration reduces discontinuation. Do not push every patient to maximum labeled dose. Most patients reach goals at intermediate doses. - Diabetic co-therapy: Insulin and sulfonylurea doses typically need reduction to avoid hypoglycemia. Coordinate with the patient’s diabetes prescriber. - Dehydration risk: All incretin therapies can reduce oral intake. Patients need explicit hydration instructions, especially in hot climates or with concurrent diuretics. - Lean mass: Document that rapid weight-loss patients were counseled on protein intake and resistance training. The number on the scale is not the only endpoint.

B.1.2 Growth Hormone Axis Table: GHRH Analogs and Secretagogue Stacks

Category-Specific Administration Notes: - DAC vs. no-DAC: These are not interchangeable. With-DAC (Drug Affinity Complex) has a much longer half-life and produces more sustained GH/IGF-1 elevation. Document which form you prescribed and why. - Empty stomach: CJC-1295 and ipamorelin are typically administered on an empty stomach (30+ minutes before food) to avoid interference with glucose and insulin. Patients need clear written instructions. -Cycling: Tesamorelin and sermorelin protocols often use cycling (5 on / 2 off, or 6-8 weeks on / 4 weeks off) to limit tachyphylaxis. Document the cycle plan. - IGF-1 monitoring: Obtain baseline IGF-1 before starting any GH-axis peptide. Recheck at 4-6 weeks, then per cycle. Stop or reduce if IGF-1 exceeds age-appropriate upper limit. - The pituitary feedback brake: Sermorelin, tesamorelin, and CJC-1295/ipamorelin work through physiologic pathways with feedback mechanisms intact. This is conceptually different from exogenous recombinant GH (somatropin), where IGF-1 can climb without restraint. Document that you understand this distinction.

B.1.3 Repair / Immune / Tissue Regeneration Table

Category-Specific Administration Notes: - BPC-157: The human evidence base is thin. Most published work is animal or cell-culture studies. Do not let patient enthusiasm outrun evidence.

Set measurable endpoints (pain scale, range of motion, imaging, function) and reassess at 4-6 weeks. If there is no measurable benefit, stop. - TB-500 vs. full-length thymosin beta-4: These are not the same compound. TB-500 is a 17-amino-acid fragment. Full-length thymosin beta-4 is a 43-amino-acid protein with different research programs. Do not use full-length safety data to validate fragment dosing. - Thymosin Alpha-1: This has the strongest non-GLP-1 human evidence base in the peptide world, with international approvals and published RCTs in hepatitis and sepsis. That still does not make it FDA-approved in the United States. Chart it as off-label/investigational with explicit consent. - Athletes: Both TB-500 and full-length thymosin beta-4 are on the WADA prohibited list at all times. Document WADA status clearly. An athlete using these compounds risks competition eligibility. - Research-use-only warning: None of these compounds should be sourced from grey-market vendors. The chart must show pharmacy dispensing, not patient-purchased vials.

B.1.4 Metabolic / Wellness / Sexual Health / Supportive Therapy Table

E Category-Specific Administration Notes: - AOD-9604: The human trial program included ~900+ participants and did not demonstrate meaningful obesity benefit. It is reasonable to discuss as an adjunct for patients who cannot tolerate GLP-1s, but do not promise dramatic fat loss. If there is no measurable benefit at 8-12 weeks, stop. - MOTS-c: This is preclinical science. The original characterization paper from USC (2015) established a plausible mechanism, but there are zero human treatment RCTs. Position it as an investigational adjunct for metabolic support, not a replacement for exercise. Cycle length is typically 4-8 weeks. -KPV: Route matters. Oral delivery targets gut-local anti-inflammatory effects through PepT1 transporters. Subcutaneous delivery is a different pharmacologic concept. Topical delivery targets local inflammation. Document why you chose the route. - PT-141: Bremelanotide (Vyleesi) is FDA-approved for a narrow indication. Anything outside that label is off-label and requires elevated documentation. Do not prescribe casually by text because a patient wants a weekend shot. The effect is not the same as sildenafil - it works centrally on desire/arousal, not peripherally on blood flow. - NAD+: This is not a peptide. It is included because peptide and wellness clinics sell it alongside peptides. The strongest honest position: mechanisms are real, but clinical claims vary greatly by route. IV NAD+ for wellness has the weakest evidence relative to its marketing. Oral NR/NMN have actual human pharmacokinetic and biomarker data. Document that the patient understood the difference.

B.2 Comparative Summary: Key Parameters at a Glance

This comparative summary is a quick orientation tool. It is not a prescribing protocol. It shows which peptide categories carry the strongest evidence, where the investigational risk is highest, what monitoring tends to matter, and what chart documentation should be strongest before a physician prescribes anything.

Parameter	GLP-1/GIP Class	GH-Axis Class	Repair/Immune Class	Metabolic/Wellness Class
Strongest human evidence	Semaglutide, Tirzepatide (Phase 3)	Tesamorelin (FDA-approved)	Thymosin Alpha-1 (international RCTs)	PT-141 (FDA-approved for HSDD)
Investigational compounds	Retatrutide	CJC-1295/Ipamorelin, Sermorelin (compounded)	BPC-157, TB-500, GHK-Cu (injectable)	MOTS-c, KPV, AOD-9604
Typical monitoring interval	2-4 weeks initially	4-6 weeks (IGF-1)	4-6 weeks with stop criteria	4-12 weeks depending on compound
Key lab monitoring	Weight, glucose, HbA1c, lipids	IGF-1, glucose/HbA1c	CBC (TA1), injury outcomes	Weight, body composition, lipids, glucose

Parameter	GLP-1/GIP Class	GH-Axis Class	Repair/Immune Class	Metabolic/Wellness Class
Highest risk patients	MEN2/MTC history, pancreatitis, gallbladder disease	Active cancer, pituitary disease, uncontrolled diabetes	Active cancer (angiogenesis concern), autoimmune risk (TA1)	Uncontrolled hypertension (PT-141), active IBD (KPV)
FDA status complexity	Approved branded products; compounding status changes	Tesamorelin approved for a narrow label; others compounded	None FDA-approved in U.S.; TA1 approved abroad	PT-141 approved for a narrow label; others not FDA-approved

B.3 Dosing Documentation Checklist

Before any patient receives a vial, the chart should confirm:

- Pharmacy concentration verified and documented (mg/mL or mcg/mL)

- Patient-specific dose calculated and documented in mg, mcg, AND units for the

prescribed syringe

- Route documented (subcutaneous, intramuscular, intravenous, intranasal, oral, topical)
- Frequency documented (daily, weekly, as needed, etc.)
- Titration plan documented (if applicable)
- Cycle length documented (if applicable)
- Administration timing documented (e.g., bedtime, empty stomach, 45 min before activity)
- Patient educated on dose calculation and administration technique
- No-self-adjustment instruction documented
- Stop criteria documented
- Monitoring schedule documented
- Rationale for dose selection documented (why this dose, why this patient, why now)

www.ingramcontent.com/pod-product-compliance
Lightning Source LLC
LaVergne TN
LVHW080004210926
848481LV00011B/2944